ESSENTIAL PAPERS IN PSYCHOANALYSIS

Essential Papers on Borderline Disorders
Michael D. Stone, M.D., Editor

Essential Papers on Object Relations
Peter Buckley, M.D., Editor

Essential Papers on Narcissism
Andrew P. Morrison, M.D., Editor

Essential Papers on Depression
James C. Coyne, Editor

Essential Papers on Psychosis
Peter Buckley, M.D., Editor

Essential Papers on Countertransference
Benjamin Wolstein, Editor

Essential Papers on Character Neurosis and Treatment
Ruth F. Lax, Editor

Essential Papers on the Psychology of Women
Claudia Zanardi, Editor

ESSENTIAL PAPERS ON THE PSYCHOLOGY OF WOMEN

Claudia Zanardi,
Editor

NEW YORK UNIVERSITY PRESS
NEW YORK AND LONDON

Library of Congress Cataloging-in-Publication Data
Essential papers on the psychology of women / Claudia Zanardi, editor
    p.   cm. — (Essential papers in psychoanalysis)
    Includes bibliographical references.
    ISBN 0-8147-9667-2 (alk. paper) — ISBN 0-8147-9668-0 (pbk. : alk. paper)
    1. Women—Psychology. I. Zanardi, Claudia, 1939–
II. Series.
HQ1206.E87   1990
155.6'33—dc20   89-13560
                  CIP

p 10 9 8 7 6 5 4 3

Book design by Ken Venezio

To my American and European women friends

Contents

Preface   ix

Introduction   1

PART I: PSYCHOANALYTIC VIEWS ON FEMALE SEXUALITY

In Europe

1. The Preoedipal Phase of the Libido Development,
   Ruth Mack Brunswick   43

2. The Oedipus Complex in the Light of Early Anxieties,
   Melanie Klein   65

3. Feminine Guilt and the Oedipus Complex,
   Janine Chasseguet-Smirgel   88

4. Creativity and Its Origins, *D. W. Winnicott*   132

5. Feminine Sexuality in Psychoanalytic Doctrine,
   Moustafa Safouan   146

6. The Dead Father: On Early Psychic Trauma and Its Relation to Disturbance in Sexual Identity and in Creative Activity,
   Joyce McDougall   159

In the United States

7. Ways of Female Superego Formation and the Female Castration Conflict, *Edith Jacobson*   187

8. A Contribution to the Psychoanalysis of Extreme Submissiveness in
   Women, *Annie Reich*   198

9. Cultural Pressures in the Psychology of Women,
   Clara Thompson   207

10. Masochism — A Defense Reaction of the Ego, *Esther Menaker*   221

11. Outside and Inside, Male and Female, *Judith Kestenberg*   234

12. The Sense of Femaleness, *Robert J. Stoller*   278

13. Penis Envy: From Childhood Wish to Developmental Metaphor, *William I. Grossman* and *Walter A. Stewart* 290

14. The Influence of Values in Psychoanalysis: The Case of Female Psychology, *Ethel S. Person* 305

PART II: FEMINISM AND PSYCHOANALYSIS

In Europe

15. Psychoanalysis and Women, *Juliet Mitchell* 331

16. This Sex Which Is Not One, *Luce Irigaray* 344

17. Inquiry into Femininity, *Michèle Montrelay* 352

18. Women's Time, *Julia Kristeva* 374

In the United States

19. "Sometimes You Wonder if They're Human," *Dorothy Dinnerstein* 401

20. Gender, Relation, and Difference in Psychoanalytic Perspective, *Nancy Julia Chodorow* 420

21. The Development of Women's Sense of Self, *Jean Baker Miller* 437

22. The Alienation of Desire: Women's Masochism and Ideal Love, *Jessica Benjamin* 455

23. Remapping the Moral Domain: New Images of the Self in Relationship, *Carol Gilligan* 480

Name Index 497

Subject Index 501

Preface

There are people I would like to thank for their help in editing this book and in the organization of the course Psychology of Women at New York University:

Elettra Nerbosi Barth, a colleague and a friend who helped me in clarifying my thinking and in choosing the various chapters through interminable theoretical and personal discussions on psychoanalysis and feminism in Europe and in the United States.

All the students who attended my courses in Psychology of Women, who had responded with their knowledge and their personal experiences to the selections I had proposed and who supported and encouraged my choices. Betty Brewer, administrator of the Graduate Program in the Department of Psychology at New York University, and the students who believed in my feminist approach of teaching.

I also would like to thank Professor Leo Goldberger for his encouragement in editing this collection as an expression of my thinking and as a result of all the material I had assembled for the course.

I am grateful to my editor Kitty Moore at New York University Press for her flexibility, her warmth, and her personal belief that she shared with me in an international approach to the subject.

In editing this anthology I thought many times of my relationship with my mother, Carla. I would like to thank her for being able to recognize and to accept sympathetically my difference from her and to encourage me to pursue my interests.

Introduction

The decision to edit an anthology on female psychology grew out of a course I taught on women's psychology at New York University. In choosing to teach this course, I was faced with many questions from my past as a participant in the feminist movement of the 1970s, and from my present as a woman in academia. My questions are similar to those of other women in academia. I wanted to accomplish a number of goals: to teach women's psychology in an institutional and patriarchal environment that has traditionally alienated women; to evaluate the feminine in its difference without creating the masculine/feminine polarity that to my way of thinking leads only to the devaluation of one or the other and perpetuates this dynamic; to find a space within the teaching environment of psychology to voice theoretical interpretations of the psychological development of women without relegating them to an exclusively feminine field of studies, either inside (women's studies) or outside the institution. Through teaching I also wanted to be able to acknowledge the classic positions, accepted by institutional psychology (although often ignored in teaching), as well as to present the theories that emerged from the women's liberation movement of the seventies, which are not recognized within the environs of institutional psychology. The feminist theories criticize patriarchal society and point out the way classical theories are relative to historical and cultural conditioning; at the same time they follow the themes and premises of earlier theorists, despite their differences.

In the search for a text that gives voice to multiple interpretations in a context of historical continuity and of cultural differences, I found different anthologies, but none that contained both classical and feminist theories within a cultural and historical perspective. The underlying themes on which I structured the anthology and the course were: history as the element that determines the evolution of theory yet at the same time emphasizes its continuity; psychoanalysis as a key to reading the female psychology; and culture as an element that differentiates orientations according to the traditions or the places where they were formulated.

History determines the evolution of theories that in their turn create a new history while acting as a framework that lends continuity to scientific thought. Theory is relative to the moment in which it is formulated. History reveals the continuity and the divergence in the formulation of successive theories. Theories on female sexuality from those of Freud to those of the 1970s and 1980s exemplify continuity in their identification of the themes, yet divergence in their interpretations, based on the specific zeitgeist of the moment in which they were formulated. At times it is difficult to determine the way reality and theory interact, but psychoanalytic interest in female sexuality during the 1920s and 1930s undoubtedly stemmed from the first feminist movements of the twentieth century and their protest against the social oppression of women. The socialist theories that preceded the feminist protest interpreted women's subordination as a result of their absence from production. Historically the reproductive role of women has kept them away from work repeatedly, making them the spiritual counterpart to men in production. Feminist theories were also based on a socioeconomic analysis, but they focused on the possibility of a sexual freedom that would remove women from the reproductive role, seemingly responsible for discrimination against them. Between the end of the nineteenth century and immediately after World War I, the feminist movement in England had a powerful impact, creating a different social position and a new image for women. Feminism was not the expression of an ideology, but rather a rebellion against the norms of Victorian bourgeois femininity, a protest that extended to all areas of cultural life and had an international impact.

Freud himself recognized "the denials of the feminists, who are anxious to force us to regard the two sexes as completely equal in position and worth" (1925, 258). In spite of the feminist's opposition to his phallocentric theory, in which they could not recognize themselves, some women were attracted to psychoanalysis because it studied sexuality and therefore represented a challenge to repressed codes and to recognized knowledge. Especially attracted to the field were culturally and politically radical women looking for a profession different from those that had traditionally been assigned to the feminine, such as Edith Jacobson, Annie Reich, Helen Deutsch, and Karen Horney. When women entered the field of psychoanalysis (Freud himself encouraged this, even though theoretically he interpreted it as a masculine deviation), their participation indicated a change in women who were present in the profession in their own femininity. This opened up new dynamics in therapeutic relationships and led to a renewed theoretical interest in female sexuality (Horney 1924, 1926, 1932, 1933; Deutsch 1925, 1930; Lampl-de Groot 1927; Brunswick 1929).

The debate between the Vienna school and the London school on female sexuality expressed this greater interest in femininity, and perhaps responded to the questions being raised by feminists in search of their identity, especially in England. Ernest Jones (1927, 1935) distanced himself from Freudian phallocentrism and supported Karen Horney's argument on women's original femininity. He considered the little girl's phallic phase to be a secondary defensive construct. Freud's 1933 publication ''Femininity'' continued to identify the libido with the masculine and to relegate female sexuality to a state of biological inferiority, definitively ending the debate on female sexuality and coinciding with a silence on women's history.

As Ray Strachey wrote in the introduction to ''Our Freedom and Its Results'' (1936): ''Modern young women know amazingly little of what life was like before the war, and show a strong hostility to the word 'feminism' and all which they imagine it to connote.'' The antifeminist culture's alignment with reactionary political changes in Europe had taught these young women to despise their own movement. The new political and cultural atmosphere of the war and the postwar period sent women back to their traditional roles.

In the 1940s, 1950s, and 1960s there were sporadic publications in the European psychoanalytic literature on female sexuality. One example is Marie Bonaparte's book, *Female Sexuality* (1953), that basically supported the Freudian theory of the biological origins of women's sexual problems. The 1964 publication of an anthology edited by Janine Chasseguet-Smirgel was an important occurrence, yet it did not receive an adequate response in the scientific community, confirming the absence of women from history. In the United States instead women continued their battle for equal rights, and received greater recognition in the workplace, partly due to industry's need to substitute the enlisted men during World War II. Yet in those years American society followed a direction on sexuality that led to the sexual conservatism of the 1950s. The publications of the 1940s and 1950s adopted the classic Freudian position, but they avoided the emphasis on sexuality. The theories of women were based on either biological or psychosocial determinism. In those years Helene Deutsch published *The Psychology of Women* (1944–45), confirming the Freudian origins of her thought and dedicating an entire volume to maternity that was so reductionist that it would provoke an outcry from the feminists in the 1960s. Clara Thompson (1941) instead distanced herself from Freud and classic psychoanalysis when she took up "the patriarchal ideal of women" maintained by Karen Horney (1935), and emphasized the importance of the cultural pressure exerted by Western patriarchal society on the psychological formation of women. By introducing cultural and social categories and emphasizing cultural factors rather than drives as determinant to psychological development, Horney and Thompson initiated the so-called culturist orientation that was rejected by traditional psychoanalysis but later revived in the 1970s by both the psychoanalysts such as Ruth Moulton and Ethel Person, and by feminist psychoanalysts such as J. B. Miller, Carol Gilligan, and Nancy Chodorow.

In the 1950s the literature was more centered on the biological dimension of female sexuality (Greenacre 1950, 1952; Kestenberg 1956a, 1956b). Kinsey's study *Sexual Behavior in the Human Female* (1953) was also published during these years. The first feminist movements of the 1960s revived interest in the feminine, as we can see in psychoanalytic discussions on the Masters and Johnson report (Sherfey 1966). In the 1960s Robert Stoller led to an innovative development in psychoanalytic theory by proposing the existence of a gender identity ("core gender identity") that precedes the awareness of sexual difference (1968a, 1968b).

Both European and American feminist psychoanalytic theories were born from the feminist movement of the 1970s (following the political movement of the 1960s) that broke the historical isolation of women. The movement led to a comparison of women's experiences and to a recognition of their common problems—a collective maladjustment of women rather than individual conflicts. The analyses of experiences led to the same questions posed by classic psychoanalytic theories. "Psychoanalysis is . . . political for feminism, political in the more obvious sense that it came into the arena of discussion in response to the internal needs of feminist debate" (Rose 1983). The feminists reacted to their own questions either by attributing full responsibility to social conditioning or by trying to interpret the conflicts in the new historical light of a greater awareness of the status of women. In the development of new theories psychoanalysis was reappropriated as an instrument of women's knowledge.

This collection treats history both as a factor of change in the evolution of thought and as a link between theories. Within its limits, it attempts to cover perspectives on the feminine from the analytic literature of the 1940s, tied to the classic debate between Freud, Horney, and Jones, to the psychoanalytic theories from the 1950s through to the 1980s and to the feminist psychoanalytic theories that followed the political question of women.

Psychoanalysis was the first science to confront the study of sexuality, not only in its biological connotations, but in individual psychological development, and to look for the origin of sexual difference in the individual unconscious. Through its studies of sexuality, psychoanalysis becomes a means of identifying female sexual repression and its psychological importance to the individual and social development of women.

The contribution of psychoanalytic discourse has been to surpass social determinism and to focus on those aspects of the real that had been (and still are) too often ignored: not the so-called objective reality of the outside world, but the subjective reality of the intrapsychic processes, fantasies, and unconscious desires and needs. Psychoanalysis augments social theories with the study of sexual difference, not through behavioristic connotations, but through individual and social history inscribed in the unconscious. Its strength lies in the concept of the unconscious, the locus of the repressed, of the unspoken, of that which cannot be said and appears only in dreams, in slips of the tongue and in symptoms of disease.

Psychoanalysis began when Freud realized that hysteria represented an unarticulated, conflicting sexuality that could only be expressed through disease. Cases of hysteria mainly concerned women, but also men in some cases. Feminist psychoanalysts such as Juliet Mitchell, Julia Kristeva, and Luce Irigaray used this clinical data to postulate a repression of femininity that cannot find a way to express itself in a society governed by masculine laws. Freud claimed that human beings were psychologically bisexual, that baby girls had a phallic stage, and that the libido was masculine; in so doing he implied a third concept, the denial of femininity by both men and women.

Freud's concept of penis envy and of the castration complex are related; both express a fear of femininity. It is only with the analysis of sexual difference (1931, 1933) that the pre-Oedipal makes its first appearance, "like the Minoan-Mycenean civilization behind the civilization of Greece" (1931, 254). The discourse on the feminine developed precisely from this focus on prehistory becoming history. The vicissitudes of the relationship with the mother produce a different access to the Oedipal drama for the two sexes. The mother is the primary love-object for both sexes. A little boy's relationship with his mother must undergo a process of disidentification and of shifting to yet another female object. The little girl, instead, keeps her mother as an identifying reference, but the father replaces the mother as the love-object in the Oedipal triangle. The absolute protagonist of the Oedipal drama is the father, the principle of both reality and differentiation, who pushes the mother into the background by silencing her. Women psychoanalysts have found the initial attachment to the mother in therapeutic relations with their patients. Freud acknowledged his difficulty in tracing the pre-Oedipal stage, "so grey with age and shadowy" (1931, 226), and he appealed to his female colleagues' experiences with transference:

It does indeed appear that women-analysts—as for instance Jeanne Lampl-de Groot and Helen Deutsch—have been able to perceive these facts more easily and clearly because they were helped in dealing with those under their treatment by the transference to a suitable mother substitute. (1931, 227)

The little girl's attachment to her mother, discovered by Lampl-de Groot (1927) and then definitively identified as a pre-Oedipal phase by Brunswick in "The Analysis of a Case of Paranoia" (1929), was later explored by women psychoanalysts (Deutsch 1930; Brunswick 1940) who recognized its importance, especially in female psychological development. The mother, as an omnipotent imago for both sexes, and the greater and more prolonged attachment of daughter to mother receive increasing attention in analytic literature.

In the evolution of psychoanalytic thought and in the greater attention paid to child analysis, the mother acquires an increasingly important role in the psychological formation of the little boy or little girl, both as an element for the child to project his or her phantasy, and as a container for phantasy and affective reality (object relations theory). (The *ph* spelling for the word *fantasy* is used to indicate that the process is unconscious.)

In this new perspective feminist psychoanalytic theories examine interactions between mother and daughter and between mother and son, analyzing the differences and the dynamics of transmission of the feminine from mother to daughter in an asymmetric social structure dominated by the masculine (Chodorow 1978). The focus on the mother-daughter relationship illustrates conflicts in femininity that social change has been unable to eliminate.

The concept of femininity is still a subject of debate and research in psychoanalysis; it remains a vague and stereotypical concept. In a society in which women have achieved greater freedom to express their sexuality and in which they have greater participation in the workplace, the conflict of femininity still repressed in the unconscious once again finds expression in disease. Anorexia and bulimia, symptoms that are manifested in women and rarely in men, may represent the silence of femininity in a society that has changed externally, but that is still dominated by male laws. The questions Lou Salomé raises in her essay on the human being as woman (1899): "Who will be stronger? The Woman or the One who denies her femininity?" are still current in our time. In 1899 she left the answer to the future. Since then women changed their social position, but femininity is still an unknown value in our society.

Psychoanalysis thus remains, despite its theoretical contradictions and differences, an instrument of research that studies the unconscious in order to trace that which social values have repressed.

Psychoanalytic theories are differentiated not only by their historical contexts, but also by their different cultural contexts. In contrast to historical chronicity, the use of cultural criteria to view psychoanalytic orientations reveals fragmentation in the development of thought. In this volume I have first presented the theoretical perspectives tied to European culture and subsequently those tied to American culture to introduce a synchronic axis that forces the reader to recapitulate any given historical period. While this removes the illusion of continuity from reading, to ignore the differences or to attribute them simply to scientific divergences, without linking them to the culture, the politics, and the social terrain in which they are rooted, would prevent real comprehension of the differences. The emphasis on the scientific differences within a cultural frame allows an opening of communication that does not polarize the divergences in the name of scientific truth. In fact only the comprehension of these ties allows one to understand the relativity of science and at the same time its dynamic value as a positive force that expresses, changes and evolves on the thrust of multiple elements.

When we interpret psychoanalysis as a science, and not as a static ideology, it becomes a discipline more aware of external values and therefore more flexible and more open to confrontation and change. The case of female psychology itself represents the influence of cultural and social values on the development of theory. The image of the feminine has gradually been transformed by the greater participation of women in the culture and by their change within society (Person 1983). The critical and interpretive differences in thought on female sexuality are tied to the varying cultural backgrounds of psychoanalytic theories in general.

The theoretical perspectives of European psychoanalysis still reflect the humanistic and philosophical features that from the beginning have made it not just a clinical instrument, but a cultural and at times political force. There are naturally variants imprinted for different cultural contexts: the English orientation is more concrete and empirical with extensive examples of clinical cases; the French orientation is more abstract and theoretical with constant literary references.

In England the empirical tradition has always provided direct and careful observation and an open-mindedness that resulted from the lack of reference to and reverence for an overarching philosophical mode of thought. The psychoanalytic orientation reflects this tradition in its careful and detailed case histories that engage in a dialectical relationship with theory. The interest in child analysis has perhaps been inspired by the central position the romantic culture assigned to childhood. Before Freud, Wordsworth wrote "the child is father to the man." This attention to the child emphasizes the figure of the mother, who has assumed a decisive role in the object relations theory for internal representations and for the psychological development of the child. Alongside the unconscious phantasies involved in object relations, a growing consideration for the real relationship of mother and child has developed (Bowlby 1958, 1969, 1973).

Even in the question of female sexuality, the British school of psychoanalysis has proved the autonomy of its thought from the school of Vienna. We have seen above how Jones's theories are different from Freud's. Melanie Klein also maintained the Horney/Jones thesis that the vagina is represented in the child's unconscious, and that a little girl has an original desire to receive her father's penis. Klein adopts a different theoretical perspective structured according to an internal world of object relations. Her approach, which includes a nonorthodox formulation of the Oedipus complex, has found fertile ground in England. Some of her followers, however, have abandoned her position on an original femininity in the little girl, regarding "the fact of bisexuality as one of the fundamental concepts on which Freud has built up his theories" (Payne 1935). They supported a sexual dedifferentiation that focuses on internal object representations and on the integration and coordination of conflicting male and female elements in the personality as a basis of ego function (Brierley 1932, 1936), on each individual's necessity of coordinating masculine and feminine impulses (Payne 1935) and on both women's and men's "predisposition towards bisexuality" (Winnicott 1966).

In France the interpretation of Freud has taken such a particular direction that it has been dubbed "French Freud." In fact, the transmission of psychoanalysis has taken place on the basis of the exegesis of written texts and not through direct and clinical contacts (the only exception is Marie Bonaparte). Furthermore surrealism, an artistic and literary movement that emphasized dreams and free associations, was one of the main channels for the spread of French psychoanalysis. This cultural context takes into account a more literary and metaphoric reading of Freud's work, and explains the development in France of Lacan's thoughts that give prominence to the problem of language in both theoretical and clinical terms. The discourse on the feminine settles on either Freudian positions on female sexuality (Chasseguet-Smirgel 1964, 1976) or Kleinian positions (Torok 1964) marked by an evocative highly metaphoric language that means to reproduce the discourse of the unconscious and stress primary process, impulse and affect over ego organization. On the other hand Jacques Lacan incites clamorous debates by illustrating the tragic relationship of women with the symbolic order (1958a, 1958b, 1975).

The articles written in the United States represent the two opposite tendencies of American psychoanalysis: on the one hand a secure orthodoxy, tied to medical practices and to scientific research within the lines of classic psychoanalysis, and on the other hand a cultural orientation that emphasizes the importance of the social, and to some viewpoints sacrifices the concept of sexuality and the unconscious. American psychoanalysis, which represents an empirical and pragmatic culture, has addressed its theoretical and clinical orientation not so much to the study of the unconscious as to the study and the reinforcement of the ego. This favors both individual autonomy and social adjustment to achieve the aim of curing the patient:

[From] the undifferentiated phase . . . of needs, impulses, and behavior patterns which can hardly be attributed either to an ego or to an id . . . the ego grows and develops into a specific organ of adaptation and organization, and the id becomes a partly separate system with its specific characteristics. (Hartmann 1948, 80–81)

Ego psychology was begun by Heinz Hartmann, who resumed and developed a concept that he had already begun to consider in Europe, and which stemmed from Freud's final concept of the ego (1940, 145–46) and from Anna Freud's theory (1936). One of the aims of ego psychology is to note social and cultural influences and the way the individual adjusts to them. This attempts to correct the previous de-emphasis of cultural forces yet avoid simple environmentalism. In this perspective psychoanalysis has changed since its inception, when the ego was simply a contravening agent against the id and against the culture.

The process of transformation of psychoanalysis reflects an adaptation to American cultural and political models, in spite of the presence of psychoanalysts who had immigrated from Europe in the 1930s and 1940s. In the United States the Anglo-Saxon empiric culture is united with a pragmatic component and a different concept of time and history. Immigration to a new country required adaptation to a new society that implies a denial of the past and of memories and a commitment to build a present and a future in order to find an identity different from the one that was abandoned. The uncertainty of the social, cultural, and political identity led to the need to affirm the I, which seeks to confirm its existence in producing and in doing. Perhaps the transformation of psychoanalysis can be attributed to the importance given to identity in America, where it is considered a dynamic entity to be constructed, rather than an identity that has been acquired through social and political history, as in Europe. This uncertain sense of identity must construct defenses toward unconscious repressed impulses that can produce a sense of disorientation and of loss of control. In ego psychology loss of control connotes ego deficiency.

The clinical practices of these psychoanalysts may have determined that which is important to the American mentality; this gave further stimulus and confirmation to their own suppositions and contributed to the propagation of a theory which found a response in the culture. Even the latest development of American psychoanalysis, Kohut's self psychology, structures the subject in a framework of object relations, but it too theorizes the importance of unity and the integration of the self. The self's goals—ambitions and ideals mediated by skills and talents—could not be more individualistic. In this version, self-self object relations lead to individual fulfillment of individual goals.

In the United States the transformation of psychoanalysis into a clinical and empirical discipline took place due to simultaneous presences that influenced each other. The prohibition of lay analysis expelled the humanistic and philosophical aspects that had made psychoanalysis a method for interpreting the world, history, and every human expression. A medical class formed in the medical schools, where recognized knowledge is only technical and specific, has reinforced the positivistic and antihumanistic factor. In addition the insertion of psychoanalysis into an institutional environment professionalized a discipline that was born instead from the private relationship between analyst and analysand. In the institutional environment psychoanalysis had to confront psychology, a discipline that the university recognized, and adapt to an academic environment of research and scientific verification.

Many women in the medical psychoanalytic world had immigrated from Europe (30 percent of the psychoanalysts), but a rapid decline in their number occurred due both to the impossibility of exercising the profession without a degree in medicine and to the inaccessibility of medical school, an exclusively male domain. In 1958 only 9 percent of the students at accredited psychoanalytic institutes were women (Fermi 1968, 170). The few women psychoanalysts who came out of these schools and contributed to the literature on women in that period did not dissent from the empirical model, due to their medical training and to their subordination to male power. The empirical responses of this literature represent the American culture's pragmatic spirit and its need for scientific proof.

American psychoanalysts confirmed or refuted Freud's concepts of female sexuality (penis envy, wish for a child, superego, masochism, passivity) in scientific verification of the research, or they analyzed his concepts in a sociocultural light that confirmed the culture's pragmatic tendencies.

Feminism in the 1970s united women in Western society behind an ideology of liberation from common oppression, and expressed the internationality and the universality of women's condition. This ideology could not, however, avoid a confrontation within the movement stemming from the social and cultural differences among women themselves. The differences between the United States and Europe is a main concern in this book.

With equal rights as its objective, the feminist movement in the United States tried to demonstrate that there are no differences between the sexes. The feminists thus analyzed the constraints of the social context more avidly than they did the contradictions within themselves. Certainly the presence of a psychoanalysis which focused on the social adaptation of the ego garnered great criticism; psychoanalysis was seen as an instrument in male hands that used therapy to lead women back into the traditional roles of patriarchal society (Firestone 1970). In the feminist movement there was, however, an emphasis on the force of the female ego—placing a value on assertiveness or standing up for one's rights—that led the feminists to share the American culture's suspicion of the unconscious.

In Europe the feminist movement aimed at discovering the inner conflicts of women in order to achieve first a knowledge of femininity and then an affirmation of women in society. Psychoanalysis, as the science of the unconscious whose philosophical and humanistic aspects are not inserted in the academic, institutional environment, became an instrument for introspective analysis in feminist self-awareness groups:

> Psychoanalysis is no longer best understood as an account of how women are fitted into place. Instead psychoanalysis becomes one of the few places in our culture where it is recognized as more than a fact of individual pathology that most women do not painlessly slip in their role of women if indeed they do at all. (Rose 1983, 91)

In Europe there were also critical attitudes toward Freud's theories. In 1974 Juliet Mitchell resumed Lacan's symbolic reading of Freud, and inspired a feminist interpretation of the unconscious as the locus where patriarchal society represses femininity. This interpretation allowed the feminists to comprehend internalized oppression, a concept which is most efficient when operating within a science of the unconscious. For Luce Irigaray and Julia Kristeva the articulation of women's difference must include the domain of the unconscious if the dominant discourse is to be revolutionized to its very core. The ideology of the culture is based on the repression of the woman's unconscious, which may perhaps be found only in the first months of life (preverbal) before entering the patriarchal symbolic world represented by language.

Femininity is a concept that is still unknown and difficult to identify; it is a question whose only answers are speculations. Despite their differences, the European orientations adopted Lacan's perspectives and emphasized the philosophical and dialectical aspects of psychoanalysis as tools of investigation rather than of treatment. These theories represent an idealistic, abstract, and absolutely theoretical culture at odds with American pragmatism. In fact, Mitchell's study of an unconscious shaped by patriarchal relations did not have great resonance in the United States due to the abstract nature of its concepts.

The American reappropriation of psychoanalysis refuted the model proposed by ego psychology, and opposed the concept of individual autonomy; they turned instead to the British object relations theory to understand the relationship between mother and children in an asymmetric family from which the father is absent (Dinnerstein 1976; Chodorow 1978). These theories analyze the consequences of this asymmetry on the little girl and the transmission of feminine values from mother to daughter in a patriarchal society that does not acknowledge those values. These theories maintain the importance of the construction of the self in relation and recognize the importance of attachment and of interdependence, values completely neglected in societies like the United States that emphasize the importance of autonomy and separation in psychological and social development. Within the same psychoanalytic framework, the American theories assume a more empirical and social orientation than does the philosophical approach of European theories.

The European philosophical approach asks questions about the repression of femininity, and points to the analysis of the individual unconscious as the sole response. The American empirical orientation asks questions about the oppression of femininity and its devaluation, and tends to find an answer in the transformation of the family and the society. While both approaches recognize a repudiation of femininity and investigate the child's initial relationship with the mother, European feminist psychoanalysts emphasize the primacy of the phallus while Americans direct their attention toward the significance of women's mothering. From the European perspectives the mother is absent from the linguistic structure that expresses the transmission of history, and femininity can be expressed only in a challenge to history and in the invention of a new language, to be sought in contact with the mother's body, the "semiotic"; "l'écriture féminine" (Kristeva 1974; Cixous 1976; Irigaray 1974, 1977). From the American perspectives the mother is present in history, although this history has ignored and devalued the language of women. The feminine values that American society had neglected for the sake of a fictitious equality of men and women can be found in the little girl's pre-Oedipal relationship with her mother. The little girl internalizes this relationship and it ultimately constitutes the woman's self.

From a mythological perspective each group represented itself differently. European feminists invoked Antigone, the rebellious daughter who became a heroine in the defiance of the patriarchal state (Feral 1978). The American feminists instead appealed to the figure of Demeter and Persephone or kore, revealing their need to reevaluate the mother-daughter relationship and its history (Rich 1976; Gilligan 1982).

The feminist psychoanalytic theories testify to a theoretical difference, stemming from different historical and cultural approaches, but demonstrating the common goal of research into and comprehension of femininity. This goal should enhance communication and confrontation, and prevent the disconnection that can only lead to a fragmentation and a polarity of scientific differences. While the feminist reappropriation of psychoanalysis may be expressed differently on either side of the Atlantic, it still shares the common purpose of giving back to psychoanalysis the political and cultural force it originally had.

The chapters in the book were chosen to illustrate the evolution of scientific thought on female sexuality, and to address the conceptual and interpretive development of the questions defined by Freud—castration, penis envy, wish for a child, homosexuality, masochism, and superego formation. Since it would be impossible to publish all the contributions important to the development of the theory of female sexuality, I will instead summarize the history and the concepts of the arguments.

Freud first alluded to female sexuality in *Three Essays on the Theory of Sexuality* (1905), in which he affirmed the theory of sexual monism which he would maintain until the end, despite arguments to the contrary by other psychoanalysts (Jones, Horney, Klein). In subsequent publications Freud explained his theories on the child's Oedipus complex (1923, 1924b, 1925). Like the little boy, the little girl has a primary masculine (phallic) sexuality; unaware of the vagina's existence, she experiences her clitoris as a small penis. When she discovers the anatomical distinction between the sexes she feels inferior and experiences penis envy. The little girl blames her mother for her genital inferiority, rejecting her and becoming her rival. She then turns to the father for reparation, desiring from him first a penis and then a child. The wish for a child is merely a substitute for her desire to have the penis, and the attachment to the father results from penis envy. Her wish to become pregnant derives from penis envy, rather than from a firm identification with the mother. Although Freud acknowledges the existence of the superego in girls, he believes that it is formed with some difficulty since the girl is already castrated and therefore has no fear of castration. External factors such as education, intimidation, and the fear of no longer being loved must be invoked, in contrast to the internalized prohibitions that form the boy's superego.

In ''Female Sexuality'' (1931), Freud confirms Brunswick's (1929) and Lampl-de Groot's (1927) concept of a pre-Oedipal phase:

It would seem as though we must retract the universality of the thesis that the Oedipus complex is the nucleus of the neurosis. We can take due account of our new findings by saying that the female only reaches the normal positive Oedipus situation after she has surmounted a period before it that is governed by the negative complex. (226)

This theory emphasizes the attachment to the mother in psychological formation and opens a highly significant chapter in the study of female sexuality. According to Freud, female psychosexual development is more problematic than male because women must go through two difficult developments. In order to become a woman, a little girl must change her leading erotogenic zone from clitoris to vagina, and her love object from mother to father. Freud recognizes the concept of bisexuality in his early writings (1905). In "Female Sexuality" (1931) he emphasizes bisexuality more in women than in men. Yet right when this concept could have been reinterpreted in the context of the earliest pre-Oedipal undifferentiated phase, Freud neglects the concept of bisexuality and identifies this phase as phallic for both sexes. In this article Freud refutes Klein's concept of an early Oedipus complex (Klein 1928) and the theses of Horney (1924) and Jones (1927) that a reactive and therefore secondary formation of the female phallic stage exists that conceals feelings toward the father.

Freud restates all of his previous viewpoints on the psychosexual development of women in "Femininity" (1933); here he further emphasizes the importance of the castration complex and the masculinity of the libido. In "Analysis Terminable and Interminable" (1937) Freud maintains that the repudiation of femininity "can be nothing else than a biological fact, a part of the great riddle of sex" (252). By affirming the existence of a biological "bedrock" which repudiates femininity, Freud prevents a discussion of female sexuality.

Freud's association of femininity with masochism derived from the inherent suppositions of his view of feminine development (1924b, 1925, 1931, 1933) and from his explicit statements about feminine masochism: "Feminine masochism . . . is the one that is more accessible to our observation and least problematical and it can be surveyed in all its relations" (1924a, 161). After introducing the concept he stated: "This feminine masochism which we have described is entirely based on the primary erotogenic masochism, on pleasure in pain" (1924a, 162).

Freud's exposition of feminine masochism was less influential than the work of Helene Deutsch (1930, 1944) and Marie Bonaparte (1935, 1953). Deutsch explains masochism as the diverting of active instincts originally cathected in the clitoris. She maintains that the erotic active/sadistic instincts are transformed into masochistic instincts: the narcissistic/masculine desire to have a penis is substituted by the desire to be castrated by the father, and fantasized as a rape. A woman's life is therefore dominated by a masochistic triad: castration = rape = parturition (1930). A woman can only achieve femininity through maternity.

The theories of Horney (1924, 1926, 1932, 1933) and Jones (1927, 1933, 1935), disagree with Freud's theoretical monism, but not with his views on the biological origin of sexuality. At the 1922 Berlin conference, Horney presented the first of numerous papers (published in 1924) which disagreed with Freudian phallocentrism and engaged in more study of women. Horney identified two causes for penis envy. The primary penis envy is related to three pregenital components: the overestimation of the excretory process in children; the exhibitionistic and scopophilic wishes in which the little boy has an advantage due to the visibility of his organ; and the boy's ability to handle his genitals during urination, which the girl perceives as a permission to masturbate. The second cause relates to the implied existence of an intrinsic feminine sexual pleasure. Horney (1924) considered fundamental the girl's basic fantasy of having suffered castration through the love relation with the father. She emphasizes the little girl's disappointed wish for her father to give her a child, resulting in a displacement in which the "penis had become the object of envy in place of the child" (47). According to her later thesis, vaginal sensations exist from the time of birth, but the little girl later represses them for fear of her mother, on whom she projected aggressive wishes, and for fear of a narcissistic wound inherent in Oedipal wishes: "The undiscovered vagina is a vagina denied" (1933). Horney (1935) explained female masochism on the basis of the socioeconomic inferiority of women and as a consequence of their restricted life:

The problem of feminine masochism cannot be related to factors inherent in the anatomical-physiological-psychic characteristics of women alone, but must be considered as importantly conditioned by the culture-complex or social organization in which the particular masochistic woman has developed. (233)

Ernest Jones confirmed the secondary defensive construction of the phallic phase (1927); he followed Horney's thesis and underlined the prejudices of analysts who shared Freud's phallocentricism and underestimated the importance of the female organs. Jones replaced the fear of castration by both sexes with the fear of complete loss of sexuality (aphanisis), which originated in the nonfulfillment of Oedipal wishes. To him, guilt and the superego are an internal defense against aphanisis rather than external formations.

Melanie Klein made an important contribution to the discourse on female sexuality (1928, 1932, 1945). To explain her position we need to mention certain revisions she brought to Freudian theory that led to a new orientation in psychoanalysis. She identified an early stage of the Oedipus complex in a child's infancy. In her psychoanalytic work with children she recognized the presence of genital excitation in the first months of life, thereby refuting Freud's sequence of stages. The oral impulses initially lead the orchestra of polymorphous urges; along with the urethral and anal zones, they over-shadow the genitals for a period, so that genital excitations are in part linked with pregenital phantasies. However in the second half of the first year genital stirrings strengthen, and the wish for genital gratification comes to include the wish to receive and to give a child. It is to this phase that Klein attributes the origin of the unconscious equation of breast, penis, faeces, child, and so forth, and the theories of infantile sexuality, which Freud had discovered and related instead to the three- to five-year-old child.

Klein acknowledges the presence of the primary instincts of life and death identified by Freud, but she gives greater importance to the death instinct, that the child manifests in aggressive and cruel impulses. Klein also develops the concept of "unconscious phantasies," which are inborn and therefore present in the infant from the beginning of its life; they are the most primitive psychic formations inherent to the operation of the instinctual urges. Unconscious phantasies are associated with the infant's experience of pleasure or pain, happiness or anxiety; they involve its relationships with objects. They are dynamic processes because they are charged with the energy of the instinctual impulses, and they influence the development of the ego mechanism. The mother, on whom the child is extremely dependent, becomes a good or a hostile image in the unconscious phantasies, depending on the projections the child develops out of the phantasy of expelling an object. Klein gives the mother greater importance than did previous theorists. The mother is an internal bodily space containing the breast, the children, and the father's penis; these elements of the masculine and the feminine are confused in the mother and differentiated only at a later Oedipal stage.

Klein approaches Jones's and Horney's theories on the differences between the sexual development of the little boy and of the little girl. Klein disagrees with Freud that the woman's wish for a child is secondary to her wish to possess a penis. The little girl's frustration at no longer having the mother's nourishing breast makes her hate the mother and want to steal the father's penis from her and introject it in herself. Contrary to Freud's theory, the little girl does not want to possess the father's penis as her own masculine attribute (for narcissistic reasons), but rather to introject the penis as an object of oral satisfaction.

The nucleus of early Oedipal conflict lies in the passage from the cathexis of the frustrating breast to that of the penis. In the genital aspects of the girl's early Oedipal phantasies the oral desire for the paternal penis is seen as belonging to the mother, who keeps it inside her body. The little girl wishes therefore to sadistically attack her mother in order to steal from her the object she desires for herself. She fears that the mother's retributions will destroy her own internal organs. The girl's grievances against her mother for withholding the penis from her and sending her in the world as an incomplete creature (penis envy) are based on her need to deny her attacks on the mother's body and on her rivalry with both parents. She protests that she never was greedy, never usurped the mother's position with father, and never robbed her of the father's love, penis, and children. Klein found that little girls at this stage have vaginal sensations and not just clitoral sensations. The phantasies that accompany the vaginal urges have a specifically feminine character: "The female child is brought under the sway of her Oedipus impulses not indirectly, through her masculine tendencies and her penis envy, but directly, as a result of her dominant feminine instinctual components" (1932, 196).

Since the little girl's phallicism is largely a secondary and defensive phenomenon, she develops penis envy at the expense of femininity. She disowns her vagina and thinks that only the penis has genital qualities. She hopes that her clitoris will grow into a penis, but she is disappointed. The devaluation of femininity underlies this overestimation of the penis. For Klein penis envy is not Freud's "biological bedrock." The way an infant first relates to the maternal breast determines penis envy. The penis can also be the object of intense aggression due to the frustration it causes the little girl; by projecting this aggression into the penis, it becomes dangerous (the bad penis), cruel and threatening. The introjection of this penis forms the nucleus of the paternal superego in both sexes. Because of her receptive female instinctual impulses the little girl tends to introject and keep the father's penis, i.e., the Oedipal object. Through submission to the introjected father the girl's superego becomes still more powerful and more severe than that of the boy. The little girl has to face more obstacles than the little boy in forming a superego through introjection of the parent of the same sex: "It is difficult for her to identify herself with her mother on the basis of an anatomical resemblance owing to the fact that the internal organs . . . do not admit of any investigation or test by reality'' (1932, 235).

For Klein ''the deepest root of feminine masochism would seem to be the woman's fear of the dangerous object she has internalized; and her masochism would ultimately be none other than her sadistic instincts turned inward against those internalized objects'' (1932, 202).

The concept of the little girl's original femininity and the concept of penis envy as a secondary formation separate Klein from Freud as do her concept of the formation of the superego and her representation of masochism.

In subsequent literature on female sexuality psychoanalysis continued its emphasis on the initial phase of the child's life, partly due to the enormous importance of Klein's object relations theory. Ruth Mack Brunswick's article (1940), written in collaboration with Freud, focuses more on the pre-Oedipal phase and on the importance of the mother as the principle of activity. The little girl's desire for a child precedes penis envy and is linked to the desire to possess the attributes of the omnipotent mother. Therefore penis envy is not motivated solely by the narcissistic urge to have that which one does not have, but also by the object-oriented cause of possessing the mother.

Janine Chasseguet-Smirgel (1964, 1976) adopts an articulate and complex Freudian perspective that incorporates Klein's concept of the child's extreme dependence on a mother experienced as omnipotent. She reaffirms the father's importance in the woman's psychosexual development, and maintains that the Oedipus complex, with all its difficulties and obstacles, is also a woman's ''crux of neurosis.'' The little girl's relationship with her father is influenced by her original relationship with her mother. Chasseguet-Smirgel (1964) identifies the features that help to form a specific sense of feminine guilt. She traces the traits of female sexuality—penis envy, masochism, superego formation, and the dissolution of the Oedipus complex—to the sense of guilt that results both from a woman's struggle to free herself of an omnipotent mother and from repressed aggressiveness toward an idealized father. Penis envy is primary; it constitutes a revolt against the omnipotent mother who inflicted a narcissistic wound that can only be healed through possession of the penis. Masochism is linked to her guilt for trying to sadoanally introject the penis. In the little girl's attempt to free herself from her mother and need to protect her father, she offers herself to him as a part-object playing the role of ''the other person's thing'' (1964, 131). In this way she refuses to take the place of her mother, whom she sadistically represents next to the father, and she denies her female sexuality. The superego is tied to an identification with the father's penis, like a heavily internalized eleventh commandment which orders "You may not have your own law, your law is the object law" (1964, 132).

Penis envy is interpreted differently by Maria Torok (1964). She instead emphasizes its metaphoric significance. The woman idealizes the penis to express an unfulfillable female sexual desire, which she would sacrifice for fear of losing the mother's love. It therefore represents an oath of faithfulness to the mother.

The British object relations school proposes that object relations, which have been internalized by the vicissitudes of affects, structure the unconscious. This perspective avoids emphasis on the biological terms of sexual differentiation. Marjorie Brierley (1932, 1936) tried to integrate her dynamic whole person approach with Freud's and Klein's formulations about early female development. Brierley addresses the problems of ego-development in women which allowed a different integration of feminine and masculine drives common to both sexes. "If we ever achieve a psychological definition of femininity it looks as if it might have to be a definition in terms of types of integration" (1932, 447). In 1936 Brierley emphasized the equation of the vagina with the mouth, pointing out that vaginal contractions were sometimes associated with suckling: "These impulses may perhaps be regarded as primary, because they arise in the genital system itself." "As far as the raw material of instinct is concerned, then, we may say tentatively that we have one determinant which is qualitatively specific to the female, and the possibility of a number of quantitative variations common to both sexes" (1936, 165). Sylvia Payne (1935) in a Kleinian framework analyzes femininity and passivity. "The sexual aims of the little girl which refer to her mother are both active and passive in kind, and they are determined by the phases of the libido through which she passes. From the child's behaviour we can judge the relative strength of the masculinity or femininity which will one day appear in its sexuality" (1935, 18). She adds: "A study of the nature of the impulses which determine cultural pursuits reveals the fact that feminine drives are as important as masculine. . . . Further, owing the fact that our present civilization regards masculine qualities as more valuable than feminine, it stands to reason that the influence of the environment favours the successful repression of feminine tendencies in man, and fosters the growth of masculine aspirations in women" (1935, 19). D. W. Winnicott (1966) analyzes the masculine and feminine elements and identifies their differences.

The male element is characterized by impulses related to objects that have the quality of "being not me," separate. The male element's relating to the object presupposes separateness and originates the experience of doing. By contrast, the pure female element relates to the breast (or to the mother) in the sense that the object is the subject. The first object is "not yet repudiated as not-me phenomenon" (80). In this treatment of the subjective object, the female element's object relating establishes "what is perhaps the simplest of all experiences, the experience of being" (80). Being, a primordial space of being created solely by the mother, is the beginning of creativity, not as a creative production, but as a real sense of one's self. In Winnicott's definition, "Masculinity does, femininity is."

The British school that followed Anna Freud's theory incorporated the viewpoint of object relatedness into a Freudian position. Rose Edgcumbe (1976) analyzed data taken from the analyses of little girls at the Hampstead Clinic and found that "the concept of a negative Oedipal phase is seldom used . . . because the concept does not accurately fit the observable clinical evidence" (45). Rose Edgcumbe and Marion Burgner suggest that "it might be more appropriate to describe the early phallic phase as narcissistic for both sexes, rather than as negative oedipal for the girl" (1975, 162). They see a difference between this early phase and the Oedipal phase. In the phallic narcissistic phase the real or fantasied use of the genitals serves primarily exhibitionistic and narcissistic purposes and "the one-to-one relationship is still dominant since the rivalry of triangular oedipal relationship is not yet developed" (162).

I have included Lacanian analysis in the book because of its centrality to thought on female sexuality by European feminist psychoanalysts. Lacan's symbolic reading of Freud helped these theorists to reappropriate the concept of the unconscious and use it as a political force for change.

Jacques Lacan (1957–58) criticizes Kleinian orientations and returns to a Freudian position. He engages in a symbolic reading of the unconscious, which in his view is structured like a language—a language that represents the values of a patriarchal society symbolized by the phallus. He believes psychoanalysis concentrated increasingly on the adequacies and inadequacies of the mother-child relationship—an emphasis that tends to comply with the idea of a maternal role—because it failed to grasp the concept of the symbolic. The concept of castration was central to Lacan because of its constant reference to paternal law. Castration means that the child's desire for the mother does not refer to her but beyond her, to an object, the phallus, whose status is first imaginary (presuming that the object satisfies her desire) and then symbolic (recognizing that desire cannot be satisfied). The mother is presumed to desire the phallus not because she contains it (Klein), but precisely because she does not. The phallus stands outside the mother-child dyad until the moment of the Oedipus complex, at which point in the child's psychic development the phallus creates a third term in the family and brings the family into the social order.

Lacan returns to the concept not of the Oedipal father, but to that of the primal father with absolute phallic power. The phallus is "the paternal metaphor: The link between the Name of the Father, insofar as he can at times be missing, and the father whose effective presence is not always necessary for him not to be missing" (Lacan 1957–58, 8).

Lacan's position presents two alternative emphases—one on the actual behavior of the mother by herself (adequacy and inadequacy), and the other on a literally present or absent father (his idealization and/or deficiency). The French reading of Freud has located a particularly troublesome textual knot in psychoanalytic investigation of sexual difference and female sexuality. Lacan has declared the need to define this problem in "Guiding Remarks for a Congress in Feminine Sexuality" (1958b). Lacan's most concise articulation of a theory of sexual difference appears in "The Signification of the Phallus" (1958a). The chapter chosen to represent Lacan in the book was published in 1975 in *Scilicet*, no. 5, but rewritten in 1976 by Moustafa Safouan of the Lacanian school. Safouan systematized the audacity out of Lacan and made his abstract theories more accessible. He emphasizes "first, that phallicism is an unconscious phenomenon . . . which has nothing natural about it for the boy any more so than for the girl, and . . . secondly, the common root of the phallic function in its relation to discourse" (1976, 135).

The last chapter in the European section deals with female homosexuality, a topic still subject to varying interpretations. Psychoanalytic theories consider homosexuality a sexual aberration. Freud explained that the negative complex in girls does not always have a normal dissolution. The little girl may stay attached to her mother and deny castration. If she is disappointed by the father, she may turn away from him and return to her previous position, to her masculine attitude. In extreme cases this can lead to homosexuality, as he demonstrated in "The Psychogenesis of a Case of Female Homosexuality" (1920). Jones (1927) believed that Freud's description of an identical phallic stage for boys and for girls, both of whom are unaware of the vagina, is nothing other than this defense of homosexual women in an attenuated form and like it, essentially a secondary phenomenon. That this defense assumes such importance as to lead to homosexuality may result from particularly intense sadism at the oral stage. Jones distinguished between two groups of homosexual women: those who are still interested in men but would like to be considered as one of them, and those who are not interested in men but in women, since women represent the femininity that they themselves have not been able to enjoy directly. Women of the first group have chosen to give up their sex but to keep the object. In this case the woman has identified with her father and desires to be loved by him by making him acknowledge her virility. The women of the second group identify with the father but then give him up as an object. But in reality their external object relation to a woman is based on the fact that their partner represents their projected femininity, which is satisfied by the internal object (the incorporated father, object of their identification).

Joyce McDougall (1964, 1978) adopts this distinction between two different expressions of female homosexuality. In both types she sees a refusal to identify with the genital mother, but she also emphasizes the differences of original family structures (1964). McDougall (1964, 1978) explains female homosexuality as an attempt to maintain a narcissistic equilibrium by conserving an unconscious identification with the father in order to escape from the dangerous symbiotic relationship claimed by the mother imago (1964). She focuses on the pregenital conflicts before the Oedipal significance of sexual differences is acknowledged (1964, 1978). For the homosexual woman, "the father (or his penis) comes to represent a protection from the all controlling 'anal' mother or from being engulfed by a devouring 'oral' mother, protection therefore against the primitive anxiety associated with these images" (1964, 172). "The idealized aspects of the maternal imago are sought in the female partner" (1964, 172). Recently (1989) McDougall changed her theoretical perspective on female homosexuality from a Kleinian perspective focused on the dyad (mother and daughter) to a Freudian approach (with some Lacanian conceptualizations) focused on the triangle (parents and child). She acknowledges Stoller's theory of core gender and sexual identity (1968b), focusing on the role played by the psychic representations of the parents as a couple on the development of homosexual identity. "Psychoanalysis has specific contribution to make on the study of aberrations in core gender identity and in the established sense of one's sexual role, in so far as these have their roots in the experiences of early childhood and the unconscious problems of parents." McDougall adopts and develops the

Freudian concept of bisexuality. She recognizes the role of the homosexual drama together with the heterosexual Oedipal crisis in the development of a sexual identity and in the establishment of one's sexual role. "But there is also the homosexual oedipal drama which also implies a double aim, that of having exclusive possession of the same sex parent and that of being the parent of the opposite sex." "Thus the psychic representation of the parental couple, as well as their words, may either help or hinder the child in its attempts to give up universal wishes of both bisexual and incestuous nature, and may indeed favour a deviant representation of the small individual's developing sense of core gender and sexual identity role" (1989, 206). McDougall presents a case history in which she analyzes the relation between the loss of the psychic representation of father in a woman and her homosexual identity. If the father is symbolically lost, absent or dead in the little girl's inner world, she becomes the lost father through a process of primitive internalization." In seeking to possess the mental representation of two parents, capable of conferring upon her the status of subjective and of sexual identity, it appeared that the price to be paid was her own castration—the loss of her femininity." (1989, 217). This perspective leaves flexible interplay for the child's sexual identification.

The articles in the American section provide an interpretation of the female psychosexual development that focuses more on ego formation than on unconscious processes, and more on the influence of culture and society on feminine identity. American psychoanalytic literature has shown a greater interest in women than has European. In addition American psychoanalysts have dedicated more attention to the direct observation of infants in their research, making an enormous contribution to psychoanalysis. The chapters chosen represent only a small part of the scientific literature.

The American section begins with a chapter by Edith Jacobson, which she wrote in Europe in 1937 and republished in the United States in 1976. Jacobson adheres to the Freudian position on the superego, but is more open to the idea of women changing themselves. She focuses on the contradictions between theory, which she herself accepts, and clinical practice, which sometimes reveal women "who show eruptions of cruel superego demands," demonstrating that "the female superego is much more complicated than we commonly assume" (525–26). She also underlines "the lack of uniformity in the female personality" (527) and stresses the changes in a woman who is acquiring a new identity. The contradictions Jacobson described led in more recent times to the criticism of the classical theories on the superego by

Schafer (1974), Blum (1976), Applegarth (1976), and Bernstein (1983). For them it is not that a woman's superego is inferior or that a man's superego is superior, but just that they are different.

Annie Reich (1940) in her article gives an interpretation of the women's extreme submissiveness as a masochistic perversion which is structured from infantile frustrations in the relationship with the mother. "The hostility which had been repressed was explosively discharged upon herself during intercourse through identification with the brutal sadistic man" (1940, 476). There is in the submissive woman an identification with the aggressor and an idealization of the partner in the attempting to recreate the sensation of ecstasy of the "magic fusion with the mother."

Clara Thompson (1941, 1942, 1943) explained the cultural complications which affect a woman's development, and she interpreted the weakness of the woman's superego "as an attitude typical of people who have found that their security depends on approval of some powerful person or group" (1942, 237). From this cultural perspective penis envy is a concept which offers women "an explanation for their feelings of inadequacy by referring it to an evidently irremediable cause. In the same way, it offers the man a justification for his aggression against her" (1943, 54). Envy is characteristic of a competitive culture. It implies comparison to one's advantage" (1943, 55).

Phyllis Greenacre gave an important contribution to the study of female sexuality. In the 1950s Greenacre used the case studies of her adult female patients to prove the existence of early vaginal sensations and prepubescent vaginal awareness. She distinguished between two phases of genital awareness in little girls. In the pregenital phase the little girl's realization of genital difference means more to her sense of self-worth and to her attempt to differentiate herself from her mother. At a later stage the problem becomes Oedipal and she conceptualizes her narcissistic injury in sexual terms (1950, 1952).

Judith Kestenberg (1956a, 1956b, 1968) acknowledges inner genital sensations in both sexes in early childhood and the anxiety-provoking nature of these sensations. The wish for a baby is based in boys and girls on the underlying desire to master the inner genital organ. The girl, however, depends more than a boy on the external objects to alleviate her inner genital sensations, being more vulnerable to fear of injury and loss of the inside genital. Like Erikson (1964), who wrote about the centrality of inner space in females, Kestenberg emphasizes the role of the inner genital awareness in the girl's development. The little girl tries to overcome her confusion about vaginal impulses externalizing them, at first to her doll-baby and later, in the phallic phase, to a penis. Kestenberg proposes "that the universal repudiation of femininity is based on the anxiety-provoking nature of the inner genital sensations" (1968, 102).

Esther Menaker analyzed the theme of moral masochism in a frame of ego development. She views "the problem of masochism from the standpoint of the self-preservative functions of the ego" (1953, 207). In her chapter she addresses the importance of the mother's attitudes in the development of the child's ego: "The potentiality of loving or hating the self is thus contained in the destiny of the development of the ego functions, which in turn depends on the mother's attitude toward them" (1953, 209). Furthermore:

The hatred of the self, originating at the earliest level of ego differentiation, and the accompanying feelings of powerlessness become the prototype for later feelings of worthlessness which characterize the moral masochist. These very feelings are used in the service of the ego to protect it from the fear to be abandoned, and to gain for it a fantasized gratification of love. (109)

Menaker does not associate masochism with femininity in her chapter, although she cites a woman's case as a clinical example. However her interpretation of masochism emphasizes the importance of the mother's attitude and the idealization that results from the child's incapacity to separate itself from the primary object. This breaks the ground for a different interpretation of female masochism tied to the feminist psychoanalytic perspectives based on the mother's transmission of different values to the daughter and to the son (Chodorow 1978). Menaker's interpretation, together with Stoller's (1975, 1979) and Khan's (1979) that focus on masochism issues as object loss and separation, and those of Kohut (1975), and Stolorow and Lachmann (1980) that focus on the merger with an ideal object as an attempt to ward off self dissolution, allow for the association of masochism with the feminine in a new feminist psychoanalytical interpretation (Benjamin 1983, 1986, 1988).

In a drive theory context on the other hand Blum's article on female masochism maintained that there is no evidence of a particular feminine pleasure in pain, pointing out that the classical views did not distinguish the willingness to bear pain in the service of a higher goal from perverse, self-destructive acquiescence to abuse. "Therefore masochism is not essentially feminine, and it is a residue of an unresolved infantile conflict representing a tolerance for a discomfort or deprivation in the service of the ego or ego ideal" (1976, 188).

Some theories on the psychosexual development of women were verified by direct observation of little girls; their findings either confirmed or disputed theoretical assumptions, and led at times to new theories. For example, the theory that the wish for a child exists prior to penis envy proposed by Kestenberg, and before her by Horney, Jones, and Klein, was confirmed by the research of Parens et al. (1976). The research of Galenson and Roiphe (1974) and Kleeman (1976) confirmed the theory of a pre-Oedipal awareness of the vagina in little girls, which had also been proposed by Horney, Jones, and Klein, and to which Greenacre (1950, 1952) had dedicated much literature.

Stoller's studies represent a very important development in the field of psychoanalysis, especially in the United States (1968a, 1968b). His theory of a "core gender identity" predating the discovery of the anatomical differences between the sexes influenced psychoanalytic literature and the new psychoanalytic thoughts of American feminists. Stoller suggested that "the earliest phases of women's identity—the core gender identity—is the simple acceptance of the body ego, 'I am a female' " (1968a, 54). Only later will this be covered over by penis envy, identification with the male, and other signs of femininity. "This core of femininity develops regardless of chromosomal state or anatomy of the genitalia so long as the parents have no doubt their infant is a female" (1968a, 54). This focus on gender identity led psychoanalysis to examine the results of "imprinting" on a woman's psychological development (Fast 1984; Person 1980).

Currently there are different perspectives on the importance and the meaning of penis envy. According to early psychoanalysis, the little girl seldom recovers from her narcissistic injury, and her subsequent female development remains secondary to penis envy (Freud 1925). Recent theories instead view penis envy as a phasic-specific developmental phenomenon. Grossman and Stewart (1976) consider penis envy "the manifest content of a symptom that needs analysis," rather than as "bedrock" or as ultimate conflict (1976, 211). They agree with Torok's earlier theory, which from a different perspective gives penis envy a metaphoric significance.

Heinz Kohut's self psychology shares the classical emphasis on the little girl's narcissistic wound, but he does not find it related to the later desire for a child:

I believe that the healthy woman's wish for a child is . . . manifestation of her nuclear self, as a manifestation of her most central ambitions and ideals, as the high point of a development that has its beginning in the archaic self's urge toward self expression. (1975, 786)

In 1984 Kohut confirmed:

The girl's rejection of femininity, her feeling of being castrated and inferior, and her intense wish for a penis arise not because the male sex organs are psychobiologically more desirable than the female ones, but because the little girl's self objects failed to respond to her with appropriate mirroring, since either no idealizable female imago was available to her, or that no alter ego gave her support during the childhood years when a proud feminine self should have established itself. (1984, 21)

These diverse interpretations demonstrate how the meaning of Freudian theories can change according to cultural and social values and how these values are expressed not only in theory, but also in therapy, by both the analyst and the analysand. The case of female sexuality exemplifies this situation and "encourages us to distinguish systematically between the contingent and the universal" (Person 1983, 49).

Person's chapter emphasizes that psychoanalysis is a science, and as such is susceptible to change from outside forces. Her chapter breaks the ground of the acceptance of new theories on female sexuality, which developed following the political question of women. The women's liberation movement had changed the feminine image, thereby requiring an interpretation of the psychosexual development of women which better corresponded to this new image not only in social and cultural changes, but also in the acquired consciousness of femininity and its conflicts.

The section on Feminism and Psychoanalysis includes both European and American contributions that reread psychoanalytic thought but also manifest theoretical continuity. The articles are psychoanalytically oriented but they do not belong exclusively to psychoanalytic literature. They aim to widen perspectives by taking an interdisciplinary approach, a principle that feminism has supported.

The feminist movement's reappropriation of psychoanalytic thought began in Europe, with the 1974 publication of Juliet Mitchell's *Psycho-Analysis and Feminism,* a new reading of Freud based on Lacanian theory. This book created the possibility of new interpretations and new uses of psychoanalytic theory. In separate works Dinnerstein (1976) and Chodorow (1978) reappropriated the object relations theory and brought a new perspective to the pre-

Oedipal issue of separation-individuation in the mother-child relationship (Mahler et al. 1975).

This book acknowledges the historical priority of Mitchell's book by considering first the European chapters and then the American ones. The European chapters refer to Lacan, who considered the unconscious to be structured like language, and therefore representative of a patriarchal society. This symbolic reading allowed feminist psychoanalysts to understand the repression of femininity that cannot be expressed through a language or through values that it does not recognize.

Within this framework, Mitchell reconsiders Freudian theory and notices a repression of femininity in his reading of the unconscious. For Mitchell the unconscious is structured in the terms of patriarchy's kinship, and it represents women's deep-rooted acquiescence to patriarchal ideology. Mitchell states that in *Totem and Taboo* (1913) and in *Moses and Monotheism* (1939) Freud's description of the unconscious:

is a concept of mankind's transmission and inheritance of his social (cultural) laws. . . . Understanding the laws of the unconscious thus amounts to a start in understanding how ideology functions, how we acquire and live the ideas and laws within which we must exist. A primary aspect of the law is that we live according to our sexed identity, our ever imperfect "masculinity" or "femininity" (1974, 403).

Mitchell identifies an unconscious which represses femininity at the same time as she reconsiders it as the only place where repressed femininity can perhaps be retraced. Mitchell studied the repression of femininity in men and women in a society dominated by the father's laws, and upholds Freud's concept of bisexuality (1984).

By contrast, Luce Irigaray views femininity as an exclusively feminine quality which a male society represses. "She is left with a void, a lack of all presentation, representation, and even strictly speaking of all mimesis of her desire for origin. That desire will henceforth pass through the discourse-desire-law of man's desire" (1974, 42). Women's femininity is provided in essence by their sexual organs. Irigaray implies that men and their needs alienate women from their specifically feminine desire, a desire rooted to their bodies. "A woman's autoeroticism," she writes, "which she needs in order not to risk the disappearance of her pleasure in the sex act, is interrupted by a violent intrusion: the brutal spreading of these two lips by a violating penis" (1977, 100). Women are not only alienated from their essential femininity by social and sexual intercourse with men, but they are also alienated from their own sexuality by the way male discourse represents it as lacking in women. Irigaray maintains that female homosexuality can be a temporary strategic necessity for women "to learn to defend their desire, especially through speech, to discover the love of other women . . . to forge for themselves a social status that compels recognition, to earn their living in order to escape from the condition of prostitute" (1977, 106). Irigaray followed Lacan but she was expelled from his school for criticizing Lacanian phallocentrism; she accused psychoanalysis of representing a male discourse in its repression/exclusion of the female subject and her desire (1974, 1977, 1987).

Michèle Montrelay (1977) followed Lacanian thought, but reinterpreted it from a feminist perspective. She returned to the debate between Freud and Jones on female sexuality, referring specifically to women's access to language and to the process of symbolization. She attempted to resolve Freud's stand on the masculine libido and Jones's stand on a specific feminine libido by equating them with two stages in feminine psychosexual development. Femininity thus becomes the passage from a concentric psychic economy (preconscious femininity) to an economy in which symbolic castration has achieved representation with the entrance of woman to the "signifying order" and with the repression of the "preconscious femininity." The access to symbolization is considered a sublimated sexual pleasure which depends on the transition from the first to the second economy. If this transition fails—it never is fully actuated—the woman remains outside significance. Sublimation allows her instead to metaphorically represent not only pleasure, but also the orgasm which helps rupture, explode the significance of discourse.

In "Women's Time" (1979) Julia Kristeva distanced herself from her earlier perspective which was focused on the search for a language outside of the symbolic order, an exclusively feminine language to be retraced in the preverbal which she called "the semiotic" (1974). She insisted on a recognition of the way sexual difference is treated by psychoanalysis, but she argues that feminism must be reconciled with femininity and motherhood (cyclical time) and with the symbolic order (linear time, historical time). Kristeva emphasizes the multiplicity of female expressions and distinguishes between two generations of feminists, those who asked for equal rights with men (a place in linear time) and those who asked (after 1968) to remain outside of history (outside linear time). Kristeva noted the danger of this second position, which could easily degenerate into an inverse form of sexism, and the need to reconcile the masculine and the feminine.

The American theorists also focused on the repudiation of femininity, but they emphasized the importance of the social construct in the devaluation of the feminine rather than the repressive dynamics of the unconscious. Based on the Oedipal complex, Freud's theory demonstrates how little boys become men by repudiating their primary identification with the mother and thereby repudiating femininity. This model presupposes an identification with paternal authority, and it is accepted by the patriarchal culture; it identifies the ideal concept of autonomy with separation and distance, excluding mutuality, dependency, connectedness, and nurture, which are linked to the relationship with the mother. American feminist psychoanalysis has focused on pre-Oedipal time, and it investigates early identifications and experiences of the children with the mother.

The American section begins with a chapter from Dorothy Dinnerstein's book *The Mermaid and the Minotaur* (1976), which constituted the first example in the United States of a feminist psychoanalytic theoretical reading. Dinnerstein adopts a Kleinian perspective which emphasizes the mother's omnipotence in an asymmetrical family structure from which the father is absent. She argues that due to our present child-care system (in which the infants are primarily looked after by women), children permanently sidestep the task of working through the persecutory and depressive anxiety which Klein believes is involved in developing a more realistic sense of themselves and of the mother, and involved in recognizing their independence and freedom from her. Children instead retain into adulthood their infantile sense of the mother as "engulfing" and "nebulously overwhelming." Rather than seize freedom, women avoid the pain it would involve by turning from the "quasi-magical" woman of their infancy to a dependency on men who, because they are relatively uninvolved in infant care, are not imbued as women are with the primitive fantasies of the child. Dinnerstein sees a solution to this situation in the greater participation of fathers in the growth and education of children.

In 1974 Nancy Chodorow proposed the same thesis from a psychosocial angle, attempting to account for "the reproduction within each generation of certain general and nearly universal differences that characterize masculine and feminine personality and roles." She attributes the differences between the sexes not to anatomy but rather to "the fact that women, universally are largely responsible for early child care" (1974, 43–44). Chodorow's book *The Reproduction of Mothering* (1978) represents an important theoretical development in understanding female difference from a feminist psychoanalytic perspective. She determines the differences of experience, identification, and transmission of values between mother and little girl and mother and little boy from the psychoanalytic perspective of the object relations theory which includes the concept of "core gender identity" (Stoller 1968b). Mothers experience their daughters because they are of the same sex, and more merged and identified with them than their sons. As a result they do not encourage them to have the same degree of "separation-individuation" (Mahler et al. 1975). A woman's gender identity is formed on a more personal basis than that of men; it is formed out of personal interaction with the women who looked after them in their infancy. "To speak of difference as a final, irreducible concept and to focus on gender differences as central is to reify them and to deny the reality of those processes which create the meaning and the significance of gender" (1979, 16). She continues the general themes presented in her book, and clarifies her theoretical differences with the European feminist psychoanalysts.

Since the beginning of the 1970s, Jean Baker Miller (1973, 1976) has dedicated herself to the study of women's psychology, trying to develop it into a clinical practice and not just a theoretical formulation (Stone Center for Developmental Services and Studies). She reaffirmed the concept of "self in relation," emphasizing "the extraordinarily important character of the interaction—that of attending to and responding to the other," noting that "it is in the basis of all continuing psychological growth, all growth occurring within emotional connections, not separate from them" (1984, 4). She accepted Erikson's concept (1950) of a psychological development which takes place throughout life, but she criticized this theory's focus on the principals of separation and self-development. She thus adopted, from a different perspective, Erikson's formulations "as a framework in the consideration of the few of the many futures in women's development" (1984, 2).

Jessica Benjamin follows Dinnerstein's and Chodorow's theories focused on the maternal identification of the girl and stresses the problem of woman's desire and the lack of its representation. She argues that what Freud saw as the little girl masculine orientation reflects the wish to identify with the father, who is perceived as a representative of the outside world, standing for freedom, separation, and desire. The early love of the father is an ideal love because he appears to be the solution of her impossibility to perceive the mother as an independent sexual subject. This idealization becomes the basis for future relationships of ideal love, the submission to a powerful other, who seems to embody the agency and desire. Masochism is reinterpreted, by Benjamin, as a feminine experience in its dimension of submission to an idealized other-ideal love. The girl, unable to create a representation of desire based on maternal identification, turns to an idealized love for a male figure, who represents desire. Benjamin challenges the structure of heterosexuality in our present gender system: "The structural conditions of gender that now exist do not allow for reconciliation of agency and desire with femininity" (1986, 134). "I believe that, given substantial alteration in gender expectations and parenting, both parents can be figures of separation and attachment for their children; that both boys and girls can make use of identifications with both parents, without being confused about their gender identity" (1988, 112).

Carol Gilligan (1977, 1982, 1986) notes the consequences of this different psychological development on the formation of the woman's superego. She believes in a feminine psychological development which takes place on the basis of the relation (self in relation). The difference of the woman's superego had already been determined by Schafer (1974), who did not accept the idea that the woman's superego was inferior. Gilligan's research described these differences from a feminist perspective grounded in a cognitive framework. In her book *In a Different Voice* (1982) she suggests that women impose a distinct construct on moral problems, and see moral dilemmas as cases of conflicting responsibilities. "In women a more complex understanding of the relationship between self and others represents a critical reinterpretation of the moral conflict between selfishness and responsibility" (1982, 515). She typifies both women's and men's moral reasoning: men supposedly reason in terms of individual rights, while women reason in terms of relational issues. She therefore believes in the presence of two predispositions which "inhere in the structure of human connection. These predispositions —toward justice and toward care—arise from the experience of inequality and attachment embedded in the relationship between child and parent" (1986, 238).

Gilligan maintains that "the elusive mystery of women's development lies in its recognition of the continuing importance of attachment in the human life cycle," and notes that "only when life-cycle theorists divide their attention and begin to live with women as they have lived with men will their vision encompass the experience of both sexes and their theories become correspondingly more fertile" (1982, 23).

BIBLIOGRAPHY

Applegarth, A. 1976. Some observations on work inhibition in women. *J. Amer. Psychoanal. Assn* 24,5 (Suppl.):251–68.
Benjamin, J. 1983. Master and slave: The fantasy of erotic domination. In *Power of desire,* edited by A. Snitow, C. Stansell, and S. Thompson, 280–99. New York: Monthly Review Press.
———. 1986. The alienation of desire: Women's masochism and ideal love. In *Psychoanalysis and women: Contemporary reappraisals,* edited by J. Alpert. Hillsdale, N.J.: Analytic Press.
———. 1988. *The bonds of love.* New York: Pantheon.
Bernstein, D. 1983. The female superego: A different perspective. *Int. J. Psycho-Anal.* 64: 187–202.
Blum, H. P. 1976. Masochism, the ego ideal, and the psychology of women. *J. Amer. Psychoanal. Assn.* 24,5 (Suppl.):157–92.
Bonaparte, M. 1935. Passivity, masochism, and femininity. *Int. J. Psycho-Anal.* 16:325–33.
———. 1953. *Female sexuality.* New York: International Universities Press.
Bowlby, J. 1958. The nature of the child's tie to the mother. *Int. J. Psycho-Anal.* 39:350–73.
———. 1969. *Attachment.* New York: Basic Books.
———. 1973. *Separation.* New York: Basic Books.
Brierley, M. 1932. Some problems of integration in women. *Int. J. Psycho-Anal.* 13:433–48.
———. 1936. Specific determinants in feminine development. *Int. J. Psycho-Anal.* 17:163–80.
Brunswick, R. M. 1929. The analysis of a case of paranoia. *J. of Nerv. and Ment. Dis.* 70:177.
———. 1940. The preoedipal phase of the libido development. *Psychoanal. Quarterly* 9: 293–319.
Chasseguet-Smirgel, J. 1964. Feminine guilt and the Oedipus complex. In *Female sexuality,* edited by J. Chasseguet-Smirgel, 94–134. Ann Arbor: University of Michigan Press, 1970.
———. 1976. Freud and female sexuality. *Int. J. Psycho-Anal.* 57:275–86.
Chodorow, N. 1974. Family structure and feminine personality. In *Women, culture, and society,* edited by M. Z. Rosaldo and L. Lamphere. Stanford: Stanford University Press.
———. 1978. *The reproduction of mothering.* Berkeley: University of California Press.
———. 1979. Difference, relation, and gender in psychoanalytic perspective. *Socialist Rev.* 9 (4):51–70. Also published as Gender, relation, and difference in psychoanalytic perspectives. In *The future of difference,* edited by H. Eisenstein and A. Jardine, 3–19. New Brunswick, N.J.: Rutgers University Press, 1985.
Cixous, H. 1976. *The laugh of the medusa.* Signs (Summer 1976):875–93.
Cixous, H., Gagnon M., and Leclerc, A. 1977. *La venue à l'écriture.* Paris: Union Générale d'editions, 10/18.
Deutsch, H. 1925. Psychology of women in relation to the function of reproduction. *Int. J. Psycho-Anal.* 6:405–18.
———. 1930. The significance of masochism in the mental life of women. *Int. J. Psycho-Anal.* 11:48–60.
———. 1944–45. *The psychology of women.* 2 vols. New York: Grune and Stratton.
Dinnerstein, D. 1976. *The mermaid and the minotaur.* New York: Harper and Row.
Edgcumbe, R. 1976. Some comments on the concept of the negative oedipal phase in girls. *Psychoanal. Study Child* 31:35–61.
Edgcumbe, R., and Burgner, M. 1975. The phallic-narcissistic phase. *Psychoanal. Study Child* 30:161–80.
Erikson, E. H. 1950. *Childhood and society.* New York: Norton.

————. 1964. Reflections on womanhood. *Daedalus* 2:582–606.

————. 1968. Womanhood and the inner space. In *Identity, youth, and crisis*, 261–95. New York: Norton.

Fast, I. 1984. *Gender identity*. Hillsdale, N.J.: Analytic Press.

Feral, J. 1978. Antigone or the irony of the tribe. *Diacritics* (Fall 1978):2–14.

Fermi, L. 1968. *Illustrious immigrants: The intellectual migration from Europe 1930–41*. Chicago: University of Chicago Press.

Firestone, S. 1970. *The dialectic of sex*. New York: Bantam Books.

Freud, A. 1936. *The ego and the mechanisms of defense*. New York: International Universities Press, 1966.

Freud, S. 1905. *Three essays on the theory of sexuality*. Standard Edition 7:135–243. London: Hogarth Press, 1953.

————. 1913. *Totem and taboo*. Standard Edition 13:1–161. London: Hogarth Press, 1961.

————. 1920. The psychogenesis of a case of female homosexuality. Standard Edition 18:145–72. London: Hogarth Press, 1955.

————. 1923. The infantile genital organization of the libido. Standard Edition 19:141–53. London: Hogarth Press, 1961.

———— 1924a. The economic problem of masochism. Standard Edition 19:159–72. London: Hogarth Press, 1961.

————. 1924b. The dissolution of the Oedipal complex. Standard Edition 19:173–82. London: Hogarth Press, 1961.

————. 1925. Some psychical consequences of the anatomical distinction between the sexes. Standard Edition 19:248–58. London: Hogarth Press, 1961.

————. 1931. Female sexuality. Standard Edition 21:225–43. London: Hogarth Press, 1961.

————. 1933. Femininity. Standard Edition 22:112–35. London: Hogarth Press, 1964.

————. 1937. Analysis terminable and interminable. Standard Edition 23:216–53. London: Hogarth Press, 1964.

————. 1939. *Moses and Monotheism: Three Essays*. Standard Edition 23:7–137. London: Hogarth Press, 1964.

————. 1940. *An outline of psychoanalysis*. Standard Edition 23:144–207. London: Hogarth Press, 1964.

Galenson, E., and Roiphe, H. 1974. The emergence of genital awareness during the second year of life. In *Sex differences in behavior*, edited by R. C. Friedman, R. M. Richard, and R. L. Vandewieli, 223–31. New York: Wiley.

————. 1976. Some suggested revisions concerning early female development. *J. Amer. Psychoanal. Assn* 24,5 (Suppl.):29–57.

Gilligan, C. 1977. In a different voice: Women's conceptions of self and morality. *Harvard Educational Review* 47:481–517.

————. 1982. *In a different voice*. Cambridge: Harvard University Press.

————. 1986. Remapping the moral domain: New images of the self in relationship. In *Reconstructing individualism*, edited by T. Heller et al. Stanford: Stanford University Press.

Greenacre, P. 1950. Special problems of early female sexual development. *Psychoanal. Study Child* 5:112–38.

————. 1952. Some factors producing different types of genital and pregenital emotional organization. In *Trauma, growth, and personality*, 293–302. New York: International Universities Press, 1969.

Grossman, W. I., and Stewart, W. 1976. Penis envy: From childhood wish to developmental metaphor. *J. Amer. Psychoanal. Assn* 24,5 (Suppl.):193–212.

Hartmann, H. 1948. Comments on the psychoanalytic theory of instinctual drives. *Psychoanal. Quarterly* 17:368–88.

Horney, K. 1924. On the genesis of the castration complex in women. *Int. J. Psycho-Anal.* 5:50–65.

———. 1926. The flight from womanhood: The masculinity complex in women as viewed by men and women. *Int. J. Psycho-Anal.* 7:324–39.

———. 1932. The dread of women. *Int. J. Psycho-Anal.* 13:348–61.

———. 1933. The denial of the vagina: A contribution to genital anxiety specific to women. *Int. J. Psycho-Anal.* 14:57–70.

———. 1935. The problem of feminine masochism. *Psychoanalytic Review* 22,3:241–57.

Irigaray, L. 1974. *Speculum of the other woman.* Ithaca: Cornell University Press, 1985.

———. 1977. This sex which is not one. In *New French Feminisms,* edited by Elaine Marks and Isabelle de Courtivron. Amherst: University of Massachusetts Press, 1980.

———. 1987. *Sexes et parentes.* Paris: Editions de Minuit.

Jacobson, E. 1937. Ways of female superego formation and the female castration conflict. *Psychoanal. Quarterly* 45 (1976):525–38.

Jones, E. 1927. The early development of female sexuality. *Int. J. Psycho-Anal.* 8:459–72.

———. 1933. The phallic phase. *Int. J. Psycho-Anal.* 14:1–33.

———. 1935. Early female sexuality. *Int. J. Psycho-Anal.* 16:263–73.

Kestenberg, J. 1956a. Vicissitudes of female sexuality. *J. Amer. Psychoanal. Assn* 4:453–576.

———. 1956b. On the development of maternal feelings in early childhood. *Psychoanal. Study Child* 11:257–91.

———. 1968. Outside and inside, male and female. *J. Amer. Psychoanal. Assn* 16:457–520.

Khan, M. 1979. From masochism to psychic pain. In *Alienation in perversions,* 210–18. New York: International Universities Press.

Kinsey, A., Pomeroy, W., Martin, C., and Gebhard, P. 1953. *Sexual behavior in the human female.* Philadelphia: Saunders.

Kleeman, J. 1976. Freud's views on early female sexuality in the light of direct child observation. *J. Amer. Psychoanal. Assn* 24,5 (Suppl.):3–27.

Klein, M. 1928. Early stages of the Oedipus conflict. *Int. J. Psycho-Anal.* 9:167–80.

———. 1932. The effects of early anxiety-situations on the sexual development of the girl. In *Psychoanalysis of children,* 194–239. New York: Free Press, 1986.

———. 1945. The Oedipus complex in the light of early anxieties. In *Love, guilt, and reparation and other works, 1921–1945,* 397–419. New York: Free Press.

Kohut, H. 1975. A note on female sexuality. In *The search for the self: Selected writings of H. Kohut: 1950–1978.* New York: International Universities Press, 1978.

———. 1984. A reexamination of castration anxiety. In *How does analysis cure?* Edited by A. Goldberg, 13–33. Chicago: University of Chicago Press.

Kristeva, J. 1974. *Revolution in poetic language.* New York: Columbia University Press, 1984.

———. 1977. *Polylogue.* Paris: Seuil.

———. 1979. Women's time. *Signs* 7, no. 1 (1981):13–35.

Lacan, J. 1957–58. Les formations de l'inconscient. *Bulletin de Psychologie* 11:1–15.

———. 1958a. The signification of the phallus. In *Ecrits: A selection,* 281–91. London: Tavistock, 1977.

———. 1958. Guiding remarks for a congress on feminine sexuality. In *Ecrits: A selection,* 725–36. London: Tavistock.

———. 1975. La sexualité féminine dans la doctrine Freudienne. *Scilicet* 5:91–104.

Lampl-de Groot, J. 1927. The evolution of the Oedipus complex in women. *Int. J. Psycho-Anal.* 9:332–45.

———. 1933. Contribution to the problem of femininity. *Psychoanal. Quarterly* 2:489–518.

McDougall, J. 1964. Homosexuality in women. In *Female sexuality*, edited by J. Chasseguet-Smirgel 170–212. Ann Arbor: University of Michigan Press, 1970.

———. 1978. The homosexual dilemma: A study of female homosexuality. In *Plea for a measure of abnormality*, 87–141. New York: International Universities Press, 1980.

———. 1989. The dead father: On early psychic trauma and its relation to disturbance in sexual identity and in creative activity. *Int. J. Psycho-Anal.* 70:205–20.

Mahler, M., Pine, F., and Bergman, A. 1975. *The psychological birth of the human infant.* New York: Basic Books.

Masters, W., and Johnson, V. 1966. *Human sexual response.* Boston: Little, Brown.

Menaker, E. 1953. Masochism—A defense reaction of the ego. *Psychoanal. Quarterly* 22:205–21.

Miller, J. B. 1973. New issues, new approaches. In *Psychoanalysis and women,* edited by J. B. Miller, 375–406. Baltimore: Penguin.

———. 1976. *Toward a new psychology of women.* Boston: Beacon Press.

———. 1984. The development of women's sense of self. *Work in Progress,* no. 12.

Mitchell, J. 1974. *Psycho-analysis and Feminism.* New York: Vintage Books, 1975.

———. 1984. The question of femininity and the theory of psychoanalysis. In *Women: The longest revolution,* 295–315. London: Virago Press.

Montrelay, M. 1977. Inquiry into Femininity. *m/f,* no. 1 (1978):83–101.

Moulton, R. 1970. A survey and reevaluation of the concept of penis envy. *Contemp. Psychoanal.* 7:84–104.

Parens, H., Pollock, L., Stern, J., and Kramer, S. 1976. On the girl's entry into the Oedipus complex. *J. Amer. Psychoanal. Assn* 24:79–107.

Payne, S. 1935. A conception of femininity. *Brit. J. Med. Psychol.* 15:18–33.

Person, E. 1974. Some new observations on the origins of femininity. In *Women and analysis,* edited by J. Strouse, 250–61. New York: Grossman.

———. 1980. Sexuality as the mainstay of identity: Psychoanalytic perspectives. *Signs* 5:605–30.

———. 1983. The influence of values in psychoanalysis: The case of female psychology. *Psychiatry Update* 2:36–50.

Reich, A. 1940. A contribution to the psycho-analysis of extreme submissiveness in women. *Psychoanal. Quarterly* 9:470–80.

Rich, A. 1971–72. Diving into the wreck. In *Diving into the wreck, Poems, 1971–1972,* 22–24. New York: Norton, 1976.

———. 1976. *Of woman born: Motherhood as experience and institution.* New York: Norton.

Riviere, J. 1927. Womanliness as a masquerade. *Int. J. Psycho-Anal.* 8:303–13.

Rose, J. 1983. *Femininity and its discontents.* In *Sexuality in the field of vision.* London: Verse, 1986.

Safouan, M. 1976. Feminine sexuality in psychoanalytic doctrine. In *Feminine sexuality,* edited by J. Mitchell and J. Rose, 123–36. New York: Pantheon Books, 1985.

Salomé L. A. 1899. Der Mensch als Weib: Neue Deutsche Rundschau. In *Die Erotik,* edited by E. Pfeiffer. Frankfurt, 1979.

Schafer, R. 1974. Problems in Freud's psychology of women. *J. Amer. Psychoanal. Assn.* 22:459–89.

Sherfey, M. J. 1966. The evolution and nature of female sexuality in relation to psychoanalytic theory. *J. Amer. Psychoanal. Assn* 14:28–128.

Stoller, R. J. 1968a. The sense of femaleness. *Psychoanal. Quarterly* 37:42–55.

———. 1968. *Sex and gender.* New York: Aronson.

——. 1975. *Perversion.* New York: Pantheon.

——. 1979. *Sexual excitement.* New York: Simon and Schuster, 1980.

Stolorow, R. D., and Lachmann, F. M. 1980. *Psychoanalysis of developmental arrests.* New York: International Universities Press.

Strachey, R. 1936. Our freedom and its results. In *The cause: A short history of the women's movement in Great Britain.* London: G. Bellad Sons.

Thompson, C. 1941. The role of women in this culture. *Psychiatry* 4:1–8.

——. 1942. Cultural pressures in the psychology of women. *Psychiatry* 5:331–39.

——. 1943. Penis envy in women. In *Interpersonal psychoanalysis,* edited by M. R. Green. New York: Basic Books.

Torok, M. 1964. The significance of penis envy in women. In *Female sexuality,* edited by J. Chasseguet-Smirgel, 137–70. Ann Arbor: University of Michigan Press, 1970.

Winnicott, D. W. 1966. Creativity and its origins. In *Playing and reality,* 72–85. London: Tavistock, 1971.

PART I

PSYCHOANALYTIC VIEWS ON FEMALE SEXUALITY

If you want to know more about femininity, enquire from your own experience of life, or turn to the poets, or wait until science can give you deeper and more coherent information.

SIGMUND FREUD

In Europe

1. The Preoedipal Phase of the Libido Development

Ruth Mack Brunswick

The material published here is the result of work begun in the summer of 1930 in collaboration with Freud. The starting point was a case of delusional jealousy which I had previously analyzed and published and which inadvertently had revealed a wealth of unsuspected information concerning a period hitherto unknown, antedating the oedipus complex and consequently termed preoedipal. The written record of this collaboration is a manuscript which consists of my notes, typed after discussions with Freud, and Freud's own marginal comments, ideas and suggestions.

We are accustomed to the postulate that the roots of neurotic illness are to be found in the oedipus complex of the individual. The normal man or woman has emerged from his infantile sexuality, of which the oedipus complex is the pinnacle, and has abandoned the love object of this period, whereas the neurotic has remained fixed to the oedipal love object.

Thus originally Freud postulated the etiology of the neuroses; but in his work on female sexuality[1] first published in 1931, he limits the role of the oedipus complex in women and attributes great importance to the preoedipal[2] period in the formation of neurotic illness. Indeed, he says that so far as women are concerned, he is obliged to retract the statement that the oedipus complex contains the nucleus of the neuroses.

When we attempt to examine the origins and precursors of the oedipus complex, we encounter among analysts an opposition not unlike the earlier opposition of the outside world to the oedipus complex itself. The use of the term *preoedipal sexuality* seems to arouse a certain loyalty to the oedipus complex as if its validity were being threatened. Evidently we have had sufficient difficulty in acknowledging the full importance of the oedipus complex: insult seems added to injury when we are asked to go beyond it.

Originally published in *Psychoanalytic Quarterly* 9 (1940):293–319. Reprinted by permission.

The admission of the importance of the oedipus complex constitutes in a sense the main distinction between the analyst and the outside world which of course has always been reluctant to accept sexuality in the children, particularly adult, genital sexuality as it is revealed in the oedipus complex. A different situation arose with the establishment of the other great complex of childhood, the castration complex. Its very nature created another fate for it. It has remained generally unknown except to analysts and has indeed proved to be the rock upon which the adherence of certain analysts to psychoanalysis has shattered. There is no doubt that the castration complex is much more foreign to our conscious mode of thought than the oedipus complex; yet if we are free to observe it, its expression in early childhood equals in directness that of the oedipus complex itself.

The importance of the castration complex in the development as well as in the relinquishment of the oedipus complex has long since become clear. However, we must now add that all these conceptions are strictly applicable only to the male child. It was assumed that the girl's development did not differ radically from that of the boy, but in the course of the last decade we have seen that male and female development, while closely resembling one another, in no sense run parallel.

The present work is a preliminary attempt to correlate our knowledge of the sexes, and to describe that earliest level of the libido development which extends from birth to the formation of the oedipus complex.

Unfortunately, correlation and precision demand the restatement of much that is known or indeed obvious. Sometimes the new formulation differs by only a nuance from the old; but frequently it is exactly this nuance which is significant. For these reasons, I ask the indulgence of the reader throughout a frequently banal and tiresome repetition of many self-evident facts of psycho-analytic theory.

A second apology concerns the apparently schematic character of this work. Only at the end have I ventured to apply the theoretical insight hereby acquired to one or two clinical problems. Yet I need hardly state that clinical observations alone were responsible for what becomes, in such a brief pre-sentation, merely a diagram of early development.

Let us define our terms at once. Under oedipus complex we understand not only the positive attachment of the child to the parent of the opposite sex, but above all the situation of the *triangle:* the child positively attached to the one parent and in rivalry with the other. The preoedipal phase, on the other hand, is for both sexes that earliest period of attachment to the first love object, the mother, before the advent of the father as a rival. It is the period during which an exclusive relation exists between mother and child. Other individuals are of course present in the outside world, especially the father who is an object of affection and admiration, as well as of annoyance when he interferes with the mother's preoccupation with the child. But he is not yet a rival, nor is the strong bond between mother and child split up, as it is destined to be, amongst the various other individuals in the environment. The only person who shares the mother-child relation is the nurse, and she merges ordinarily, though not invariably, into the mother figure.

Examination of the early phase of exclusive mother attachment is beset with difficulties. First of all, this period is the most ancient, the most archaic, and the most foreign to our usual mode of thought. Second, it is overlaid with material from other phases, and is therefore not readily discernible. Third, it is the period of greatest inarticulateness, so that even direct nursery observations are not easy to make. And finally, the forces of repression have mutilated and indeed often destroyed to the point of making unrecognizable much of this very epoch which contains the roots of all later development.

The complicated chronological relations of the preoedipal phase, oedipus complex, and castration complex vary both according to the sex of the child and, individually, according to the time and incidence of traumata, childish observations of the primal scene, the perception of the sexual difference, the birth of another child, etc. In the boy, the preoedipal mother attachment is apparently of much shorter duration than in the girl, merging very early into the oedipus complex. This in turn is followed by the castration complex on the basis of which the oedipus complex is destroyed. It is otherwise with the girl. Here too the preoedipal mother attachment develops into something surprisingly like the oedipus complex of the boy, with the mother as love object and the father as rival.[3] As we shall see, this active oedipus complex of the girl also is destroyed by the discovery of castration although for reasons which differ radically from those of the boy. But out of the castration complex and the ruins of this primitive oedipus complex, there now develops the positive, or passive, oedipus complex of the little girl in which the father is the new love object and the mother the rival.

Thus we see that the little girl traverses a long and complicated route before entering the oedipus complex. Indeed, during the examination of the preoedipal phenomena we become uncertain as to the comparative importance of preoedipal and oedipal phenomena in feminine development.

At the beginning of her sexual life the little girl is to all intents and purposes a little boy. Her relation to her first love object, the mother, is precisely that of the boy, with similarly conflicting passive and active libidinal strivings. But unlike the boy, the girl must relinquish this love and transfer it to the father, a difficult process which we now know to be at times only partially achieved. Once in the oedipus complex, the normal woman tends to remain there; the oedipus complex of the woman undergoes no such widespread destruction as that of the man. On the contrary, it remains and forms the normal basis of the erotic life of the woman. The resistance of the female oedipus complex to the powers of destruction accounts for the differences in structure of the male and female superego.

It is evident that the sexual development of the woman in contrast to that of the man is complicated by the fact that the woman must give up her first love object, the mother, and transfer her libido to the father, whereas the boy, in passing from the preoedipal to the oedipal stage, makes no change of object. But the woman has not only two love objects: she possesses also two sexual organs, the clitoris and the vagina, whereas again the boy has only one. A possible parallel between the love object and the sexual organ will be sought later. We can, however, now make the following statement: that although the woman is obliged to give up one sexual object for another, and one sexual organ likewise for another, the boy is faced with the almost equally arduous task of changing, not love objects or sexual organs, but his own attitude to the original love object, the mother. That is to say, the originally passive male is obliged to develop that full degree of activity toward the woman which is the token of his psychic health.

The phenomena of the preoedipal phase should be described in their own terms and not in the terms of the oedipus complex. Inasmuch as the preoedipal phase extends from the beginning of life to the formation of the oedipus complex, it is obvious that the discovery of the sexual difference ordinarily falls within its scope, especially in the case of the girl, in whom the preoedipal phase is so much more extensive than that of the boy. Previous to this discovery the child makes personal but not sexual differentiation between the individuals of its immediate world. It must be remembered that until approximately three years of age, the pregenital zones outweigh the genital in importance. Similarly the boy, judging others by himself, takes for granted the universal possession of the penis, like the mouth, the anus, etc. The girl who has not yet discovered the existence of the penis believes her sexual constitution to be universal.

Three great pairs of antitheses exist throughout the entire libido development, mingling, overlapping, and combining, never wholly coinciding, and ultimately replacing one another. Infancy and childhood are characterized by the first two, and adolescence by the third. These are (1) *active-passive*, (2) *phallic-castrated* and (3) *masculine-feminine.* Schematically, but schematically only, these follow upon one another, each characteristic of a given stage of development. We shall attempt to define each stage within its own terms rather than in the terms of a later stage.

The first great pair of antitheses, *active-passive,* governs the beginning of life. That the infant is largely passive is evident; often it must be taught even to breathe and to suckle. One is tempted to state that development consists largely in the supervention of activity over a prior passivity. One is restrained from any such generalization by the fact that not only do we know almost nothing of the essential nature of passivity and of activity, or of their relation to one another, but in addition, it is a matter of speculation whether passivity is converted into activity, or whether certain developmental strivings are specifically active and others passive, and whether in the course of development the active strivings increase in number and intensity and therefore occupy more place. What we do see, and what we are able in some measure to trace at least descriptively and perhaps dynamically, is a constantly growing activity on the part of the child. It learns to sit instead of being held; it reaches out for its own bottle instead of merely receiving it, etc. What we learn is that each bit of activity is based to some extent on an identification with the active mother, an identification which provides a form for the activity inherent in the child who does for and to itself what the mother has done for it, playing the roles of both mother and child in the manner typical of childhood. Indeed, the child plays the role of the mother not only toward itself but also toward other children, animals, and toys, and ultimately and above all toward the mother herself.

The active-passive phase is prephallic, what Jones calls deuterophallic. As I have remarked before, the child takes for granted the likeness of its own sexual organization to that of others, and the genital is a matter of no greater concern than the other erogenous zones, notably, at this early age, the mouth. Thus the sex of the child is immaterial; and it is to be noted that the role of the mother, at this time prior to sexual differentiation, is not feminine but active.

A new epoch begins with the discovery of castration, which establishes the sway of the second pair of antitheses, *phallic-castrated.* This still does not coincide with masculine and feminine although by taking cognizance of the presence or absence of the exclusively phallic genital it more nearly approaches the final pair than does its predecessor. However the lack of the phallus is at first considered individual or accidental, in no sense irremediable. With the exception of the clitoris, the female genital, including the vagina, is still essentially unknown. We are all familiar with the reactions of the child to the discovery of castration. We know that the boy does not immediately question the sex of the most important person in his environment, the mother. On the contrary, he takes it for granted that she at least is phallic. Thus castration as an irretrievable fact affecting all females is not immediately accepted by the child. With the final recognition of the mother's castration and the possibility of his own at the hands of the father, the oedipus complex of the little boy is destroyed.

But whereas the normal male gives up the mother and saves himself from castration, the neurotic faces two possibilities: first, he represses but fails to give up his love for the mother; and, second, frequently in combination with the first possibility, he accepts in fantasy castration by the father, gives it a libidinal significance, and takes the father as a love object. This we call the negative or passive oedipus complex.

I should like to offer a suggestion made by Freud in our early discussions of these problems. The terms *active* and *passive oedipus complex* are more comprehensive and accurate in their application to both sexes than the usual *positive* and *negative oedipus complex*. According to this new terminology, the preoedipal sexuality of the girl becomes her active oedipus complex with the mother as its object. Her passive oedipus complex has the father as its object. For the boy, the active oedipus complex denotes what we ordinarily call the positive oedipus complex with the mother as the object. His passive oedipus complex which we ordinarily term the negative oedipus complex has as its object the father, and is a neurotic phenomenon when occurring to any marked extent. However I shall retain the older terminology here because of the otherwise inevitable confusion between the terms *preoedipal* and *oedipal*.

The man in the passive oedipus complex so closely resembles the woman in her oedipal attachment to the father that it seems as if our new understanding of female development should aid us in our examination of the problems of the neurotic man. Freud suggests that on the basis of this new concept of early female sexuality, the preoedipal phase of the boy should be thoroughly investigated.[4] The present work is an attempt in this direction. I should like to add that it has been necessary to repeat much of the material contained in Freud's two papers on female sexuality because those findings form the background essential both to the study of the corresponding development of the boy, and to the further examination of these phenomena in the girl.

Let us now return to the first position of the child in which it is passive to the active mother. Normal development demands that activity supervene over passivity. Whether the passivity remains, is given up, or is converted, we do not know. Clinically it appears to give place to activity. The degree to which this occurs is immensely variable. The process is more vigorous in boys than in girls and the actual quantity of activity is undoubtedly greater. The early character of the child depends largely upon the relative proportions of activity and passivity.

It is apparent that the child's earliest activity is, in its outward form at least, a copy of the mother. This is the most fundamental and primitive kind of identification, dependent for its existence solely upon the replacement of passivity by activity and consequently of mother attachment by mother identification, irrespective of any other emotional bond.

One might state that a young child's inability to produce an adequate activity is one of the earliest abnormalities. Passivity then predominates. But what besides constitutional elements interferes with the normal production of activity at this early age? Observations in the nursery have proved useful here. Briefly one may state that every successful act of identification with the mother makes the mother less necessary to the child. As she becomes less necessary, the restrictions and demands which she is obliged to make are increasingly resented. The child, which has just succeeded in the difficult task of reliving actively what it has until now passively experienced—and here the repetition compulsion acquires its full significance—is particularly on the defensive in regard to this freshly acquired activity. It is a newly won libidinal position which the child guards zealously. Any activity on the part of the mother is likely to be resented. Therefore unless the mother accepts a more or less passive role, she becomes at best superfluous. The child reacts to her very presence with a kind of primitive, defensive aggression which is a by-product and protection of its activity as well as the defense against its original, barely overcome passivity. The pull of any earlier libidinal position is profound; every step of development is hard-won, and bound therefore to be defended. True aggression inevitably arises when the mother is obliged to hamper this budding activity either by forbidding or compelling certain acts. It is apparent that the resultant aggression derived from the original activity is now directed specifically against the mother who at this time is vested with the authority to restrict, prohibit and command, according to the requirements

of the situation and by virtue of the fact that, until her subsequent depreciation because of her castration, she is not only active, phallic, but *omnipotent*.

This is perhaps the simplest of the various ways in which aggression
arises. In reality we have to deal with far more ominous situations. Early
narcissistic injuries on the part of the mother enormously increase the child's
hostility. Conspicuous among these injuries which I shall not attempt to
enumerate in detail are weaning, the birth of a brother or sister, the relation
between father and mother, the sexual rejection of the child of either sex by
the mother; and finally, the depreciation of the mother as the result of her
castration. On the basis of these injuries a conflict ensues which demands
that the aggression toward the mother be repressed. But inasmuch as every
new activity is associated with the repressed hostility, a large amount of
normal activity must often be forfeited to insure the success of the repression.
An individual hampered in his development ordinarily regresses; when further activity as demanded by development is blocked, a deeper regression to
a still earlier, more passive, level takes place. We know that the interest in
the genital and the discovery of the sexual difference coincide with a biological "push" which occurs at about the end of the third year of life when the
phallic period begins. The organic awakening of the phallic genital leads to
the great period of infantile sexual activity. The libidinal desires of the child
toward the mother, both passive and more especially active, become intense.
They are accompanied by phallic masturbation with the clitoris as the executive organ of the girl. The boy seems to pass with relative ease out of his
predominantly passive, preoedipal attachment to the mother into the characteristically active, normal oedipus complex. The corresponding phase in the
little girl is of course still preoedipal. While the genital libido is at its height
the castration of the mother is perceived and finally acknowledged with all
its implications. Under the threat of castration by the father, the boy abandons the mother as his love object and turns his activity to the formation of
his superego and his sublimations, aided undoubtedly by a mildly contemp-
tuous attitude toward the castrated sex, and by the fact that, possessing the
phallus himself, he has far less need of it in his love object than the little girl
has. Not the mother's castration, but the threat to the boy's own penis results
in the destruction of the male oedipus complex.

It is otherwise with the little girl. Here the mother's castration means not
only the depreciation of the love object and the possibility of the girl's own
castration as in the case of the boy; the mother's castration is above all the
doom of the girl's hopes of ever acquiring possession of a penis. The girl

abandons the mother as a love object with far more embitterment and finality than the boy. She seeks to transfer her libido to the father, a transference beset by difficulties arising from the tenacity of the active and passive preoedipal mother attachment. In the normal girl it is essentially the passive strivings which in the identification with the castrated mother, are successfully transferred to the father in the oedipal phase, and in adult life to the husband. The active strivings are sublimated at this time and only much later find their real scope in the relation of the woman to her own child, in her final and complete identification with the active mother.

Here I should like to call attention to one small clinical observation. Between the girl's attachment to the mother and the attachment to the father there may sometimes be observed a brief interregnum resembling the latency period. One might call it a preoedipal latency period. It is a kind of suspension of the libido which has been detached from the mother and has not yet found its connection with the father. It is to be found or at least to be observed especially in girls with a somewhat retarded libido development, in whom the attachment to the mother has persisted beyond the usual length of time. It precedes the fresh wave of sexuality of the passive or positive oedipus complex.

The final pair of antitheses, *masculine-feminine,* comes at puberty. In the boy, the flood of virile libido brings with it for the first time the desire to penetrate the newly discovered vagina. A new relation to the woman is established which however has its roots in those remnants of the oedipus complex which have not been destroyed. These vary in quality and quantity. A healthy amount of activity toward the mother in the preoedipal and oedipal phases is of immeasurable value to the ultimate relation of the man to the woman.

In the adolescent girl the wave of passive libido, libido, that is to say with passive aim called forth by the menses and the awakening of the vagina, is directed toward the father in an intensification of the oedipal libido position which we may now call feminine.

So much for the investigation of the course of our three pairs of antitheses. We now return to our starting point in an attempt to examine that major phenomenon of the preoedipal period, the exclusive mother-child relationship. The relation of the child to the mother is obviously the fundament of its psychic life, the basis and prototype of all later love relationships. We may examine it from two points of view: first, in relation to the zones involved: oral, anal, and genital; and second, from that other angle of the libido development which we have been considering: first and foremost, at this early time, from the active-passive point of view, and, later, from the phallic-castrated.

I should like to say a word here about the concept of the phallic mother, a concept familiar to us from the fantasies of neurotics, psychotics, and both normal and abnormal children. Whereas both the active and the castrated mother exist in point of fact, the phallic mother is pure fantasy, a childish hypothesis elaborated after the discovery of the penis and the possibility of its loss or absence in the female. It is a hypothesis made to insure the mother's possession of the penis, and as such probably arises at the moment when the child becomes uncertain that the mother does indeed possess it. Previously, in the active-passive phase, it seems more than probable that the executive organ of the active mother is the breast; the idea of the penis is then projected back upon the active mother after the importance of the phallus has been recognized. Thus it is a fantasy of regressive, compensatory nature. We shall continue to use the term *phallic mother*, first because of the prevalence of the idea in the neuroses and psychoses, and second because whether the idea is primary or regressive, the term is one which best designates the all-powerful mother, the mother who is capable of everything and who possesses every valuable attribute.

At this early age the only possible contact with the child is a physical one; therefore probably nothing equals in importance the physical care of the infant by the mother or nurse. The entire infantile psychic life runs parallel to this care. The child's role is mainly passive, becoming active only in direct response to certain stimuli. The body as a whole, with the erogenous zones in particular, including the skin which plays so important a part at this time, must necessarily be cleansed and handled. We know that well-managed physical care is a source of intense pleasure to the infant and, equally, that rough or unexpected handling has a traumatic effect. It would appear that the first attachment to the mother which is so passive in nature, derives its strength and tenacity in great part from her physical care, and of course above all from her feeding of the child. There is no doubt about the sexual nature of the child's response. Only because at this very early age the genital plays so small a part does the mother-child relationship seem so innocent; then, too, the nature of infantile love is aimless and diffuse, appearing "harmless." Pleasure is obtained from innumerable sources; the child's appetite for it is random and without a particular goal, one reason perhaps, why that appetite remains unsatiated.

We have said that development brings with it increasing activity; so we may expect to find, as is indeed the case, that the child attempts to repeat actively every detail of physical care which it has experienced passively. Here, too, I am obliged to omit concrete examples with one important exception: the mother in the course of bathing and caring for the child is obliged to touch its genitals. A new bit of activity appears when the child, instead of allowing its genitals to be touched by the mother and experiencing pleasurable sensations from this passive experience, touches its own genitals not to wash them but purely for the sake of those pleasurable sensations with which it has become familiar from the mother's care. Here we have the first basis in fact for infantile masturbation, the first experience of which that masturbation is the voluntary repetition. The child's earliest phallic fantasy is undoubtedly one of playing the role of the mother toward itself by touching its genitals and eliciting thereby the same pleasurable sensations originally called forth by the mother. Thus the mother's physical care of the genitals has constituted a true seduction, and is so viewed by the child. The blame incurred by the mother is doubled when later she forbids what she has herself provoked: phallic masturbation. Observations of young children, as well as of a certain primitive type of adult in the course of analysis, make it appear probable that the passive genital aim persists long after the mother's role has been largely taken over by the child. Despite a great display of activity, the child at the beginning of the phallic phase still primarily wishes to have its genitals touched by the mother.

When the statement is made that the physical care of the child by the mother constitutes the basis in fact for infantile masturbation, the significance of the primal scene as the sexual stimulus which frequently initiates the masturbation is in no way diminished or disregarded. The point is that the mother's physical care provides the pattern according to which the child can then react to the stimulus of the primal scene.

It is easier to discern the phallic phase than the oral and anal phases. The true oral phase is traversed while the infant is still too inarticulate to afford us much material. The anal stage, beginning at approximately two years of age, is more expressive. Here *giving* is initiated in contradistinction to the earlier and more passive *receiving*. The active giving has of course been present in some measure from the very first day of life, as manifested by spontaneous defecation or urination. In the phallic phase the active attitude takes the lead. In the regression which usually follows the acceptance of castration of the woman at the end of the phallic phase, it is possible to observe both oral and anal phases quite clearly because of our greater similarity to an older child as well as its own increased articulateness.

We have said that the physical care of the child provides the basis for infantile masturbation, with its oral, anal, and phallic fantasies, and its interchanging passive and active roles. But as has also been stated, there is something else with which we are accustomed to associate infantile masturbation, and that is the primal scene. So long as the exclusive mother-child relation obtains, the relations of the parents are of minor interest to the child. But the moment the active oedipus complex of the boy or girl is formed, the relations between the parents become the object of intense and jealous interest. We know that the child takes every opportunity to observe the sexual life of the parents and that when the opportunity is lacking some substitute is found even if only in fantasy. We have always asked ourselves how the child is able to understand the sexual relations of the parents. The answer may be found in the early physical relation of the child to the mother.

We frequently observe that not only does the child identify itself with the rival father in its love of the mother; it also identifies the father with itself. What does the father do with the mother? The child's answer is that he undoubtedly performs those acts which have been the source of intense pleasure to the child itself: in the oral fantasy, for example, the mother suckles the father. Now while suckling is in part active, every human act being mixed, it is nevertheless originally largely passive, doubtless because it occurs at a time of life when the child is overwhelmingly passive. It must be remembered that there is as yet no sexual difference between parents. Thus in the fantasy of the oral relation of the parents, the role of the father is in part passive. A passive father role sounds contradictory to the point of absurdity. But the child's capacity for projecting its own desires upon others should be borne in mind, as well as the fact that active and passive at this time are not associated with the sexual distinction in as much as the latter does not yet exist. The counterpart of the passive fantasy of being suckled is the active oral fantasy of suckling. Here the mother is suckled by the child, or by the father.[5] One must never lose sight of the fact that every passive fantasy acquires its active counterpart, and that this play of interchanging roles is one of the chief characteristics of childhood. I recall one particularly infantile patient whose sole conscious masturbation fantasy was suckling her doll. Just beneath this manifest fantasy in which the mother role is dominant was the fantasy of nursing at the mother's breast.

We are aware of the importance of the child's bowel training and how easily it may become traumatic. We speak of the anal-sadistic level of development, and note that the awakening of the anal zone corresponds in point of time to the production of intense aggressive impulses in an individual who has by this time become more capable of expression than he had been during the oral phase. In the nursery one can observe that during the anal period any stimulation of the anal zone (or in the course of an adult analysis, any simulation of anal mechanisms or material) may cause a violent outburst of rage. There is an etiological connection between anal stimulation and the production of anger. The enemas so frequent in childhood have all the appearance of rape; the child reacts with a tempestuous although helpless outburst of rage which can only be likened to orgasm. Rage appears to be the true motor expression of anal erotism, the anal equivalent of genital orgasm.[6]

In the phallic phase, the original passive desire of the child is to be masturbated by the mother. This passive wish is also ascribed by the child to the father, according to the mechanism described in the suckling fantasy. By the time the active wish to touch the mother's genital is formed, inhibiting influences and prohibitions have usually become sufficiently strong to limit the child in fact though not in fantasy, and not even always in fact to a wish to see the mother's genital. Consequently the most usual coitus concept or equivalent of the phallic phase, in which the vagina is still unknown and the need of penetration not yet formed, is the mutual touching of the genitals. This is indeed what children often do among themselves when attempting to imitate the coitus of the parents.

Thus we see that while the parental coitus is incorporated into the oedipal fantasy life of the child and into its masturbation, nevertheless the understanding and interest which the child brings to the parental coitus are based on the child's own preoedipal physical experiences with the mother and its resultant desires. The biological factor obviously outweighs all others; animals are able to perform the sexual act without any apparent learning process. Undoubtedly at puberty forces come into play which enable the individual to have sexual relations regardless of his prior observations or experiences. But what has always surprised us is not the adolescent's capacity for sexual intercourse, but the amazing understanding which the three- or four-year-old child shows for the sexual relations of its parents. This understanding becomes less mysterious if we consider not only inherited and instinctual knowledge, but also the actual physical experiences of the child at the hands of the mother or nurse.

I should now like to describe chronologically and in relation to one another the two great wishes of childhood: the wish for a baby, and the wish for a penis. The original, asexual, "harmless" wish for a baby arises very early, is based wholly on the primitive identification of the child of either sex with the active mother, and in the absence of a true object relation to the mother is neither passive nor active. The child wants everything the omnipotent and all-possessing mother has in order to do everything the mother does; and a mother is above all the possessor of a baby. In the anal phase with its new concept of giving and receiving and of increasing object relation to the mother, the wish for a baby acquires a second root: both boy and girl then desire a baby from the mother. This originally passive wish like every other acquires an active form: the wish to present the mother with a baby. The boy gives up the passive baby wish when his activity predominates. As his oedipus complex develops, a father identification replaces the earlier identi-fication with the active mother. The girl, on the other hand, gives up her active baby wish when she accepts her own castration and consequent inabil-ity to impregnate the mother; the passive wish however is retained and is normally transferred from the mother to the father where as we know it assumes the greatest importance. Normality demands that the boy give up his passive wish for a child, and the girl her active wish.

It may be tentatively stated that three types of infantile activity exist. The first, familiar type is the activity of the all-providing mother, seen in the child's earliest identification with the mother. The second, also familiar and much later type arises from the identification with the oedipal father. This type the girl is incapable of achieving in full, try as she may. (These attempts and failures are best known to us from the homosexual relations of women and their rivalry with men.) The little boy with temporary developmental rather than irremediable anatomical inadequacies, and therefore in possession of a full potential father identification, actually achieves an adequate father role toward the mother which he relinquishes only under the oedipal threat of castration by the father.

But there exists a third, unfamiliar type of activity in the young child of either sex, apparently inherent in the individual and independent of identifi-cation mechanisms. Our ignorance of the nature of activity makes description difficult and we are obliged to resort to analogy. The young page in an opera, a part almost always taken by women, personifies this type of activity and is characteristic of the uncastrated, or rather sexually undifferentiated child. Recently a female patient with a strong mother attachment remarked: "It isn't that I want to be a man. I think I really want to be a little boy.'' The favorite childhood fantasy of this girl was to be a page to royalty.

The activity required for the father identification doubtless utilizes every preexisting form and then adds the final stamp of masculinity. This ultimate and all-inclusive type of activity is never fully achieved by the girl.

The active wish for a penis of the little girl arises with the observation of the difference between the sexes and the determination to have what the boy has. This original basis is narcissistic. An object root is formed when the little girl realizes that without the penis she is unable to win the mother. Normally the relinquishment of the active penis wish and of the attachment to the mother coincide. Contrary to our earlier ideas, the penis wish is not exchanged for the baby wish which, as we have seen, has indeed long preceded it. In the course of normal development the impossible is given up and the possible retained. The little girl concentrates her energy on the permissable and legitimate desire for a baby. The active penis wish, the wish for the full and permanent possession of a penis, makes way for the passive penis wish, the wish to receive the penis from the man in coitus. Out of this as the little girl knows, she will receive a child. Thus the two wishes finally unite. Originally narcissistic, both wishes next find transient root in the mother relation before finally and permanently attaching themselves to the father.

Let us now examine the phallic masturbation of the little girl, so much less familiar to us than that of the boy. It is a surprising fact that many adult women are unacquainted with both masturbation and orgasm. It is perhaps not correct to call these women frigid; they are responsive in coitus and their pleasure, though difficult to describe, is undeniable. But it is diffuse rather than specific, and it lacks the high, sharp curve typical of true orgasm.

We know that the clitoris is the executive organ of the infantile sexuality of the girl. We know too that the first object of this sexuality is the mother. One of the greatest differences between the sexes is the enormous extent to which infantile sexuality is repressed in the girl. Except in profound neurotic states, no man resorts to any similar repression of his infantile sexuality. The little girl's repression frequently results in a severe limitation of her entire sexuality, with permanent psychic injury. Freud has explained the female distaste for masturbation on the basis of the castration trauma: every act of masturbation reveals anew to the little girl the physical fact of her own castration. Girls seem to give up the use of the hands in masturbation earlier and more frequently than boys, although the same phenomenon is of course to be found in boys. Masturbation is then accomplished by pressure of the thighs. The use of the hands reveals with too much tactile accuracy the actual nature of the little girl's genital, and is consequently discarded.

Undoubtedly castration is the narcissistic basis for the repression of masturbation in women. But there is another reason. We have seen that the relinquishment of the first love object of the girl is accompanied by tremendous embitterment. While the little boy acquires what we have come to consider the normal male contempt for women, the little girl, incapable of such contempt because of her own identical nature, frees herself from the mother with a degree of hostility far greater than any comparable hostility in the boy. The mother and the phallic masturbation of the girl are so intimately connected that it seems reasonable to believe that the loss of one is somehow connected with the loss of the other. While the clitoris is undoubtedly used during the positive oedipus complex because the child is obliged to utilize whatever means it possesses, it remains true that the original and, one might say, more appropriate object of the clitoris activity is the mother. Therefore, although the little girl later uses her clitoris in masturbation with passive oedipal fantasies, its original role has been lost, in other words, repressed with the original object. We are all familiar with those difficult cases where masturbation has been repressed so vigorously and at such an early age that its recovery in the course of analysis seems almost impossible. These women may nevertheless present strong father fixation, expressed in diverse oedipal fantasies which however, are unaccompanied by any physical masturbatory activity. I recall one especially instructive case of a woman with a strong father attachment and no ascertainable physical masturbation whatsoever. Her analysis showed that she had been deeply attached to a nurse who had been dismissed when the patient was two years old. The patient had immediately shifted her love of the nurse to her father to whom she became inordinately attached. But masturbation so thoroughly repressed at the age of two years was only recovered at the end of an extensive and successful analysis, in the course of which it became clear that its repression coincided precisely with the repression of the attachment to the mother, or in this case mother substitute.

The vagina as we know derives its sensitivity primarily from the clitoris and secondarily from the anus. It has become a question whether, as heretofore stated, the vagina is always, or even usually, a "silent organ" until adolescence. It now seems probable that an early vaginal sensitivity of anal origin frequently exists. A marked degree of anal sensitivity seems to favor the development of early vaginal sensations, probably because the anus like the vagina is a receptive organ and as such transfers its passive sensitivity to the vagina much more readily than does the active clitoris. Needless to say even when such vaginal sensitivity exists, its role is decidedly minor and secondary to that of the clitoris as the organ of the infantile sexuality. A correlation of the periods of clitoris and vaginal sensitivity, with the age of the little girl when she gives up the mother and attaches herself to the father should throw valuable light on the relation between the nature of the sexual organ and its love object.

As we know, not every little girl gives up masturbation along with her attachment to the mother. The reasons for the continuance of masturbation are manifold and need not be entered into here. But it is important to note that the repression of masturbation in girls does in reality frequently coincide with the relinquishment of the mother as the love object. When one remembers how difficult it is to penetrate the repressions which surround the little girl's first love object, one arrives at a clue in the equally difficult search for the lost sexuality of some women.

We know that the exclusive mother-child relationship is doomed to extinction. Many factors militate against it, the most potent perhaps its primitive, archaic nature. Ambivalence and passivity characterize every primitive relation and ultimately destroy it. Hostility and rebellion prevail when the passive pull is too strong, or when outside factors hamper the desired activity.

The oedipal attitude of the small boy frequently affords us insight into his preoedipal attitude. An unduly strong, persistent oedipus complex combined with exceptional difficulty in giving it up, even at the risk of castration by the father, almost always signifies the existence of obstacles in the production of the normal oedipal activity. Either there has been too much aggression against the mother for any of the reasons familiar to us, or for reasons unknown the passive bond has been too strong. In these cases the little boy clings stubbornly to his active oedipal relation which he has attained with such difficulty. The clinical picture is that of a profound mother fixation at the oedipal level, but closer study reveals that much of the fixation is passive instead of active, and preoedipal instead of oedipal.

We have already investigated the fate of the girl's relation to the mother, and have seen that the frustrations of the preoedipal period provide the foundation for the jealousy and antagonism manifested by the girl in the normal oedipus complex. In addition to the fact that these earliest levels of development are most threatened with change, repression, and extinction, there are definite grudges which the child bears the mother which are usually the outcome of traumatic external events. In our consideration of the causes of aggression against the mother these grudges have already been mentioned. But in addition to being an early source of aggression against the mother, they play a further role in the final dissolution of the mother attachment.

Weaning is doubtless the first major interference in the relationship between mother and child. It is probably true that no matter how early weaning occurs, the infant reacts emotionally not only to the loss of food which can be compensated for in other ways, but to the loss of the breast itself. The disappointment in the mother at this early time constitutes a latent weakness in the relationship, a weakness which later traumata successively reactivate.

We know that an ensuing pregnancy ordinarily so changes the mother's milk that weaning becomes necessary. Later, the birth of a brother or sister further occupies the mother who in fantasy at least has up to now been the exclusive possession of the child. The jealousy and hostility at first directed toward the newborn brother or sister are later referred back to the mother who is of course responsible for the presence of the intruder. The role of the father now begins to be perceived and related to the birth of the younger brother or sister. Competition with the father proves futile to the child of either sex; thus its sexual rejection by the mother is inevitable.

It will be recalled that the mother who by means of her physical care of the child has stimulated or indeed initiated its phallic activity, now attempts to forbid the infantile masturbation which she herself has provoked and of which she is the object. We are all familiar with the more or less traumatic reactions of the child to any attempt on the part of the mother to suppress masturbation, whether accompanied by the usual castration threats or not. Almost invariably it is the mother who expresses the threat of castration; but despite this practical fact it is the father who, out of some biological necessity, becomes the castrator of the boy while the mother retains this power over the girl. The castration of the girl by the father seems, like so many things, to be merely a second edition of the original castration by the mother.

The hostile reaction of the child to the threat of castration is well known. But there is another reaction due doubtless to the child's own guilty fear of the dangers of masturbation. The child, fearing masturbation and nevertheless unable to give it up, forms an unspoken pact with the forbidding mother or nurse. These are the children who cannot go to sleep unless the mother is with them, whose life is made miserable by the nurse's day off. They cling to the mother or nurse in the hope that hereby the dreaded consequences of masturbation will be averted. They rebel at being forbidden to masturbate but they are grateful for the aid given in the struggle against masturbation. It is obvious in these cases that the relinquishment of masturbation at the mother's demand has resulted in an undue degree of regressive, passive dependence upon the mother.

But not only does the mother reject and neglect the child and forbid its masturbation. Her culminating crime is her depreciation as a love object due to her castration. To this castration the normal boy reacts with a degree of contempt which, modified, persists through his later attitude toward women.

We have already seen that the little girl reacts far more traumatically than the boy to the mother's castration. On the one hand the mother has failed to provide the girl with an adequate genital; on the other hand the girl is obliged to admit that this omission is doubtless due to the mother's own lack of a penis. The mother who is held responsible for the sexual inadequacy, simultaneously ceases to be a love object because of her inferiority. When the girl becomes to a greater or lesser degree reconciled to her own lack of a penis, she determines to take as her love object an individual whose possession of the penis is assured and for whose love it may even be worthwhile to undergo or, in reality, to accept castration. Castration by the father acquires a libidinal value and a virtue is made out of a necessity. Here the girl identifies herself with the castrated mother; and this indeed is her role throughout the passive oedipus complex.

It is impossible to trace the influence of the preoedipal phase on later development without a full and detailed description of the entire infantile sexuality. Let us therefore consider briefly one or two clinical pictures in which preoedipal influences are particularly striking.

The first patient in whom the preoedipal sexuality revealed itself unmistakably was the paranoid woman to whom I have repeatedly referred. The remarkable aspect of this case is the total absence of the normal oedipus complex. The traumatic seduction had so fixed the patient to her first homosexual love object that all further development was blocked. The poverty of psychic growth produced a simple, childlike individual, in whom preoedipal attitudes and mechanisms, normally overshadowed by the complications of the oedipus complex were outstanding. I judged this case to be extremely rare, dependent for its existence on the unusual nature and circumstances of the trauma.

But the insight gained in this analysis and applied to other patients demonstrated that the difference was merely one of degree, and further that no particular trauma such as seduction is essential for the production of this clinical picture which instead of being exceptional has proved to be extraordinarily common. The undeveloped, primitive woman with scant heterosexuality and a childish, unquestioning attachment to the mother, presents herself almost regularly to a woman analyst. This type of individual does not consult the male analyst because of a total lack of contact with the man. The degree to which a woman is successful in giving up her first love object and concentrating her libido upon the father determines her entire later life. Between the exclusive attachment to the mother on the one hand and the complete transfer of the libido to the father on the other hand, the innumerable gradations of normal and abnormal development are to be found. It might almost be said that partial success is the rule rather than the exception, so great is the proportion of women whose libido has remained fixed to the mother.

The preoedipal phase of the male, despite its comparative brevity, is perhaps less dramatic than the woman's, but equally far-reaching. It results in what we have come to consider the typical neurosis of the man: his passive attachment to the father in the so-called negative oedipus complex. In this presentation I am obliged to confine myself to those observations which have led me to believe that the submissive attitude of the man to the father has its origin in the preoedipal phase. The consideration of other important etiological factors, such as masochism, is necessarily omitted.

We have seen how closely the little girl in her active preoedipal attachment to the mother resembles the little boy in his active oedipus complex. We now see that the boy in the negative or passive oedipus complex closely resembles the little girl in her passive, positive oedipal relation to the father. Unable to achieve the full activity of the male in the father identification, the girl falls back upon her identification with the active mother. Under the influence of castration, she shifts her passivity from the mother to the father. But the boy too may come upon obstacles in his oedipal father identification. The first of these is the presence of what I should like to call the "nuclear passivity" of the child, that original passivity of wide constitutional variation with which it is born into the world. Somehow, either as the result of a strong tendency to regress, or because of the presence of an unknown point of fixation at the preoedipal level, or because of some constitutional inability to overcome the primary inertia, the development of activity is impaired. An additional hindrance is undue aggression toward the mother. The external causes of hostility are manifold, but in addition certain human beings probably possess, actually or potentially, a greater number of aggressive impulses than the normal. When activity is thus impaired at its origin it seems highly probable that traces of this impairment, like those somatic evidences of injury to the germ plasm itself, become evident somewhere in the course of later development.

During the active oedipus complex of the boy, aggression toward the mother may manifest itself as sadistic love. But a fundamental hostility seriously interferes with the full formation of normal oedipal love, and persisting ambivalence further undermines the relation. These individuals are sensitized to traumata, and the oedipal rejection and disappointment frequently result in a regression to the earlier mother attachment which as we know belongs to the active-passive rather than the phallic-castrated level. This regression makes it possible for the neurotic boy to avoid the entire topic of castration. Inability to accept the castration of the mother is in itself a usual cause of regression. Under these circumstances only phallic individuals are acceptable as love objects. In this clinical picture of manifest male homosexuality, the influence of the preoedipal phase is unmistakable.

But the main neurotic type which results from preoedipal fixation is that of the man with a passive oedipus complex. Under the stress of the maternal castration, the little boy has identified himself with the mother and has taken the father as his love object. We have described the manner in which the girl shifts her passivity from the mother to the father, and have seen that the neurotic boy pursues a similar course. But the boy who because of the mother's castration has shifted his passivity from the mother to the father has not gained by the transaction. His possession of the phallus is further threatened by his love of the father. The various methods of solving this dilemma are reflected in the innumerable clinical manifestations of the neuroses. A paranoid psychosis may result when the love of the father is so strong as to become intolerable. Sometimes, on the other hand, the individual succeeds in shifting his passivity from the father back to its original object, the mother, thus avoiding the paranoid sphere of the father. In these cases a neurosis results which is characterized throughout life by a pendulum-like swing from one parent to the other. Where these individuals have succeeded in more or less permanently attaching themselves to the mother, a so called mother-fixation results. It has always been assumed that these individuals could not relinquish their oedipal object. But closer examination reveals that the mother who cannot be given up is the phallic mother, and that the relationship is dominated not by the usual active oedipal love but by an attachment which is to a large extent preoedipal and passive. Because of the primitive nature of this passive, tenacious attachment to the mother, an intensely ambivalent relationship between the man and his mother substitute results. His passivity and his dependence upon the phallic mother are resented and rebelled against by his entire masculinity. Here it is evident that the persistence of the preoedipal passivity has led to a malformation of the oedipus complex itself, and has played a major role perhaps in the genesis and certainly in the maintenance of the passive love of the man for his father.

While I am inclined to believe that unresolved, unassimilated passivity is in large measure responsible for these abnormalities of development, there exists also a primitive activity whose nature and possible pathogenic role has not yet been studied.

It is axiomatic that the difficulties of investigation and the tentativeness of our findings vary inversely with the age of the child under examination. This axiom is my excuse for the fragmentary nature of this work.

NOTES

1. Freud: *Über die weibliche Sexualität,* Ges. Schr., XII, p. 120.
2. To the best of my knowledge, the term *preoedipal* was first used by Freud in 1931 in this work, p. 126, and by this author in *The Analysis of a Case of Paranoia.* J. of Nerv. and Ment. Dis., LXX, 1929, p. 177.
3. This situation is described by Jeanne Lampl-de Groot in *Zur Entwicklungs-geschichte des Oedipuskomplexes der Frau,* Int. Ztschr. Psa., XIII, No. 3, 1927.
4. Freud: *Über die weibliche Sexualität,* Ges. Schr., XII, p. 132.
5. In order to avoid undue confusion on the part of the reader, it should be remembered that suckling is always a transitive verb, although it is frequently used in the opposite sense with a resultant confusion typical of this early phase.
6. Freud: *Über die weibliche Sexualität,* Ges. Schr., XII, p. 134.

2. The Oedipus Complex in the Light of Early Anxieties

Melanie Klein

INTRODUCTION

I have two main objectives in presenting this paper. I intend to single out some typical early anxiety situations and show their connection with the Oedipus complex. Since these anxieties and defences are part of the infantile depressive position as I see it, I hope to throw some light on the relation between the depressive position and libidinal development. My second purpose is to compare my conclusions about the Oedipus complex with Freud's views on that subject.

I shall exemplify my argument by short extracts from two case histories. Many more details could be adduced about both analyses, about the patients' family relationships and about the technique used. I shall, however, confine myself to those details of the material which are most essential from the point of view of my subject-matter.

The children whose case histories I shall use to illustrate my argument were both suffering from severe emotional difficulties. In making use of such material as a basis for my conclusions about the normal course of the Oedipus development, I am following a method well tried in psycho-analysis. Freud justified this angle of approach in many of his writings. For instance in one place, he says: 'Pathology has always done us the service of making discernible by isolation and exaggeration conditions which would remain concealed in a normal state' (*S.E.* 22, p. 121). . . .

Adapted with permission of the author and The Free Press, a Division of Macmillan, Inc., from *Love, Guilt, and Reparation and Other Works*, by Melanie Klein. © 1975 by The Melanie Klein Trust. First published in 1945.

EXTRACTS FROM CASE HISTORY ILLUSTRATING THE BOY'S OEDIPUS DEVELOPMENT

[The author illustrates her views about the boy's Oedipus development with clinical material taken from the analysis of Richard, a ten-year-old boy. Richard's Oedipal anxieties in the early stages of his development are illustrated by the interpretation of a series of his drawings. Klein analyzes Richard's feminine position which is under the dominance of oral, urethral, and anal impulses and phantasies and is closely linked with the boy's relation to his mother's breasts. These feminine desires are at the root of his inverted Oedipus complex and of his first homosexual position. The boy's capacity to turn some of his love and libidinal desires from his mother's breast toward his father's penis, while retaining the breast as a good object, will determine the representation in the boy's mind of his father's penis as a good and creative organ that will give him libidinal gratification as well as give him children as it does to his mother. The belief in the ''goodness'' of the male genital allows the boy to experience his genital desires toward his mother and to develop positive Oedipus tendencies. — ED.]

EXTRACTS FROM CASE HISTORY ILLUSTRATING THE GIRL'S OEDIPUS DEVELOPMENT

I have discussed some of the anxieties which disturb genital development in the boy and I shall now put forward some material from the case history of a little girl, Rita, which I have already described from various angles in earlier publications. This material has certain advantages for purposes of presentation, for it is simple and straightforward. Most of this case material has been published previously; I shall however add a few details so far unpublished as well as some new interpretations which I could not have made at the time but which, in retrospect, seem to be fully borne out by the material.

My patient Rita, who was two years and nine months old at the beginning of her analysis, was a very difficult child to bring up. She suffered from anxieties of various kinds, from inability to tolerate frustration, and from frequent states of unhappiness. She showed marked obsessional features which had been increasing for some time, and she insisted on elaborate obsessional ceremonials. She alternated between an exaggerated 'goodness', accompanied by feelings of remorse, and states of 'naughtiness' when she attempted to dominate everybody around her. She also had difficulties over eating, was 'faddy', and frequently suffered from loss of appetite. Though she was a very intelligent child, the development and integration of her personality were held back by the strength of her neurosis.

She often cried, apparently without cause, and when asked by her mother why she was crying answered: 'Because I'm so sad,' To the question: 'Why are you so sad?' she replied: 'Because I'm crying.' Her feelings of guilt and unhappiness expressed themselves in constant questions to her mother: 'Am I good?' 'Do you love me?' and so on. She could not bear any reproach and, if reprimanded, either burst into tears or became defiant. Her feeling of insecurity in relation to her parents showed itself for instance in the following incident from her second year. Once, so I was told, she burst into tears because her father uttered a playful threat against a bear in her picture book with whom she had obviously identified herself.

Rita suffered from a marked inhibition in play. The only thing she could do with her dolls, for instance, was to wash them and change their clothes in a compulsive way. As soon as she introduced any imaginative element, she had an outbreak of anxiety and stopped playing.

The following are some relevant facts from her history. Rita was breast-fed for a few months; then she had been given the bottle, which she had at first been unwilling to accept. Weaning from the bottle to solid food was again troublesome, and she was still suffering from difficulties over eating when I began her analysis. Moreover, at that time she was still being given a bottle at night. Her mother told me that she had given up trying to wean Rita from this last bottle because every such attempt caused the child great distress. With regard to Rita's habit training, which was achieved early in her second year, I have reason to assume that her mother had been rather too anxious over it. Rita's obsessional neurosis proved to be closely connected with her early habit training.

Rita shared her parents' bedroom until she was nearly two, and she repeatedly witnessed sexual intercourse between her parents. When she was two years old, her brother was born, and at that time her neurosis broke out in full force. Another contributory circumstance was the fact that her mother was herself neurotic and obviously ambivalent towards Rita.

Her parents told me that Rita was much more fond of her mother than of her father until the end of her first year. At the beginning of her second year she developed a marked preference for her father, together with pronounced jealousy of her mother. At fifteen months Rita repeatedly and unmistakably expressed the wish, when she sat on her father's knee, to be left alone with him in the room. She could already put this into words. At the age of about eighteen months there was a striking change, which showed itself in an altered relation to both her parents, as well as in various symptoms such as night terrors and animal phobias (particularly of dogs). Her mother once again became the favourite, yet the child's relation to her showed strong ambivalence. She clung to her mother so much that she could hardly let her out of her sight. This went together with attempts to dominate her and with an often unconcealed hatred of her. Concurrently Rita developed an outspoken dislike of her father.

These facts were clearly observed at the time and reported to me by her parents. In the case of older children, parents' reports about the earlier years are often unreliable, since, as time goes on, the facts are apt to be increasingly falsified in their memory. In Rita's case the details were still fresh in her parents' minds, and the analysis fully confirmed all the essentials of their report.

Early Relations to the Parents

At the beginning of Rita's second year some important elements of her Oedipus situation were plainly observable, such as her preference for her father and jealousy of her mother, and even the wish to take her mother's place with her father. In assessing Rita's Oedipus development in her second year we have to consider some outstanding external factors. The child shared her parents' bedroom and had ample opportunity for witnessing sexual intercourse between them; there was therefore a constant stimulus for libidinal desires and for jealousy, hatred and anxiety. When she was fifteen months old her mother became pregnant, and the child unconsciously understood her mother's condition; thus Rita's desire to receive a baby from her father, as well as her rivalry with her mother, was strongly reinforced. As a consequence, her aggressiveness, and the ensuing anxiety and feelings of guilt increased to such an extent that her Oedipus desires could not be maintained.

The difficulties in Rita's development cannot be explained, however, by these external stimuli alone. Many children are exposed to similar, and even to much more unfavourable, experiences without becoming seriously ill in consequence. We have therefore to consider the internal factors which, in interaction with the influences from without, led to Rita's illness and to the disturbance of her sexual development.

As the analysis revealed, Rita's oral-sadistic impulses were exceedingly strong and her capacity to tolerate tension of any kind was unusually low. These were some of the constitutional characteristics which determined her reactions to the early frustrations she suffered and from the beginning strongly affected her relation to her mother. When Rita's positive Oedipus desires came to the fore at the end of her first year, this new relation to both parents reinforced Rita's feelings of frustration, hatred and aggressiveness, with their concomitants of anxiety and guilt. She was unable to cope with these manifold conflicts and therefore could not maintain her genital desires.

Rita's relation to her mother was dominated by two great sources of anxiety: persecutory fear and depressive anxiety. In one aspect her mother represented a terrifying and retaliating figure. In another aspect she was Rita's indispensable loved and good object, and Rita felt her own aggression as a danger to this loved mother. She was therefore overwhelmed by the fear of losing her. It was the strength of these early anxieties and feelings of guilt which largely determined Rita's incapacity to tolerate the additional anxiety and guilt arising from the Oedipus feelings—rivalry and hatred against her mother. In defence she repressed her hatred and over-compensated for it by excessive love, and this necessarily implied a regression to earlier stages of the libido. Rita's relation to her father was also fundamentally influenced by these factors. Some of the resentment she felt towards her mother was deflected on to her father and reinforced the hatred of him which derived from the frustration of her Oedipus desires and which, towards the beginning of her second year, strikingly superseded her former love for her father. The failure to establish a satisfactory relation to her mother was repeated in her oral and genital relation to her father. Strong desires to castrate him (partly derived from frustration in the feminine position, partly from penis envy in the male position) became clear in the analysis.

Rita's sadistic phantasies were thus closely bound up with grievances derived from frustration in various libidinal positions and experienced in the inverted as well as in the positive Oedipus situation. The sexual intercourse between her parents played an important part in her sadistic phantasies and became in the child's mind a dangerous and frightening event, in which her mother appeared as the victim of her father's extreme cruelty. In consequence, not only did her father turn in her mind into someone dangerous to her mother but—in so far as Rita's Oedipus desires were maintained in identification with her mother—into a person dangerous toward herself. Rita's phobia of dogs went back to the fear of the dangerous penis of her father which would bite her in retaliation for her own impulses to castrate him. Her whole relation to her father was profoundly disturbed because he had turned into a 'bad man'. He was all the more hated because he became the embodiment of her own sadistic desires towards her mother.

The following episode, reported to me by her mother, illustrates this last point. At the beginning of her third year Rita was out for a walk with her mother and saw a cabman beating his horses cruelly. Her mother was extremely indignant, and the little girl also expressed strong indignation. Later on in the day she surprised her mother by saying: 'When are we going out again to see the bad man beating the horses?' thus revealing the fact that she had derived sadistic pleasure from the experience and wished for its repetition. In her unconscious the cabman represented her father and the horses her mother, and her father was carrying out in sexual intercourse the child's sadistic phantasies directed against her mother. The fear of her father's bad genital, together with the phantasy of her mother injured and destroyed by Rita's hatred and by the bad father—the cabman—interfered both with her positive and with her inverted Oedipus desires. Rita could neither identify herself with such a destroyed mother, nor allow herself to play in the homosexual position the role of the father. Thus in these early stages neither position could be satisfactorily established.

Some Instances from the Analytic Material

The anxieties Rita experienced when she witnessed the primal scene are shown in the following material.

On one occasion during the analysis she put a triangular brick on one side and said: 'That's a little woman.' She then took a 'little hammer', as she called an oblong brick, and she hit the brickbox with it saying: 'When the hammer hit hard, the little woman was *so* frightened.' The triangular brick stood for herself, the 'hammer' for her father's penis, the box for her mother, and the whole situation represented her witnessing the primal scene. It is significant that she hit the box exactly in a place where it happened to be stuck together only with paper, so that she made a hole in it. This was one of the instances when Rita showed me symbolically her unconscious knowledge of the vagina and the part it played in her sexual theories.

The next two instances relate to her castration complex and penis envy. Rita was playing that she was travelling with her Teddy-bear to the house of a 'good' woman where she was to be given 'a marvellous treat'. This journey, however, did not go smoothly. Rita got rid of the engine-driver and took his place. But he came back again and again and threatened her, causing her great anxiety. An object of contention between her and him was her Teddy-bear whom she felt to be essential for the success of the journey. Here the bear represented her father's penis, and her rivalry with her father was expressed by this fight over the penis. She had robbed her father of it, partly from feelings of envy, hatred and revenge, partly in order to take his place with her mother and—by means of her father's potent penis—to make reparation for the injuries done to her mother in phantasy.

The next instance is linked with her bed-time ritual, which had become more and more elaborate and compulsive as time went on and involved a corresponding ceremonial with her doll. The main point of it was that she (and her doll as well) had to be tightly tucked up in the bed clothes, otherwise —as she said—a mouse or a 'butzen' (a word of her own) would get in through the window and bite off her own 'butzen'. The 'butzen' represented both her father's genital and her own: her father's penis would bite off her own imaginary penis just as *she* desired to castrate *him*. As I see it now, the fear of her mother attacking the 'inside' of her body also contributed to her fear of someone coming through the window. The room also represented her body and the assailant was her mother retaliating for the child's attacks on her. The obsessional need to be tucked in with such elaborate care was a defence against all these fears.

Super-ego Development

The anxieties and feelings of guilt described in the last two sections were bound up with Rita's super-ego development. I found in her a cruel and unrelenting super-ego, such as underlies severe obsessional neuroses in adults. This development I could in the analysis trace back definitely to the beginning of her second year. In the light of my later experience I am bound to conclude that the beginnings of Rita's super-ego reached back to the first few months of life.

In the travelling game I have described, the engine-driver represented her super-ego as well as her actual father. We also see her super-ego at work in Rita's obsessional play with her doll, when she went through a ritual similar to her own bed-time ceremonial, putting the doll to sleep and tucking her up very elaborately. Once during the analysis Rita placed an elephant by the doll's bedside. As she explained, the elephant was to prevent the 'child' (doll) from getting up, because otherwise the 'child' would steal into its parents' bedroom and either 'do them some harm or take something away from them'. The elephant represented her super-ego (her father and mother), and the attacks on her parents which it was to prevent were the expression of Rita's own sadistic impulses centering on her parents' sexual intercourse and her mother's pregnancy. The super-ego was to make it impossible for the child to rob her mother of the baby inside her, to injure or destroy her mother's body, as well as to castrate the father.

A significant detail from her history was that early in her third year Rita repeatedly declared, when she was playing with dolls, that she *was not the doll's mother*. In the context of the analysis it appeared that she could not allow herself to be the doll's mother because the doll stood for her baby brother whom she wanted and feared to take away from her mother. Her guilt also related to her aggressive phantasies during her mother's pregnancy. When Rita could not play at being her doll's mother, this inhibition derived from her feelings of guilt as well as from her fear of a cruel mother-figure, infinitely more severe than her actual mother had ever been. Not only did Rita see her *real* mother in this distorted light, but she felt in constant danger from a terrifying *internal* mother-figure. I have referred to Rita's phantasied attacks on her mother's body and the corresponding anxiety that her mother would attack her and rob her of her imaginary babies, as well as to her fear of being attacked and castrated by her father. I would now go further in my interpretations. To the phantasied attacks on her body by her parents as external figures corresponded fear of inner attacks by the internalized persecuting parent-figures who formed the cruel part of her super-ego.[1]

The harshness of Rita's super-ego often showed in her play during the analysis. For instance, she used to punish her doll cruelly; then would follow an outbreak of rage and fear. She was identified both with the harsh parents who inflict severe punishment and with the child who is being cruelly punished and bursts into a rage. This was not only noticeable in her play but in her behaviour in general. At certain times she seemed to be the mouthpiece of a severe and unrelenting mother, at other times of an uncontrollable, greedy and destructive infant. There seemed to be very little of her own ego to bridge these two extremes and to modify the intensity of the conflict. The gradual process of integration of her super-ego was severely interfered with, and she could not develop an individuality of her own.

Persecutory and Depressive Anxieties Disturbing the Oedipus Development

Rita's depressive feelings were a marked feature in her neurosis. Her states of sadness and crying without cause, her constant questions whether her mother loved her—all these were indications of her depressive anxieties. These anxieties were rooted in her relation to her mother's breasts. In consequence of her sadistic phantasies, in which she had attacked the breast and her mother as a whole, Rita was dominated by fears which profoundly influenced her relation to her mother. In one aspect she loved her mother as a good and indispensable object and felt guilty because she had endangered her by her aggressive phantasies; in another aspect she hated and feared her as the bad, persecutory mother (in the first place, the bad breast). These fears and complex feelings, which related to her mother both an an external and internal object, constituted her infantile depressive position. Rita was incapable of dealing with these acute anxieties and could not overcome her depressive position.

In this connection some material from the early part of her analysis is significant. She scribbled on a piece of paper and blackened it with great vigour. Then she tore it up and threw the scraps into a glass of water which she put to her mouth as if to drink from it. At that moment she stopped and said under her breath: 'Dead woman.' This material, with the same words, was repeated on another occasion.

The piece of paper blackened, torn up and thrown into the water represented her mother destroyed by oral, anal, and urethral means, and this picture of a dead mother related not only to the external mother when she was out of sight but also to the *internal* mother. Rita had to give up the rivalry with her mother in the Oedipus situation because her unconscious fear of loss of the internal and external object acted as a barrier to every desire which would increase her hatred of her mother and therefore cause her mother's death. These anxieties, derived from the oral position, underlay the marked depression which Rita developed at her mother's attempt to wean her of the last bottle. Rita would not drink the milk from a cup. She fell into a state of despair; she lost her appetite in general, refused food, clung more than ever to her mother, asking her again and again whether she loved her, if she had been naughty, and so on. Her analysis revealed that the weaning represented a cruel punishment for her aggressive desires and death wishes against her mother. Since the loss of the bottle stood for the final loss of the breast, Rita felt when the bottle was taken away that she had actually destroyed her mother. Even the presence of her mother could do no more than temporarily alleviate these fears. The inference suggests itself that while the lost bottle represented the lost good breast, the cup of milk which Rita refused in her state of depression following the weaning represented the destroyed and dead mother, just as the glass of water with the torn paper had represented the 'dead woman'.

As I have suggested, Rita's depressive anxieties about the death of her mother were bound up with persecutory fears relating to attacks on her own body by a retaliating mother. In fact such attacks always appear to a girl not only as a danger to her body, but as a danger to everything precious which in her mind her 'inside' contains: her potential children, the good mother, and the good father.

The incapacity to protect these loved objects against external and internal persecutors is part of the most fundamental anxiety situation of girls.[2]

Rita's relation to her father was largely determined by the anxiety situations centring on her mother. Much of her hatred and fear of the bad breast had been transferred to her father's penis. Excessive guilt and fear of loss relating to her mother had also been transferred to her father. All this—together with the frustration suffered directly from her father—had interfered with the development of her positive Oedipus complex.

Her hatred of her father was reinforced by penis envy and by rivalry with him in the inverted Oedipus situation. Her attempts to cope with her penis envy led to a reinforced belief in her imaginary penis. However, she felt this penis to be endangered by a bad father who would castrate her in retaliation for her own desires to castrate him. When Rita was afraid of her father's 'butzen' coming into the room and biting off her own 'butzen', this was an instance of her castration fear.

Her desires to annex her father's penis and to play his part with her mother were clear indications of her penis envy. This was illustrated by the play material I have quoted: she travelled with her Teddy-bear, representing the penis, to the 'good woman' who was to give them a 'marvellous treat'. The wish to possess a penis of her own, however, was —as her analysis showed me—strongly reinforced by anxieties and guilt relating to the death of her loved mother. These anxieties, which early on had undermined her relation to her mother, largely contributed to the failure of the positive Oedipus development. They also had the effect of reinforcing Rita's desires to possess a penis, for she felt that she could only repair the damage done to her mother, and make up for the babies which in phantasy she had taken from her, if she possessed a penis of her own with which to gratify her mother and give her children.

Rita's excessive difficulties in dealing with her inverted and positive Oedipus complex were thus rooted in her depressive position. Along with the lessening of these anxieties, she became able to tolerate her Oedipus desires and to achieve increasingly a feminine and maternal attitude. Towards the end of her analysis, which was cut short owing to external circumstances, Rita's relation to both parents, as well as to her brother, improved. Her aversion to her father, which had until then been very marked, gave place to affection for him; the ambivalence towards her mother decreased, and a more friendly and stable relationship developed.

Rita's changed attitude towards her Teddy-bear and her doll reflected the extent to which her libidinal development had progressed and her neurotic difficulties and the severity of her super-ego had been reduced. Once, near the end of the analysis, while she was kissing the bear and hugging it and calling it pet names, she said: 'I'm not a bit unhappy any more because now I've got such a dear little baby.' She could now allow herself to be the mother of her imaginary child. This change was not an altogether new development, but in some measure a return to an earlier libidinal position. In her second year Rita's desires to receive her father's penis and to have a child from him had been disturbed by anxiety and guilt relating to her mother; her positive Oedipus development broke down and there was a marked aggravation of her neurosis. When Rita said emphatically that she was not the mother of her doll, she clearly indicated the struggle against her desires to have a baby. Under the stress of her anxiety and guilt she could not maintain the feminine position and was driven to reinforce the male position. The bear thus came to stand predominantly for the desired penis. Rita could not allow herself the wish for a child from her father, and the identification with her mother in the Oedipus situation could not be established, until her anxieties and guilt in relation to both parents had lessened.

GENERAL THEORETICAL SUMMARY

Early Stages of the Oedipus Complex in Both Sexes

The clinical pictures of the two cases I have presented in this paper differed in many ways.* However, the two cases had some important features in common, such as strong oral-sadistic impulses, excessive anxiety and guilt, and a low capacity of the ego to tolerate tension of any kind. In my experience, these are some of the factors which, in interaction with external circumstances, prevent the ego from gradually building up adequate defences against anxiety. As a result, the working through of early anxiety situations is impaired and the child's emotional, libidinal, and ego-development suffers. Owing to the dominance of anxiety and guilt there is an over-strong fixation to the early stages of libidinal organization and, in interaction with this, an excessive tendency to regress to those early stages. In consequence, the Oedipus development is interfered with and the genital organization cannot be securely established. In the two cases referred to in this paper, as well as in others, the Oedipus complex began to develop on normal lines when these early anxieties were diminished.

The effect of anxiety and guilt on the course of the Oedipus development is to some extent illustrated by the two brief case histories I have given. The following survey of my theoretical conclusions on certain aspects of the Oedipus development is, however, based on the whole of my analytic work with child and adult cases, ranging from normality to severe illness.

A full description of the Oedipus development would have to include a discussion of external influences and experiences at every stage, and of their effect throughout childhood. I have deliberately sacrificed the exhaustive description of external factors to the need to clarify the most important issues.[3]

My experience has led me to believe that, from the very beginning of life, libido is fused with aggressiveness, and that the development of the libido is at every stage vitally affected by anxiety derived from aggressiveness. Anxiety, guilt, and depressive feelings at times drive the libido forward to new sources of gratification, at times they check the development of the libido by reinforcing the fixation to an earlier object and aim.

In comparison with the later phases of the Oedipus complex, the picture

---

*[The boy's case history has not been reprinted here.]

of its earliest stages is necessarily more obscure, as the infant's ego is immature and under the full sway of unconscious phantasy; also his instinctual life is in its most polymorphous phase. These early stages are characterized by swift fluctuations between different objects and aims, with corresponding fluctuations in the nature of the defences. In my view, the Oedipus complex starts during the first year of life and in both sexes develops to begin with on similar lines. The relation to the mother's breast is one of the essential factors which determine the whole emotional and sexual development. I therefore take the breast relation as my starting point in the following description of the beginnings of the Oedipus complex in both sexes.

It seems that the search for new sources of gratification is inherent in the forward movement of the libido. The gratification experienced at the mother's breast enables the infant to turn his desires towards new objects, first of all towards his father's penis. Particular impetus, however, is given to the new desire by frustration in the breast relation. It is important to remember that frustration depends on internal factors as well as on actual experiences. Some measure of frustration at the breast is inevitable, even under the most favourable conditions, for what the infant actually desires is *unlimited* gratification. The frustration experienced at the mother's breast leads both boy and girl to turn away from it and stimulates the infant's desire for oral gratification from the penis of the father. The breast and the penis are, therefore, the primary objects of the infant's oral desires.[4]

Frustration and gratification from the outset mould the infant's relation to a loved good breast and to a hated bad breast. The need to cope with frustration and with the ensuing aggression is one of the factors which lead to idealizing the good breast and good mother, and correspondingly to intensifying the hatred and fears of the bad breast and bad mother, which becomes the prototype of all persecuting and frightening objects.

The two conflicting attitudes to the mother's breast are carried over into the new relation to the father's penis. The frustration suffered in the earlier relation increases the demands and hopes from the new source and stimulates love for the new object. The inevitable disappointment in the new relation reinforces the pull-back to the first object; and this contributes to the lability and fluidity of emotional attitudes and of the stages of libidinal organization.

Furthermore, aggressive impulses, stimulated and reinforced by frustration, turn, in the child's mind, the victims of his aggressive phantasies into injured and retaliating figures which threaten him with the same sadistic attacks as he commits against the parents in phantasy.[5] In consequence, the infant feels an increased need for a loved and loving object—a perfect, an ideal object—in order to satisfy his craving for help and security. Each object, therefore, is in turn liable to become at times good, at times bad. This movement to and fro between the various aspects of the primary imagos implies a close interaction between the early stages of the inverted and positive Oedipus complex.

Since under the dominance of the oral libido the infant from the beginning introjects his objects, the primary imagos have a counterpart in his inner world. The imagos of his mother's breast and of his father's penis are established within his ego and form the nucleus of his super-ego. To the introjection of the good and bad breast and mother corresponds the introjection of the good and bad penis and father. They become the first representatives on the one hand of protective and helpful internal figures, on the other hand of retaliating and persecuting internal figures, and are the first identifications which the ego develops.

The relation to internal figures interacts in manifold ways with the child's ambivalent relation to both parents as external objects. For to the introjection of external objects corresponds at every step the projection of internal figures on to the external world, and this interaction underlies the relation to the actual parents as well as the development of the super-ego. In consequence of this interaction, which implies an orientation outwards and inwards, there is a constant fluctuation between internal and external objects and situations. These fluctuations are bound up with the movement of the libido between different aims and objects, and thus the course of the Oedipus complex and the development of the super-ego are closely interlinked.

Though still overshadowed by oral, urethral and anal libido, genital desires soon mingle with the child's oral impulses. Early genital desires, as well as oral ones, are directed towards mother and father. This is in line with my assumption that in both sexes there is an inherent unconscious knowledge of the existence of the penis as well as of the vagina. In the male infant, genital sensations are the basis for the expectation that his father possesses a penis which the boy desires according to the equation 'breast = penis'. At the same time, his genital sensations and impulses also imply the search for an opening into which to insert his penis, i.e., they are directed towards his mother. The infant girl's genital sensations correspondingly prepare the desire to receive her father's penis into her vagina. It appears therefore that the genital desires for the penis of the father, which mingle with oral desires, are at the root of the early stages of the girl's positive and of the boy's inverted Oedipus complex.

The course of libidinal development is at every stage influenced by anxiety, guilt and depressive feelings. In the two earlier papers I have repeatedly referred to the infantile depressive position as the central position in early development. I would now rather suggest the following formulation: the core of infantile depressive feelings, i.e., the child's fear of the loss of his loved objects, as a consequence of his hatred and aggression, enters into his object relations and Oedipus complex from the beginning.

An essential corollary of anxiety, guilt, and depressive feelings is the urge for reparation. Under the sway of guilt the infant is impelled to undo the effect of his sadistic impulses by libidinal means. Thus feelings of love, which co-exist with aggressive impulses, are reinforced by the drive for reparation. Reparative phantasies represent, often in minute detail, the obverse of sadistic phantasies, and to the feeling of sadistic omnipotence corresponds the feeling of reparative omnipotence. For instance, urine and faeces represent agents of destruction when the child hates and gifts when he loves; but when he feels guilty and driven to make reparation, the 'good' excrements in his mind become the means by which he can cure the damage done by his 'dangerous' excrements. Again, both boy and girl, though in different ways, feel that the penis which damaged and destroyed the mother in their sadistic phantasies becomes the means of restoring and curing her in phantasies of reparation. The desire to give and receive libidinal gratification is thus enhanced by the drive for reparation. For the infant feels that in this way the injured object can be restored, and also that the power of his aggressive impulses is diminished, that his impulses of love are given free rein, and guilt is assuaged.

The course of libidinal development is thus at every step stimulated and reinforced by the drive for reparation, and ultimately by the sense of guilt. On the other hand, guilt which engenders the drive for reparation also inhibits libidinal desires. For when the child feels that his aggressiveness predominates, libidinal desires appear to him as a danger to his loved objects and must therefore be repressed. . . .

The Girl's Oedipus Development

I have already described the early stages of the girl's Oedipus development insofar as it is in line with the boy's development. I shall now point out some essential features which are specific to the girl's Oedipus complex.

When genital sensations in the infant girl gain in strength, in keeping with the receptive nature of her genitals, the desire to receive the penis arises.[6] At the same time she has an unconscious knowledge that her body contains potential children whom she feels to be her most precious possession. The penis of her father as the giver of children, and equated to children, becomes the object of great desire and admiration for the little girl. This relation to the penis as a source of happiness and good gifts is enhanced by the loving and grateful relation to the good breast.

Together with the unconscious knowledge that she contains potential babies, the little girl has grave doubts as to her future capacity to bear children. On many grounds she feels at a disadvantage in comparison with her mother. In the child's unconscious the mother is imbued with magic power, for all goodness springs from her breast and the mother also contains the father's penis and the babies. The little girl—in contrast to the boy, whose hope for potency gains strength from the possession of a penis which can be compared with his father's penis—has no means of reassuring herself about her future fertility. In addition, her doubts are increased by all the anxieties relating to the contents of her body. These anxieties intensify the impulses to rob her mother's body of her children as well as of the father's penis, and this in turn intensifies the fear lest her own inside be attacked and robbed of its 'good' contents by a retaliating external and internal mother.

Some of these elements are operative in the boy as well, but the fact that the girl's genital development centres on the feminine desire to receive her father's penis and that her main unconscious concern is for her imaginary babies, is a specific feature of the girl's development. In consequence, her phantasies and emotions are predominantly built round her inner world and inner objects; her Oedipus rivalry expresses itself essentially in the impulse to rob her mother of the father's penis and the babies; the fear of having her body attacked and her inner good objects injured or taken away by a bad retaliating mother plays a prominent and lasting part in her anxieties. This, as I see it, is the leading anxiety situation of the girl.

Moreover, while in the boy the envy of his mother (who is felt to contain the penis of his father and the babies) is an element in his inverted Oedipus complex, with the girl this envy forms part of her positive Oedipus situation. It remains an essential factor throughout her sexual and emotional development, and has an important effect on her identification with her mother in the sexual relation with the father as well as in the maternal role.

The girl's desire to possess a penis and to be a boy is an expression of her bisexuality and is as inherent a feature in girls as the desire to be a woman is in boys. Her wish to have a penis of her own is secondary to her desire to receive the penis, and is greatly enhanced by the frustrations in her feminine position and by the anxiety and guilt experienced in the positive Oedipus situation. The girl's penis envy covers in some measure the frustrated desire to take her mother's place with the father and to receive children from him.

I can here only touch upon the specific factors which underlie the girl's super-ego formation. Because of the great part her inner world plays in the girl's emotional life, she has a strong urge to fill this inner world with good objects. This contributes to the intensity of her introjective processes, which are also reinforced by the receptive nature of her genital. The admired internalized penis of her father forms an intrinsic part of her super-ego. She identifies herself with her father in her male position, but this identification rests on the possession of an imaginary penis. Her main identification with her father is experienced in relation to the internalized penis of her father, and this relation is based on the feminine as well as on the male position. In the feminine position she is driven by her sexual desires, and by her longing for a child, to internalize her father's penis. She is capable of complete submission to this admired internalized father, while in the male position she wishes to emulate him in all her masculine aspirations and sublimations. Thus her male identification with her father is mixed with her feminine attitude, and it is this combination which characterizes the feminine super-ego.

To the admired good father in the girl's super-ego formation corresponds to some extent the bad castrating father. Her main anxiety object, however, is the persecuting mother. If the internalization of a good mother, with whose maternal attitude she can identify herself, counterbalances this persecutory fear, her relation to the good internalized father becomes strengthened by her own maternal attitude towards him.

In spite of the prominence of the inner world in her emotional life, the little girl's need for love and her relation to people show a great dependence on the outer world. This contradiction is, however, only apparent, because this dependence on the outer world is reinforced by her need to gain reassurance about her inner world.

Some Comparisons with the Classical Concept of the Oedipus Complex

I now propose to compare my views with those of Freud on certain aspects of the Oedipus complex, and to clarify some divergences to which my experience has led me. Many aspects of the Oedipus complex, on which my work fully confirms Freud's findings, have been to some extent implied in my description of the Oedipus situation. The magnitude of the subject, however, makes it necessary for me to refrain from discussing these aspects in detail, and I have to limit myself to clarifying some of the divergences. The following summary represents in my opinion the essence of Freud's conclusions about certain essential features of the Oedipus development.[7]

According to Freud, genital desires emerge and a definite object choice takes place during the phallic phase, which extends from about three to five years of age, and is contemporaneous with the Oedipus complex. During this phase 'only one genital, namely the male one, comes into account. What is present, therefore, is not a primacy of the genitals, but a primacy of the *phallus*' (*S.E.* 19, p. 142).

In the boy, 'what brings about the destruction of the child's phallic organization is the threat of castration' (*S.E.* 19, p. 175). Furthermore, his super-ego, the heir of the Oedipus complex, is formed by the internalization of the parental authority. Guilt is the expression of tension between the ego and the super-ego. It is only when the super-ego has developed that the use of the term 'guilt' is justified. Predominant weight is given by Freud to the boy's super-ego as the internalized authority of the father; and, though in some measure he acknowledges the identification with the mother as a factor in the boy's super-ego formation, he has not expressed his views on this aspect of the super-ego in any detail.

With regard to the girl, in Freud's view her long 'pre-Oedipal attachment' to her mother covers the period before she enters the Oedipus situation. Freud also characterizes this period as 'the phase of exclusive attachment to the mother, which may be called the pre-Oedipus phase' (*S.E.* 21, p. 230). Subsequently during her phallic phase, the girl's fundamental desires in relation to her mother, maintained with the greatest intensity, focus on receiving a penis from her. The clitoris represents in the little girl's mind her penis, clitoris masturbation is the expression of her phallic desires. The vagina is not yet discovered and will only play its part in womanhood. When the girl discovers that she does not possess a penis, her castration complex comes to the fore. At this juncture the attachment to her mother is broken off with resentment and hatred because her mother has not given her a penis. She also discovers that even her mother lacks a penis, and this contributes to her turning away from her mother to her father. She first turns to her father with the wish to receive a penis, and only subsequently with the desire to receive a child from him, 'that is, a baby takes the place of a penis in accordance with an ancient symbolic equivalence' (S.E. 22, p. 128). In these ways her Oedipus complex is ushered in by her castration complex.

The girl's main anxiety situation is the loss of love, and Freud connects this fear with the fear of the death of her mother.

The girl's super-ego development differs in various ways from the boy's super-ego development, but they have in common an essential feature, i.e., that the super-ego and the sense of guilt are sequels to the Oedipus complex.

Freud refers to the girl's motherly feelings derived from the early relation to her mother in the pre-Oedipus phase. He also refers to the girl's identification with her mother, derived from her Oedipus complex. But he has not linked these two attitudes, nor shown how the feminine identification with her mother in the Oedipus situation affects the course of the girl's Oedipus complex. In his view, while the girl's genital organization is taking shape, she values her mother predominantly in the phallic aspect.

I shall now summarize my own views on these essential issues. As I see it, the boy's and girl's sexual and emotional development *from early infancy onwards* includes genital sensations and trends, which constitute the first stages of the inverted and positive Oedipus complex; they are experienced under the primacy of oral libido and mingle with urethral and anal desires and phantasies. The libidinal stages overlap from the earliest months of life onwards. The positive and inverted Oedipus tendencies are from their inception in close interaction. It is during the stage of genital primacy that the positive Oedipus situation reaches its climax.

In my view, infants of both sexes experience genital desires directed towards their mother and father, and they have an unconscious knowledge of the vagina as well as the penis.[8] For these reasons Freud's earlier term 'genital phase' seems to me more adequate than his later concept of the 'phallic phase'.

The super-ego in both sexes comes into being during the oral phase.

Under the sway of phantasy life and of conflicting emotions, the child at every stage of libidinal organization introjects his objects—primarily his parents—and builds up the super-ego from these elements.

Thus, though the super-ego corresponds in many ways to the actual people in the young child's world, it has various components and features which reflect the phantastic images in his mind. All the factors which have a bearing on his object relations play a part from the beginning in the building-up of the super-ego.

The first introjected object, the mother's breast, forms the basis of the super-ego. Just as the relation to the mother's breast precedes and strongly influences the relation to the father's penis, so the relation to the introjected mother affects in many ways the whole course of super-ego development. Some of the most important features of the super-ego, whether loving and protective or destructive and devouring, are derived from the early maternal components of the super-ego.

The earliest feelings of guilt in both sexes derive from the oral-sadistic desires to devour the mother, and primarily her breasts (Abraham). It is therefore in infancy that feelings of guilt arise. Guilt does not emerge when the Oedipus complex comes to an end, but is rather one of the factors which from the beginning mould its course and affect its outcome.

I wish now to turn specifically to the boy's development. In my view, castration fear starts in infancy as soon as genital sensations are experienced. The boy's early impulses to castrate his father take the form of wishing to bite off his penis, and correspondingly castration fear is first experienced by the boy as the fear lest his own penis should be bitten off. These early castration fears are to begin with overshadowed by anxieties from many other sources, among which internal danger situations play a prominent part. The closer development approaches to genital primacy, the more castration fear comes to the fore. While I thus fully agree with Freud that *castration fear is the leading anxiety situation in the male,* I cannot agree with his description of it as the *single factor* which determines the repression of the Oedipus complex. Early anxieties from various sources contribute all along to the central part which castration fear comes to play in the climax of the Oedipus situation. Furthermore, the boy experiences grief and sorrow in relation to his father as a loved object, because of his impulses to castrate and murder him. For in his good aspects the father is an indispensable source of strength, a friend and an ideal, to whom the boy looks for protection and guidance and whom he therefore feels impelled to preserve. His feelings of guilt about his aggressive impulses towards his father increase his urge to repress his genital desires. Again and again in the analyses of boys and men I have found that feelings of guilt in relation to the loved father were an integral element of the Oedipus complex and vitally influenced its outcome. The feeling that his mother too is endangered by the son's rivalry with the father, and that the father's death would be an irreparable loss to her, contributes to the strength of the boy's sense of guilt and hence to the repression of his Oedipus desires.

Freud, as we know, arrived at the theoretical conclusion that the father, as well as the mother, is an object of the son's libidinal desires. (Cf. his concept of the inverted Oedipus complex.) Moreover, Freud in some of his writings (among his case histories particularly in the 'Analysis of a Phobia in a Five-Year-Old Boy', 1909) has taken account of the part which love for his father plays in the boy's positive Oedipus conflict. He has, however, not given enough weight to the crucial role of these feelings of love, both in the development of the Oedipus conflict and in its passing. In my experience the Oedipus situation loses in power not only because the boy is afraid of the destruction of his genital by a revengeful father, but also because he is driven by feelings of love and guilt to preserve his father as an internal and external figure.

I will now briefly state my conclusion about the girl's Oedipus complex. The phase in which, according to Freud, the girl is exclusively attached to her mother already includes, in my view, desires directed towards her father and covers the early stages of the inverted and positive Oedipus complex. While I therefore consider this phase as a period of fluctuation between desires directed towards mother and father in all libidinal positions, there is no doubt in my mind as to the far-reaching and lasting influence of every facet of the relation to the mother upon the relation to the father.

Penis envy and the castration complex play an essential part in the girl's development. But they are very much reinforced by frustration of her positive Oedipus desires. Though the little girl at one stage assumes that her mother possesses a penis as a male attribute, this concept does not play nearly as important a part in her development as Freud suggests. The unconscious theory that her mother contains the admired and desired penis of the father underlies, in my experience, many of the phenomena which Freud described as the relation of the girl to the phallic mother.

The girl's oral desires for her father's penis mingle with her first genital desires to receive that penis. These genital desires imply the wish to receive children from her father, which is also borne out by the equation 'penis = child'.

The feminine desire to internalize the penis and to receive a child from her father invariably precedes the wish to possess a penis of her own.

While I agree with Freud about the prominence of the fear of loss of love and of the death of the mother among the girl's anxieties, I hold that the fear of having her body attacked and her loved inner objects destroyed essentially contributes to her main anxiety situation.

FINAL REMARKS

Throughout my description of the Oedipus complex I have attempted to show the interdependence of certain major aspects of development. The sexual development of the child is inextricably bound up with his object relations and with all the emotions which from the beginning mould his attitude to mother and father. Anxiety, guilt and depressive feelings are intrinsic elements of the child's emotional life and therefore permeate the child's early object relations, which consist of the relation to actual people as well as to their representatives in his inner world. From these introjected figures—the child's identifications—the super-ego develops and in turn influences the relation to both parents and the whole sexual development. Thus emotional and sexual development, object relations, and super-ego development interact from the beginning.

The infant's emotional life, the early defences built up under the stress of the conflict between love, hatred, and guilt, and the vicissitudes of the child's identifications—all these are topics which may well occupy analytic research for a long time to come. Further work in these directions should lead us to a fuller understanding of the personality, which implies a fuller understanding of the Oedipus complex and of sexual development as a whole.

NOTES

1. In my General Theoretical Summary below I deal with the girl's super-ego development and the essential part the good internalized father plays in it. With Rita this aspect of her super-ego formation had not appeared in her analysis. A development in this direction, however, was indicated by the improved relation to her father toward the end of her analysis. As I see it now, the anxiety and guilt relating to her mother so much dominated her emotional life that both the relation to the external father and to the internalized father-figure were interfered with.
2. This anxiety situation entered to some extent into Rita's analysis, but at that time I did not

realize fully the importance of such anxieties and their close connection with depression. This became clearer to me in the light of later experience.

3. My main purpose in this summary is to provide a clear presentation of my views on some aspects of the Oedipus complex. I also intend to compare my conclusions with certain of Freud's statements on the subject. I find it impossible, therefore, at the same time to quote other authors or to make references to the copious literature dealing with this subject. With regard to the girl's Oedipus complex, however, I should like to draw attention to chapter 11 in my book, *The Psycho-Analysis of Children* (1932), in which I have referred to the views of various authors on this subject.

4. In dwelling on the infant's fundamental relation to the mother's breast and to the father's penis, and on the ensuing anxiety situations and defences, I have in mind more than the relation to part-objects. In fact these part-objects are from the beginning associated in the infant's mind with his mother and father. Day-to-day experiences with his parents, and the unconscious relation which develops to them as inner objects, come increasingly to cluster round these primary part-objects and add to their prominence in the child's unconscious.

5. Allowance must be made for the great difficulty of expressing a young child's feelings and phantasies in adult language. All descriptions of early unconscious phantasies—and for that matter of unconscious phantasies in general—can therefore only be considered as pointers to the contents rather than to the form of such phantasies.

6. The analysis of young children leaves no doubt as to the fact that the vagina is represented in the unconscious of the child. Actual vaginal masturbation in early childhood is much more frequent than has been assumed, and this is corroborated by a number of authors.

7. This summary is mainly derived from the following of Freud's writings: *The Ego and the Id* (*S.E.*19), 'The Infantile Genital Organization' (*S.E.* 19), 'The Dissolution of the Oedipus Complex' (*S.E.* 19), 'Some Psychical Consequences of the Anatomical Distinction between the Sexes' (*S.E.* 19), 'Female Sexuality' (*S.E.* 21) and *New Introductory Lectures* (*S.E.* 22).

8. This knowledge exists side by side with the infant's unconscious, and to some extent conscious, knowledge of the existence of the anus which plays a more frequently observed part in infantile sexual theories.

3. Feminine Guilt and the Oedipus Complex

Janine Chasseguet-Smirgel

This is in disagreement with Freud's formidable statement that the concept of the Oedipus complex is strictly applicable only to male children and "it is only in male children that there occurs the fateful conjunction of love for the one parent and hatred of the other as rival." [1] We seem compelled here to be *plus royaliste que le roy.* . . . I can find no reason to doubt that for girls, no less than for boys, the Oedipus situation in its reality and phantasy is the most fateful psychical event in life. —Jones ("The Phallic Phase," 1932)

It is troubling to note that Freudian theory gives the father a central role in the boy's Oedipus complex but considerably reduces that role in the girl's. In fact, in considering Freud's article "Female Sexuality" (to which Jones replies in his article "The Phallic Phase") it is suggested that the girl's positive Oedipus complex may simply not exist. If it exists, it is usually an exact replica of her relationship to her mother. Freud says in the same article, "except for the change of her love object, the second phase had scarcely added any new feature to her erotic life" (this second phase being the positive Oedipus complex).

Freud maintains that it is not because of her love for her father nor because of her feminine desires that the little girl arrives at the positive Oedipus position but because of her masculine desires and her penis envy. She tries to get what she wants from her father, the possessor of the penis. When the Oedipus position is reached, it tends to last some time as it is essentially a "haven" ("The Dissolution of the Oedipus Complex," 1924). "She enters the Oedipus situation as though into a haven or refuge." As the little girl has no fear of castration, she has nothing to give up, and she does not need a powerful superego.

During the period preceding the change of object, if it occurs at all, the

Reprinted from Janine Chasseguet-Smirgel, ed., *Female Sexuality: New Psychoanalytic Views* (London: Karnac Books, 1988), by permission of Karnac Books (London), Payot (Paris), and the University of Michigan Press (Ann Arbor). First published in 1964.

father is "scarcely very different from an irritating rival" ("Female Sexuality," 1931), but at the same time the rivalry with the father in the negative Oedipus complex is not so strong and is not in any way symmetrical with the boy's Oedipus rivalry accompanying his desire to possess his mother. The little girl in her homosexual love for the mother does not identify with the father.

If we turn from the study of normal or neurotic behavior to that of psychotics, we note the importance Freud gave to the role of homosexuality in his theories of delusion formation. Desires of passive submission to the father, dangerous for the ego, play the main role in masculine delusions. One of the most important of these wishes is the desire to have a child from the father. It is surprising that Freud, when he considered this desire in the context of a little girl's normal development, did not believe it to be a primary desire arising from her femininity but, on the contrary, a secondary desire, a substitute for penis envy.

Paradoxically, the father seems to occupy a much more important place in the psychosexual development of the boy than of the girl, be it as a love object or as a rival. I would even say that Freud, if one accepts all the implications of his theory, believes the father to be much more important in general for the boy than for the girl. However, Freud, with the open, scientific mind and concern for truth which characterize genius, never considered his studies of femininity to be complete or definitive, and he encouraged his disciples to continue their exploration of "the dark continent." One need only refer to the final sentence of one of his last works on the psychology of women: "If you want to know more about femininity, enquire from your own experience of life, or turn to the poets, or wait until science can give you deeper and more coherent information" (in "Femininity," 1933).

My aim in this study is to discuss certain specifically feminine positions in the Oedipal situation which are not found in that of the male. Perhaps I shall be able to reveal a little of their deeper motivation and describe their eventual consequences. Time will prevent our studying in detail many problems of woman's psychosexual life on which this study will inevitably touch, such as penis envy, female masochism, the superego, and the resolution of the Oedipus complex in girls. I shall treat of them only inasmuch as they relate to my central theme. Because of the numerous difficulties involved in this type of study a somewhat artificial presentation becomes unavoidable. I have placed greater emphasis on the particular characteristics of the girl's relation to her father, without taking into consideration, as one should, the significant early history of this relationship; neither have I touched on the particular problems of identification so important in homosexual development, as Joyce McDougall has treated more fully in "Homosexuality in Women" (1964). Whenever one discusses "the specificity" of certain female attitudes one should compare them to male ones. In this study such a comparison can be no more than implied.

Most psychoanalytical authors have noted that women on the road to genital and Oedipal maturity are faced with greater difficulties than men, so much so that Freud, as we know, was led to reconsider his belief in the universality of the Oedipus complex as the nucleus of the neuroses. Those authors who do not agree with Freud generally believe that the difficulties the little girl encounters in her psychosexual development are due mainly to the fears for the ego—*narcissistic anxieties* awakened by the feminine role.

For my part, I shall concern myself with aspects of the female Oedipus complex which have no counterpart in the male, and which are the source of a specific form of feminine *guilt* inherent in a specific moment in woman's psychosexual development: the change of object.

I. OBJECT IDEALIZATION IN THE GIRL'S RELATION TO HER FATHER

The theories of Freud and those who have followed him, as well as the theories of those who oppose him (Melanie Klein and Ernest Jones in particular), all agree on one point about the girl's development: the *change of object* inherent in the Oedipal development of women is based on *frustration*.

Thus, for Freud, the girl's Oedipus complex is due to a double misapprehension, having to do first with objects, then with her own narcissism. This disappointment is caused mainly by the fact that the little girl discovers her "castration"—the mother has given her neither the love nor the penis she wanted. According to Freud, this frustrated penis envy, replaced by a desire for a penis substitute, a child, prompts the little girl to turn to her father. Melanie Klein and Ernest Jones, on the other hand, thought that "the girl is brought under the sway of her Oedipus impulses, not indirectly, through her masculine tendencies and her penis envy, but directly, as a result of her dominant feminine instinctual components" (Melanie Klein, *The Psychoanalysis of Children*, 1932). Most of all the little girl wants to incorporate a penis, not for itself but in order to have a child by it. The desire to have a child is not a substitute for the impossible desire to have a penis (Jones, "The Phallic Phase," 1932). These authors, in spite of their refusal to admit the secondary quality of the feminine Oedipus complex, believe that the little girl's Oedipal desire is activated and awakened precociously by the *frustration* caused by the maternal breast, which then becomes "bad." It is, therefore, *the bad aspect of the first object* which (in both these views opposing Freud) lies at the basis of the change of object, the little girl seeking a good object capable of procuring for her the object-oriented and narcissistic satisfactions she lacks. The second object—the father or the penis—will be *idealized* because of the disappointment with the first object.

Indeed, a belief in the existence of a good object capable of alleviating the shortcomings of the first one is vital in order for any change of object to take place. This belief is accompanied by a projection of all the good aspects of the primary object onto the secondary object, while at the same time projection onto the original primitive object is maintained (temporarily at least) of all the bad aspects of that (new) object. This splitting is the indispensable condition leading to the change of object which would otherwise have no reason to occur. It is at the base of the girl's triangular orientation, as Catherine Luquet-Parat has emphasized in "The Change of Object" (1964). But the splitting of the maternal image implies an *idealization* of the second object, if one may so refer to the projection of qualities all of which are exclusively good.

Several authors have stressed the importance of the idealization of this second object in girls. Thus, in *Envy and Gratitude,*[2] Klein refers to the exacerbation of negative feelings toward the mother, which turn the little girl away from her: "But an idealization of the second object, the father's penis and the father, may then be more successful. This idealization derives mainly from the search for a good object."

The idealization process on which the change of object is founded weighs heavily on women's future psychosexual development. In fact it implies an *instinctual disfusion,* each object being, at the time of the change of object, either entirely negatively cathected (the mother, her breast, her phallus) or entirely positively cathected (the father and his penis). Because of this the little girl will tend to *repress and countercathect* the aggressive instincts which exist in her relation to her father in order to maintain this instinctual disfusion. As a result there arises *a specifically feminine form of guilt attached to the anal-sadistic component of sexuality,* which is radically opposed to idealization.

The conflicts the little girl experiences in her relation with her father are, of course, linked to her first experiences with the maternal object as well as the peculiarities of the second object.

If positive experiences and progressively dosed "normal frustrations" (those which are necessary for the development of a strong and harmonious ego) prevail in the girl's relation to her mother, if the father's personality offers an adequate basis for the projection of the object's good aspects onto him, and if at the same time he is solid enough, the little girl will be able to go through that change of object when prompted by these frustrations, achieving thereby a nonconflictual identification with the mother without the idealization of the second object becoming unduly important at this particular moment of her development.

The need to make permanent the idealization of the object concomitant with an instinctual disfusion is in this situation less pressing, and feminine psychosexuality can now progress under more satisfactory conditions. On the other hand, if the first attempts turn out badly, and if the second object does not offer the attributes necessary for the projection of good qualities, then character problems, perversions, and psychoses may develop.

Nevertheless, in most cases—and this seems practically inherent in woman's situation—the change of object coincides with dosages of maternal frustration at the wrong times. The father then becomes the last resort, the last chance of establishing a relation with a satisfying object. Indeed, the relation between mother and daughter is handicapped from the start; one might even say intrinsically so since, as Dr. Grunberger points out in his article on female narcissism, "Outline for a Study of Narcissism in Female Sexuality" (1964), this state is due to the sexual identity between mother and daughter. Freud himself stressed that the only relation that could avoid "the ambivalence characterizing all human relations" is that of mother and son. Later, I shall try to show some aspects of the father-daughter relationship which may help to explain why the idealization of the second object can be induced by the paternal attitude itself.

In most cases the father-daughter relation is characterized by the persistence of instinctual disfusion; the aggressive and anal-sadistic components are countercathected and repressed, since the second object must be safeguarded. At the same time the counteridentifications with the bad aspects of the first object are maintained.

The fact that the girl encounters greater difficulties in her psychosexual development than the boy is stressed by all authors. The frequency of female frigidity shows this. The guilt toward the mother alone is not sufficient to explain it; if it were, there ought to be something in the male that corresponds to it.

When Marie Bonaparte says that the cause of frigidity is to be found in the fact that woman has less libidinal energy, while Hélène Deutsch believes it to be linked to "constitutional inhibitions," [3] or when other authors believe it to be due to bisexuality, then it seems to me that they are sidestepping the discovery and interpretation of unconscious factors which, as Jones stressed in "Early Female Sexuality," form the main part of the analyst's task.

Many writers have noted, on the other hand, that woman's tendency toward idealization of sexuality is commonplace. One has only to think of adolescents or even of mature women who live in a romantic dream à la Madame Bovary waiting for Prince Charming, for eternal love, etc. (In a recent sociological study Evelyne Sullerot mentions that the publishers of romantic pulp sell sixteen million copies a year.) Thus, in *The Psychology of Women* (1944), Hélène Deutsch notes:

> As a result of a process of sublimation, woman's sexuality is more spiritual than man's. . . .
> This process of sublimation enriches woman's entire erotic affective life and makes it more individually varied than man's, but it endangers her capacity for direct sexual gratification. The constitutional inhibition of woman's sexuality is all the more difficult to overcome because, as a result of sublimation, it is more complicated (and the conditions for its gratification more exacting) than the primitive desire to get rid of sexual tension that more commonly characterizes masculine sexuality.

Hélène Deutsch stresses the "spiritualized" character of female sexuality and speaks of "sublimation" when she refers to it. But if this were a true sublimation the process would not end in inhibition. On the contrary, it seems to me that this is a reaction formation based on repression and counter-cathexis of those instinctual components opposed by nature to idealization or to anything spiritual or sublime; in other words, the anal-sadistic component instincts.

I shall now try to show the consequences of the repression of the anal-sadistic component for woman's psychosexual development. I shall make no attempt here to reconsider the concepts of activity and passivity, let alone the death instinct, but I would still like to quote certain statements by Freud about these concepts inasmuch as they concern the subject of this paper.

Discussing sexuality in general (not simply masculine sexuality) and refer-ring to the *Three Essays,* Freud says in *Beyond the Pleasure Principle:*

"From the very start we recognized the presence of a sadistic component in the sexual instinct . . . later, the sadistic instinct separates off, and finally, at the stage of genital primacy, it takes on, for the purposes of reproduction, the function of overpowering the sexual object to the extent necessary for carrying out the sexual act."[4]

In this passage Freud identifies sadism with destructive and death instincts, pointing out that in the sexual act these instincts are subordinated to Eros in order to secure control of the object. This instinctual control explicitly links Freud, in *Three Essays* (1905), to the anal-sadistic stage and to mobility. In the 1915 revision he adds: "It may be assumed the impulse of cruelty arises from the instinct for mastery and appears at a period of sexual life at which the genitals have not yet taken over their later role."

In *The Ego and the Id*[5] (1923), Freud repeats this idea but this time insists on the importance of instinctual disfusion:

The sadistic component of the sexual instinct would be a classical example of a serviceable instinctual fusion. . . . Marking a swift generalization, we might conjecture that the essence of a regression of libido (e.g., from the genital to the sadistic-anal phase) lies in a disfusion of instincts.

Freud shows, in *Inhibitions, Symptoms, Anxiety,*[6] that Eros desires contact because it strives to make the ego and the loved object one, "to abolish all spatial barriers between the Ego and the loved object"; "the aggressive object cathexis has the same aim." Here again we see that aggression, according to Freud, is put in the service of Eros, desiring close contact with the object.

In these quotations we can see a sequential chain: mastery-sadism-anality; this chain is indispensable for sexual maturity, and its effective formation is a sign of genital maturation. Does the fact that this chain also has another link, "activity," mean that female sexuality is excluded from the Freudian concept of instinctual fusion which I have just mentioned? Once more, it is beyond my purpose to consider the concepts of activity and passivity in general. I merely wish to recall that one can follow Freud's thought and its numerous variations through all his writings on female sexuality in terms of antagonistic pairs of "masculine-feminine" and "active-passive." Whenever Freud attempts to liken these pairs of concepts he feels compelled to retract what he has said. In spite of his attempt to avoid equating these terms, other authors have completely identified activity with masculinity, passivity with femininity, and have reached doubtful conclusions as a result, especially as they have taken passivity to mean inertia or inactivity.

Thus, J. Lampl-de Groot, in her article "Contribution to the Problem of Femininity" (1933), equates masculinity with activity and passivity with femininity. She draws a series of conclusions to the effect that "feminine" women do not know object love, activity under any guise, nor aggression. Since activity and love undoubtedly play a role in maternity, Lampl-de Groot makes her famous postulate that it is women's *masculinity* which is expressed in the experience of pregnancy; and as this masculinity is opposed to female sexuality, "good mothers are frigid wives." This is not really proved because the postulate with which the article begins is merely repeated throughout in various tautological ways. Her essay ends with the statement that *introjection,* because it activates aggression, does not exist in truly "feminine" women.

Hélène Deutsch emphasized[7] the idea of a typically feminine activity "directed inward," and the amphimixis of oral, anal, and urethral instincts connected with the vagina during coitus and orgasm. Yet in a symposium on frigidity (1961) at which she presided, she held that orgasmic climax could only occur in men, because it is a sphincter activity typical of the male.

As early as 1930 authors like Imre Hermann, Fritz Wittels, and Paul Schilder had warned against the theoretical and therapeutic dangers of identifying femininity with passivity, or even inertia. Therefore, in order to avoid ambiguity in the use of such terms as "passivity" and "activity," I shall refer instead to the anal-sadistic component, whether it is the aggressive component of incorporative impulses or the aggressiveness linked to all attempts at achievement, for these two seem to me especially charged with conflict for women.

How Incorporation Becomes Charged with Conflict

Referring in the *Three Essays* to infantile masturbation Freud states that the girl often masturbates by pressing her thighs together, whereas the boy prefers to use his hand. "The preference for the hand which is shown by boys is already evidence of the important contribution which the instinct for mastery is destined to make to masculine sexual activity." In fact I believe that Freud is also indicating the importance this same instinct will have in female sexual activity. In coitus the vagina replaces the hand and like the hand it grasps the penis; this is reflected in the fantasies and problems characteristic for female sexuality, to the point that the anal component in the control of the vagina causes conflict. Psychoanalytical writings frequently refer to man's fear of the vagina (Freud, "The Taboo of Virginity," 1918;[8] Karen Horney, "The Dread of Women," 1932), but they rarely mention the other side of the problem, which is the attitude of the woman (her superego) toward her own aggression to the penis; if the problem is mentioned, the aggression is usually attributed to penis envy, or to defense against the penis considered dangerous because of certain projections, but the problem is never linked to the anal-sadistic component—as though female sexual desire contained no aggressive or sadistic elements.

In general, women's aggression toward the penis is never seen as a source of guilt. I do not wish in any way to deny the existence of the forms of female aggression which are frequently discussed, but I should like to insist particularly on the problems implied in *a basically feminine wish to incorporate the paternal penis,* which invariably includes the anal-sadistic instinctual components.

One must remember that during sexual intercourse, the woman does actually incorporate the man's penis. Although this incorporation is only partial and temporary, women desire in fantasy to keep the penis permanently, as Freud pointed out in his article "On Transformations of Instincts as Exemplified in Anal Erotism" (1924).[9]

I shall illustrate the problems connected with wishes of incorporation toward the paternal penis through one case only, though in my experience the same conflicts are to be found in all women's analyses.

The patient, whom I shall call Ann, had idealized the image of her father. In order to protect this image she split her erotic objects into two very distinct types.

The first, a substitute for the father, is represented by a man, far older than she is, whom she loves tenderly and purely. This man is impotent. He loves her, protects her, encourages her career. She speaks of him in the same terms as she speaks of her father, who would give her a warm stone in winter to prevent the chilling of her fingers while going to school, kiss her tenderly, or sit with her on a bench in front of the house, offering wine to the neighbors passing by. The other man is represented by a Negro, to whom she feels she could show her erotic impulses, which are *linked* to the anal impulses.

During analysis, she says, "Before, black and white were separate, now they are mixed together."

Ann is in her forties, she is an opthalmologist, married and with two children, full of vitality and spirit, but paralyzed by deep conflicts which reveal themselves in strong anxieties, depersonalization, and the impulse to throw herself into the river or off a building. The theme of *engulfment* in water is frequent in her associations in the transference.

In the first session she is already very anxious and sees the green wall of my consulting room as an aquarium. *She feels she is in this aquarium herself* and says:

"I am very frightened. . . . These ideas of aquaria are fetal. . . . I feel I am becoming schizophrenic."

Several times during the analysis she expressed her anxiety in the following terms:

"I am cracking up, I am *drowning*. I need a branch to save me. Will you be that branch?"

She often expressed the fear that I might become pregnant.

She also suffered from claustrophobia: fear of being alone in a room with no exit, fear of elevators. She dreams she is enclosed in a very tiny and very dark room similar to a coffin from which she cannot escape.

Ann's parents were farmers. She was, along with her sister, brought up by a severe and castrating mother. The father, much older than the mother, was "gentle and kind."

"My mother bossed him around. She was the ruler of the home. She ruled us all with a rod of iron. . . . Father was good; he forgave her everything. She took advantage of it."

Ann often recalled incidents which represented the father's castration by the mother. For example, one day her father comes back from the fair where he had been drinking a little, lies down, and goes to sleep. The mother takes advantage of this occasion by stealing his wallet and then accusing him of having lost it. The primal scene which reveals itself through Ann's association is fantasied as a sadistic act during which the mother takes the father's penis.

I cannot give the whole development of Ann's analysis, but her treatment was centered on her difficulty in identifying with her mother. This difficulty was the major obstacle to a satisfactory Oedipal development. It was as though loving her father meant becoming like the castrating mother, sadistically incorporating his penis, and keeping it within her. But her love for her father could not allow her to adopt such a role.

Very early in the analysis, Ann expressed this conflict in the form of a dream:

"This is a very frightening dream. *I was* walking with *my mother* (an attempt to identify with the mother) in the river where I had my first impulse to throw myself into the water. We were looking for eel traps. It reminds me of the penis in the vagina (sadistic and castrating aspect of intercourse). My mother was mean to my father. This dream frightens me."

Another dream of the same night: "My mother was coming back from the river with my father's jacket on her shoulders. She had gone mad. In real life it is I who am afraid of going mad, of giving in to my impulses."

Behind her impulses of throwing herself into the river or off a building lies the unconscious fantasy of identification with the mother who castrates her father during intercourse (the mother coming back from the river with the father's jacket). She expresses her castration wishes in the transference in many ways, sometimes even in a quasi-delirious way. She feels guilty because she is sure that *by shaking hands with me* (to bid good-bye) *she has strained my wrist* (she associates this with the paternal penis).

The transference expressions of her anal-sadistic impulses directed toward the penis were predominant in her relation with me and were mixed with anxiety and guilt. One day she associated the following recollection with her feeling of cracking up and *drowning:*

"In the River Gave there are potholes, you know, and deep eddies. One day my father nearly drowned in one; he was carried away by the current but caught hold of a branch at the last minute. . . . I am afraid of elevators. The elevator could fall in its shaft, and I would fall with it. I have the image of a penis drawn in by a vagina."

I believe Ann's conflict appears clearly in these associations of her fear of the impulse to throw herself into the river or off a building. The parents' intercourse signified for Ann an aggressive incorporation of the father's penis by the mother (the father's jacket on the mother's shoulders, the eel in the trap, the father engulfed by the eddy). In order to arrive at the Oedipal phase she must identify with the castrating mother, that is to say, *engulf the father's penis* in her vagina.

Yet, behind the patient's symptoms (her phobic impulses) there is a *reverse fantasy:* she is the contents (father's penis or father) of a destructive container (mother or mother's vagina). Her own body or vagina is identified with the mother or the mother's vagina. The destructive feature of the vagina is linked with the sphincteral anal component. The first fantasy hidden behind the symptom is therefore a compromise between the fulfillment of a desire and its punishment.

Ann achieves through guilt in fantasy the genital Oedipal desire to "engulf" the father's penis (as the mother did), but she does this by *turning the aggression* against herself, her whole body identified with the paternal penis, whereas her destructive vagina, projected onto the outer world, is experienced as a cavity into which she disappears.

The contents and the container are reversed. Ann herself becomes the contents, which have disappeared into the container.

We realize that the first fantasy (the most superficial one), in which the punishment (superego) occurs, resulting in a compromise between the instinct and the defense, merely conceals another more primitive fantasy, which directly expresses the instinct: "I am the hole in which my father (his penis) is engulfed."

Her phobic symptom contains a double unconscious fantasy which is in accord with the Freudian theory of symptoms: a compromise concealing a primitive instinct.

It is important to add that one of the precipitating factors in mobilizing Ann's neurosis was her father's death just before her analysis, when she herself was pregnant. When she spoke of her father's death it was always in relation to her pregnancy. It became obvious during the analysis that the fantasy underlying this was that of the father's destruction by incorporation. Her fear that I should become pregnant, her projection of an aquarium onto the green wall of my consulting room, along with her fantasy of fetal regression, manifested the same symptomatic reversal of her fantasy: the fear of being engulfed and shut up inside me, like the fetus in its mother's womb, the fecal stool in the anus, or the penis in the vagina.

Having had a number of female patients with phobias of being engulfed by water, claustrophobia, compulsive ideas of throwing themselves into water or from a great height, vertigo, and phobias of falling, I came to realize that they all had a common meaning. In my experience they signify reversal of contents and container. The patient, by turning the aggression onto herself, experiences the sensation that she is the contents threatened by a dangerous container.

The genital level of these phobias does not mean that the ego is not severely affected; as we have seen the guilt involved in the relation with the idealized father often results from early conflicts with the primary object, since these conflicts are numerous and dangerous.

The sexual problems of these patients are of various kinds. Sometimes the splitting of the desired objects is enough to maintain a normal sexual appearance, but sexual pleasure is often restricted to the *clitoris* only. This particular sexual problem should be related to the same incorporation-guilt that forbids the erotic cathexis of the vagina, the organ of incorporation displacing its cathexis then onto an external organ, the clitoris. The analysis of this incorporation-guilt often allows for a more or less rapid extension of the clitoris's erotic cathexis to the vagina. This happens through the liberation of anal erotic and aggressive drive components which are then invested in the vagina. In some cases active homosexual wishes carry the same meaning of defense when conflict over incorporation is the issue.

A patient suffering from dyspareunia manifested this by a lack of vaginal stricture during intercourse. This symptom, which is in some way the reverse of vaginismus, is relatively frequent, but the patients who suffer from it believe it to be due to their anatomical make-up and become conscious of its psychogenic character only when it disappears during treatment. This symptom is the one which expresses most clearly the countercathexis of the anal-sadistic instinct of control. When this component is well integrated the vagina can allow itself to close around [10] the penis. In Freudian terms, one could say that desire of the Eros to unite with the object is satisfied, due to the instinct of control's subordinating itself to the former.

Guilt Concerning Feminine Achievement

A girl's guilt toward her father does not interfere merely with her sexual life but extends to her achievements in other fields if they take on an unconscious phallic significance. Inhibition related to this guilt seems to me chiefly responsible for women's place in culture and society today. Psychoanalysts have noticed that Oedipal guilt, linked to the guilt of surpassing the mother, is associated in many intellectual, professional and creative activities with a feeling of guilt toward the father, a guilt which is specifically feminine. Indeed, I found that in patients suffering from chronic headaches their guilt over surpassing their parents on an intellectual level (which is so often the origin of cephalic symptoms, as though reproducing an autocastration of the intellectual faculties) was usually linked to the father, in both male and

female patients. For both sexes successful intellectual activity is the unconscious equivalent of possessing the penis. For women this means they have
the father's penis and have thus dispossessed the mother, the Oedipal drama.
In addition they have also *castrated the father*. Moreover, the adequate use
of such a penis also involves from the unconscious point of view the fecal
origin of this image, ultimately, that of retaining an anal penis, which in turn
engenders guilt.

One of my patients, a young girl of fifteen and a half who had severe
migraine as well as school problems, was particularly poor in spelling and
always had low marks on oral tests. When she tried to think, her thoughts
blurred. She felt as though she were in a fog. Her ideas would become
imprecise, she grew muddled and felt stumped—in other words her ideas
lost their anal component. Her headaches began while she was preparing
for an examination which she kept failing. The diploma she was trying to
obtain was exactly the same as the one her father had.

This inhibition concerning the intellectual field she shared with her
father was analyzed in relation to her Oedipal guilt about her mother, but
it was soon obvious that interpretations on these levels were insufficient to
bring to light the meaning of her symptoms.

She had a dream in which she wanted to hold her hand up, as a sign
that she could answer the questions in the tests, but she felt it was
"forbidden"; she had another dream in which she had a snake in her hand
which turned into a pen, so she took it to the police station because "the
man to whom it belonged could not write without his pen"; . . . these
dreams led to interpretations in relation to her guilt about castrating her
father and resulted in the cessation of her school inhibitions as well as a
satisfactory Oedipal evolution. Indeed, once her aggression toward the
paternal penis was accepted she was able to create fantasies about an
Oedipal sexual relation with the father. The last dream she brought was
one in which she received an attractive pen as a present from her father
and then went with him for a walk along a sunken road, while her mother,
who in the dream looked like me, was away on holiday.

Ann, the patient whom I formerly discussed, though all her problems
were due to her professional promotion. "I am classless," she would say,
"I am neither peasant nor bourgeois. I would have done better to have
stayed working on the farm like father." With the people who praised her

for her professional success she suddenly felt like "shouting, saying stupid things, acting like a mad woman." Before her analysis she had had a period of anxiety during which she could not write any prescriptions, all the formulas blurring in her mind. Having a profession meant having a penis which she had stolen from her father just as her mother had done during the primal scene.

This meaning is expressed clearly in the following dream: "I am beside an operating table. The surgeon is operating on the brain of an elderly man who could be my father. He ablates the whole frontal part of his brain away. I think to myself, 'Poor man, he is going to be abnormal.' When the surgeon has finished, he addresses the people who are there and says of me: 'She is extremely intelligent and an excellent doctor, and she has a very pretty little girl with dark hair.' "

Her associations about this dream are:

"I worked for that surgeon when I was a student. He used to congratulate me on doing my medical studies simultaneously with working as a nurse. Oh! *What a headache I've got.* . . . I had another dream:

"I was at your place and I was cutting bread. A patient came in. You diagnosed him and phoned the diagnosis to someone. I admired how fast and sure you were in your diagnosis. Then you came up to me and said, 'What is the diagnosis?' I gave the same diagnosis as you had. Then I felt embarrassed because it is as though you thought I hadn't overheard your conversation on the phone and that I thought of that diagnosis myself. So for the sake of intellectual honesty I told you that I had overheard your diagnosis. I thought I would have no difficulty in telling you this dream, but on the contrary I feel embarrassed as though I had cheated you. In the dream I had the feeling I was lying, and stealing something. One day I made a girl-friend of mine steal a toy. We were little then. When I said good-bye to you last time I again had the feeling that I had sprained your wrist. I have the feeling you are fragile."

For Ann professional capability had the meaning of castrating the father, or the analyst in the paternal transference, and this castration represents an identification with the mother who steals the father's power. This is an anal castration as one can see by her feeling that she is telling lies and cheating me, analogous to her fantasy of the Primal Scene as shown in the screen memories: the mother stealing the father's money after he had come back drunk from the fair, followed by her accusation that the father had lost the money; the mother ordering him about, hiding for hours to frighten him, making him believe that she was working all the time, while in fact she did nothing. She seemed to be like Delilah, taking advantage of Samson's trusting sleep to cut off his hair.

The guilt linked with this desire to identify with the sadistic mother leads Ann to castrate herself (have headaches, fantasies in which she "loses her mind," professional inhibitions) and to perform acts which restore what has been taken away (she gives me back the diagnosis she has stolen, she worries about my sprained wrist). This fantasy of possessing a phallus is so conflict-laden that any small intervention touching on it stimulates guilt in women who otherwise seem quite free of work inhibitions.

I had a patient who, before she came to analysis, gave lectures on a rather feminine topic—children's education. At the end of one of her lectures, someone came up to her and said:

"All that is very well but, you know, the sight of a woman carrying a brief case and a whole lot of files—really, that just isn't a woman's role!" [11]

From that day on, this patient never gave another lecture!

Analytical interpretation of these conflicts brings relief to women involved in fields they feel belong to men and which have an obvious phallic meaning (for example, taking exams, driving a car) as well as in those which are specifically feminine, such as pregnancy. Here again guilt toward the mother, the Oedipal rival, is coupled with the guilt of having taken the father's penis in order to make a child with it. This attack against the essence of the love object applied in transformation is experienced as anal guilt.

The symbolic connection "child-penis" becomes significant in this context. Uncontrollable vomiting during pregnancy, and all the psychosomatic difficulties linked with the problems of accepting motherhood are often related to this guilt, as one can see in the analytical material of pregnant women.

Creativity. It is commonplace that women (with few exceptions) are not great creators, scientific or artistic. Man's creativity has been attributed to a desire to compensate for the fact that he cannot bear children (K. Horney) and thus create life. I believe that this is indeed one of the deep motives of creative work.

Yet creating is a means of alleviating deficiencies at various levels of instinctual maturity, and this results in attempts to achieve narcissistic integrity—represented in the unconscious by the phallus (Grunberger 1964).

The phallic significance of creativity is emphasized in Phyllis Greenacre's article dealing with women who are creative artists. She believes that this sometimes results in inhibitions due to fear that a phallic achievement might interfere with the fulfillment of feminine desires. I agree with the author about the phallic meaning of creativity, but I would here again stress the part played by feminine guilt concerning possession of the penis and aggression toward the idealized father.

Women who have not idealized their fathers usually have no urge to create, because creation implies the projection of one's narcissism onto an ideal image which can be attained only through creative work.

If creative work signified only the act of parturition, then women with children would lack any desire to create, but analysis proves this to be untrue. The giving of life is not the same thing as being creative. To create is to do something other and something more than what a mother does, and it is in this respect that we see the phallic meaning of creation and its relation to penis envy.

That so many different achievements are symbolized by the possession and use of a penis results from the unconscious meaning of the phallus for both men and women. Whatever works well is represented in the unconscious by the phallus. Grunberger demonstrates in his essay on "The Phallic Image" that the phallus is the symbol of narcissistic wholeness. Why is it that valor, creativity, integrity, and power are all, on different levels, symbolized by the male sex organ? In order to attempt to answer this question we shall consider the problems of castration and penis envy in women.

II. THE FEMALE CASTRATION COMPLEX AND PENIS ENVY

"I've got one, and you've got none!" (Gay little song sung by a three-and-a-half-year-old boy to his six-year-old sister.)

On the subject of penis envy Freud's views are opposed to those of Josine Müller, Karen Horney, Melanie Klein, and Ernest Jones. Freud holds that, until puberty, there is a *phallic sexual monism,* and therefore a total sexual identity between boys and girls up till the development of the castration complex. According to Hélène Deutsch, who agrees with Freud on these points, the little girl has no complete sexual organ from the age of four (age of the castration complex) to puberty—she has only her clitoris, which is seen as a *castrated penis*. She has no vagina as she has not yet discovered it and does not even know of it *unconsciously*.[12] We can understand easily why Freud and those who followed him in his theory on female sexuality believed *penis envy to be a primary phenomenon* and fundamental to women's psychosexuality, since the little girl wants to compensate for the instinctual and narcissistic defects which mark most of her childhood.

Authors who do not agree with Freud's theory of female sexuality refuse to consider woman as *"un homme manqué"* (Jones). According to these authors the vagina is the first sexual organ to be libidinally cathected. The little girl is a woman from the start. The cathexis of the clitoris is secondary and serves a defensive function with regard to conflicts concerning genital impulses linked to the vagina: "The undiscovered vagina is a vagina denied" (Karen Horney).

These authors agree that repression of vaginal impulses is due to narcissistic anxieties concerned with attacks against the inside of the body. Therefore, the erotic cathexis is transferred to the clitoris, a safer, external sexual organ.[13] This throws a new light on the theory of penis envy.

Josine Müller believes that self-esteem is linked to the satisfaction of the impulses peculiar to one's own sex. Penis envy, therefore, is due to the narcissistic wound resulting from unsatisfied genital (vaginal) desires, which have been repressed.

For Karen Horney penis envy results from certain characteristics of the penis (its visibility, the fact that its micturition is in the form of a jet, and so on),[14] but also from a fear of the vagina which exists in both sexes. In the girl such fears are related to her Oedipal desire to be penetrated by the father's penis, which becomes fearful because she attributes to it a power of destruction.

According to Melanie Klein, *the libidinal desire for the penis* is a primary one. It is first of all an oral desire, the prototype of vaginal desire. The fulfillment of this desire is linked to the fantasy of sadistically taking the paternal penis from the mother, who has incorporated it. This results in fear of retaliation from the mother, who might try to wound or destroy the inside of the girl's body. Therefore, penis envy can be related to the following ideas in the girl's unconscious: By using the external organ she demonstrates her fears are unfounded, testing them against reality. She regards the penis as a weapon to satisfy her sadistic desires toward her mother (cleaving to her so as to tear away the penis which is hidden inside her, to drown her in a jet of corrosive urine, etc.). The guilt resulting from these fantasies may make her wish to return the penis which she has stolen from the mother, and thus restitute her by regressing to an active homosexual position for which the possession of a penis is necessary.

Ernest Jones follows Melanie Klein's theory of penis envy in his article "The Phallic Phase" (1932) centering his ideas on the primary characteristic of the "receptive" cathexes of all the orifices of a woman's body (her mouth, anus, vagina).

All these authors attribute a large part in female psychosexuality to the father and to penis envy, whereas Freud believed the Oedipus complex to be mainly masculine. Ruth Mack Brunswick thought female neuroses lack an "Oedipus complex" and J. Lampl-de Groot claims that the paternal image really exists for the little girl only after she is six, and maintains, that until that age, the relation with the father is the same as the child's relation with any other member of the household: sometimes friendly, sometimes hostile, according to her mood.

In his article on "Female Sexuality" (1931) Freud argues against the *secondary* nature of penis envy, because the woman's envy is so violent that it can only have drawn its energy from *primary* instincts.

I believe that the fact that there may be primary receptive instincts in women, be they oral, anal, or vaginal,[15] does not prevent penis envy from being primary, too. However, even if one holds that a female sexual impulse exists right from the start, that the little girl has an adequate organ of which she has some certain knowledge, in other words, that she has all the instinctual equipment, yet we learn from clinical experience that from a narcissistic point of view the girl feels painfully incomplete. I believe the cause of this feeling of incompleteness is to be found in the primary relation with the mother and will therefore be found in children of both sexes.

The Omnipotent Mother

In the article she wrote with Freud, "The Pre-Oedipal Phase of the Libido Development" (1940), Ruth Mack Brunswick insists on the powerful character of the primitive maternal imago ("She is not only active, phallic, but *omnipotent*"). She shows that *the first activity to which the child is submitted is the mother's*. The transition passage from passivity to activity is achieved by an *identification with the mother's activity*. Because of his dependence on the omnipotent mother "who is capable of everything and possesses every valuable attribute'' the child obviously sustains ''early narcissistic injuries from the mother'' which ''enormously increases the child's hostility.''

I believe that a child, whether male or female, even with the best and kindest of mothers, will maintain a terrifying maternal image in his unconscious, the result of projected hostility deriving from his own impotence.[16] This powerful image, symbolic of all that is bad, does not exclude an omnipotent, protective imago (witch *and* fairy), varying according to the mother's real characteristics.

However, the child's primary powerlessness, the intrinsic characteristics of his psychophysiological condition, and the inevitable frustrations of training are such that the imago of the good, omnipotent mother never covers over that of the terrifying, omnipotent, bad mother.

It seems to me that when the little boy becomes conscious[17] that this omnipotent mother has no penis and that he, subdued so far by her omnipotence, has an organ which she has not, this forms an important factor in his narcissistic development.

Analysts have mainly stressed the horror (the *''Abscheu''*) the little boy feels when he realizes that his mother has no penis, since it means to him that she has been castrated, thus confirming his idea that such a terrifying possibility exists. This in turn may lead to fetishistic perversion and certain kinds of homosexuality. Few people take note of Freud's other statements stressing the narcissistic satisfaction felt by the little boy at the thought that he has an organ which women do not have. Thus, Freud says (in a note on exhibitionism added to the *Three Essays* in 1920): ''It is a means of constantly insisting upon the integrity of the subject's own (male) genitals and it reiterates his infantile satisfaction at the absence of a penis in those of women.'' Elsewhere, Freud mentions the little boy's triumphant disdain for the other sex. He believes that this feeling of triumph (a note in *Group Psychology and the Analysis of the Ego*)[18] always arises from a convergence of the ego and the ego ideal. So it is indeed a narcissistic satisfaction, a triumph at last, over the omnipotent mother.

In his 1927 article on ''Fetishism'' Freud pointed out the ambivalent role of the fetish. It is supposed to conceal the horrifying castration while it is at the same time the means of its possible reparation. Freud says of the fetishist that ''to point out that he reverses his fetish is not the whole story; in many cases he treats it in a way which is obviously equivalent to a representation of castration,'' and at this point Freud refers to the people who cut off braids. When considering the Chinese custom of mutilating women's feet and then venerating them, which he believes to be analogous to fetishism, Freud states: "It seems as though the Chinese male wants to thank the woman for having submitted to being castrated."

Countless clinical details relating to both sexes testify to the frequency and wealth of wishes to castrate the mother of her breast and of her phallus. If it were not for this deep satisfaction and its associated horror, the fantasy of the castrated mother would probably be less forceful.

Is it not at this point that myths begin to prevail over scientific thought? Are we not all tempted to talk as Freud did of "the castrated condition of women," or of "the necessity for women to accept their castration," or as Ruth Mack Brunswick put it, "The real quality of the representation of the castrated mother and the fantasy quality of the phallic mother," instead of putting these two representations back under the sway of the pleasure principle?

Images of woman as deficient, as containing a hole or wound, seem to me to be a denial of the imagoes of the primitive mother; this is true for both sexes, but in women identification with such an imago leads to deep guilt.

The protective imago of the good omnipotent mother and the terrifying imago of the bad omnipotent mother are both in opposition to this representation of the castrated mother.

Generous breast, fruitful womb, softness, warmth, wholeness, abundance, harvest, the earth, all symbolize the mother.

Frustration, invasion, intrusion, evil, illness, death, all symbolize the mother.

In comparison with the ideal qualities attributed to the early mother-image, the fall of the "castrated" mother appears to result from a deep desire to free oneself from her domination and evil qualities.

The little boy's triumph over the omnipotent mother has many effects on his future relations with women. Bergler points out that man attempts to reverse the infantile situation experienced with the mother and live out actively what he has endured passively, thus turning her into the dependent child he had been. This idea seems to be supported by certain aspects of woman's role, often noted by other authors. One also observes in patients the narcissistic effect of a man's realization that his mother does not possess a penis.

If the little boy has not been traumatized by the omnipotent mother, if her attitude has been neither too restraining, nor too invasive, he will be sufficiently reassured by the possession of his penis to dispense with constant reiteration of the triumphant feeling he once experienced. The need to reverse the situation might be restricted to a protective attitude toward women (this is not necessarily a reaction formation; it might be a way of linking his need for mastery to his love). But if the child was a fecal part-object serving to satisfy the mother's desire for power and authority, then the child's future object-relations with women will be deeply affected.[19]

In analysis we rarely encounter male patients who show defused anal-sadistic impulses in a pure state, nor do we find mothers in *analyses* who satisfy perverse desires through their children. But many male patients present contained sexual and relational problems, linked to a need for a specific form of narcissistic gratification which we regard as being the result of regression to the phallic-narcissistic phase.

It seems that Jones's description of the deutero-phallic phase in boys (with narcissistic overestimation of the penis, withdrawal of object-libido and lack of desire to penetrate sexually and certain aspects of ejaculatio praecox noted by Abraham) are to be found in these narcissistic-phallic men who have been disturbed in their early relation with the mother. They lack confidence in the narcissistic value of the penis and constantly have to put it to the proof; theirs is the "little penis" complex, they regard a sexual relation as narcissistic reassurance rather than an object relationship of mutual value.[20]

Such men constantly doubt their triumph over women, as they doubt the fact that she has no penis, and are always fearful of finding one concealed in the vagina. This leads to ejaculation *ante portas,* in order to avoid such a dangerous encounter. The fantasy represents not only the paternal phallus but also (as Jones pointed out) the destructive anal penis of the omnipotent mother.[21]

But, in general, possessing the penis proves to be the satisfactory narcissistic answer to the little boy's primary relation with his mother.

Like the boy, the little girl, too, has been narcissistically wounded by the mother's omnipotence—maybe even more than he, for the mother does not cathect her daughter in the same way that she cathects her son. But the girl cannot free herself from this omnipotence as she has nothing with which to oppose the mother, no narcissistic virtue the mother does not also possess. She will not be able to "show her" her independence (I think this expression relates to phallic exhibitionism). So she will envy the boy his penis and say that he can "do everything." I see penis envy *not as "a virility claim" to something one wants for its own sake, but as a revolt against the person who caused the narcissistic would: the omnipotent mother.*

Clinical experience often shows that penis envy is stronger and more difficult to resolve when the daughter has been traumatized by a domineering mother. The narcissistic wound aroused by the child's helplessness and by penis envy are closely related.

Realization that possession of the penis presents the possibility of healing the narcissistic wound imposed by the omnipotent mother[22] helps to explain some of the unconscious significance of the penis, whether it is that of a treasure of strength, integrity, magic power, or autonomy. In the idea connected with this organ we find condensed all the primitive ideas of power. This power becomes then the prerogative of the man, who by attracting the mother destroyed her power. Since women lack this power they come to envy the one who possesses the penis. Thus, woman's envy has its source in her conflict with her mother and must seek satisfaction through aggression (that is, what she considers to be aggression) toward her love object, the father. Any achievement which provides her with narcissistic pleasure will be felt as an encroachment on the father's power, thereby leading to many inhibitions, as already mentioned. In fact there is often an unfortunate connection between violent penis envy and the inhibition or fear of satisfying this envy. The connection arises because penis envy derives from conflict with the mother, giving rise to idealization of the father, which must be maintained thereafter.

I think that women's fear of castration can be explained by this equation of the narcissistic wound and the lack of a penis. Freud could see no reason for the little girl to fear castration as she had already undergone it. This led him to alter his proposition that all anxieties were castration fears to that in *Inhibitions, Symptoms, Anxiety* (1936), in which he claimed that woman's fear of losing love is the equivalent of castration anxiety.

Jones pointed out that fears of castration do exist in women since they have as many fears about the future as men have; he also stressed the importance of fears about the integrity of their internal organs. In fact, the fears of both sexes are similar (fear of going blind, being paralyzed, becoming mad, having cancer, having an accident, failing, and so on). In the unconscious, all narcissistic fears at any level are equivalent to castration, because of the narcissistic value given to the phallus by both sexes. Thus, women as well as men constantly fear castration; even if they already have lost the *penis,* there are still many other things with a phallic meaning which one might lose. And men as well as women experience penis envy because each attempt to compensate a deficiency implies a phallic acquisition. The fear of loss or of castration centers in the mother as it is from her the daughter wishes to escape, *at the same time that she gives herself a penis and turns to the father.*

During the change of object even though retaining the unconscious image of the phallic mother the daughter fully realizes that *the father is the only true possessor of the penis.* The change of object and the development of the Oedipal situation come about only when the imago of the phallic mother has become that of a mother who has dispossessed the father of his penis. In order to acquire the penis the girl now turns to her father *just as her mother did;* she does this with all the guilt we have discussed earlier, grappling with both her parents at the same time, and also attacking the loved object.

As Freud said, she turns to the father to acquire the penis, but her fears, owing to the temporary split between her libidinal and aggressive cathexes *at the time of the change of object,* are tied to the mother, the guilt to the father.

I believe that it is at this stage that the imago of the phallic mother *who holds in herself the paternal penis* (Melanie Klein) becomes much more important than the imago of the phallic mother who on her own possesses a phallus. Even if this latter imago persists in the unconscious it is not the prevailing one. But the father's penis, the mother's property, loses its genital and positive characteristics and acquires the same intrusive, destructive, anal properties of the phallic mother's own penis, thereby being cathected in the same way as its owner.

If the imago of the phallic mother as possessor of a penis remains the more important one, then the homosexual situation threatens to establish itself permanently, but if the imago of the mother as holder of the paternal penis dominates, the triangular situation begins in outline.

In Freud's view, then, *the girl turns away from her mother in order to acquire a penis;* and by turning to the father enters the positive Oedipus phase.

If, however, *penis envy is caused by the desire to liberate oneself from the mother,* as I propose, the sequence of events is somewhat different: the girl will *simultaneously* be envious of the penis *and* turn to her father, powerfully aided by a basic feminine wish to free herself from the mother. Thus, penis envy and the erotic desire for a penis are not opposed to each other but complementary, and if symbolic satisfaction of the former is achieved this becomes a step forward toward integration of the latter.

In his article on "Manifestations of the Female Castration Complex" (1921), Karl Abraham states that women who have professional ambitions thereby manifest their penis envy.[23] This can be demonstrated clinically,[24] but I think the desire to fulfill oneself in any field, professional or otherwise, as well as penis envy, springs from the same narcissistic wound, and is therefore an attempt at reparation. Freud in his essay on narcissism states that once the primary stage of narcissism is passed, personal achievement provides narcissistic rewards. It is important to take this into account in analytic treatment. If one interprets desire for achievement as the manifestation of "masculine demands" (as Abraham did with regard to professional activities), if women's professional desires are invariably interpreted as penis envy, there is a risk of awakening profound guilt feelings. I believe that if one accepts that penis envy is caused by a deep narcissistic wound, then one is able to bind this wound as well as open the way to a normal Oedipus conflict. Sexuality itself is often seen as men's prerogative and, in fact, from a symbolic point of view *normal female sexuality* (a vagina which functions normally) can be regarded as the possession of a phallus, due to the fact that the penis represents wholeness even in regard to orgasm. Certain analysts, basing their views on this fantasy go so far as to say that normal women never have an orgasm. This is tantamount to acquiescing to the patients' guilt, leading indeed to castration not only of the penis but also of the vagina and of the whole of femininity. Basically, penis envy is the symbolic expression of another desire. Women do not wish to become men, but want to detach themselves from the mother and become complete, autonomous *women*.

Penis Envy as a Defense and Fears for the Integrity of the Ego

I do not wish to ignore *the role of penis envy* as a feminine defense. I have insisted upon *guilt* because this aspect of female psychosexuality seems to have been more neglected than that of *the narcissistic fears for the ego's integrity*.

Many women want a penis *to avoid being penetrated,* since penetration is felt as a threat to their integrity;[25] they want to castrate this dangerous penis in order to prevent it from approaching them. But then one wonders, *which* penis?

In the 1964 article "The Change of Object," Luquet-Parat suggests that, if penetration is desired and imagined as a danger for body as well as ego integrity, that is, if the penis continues to represent exaggerated phallic power (the immense penis the little girl desires, too big in comparison with her, is the heir to the invading, destructive, annihilating phallic power of the *primitive maternal* phallus), then sexual penetration is experienced as an intolerable desire which the ego cannot accept, since it is in contradiction to self-preservation.

I agree with Dr. Luquet-Parat that this destructive penis is the equivalent of the maternal phallus of the anal phase; this, in turn, is linked for the girl with persecution and passive homosexual attitudes and provides the basis for paranoia in women. In these cases I wonder if one can truly speak of a "change of object" (since emotions concerning the paternal penis are the same as they had been for the mother's phallus). It may be more correct to say that this was already part of the positive Oedipal situation.

The "transfer" to the father of what was invested in the mother and the fact that these cathexes are equal (as the projections have simply been displaced) seem to point to the creation of a mechanism of defense aimed at escaping the dangerous relation with the phallic mother by establishing a relation with the father. But this mechanism of defense fails because the projections remain the same while the two objects are insufficiently differentiated.

It seems as if in these cases the father did not adequately support the projection of the good aspects of the object, because the primitive object itself was particularly bad. The process of idealization could not be established and thus could not allow for the true triangular situation. Castration as a defense and penis envy which prevents penetration seem to me to be linked mainly to the phallic maternal imago even though they appear to take the father as their aim. The latter does not yet have *the attributes of the paternal role* and only plays the role of a substitute for the mother, who possesses the destructive anal phallus.[26]

Fears for ego integrity are best analyzed from the angle of passive homosexuality and identifications and provide a deeper understanding of the meaning of this narcissistic defense against penetration by the penis (unconsciously, the mother's phallus), which causes so many conjugal difficulties. Women who attack and castrate their husbands have unconsciously married the bad mother, and this is often equally true for the husband. Freud noticed that many women marry mother substitutes and act ambivalently toward them.

I believe this results both from Oedipal guilt (one must not take the father from the mother, not incorporate the father's penis) and the repetition compulsion. The issue here is to master the traumatic childhood situation, to live out actively what has been passively experienced, rather than integrated, in relation to the mother. In this case the relationship is homosexual.

It does happen—and this is a proof that the husband does not represent the father in this case—that the idealized paternal imago remains untouched and identical with the ideal portrait created by the little girl.

For example, Adrienne, a young and pretty mother, who has made an important advance in the social and financial scale, has retained a genuine simplicity. She tells me that she married her husband on the spur of the moment. At the time she was "going out" with a young man whom she loved, but for some reason which she cannot explain she yielded to her present husband's proposal. He is a rather sadistic man who beats her and makes perverse demands upon her. At the same time he is very attentive to her, which gives him an eminently ambiguous position in her eyes. She is full of bitterness toward him and grievances: he deprives her of her freedom; he does not let her gad about, or hum to herself, or whistle; he demands that she wear a girdle, etc. On top of this he is unfaithful to her. It soon became obvious that this husband was an equivalent of Adrienne's mother, who used to take her things away, keep her under her control, force her to work, and never stop pestering her.

When the mother was angry at mealtimes she would throw forks at the children's heads.

From the very beginning this aspect of the mother was projected onto me, and at the outset the analysis was very difficult, especially as she had not come of her own accord but only because her husband insisted on it. Yet she found sufficient satisfaction in the treatment to keep up the analysis despite her pointedly hysterophobic character.

Thus, when she leaves at the end of her session, she feels that she has become very small, her handbag has become a satchel, she senses that I follow her everywhere: into the subway, the streets and even her bedroom. The smell of my flat follows her everywhere, too. I am always behind her, etc. (In spite of the content of her feelings, their relation and structure are not at all paranoiac, there is a true possibility of insight.)

She liked her father but it was always the mother "who wore the trousers," who took the father's pay, controlling even the smallest expenditure, shutting him out if he came home late, etc.

Adrienne made an attempt at suicide the day her grandfather had his leg amputated. Later, she visited him in the hospital, went to much trouble for him, pampered him, even wished to become a nurse. To this day, every month she goes and gives her blood at the hospital (the links between the suicide attempt, the grandfather's amputation, and the efforts to put it right only became clear late in the analysis; they came up as separate facts, because they were unconscious). This grandfather is the mother's father whom the mother treats with indifference, hardly bothering or worrying about him, unlike Adrienne. When he died, after a second amputation, Adrienne described her mother's attitude at the grandfather's deathbed (the mother had stolen his cigarettes and his money) in the following words:

"How can she think of profiting from him? . . . I can see an animal in the forest, something like a huge wild boar surrounded by hunters. They are trying to strip him of everything he has."

Her husband had then gone hunting. He had sent her some game which she could not bring herself to eat. Adrienne's attitude to her husband is quite different from her attitude to her father or grandfather. She openly attacks him, forces him to give her money, a personal car, etc., without any inhibition whatsoever. She ridicules him, thinks he looks like a clown and says so in front of him.

One day, the imago she had projected onto her husband became clear:

"In his dressing-gown he looks amazingly like my mother-in-law."

Not long before this, she had a dream in which her mother was dressed up as a priest in a robe.

She sometimes projects onto me the good image of the idealized father, the victim of the mother's castration, at other times the image of the phallic mother, with whom she wishes and fears an anal relation, experiencing once again the intrusive sphincter-training period.

"I can still feel you behind me, I am frightened. . . . I don't want to speak. I can feel you're going to interrogate me and I'm frightened. It's stupid; in fact, you never do ask questions . . . or, at least, not in that way. . . . I shall say nothing."

"The image of my husband is haunting me. I keep thinking of him, and yet he infuriates me. I don't want to make love to him. . . . I dreamed of a rat whose claws were pinching my daughter's bottom."

It seems to me obvious that the relationships to the husband and to me in the transference express a defense against a passive homosexual relation with the phallic mother, whom she attacks, whom she defies, whom she castrates in order to prevent her approach and in order to prove that there is no collusion between them; whereas her relation with her father is based on a counteridentification with the phallic mother and so on an idealization of the paternal image she is trying to restore.

The relation with the phallic husband-mother is connected with *narcissistic fears for the body ego*, whereas the relation to the father-grandfather is connected with guilt.

III. A CONFLICTUAL OUTCOME OF FEMININE PROBLEMS: THE DAUGHTER'S IDENTIFICATION WITH THE FATHER'S PENIS

OEDIPUS: This girl is my eyes, stranger, my daughter.
. . . .
ANTIGONE: Father, we are yours.
OEDIPUS: Where are you?
ANTIGONE: Near you, father. (They go toward him.)
OEDIPUS: Oh, my torches!
ISMENE: Of your light, father.
ANTIGONE: In suffering and in joy.
OEDIPUS: Let death come, I shall be alone at the time of my extinction, resting on these columns like a Temple.
(Translated from Jean Gillibert's French version of Sophocles' *Oedipus at Colonus*.)

I have tried to show that the idealization of the father, a process which underlies the change of object, can result in a specific conflict for the woman in the area of sadistic-anal instinctual components, thereby rendering difficult the instinctual fusion required for normal sexuality, as well as interfering with any achievement necessary to healthy narcissistic equilibrium.[27]

We have already referred to Freud's idea in "On Narcissism, An Introduction,"[28] according to which "everything a person possesses, or achieves, every remnant of the primitive feeling of omnipotence which his experience has confirmed, helps to increase his self-regard."

But in the same work Freud also suggested another possibility for narcissistic support: the object's love for us: "In love relations not being loved lowers the self-regard, while being loved raises it." It seems that many women unconsciously choose Freud's second solution to the need for narcissistic gratifications, because they cannot freely and without guilt fulfill themselves through their personal achievements.

I do not think this choice necessarily implies an incapacity for object love. Indeed, according to Freud ("Instincts and Their Vicissitudes"),[29] "If the object becomes a source of pleasurable feelings, a motor urge is set up which seeks to bring the object closer to the ego and to incorporate it into the ego. We then speak of the 'attraction' exercised by the pleasure-giving object, and we say that we 'love' that object.''

Thus, love is first of all a response to satisfaction, that is, an answer to the love which the object gives us. The two states—loving and being loved—are therefore correlative, and loving implies the desire to renew, to perpetuate the agreeable experience and the love one has received, by incorporating the object in the ego. In fact one often gives love in order to be loved by the object. Further discussion of this subject would lead us to examine the essence of love itself, but that would take us far beyond our present purpose. Here I wished to state above all that the conflictual outcome, when partly based on guilt, necessarily implies consideration for the object, and therefore love, even if the aim is at the same time to find satisfaction for narcissistic needs.

I believe this to be a very common female attitude, and one which can be interpreted as an identification with the part-object, the father's penis. I am not referring to woman's identification with an *autonomous phallus,* but to an identification with the *penis* as such, that is a complementary and totally dependent part of the object.

Identification of oneself with an autonomous phallus results in a pathological form of secondary narcissisim. The ego is libidinally overcathected and shielded from external objects without which the link with reality is broken. Favreau (personal communication) stresses the importance of the narcissistic characteristics peculiar to this situation: the woman who identifies with the phallus *desires only to be desired.* She establishes herself as a phallus; this implies impenetrability and therefore withdrawal from any relation with an external erotic object. Some of these characteristics can be compared with those found in masculine narcissistic-phallic regression.

This sort of phallic identification is traceable in models (''mannequins''), ballerinas (though, of course, many other components make up a true artist's character), vamps, etc. The phallus woman resembles, more than any other woman, what Freud described as the narcissistic woman whose fascination, similar to that of a child, is linked with her *''inaccessibility''* like ''the charm of certain animals *which seem not to concern themselves about us,* such as cats and the large beasts of prey'' (''On Narcissism, An Introduction,'' 1925). Further on Freud mentions the ''enigmatic nature'' and the ''cold and narcissistic'' attitude these women have toward men. Rather than seeing in this the essence of women's object relations, I see it as an identification with an autonomous phallus. Is it not true that men admire the phallus in these women more than the women themselves?

If I have dwelt at such length on this description of woman's identification with the autonomous phallus, it is because I wish to avoid confusing it with the position I am now going to discuss—that of the paternal-penis woman. Far from being autonomous with regard to the object, she is closely dependent on it and is also its *complement*. She is the *right hand*, the assistant, the colleague, the secretary, the auxiliary, the inspiration for an employer, a lover, a husband, a father. She may also be a companion for old age, guide, or nurse. One sees the basic conflicts underlying such relationships in clinical practice.

The autonomous phallus-woman, is similar to the woman described in Conrad Stein's article "La Castration comme négation de la féminité" (*Revue française de psychanalyse*, 1961). Stein relates this problem to bisexuality and to the dialectic of "being" and "having." I think it is necessary to distinguish in metapsychology between "being" as identification with the total object one would like to "have," and "being" the other person's "thing," as an identification with the part-object. This latter position seems to be linked with the subject's reparative tendencies and results from a counteridentification with the mother's castration of the father during the primal scene. In this case the daughter remains closely dependent on the object she makes complete.

Alice is a thirty-eight-year-old woman, small, lively, and full of humor. She is the best friend of a colleague who entrusted her to me, saying that she was "the apple of his eye."

In Alice's case this expression was full of meaning. Alice came to analysis after undergoing an operation for the removal of a neoplastic tumor. The illness naturally aroused deep narcissistic fears, but even more important was the fact that the seriousness of her illness had allowed her to do something for herself for once. Her marriage situation suddenly became unbearable. She was an only child. Her mother was a severe and demanding school teacher, her father a kind and sentimental man who grew flowers and vines in his garden and wrote naive and delicate poems. He would say to Alice when she was little, "You are the prettiest little girl in the world." Even today Alice sometimes wakes up and asks her husband if she really is "the prettiest little girl in the world."

But Alice did not recognize her love for her father. She said her father "revolted" her, she did not like his kisses, he annoyed her, she felt like pushing him down the stairs, especially when he had had a bit too much homemade wine. "At those time," said Alice, "his eyes were very very small." He was clumsy and missed the glass as he poured out the wine. Alice did not understand why she felt irritated by this father whose love could also bring her to tears.

Alice's relation with her mother was based on a mixture of fear and the desire to be held on her lap again and have body contact with her as she was when very small. Alice avoided telling her mother that she had a malignant tumor because her mother despised illness and weakness. When Alice was little she never dared complain nor tell her mother for instance that her sweater made of rough wool itched nor that her socks were too tight.

Alice's fantasy of the primal scene was a sadistic one, the mother playing the role of a castrating and sadistic person.

She studied at the National Academy of Music and married a gifted composer. Once married she gave up her career, saying that "one artist in the family is enough."

She suffered from eczema, particularly at her son's birth; she feels the need for a nonconflictual fusion with the object (the analyst in the transference; the "allergic object relation" described by Pierre Marty). At one point in the treatment she express the need for fusion in the following fantasy:

She is on a lake in a foam-rubber boat with an opening only big enough to let in a little air. But when she thinks of this opening she sees flies and insects coming to bother her.

It became clear that these were her aggressive instincts which she had to leave outside the world of fusion. She associated the boat with a cradle and the mother's womb. But on the level of the triangular relationship the fusion was between her and the gentle, kind father (heir to the mother upon whose lap it was so nice to sit), the mother representing her own aggressive instincts which needed to be repressed. Before and at the beginning of the analysis, Alice dreamed of empty flats; she associated them with the parcels she used to receive from her father's house, which annoyed her and which she did not want to open. Yet one day, opening a parcel from her father, she cried because she was so touched and thus expressed the pleasure she could have felt at accepting her father's love and presents. It became obvious that her rejection of her father was only a superficial defense and that her difficulties with incorporation (empty houses) were not related solely to narcissistic fears of damage.

I cannot give a detailed account of Alice's analysis, but she did express strong guilt about her anal-sadistic instinctual impulses toward the father and his penis. Thus, she dreamed she had a shrimp-child which had dried up between the pages of a book. She felt very guilty at having killed him. She associated this with her father's body. In another dream a baby put in her mother's care was dying of dehydration. After a frantic race she managed to arrive just in time to save him. She noticed her mother was feeding the baby with a bottle full of dirty water. Etc.

This guilt became increasingly obvious in the transference. For example, she thought of offering me a reproduction of a painting by Chagall which represented a rooster. She associated this with childhood fantasies in which a woman wandered the roads with a rooster on a leash. In the sessions I am about to discuss this appears as a penis which has to be restored to the father.

For some time Alice had been feeling guilty toward me, thinking she was not paying me enough money. Her husband, also in analysis, was paying a much higher fee. Alice arrives at her session at 11:30, lies down, and wonders if she is on time. Is her session at 11:20 or 11:40? She cannot remember even though she has come at the same time since the beginning of her analysis and is on time today. She continues by listing a series of things "which are not going well." The windows in her apartment are broken, and she cannot get the caretaker to send someone round to repair them (this question of windows has taken up a great deal of the analysis lately); with her husband things are not going well, she cannot stand it any longer. She fails in what she attempts. She asks me if she has arrived early or late. I say: "It seems as if one of us must give up something (ten minutes from you or ten minutes from me) and you are trying to show me that it is *you* who loses, that you are diminished by everyone in every way."

At the next session Alice gets muddled about the time of her appointment and arrives half an hour early. After going away and coming back at the usual time she lies down and says:

"One of my eyes is running, it stings. By the way my eye always runs when I come here." Silence. "Oh! Well what do you know! But I never told you that my father had his eye put out, right in front of me when I was little. I don't remember how old I was . . . maybe eight. We used to go together in the fields and he suddenly put his foot down on some barbed wire which flew in the air and hit him in the eye. How amazing that I never told you about that. My running eye is on the same side as my father's. Now I suddenly understand why I was fascinated for so long by the Galton portrait game, in which one glues both left sides and both right sides together. Because of his eye my father has two very different profiles. When I was little I used to imagine the story of a little girl who had one dark and one light eye.'' Her dark eye was due to the fact that she went to school by a path sunk between two very dark walls and the light eye was due to the fact that these walls suddenly gave way to a dazzling courtyard full of bits of glass, etc.

This session was one of the most important in Alice's analysis as it allowed her to understand better and experience certain aspects of her object relations through the specially symbolized details in her fantasy (her love of big, transparent, amber pearls, her worry about the windows in her flat, her hatred of symmetry, etc.). This historical event is important inasmuch as it ''crystallized'' a series of emotions linked to the father and his penis; the event was traumatic because Alice's aggressive fantasies had been confirmed in reality.

Her annoyance with her father, with his ''small eyes'' when he was drunk, with his clumsiness (Alice never associated the ''small eyes'' with the event of his eye being put out), were struggles against guilt: ''It is not my fault my father had this accident, in fact there was no accident, he had only drunk a little and that is why he had those ''small eyes.'' He can see perfectly well, he is only clumsy. I must not approach him, accept his love, because any contact between us is dangerous. I must reject my father, that is the only desire I have toward him.'' But unconsciously all Alice's object relations are dominated by the desire to *heal* her father, as an atonement for her guilty desires toward him.

Alice, who never took full advantage of her musical knowledge, is very clever with her hands and can achieve amazing things in carpentry and handiwork. She is proud of these activities, even though she deprecates herself in so many others. During her analysis, she thinks of taking up some professional activity. At the beginning of his career her husband had written some commercial songs to earn money. She had contributed the main ideas for these, so he now suggested that she write her own songs. But she says she is incapable of doing that—she could never be inspired *unless the song could be considered as his creation.*

During one session the unconscious meaning of her handicraft becomes clear. First of all she mentions her present difficulty over driving a car, a difficulty in total contrast to the facility with which she drove her father in a car, since he was incapacitated by the accident to his eye. "Daddy was very proud of me then." She associated this with her difficulty in remembering what I had told her during the previous session, yet she had fully understood what I had said. She said that if I were to repeat the beginning of what I had said, she would remember the rest of it. In other words, if I were beside her she could drive but she could not take the initiative alone: that would have meant driving for oneself, and she could not do that any more than she could write a song if it were not to become her husband's.

Then she mentioned a disagreeable woman who had annoyed her the previous day until she had suddenly learned that this woman did a lot of handicraft. "All my irritation with her vanished, she did not seem aggressive or disagreeable any more. I thought she was very sweet." In Alice's mind handicraft seemed to make the lady as *innocent* as it made Alice herself.

One of her fantasies clarified the meaning of her attitudes and activities. She was going to Lourdes to sell miraculous, pious objects, virgins with luminous eyes. She also invented medicines for sick animals. One can see that Alice's activities are aimed at *replacing the eye lost by her father.* She is entirely involved in her prosthetic function. She can only create, act, live, *for* someone of whom she becomes the complementary part, the penis.

Her love for her father meant that she could not take on an identification with the mother, castrating the father during the primal scene. All activity, all means of existing which could be symbolized in the unconscious as a penis, were forbidden her. Indeed, acting for oneself, being autonomous, creating for oneself meant possessing the paternal penis and thus castrating the father. Alice has disfused her instinctual impulses, countercathected her aggression and offered herself as a replacement for the lost paternal penis, thus making the loved object complete. The position is therefore a *reaction formation.*

Alice's sexuality follows the same pattern. She seems free, but her choice of erotic objects shows that she is not. She is loved by several charming, cultivated gentlemen, much older than herself. They court her in a slightly discreet melancholic way. Alice only shows them kindness and friendship. One of them, who is married, has even decided, with his wife's agreement, to adopt her as his daughter.

Thinking about these "affairs," Alice remembers that ten years ago, while being courted by one of these men, she went to the café where they usually met and encountered some young men, her "little brothers," seeing them for an obvious sexual purpose. These adventures always occurred during her father's absence from Paris. This is a classical defense against the Oedipus complex. But another fact more precisely locates the level of this defense: these gentlemen, Alice realizes, are nearly all Jewish. In fact she only gets on well with Jews. Even a badly educated man, if he is Jewish, attracts her. Perhaps it is because of their sense of humor, or their sadness, or their persecution. Sometimes, when Alice sees beggars, she is very upset. Once, with a lump in her throat, she gave one a lot of money, the notes rolled up in a ball. Then she realized he looked like her father.

These conflicts were analyzed at great length. Alice, whose dream life had been poor, as though paralyzed, suddenly began to have many dreams and started recalling all her childhood. One series of dreams is particularly important. Having recalled the erotic games of her childhood, especially her favorite one of taking people's temperatures,[30] she remembers an adolescent dream: she was looking at the stars with her mother and one constellation looked like an agitated man. She was the only one to see this in the stars and she was going to go mad because her head kept flopping onto her shoulder. She associated this with the memory of witnessing a friend's epileptic fit. She feared that she too might have those terrible convulsions.

Next, a transference dream. A faith healer noticed that she was emitting an excessively dangerous electric vibration. The next night the healer died, very probably of this vibration.

Thereafter, every night Alice dreamed of corpses. The first one was that of the kindest of her old gentlemen; he was all broken up and was about to die when Alice called for a doctor. Strangely, the dying man was taken to a sordid barn; the next night she dreamed that her husband was taken to a sinister clinic on the outskirts of Paris, with the side of his body all black. The following night she dreamed that she was crying during a session while I was explaining that the police were coming, and I showed her a man's corpse which I kept in a coffin. The police arrived and, quite unexpectedly—that was the worst punishment of all—they took away her father while she cried, and then she had to see him die in a prison cell, while she stood by powerless, seeing his abject poverty.

This dream, in which the id disguises itself as the superego in order to fulfill the desire of anally incorporating the paternal penis, was followed by a number of memories: sex play with a farmhand who had shown her his penis, games with a cousin in the hayloft, the exciting smell of the granaries and cellars where the hams were hung and the cheese and wines matured. At the same time Alice tells me that, for some incomprehensible reason, she has deliberately omitted telling me one fact: a good-looking rag-and-bone man, with dark eyes, came to empty their cellar. He made advances to her, but although she refused them she was not indifferent to them. As the price he was asking for emptying her cellar was too steep, she decided to do it herself. Once the cellar was empty, there was a huge carpet rolled up on the ground. With a great effort Alice unrolled the carpet and very cleverly managed to hang it vertically from the cellar ceiling and leave it there.

Of course I cannot discuss here all the material from this series of sessions nor give details of the transference. I shall merely recount the two dreams which followed this last session, as they show in an abbreviated form the shape of her development.

Alice is going up the staircase in my building. She meets a handsome man who flirts with her. He is my husband. He asks her when he can see her again, and Alice replies: "I come here three times a week."

The following night Alice dreams that her father and mother are sleeping in her flat. In the middle of the night Alice's mother throws the father out of her room and he goes and sits on a stool in the kitchen. Grieved because he cannot spend the whole night there, Alice offers to let him sleep with her.

As the anal-sadistic incorporative desires toward the father's penis become conscious a true Oedipal situation is able to develop. The disfused instinct begins to appear under its own disfused aspect only to merge with the cluster which makes up genital primacy.

When the sadistic-anal instincts of incorporating the paternal penis result in guilt (as discussed at the beginning of this article) they increase the possibility of the girl's identifying with the father's penis. As we have shown, there is then an inversion of content and container, the woman identifying herself with the penis in the dangerous vagina—dangerous because of the sadistic-anal component, the fecal stool in the rectum. (This inversion is the main symptom of claustrophobia; it also exists in other structures.) The girl thus becomes the father's anal penis, she is a part of him and offers herself to his handling and mastery. Mastery, possession, or domination of the father, or of his substitutes (generally masculine ones), are forbidden to her. Thus, Alice, asked to compose the music for a ballet, is very pleased and says: "The person who asked me to do it is a friend; I know his taste. There will be no problem in doing it. But I would never dare accept a job from a stranger. He might not like what I did. I would never dare impose my taste on anybody."

I would readily see this as the source of one of woman's main conflicts, that of being *relative* to men, just as nearly all of woman's cultural or social achievements are. Women are said to produce few original works; they are often the brilliant disciple of a man or of a masculine theory. They are rarely leaders of movements. This is surely the effect of a conflict specific to women.

I believe it is important, both from a clinical and from a technical point of view, to discuss this position which can be scotomized because of the countertransference it causes. (I am here thinking of my own clinical experience.) Certain patients, and this seems to be peculiar to women—for when this happens in men the conflictual aspect of it is immediately obvious—are cured of their symptoms only in order to make publicity for their analyst; they feel they are a successful product, and experience their analysis as though the future and the reputation of the analyst depended on it. (The aggression toward the object becomes self-destructive.)

Thus, one of my patients imagined she was a sandwichman advertising my name and address. This reminded her of a brand of coffee whose advertising had taken the form of men disguised as coffee packets walking through Paris.

Certain aspects of *female masochism* seems to be related to this position. One of the main aspects of the masochistic character is the role of being "the other person's thing." "I am your thing. Do whatever you want to with me," says the masochist to his partner. In other words I am your fecal stool and you can deal with me as you wish. One explanation of female masochism is to be found in its link with the guilt of incorporating the penis in a sadistic-anal way, as though women, in order to achieve this incorporation, had to pretend to offer themselves entirely, in place of the stolen penis, proposing that the partner do to her body, to her ego, to herself, what she had, in fantasy, done to his penis.

Grunberger had based his study of masochism (in both sexes) on the guilt associated with anal introjection of the paternal penis, but the mechanism he discussed is not quite the same as the one I am here describing.

The woman's superego seems also to be linked to her identification with the paternal penis. Without entering the discussion of whether her superego is stronger than man's (Melanie Klein), or weaker (Freud), or quasi-non-existent (J. Lampl-de Groot), I wish to discuss one of the aspects of the female superego described by Freud. He states that woman's superego is more impersonal than man's. This is a common observation. Women have, at least in appearance, a superego which constantly changes, taking on new aspects, giving up old ones, according to their sexual partners. One frequently says that women are easily influenced, that they have no fixed opinions, that they readily change their principles. One of my patients, the one who gave up her lectures because of a disagreeable criticism, seems to be this type of woman who judges her acts and thoughts according to the object's judgments. She seems to hear only the rules she is told of, while being ignorant of the law. But this "malleable" character of her thought is linked only to her conscious guilt. Beyond these variations, the internalized prohibitions are very strong. One of them dominates all the others, as if it were some sort of Eleventh Commandment: "You may not have your own law—your law is your object's law." It seems as though many women have internalized this commandment, making them eternally dependent.

Here again, man's conflict with the omnipotent mother and woman's conflict with the cathexis of the loved object both contribute to this situation in which woman plays the role of a part-object.[31]

CONCLUSION

The cases which I have chosen to discuss, despite different nosological data, all have one feature in common: the mother was sadistic and castrating, the father was good and vulnerable. Of course, many families do not have this structure. There are families where the opposite is true, where the mother is the good element and the father the sadistic one. It is interesting that in these latter cases the paternal figure becomes ambiguous and is identified once again, in woman's unconscious, with the phallic mother. Therefore, the family structure, in the cases discussed here, even though it seems exaggerated, is nevertheless an objective one inasmuch as it represents the normal unconscious structure at the time of the change of object, the bad object being projected onto the mother, the good onto the father. When reality cannot correct this unconscious image, severe problems are bound to arise. Then the Primal Scene represents a mixture of the destructive bad object and the good object which must be safeguarded, or, in other words, a terrifying fusion of the aggressive and erotic instincts. To deny the necessity of instinctual fusion in female sexuality corresponds to ignoring men's terrifying fantasies about femininity and women's guilty fantasies about their instinctual impulses, which is rather like trying to transform black Eros into a cherubic cupid.

It seems to me that one cannot base all female conflicts with the father and his penis on primitive conflicts with the mother and her breast; that would be shortcircuiting the total transformation which occurs during the change of object inherent in the path to womanhood.

Freud has shown that the little girl's Oedipus complex, caused by penis envy, is a *haven* for her inasmuch as the girl, whose castration has already been effected, has nothing more to fear from the mother. This results in *a tendency to prolong the Oedipal situation*. It is interesting that the female Oedipus complex is not resolved in the way that the male Oedipus complex is. (Parents readily say that "a son's your son till he gets a wife; a daughter's your daughter all her life.")

Is this not related to the fact that the girl, in seeking to free herself from the mother during the change of object, and in her need to safeguard the father, offers herself to him as a part-object, protected from the mother, loved by the father, and forever dependent?

It seems as if the girl who prolongs this situation feels it to be a *haven* only inasmuch as she is not taking the mother's place beside the father because she is not identifying with her and because she stays a child rather than becomes a woman. I believe that she is, at the same time, protecting herself from castration threatened by the mother by refusing to take her place. An Oedipal situation in which the girl truly identifies with the mother in order to take her place beside the father is never a comfortable one. The obstacles which the girl encounters in her love for her father and in the rivalry with her mother are frightening enough for the girl's Oedipus complex to be just what the boy's Oedipus complex was, "the crux of neuroses."

Man and woman are born of woman: before all else we are our mother's child. Yet all our desires seem designed to deny this fact, so full of conflicts and reminiscent of our primitive dependence. The myth of Genesis seems to express this desire to free ourselves from our mother: man is born of God, an idealized paternal figure, a projection of lost omnipotence. Woman is born from man's body. If this myth expresses the victory of man over his mother and over woman, who thereby becomes his own child, it also provides a certain solution for woman inasmuch as she also is her mother's daughter: she chooses to belong to man, to be created *for* him, and not for herself, to be part of him—Adam's rib—rather than to prolong her "attachment" to her mother. I have tried to show the conflicts which oblige so many women to choose between mother and husband as the object of dependent attachment.

NOTES

1. Sigmund Freud, "Female Sexuality," 1931.
2. Melanie Klein, *Envy and Gratitude* (New York, 1957).
3. "Our understanding of feminine frigidity . . . can be complete only if we take into consideration the fact that there is a constitutional inhibition that has no parallel in men" (Hélène Deutsch, *The Psychology of Women,* New York, 1944).
4. Sigmund Freud, *Beyond the Pleasure Principle* (London, 1950).
5. Sigmund Freud, *The Ego and the Id* (London, 1927).
6. Sigmund Freud, *Inhibitions, Symptoms, Anxiety* (London, 1936).
7. Deutsch, *Psychology of Women.*
8. Sigmund Freud, *Collected Papers,* 4 (London, 1918), 217–35.
9. "I have had occasional opportunities of being told women's dreams that had occurred after their first experience of intercourse. They revealed an unmistakable wish in the woman to keep for herself the penis which she had felt" (Sigmund Freud, "On Transformations of Instincts as Exemplified in Anal Erotism," 1924).

   I believe that this desire, which Freud thinks is a regressive one, is, in fact, the manifestation of a desire more authentically feminine, that of keeping the penis in order to be *impregnated* by it. The female sexual desire to be penetrated seems to me to be inseparably linked in the unconscious with the biological consequence of that desire—impregnation, that is to say the desire, as Ernest Jones said, to keep the penis in oneself in order to turn it into a child. Also, the instinctual drive at the level of the primary processes is absolute and unlimited and cannot be set in a spatio-temporal framework. The complementary masculine desire is similar in that it is not limited to penetrating one particular part of the woman's body at a given moment, but, as Ferenczi said in *Thalassa,* it is a desire to return one's whole body to the mother's womb.
10. *"Epouser"* = "to take the exact shape of" *and* "to marry." (Tr. note.)
11. It is not sufficient to give purely sociological reasons for women's difficulties in professional or creative fields; we need to seek out the deep unconscious roots of these difficulties. But

neither would it be exact to say that there is no sociocultural factor. Women's internal guilt is constantly encouraged by real external factors. Psychoanalysts rightly emphasize the role of these external factors in creating neuroses—by being particularly favorable to unconscious conflicts common to many people.

12. This assertion was maintained by Freud even in his "Short Account of Psychoanalysis" (1924), after many people had opposed him in theory and by clinical observation. Yet in the article Ruth Mack Brunswick wrote with him ("The Pre-Oedipal Phase," 1940), he seems to have more or less accepted that early sensations do exist in the vagina.

13. I think this transfer of cathexis is due to the guilt associated with the anal-sadistic incorporative drives.

14. The narcissistic cathexis of these characteristics is linked, according to Grunberger, with the anal-sadistic phase, and thus the only objects of value are those which can be measured, compared, and precisely graded.

15. Freud not only ignores the vagina but, until the castration complex, that is, the Oedipus complex, he believes the girl's sexuality to be identical with that of the boy. She merely hopes for receptive satisfactions from her mother, but she does not expect them to be phallic and denies the penis as well as the vagina. When she turns to the father wanting a child by him, it is not yet a desire for incorporation of the paternal penis. For Freud, the girl's Oedipus complex occurs without interfering with incorporation desires (or desires of being penetrated in any manner); in a similar way the boy has no desire to penetrate the mother. He is ignorant of her possessing an organ complementary to his own. It is only at puberty that erection of a penis indicates a new aim—the penetration of a cavity. Apart from numerous indications that there are early desires of penetration (which many people have noted), erections are frequent before puberty, and one finds babies having erections, particularly while being suckled. E. Jones, Melanie Klein, Josine Müller, Karen Horney, and, more recently, Phyllis Greenacre, in discussing the girl's discovery of the vagina, stress the fact that we are used to talking about external and visible organs without taking deep coenesthetic sensations into consideration. Girls' ignorance of their vaginas does not prove the nonexistence of a genital desire to incorporate the penis, just as a congenital malformation obstructing the mouth would not deny the existence of hunger. Indeed, the impossibility of satisfying the instinct increases guilt, in face of the "condemned" vagina.

16. Once frustration has brought the primary narcissistic phase to an end.

17. Unconsciously, he has probably always known she had no penis just as, unconsciously, he always knew she had a vagina. But this does not exclude representation of a phallic or castrated mother, since the primary processes readily admit contradiction.

18. Sigmund Freud, *Group Psychology and the Analysis of the Ego,* 1922.

19. Of course other causes also dictate a man's future attitude to women, one of which is an identification with the real father in his relation to the mother.

20. See Karen Horney, "The Dread of Women." The little boy feels an aggressive desire for his mother. In her role as educator she is obliged to dominate him and frustrate him. He desires to penetrate her, but feels humiliated at being small and incapable of achieving this, which leads to his feeling narcissistically wounded and immensely inferior, but he also feels a violently aggressive desire for revenge, which is projected, along with those desires caused by the first frustrations, onto the mother and her vagina.

21. One patient suffering from ejaculatio praecox was content in his first sexual relations at the age of twenty-two with merely external contact "because he did not know" that the vagina existed. Such "ignorance" is due to frightening sexual fantasies. For him the female organ was a threat, full of fecal content (crumbling caves full of garbage, cow's cloaca blocked with dung "as hard as granite," corpses found in rooms, crashed cars spread across an icy

road, etc.). Therefore, penetration is dangerous: in order to avoid it one must "fill the vagina with powdered glass, use it as a chamber pot and fill it to the brim," think of it as a john where one puts the lid down before urinating or else tries to get rid of the contents first. Thus, at puberty, this patient spent a lot of time disembowelling flies; one of his favorite fantasies was the following: he was master of a harem and ruled women of all ages with a whip. He had established very strict rules in which the women had to defecate by orders and under close scrutiny. This illustrates the child's inversion of sphincter education and his victory over the anal penis of the intrusive mother. (This patient also had fantasies about excision of the clitoris.)

Men fear the mother's power, and her anal penis in particular. Later they try to stop women from using their anal impulses. As woman is guilty about her own anal wishes toward the father, she becomes an accomplice to the man's defenses. This conjunction results in the visible inhibition of women's anality in society: a woman must never swear, spit, eat strong food or wine, and, until recently, discuss money or business. Charm and grace are on the whole either reaction formations or sublimations of anal impulses (the opposite of vulgarity). At the same time, women are represented as illogical, vague, incapable of the rigors of science, engineering, etc.—all signs of successful integration of the anal components.

(Owing to the enforced repression it undergoes, the anal instinct may become somewhat "corrosive." The weaker muscular structure of women also favors this corrosive aspect of feminine aggression, as it does not allow for adequate motor discharge. Women are said to scratch, bite, or poison, whereas men punch or knock down.) In fact this desire for victory over the omnipotent mother is often displaced by men onto all women. An exception is the *daughter,* perhaps because she in a dependent situation. The father projects onto her an *idealized image* which is opposed to the *"normal lasting contempt"* (Freud, Ruth Mack Brunswick, Hélène Deutsch) he feels for other women. His daughter often represents the best part of himself and of the good, primitive object. She is tenderness, purity, innocence, and grace and represents for him a privileged relationship which escapes his ambivalence.

Of course, this relation is not always there, as some men extend their maternal conflicts onto their daughters, too. An obsessional patient suffering from ejaculatio praecox was discussing his six-year-old daughter who was working hard at school in order to attract his attention, a fact he was well aware of: "I push her away from me but, being truly feminine, she still tries to attract my attention"; but the relation I have described exists frequently enough for it to be noticeable. Three patients told me at the outset of their treatment that one of their reasons for coming to analysis was a desire to help their daughters.

22. In her article "The Pre-Oedipal Phase" (written with Freud), Ruth Mack Brunswick reconsiders the idea that the desire for a child is a substitute for penis envy: the desire for a child expresses mainly the desire to have what the mother possessed: a child.

   I believe that if the child's desire is linked both with penis envy and with the omnipotent mother, it is because of a certain connection between penis envy and the omnipotent maternal imago.

23. For Freud (in "Femininity," 1933), if a woman comes to analysis in order to be more successful in her profession she is by the same token displaying her penis envy.

24. The same is true of men: for a man to achieve his professional ambitions is symbolically to have a penis *like the father*.

25. Protecting oneself from penetration is also a way of safeguarding the object. A whole series of aggressive acts toward the father can be understood as an attempt to protect him from *contact*.

26. Of course, this may also be due to regression.

27. Space prevents our considering here the child's role as a narcissistic support. Joyce Mc-Dougall noted that penis envy plays as important a role in mothers as in women who are childless.

It is a fact that many mothers castrate their children psychologically, which indicates that their penis envy is not satisfied by maternity.

It is no solution to the problem to say that in these cases the women have not been able to transform their desire for a penis into a desire for a child.

Having a child may mean possessing what the omnipotent mother had (Ruth Mack Brunswick), but it does not yet mean having *something different* from what she had, and this, I believe, is the true aim of narcissistic achievements.

28. Freud, *Collected Papers,* 4 (1925), 39–59.
29. Freud, *Collected Papers,* 4 (1925), 60–83.
30. Taken anally in France. (Tr. note.)
31. This is similar to the situation described by Simone de Beauvoir in *The Second Sex* (New York, 1952).

4. Creativity and Its Origins

D. W. Winnicott

THE SPLIT-OFF MALE AND FEMALE ELEMENTS TO BE FOUND IN MEN AND WOMEN

There is nothing new either inside or outside psychoanalysis in the idea that men and women have a 'predisposition towards bisexuality'.

I try here to use what I have learned about bisexuality from analyses that have gone step by step towards a certain point and have focused on one detail. No attempt will be made here to trace the steps by which an analysis comes to this kind of material. It can be said that a great deal of work usually has had to be done before this type of material has become significant and calls for priority. It is difficult to see how all this preliminary work can be avoided. The slowness of the analytic process is a manifestation of a defence the analyst must respect, as we respect all defences. While it is the patient who is all the time teaching the analyst, the analyst should be able to know, theoretically, about the matters that concern the deepest or most central features of personality, else he may fail to recognize and to meet new demands on his understanding and technique when at long last the patient is able to bring deeply buried matters into the content of the transference, thereby affording opportunity for mutative interpretation. The analyst, by interpreting, shows how much and how little of the patient's communication he is able to receive.

As a basis for the idea that I wish to give in this chapter I suggest that creativity is one of the common denominators of men and women. In another language, however, creativity is the prerogative of women, and in yet another language it is a masculine feature. It is this last of the three that concerns me in what follows here.

Adapted with permission from D. W. Winnicott, *Playing and Reality* (London: Tavistock, 1971), 72–85. First published in 1966.

Clinical Data

Illustrative Case. I propose to start with a clinical example. This concerns the treatment of a man of middle age, a married man with a family, and successful in one of the professions. The analysis has proceeded along classical lines. This man has had a long analysis and I am not by any means his first psychotherapist. A great deal of work has been done by him and by each of us therapists and analysts in turn, and much change has been brought about in his personality. But there is still something he avers that makes it impossible for him to stop. He knows that what he came for he has not reached. If he cuts his losses the sacrifice is too great.

In the present phase of this analysis something has been reached which is new *for me*. It has to do with the way I am dealing with the non-masculine element in his personality.

On a Friday the patient came and reported much as usual. The thing that struck me on this Friday was that the patient was talking about *penis envy*. I use this term advisedly, and I must invite acceptance of the fact that this term was appropriate here in view of the material, and of its presentation. Obviously this term, 'penis envy', is not usually applied in the description of a man.

The change that belongs to this particular phase is shown in the way I handled this. On this particular occasion I said to him: 'I am listening to a girl. I know perfectly well that you are a man but I am listening to a girl, and I am talking to a girl. I am telling this girl: "You are talking about penis envy." '

I wish to emphasize that this has nothing to do with homosexuality.

(It has been pointed out to me that my interpretation in each of its two parts could be thought of as related to playing, and as far as possible removed from authoritative interpretation that is next door to indoctrination.)

It was clear to me, by the profound effect of this interpretation, that my remark was in some way apposite, and indeed I would not be reporting this incident in this context were it not for the fact that the work that started on this Friday did in fact break into a vicious circle. I had grown accustomed to a routine of good work, good interpretations, good immediate results, and then destruction and disillusionment that followed each time because of the patient's gradual recognition that something fundamental had remained unchanged; there was this unknown factor which had kept this man working at his own analysis for a quarter of a century. Would his work with me suffer the same fate as his work with the other therapists?

On this occasion there was an immediate effect in the form of intellectual acceptance, and relief, and then there were more remote effects. After a pause the patient said: 'If I were to tell someone about this girl I would be called mad.'

The matter could have been left there, but I am glad, in view of subsequent events, that I went further. It was my next remark that surprised me, and it clinched the matter. I said: 'It was not that *you* told this to anyone; it is *I* who see the girl and hear a girl talking, when actually there is a man on my couch. The mad person is *myself.*'

I did not have to elaborate this point because it went home. The patient said that he now felt sane in a mad environment. In other words he was now released from a dilemma. As he said, subsequently, 'I myself could never say (knowing myself to be a man) "I am a girl". I am not mad that way. But you said it, and you have spoken to both parts of me.'

This madness which was mine enabled him to see himself as a girl *from my position.* He knows himself to be a man, and never doubts that he is a man.

Is it obvious what was happening here? For my part, I have needed to live through a deep personal experience in order to arrive at the understanding I feel I now have reached.

This complex state of affairs has a special reality for this man because he and I have been driven to the conclusion (though unable to prove it) that his mother (who is not alive now) saw a girl baby when she saw him as a baby before she came round to thinking of him as a boy. In other words this man had to fit into her idea that her baby would be and was a girl. (He was the second child, the first being a boy.) We have very good evidence from inside the analysis that in her early management of him the mother held him and dealt with him in all sorts of physical ways as if she failed to see him as a male. On the basis of this pattern he later arranged his defences, but it was the mother's 'madness' that saw a girl where there was a boy, and this was brought right into the present by my having said 'It is I who am mad'. On this Friday he went away profoundly moved and feeling that this was the first significant shift in the analysis for a long time (although, as I have said, there had always been continuous progress in the sense of good work being done).

I would like to give further details relative to this Friday incident. When he came on the following Monday he told me that he was ill. It was quite clear to me that he had an infection and I reminded him that his wife would have it the next day, which in fact happened. Nevertheless, he was inviting me to *interpret* this illness, which started on the Saturday, as if it were psychosomatic. What he tried to tell me was that on the Friday night he had had a satisfactory sexual intercourse with his wife, and so he *ought* to have felt better on the Saturday, but instead of feeling better he had become ill and had felt ill. I was able to leave aside the physical disorder and talk about the incongruity of his feeling ill after the intercourse that he felt ought to have been a healing experience. (He might, indeed, have said: 'I have 'flu, but in spite of that I feel better in myself.')

My interpretation continued along the line started up on the Friday. I said: 'You feel as if you ought to be pleased that here was an interpretation of mine that had released masculine behaviour. *The girl that I was talking to, however, does not want the man released,* and indeed she is not interested in him. What she wants is full acknowledgement of herself and of her own rights over your body. Her penis envy especially includes envy of you as a male.' I went on: 'The feeling ill is a protest from the female self, this girl, because she has always hoped that the analysis would in fact find out that this man, yourself, is and always has been a girl (and "being ill" is a pregenital pregnancy). The only end to the analysis that this girl can look for is the discovery that in fact you are a girl.' Out of this one could begin to understand his conviction that the analysis could never end.[1]

In the subsequent weeks there was a great deal of material confirming the validity of my interpretation and my attitude, and the patient felt that he could see now that his analysis had ceased to be under doom of interminability.

Later I was able to see that the patient's resistance had now shifted to a denial of the importance of my having said 'It is I who am mad'. He tried to pass this off as just my way of putting things—a figure of speech that could be forgotten. I found, however, that here is one of those examples of delusional transference that puzzle patients and analysts alike, and the crux of the problem of management is just here in this interpretation, which I confess I nearly did not allow myself to make.

When I gave myself time to think over what had happened I was puzzled. Here was no new theoretical concept, here was no new principle of technique. In fact, I and my patient had been over this ground before. Yet we had here something new, new in my own attitude and new in his capacity to make use of my interpretative work. I decided to surrender myself to whatever this might mean in myself, and the result is to be found in this paper that I am presenting.

Dissociation. The first thing I noticed was that I had never before fully accepted the complete dissociation between the man (or woman) and the aspect of the personality that has the opposite sex. In the case of this man patient the dissociation was nearly complete.

Here, then, I found myself with a new edge to an old weapon, and I wondered how this would or could affect the work I was doing with other patients, both men and women, or boys and girls. I decided, therefore, to study this type of dissociation, leaving aside but not forgetting all the other types of splitting.

Male and Female Elements in Men and Women.[2] There was in this case a dissociation that was on the point of breaking down. The dissociation defence was giving way to an acceptance of bisexuality as a quality of the unit or total self. I saw that I was dealing with what could be called a *pure female element*. At first it surprised me that I could reach this only by looking at the material presented by a male patient.[3]

A further clinical observation belongs to this case. Some of the relief that followed our arrival at the new platform for our work together came from the fact that we now could explain why my interpretations, made on good grounds, in respect of use of objects, oral erotic satisfactions in the transference, oral sadistic ideas in respect of the patient's interest in the analyst as part-object or as a person with breast or penis—why such interpretations were never mutative. They were accepted, but: so what? Now that the new position had been reached the patient felt a sense of relationship with me, and this was extremely vivid. It had to do with identity. The pure female split-off element found a primary unity with me as analyst, and this gave the man a feeling of having started to live. I have been affected by this detail, as will appear in my application to theory of what I have found in this case.

Addendum to the Clinical Section. It is rewarding to review one's current clinical material keeping in mind this one example of dissociation, the split-off girl element in a male patient. The subject can quickly become vast and complex, so that a few observations must be chosen for special mention.

(a) One may, to one's surprise, find that one is dealing with and attempting to analyze the split-off part, while the main functioning person appears only in projected form. This is like treating a child only to find that one is treating one or other parent by proxy. Every possible variation on this theme may come one's way.

(b) The other-sex element may be completely split off so that, for instance, a man may not be able to make any link at all with the split-off part. This applies especially when the personality is otherwise sane and integrated. Where the functioning personality is already organized into multiple splits there is less accent on 'I am sane', and therefore less resistance against the idea 'I am a girl' (in the case of a man) or 'I am a boy' (in the case of a woman).

(c) There may be found clinically a near-complete other-sex dissociation, organized in relation to external factors at a very early date, mixed in with later dissociations organized as a defence, based more or less on cross-identifications. The reality of this later organized defence may militate against the patient's revival in the analysis of the earlier reactive split.

(There is an axiom here, that a patient will always cling to the full exploitation of personal and *internal* factors, which give him or her a measure of omnipotent control, rather than allow the idea of a crude reaction to an environmental factor, whether distortion or failure. Environmental influence, bad or even good, comes into our work as a traumatic idea, intolerable because not operating within the area of the patient's omnipotence. Compare the melancholic's claim to be responsible for *all* evil.)

(d) The split-off other-sex part of the personality tends to remain of one age, or to grow but slowly. As compared with this, the truly imaginative figures of the person's inner psychic reality mature, interrelate, grow old, and die. For instance, a man who depends on younger girls for keeping his split-off girl-self alive may gradually become able to employ for his special purpose girls of marriageable age. But should he live to ninety it is unlikely that the girls so employed will reach thirty. Yet in a

man patient the girl (hiding the pure girl element of earlier formation) may have girl characteristics, may be breast-proud, experience penis envy, become pregnant, be equipped with no male external genitalia and even possess female sexual equipment and enjoy female sexual experience.

(e) An important issue here is the assessment of all this in terms of psychiatric health. The man who initiates girls into sexual experience may well be one who is more identified with the girl than with himself. This gives him the capacity to go all out to wake up the girl's sex and to satisfy her. He pays for this by getting but little male satisfaction himself, and he pays also in terms of his need to seek always a new girl, this being the opposite of object-constancy.

At the other extreme is the illness of impotence. In between the two lies the whole range of relative potency mixed with dependence of various types and degrees. What is normal depends on the social expectation of any one social group at any one particular time. Could it not be said that at the patriarchal extreme of society sexual intercourse is rape, and at the matriarchal extreme the man with a split-off female element who must satisfy many women is at a premium even if in doing so he annihilates himself?

In between the extremes is bisexuality and an expectation of sexual experience which is less than optimal. This goes along with the idea that social health is mildly depressive—except for holidays.

It is interesting that the existence of this split-off female element actually prevents homosexual practice. In the case of my patient he always fled from homosexual advances at the critical moment because (as he came to see and to tell me) putting homosexuality into practice would establish his maleness which (from the split-off female element self) he never wanted to know for certain.

(In the normal, where bisexuality is a fact, homosexual ideas do not conflict in this way largely because the anal factor (which is a secondary matter) has not attained supremacy over fellatio, and in the fantasy of a fellatio union the matter of the person's biological sex is not significant.)

(f) It seems that in the evolution of Greek myth the first homosexuals were men who imitated women so as to get into as close as possible a relationship with the supreme goddess. This belonged to a matriarchal era out of which a patriarchal god system appeared with Zeus as head. Zeus (symbol of the patriarchal system) initiated the idea of the boy

loved sexually by man, and along with this went the relegation of women to a lower status. If this is a true statement of the history of the development of ideas, it gives the link that I need if I am to be able to join my clinical observations about the split-off female element in the case of men patients with the theory of object-relating. (The split-off male element in women patients is of equal importance in our work, but what I have to say about object-relating can be said in terms of one only of the two possible examples of dissociation.)

Summary of Preliminary Observations

In our theory it is necessary to allow for both a male and a female element in boys and men and girls and women. These elements may be split off from each other to a high degree. This idea requires of us both a study of the clinical effects of this type of dissociation and an examination of the distilled male and female elements themselves.

I have made some observations on the first of these two, the clinical effects; now I wish to examine what I am calling the distilled male and female elements (not male and female persons).

Pure Male and Pure Female Elements

Speculation about Contrast in Kinds of Object-relating. Let us compare and contrast the unalloyed male and female elements in the context of object-relating.

I wish to say that the element that I am calling 'male' does traffic in terms of active relating or passive being related to, each being backed by instinct. It is in the development of this idea that we speak of instinct drive in the baby's relation to the breast and to feeding, and subsequently in relation to all the experiences involving the main erotogenic zones, and to subsidiary drives and satisfactions. My suggestion is that, by contrast, the pure female element relates to the breast (or to the mother) in the sense of *the baby becoming the breast (or mother), in the sense that the object is the subject.* I can see no instinct drive in this.

(There is also to be remembered the use of the word 'instinct' that comes from ethology; however, I doubt very much whether imprinting is a matter that affects the newborn human infant at all. I will say here and now that I believe the whole subject of imprinting is irrelevant to the study of the early object-relating of human infants. It certainly has nothing to do with the trauma of separation at two years, the very place where its prime importance has been assumed.)

The term 'subjective object' has been used in describing the first object, the object *not yet repudiated as a not-me phenomenon.* Here in this related-ness of pure female element to 'breast' is a practical application of the idea of the subjective object, and the experience of this paves the way for the objective subject—that is, the idea of a self, and the feeling of real that springs from the sense of having an identity.

However complex the psychology of the sense of self and of the establish-ment of an identity eventually becomes as a baby grows, no sense of self emerges except on the basis of this relating in the sense of BEING. This sense of being is something that antedates the idea of being-at-one-with, because there has not yet been anything else except identity. Two separate persons can *feel* at one, but here at the place that I am examining the baby and the object *are* one. The term 'primary identification' has perhaps been used for just this that I am describing and I am trying to show how vitally important this first experience is for the initiation of all subsequent experiences of identification.

Projective and introjective identifications both stem from this place where each is the same as the other.

In the growth of the human baby, as the ego begins to organize, this that I am calling the object-relating of the pure female element establishes what is perhaps the simplest of all experiences, the experience of *being.* Here one finds a true continuity of generations, being which is passed on from one generation to another, via the female element of men and women and of male and female infants. I think this has been said before, but always in terms of women and girls, which confuses the issue. It is a matter of the female elements in both males and females.

By contrast, the object-relating of the male element to the object presup-poses separateness. As soon as there is the ego organization available, the baby allows the object the quality of being not-me or separate, and experi-ences id satisfactions that include anger relative to frustration. Drive satisfac-tion enhances the separation of the object from the baby, and leads to objec-tification of the object. Henceforth, on the male element side, identification needs to be based on complex mental mechanisms, mental mechanisms that must be given time to appear, to develop, and to become established as part of the new baby's equipment. On the female element side, however, identity requires so little mental structure that this primary identity can be a feature from very early, and the foundation for simple being can be laid (let us say) from the birth date or before or soon after or from whenever the mind has become free from the handicaps to its functioning due to immaturity and to brain damage associated with the birth process.

Psychoanalysts have perhaps given special attention to this male element or drive aspect of object-relating, and yet have neglected the subject-object identity to which I am drawing attention here, which is at the basis of the capacity to be. The male element *does* while the female element (in males and females) *is*. Here would come in those males in Greek myth who tried to be at one with the supreme goddess. Here also is a way of stating a male person's very deep-seated envy of women whose female element men take for granted, sometimes in error.

It seems that frustration belongs to satisfaction-seeking. To the experience of being belongs something else, not frustration, but maiming. I wish to study this specific detail.

Identity: Child and Breast. It is not possible to state what I am calling here the female element's relation to the breast without the concept of the good-enough and the not-good-enough mother.

(Such an observation is even more true in this area that it is in the comparable area covered by the terms transitional phenomena and transitional objects. The transitional object represents the mother's ability to present the world in such a way that the infant does not at first have to know that the object is not created by the infant. In our immediate context we may allow a total significance to the meaning of adaptation, the mother either giving the infant the opportunity to feel that the breast is the infant, or else not doing so. The breast here is a symbol not of doing but of being.)

This being a good-enough purveyor of female element must be a matter of very subtle details of handling, and in giving consideration to these matters one can draw on the writing of Margaret Mead and of Erik Erikson, who are able to describe the ways in which maternal care in various types of culture determines at a very early age the patterns of the defences of the individual, and also gives the blueprints for later sublimation. These are very subtle matters that we study in respect of *this* mother and *this* child.

The Nature of the Environmental Factor. I now return to the consideration of the very early stage in which the pattern is being laid down by the manner in which the mother in subtle ways handles her infant. I must refer in detail to this very special example of the environmental factor. Either the mother has a breast that *is,* so that the baby can also *be* when the baby and mother are not yet separated out in the infant's rudimentary mind; or else the mother is incapable of making this contribution, in which case the baby has to develop without the capacity to be, or with a crippled capacity to be.

(Clinically one needs to deal with the case of the baby who has to make do with an identity with a breast that is active, which is a male element breast, but which is not satisfactory for the initial identity which needs a breast that *is,* not a breast that *does.* Instead of 'being like' this baby had to 'do like', or to be done to, which from our point of view here is the same thing.)

The mother who is able to do this very subtle thing that I am referring to does not produce a child whose 'pure female' self is envious of the breast, since for this child the breast is the self and the self is the breast. 'Envy' is a term that might become applicable in the experience of a tantalizing failure of the breast as something that *is.*

The Male and Female Elements Contrasted. These considerations have involved me then in a curious statement about the pure male and the pure female aspects of the infant boy or girl. I have arrived at a position in which I say that object-relating in terms of *this pure female element has nothing to do with drive (or instinct).* Object-relating backed by instinct drive belongs to the male element in the personality uncontaminated by the female element. This line of argument involves me in great difficulties, and yet it seems as if in a statement of the initial stages of the emotional development of the individual it is necessary to separate out (not boys from girls but) the uncontaminated boy element from the uncontaminated girl element. The classical statement in regard to finding, using, oral erotism, oral sadism, anal stages, etc., arises out of a consideration of the life of the pure male element. Studies of identification based on introjection or on incorporation are studies of the experience of the already mixed male and female elements. Study of the pure female element leads us elsewhere.

The study of the pure distilled uncontaminated female element leads us to BEING, and this forms the only basis for self-discovery and a sense of existing (and then on to the capacity to develop an inside, to be a container, to have a capacity to use the mechanisms of projection and introjection and to relate to the world in terms of introjection and projection).

At risk of being repetitious I wish to restate: when the girl element in the boy or girl baby or patient finds the breast it is the self that has been found. If the question is asked, what does the girl baby do with the breast?—the answer must be that this girl element *is* the breast and shares the qualities of breast and mother and is desirable. In the course of time, desirable means edible and this means that the infant is in danger because of being desirable, or, in more sophisticated language, exciting. Exciting implies: liable to make someone's male element *do* something. In this way a man's penis may be an exciting female element generating male element activity in the girl. But (it must be made clear) no girl or woman is like this; in health, there is a variable amount of girl element in the girl, and in a boy. Also, hereditary factor elements enter in, so it would easily be possible to find a boy with a stronger girl element than the girl standing next to him, who may have less pure female element potential. Add to this the variable capacity of mothers to hand on the desirability of the good breast or of that part of the maternal function that the good breast symbolizes, and it can be seen that some boys and girls are doomed to grow up with a lop-sided bisexuality, loaded on the wrong side of their biological provision.

I am reminded of the question: what is the nature of the communication Shakespeare offers in his delineation of Hamlet's personality and character?

Hamlet is mainly about the awful dilemma that Hamlet found himself in, and there was no solution for him because of the dissociation that was taking place in him as a defence mechanism. It would be rewarding to hear an actor play Hamlet with this in mind. This actor would have a special way of delivering the first line of the famous soliloquy: 'To be, or not to be . . .' He would say, as if trying to get to the bottom of something that cannot be fathomed, 'To be, . . . or . . .' and then he would pause, because in fact the character Hamlet does not know the alternative. At last he would come in with the rather banal alternative: '. . . or not to be'; and then he would be well away on a journey that can lead nowhere. 'Whether 'tis nobler in the mind to suffer / The slings and arrows of outrageous fortune, / Or to take arms against a sea of troubles, / And by opposing end them?' (Act III, Sc. 1). Here Hamlet has gone over into the sado-masochistic alternative, and he has left aside the theme he started with. The rest of the play is a long working-out of the statement of the problem. I mean: Hamlet is depicted at this stage as searching for an alternative to the idea 'To be'. He was searching for a way to state the dissociation that had taken place in his personality between his male and female elements, elements which had up to the time of his death of his father lived together in harmony, being but aspects of his richly endowed person. Yes, inevitably I write as if writing of a person, not a stage character.

As I see it, this difficult soliloquy is difficult because Hamlet had himself not got the clue to his dilemma—since it lay in his own changed state. Shakespeare had the clue, but Hamlet could not go to Shakespeare's play.

If the play is looked at in this way it seems possible to use Hamlet's altered attitude to Ophelia and his cruelty to her as a picture of his ruthless rejection of his own female element, now split off and handed over to her, with his unwelcome male element threatening to take over his whole personality. The cruelty to Ophelia can be a measure of his reluctance to abandon his split-off female element.

In this way it is *the play* (if Hamlet could have read it, or seen it acted) that could have shown him the nature of his dilemma. The play within the play failed to do this, and I would say that it was staged by him to bring to life his male element which was challenged to the full by the tragedy that had become interwoven with it.

It could be found that the same dilemma in Shakespeare himself provides the problem behind the content of the sonnets. But this is to ignore or even insult the main feature of the sonnets, namely, the poetry. Indeed, as Professor L. C. Knights (1946) specifically insists, it is only too easy to forget the poetry of the plays in writing of the *dramatis personae* as if they were historical persons.

Summary

1. I have examined the implications for me in my work of my new degree of recognition of the importance of dissociation in some men and women in respect of these male or female elements and the parts of their personalities that are built on these foundations.

2. I have looked at the artificially dissected male and female elements, and I have found that, for the time being, I associate impulse related to objects (also the passive voice of this) with the male element, whereas I find that the characteristic of the female element in the context of object-relating is identity, giving the child the basis for being, and then, later on, a basis for a sense of self. But I find that it is here, in the absolute dependence on maternal provision of that special quality by which the mother meets or fails to meet the earliest functioning of the female element, that we may

seek the foundation for the experience of being. I wrote: 'There is thus no sense in making use of the word "id" for phenomena that are not covered and catalogued and experienced and eventually interpreted by ego functioning' (Winnicott 1962).

Now I want to say: 'After being—doing and being done to. But first, being.'

Added Note on the Subject of Stealing

Stealing belongs to the male element in boys and girls. The question arises: what corresponds to this in terms of the female element in boys and girls? The answer can be that in respect of this element the individual usurps the mother's position and her seat or garments, in this way deriving desirability and seductiveness stolen from the mother.

NOTES

1. It will be understood, I hope, that I am not suggesting that this man's very real physical illness, 'flu, was brought about by the emotional trends that coexisted with the physical.
2. I shall continue to use this terminology (male and female elements) for the time being, since I know of no other suitable descriptive terms. Certainly 'active' and 'passive' are not correct terms, and I must continue the argument using the terms that are available.
3. It would be logical here to follow up the work this man and I did together with a similar piece of work involving a girl or a woman patient. For instance, a young woman reminds me of old material belonging to her early latency when she longed to be a boy. She spent much time and energy willing herself a penis. She needed, however, a special piece of understanding, which was that she, an obvious girl, happy to be a girl, at the same time (with a 10 per cent dissociated part) knew and always had known that she was a boy. Associated with this was a certainty of having been castrated and so deprived of destructive potential, and along with this was murder of mother and the whole of her masochistic defence organization which was central in her personality structure.

   Giving clinical examples here involves me in a risk of distracting the reader's attention from my main theme; also, if my ideas are true and universal, then each reader will have personal cases illustrating the place of dissociation rather than of repression related to male and female elements in men and women.

REFERENCES

Knights, C. L. 1946. *Explorations*. London: Chatto and Windus. Harmondsworth: Penguin Books (Peregrine series), 1964.
Winnicott, D. W. 1962. "Ego Integration in Child Development". In *The Maturational Processes and the Facilitating Environment*. London: Hogarth Press and the Institute of Psycho-Analysis, 1965.

5. Feminine Sexuality in Psychoanalytic Doctrine

Moustafa Safouan

During her sexual evolution, the little girl must, according to Freud, resolve two problems, whose analytic formulation he first advanced after he had noticed that this evolution comprises a time, or stage, during which everything happens for the girl exactly as it does for the boy.

This similarity indicates:

(1) that it is the mother who is the object of her desire[1] while rivalry, or the death wish, falls on the father;

(2) that equally for the girl, the only organ or, to be more precise, the only kind of sexual organ which exists is the phallus—which, as Freud makes clear, does not mean the penis, unless we were to talk of a penis with the remarkable characteristic of not admitting to a vagina. This point is worth stopping at.

It is of course obvious that the idea of an organ in glorious, monadic isolation, rejecting any tie or relation (whether complementary or antagonistic) in favour of the sole alternative of being or of not being, must refer to an essentially imaginary organ, even if this image is that of a real organ, namely the penis, or, more precisely, the penis in its privileged state of tumescence and erection.

Secondly, it is no less obvious that the playing out of this alternative must bring about a subtle nuancing of the category of sex or of the other sex, even before it has appeared. For beings are to be divided up, not into men and women or males and females, but only into those who have the phallus and those who do not, meaning in this last case (since only the phallus exists)

"Feminine Sexuality in Psychoanalytic Doctrine," by Moustafa Safouan, is reprinted from *Feminine Sexuality: Jacques Lacan and the Ecole Freudienne,* edited by Juliet Mitchell and Jacqueline Rose, translated by Jacqueline Rose, with the permission of Macmillan, London and Basingstoke, and of W. W. Norton and Company, Inc. English translation copyright 1982 by Jacqueline Rose. Selection, editorial matter, and introductions copyright 1982 by Juliet Mitchell and Jacqueline Rose. First published in 1975.

those who are castrated, or rather, eunuchs. Where, then, should we look for the woman?

One look at common parlance or common modes of reasoning is enough to establish that the phallic division cannot be superimposed onto sexual division. For example, a certain society might decide to make a certain activity, quality or distinguishing mark a characteristic of man or of woman, that is, a difference according to which men and women should be recognised. There will always be one woman, not incidentally lacking in supporters, to show that this difference is no difference: for instance, a woman learned in Greek, in a society which restricts the study of this language to young boys, as was indeed the case during the Renaissance. But the point of this effective demonstration is always missed, for instead of admitting that being a woman is no handicap for learning Greek—which after all has no need of demonstration—it is concluded that because she is learned in Greek she must be a man. Furthermore, women are not second to men in this kind of reasoning. What is more common than to hear our women analysands expressing the fear that by becoming 'theoreticians' they cease to be women? It is not enough simply not to be a feminist to ensure that one knows one's place in the business of sex.

If, therefore, it is the case that, contrary to all common sense, phallicism, or the belief in one single type of sexual organ, is the one thing in the world most equally shared between the sexes, and if there is only one basic form of incest—that which takes the mother as its object—then two problems clearly arise for the girl which the boy is spared, one of which concerns her relation to the object, and the other her relation to her own body.

For while the boy must of course give up the first object of his desire, it is for another woman; whereas the girl must manage the same renunciation for the sake of an object of the opposite sex. Likewise, both before and after this renunciation, the phallus remains, so to speak, on the side of the boy; the girl first thinks that it can be found in that part of her body bearing the closest resemblance to its form, that is, the clitoris, and then has to give up her investment in this erotogenic zone in favour of the vagina. Freud even goes so far as to make the criterion for the successful sexual normativisation of the woman a restricting of orgasm to the vaginal orgasm alone. This calls for a number of wide-ranging remarks, but it is a crucial issue which has been fiercely debated within analytic doctrine.

In actual fact, according to this criterion, all the evidence goes to show that the normal woman is a somewhat rare phenomenon, and, when we do come across her, it would seem that she does not stand out as a model of normality. I am saying 'it would seem' because my reference is to recently published case-studies, whose author, following the method dear to the United States, proceeds by way of correlations established by the most dubious of methods—dubious, that is, for everyone except the author, who believes, with disarming naïvety, that he is 'letting the facts speak' for themselves.[2] Nothing stops us, however, from making the most remarkable findings in a collection of this kind, such as the fact that women who have exclusively vaginal orgasms show a strongly marked propensity to anxiety. An observation for what it's worth, but one which is by no means indispensable, since the fictive nature of the criterion laid down by Freud is obvious without this false appeal to 'scientific data'. So is this a case of prejudice on the part of Freud? One thing we can be sure of, there is a theoretical reason involved which is in urgent need of clarification.

In point of fact, phallicism for the girl has always seemed difficult to explain, if not incredible. What tends to be overlooked is that it is no less so in the case of the boy. It only *appears* more easy to explain in his case, and I would argue that this apparent ease is a function of phallicism itself. So how does Freud explain it for the boy?

According to Freud, the boy manages from a very early age to distinguish between men and women by going on all kinds of indications, clothes in particular, without it occurring to him to relate these perceived differences on which he bases his distinction to a difference between the genital organs of the two parties. This is due to his ignorance, since at that stage he has had no chance of observing the anatomical distinction between the two sexes. Not that he reserves judgement for all that—for him, everyone is equipped with a phallus. Why? This is where his narcissism comes in. Such is the importance which the little boy attaches to an organ which is so rich in sensations and whose significance he obscurely grasps, that he loves himself precisely as a boy. One might as well say, even if Freud doesn't do so explicitly, that from then on narcissism can only work on this condition, that the little boy does, or does not, love himself according to whether he is sufficiently in possession of the phallus or not. From that point, the very idea that this organ might be lacking becomes intolerable to him. In defiance of his sexed being, for want of a better expression, he imagines everyone to be made in his own image, that is, in his image such as he loves it. If we now assume the existence of an analogous organ for the girl, and take this to be the clitoris, which acquires the same importance for her as the condition for her loving herself, then an identical explanation would be made a lot easier. Only, is such an explanation tenable?

As far as the boy's ignorance is concerned, a young boy can be seen to have very early visual access to a differently made body from his own, such as that of a mother with few scruples about having her bath in front of him, or a sister dressed and undressed before his eyes. This won't stop things from proceeding for him in exactly the same way, meaning that at no point is his relation to anything which might be termed another sex, but only to a covering behind which it is impossible for there not to be a phallus. Thus ignorance can explain nothing, since knowledge, the lifting of this ignorance, is no obstacle to occult science. As for narcissism, are we providing an explanation or merely setting up the most inscrutable of enigmas when we talk of a love of self which implies one's own liquidation as sexed being?

The fact remains, however, that the enigma is there, in that whatever the sex of the subject, the only conceivable pleasure in his or her image depends on finding in that image or thinking that he or she finds there (which means if only in the mind) something withdrawn from sight which answers or corresponds to what we have called the monadic phallus. Narcissism is henceforth a 'phallo-narcissism', which means, and the expression has no other meaning, that the subject loves himself or herself as phallus, in the two senses that grammatical analysis gives to this phrase. Once this fact has been put like this, we are in a position to throw some light on a famous quarrel.

In point of fact, when Karen Horney disputes the anatomical priority of the clitoris, which according to Freud, is facilitated by its being within reach of the girl's knowledge and her hand, and when she states that the girl knows of the existence of the vagina, for our part we see no reason to disagree. Only this in no sense detracts from Freud's basic thesis on the phallic conditioning of narcissism in the subject irrespective of its sex, a thesis which no direct observation could either invalidate or confirm, since it is established in, and only in, analytic practice. So-called 'direct' observation is as useless here as it is in relation to the Oedipus complex. For example, one may think one is 'ascertaining' Oedipal desire on hearing a child say to its mother: 'When I grow up, I will marry you.' Whereas, in saying this, the child is simply on the way to becoming more stupid than a half-wit, by giving in to the presence of a maternal desire felt by the child as overwhelming. The field of analytic experience is not that of perception—the perception the subject might have of anatomical difference. Nor is it that of consciousness—the consciousness the subject gains of his or her sex as a boy or girl on the basis of that perception. Its field is that of the thought which slides between perception and consciousness. This is where Freud situates himself, unlike Karen Horney, analyst as she claims to be. And that alone refutes all her objections and gives them their true weight as mere quibbles. What, then, does analytic experience alone teach us?

Is some female patients the clitoris does indeed function as the fantasmatic equivalent of a 'little penis' and such cases were certainly not foreign to Freud's thesis. But it is equally certain that other cases show us the girl remaining free, at the whim of her fantasy, to throw the phallic image back onto any other zone of her own body, not excluding the vagina which she would then think of as a hollowed-out phallus. On occasions this is proved by this fantasy of women analysands — that merely by turning inside out like a glove she would turn into the still form of her rivalry, which also represents the most intimate and inadmissable nucleus of her identity.

Where this fantasy predominates, and it comes out in subjects strongly inclined to sublimations as hazy as they are unproductive, it induces, not frigidity, but more precisely a quasi-total extinction of sexual life, except possibly in the domain of verbal parade. An extinction which the women in question are not even aware of, but which strikes them as quite normal, that is, as belonging in the order of things. In short, they do not see it as having the value of a symptom but rather as adding to their 'value'. Which makes us ask: why does the equation 'vagina = phallus or hollowed-out phallus' give rise to a half-suspected, half-tolerated frigidity, whereas the equation 'clitoris = little penis' detracts nothing from the sensitivity of this part of the body, to which, what is more, erotogenicity tends to become confined?

The only answer to this question I can think of is that the two equations or two identities have neither the same meaning nor the same weight. The equation 'vagina = hollowed-out phallus' involves, at the level of fantasy or belief, such a reduction of the phallic image to one's own body, or to that particular region of the body, that the subject no longer hesitates, so to speak, to draw the inference. Her desire is then reabsorbed into the sole desire of displaying 'it', as was the case of the little girl reported by Anna Freud in her work, *The Ego and the Mechanisms of Defence* [1937, pp. 92–93]. This type of case shows the subject of the female sex so convinced of having it that one starts to wonder whether one can still talk of a division of the subject; the least that one can note is that there is no apparent division. And it is precisely this abolition of sexual life, which threatens to come about with the abolition of lack, that incites certain other women to fall back on the equation 'clitoris = little penis', which, as its formula indicates ('little penis'), leaves the field open, if you will pardon the expression, to some hope. There is, however, a close link between this equation and the first, which can be sensed in the worry, not to say the genuine 'state' that the woman gets into over her vaginal frigidity. This is especially so when, as is often the case nowadays, she is familiar with what has become the commonplace Freudian thesis that elimination of clitoral orgasm is the criterion of femininity, or of the woman's successful sexual normativisation—which doesn't make our task as analysts any easier. Freud, that is, Freud himself, demands that the woman analysand come—vaginally. Hardly an injunction to which it would be easy to respond; indeed, on the contrary, it can only reinforce, in some cases *beyond recovery* [English in the original], a purely anal subjective integration of sexuality. It is hardly surprising that analysts, notably Helene Deutsch, are stressing more and more the resistance of an increasingly widespread clitoral fixation to all therapeutic efforts.

The preceding outline will not, I hope seem too long in relation to the conclusion that I wish to draw from it—that while the erotogenicity of the vagina strikes me no more as a sign of normality than that of the clitoris a sign of abnormality, the fact none the less remains that frigidity constitutes a definite symptomatic disturbance of sexual life in the woman, in the full psychoanalytic sense of the term symptom. I am deliberately avoiding the term orgasm, which raises problems too complex to be dealt with here. We need only think back to the observations of Masters and Johnson, which I consider to be highly dubious, and to the bold conclusions—to say the least —which Mary Jane Sherfey drew from them [Sherfey, 1966]. Without espousing all her arguments, I would concede to this author that the transference of orgasmic capacity from the clitoris to the vagina is a mythical concept of femininity, even from the biological point of view. From the point of view of psychoanalysis, what matters is not the transformation of the clitoral into the vaginal, but that of auto-erotic libido into object libido. Both girl and boy have to undergo a double renunciation: of the mother, on the one hand, of masturbation, on the other. The only feature which is specific to the sexual evolution of the girl resides in her directing her desire towards an object of a different sex to her mother. How does she make this step? In other words, how does she enter into the specifically feminine Oedipus complex?

To answer this question, Freud says that we must start by examining the nature of the ties attaching the girl to her mother, which does seem the correct way to proceed. What does the little girl want from her mother? Or again, what does she demand of her? That is the key question, whose answer is the precondition for solving the problem. But, as the father of psychoanalysis goes on to add, this is precisely where we find ourselves in a region where everything is cloaked in obscurity. The ties in question seem to have succumbed to such an inexorable repression and to belong to such a far-off and deeply buried epoch, that we will no doubt have to wait for the results of later investigations before any light can be shed on this 'dark continent'.

Now, the fact of the matter is that later investigations have not produced the clarification that Freud hoped for, and they have failed to do so precisely to the extent that they have been carried out along the paths traced by Freud's dearly loved metaphors (which I would call archaeological). To devote oneself to such investigations with the naïve idea that one will discover something if one only goes back far enough, as if desire were daughter of an epoch, is a blind alley. It can only lead away from the understanding dawning on anyone who has the not so naïve idea of pondering on the very wording of the question. I am thinking of Lacan, since it is he who has brought out the full impact of Freud's question.

'What does the little girl demand of her mother?' But it's easy! She has no shortage of words for telling us: to dress her, to make her hurt go away, to take her for a walk, to belong to her, or to her alone, in short all sorts of demands, including at times the demand to leave her alone, that is, the demand to take a rest from all demand. If, therefore, Freud's question has any meaning, it must signify something else, that is, not so much 'What is she demanding *of her?*', as 'What is she *demanding,* what is she really demanding, by demanding of her mother all that?'

In other words, Freud's question implies the separating out of demand onto two planes: that of the demands effectively spoken, or enounced, and that of Demand (with a capital D) which subsists within and beyond these very demands, and which, because it remains resistant to articulation, incites the little girl to make those demands at the same time as rendering them futile, both the demands and any reply they might receive.

Is it desire?—this Demand, this unknown Demand, which language does not allow to be spoken and for which there are no words. Definitely not. Freud's question can be put either of two ways: what does the little girl *demand* of her mother or what does she *want* from her? It refers, therefore, to a field appearing first as the field of a pure and empty want, one which is not yet inhabited unless it be by the very idea of the Thing, the Thing on which Freud is interrogating the little girl by asking her what she wants. As we will see, desire is precisely what comes to inhabit this field of empty want. By inhabiting this field as the Thing itself, it takes on the structure of demand. Not that this makes it into a demand, since this coming of the Thing does not necessarily leave the subject in a position to say what thing it is. A thing in itself, a thing with its mouth sealed. How does this Thing come into being? How does desire come to inhabit this field?

Here we need to make a fairly simple point: that the question of what she wants is as much the question of the girl herself as it is that of the Other, whether this be Freud, ourselves, or again and in the first instance, the Mother. It is, therefore, a question which can apparently be formulated either way, as 'What do I want?', or as 'What do you want?' In fact only the second formula is tenable. For in the last analysis, what is involved is a question which comes to her as in echo to her own demand. At the moment when she says 'milk' or 'it hurts' or 'walk', at that very moment the question resounds back to her from the place from which she draws these functional signifiers, in the form 'what do you want?' The 'you' descends on her with no possibility of error, since it is a 'you' not addressed to her as a person or as second person, but one which strikes her at the very roots of her want. There is no 'you' unless it comes from the Other with a capital O. Once the little girl is in a position to receive its message in the inverted form of 'I', once she can refer to her image with this 'I' and effectively articulate the question 'What do I want?', then she is already in the realm of 'intersubjectivity', which may soon become that of 'personalism', but which in any case is beyond the pale.

If we, on the other hand, stay on this side of it, it is easy to see that what we have just stated can be written as the question mark of Lacan's graph (reproduced below).[3]

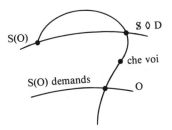

I had reached the point in my argument when the girl finds herself barred in the face of Demand. To be *Barred* means to have no possibility of saying which demand. The result is that she can only constitute herself as not-knowing. Insofar as she is not purely and simply reduced to what is designated at the time as 'I', in the statements which unfold along the bottom line, that is, to the pure claim of being there, then the girl speeds, so to speak, towards the line above, where we rediscover her as subject, but as a subject which does not know. This implies that knowledge is presupposed—or even posed. The reply *is,* because there is the question. And it is somewhere other than in the subject, in another place: the place of the Other where the question mark comes to an end.

But it only needs someone, not excluding our little girl turned chatterbox, to put themselves in this place and from there to strive to answer, for them to discover that their reply necessarily misses the point. The only valid way of filling this place is to hold on, as Freud did, to the question itself—what does she want? Is there anything more ridiculous than hearing an analyst express his regret, or fear, that the conditions of our century are standing in the way of woman's natural fulfilment, her true desire for maternity (Nacht, 1973)? If we can be so sure that this is woman's desire or the desire of every woman, then why not go and open a marriage counsel bureau or practice artificial insemination instead of bothering with psychoanalysis? The anguish of such analysts will not blind us to the fact that no answer could be the Answer. The Other is barred, just as much as the girl. The Other of truth *is-without* truth. Truth is involved only insofar as it is excluded from the utterance and simultaneously declares it false. Corresponding to the message on the bottom line of statements *[énoncés],* there is, on the line of enunciation *[énonciation]* above, an 'I am lying'. But, surely this undermines the very possibility of speaking since I can say nothing, not even a lie, without believing in it a little. And then, what is there to say? What is there to want when want persists as pure want? We are back to our earlier question in a slightly different form: how has a desire come to inhabit this field of pure want, at the moment when the subject starts to speak?

Our argument will be easier to follow here if we appeal to an experience, one which is moreover fairly banal. The experience we go through, for example, when we want to buy a piece of antique furniture. Who will authenticate it? The dealer's word is not gospel. We therefore need a stamp to guarantee both the good faith of the dealer and that of the piece of furniture. It is a rescindable guarantee, since we can ask whether it is false; it is even useless, since not all pieces of antique furniture are necessarily stamped. Not that this stops us from demanding it; and the demand couldn't have arisen were it not laid down somewhere, whether explicitly or not, that no piece of furniture can guarantee its own authenticity.

Imagine now a piece of furniture which, struck by this inability to certify its own authenticity, lights on the idea of the stamp, which the other pieces of furniture, its neighbours in the same gallery, seem equally deprived of— its feeling would be one of irremediable loss. But it would only need one piece of furniture to bear the stamp for the situation of all the others to change completely. Each one would rig itself out with the same stamp and from then on, like the table Marx talks about in one of the first chapters of *Capital,* would never tire of the oratorial flight in which it sings out its own exchange value, its use value incidentally remaining unaltered.

It is obvious what this fable is about—nothing less than the experience of our being or of what we are, for none of us are dispensed from thinking of ourselves as a piece of furniture. It is Lacan who first brought to light the effects which demand has in bringing whoever articulates it, even if they are a piece of furniture, up against a place which is the place of language and of Truth (with a capital T). Only by examining these effects, has it at last become possible to dispel the mystery surrounding the phallic function, which is the most disturbing of all functions, and not only for the analysts (but above all for the analysts). Here we leave the plane of deduction for that of analytic experience. And what, precisely, does this experience teach us about the phallus, if not that it makes a joke of phallicism? The phallicism which extends to those theories which ring out like so many empty hymns in praise of the divine phallus, of the phallus as the symbol of life, of creation or procreation, or as a symbol of the unity and cohesion of the body, etc. To be more rigorous, what is the phallus if not that which renders vain and derisory the regressive positionings of the ego ideal, which start from the ideal ego, whether these positions are oral, anal or phallic? In other words, the phallus is the very point where the Other of Truth (capital T) is seen to be without truth (small t); at which point, precisely, objects start performing like stamps. These objects are taken from the body itself. For what is the phenomenal being of the subject, if not to all intents and purposes a body? And what, therefore, could be the subject's noumenal being, if not that aspect of the same body which remains invisible to the subject? At the moment when the subject articulates the first demands, the field of pure want has already been transformed by these objects into the field of the drives: $ \diamond $ D.

How does this phallic function come into play? That much we know— who hasn't heard of the paternal metaphor? What we perhaps don't know so well is the link between this effect of the paternal metaphor and the production of a lying subject, that is, of a subject who is marked with a bar which refutes any ontology.

Why does this indication (that the Other is barred) take on an imaginary form, and especially a form drawn from the most salient and, so to speak, the most conspicuous organ of procreation? For the moment the important thing to note is that if the function of this phallus ($- \phi$), which we lend wings to not only on account of its erectibility, is an undeniable fact of Freud's experience, this fact stands less in the way of our understanding as soon as it is related, not to the sex of the girl but to her status or condition as speaking subject. The problem then is that the same function has to be explained similarly or along the same lines for the boy: since he too shares that condition.

Thus our puzzlement has turned inside out or almost. The question of how it can be the case that the girl experiences the same phallicism as the boy hands over to the question of what it can still mean for them to call themselves boy or girl, or, to be more precise (since they don't call themselves boy or girl so much as repeat it) for us to call them different. An additional question to the one which was set aside but not forgotten in the course of the argument, that is, how does the little girl manage to transfer, not the erotogenicity of the clitoris to the vagina, but her desire or preference to an object of another sex than that of her mother?

It seems to me that the correct procedure would be to take up the second question first, which is a task I will have to come back to later. For the moment, I should just point out that as a preliminary it calls for a revision of Freud's theses on the dissolution of the Oedipus complex, as well as a close examination of what he calls the appearance of the one or the single object during the period of early or infantile sexuality, and also of the way in which the boy himself struggles with the phallicism which appears at this same period. My objective in this article, intended after all only as an introduction, was simply to show: *first,* that phallicism is an 'unconscious phenomenon', if this somewhat risky expression be permitted, which has nothing natural about it for the boy any more so than for the girl, and to show, *secondly,* the common root of the phallic function in its relation to discourse. This path, marked out by Lacan, could already be glimpsed in the ancient paradox of the phallus, which appeared alternatively as the principle of madness and of reason.

If this objective has been achieved, as I hope it has, it should enable us to dispense with a certain number of questions, such as the following:

There is a book which came out recently under the title *Woman as Sex Object* (Hess and Nochlin, 1973). It is a collective work whose authors, mostly women, are all art historians. The central idea of this work consists of noting that it has been men, or almost exclusively men, in modern times at least, who have produced and elaborated at all levels, from the pornographic photo to high art, what the authors call the common places of desire —a reference not to brothels, but to dead metaphors such as eyes in the shapes of cups or fountains, cherry lips or apple breasts, etc. This to such an extent that it is redundant to speak of *masculine* eroticism or *feminine* object, and equally for the authors to regret the fact that women, whether this be their doing or that of the men, have not had the same opportunity to elaborate the common places of their desire. The basic question which I would like to put to these authors is the following: can one speak of the common places, the *topoi,* of a desire which might be feminine?

NOTES

1. Not to be confused, as Strachey thinks, with the object 'of her love'; cf. his note (Freud, xix, 1925, p. 246), to the effect that this was not an entirely new discovery by Freud, since he had said in the *Three Essays* that the girl's first love-object was her mother.
2. Fisher (1973), in which we equally learn that college girls have more highly developed orgasmic capacities than their maids, and than the women workers employed by their fathers.
3. The graph is a modified version of the graph given in four stages in 'Subversion of the Subject and Dialectic of Desire' (Lacan, 1960). It represents the radical division/inversion which constitutes the subject in its relation to the signifying chain—division between the subject of the enunciated (the demands it utters) and the subject of the enunciation (its fading before the very process of demand); inversion of the query which the subject sees as emanating from the Other ('What do you want?') and which the subject must reverse or take up in its own place ('What does it want from me?') (tr.).

REFERENCES

Fisher, S. 1973. *Understanding the Female Orgasm.* Harmondsworth: Penguin Books.
Freud, Anna. 1937. *The Ego and the Mechanisms of Defence.* London: Hogarth.

Freud, Sigmund. 1925. "Some Psychical Consequences of the Anatomical Distinction Between the Sexes." *SE* 19:243–58.

Hess, T. B., and Linda Nochlin. 1973. *Woman as Sex Object: Studies in Erotic Art 1730–1930.* London: Allen Lane.

Lacan, Jacques. 1960. "Subversion du sujet et dialectique du désir dans l'inconscient freudien." In *Les écrits techniques de Freud: le séminaire I, 1953–54.* Paris: Seuil, 1975.

Nacht, S. 1973. "Introduction au séminaire de perfectionnement sur la sexualité féminine." *Revue Française de Psychanalyse* 37:155–63.

Sherfey, Mary Jane. 1966. *The Nature and Evolution of Female Sexuality.* New York: Random House.

6. The Dead Father: On Early Psychic Trauma and Its Relation to Disturbance in Sexual Identity and in Creative Activity

Joyce McDougall

Psychoanalysis has as yet no comprehensive theory of core gender and sexual identity (in the sense in which Stoller (1968) defines these terms). As a psychic construction, gender and sexual identity have both biological and acquired origins and are thus at the research crossroads of several scientific disciplines. Nevertheless psychoanalysis has a specific contribution to make to the study of aberrations in core gender identity and in the established sense of one's sexual role, in so far as these have their roots in the experiences of early childhood and the unconscious problems of parents.

THE ORIGINS OF SEXUAL KNOWLEDGE

It is well known that the genital organs, from the time that they form a manifest mental representation in the mind of the small child, have a special relationship with the visual discovery of the difference between the sexes. The toddler's eye, avid to acquire new knowledge, seizes very early, usually between the twelfth and the eighteenth month of life, this striking visible difference in the observable bodies of other children, bodies which from this time onward are for ever identified sexually. Children of both sexes display manifest anxiety about this surprising discovery and this in turn brings about a reorganization of both their relationship to and interest in their own bodies as well as in their play activities (Roiphe and Galenson, 1981). Until this disquieting revelation, every child has an intuitive knowledge of its own sexual body, based on the mother's touch and the overall bodily contact with both parents, as well as the coexcitation aroused by affective experiences both pleasurable and unpleasurable. But following the discovery of anatomi-

Reprinted by permission from *Int. J. Psycho-Anal.*, vol. 70, pt. 2, 1989, pp. 205–20.

cal difference, the genital suddenly becomes an object that can be pointed out and named, and that marks you as belonging ineluctably to one clan only and excluded for ever from the other. It is evident that his knowledge will not be acquired without conflict, for the narcissistic and megalomanic child inevitably wishes to possess both sexes as well as the powers and privileges attributed to the personalities and genital organs of each parent (McDougall, 1986a). Much psychic work is required in order to carry out the task of mourning that will eventually allow the child to accept the narcissistically unacceptable difference and assume its monosexual destiny.

In this respect I recall the analytic session of a 5-year-old on return from a summer vacation, who rushed into the consulting room in a state of evident excitement to announce an unusual event: 'During the holidays we were in a camp where all the kids bathed together, *naked!*' 'You mean boys and girls together?' Looking startled, he shouted: 'Don't be stupid! How could I tell? I've already told you, they didn't have their *clothes* on!'

Faced with the scandalous evidence of humanity's monosexual status and its anxiety-arousing consequences, children are not the only ones to maintain a split between knowing and not-knowing (the phenomenon that Bion (1963) named 'minus-K'). Certain adults also disavow and render meaningless their biological sex—as witnessed in the extreme remedies to which transsexuals of both sexes are willing to submit. Others again, while accepting their biological sex as an inescapable reality, refuse the sexual role that society attributes to masculine or feminine identity. This is the homosexual response to an internal conflict regarding sexual role and object choice. The reasons for this deviation in gender identity are various and highly complex. In part, the so-called homosexual choice can be understood, in the light of psycho-analytic experience, as a construction that is founded on what the child during its formative years has interpreted of the parental discourse concerning the significance to be attached to the mysterious difference, as well as the model of a sexual couple that the parents unwittingly offer to the child's alert eye (McDougall, 1978, 1982, 1986b). Thus the psychic representation of the parental couple, as well as their words, may either help or hinder the child in its attempt to give up universal wishes of both a bisexual and an incestuous nature, and may indeed favour a deviant representation of the small individ-ual's developing sense of core gender and sexual identity role.

With the help of a clinical illustration, I hope to throw some light on certain fundamental factors that contribute to sexual identity formation and its inversions, in particular the importance of the different identifications with *both* parents that essentially structure the sense of sexual identity for all children. Here several psychic dramas intertwine: the one to receive most attention in our psychoanalytic literature is the heterosexual oedipal crisis which involves, among other important factors, the wish to possess in the most literal sense of the word the parent of the opposite sex while wishing death upon the same-sex parent. But there is also the homosexual oedipal drama which also implies a double aim, that of *having* exclusive possession of the same-sex parent and that of *being* the parent of the opposite sex. This twofold dilemma has been explored elsewhere (McDougall, 1986a).

THE LOST FATHER

The vignette that I am about to present raises a number of questions of both a clinical and a theoretical order with regard to disturbance in sexual identity, but before formulating these I should like to introduce my patient and give a glimpse into our first meeting.

Benedicte grew up in a large city in the south of France where all her close relatives also lived. A writer by profession, she sought help because of an almost total blockage in her work. She felt unable to terminate a novel she was working on in spite of considerable talent and the fact that she had already gained a certain reputation for her writing. I opened my waiting-room door to discover a woman who appeared to be in her middle thirties: her face, framed by short curly hair, bore not a trace of make-up; her tight blue jeans and well-cut cashmere sweater revealed an attractive feminine silhouette. She nodded gravely and walked into my consulting-room in a hesitant manner. With extreme caution she lowered herself into the chair facing mine, watching me all the while like a sleuth-hound seeking to surprise in the eyes of the other some secret knowledge. After a long moment's silence she began to speak haltingly, almost stammering, in a voice so soft that I had difficulty in hearing her. She would stop abruptly in the middle of a sentence, as though unwilling to allow her words to reach me, or as though each phrase had to be checked before being uttered.

Benedicte: I don't . . . er . . . don't know if analysis can help . . . er . . . me. Also I don't . . . er . . . have confidence in it. But I read something . . . er . . . written by . . . er . . . you. My writing . . . something's wrong . . . I can no longer . . . er . . . create . . . I don't like that word . . . you might be able . . . er . . . to help me.

I asked her what kind of help she had in mind.

B: Perhaps you could collaborate with . . . er . . . me . . . that is . . . er . . . I don't think it's a real analysis that . . . er . . . I need . . . but someone like . . . er . . . you . . . who writes as well.

J: But I'm an analyst rather than a writer.

B: I'm completely blocked . . .

J: Perhaps we might discover what is blocking you.

B: I've accomplished nothing in my life. I'm ashamed . . . er . . . to be still alive . . . to have done so little. (Long pause) I shall be . . . er . . . forty next week. (Another long pause) My . . . er . . . father died . . . at forty.

Benedicte stared intently at me for some minutes in anguished silence. In order to break it I made a meaningless comment.

J: So you have reached the age at which your father died.

B: Yes . . . but . . . I never knew him. I was only about fifteen months old at the time. (A further long tense silence)

J: Perhaps people talked to you about him?

B: Yes . . . and . . . no. No one told me he was dead.

Benedicte stopped abruptly and appeared this time to sink into an interminable silence. I began to feel ill at ease and to wonder if she were suffering from some form of thought disorder. However, her expression was most communicative, a desperate expression as though no words could hope to transmit what she was feeling. In an attempt to re-establish communication I remarked that it must be difficult to talk of a father whom one had the impression one had never known.

B: It's just that my . . . er . . . mother hid his death from me. She always said when I asked about him 'He's in the hospital'. She made everyone in the family lie to me also. I was more than 5 . . . when a neighbour . . . er . . . told me the . . . the truth.

Benedicte did not believe that this discovery had upset her unduly. (No doubt because she already knew the truth, for it seems unlikely that a child of 5 would not have suspected that there was some mystery about her supposedly alive but invisible father.) I thought to myself that possibly the mother had invented the fiction of the eternally-ill father because she herself could not deal with her bereavement and thus, to the little girl, the father's death might have been experienced as forbidden knowledge. Benedicte went on to say that when she confronted her mother with the neighbour's news her mother burst into tears causing Benedicte to feel upset at having made her suffer. She added that her mother never spoke to this neighbour again.

Benedicte's thoughts now turned to a fictitious aspect of her mother's personality.

B: My mother's an unreal person. Everything about her is false . . . even her nose that she had remade. Whenever I was worried about anything she'd say: 'Don't frown! You'll get wrinkles on your forehead'. My worries didn't interest her, only my appearance . . . er . . . that is, only what the 'others' would think if they . . . er . . . saw me.

Benedicte frowned at me as though seeking to reassure herself that I would be more interested in her anxiety than her wrinkles.

B: She never understood why I didn't want to be what she called . . . er . . . feminine. We have nothing in common, my mother and I. She . . . er . . . she can keep it . . . her . . . er . . . femininity! It's totally inauthentic. Only what she thinks the others think you're supposed to be like. Her infallible system for getting through life. (Long silence)
J: So you resisted her system?
B: I only like . . . er . . . authentic women.
    There followed another extremely long mute interval before Benedicte could continue.
B: To resemble her would have been . . . er . . . to stop existing . . . to be . . . nothing.

Although Benedicte spoke slowly and softly, every word and every bodily movement revealed an inexpressible tension. After much hesitation she said she felt she had some difficult life-situations to face and to resolve. She then asked if she might see me from time to time. Sensing her extreme anxiety I proposed a second consultation for the following week—the day of her fortieth birthday. She smiled and replied gravely: 'Thank you. I shall stay alive until then'.

At our second meeting Benedicte talked of her love-relationships, the difficult 'life-situations' at which she had hinted the previous week.

B: There is a woman who has meant a great deal to me. Fredrika and I have been lovers for many years—ever since the . . . er . . . death of her husband. Her presence was always . . . vitally important to me. But now . . . I've lost interest in the . . . er . . . passionate side of our relationship. We're still very close friends, and see each other every day . . . but I can't bear the pain that I'm causing her. And yet I can't go back either . . .

Benedicte went on to describe a love-relationship of the past three years with Marie-Christine. She hid all knowledge of this friendship from Fredrika, adding it was the first time she had ever deceived or lied to her. Outwardly there appeared to be some similarity between Benedicte's two lovers. In each case it was the other woman who initiated the love relationship. Both women were mothers and both were widowed. Perhaps Benedicte read in my expression the thought that a dead man always appeared on the scene in her life-story. In any case she continued with a statement that could have been a negation of my unspoken thought.

B: Neither of these two . . . er . . . important women in my life has the slightest resemblance to my . . . er . . . mother.

Benedicte threw me a wary glance as though fearing I might not be in agreement. A few weeks later, before regular sessions had begun, she believed she had the proof of this. She had just bought a book on female sexuality to which I had contributed a chapter entitled 'On homosexuality in women' (McDougall, 1964). Benedicte mentioned this as soon as she arrived saying, with much stumbling and circumlocution, that she disagreed with what I had written. I encouraged her to express her criticism. (I might add that today I am no longer in agreement with myself with many of the ideas expressed in this article written some twenty years ago. However, I still feel the importance I attributed to the role of the father in the girl's inner universe is pertinent.)

B: You say that the . . . er . . . homosexual girl has an idealized image of her . . . er . . . mother as an unattainable model and therefore gives up all hope of rivalry with her. I loathed my mother. No rivalry with her! As for my . . . er . . . father, since I never knew him it's improbable that he could have been a model for me, beneficial or otherwise.

Indeed, in view of the parental imagos that Benedicte had brought to our initial interviews (and of which I have given the salient features) she appeared to be something of a psychic orphan. Her internal world, as she presented it, was inhabited only by an 'unreal' mother regarded as a mannequin and a dead father experienced as never having existed.

Although she was reticent about engaging in a 'real analysis' Benedicte asked if she could come to see me regularly since she now had a clearer vision of what she was seeking to discover about herself. Eventually the analysis began on a four-times weekly basis and continued for eight or nine years.

The notes of my first sessions with Benedicte and the questions they aroused in my mind may be summarized under three major headings:

1) Would this psychoanalytic adventure be dedicated to the search for the

lost father? Early parent loss is almost inevitably traumatic. A fifteen-month-old child has little capacity to carry out the work of mourning. Where, in a small child's psyche, might we hope to find the buried trace of a dead father?

2) How would a little girl of this age construct her image of her core gender and sexual identity under the circumstances described by Benedicte: a father presented to the growing child as alive but invisible and a mother whose behavior was interpreted by the daughter to mean that she was little more than a mere narcissistic extension of her mother?

3) What might Benedicte be able to teach me about the creative process and its vicissitudes? When these give rise to work inhibitions, there ensues a complicated inner drama that has interested me for a number of years.

WHAT CONSTITUTES PSYCHIC TRAUMA?

The first question, of both clinical and technical interest, brings up the issue of early psychic trauma and a traumatic event that is frequently revealed in analytic practice. The number of patients in psychoanalytic therapy whose fathers (whether due to abandonment or death) disappeared during childhood appears to be greater than that found in the population at large. Should this potentially traumatic disappearance occur in early childhood it tends to be compensated by defensive structures that are different from those constructed by the already verbal child.

Early psychic trauma of this kind plays an evident role in the life of any child. It must nevertheless be emphasized that the long-range traumatic impact of a catastrophic event depends to a large degree on the *parental reactions* to the trauma in question. An event can be judged traumatic (that is to say as having left lasting psychological scars) only to the extent that the child's psychic reality has been reorganized in such a way as to prevent the return of the helpless state experienced at the time of the traumatizing event. The way in which the potential trauma is handled by the environment is therefore a crucial factor in determining the extent to which the child will suffer future pathological consequences (McDougall, 1986c).

The fact that Benedicte's father died unexpectedly when she was fifteen months old, although it certainly contributed to her disturbed sense of sexual identity, could not be considered as a sufficient explanation. With regard to early parent loss it should also be emphasized that a father who is dead may be carried within the child's mind as a very alive figure, depending on the mother's way of talking about the father, and on the nature of his own former relationship to the child. Concomitantly, a father who is physically present might nevertheless be lived as symbolically lost, absent or dead in the child's inner world depending once again on the father's own personality and on the way the mother invests and speaks of him to the child. In this respect it seemed evident that Benedicte's mother had not handled the father's death in such a way as to mitigate its traumatic potential for her daughter.

It should be added that the earlier a child is exposed to traumatic loss of any kind the greater will be the tendency to overinvest the external and the visible world, in the search for reassuring points of identification to shore up a feeling of uncertainty with regard either to subjective or sexual identity feeling. Thus, early psychic trauma stemming from the parents' unconscious problems, whether exacerbated or not by external catastrophes, will frequently favour deviant sexuality in an attempt not only to preserve the right to sexual and love relations in adult life but also to stem a rising tide of panic at any threat to the feeling of subjective identity. The individual concerned will sometimes feel compelled to seek his or her own image in the mirror provided by another of the same sex. The importance of the narcissistic dimension in homosexual relationships is self-evident.

ON THE ORIGINS OF SEXUAL IDENTITY

Question two, of a theoretical order, concerns the infantile roots of sexual identity-feeling. What are the leading elements that contribute to structure an individual's representation of his or her own gender identity and sexual role? These psychic acquisitions, as Freud was the first to point out, cannot be taken for granted. They have to be created by the growing child, using information received from the parents. A quarter of a century in psychoanalytic practice, including the analysis of a number of homosexual patients, has led me to give considerable weight to the importance of the mother's unconscious projections upon her infant in the first year of life. These influence her ways of handling and talking to her baby and her future wishes for this baby. Of crucial importance is the place given to the baby's father in the mother's mind. From birth, babies of both sexes begin to create intense sensuous and libidinal ties to both parents. Every infant experiences in its mother's arms the earliest schema of sexual and love relationships to come and thus the beginnings of a sense of sexual identity. The attitude of the tiny infant's father is equally vital to the transmission of early erotic investments. If the father's personality and sexuality are devalued or play little role in the mother's life, and if in addition the father himself is uninterested in his small offspring and accepts being excluded, then there is a strong risk that he may be leaving the infant to fulfil a role arising from the mother's unconscious problems. A mother who regards her baby as a narcissistic extension of herself, or who puts her children in the place of their father as her libidinal complement, may be laying the groundwork for future deviant sexual development. If on the other hand children see their parents as a loving couple who desire and respect each other, they will tend to follow the parental model in their own adult sexual and love lives. Even a mother who brings her children up alone will not necessarily incur the risk of pathological maturation provided she does not regard her children as a substitute for adult love relationships.

After the first year of life the endogenous perceptions of sexual awareness become highly significant following the discernible difference between boys and girls. Most authors who have dealt with the establishment of gender identity (Stoller, 1968; Roiphe and Galenson, 1981) agree that the most critical period for the establishment of gender identity occurs in the second half of the second year.

From this point of view my patient suffered the loss of her father at a highly important period in the development of her sense of identity.

CREATIVITY AND THE INTEGRATION OF BISEXUAL WISHES

My third question arises from observations made over a number of years with creative analysands (in artistic, scientific and other fields requiring the capacity for original thought and imagination) whose work had become sterile. Homosexual libido, once deflected from its original twofold aim (namely, to *have* the same-sex parent for oneself in a world in which all members of the opposite sex are excluded, and to *be* the opposite-sex parent with this parent's genitals and supposed powers), finds many paths of integration in the adult personality. It enriches not only each individual's narcissistic self-image but also the heterosexual love-relationship through identification with the pleasure of one's partner. Reflection has led me to the conviction that the creative process also depends to a considerable extent on the integration of bisexual drives and fantasies. Our intellectual and artistic creations are, so to speak, parthenogenetically created children. A breakdown in the capacity to work creatively frequently involves an interdiction concerning unconscious homosexual identifications, as well as unresolved conflicts attached to the significant inner objects involved (McDougall, 1986a).

One further point, the necessity for a writer to be able to identify profoundly with characters of both sexes, has been immortalized by Flaubert who, when questioned about the source of his inspiration in writing *Madame Bovary,* replied: 'Madame Bovary, c'est moi!' An unconscious refusal to become aware of and explore one's capacity for ambisexual identifications may well involve the risk of producing writer's block.

THE BEGINNING OF THE ANALYTIC ADVENTURE

Before quoting a few fragments from Benedicte's analysis to illustrate the above themes, I shall give an over-all impression of our first two years' work together.

Benedicte became rapidly and intensely involved in her psychoanalytic adventure, bringing dreams, daydreams, thoughts and feelings with an unusual richness of metaphor. At the same time her verbal expression was laborious, stumbling and often inaudible or interspersed with long periods of silence. Every gesture, every word was retained and carefully checked before being released. In the early months of our work I did not interpret the possible significance of this inaudibility, convinced as I was that Benedicte could not communicate otherwise without doing violence to her own way of relating to another human being. There were glimpses also of a fantasy that any rapprochement between us was potentially dangerous. Benedicte kept an avid eye on me as though drinking in my surroundings, but at the same time like a thirsty wanderer searching the desert for fear that the oasis would become a mirage. Thus she would suddenly break off her staring as she did her words. In a painfully halting manner she would comment on the slightest modification in the haphazard arrangement of a pile of reviews, or the displacement of a lamp or an art object. The same close scrutiny was applied to my appearance or the exact position of my chair in relation to the couch. These infinitely small changes, of which I was rarely aware, gave rise to timid but insistent questioning on Benedicte's part. Faced with my silence she constructed highly improbable theories to explain the insignificant changes, usually leading to the conviction that 'her presence bothered me since I preferred to be with someone else or engaged in some other occupation'. In other words, she constantly sought some sign that would confirm the contrary, namely, that would dispel her uncertainty as to whether her existence counted for me.

This incessant search for meaning, which, once found, resembled a child's reasoning, was of course intimately connected with her attempts in the past to make sense out of her mother's fabulations and incoherent communications. Benedicte seemed to believe, much as psychotic children tend to do, that she must discover the truth alone or otherwise invent her version of the truth. This concerned not only her father's death but also her mother's frequent absences, for, once widowed, Benedicte's mother conducted a feverish search for a new mate. Transposed on to the psychoanalytic stage, these preoccupations added their weight to my patient's difficulty in talking without having to chop her phrases or muffle the sound of her voice.

Quite apart from the fantasy of danger attached to communication with others, Benedicte was frightened of words in themselves. She handled them like concrete objects capable of turning into dangerous instruments. Her way of using language also created confusion as though the inter-penetration of primary and secondary process thinking that leaves its mark on the free-associative analytic discourse was, in Benedicte's case, closer to dream-work.

The following notes, taken from two consecutive sessions in the third year of our work together, give a glimpse into the relationship that my patient maintained with a constraining and implosive representation of her mother. At the same time, this vignette illustrates some of the reasons for which all interchange with others, verbal or otherwise, filled Benedicte with anxiety.

B: I dreamed that I was getting on a city bus. I had to . . . er . . . stamp a one-hundred franc note that was for . . . er . . . you. But the machine was blocked. Something was missing on the note. Someone behind me said 'Go on! It'll work' and I . . . er . . . woke up.

Benedicte's associations, announced in a low stifled voice, led her to think of her friend Fredrika and of the pleasure she felt in giving her money for herself and her children, in spite of the fact that Benedicte had little money for her own needs.

B: I . . . er . . . suppose I'd like to be the father of your family too . . . instead all I can give you is money. But there's something . . . er . . . missing. I dare not imagine I could give you something more valuable.

J: This sounds like a certain image of your mother; you said it was impossible to know what she really wanted from you.

B: Oh! She wanted me not to exist—outside of herself! *The machine in my dream*

. . . it made a crunching noise as though it were chewing off a bit of the note. 'Oblitérer votre billet' (cancel your ticket)—that's what you have to do as you get in the bus. I have trouble pronouncing that word because it's so violent. 'Oblitérer' only means stamp your ticket, but it's like stamping out, obliterating a person. Total destruction. That machine is . . . my mother. The infernal, maternal machine.

Benedicte had easy access to her hatred of her mother as a dangerous and destructive introject, but this got in the way of her recognizing her own primitive wishes of a violent and destructive kind, for she too is the 'blocked machine', as well as myself for whom the note is intended. I therefore redirected her associations to the transference situation.

J: But in the dream the destructive exchange took place between *us*.
B: That idea displeases me. Billet . . . billet-doux . . . I can recognize tender feelings for you. But violence, even in words, hurts me.

Benedicte then goes on in a dream-like way to examine other words and play on words associated with the dream images in which violent, then erotic thoughts occurred in rapid succession. I interpreted her fear that destructive and erotic desires might become confused.

B: My mother made everything seem dirty. That's why I couldn't even pronounce some of the words that came to mind just now. They had to do with excrement.

BENEDICTE'S STRUGGLE WITH WORDS

Benedicte's chain of anal-erotic and anal-sadistic signifiers revealed classic fantasies underlying infantile sexual theories. However, I did not interpret these since her dominant anxiety at this point centered around *symbolic equivalents* (Segal, 1957) in which word and thing became confused. (We see here certain factors that underlie speech defects. Although Benedicte did not suffer from stammering, a casual meeting with her might have given this impression.) I pointed out to Benedicte her fear of words.

B: You're right. I'm as terrified of words as children are of ghosts.

At that moment I felt as though I too were meeting a ghost on Benedicte's psychoanalytic voyage. The strange silence that surrounded her father, his never-mentioned illness and his zombie-like existence that the mother's fabulations had created in the little girl's mind continued on the analytic stage. I invited Benedicte to tell me more about 'ghost stories' that children might fear.

B: Stories of people returning from the tomb always fascinated me for some reason . . . especially those about ghosts with visible wounds that still continued to bleed.
J: Do you have any particular ghost in mind?
B: Oh! You mean . . . *him?* Yes . . . I think I waited for . . . him to come back.

Thus Benedicte was able to tell me at last, after three years of silence, the cause of her father's death. The word as well as its referent had seemed until then literally unspeakable. Benedicte's father died at the age of 40 of a rectal cancer.

At the following session, Benedicte's metaphors and the fantasies they evoked in me were still vivid in my mind: an excited-and-terrified little girl awaiting the return of her father from beyond the tomb; the father's death in terms of anal implosion; fantasies of the primal scene in anal-sadistic terms; the conflictual dream-images in which traces of an archaic primal scene may be detected in the meeting between the machine and the hundred-franc note, a phallic-anal signifier in Benedicte's associations, and destined to be 'obliterated' while at the same time representing a love-gift, the 'billet-doux''. The session brought some confirmation of these hypotheses as well as giving a glimpse into new elements.

Benedicte began with an association concerning her distrust of verbal communication and her urgent need to 'close herself up' against eventual invasion from others.

B: My mother never took her eye off me. She believed she had the right to know everything I did and everything I thought.

At this stage of our work together Benedicte could not accept that I too might be experienced as an anally implosive and controlling mother who watched her every gesture and her every word. When this aspect of the transference became interpretable, and recognizable to Benedicte herself, along with the exploration of the fantasies of mutual destruction, she began for the first time to speak easily and audibly, not only in the session but also with her friends who commented on the fact that she no longer 'mumbled'. (Fredrika had always accused Benedicte of 'swallowing her words'.)

B: As an adolescent I never dared open my mouth . . . as though my mother might fly into it. And I could never close a door. She would surge after me and throw it open. Even now, on my rare visits back home she listens in to all my telephone conversations.

Underlying fantasies of oral as well as anal sadistic penetration became transparent. The little girl of the past had believed that it was forbidden to close either the doors of her body or her mind against the invasive representation of her mother. (A year later fantasies of her mother killing the father in primitive oral and anal terms were able to be reconstructed.)

B: My mother constantly tidied up after me. My papers, my notes, my cigarettes were all put away the moment my back was turned. I would no sooner get out of a chair than she rushed forward to smooth away the trace of my body on the cushions. I was not to leave the slightest sign of my presence.

THE UNWELCOME TRACE

This question of the 'trace' and its effacement was destined to become a leitmotiv rich with significance.

B: Then I had to look at her too. She would put on a sort of erotic spectacle for me, dressing and undressing in front of me, asking which of her clothes I found the most seductive and so on. This was part of her ritual for catching a new husband. She would insist that 'we' must look nice, that 'we' must dress to impress eventual suitors. Violence was the only way out. I closed myself off in stony silence. She complained for years that I wouldn't talk to her.

I asked Benedicte to tell me more about the fantasies of violence in the face of her mother's demands. Her associations led her to recount hesitantly, and for the first time, some of her erotic fantasies.

B: This is the most exciting scene I can imagine . . . I'm a young man and I'm having a violent sodomic relationship with a much older man.

My own associations went as follows: the fantasy of the father killed through anal penetration is transformed into a scene in which the father becomes a live and phallic representation while anal penetration becomes erotically exciting and no longer mortally dangerous. The scene implies a literal fantasy of incorporating the father's penis and phallic strength, much as small children may imagine the narcissistic and libidinal possession of their parents could take place. I then thought of the predicament of a little girl of fifteen months whose father is suddenly missing when she needs him. At this age most children turn to their fathers in an attempt to detach themselves from their wish-for-and-fear-of fusional dependence upon their mothers (Roiphe and Galenson, 1981). Thus, they strengthen not only their sense of subjective but also of sexual identity. Where did Benedicte turn to accomplish this task?

J: You say the only response to your mother's seductive attitude was violence. Could the violent sodomy also be a way of protecting yourself against her?

B: That reminds me, I had to hide all my childhood games from her . . . Superman, Batman and the others were my constant companions. I was always a boy amongst men. She would never have allowed that.

J: You had to hide your wish to be a boy as well as your wish to have a man as a friend?

B: Yes . . . I'm beginning to see . . . this was the only way to have a secret relationship with my father . . . in spite of her! If she'd found out she'd have taken him away from me again. I used to spend hours dreaming and writing stories about these powerful men who were my friends. Oh, I'd forgotten . . . when I was adolescent I wrote what I called an 'opera'. Months of work. Then one day the book disappeared from my room. I never found it again. She destroyed it. It was something that took me away from her.

The theme of Benedicte's 'opera' was revealing. The whole action takes place in a subway station. An all-male cast, the central characters were a little boy, a gang of bad boys and a villainous old man. The little boy is betrayed by the old man and, broken-hearted, at the end of the opera he throws himself under a train! Benedicte linked the intriguing idea of calling her play an opera to 'operation' fantasies of her father 'in the hospital'. She must surely have felt betrayed by the absent father who, imprisoned in her mother's words, gave her no sign of recognition or remembrance. Did she have a little girl's fantasy that her father, in abandoning her, had castrated her? That he had left her to the mercy of her mother so that she was driven to keep him alive in fantasy, in games and, later, in her written stories? And was she able thus to maintain her own feeling of integrity and identity?

THE WRITER'S RELATION TO WORDS

I should like to emphasize at this point the extent to which words began to reveal themselves in Benedicte's analysis as the embodiment of paternal power and presence.

In a sense this unconscious significance is true for everyone in that it is through words that bodily perceptions and fantasies become organized as verbal constructs, aiding the child to maintain a clear representation of the difference between its own and its mother's body. This becomes a protection against the *voice* of the siren (rather than her words) since her voice and presence awaken fantasies of the wish for fusion with the consequent loss of both subjective and sexual identity. It seems evident that the transitional objects of infancy (Winnicott, 1951) give way to language as an important internal possession, capable eventually of replacing the need for the external object with thoughts about the object.

Thus, words always leave in the shadow not only the 'thing' presentation for which they are the symbol, but also half of the meaning that they are purporting to transmit. In this sense they are doubly symbolic. Over and beyond the essential importance of the role of language in structuring the human psyche, for someone who is a writer, words may come to play a specifically privileged role due to their link with unconscious bisexual fantasies.

In Benedicte's case, the paralysis of her creative possibilities represented, among other aspects, an imaginary way of renouncing her secret link with her father through language and story-building, a link that was forbidden by her mother. In destroying her 'opera', Benedicte's mother may well have sensed in a confused way that this work incorporated a serious rival and that her only child was escaping her. On the psychoanalytic stage, as the image of the internal father slowly came alive, mobilizing dynamic thoughts and fantasies in its wake, Benedicte began to write again. Her first book published after the beginning of her analysis led to her being invited to participate in a national television programme devoted to present-day authors whose work attracts attention. During this broadcast a member of the panel asked Benedicte a question concerning the sophisticated and somewhat impalpable impression conveyed by the novel. Benedicte replied: 'It's because . . . this is a book written by a child'.

THE FATHER, LOVED AND HATED

However, the search for the lost father did not proceed easily, for there was in Benedicte, as in every child, an internal father to be eliminated as a stumbling-block to the illusory hope of taking full possession of the mother. In addition, the apparent determination of Benedicte's mother to create in her child's mind an illusory family where only females counted suggests that oedipal interdictions were transmitted at an unduly young age, perhaps before the age at which the sense of sexual identity is normally well established. Thus, the mother's unconscious fears and wishes coincided with that part of the little Benedicte who wanted an exclusive relationship with her mother. It

was not surprising that dreams and daydreams came to light in which Benedicte herself was responsible for the death of her father. A dream-theme that
had persisted for many years depicted her being pursued for a crime she had
committed.

One day when Benedicte was struggling in a confused way with these
various internal fathers and mothers, I decided to interpret the different 'I's
seeking to express themselves in her associations.

J: There are several Benedictes talking at the same time. First of all there's the little
boy trying to keep alive an absent father, then the young man who is protecting
himself 'violently' from his omnipresent mother. And then there's the woman in
you who seeks to repair another woman with her love, as well as trying to be
different in every way from her own mother. But you seem to be having difficulty
with the *little girl* who longed for both her parents so that she might know her
place in the family—who she was, and for whom. You're still struggling with the
incoherent images of your parents as a couple.

The latter statement aroused a massive reaction.

B: It's absurd to hear you say 'your parents'. No child ever wished for two parents
. . . In that way at least I was lucky. That little girl had no father!

Benedicte's anger over my interpretation continued for many weeks during
which time she accused me of being the victim of social bunkum, of second-
hand ideas and of sentimentality over the death of an unknown father.

THE FIRST 'TRACE' OF MOURNING

An unforeseen incident provided us with the opportunity of crystallizing the
first trace of the dead father and the undoubtedly catastrophic consequences
of his sudden disappearance. One day, a sound from the office next to my
consulting-room alerted me to the fact that I had forgotten to switch on my
answering machine. For the first time in some four years of analytic work
with Benedicte, I got up in the middle of the session and left the room.

B: While you were out I dreamed up an amusing scene. I had an impulse to leave the
room myself and began to imagine what you would think on coming back and
finding the room empty.
J: What was I going to think?
B: Well first of all you wouldn't be sure if I'd really been there or not before you left
the room. But then, just as I imagined myself running away, I remembered that
I'd left so quickly I'd forgotten my jacket on the chair! So the whole scene was
ruined.

Thinking of Benedicte's mother who 'could not tolerate the slightest trace' of Benedicte's bodily presence, plus the sudden disappearance of her father, I answered without reflecting.

J: You would have left a trace behind?

B: The jacket. His jackets! He must have left his jackets. My cousins told me it was a lightning illness. No one expected him to die. The jackets . . . I remember the smell of them. Not my father's . . . my uncle's. When I was six or seven, after we went back to live with my grandmother, I would spend hours playing in his wardrobe, smelling and touching his jackets. It was one of my favourite games, but I was very careful to hide it from my mother.

Later Benedicte came to tell me how, in her early adolescence, she played for some years a game in which she imagined that it was her job to select and buy men's clothes for an important enterprise. She would spend hours in clothing stores, examining the cut, the quality and so on of the suits and jackets. When her adolescent girlfriends pretended they were adult women picking out the clothes they would buy for themselves, Benedicte would say that she was a married woman and had to choose her husband's clothes. She was well aware that she did not dream of a future husband but was totally unaware that she sought to keep alive a link with her lost father.

Thus we found the first signs of the work of mourning, instituted by a small girl who sought some trace of her father through his clothes, in the way that many children create their first transitional objects, demanding to sleep with a handkerchief or piece of clothing belonging to their mothers.

B: All my childhood games . . . I've never thought of their meaning nor why they were different from other children's games. I only knew that my mother would disapprove. I had to play her games, not mine!

A recurring screen memory acquired additional poignancy around this time.

B: Those two dolls that someone gave me when I was nearly 3, a boy and a girl . . . I only ever played with the boy, talking to him, dressing and undressing him . . . then one day my mother said they needed repairing. When they came back, both were girls. The boy . . . my mother killed him! I still recognized him by a tiny little trace, but I never touched the dolls again.

Shortly after the session in which Benedicte announced the assassination of the boy-doll, a new version of her repetitive crime-dream came forth in which she was merely the witness. *Benedicte dreamed that she watched a scene in which a man was killed in a neighbour's kitchen.* Her associations led her to think of the film *La Grande Bouffe* in which a dead man is laid out amidst the food that has been prepared for the funeral celebration. The principal characters were men but Benedicte sought to remember the role of the woman in this film. Her various associations to the dream and the film led me to suggest that as a little child she had perhaps believed that her mother had killed her father by devouring him.

This interpretation created a shock-effect and led Benedicte to bring forth a stream of memories . . . of mother eating more than her share of Benedicte's ice-creams, or displaying lengthily her constant digestive and eliminatory problems.

The following day Benedicte brought another dream in which heterosexual desire and love would lead to death. For some time she had talked of her strong attraction to and admiration for a young man who was a clarinet player. Although the attraction appeared to be shared, Benedicte forbade herself any realization of her desire on the grounds of her friend's age and the fact that she had known his mother in the past which she felt made him something like a son. In other words she lived the relationship as an incestuous one. Here is the dream.

B: *I was admiring a rare and beautiful bird . . . it was enclosed in a clarinet. I watched it with fascination. Then I turned to tell you about it and saw on your face a look of absolute horror, because the bird was being crushed inside the musical instrument. His blood was flowing through all the holes and his body was being torn to pieces. I realized suddenly that he was going to die and . . .* I woke up.

A chain of associations formed in my own mind while listening to Benedicte's account of her dream: the bird whose body was being crushed while it lost its blood through the holes seemed to point to fantasies of the father's rectal cancer and death, and was confirmed in a sense by the incest taboo associated in Benedicte's mind with the young clarinet player. The instrument then became a dream representation of Benedicte's own sex as an organ that would be dangerous for any man she desired. Once again there is a glimpse into a strange and terrifying primal scene, as imagined by a child. My role in the dream is to reveal its horror to Benedicte. Her associations took this as their starting-point.

B: My first thought . . . I want you to shock me, perhaps batter my mind, with your interpretations. Like yesterday . . . about my mother having killed my father by eating him.

Thus Benedicte now invites me to commit violence; through my words I am to embody the castrative and murderous image that the small Benedicte of the past attributed to her mother. While examining her transference feelings, Benedicte began to think of her own violence and fierce jealousy of my other patients, as well as her anger at having discovered my husband's name on a letter-box at the entrance to my building.

B: In fact I want to be not only your sole patient but the only person in your life.
J: To devour me?
B: Yes . . . to crush the life out of you. I'm . . . exactly like my mother!

We see here that the phallic castration represented in the dream hides a prototypic castration-fantasy in which life itself is endangered.

B: Under the mask of love my mother sucked the blood from my veins . . . and I'm shocked to discover that there's a part of myself that wants to do exactly that with the people I love. But there's something different. In love I refind my body through the body of another woman, provided she herself loves her body and takes pleasure in love-making. Then there's no murderous exchange. That's one thing my mother did not manage to crush and obliterate.

Benedicte remained silent as she reflected over the changing images in the dream and the thoughts that followed. Just before the end of the session she posed, for the first time, the following question.

B: But whose body do I live in?

Her father's? Her mother's? Which is hers? Here my patient touched upon her confusion since childhood as to her sexual identity and even her identity as a separate individual. A final fragment from her analysis may serve to illustrate the theme of sexual identity as it relates to a small child's identification to both parents. In Benedicte's case, the task was rendered more difficult due to the specific circumstances in which the sudden loss of her father had constituted an early psychic trauma that could not be elaborated mentally because Benedicte's mother herself was unable to deal with it. The following sessions were noted in the fifth year of our work together.

BENEDICTE'S TRANSFORMATION

B: I study you attentively . . . your way of holding yourself . . . the way you walk and sit . . . your clothes, your hair-style, your make-up . . .
   I asked her what she sought to learn from this careful study.
B: I want to know how you see yourself as a woman . . . and what it feels like to be

a woman. I don't know what a woman is . . . nor a man either. This weekend I tried, for the first time in five years, to imagine your body under your clothes.

There followed a heavy silence as though Benedicte were afraid to continue. I also was struck by her emphasis on the 'five years', thinking of the secret calendar we all carry in our preconscious minds, and of the fact that Benedicte was 5 years old when the truth of her father's death could no longer be denied.

B: But I could not go any further with the thought of your body, as though . . . I were afraid you would . . . disapprove.
J: What would I disapprove of?
B: The idea comes to me that you might have something to hide. (A long silence)
J: And what am I hiding?
B: Something like . . . a mutilation . . . or a shameful deformity.

The fact that on several occasions we had already discussed the fantasy of woman as a castrated man led me to feel that the present associations had to do with something more primitive, or more specific to Benedicte, than the quasi-universal fantasy of feminine 'castration'. I invited her therefore to try to imagine further the nature of my deformity.

B: It'll be difficult to tell all my thoughts since last Friday . . . things I have carefully avoided telling from the very beginning of my analysis.

Benedicte then went on to recount that her friend Marie-Christine had once told her, many years ago, that Benedicte's pubic hair was distributed in a masculine way. Her lover claimed she found it attractive, but it evoked in Benedicte a feeling of explosive rage and hatred towards her. She had suffered all her life from an impression that her body was monstrous and, as she put it, 'ambiguous' and that it had become more so as she advanced into adulthood. Marie-Christine's words suddenly confirmed this fantasy.

B: That's the reason I always wear tight-fitting jeans and clinging sweaters . . . if anything is floating around my body it might give the impression I have something to hide . . . as though my female shape might not be evident or as though I might be afflicted with a man's sex . . . even if I may have wished this as a child, it's certainly not true today. But the sudden appearance of these secondary sexual characteristics is just as terrifying to me. I've not worn shorts or a bathing suit for over ten years and I've given up swimming and sunbathing altogether.

In reply to a question on my part concerning the 'sudden' appearance of this masculine pubic hair Benedicte explained in detail that as far as she could make out it had occurred shortly after the death of Fredrika's husband.

For a number of years before his (quite unexpected) death Benedicte, knowing Fredrika was very unhappy with her husband, desired ardently to take his place, and had frequently imagined ways of killing him. She had often wondered since then whether the shock of his actual death may have produced this hormonal change. Just before the end of this session I pointed out to Benedicte that she had talked of her own feeling of being mutilated but had not been able to explore further her fantasy of my shameful deformity. The thought that our bodies were both feminine and could be compared apparently gave Benedicte the feeling, after the session, that she had a right to study her own body in more detail, perhaps in the manner of a little girl seeking to glean knowledge about her feminine self from her mother's body and way of being.

B: Last night I tried to imagine your body and to grasp what was so forbidden about this thought. This allowed me to stand in front of the mirror and for the first time in ten years look at myself in the nude. Would you believe it—there's nothing at all wrong with my pubic hair. Absolutely nothing! It isn't the neat and pretty triangle it could be, but there's no hint of anything masculine. And to think of all those years I have hidden my monstrosity from everybody!

We then spent some time examining Benedicte's conflictual feelings following the death of Fredrika's husband. On the one hand, a husband had to die before she could feel sure of her place in the world; in her imagination this would allow her to possess her own femininity through the femininity of the other woman. At the same time, a deeply unconscious fantasy prompted her to seek any possible trace of a living father-figure that she could keep as a vital part of herself. In her totally illusory 'hormonal change', she had carried out a fantasy of *incorporating* the dead husband of her lover. As a very small child she would seem to have believed that she had *become her lost father by a similar process of primitive internalization.* In seeking to possess the mental representation of two parents capable of conferring upon her the status of subjective and of sexual identity, it appeared that the price to be paid was her own castration—the loss of her femininity.

B: You were the first person ever to tell me that I had had two parents. I now see that I had kept traces of my father alive everywhere, both outside and inside myself.

Indeed this seemed to me to be profoundly true, for Benedicte's professional life as well as her love-life were both living monuments to her dead father.

B: And I also thought that you, or any woman, should be wary of me . . . because I do not possess my own female body. It's only through the body of another woman that I regain mine.

J: In order to possess your own body, in order to be a woman, you have to dispossess me? There cannot be two women?

I thought to myself that unconscious identifications are something like one's liberty. The latter cannot be handed out with permission; one has, at some time, to reach out and assume it for oneself. It requires the sexual representation of two parents in order to acquire a firm sense of one's own sexual identity, but the confusing and traumatic circumstances that surrounded Benedicte's understanding of what constituted her own sexual identity had left her with only partial identifications concerning her gender and sexual role.

B: Yes! It's as though I have to take something away from you but I don't know why. Also I still can't imagine what your deformity might be . . . but I had an important thought about that. I said to myself that I love you and that no matter what monstrosity or what bodily deformity you might hide, it would make absolutely no difference to my feelings for you.

J: In other words you have never been sure that this is also true for you . . . that you too could be loved no matter what body, no matter what sex, you have?

There followed an astonished silence before Benedicte was able to reply and when she did her voice trembled through her tears.

B: How strange . . . I never believed I could be loved, with my body, with my sex . . . just as I am . . . just because I am . . . me.

I shall leave the story of Benedicte's analysis at this point, simply adding that, among other changes, her analysis permitted her to refind and truly liberate her creative potential. Within a relatively short span of time Benedicte produced several intense and fascinating works and I feel confident that this creative source will not dry up again in the future. She also found the courage to ask her mother to give her more details of her father and her relationship with him before his death. The mother replied that it could not possibly have any meaning for Benedicte because children of that age are unaware of their fathers! She did however add, in the face of Benedicte's insistence, that her father had been the one who principally cared for her when she was teething or restless in her sleep. He also frequently helped with her bodily care, since he did not suffer, as did her mother, from any repugnance about soiled diapers. 'There you were, so excited, jumping up and down at the sight of him, with your diaper full of shit, and he would grab you up and hold you in his arms as though it didn't matter. You see, he wasn't a classical father.'

CONCLUDING REMARKS

In this chapter my primary object has been to trace, with the aid of a pertinent clinical example, the early elements that contribute to the origins of one's sense of sexual identity and the factors that may hinder the psychic process essential to the establishment of a secure sense of core gender and sexual role. These include identifications to both parents and therefore require the capacity to resolve the universal bisexual and incestuous wishes of childhood as well as institute the mourning processes needed to assume one's monosexuality without neurotic, characterological or sexual distortions. The integration of the bisexual longings of childhood enriches the personality in many ways, strengthening one's narcissistic self-image and sense of sexual identity, as well as contributing to the capacity to be creative in intellectual, scientific or artistic fields. In the clinical illustration to these themes, the role of early psychic trauma played an essential role for Benedicte who lost her father at the age of fifteen months and was thus left a prey to her mother's internal confusions and inability herself to face the traumatic loss of her husband. Her attempt to deny that the father had ever truly existed for her daughter had forced the latter to accomplish a magical mourning for her lost father by, in a sense, becoming him.

It is my hope that I have been able to communicate something of the struggle that a little girl, in traumatizing circumstances, felt obliged to maintain, in order to protect her feeling of identity and her sexuality.

Perhaps this analytic vignette might at the same time throw some light upon the struggle of every little girl in her attempt to safeguard her sense of integrity and the conviction of her personal and sexual value.

SUMMARY

This chapter explores the origins of two clinical phenomena which are frequently related in analytic practice, namely sexual deviancy and inhibition in creative or intellectual work. The analysands in question seek psychoanalytic help not for their sexual acts and object-choices but because of blockage in their professional activities.

In the author's opinion the roots of both sexual deviancy and creativity may often be traced back to early psychic trauma. The sexual 'solution' and the creative activity both represent ways of attempting to overcome the traumatic situation of infancy.

These propositions are illustrated by the case of an author who sought help because her writing was completely blocked and because her homosexual love-relations caused tension and concern. The sudden death of her father when she was fifteen months old and her mother's disturbed way of handling the tragic situation were decisive factors in both the patient's sexual and professional life.

REFERENCES

Bion, W. (1963). *Elements of Psychoanalysis.* London: Heinemann.
McDougall, J. (1964). Homosexuality in women. In *Female Sexuality: New Psychoanalytic Views,* ed. J. Chasseguet-Smirgel. Ann Arbor: Michigan Univ. Press, 1970.
——— (1978). *Plea for a Measure of Abnormality.* New York: Int. Univ. Press, 1982.
——— (1982). *Theatres of the Mind.* New York: Basic Books, 1985.
——— (1986a). Eve's reflection: On the homosexual components of female sexuality. In *Between Analyst and Patient,* ed. H. Meyers. Hillsdale, N.J.: Analytic Press.
——— (1986b). Identifications, neoneeds and neosexualities. *Int. J. Psychoanal.,* 67: 19–31.
——— (1986c). Parent loss. In *The Reconstruction of Trauma,* ed. A. Rothstein, New York: Int. Univ. Press.
Roiphe, H., and Galenson, E. (1981). *Infantile Origins of Sexual Identity.* New York: Int. Univ. Press.
Segal, H. (1957). Notes on symbol formation. *Int. J. Psychoanal.,* 38:391–397.
Stoller, R. (1968). *Sex and Gender.* New York: Jason Aronson.
Winnicott, D. W. (1951). Transitional objects and transitional phenomena. In *Collected Papers.* New York: Basic Books, 1958.

In the United States

7. Ways of Female Superego Formation and the Female Castration Conflict

Edith Jacobson

Freud (1925) has repeatedly expressed the opinion that on the average, the female superego, compared with that of the male, is organized rather weakly, is unstable, and has no independence. In his last work on *Female Sexuality* (1931) he again expresses the same opinion. Convincingly, he explains the imperfect formation of the female superego by referring to the different development of the female castration conflict. The little girl does not develop real 'castration fear', which is the strongest causal factor in the overcoming of the oedipal conflict. Since the fear of loss of love does not have the same dramatic significance as the boy's castration fear, her oedipal wishes are only slowly and incompletely given up and do not leave behind a stable superego as the heir of the oedipus complex.

Studies of the female personality and clinical analytic experiences with female patients appear to confirm this view. We know, for example, about the greater frequency of compulsive narcissism in men and of hysteria in women. However, we have to question why the illness which is characterized by the merciless cruelty of the superego, the melancholic depression, occurs so predominantly in females.

Even more surprising is the fact that in the treatment of women whose superego appears to be weak and anaclitic, whose moral judgments seem to vacillate and to depend on those of the environment, the patients may suddenly show eruptions of cruel superego demands which had been formerly warded off. Such cases compel us to suspect that the formation of the female superego is much more complicated than we commonly assume.

Translated by Paula Gross.

This is the first English translation of *Wege der weiblichen Über-Ich-Bildung* which was originally published in the International Zeitschrift für Psychoanalyse, XXIII, 1937, pp. 402–412. It complements the author's paper, *On the Development of the Girl's Wish for a Child*, *Psychoanalytic Quarterly*, XXXVII, 1968, pp. 523–538.

"Ways of Female Superego Formation and the Female Castration Conflict" is reprinted with permission from *Psychoanalytic Quarterly* 45 (1976): 525–38.

Similar to the neuroses in general, we can also observe in the course of the last decades a change in the psychic structure in women at all social levels. This finds expression in their love lives as well as in the organization of their egos and superegos.

We may question how far the frequency of female frigidity has decreased. But there is very clearly a trend toward an expansion of the formerly rather limited female love life and the onset of the growth of an ego that is richer in sublimations and of a more independent and more stable, but by no means stricter, superego.

Of course, these developments have their roots in sociological changes whose discussion is not within the scope of this paper. These processes do not take the same course and do not present the same values in all countries. In any case, the liberation of women from old ties must result in a characteristic new form of feminine nature, which we cannot simply conceive of in terms of a 'masculinization' of females.

Certainly we may say that the modern woman would like to have the privileges of a more expansive sexuality; that having entered professional life, she aims at cultural sublimations which at an earlier time were left to men; and that she acquires a critical judgment and ego ideal of her own, which were uncommon in women of earlier times. To be sure, the emancipation of women in what Marianne Weber (1917) called 'heroic types' first produced a generation of 'masculine' women. However, we question how far feminine progress actually aims at a phallic development. I should regard such an interpretation as faulty, at least in many cases.

We recall in the paper by Sachs (1928), *One of the Motive Factors in the Formation of the Superego in Women,* that the oral type with *unsuccessful* superego formation, which he describes, was found very frequently among women of former generations. His other case, in which an independent superego had developed, was a modern career woman, but not unfeminine and with a healthy feminine love life.

At any rate, in examining the female superego we must keep in mind the lack of uniformity in the female personality of our time.

If we want to probe more closely into the ways of female superego formation, we shall first have to deal with the problem of female 'castration fear', which is crucial for the understanding of superego formation, as stressed at the beginning of this paper. This seems to be at variance with the fact cited by Rado (1933), in *Fear of Castration in Women,* that in the mental life of women one can observe only derivatives of 'castration fear'. Also, I cannot share Rado's opinion that the castration fear of women reflects exclusively the fear, projected outside, of masochistic instinctual danger. The study of adult women, as well as observations of young children, has convinced me that, as already shown by other authors, for instance, Horney (1926), the little girl, too, has an original fear of bodily, especially genital, impairment. This fear, unlike the boy's, is not dictated by the oedipal relationship but develops during the preoedipal relation to the mother and undergoes certain modifications during later stages of development.

Melanie Klein (1929) has advanced the opinion that the most profound fear of the girl is that of 'destruction' of the inside of her body, a talionic fear based upon destructive impulses directed against the mother's body. This finding, however, can only be made fruitful by a close examination of the vicissitudes of the content of the fear during infantile instinctual development.

The fear of being robbed of the inside of the body occurs—in the boy as well as the girl—in the first years of life, in which pregenitality prevails. To the degree that the genitality of the little girl is exercised in clitoris masturbation and phallic strivings toward the mother, her fears of punishment are likewise concentrated on the genital organ, reaching their highest point with the discovery of the difference between the sexes. This discovery generally leads the little girl, although by no means directly, to the simple horrifying conclusion: 'I am castrated'.

This traumatic experience is, of course, usually more diffuse and differentiated and extends over a much longer time. The painful discovery is often followed by greater preoccupation with the genital, and frequently by a period of increased masturbation. The terrified little girl, who begins to doubt her normal genitality, first tries to continue believing that everything is still all right and to prove it—for example, by masturbation and genital exploration. She grasps at assumptions and consolations of the same kind the boy uses in trying to fend off the impression of the female genital: the penis is merely too small as yet, it will surely grow bigger, and, above all, it may merely be hidden inside the body and it will surely come out.

This notion of an inner, invisible penis, which is linked to introjections connected with wishes and fantasies concerning the inside of the mother's body, seems to occur regularly and is fused later on with fantasies of pregnancy. Thus in female patients at a corresponding stage of treatment we may understand a demonstrative protrusion of the abdomen, not only as a miming of pregnancy but also, at a deeper level, as an exhibition of the penis lodged inside the body (see, Weiss, 1924). The fantasied displacement of the penis inside the body, in its turn, changes the castration fear into a fear of destruction of this internal genital. It further enhances phallic and urethral as well as exhibitionistic strivings. The little girl tries desperately to force out the imaginary inner penis with the jet of urine; in that way she will be able to show it. For example, a patient preoccupied with masculine illusions hoped that at least after her death the autopsy would finally reveal her hidden penis.

The assumption of an inner organ can, however, also be a favorable preparation for the development of normal genitality. I shall come back to this later.

For the time being, the little girl is roughly in the anxious situation of a person who concludes from certain symptoms that he is afflicted by an ominous illness. The fear of impairment of the illusional inner penis combines with pregenital fears of damage to the body. I could find no characteristic difference in this reaction of the female when compared to the inner situation of the male neurotic who experiences, besides castration fear, anxieties lest he already be castrated. Such female 'castration fear' may well provide the motive for giving up masturbation; the little girl now makes efforts in this direction, sometimes after a phase of intensified sexual activity. These efforts are strongly supported by the increasing devaluation of the genital, corresponding to her narcissistic injury (Freud, 1931).

It often takes a considerable time for the anxious excitement of this period to turn into a depression indicating the final conviction of having been robbed genitally. Only then does the aggressive rebellion of the child fully set in. Vengeful impulses and wishes to recover the organ snatched away by the mother arise, the frustration of which leads to a final disappointment with the mother and to her derogation. Turning away from her, the child approaches the father, but with great ambivalence. This is the beginning of the oedipal relationship.

I cannot share the opinion of Melanie Klein (1932) that the wish for a penis accompanies the female oedipal wishes a priori. Neither the early infantile equation of the penis with the breast nor the regular occurrences of fantasies of getting the paternal penis out of the mother's body are to be disputed. But Klein's conception does not do justice to the influences exerted on the development of the female oedipal situation by the preceding narcissistic blow due to the trauma of being castrated.

The child's relation to her own genital during the ensuing period is marked by a derogation of the genital organ which predisposes her to frigidity and, in cases where it leads to a distinct reactive narcissism, may even threaten the establishment of object relations to men. The narcissistic wound will be healed with the help of the libidinal displacements to other parts of the body or to the body as a whole. Narcissistic compensations are initiated, such as the development of feminine virtue or the cultivation of feminine beauty, described by Harnik (1923); or the impaired self-esteem may be relieved by the development of 'masculine' distinctions in other physical or mental areas.

What is decisive for the sexual vicissitudes and the recovery of genital self-esteem and feeling, however, is whether and how successfully the love relationship to the father develops. It must help the girl gradually to renounce her aggressive-masculine desire, to resign herself to the lack of a penis, to overcome the oral impulses to acquire the penis forcibly and to transform them into vaginal desires.

If female development proceeds in this way, we usually describe it as normal; in a certain percentage of cases, although it allows a healthier feminine future to the woman than if she were phallicly fixated, there is no greater capacity for sexual enjoyment. Helene Deutsch (1930) has aptly described this type of frigid but otherwise quite normal feminine woman. Such sexual frigidity is undoubtedly so prevalent, it is not surprising that Freud, too, assumes that in some cases frigidity may be due to an anatomical-constitutional factor (Freud, 1933). I am convinced, on the contrary, that the frequency of frigidity is determined experientially—i.e., given the typical current nature of causative experiences, it is socially determined. Influenced by contemporary values, such as fears of pregnancy, frigidity is generally the result of inadequate solutions of the castration conflicts which, aggravated by the oedipal prohibition, lead to a regressive fixation on phallic or pregenital positions.

Indeed the little girl's situation after the castration trauma is not designed to restore her healthy self-esteem. No amount of helpful explanation convinces the child of the existence of a fully valid female organ of pleasure; the hope for a future child is insufficient consolation in the present, and the higher social valuation of the male sex is not conducive to a healing of the narcissistic injury.

Thus I also found in patients who had reached a relatively normal feminine position that the vagina, even though libidinally cathected later on, had not become fully equivalent to the sexual forces preceding the castration trauma. This was due to the fact that the female sexuality had been diverted into masochism by the castration trauma. The warding off of the revived oral-sadistic wishes for incorporation had led to a renunciation not only of the penis but of the patient's own genital organ. The phallus was yielded to the man—in expiation, as it were; on him it could now be loved, preserved intact, and only received in the sexual act, over and over again, like the maternal breast at an earlier time. Although with this development, the vaginal zone had begun to be erotized, at first the narcissistic compensation for the devalued genital became not the vagina but the paternal penis, or the entire love object equated with it, i.e., the father. The narcissistic cathexis had been displaced from the woman's own genital to the love object, and was reflected in a change of anxiety contents: following acceptance of their own castration and establishment of the oedipal relationship, the castration fear could be regressively equated with the fear of the loss of love. Fear of loss of the penis had been replaced by fear of losing the phallic love object, thus establishing an orally determined, narcissistic and often masochistic attitude toward the latter.

Not all women with such a sexual organization are frigid. As already mentioned, a displacement of the oral libidinal cathexis can cause the vagina to become the organ of pleasure in their later love life. As long as they feel secure in the possession of the man they love, these women are capable of vaginal pleasure and orgasm, but they react with frigidity, vaginismus, and pathological depression to any danger of losing the love object to whom they cling anxiously. It is striking, moreover, that although such women experience vaginal pleasure in coitus, they are often completely inhibited as far as masturbation is concerned, as I was able to observe in four cases. Lacking 'a genital of their own', they are absolutely dependent on the partner's penis for sexual excitement. Thus even though they experience pleasure in coitus, their genitality is really a sham since they experience the partner's genital as belonging to their own bodies. Such love relationships are marked by a narcissistic identification with the man and his penis. The further the masochistic mastery of oral aggression against the man has gone—i.e., the stronger the impulses to rob him of his genital—the more complete the frigidity; erotization of the receptive organ, the vagina, thus may become totally impossible.

With necessary caution we may say that the mechanisms here described were almost regularly found in the normal married women of the last generation. But nowadays we observe—beside many phallic types, with which I shall not deal here—the beginnings of a development that is healthier from the libidinal-economical point of view.

The castration conflict then is resolved as follows. Renunciation of the penis is made possible by the more rapid and direct discovery of the female genital, and the child's female self-esteem is restored with the belief that she possesses an equally valuable organ of her own. The libidinal cathexis of the vagina likewise takes place directly and not merely through displacement of oral strivings. As I indicated above, the fantasies about an internal penis provide a bridge in the formation of the symbolic equations, penis = vagina and penis = child, since her belief in the hidden organ can spur the little girl to energetic investigation of her genital, leading to satisfactory knowledge about the vagina and vaginal masturbation. This is particularly successful in cases where masturbation is not prohibited and suitable explanation of the difference between the sexes furthers the process. Characteristic for women whose female genital feeling grows out of the assumption of a penis inside the body is a stronger fantasy of erotization of the deeper parts of the vagina, as well as of a general participation of the uterus in genital excitation and orgastic satisfaction.

Once female development has been set upon this path, it will also place the relation to the love partner on a different basis than exists in the type I have described. This relation is not oral, narcissistic, and masochistic but active-genital. It permits a choice of the 'anaclitic type' (Freud, 1914) and vouchsafes a certain independence of the love object since it is less influenced by the fear of loss of love. Rather it is influenced by a fear of vaginal injury (analogous to the male's castration fear), as Karen Horney (1926) has stressed. Insofar as this fear refers also to the inner, deep-seated parts of the genital organ, Melanie Klein's opinion that the deepest female fear is a fear of destruction of body contents would again apply.

The complex character of female instinctual life, due to the peculiarity and depth of the castration conflict, of course affects female ego and superego formation as well.

For the sake of clarity I may remark that I do not share Melanie Klein's (1932) view that the earliest introjections of the parental figures should be regarded as the beginning of superego formation. Although the early identifications and anxieties are the foundation of the later superego and are therefore especially important for the understanding of superego formation, the fact that the formation of the superego as a distinct part of the personality is closely connected with the dissolution of the Oedipus complex should not be obscured. We should speak of a superego only when a uniform, consolidated structure becomes observable (cf., Fenichel, 1926). To be sure, this comes earlier in the little girl than in the boy—approximately at age three, precisely in the phallic phase in which the castration fear, intensified by her beginning doubts as to the normal character of her genital, drives the child to struggle against masturbation and detachment from the mother.

Thus one might describe the first stage of the female superego as 'heir of the negative Oedipus complex'. With the passing of the preoedipal tie to the mother, the nucleus of the female superego—and to a certain degree also of the male superego—is 'maternal-phallic'. After all, during the first years of life the mother takes precedence in all respects; she takes first place as the object of love and identification. The spur to superego formation persists— at first becomes even stronger—when the little girl can no longer avoid the fact of being 'castrated'. At a time when the greatest demands on her psychic strength are made, one can observe the development of intense efforts to be good and to build up the ego ideal of a modest, gentle, obedient, clean little girl, perhaps in opposition to an unruly, cheeky, dirty little boy.

The content of this first, typically feminine ideal of virtue is determined, of course, by the experience of 'castration'; it militates particularly against the revived oral-sadistic and phallic-aggressive strivings toward mother and father, as well as against the anal devaluation of her own and the mother's genital organs. We also see here the substantial contribution of orality to female superego formation, which Sachs (1928) pointed out. Not only the features of resignation, which he cites as characteristic of the female super-ego, are shaped at this time, but all the cardinal female virtues of bodily and mental purity and of patient resignation are ideals which the woman acquires through the usual course of her castration conflict.

During the next period of development, however, the organization of the female superego does not progress with the same intensity. The little girl's moral efforts seem to be so exhausted by her acceptance of castration that we observe instead a retrogression in her superego formation. The inhibition is closely connected with the child's relation to the paternal penis. A comparison with male development is relevant here: the process of superego formation in the boy might be characterized by saying that instead of taking possession of the paternal penis (in order to have intercourse with the mother) —i.e., instead of 'castrating' the father—he incorporates certain phallic qualities of the father. The female superego formation proceeds analogously at first, with the mother as the object of identification. However, the situation changes in the little girl when the castration conflict is resolved and her relation to the father begins to flourish. He now replaces the mother as the center of object-libidinal as well as narcissistic strivings. In the struggle between them, the phallic narcissism of the girl gives way to object libido, while the boy sacrifices his oedipal wishes in order to preserve his penis.

Incidently, this characterizes the peculiarities of male and female narcissism. The latter merges into object love, finding its expression in it; the former takes precedence over object love.

Thus, if the girl adopts the female position, the castrative wishes directed at the father are not warded off with the aid of phallic partial identification with the father in a superego, but by an elaboration of object relationship in which the possession of the father as love object—ensured by reception of the penis in the sexual act—compensates her for giving up the genital. The projective process furthering this development, in which one's own genital is renounced and the narcissistic genital cathexis transferred to the father, also results in a projection of the superego (equated with the desired phallus) upon the love object which is thereby elevated to serve as superego. From then on the female anxiety of conscience becomes to a certain extent a secondary 'social anxiety'; above all, the opinions and judgments of the love object become decisive and—like his penis—can always be taken from him again. On the other hand, from the libidinal-economical point of view, the superego's projective dependence on the father provides relief to the little girl's ego which was overtaxed by her castration conflict.

A brief example may illustrate the process of such superego projection. A patient asserted at the beginning of treatment that she was a typical case of social anxiety. She stated that she had no value judgment of her own, but adopted the values of her current environment. The patient seemed to be right. Notwithstanding outstanding intelligence, in her judgment and behavior she displayed a striking dependence on her love objects. But in the course of her treatment it became clear that her assertion of lacking any value judgment meant to her lacking a penis, being 'castrated'. This open admission of her deficiency was intended to deny her wishes to introject the penis —her fantasy of having one of her own. She then revealed the masochistic elaboration of her vehement, aggressive incorporation impulses toward the father's phallus and, respectively, on a deeper level, toward the mother's body. To her love object she surrendered not only her 'penis' and all the genital activity, but also her superego. In spite of her cleverness, she developed an infantile-oral attitude toward her lovers who had to confide their love experiences to her—i.e., share their riches with her—and also to dictate every step of her life. Only after understanding these connections did the patient reveal the desire not only for a genital organ and a sexual life of her own but also those manifestations of her superego which she had denied, repressed, and warded off by projection.

This mechanism, which was unusually obvious in my patient, seems to be typically female. Thus the development of a female-masochistic and orally determined attitude to the object leads in many cases to warding off the superego, and especially to a projective dependence of the superego on the father as well as on the mother when, as rival, she again becomes the object of identification. This process is contrary to the further development of an independent female superego. To the woman's sexual dependency on the love object is added the female tendency to love the embodiment of her own sacrificed ego ideal in the man, or to acquire his superego through her love. This is illustrated by Sachs (1928) in his description of the oral type of woman who depended upon the opinions and standards of her former lovers —i.e., she required the real incorporation of the penis for her development of a pseudo-superego.

It is not surprising that women with such libidinal organization may become melancholic despite an apparently weak superego; indeed they are predisposed to it by their orality. A later prevalence of introjective mechanisms causes the projection of the superego to be withdrawn again, and the repressed early infantile superego makes a cruel reappearance, flooding the ego with archaic fears.

The formation of the superego is much more successful when the vagina is accepted as a fully valued genital. The more genital the attitude of the little girl is during the oedipal phase, the more analogous is her ego and superego development to that of the male.

Castration fear has its counterpart in the female fear of injury to the genital. An independent ego ideal is formed in which traits of the father are included when the maternal model is insufficient, but this would not necessarily be described as a 'male superego'. Under the influence of heightened female self-esteem and a better organized superego, the ego of course is also expanded and enriched. The objection may be raised that the ego and superego development outlined here would be characteristically 'phallic'. The decisive difference, however, lies in the different libidinal organization, which finds expression in the lack of rivalry with the man, in healthy social and love relationships, and in the development of an ego and superego qualitatively different from the male's. I refer once more to the second female character described by Sachs (1928), which he defines as normally female.

To this translation of my 1937 paper, I now add a note. The difficult delimitation of the 'masculine woman' can be explained by the fact that the image of a 'truly feminine' woman is rooted in traditional standards. Furthermore, the female 'vaginal' character with an independent superego, a strong, effective ego, and healthy expansive sexuality—historically originating from the oral-narcissistic and masochistic woman by way of the phallic woman— is only beginning to prevail. Hence a 'future female type' remains even now, forty years after this paper was written.

REFERENCES

Deutsch, H. (1930): *The Significance of Masochism in the Mental Life of Women; Part I, 'Feminine' Masochism and Its Relation to Frigidity.* Int. J. Psa., XI, pp. 48–60.

Fenichel, O. (1926): Identification. In: *The Collected Papers of Otto Fenichel, Vol. I.* New York: W. W. Norton & Co., Inc., 1953, pp. 97–112.

Freud, S. (1914): *On Narcissism: An Introduction.* Standard Edition, XIV, pp. 73–102.

———— (1925): *Some Psychical Consequences of the Anatomical Distinction Between the Sexes.* Standard Edition, XIX, pp. 248–258.

———— (1931): *Female Sexuality.* Standard Edition, XXI, pp. 225–243.

———— (1933): *New Introductory Lectures on Psycho-Analysis.* Standard Edition, XXII, pp. 5–182.

Harnik, J. (1923): *The Various Developments Undergone by Narcissism in Men and Women.* Int. J. Psa., V, 1924, pp. 66–83.

Horney, K. (1926): *The Flight from Womanhood: The Masculinity-Complex in Women, as Viewed by Men and by Women.* Int. J. Psa., VII, pp. 324–339.

Klein, M. (1929): *Infantile Anxiety-Situations Reflected in a Work of Art and in the Creative Impulse.* Int. J. Psa., X, pp. 436–443.

———— (1932): *The Psycho-Analysis of Children.* New York: W. W. Norton & Co., Inc.

Rado, S. (1933): *Fear of Castration in Women.* Psychoanal. Q., II, pp. 425–475.

Sachs, H. (1928): *One of the Motive Factors in the Formation of the Superego in Women.* Int. J. Psa., X, 1929, pp. 39–50.

Weber, M. S. (1917): *Vom Typenwandel der studierenden Frau: Die Formkräfte des Geschlechtslebens.* Berlin: W. Moeser, 1918.

Weiss, E. (1924): *A Contribution to the Psychological Explanation of the 'Arc de Cercle'.* Int. J. Psa., VI, 1925, p. 323.

8. A Contribution to the Psychoanalysis of Extreme Submissiveness in Women

Annie Reich

The aim of this contribution is to further our understanding of a morbid development in the character of the woman who is extremely submissive to men and to explain a certain neurotic aspect of her love life. An investigation of this type of disturbance of the relationship to objects may also throw some light on certain properties of immature object relationships in general.

In the German language there exists the special expression *Hörigkeit* for which there seems to be no precise English equivalent; the term 'extreme submissiveness' will serve. By this term we understand a special dependency of one adult upon another: the impossibility of living without the partner, the willingness to comply with all the partner's wishes thereby sacrificing all interests of one's own, all independence and self-reliance. I think that such extreme submissiveness is a clear-cut clinical picture which may best be regarded as a perversion. It is found in men as well as in women but since my clinical material happens to comprise only female cases I will restrict myself to discussing the mechanisms at work in women. It is possible that the mechanisms in men are similar.

Susan, twenty-nine years of age, had been living in such a submissive relationship with a very brilliant but very narcissistic man for nine years. This man was very disturbed sexually and had deep objections to intercourse. It took six years before he finally gave in to Susan's importunate sexual needs, but even after that he was willing to have intercourse only on very infrequent occasions. Life with this man was a perpetual courtship on Susan's part. Notwithstanding the fact that her life had become a long chain of disappointments and rejections, she lived for this man only. Before him Susan had had several intimate friends, but somehow he was the 'right' one. She wanted only to be near him, to share his life. She followed him everywhere to the neglect of her vocation, her family, all her former interests.

For all this Susan felt recompensed by the overwhelming happiness which

Reprinted with permission from *Psychoanalytic Quarterly* 9 (1940):470–80.

she experienced whenever she succeeded in sleeping with her lover; then she was utterly happy and had the feeling of being completely fused with him. 'We become one person', she said. 'He is I and I am he.'

The overvaluation of sexual intercourse seen in Susan is typical of all similar cases. Another example of this was Mary, thirty-one years old, married to a narcissistic man who maltreated her and went around with other women. Like Susan, Mary was deeply bound to her husband in an extremely submissive way. She endured all his insults and brutalities only to feel the bliss of having intercourse with him. Describing her feelings during intercourse, she said: 'The walls between him and me do not exist any more. I feel what he feels; I even think what he thinks. We are one person, and the only wish I have is to die that very minute.'

Intercourse is an experience of extraordinary intensity in these cases of extreme submissiveness in women. Since the feeling of bliss in this *unio mystica* cannot be explained by the orgastic sensation alone, let us try to probe the matter a little deeper.

In the submissive woman the special ecstasy of intercourse must be viewed against the background of anxiety, despair and helplessness which are experienced when she is separated from the object of her love or when her lover turns away from her. Mary described this in the following way: 'I am quite disturbed, as if I were poisoned. It is as if I were in an empty, cold and dark world all by myself. It is absolute solitude.' The description given by Susan was somewhat similar: 'I feel as though I were in a dark hole, all alone. All other men are dead. I am unable to do anything.'

It is worthy of note that the self-esteem of the submissive woman falls to a strikingly low level when she is away from her lover. The man, on the other hand, is overrated; he is considered to be very important, a genius. He is the only man worthy of love.

The submissive woman seems completely to have renounced her own narcissism. It is as if she had projected her narcissism onto the man; she develops a sort of megalomania in regard to him. In the magic of the *unio mystica* she finally regains through identification the narcissism which she had renounced.

Susan's history shows this clearly. She was a very ambitious girl with a wild urge towards perfection. She was characteristically compulsive in her work: for instance, she felt that she could never find a composition book of the 'right' size in which to copy the most complicated matters of science in the 'right' order. If after innumerable struggles she once managed to do so, she would then fall into a state of narcissistic enthusiasm. She began to study philosophy but finally gave it up as too difficult. A short time afterward she became acquainted with the man who later became her husband. He was a philosopher, and she fell helplessly in love with him. She was quite conscious of the fantasy that she would come to understand philosophy through her love for this man. In her analysis it became quite clear that the perfection which Susan could not achieve through her own efforts but only through having a man in intercourse was the penis.

Mary, our other submissive patient, had also fought for masculinity desperately and unsuccessfully. She too found vicarious satisfaction in her husband's greatness. Speaking of her handsome husband, she said: 'He is tall, slender, sinewy and muscular. His body is like a large penis!'

As children both women had imagined that during intercourse the woman would get the penis from the man and keep it. But the presence of this fantasy alone does not clarify the problem of submissiveness. The process of achieving the desired penis in a magic way through intercourse seems frequently to be the solution of the masculine conflicts of normal girls. The normal girl too has to renounce her masculine desires of puberty and is also partially recompensed by the love of a man. Hence we have to look for factors more specifically determining the development of extremely submissive conduct. The question as to what distinguishes the normal woman from the submissive one is the more important inasmuch as under certain social conditions, for example those prevailing in the nineteenth century, the obedient wife who was submissively dependent upon her husband represented the ideal of society.

A factor more specifically bearing upon the question of submissiveness in certain women is their tendency to fall in love with men who abuse and humiliate them. If we suppose that these humiliations are an inseparable part of their love life, we must look for further signs of masochistic tendencies. These signs are indeed to be found. For one thing, these women consider intercourse an act of violence, or in a more sublime way the act may be experienced as a mystic dissolution of the person which has its climax in death during orgasm. Likewise, the humiliations to which the submissive woman is subjected are obviously a part of the love play: the deeper the despair resulting from abuse or separation from the lover, the greater the happiness of the reunion. There seem to be two parts to the process: that which is destroyed in the first part is restored in the second. The masochistic nature of yielding to the great can also be seen clearly in the masturbation fantasies of childhood. Little Mary dreamed: 'A father operates on the penis of a little boy. Then he loves the boy very much.' Intercourse in later life is a living out of this fantasy: the woman has first to be castrated and destroyed by the man in order to be loved afterwards. In that ecstatic experience we find a unification of contradictory trends and emotions. The ecstasies represent at the same time castration and the restitution of the penis as well as death and resurrection.

Before we can fully understand this strange process we must examine another aspect of the behavior of the submissive women: their extreme passivity. The submissive woman is helpless if she has to accomplish something unaided and alone. This is not because she lacks ability—all the submissive women I have analyzed were intelligent, distinguished and highly developed—but because the impulse towards activity was missing. The submissive woman wants to remain passive far beyond the realm of sexuality. The man has always to take the first step; she wants only to be his executive organ. If the man inspires or orders something she can do it, but independent action has no such pleasure attached to it.

The main symptom for which Susan came to analysis was her incapacity to do anything by herself. During the analysis she came to understand that every action undertaken by herself was initiated against great resistance because it showed that she was all alone and without her friend. Mary too was full of complaints about her lack of initiative and her unproductiveness. Only if someone else gave orders was she capable of doing anything. In conversation she always had to agree with her partner because, as she put it, she did not have brains enough to make independent evaluations. In fact she found pleasure in this type of intellectual subordination and she built up in each conversation a kind of submissiveness in miniature.

The inclination to be passive reveals a very intense sexualization of the whole life. Women showing this type of submissiveness continually want attention and love from their men. The necessity of independent action already represents for them loneliness and lack of love. They only partly learn to renounce continuous gain of pleasure and to adjust themselves to the requirements of reality. Their very childish attitude is clearly crystallized in the fantasy: 'I have no penis; I cannot do anything alone; you must continually give me something; you must always do something for me'.

Further analysis of the submissive woman characteristically reveals that her problems arise earlier than the phallic phase. They are rooted in a childish fixation to the mother. From her the child expects protection, tenderness, food—in short, all kinds of attention. This was most clearly seen in the analysis of another submissive woman. Frances, thirty years old, had lost her mother when she was four, after which she was sent from one foster home to another for a year until her father finally provided a new mother by marrying again. The child clung to her new mother desperately and wanted all the time to be cleaned, fed, loved and cared for. In her later life the same continual demand for attention of all kinds was seen. In masochistically yielding to a very brilliant man she tried to find fulfilment of these desires through the bliss of an ecstatic union.

In Mary's childhood this special dependency on the mother played a large role. She did not want to do anything without the help of her mother. She had a daydream of a mighty being who knew exactly what she needed and who fulfilled her every need without her asking. What in later childhood she hoped to get from her mother was the penis. Originally her desires had been anal and oral ones. Those tendencies remained unchanged, crossing each other, overlapping, and both extending into her submissive relationship to her husband. Desires that were originally meant for the mother reappear in an ecstatic love relationship to a man.

In describing this ecstatic state we emphasize repeatedly that individuality is dissolved in complete union with the man. We might also understand this union with the great and mighty as a magic fusion with the mother. It is like relapsing to a time in which the ego is about to be formed and when the boundaries between the ego and the outer world were still blurred and only painfully experienced in moments of frustration and tension. Helene Deutsch[1] believes that the sensation of ecstasy is based upon the restitution of some larger unit in the ego when she describes the ecstatic orgastic experience in terms of the fusion of the ego instincts and superego and at the same time with an otherwise hostile, denying outer world.

That the ecstatic experience of orgasm meant a fusion with the mother was substantiated in Mary's analysis. Whenever she was separated from her mother in childhood, Mary feared that her mother had died. She suffered terribly when her mother was dissatisfied or angry with her. On seeing her mother again after an absence or at reconciliation, she felt the same intense happiness she later experienced in her union with a man. She recalled having fallen asleep in her mother's bed with an indescribable feeling of bliss, cuddled up to the warm back of the mother. She used later to fall asleep in the same position after intercourse.

The fear which hung over Mary's childhood that the mother might die we recognize of course to be an expression of the repressed hostility directed against that at times callous fountainhead of all fulfilment. This hostility was later diverted from the mother and directed towards the husband, but it remained repressed. Thus the extreme infantile ambivalence was not overcome by the later change of object but merely directed into other forms. The most important transformation was into masochism. The hostility which had been repressed was explosively discharged upon herself during intercourse through identification with the brutal, sadistic man. At these times she would feel intense lust but would experience a sort of split of her personality. At the same time that she was feeling sexual pleasure as a woman she would also feel like a bystander watching the conquest of a woman. She frequently had the fantasy of being a man and doing the same thing to a young girl. Likewise some of her masturbation fantasies revealed this coexistence of active and passive attitudes: first, a boy is castrated by his father; then the grandfather performs the same operation upon the father.

The anxiety and despair which Mary experienced when separated from her husband were secondarily erotized to increase the intensity of the later sexual gratification. During analysis she realized that in such a state of despair she really felt hatred and envy towards the man who denied her his greatness, his penis. In such a state she once bit savagely into her husband's shaving brush, and her subsequent dreams showed clearly that she wanted to bite off his penis. But such an undisguised outburst of rage could occur only when her marriage was about to end in failure. This expression of rage signified a breakdown of the whole mechanism of submissiveness. So long as the marriage was working, her basic hostility was sufficiently neutralized by its secondary erotization; she was able to endure the torture of being alone in order to increase the bliss of the ensuing reconciliation. When the marriage started to go on the rocks, repression failed.

Although a certain overvaluation of the object is characteristic of a normal love relationship, the submissive woman tends to endow her object with a special greatness. Only with such an object is the *unio mystica* possible, the ecstatic intercourse in which all secret wishes are fulfilled, all aggression, all anxiety and all guilt neutralized.

What happens if this type of woman is thrown into a relationship with an 'average' man? Here, in contrast to her behavior with an admired man, her aggression breaks through. This can be illustrated in the case of Frances, cited earlier, whose fixation was determined by her mother's death when she was four. Frances had been bound submissively to an 'important' man for ten years. This liaison came to a sudden end when her lover's child died. A little later Frances began a new sexual relationship but of a very different kind. Her new lover, many years younger than she, was a nice, plain fellow who felt great love and admiration for her. From him she demanded and got economic security. But in this relationship there was nothing of her former devoted yielding. Here she dominated, but she had to struggle with intense feelings of guilt. 'I don't love this man', she would muse. 'I abuse his young body, his tenderness, his money. If I don't want him I put him in the ice-box, so to speak, to have him ready when I need him again.' She used the man like a tool. To her he was not a human being but only a penis conveniently at her disposal. She dreamed of satisfying herself with a detached penis.

Susan likewise felt egotistic and guilty when she had a sexual relationship with a man who was not the 'right' one. 'I do not love him', she felt; 'I just abuse him'.

In this form of sexual relationship the object is not intact; the man does not figure as a human being but only as a means of gratifying an instinct.

This lack of consideration for the object is characteristic of the prostitute. She may be submissive and masochistic in the hands of a bully while she abuses, exploits and destroys numerous other men. Here there is no identification with the object, no sentiment, no interest in individuality.

The relentless, destroying attitude which the prostitute lives out in her love life, the submissive woman attempts to master by repression. She tries hard to preserve her faith in the greatness and singularity of her man because this overvaluation alone enables her to maintain the underlying hatred in repression. A blind, unqualified glorification of the object insures a lasting relationship to it.

This strained repression, however, is frequently difficult to maintain. Mary, for instance, was always furtively and anxiously evaluating her admired husband to see whether he was really as great, as brilliant and as beautiful as she had made him out to be. She had continual anxiety that she might discover in him something that was stupid, ugly, ridiculous. To stifle this dread she naturally had to pump hard in order to maintain her object in a perpetual state of inflation. Were this bubble to break there would emerge the primitive, aggressive, coprophagic and cannibalistic impulses which in early childhood were predominant in relation to the mother.

The struggle to maintain this balance is characteristic of all object relationships in submissive women. There is towards all things a tendency to sham kindliness, sham warmth, sham attachment.

This inclination to destroy, present as a chronic tendency, is not in this form characteristic of the early infantile attitude from which it is in fact derived. This impulse dominates the emotional state of the infant only if its feeling of well-being is interrupted by pain and frustration. Then the denying object is wanted intensely but only then is it at the same time hated and destroyed.

This alternation between unlimited love and the wish to destroy, depending on whether or not immediate wishes were gratified, was observed clearly in the analysis of a schizophrenic patient. At one moment the world was wonderful, its beauty entering his body like a stream of warm milk; in the next instant everything was gray, colorless, hateful. The development of a minor internal tension was sufficient to produce this change: for instance, if he became thirsty and the desired drink did not come to him magically without the necessity of his getting up and getting it. Or if his girl kept him waiting two minutes his love vanished; there was nothing left but hatred and the wish to destroy.

This patient behaved like a baby in its first month of life. At this stage there is a complete intolerance of tension and frustration. The object is beloved only so long as it fulfils every need. Life is a succession of discrete moments; there is no recollection of any kind. The fact that the object was kind until now is emotionally meaningless. The infant cannot remember nor can it wait or understand that there may be a later gratification. All it can do is rage.

Conformity to the reality principle, emotional continuity and the minimization of mood swings is achieved in a variety of ways in the course of normal development. In submissive women this is attempted by the narcissistic elevation of the object, by the pleasure gratification of the ecstatic love experience, and finally by the transformation of aggression into masochistic behavior. Instead of the loose, unstable relationships of the early stage there is developed a single, unchangeable, exaggerated fixation to the object.

This solution of an infantile conflict is not the most successful one which could be achieved. The 'phallic girl' described by Fenichel,[2] for instance, has worked out a somewhat similar but more stable arrangement. This woman indentifies herself with the desired organ of the object by magic incorporation. She is now a part of the man—his penis. The 'phallic girl' is not driven to masochism and is not so much threatened by an unstable ambivalence towards the object as is the submissive woman. By incorporating the desired organ of the object she is enabled to live always in a state of satisfied narcissism.

SUMMARY

A healthy relationship to objects is one where the love of an object can be maintained even if the object be the agent of temporary disappointments or frustrations. This is possible by the development of an ego that is capable of mastering reality. Where there is interference with this development a perpetuation of early infantile conflicts results. Masochistic submissiveness in women is one way of attempting to solve these conflicts.

NOTES

1. Deutsch, Helene: *Zufriedenheit, Glück, Ekstase*. Int. Ztschr. f. Psa., XIII, 1927.
2. Fenichel, Otto: *Die symbolische Gleichung: Mädchen-Phallus*. Int. Ztschr. f. Psa., XXII, 1936, pp. 299–314.

9. Cultural Pressures in the Psychology of Women

Clara Thompson

In my study of "The Role of Women in This Culture"[1] I presented a survey of the present status of women in the United States. I pointed out the basic situation and the changes which are going on. Although the paper was chiefly concerned with the positive aspects of woman's evolution, I spoke also of the problems still remaining, and the new problems arising in the new situations.

It is this problem aspect of woman's present cultural situation which I shall now discuss. I shall approach this through a consideration of Freud's theories about women, viewing these in the light of cultural factors.

The importance of cultural influences in personality problems has become more and more significant in psychoanalytic work. A given culture tends to produce certain types of character. In *The Neurotic Personality of Our Time*[2] Karen Horney has described well certain trends found in this culture. Most of these neurotic trends are found working similarly in both sexes. Thus, for example, the so-called masochistic character is by no means an exclusively feminine phenomenon. Likewise the neurotic need to be loved is often found dominating the life of men as well as women. The neurotic need of power and insatiable ambition drives are not only found in men, but also in women.

Nevertheless, in some respects the problems of women are basically different from those of men. These fundamental differences are due to two things. First, woman has a different biologic function and because of this her position in society necessarily differs in some respects from that of the man. Second, the cultural attitude toward women differs significantly from that toward men for reasons quite apart from biological necessity. These two differences present women with certain problems which men do not have to face.

The biologic problems of a woman's life cannot be ignored, although it would seem that in most cases biology becomes a problem chiefly when it

Reprinted with permission from *Psychiatry* 5 (1942):331–39.

produces a situation which is unsatisfactory in the cultural setup. Menstruation, pregnancy, and the menopause can bring to a woman certain hazards of which there is no comparable difficulty in the male biology. Freud was so impressed with the biologic difficulties of woman that, as is well known, he believed all inferiority feelings of woman had their root in her biologic inadequacies. To say that a woman has to encounter certain hazards that a man does not, does not seem to be the same thing as saying woman is biologically inferior, as Freud implies.

According to his theory woman has a lasting feeling of inferiority because she has no penis. The discovery of this fact at about the age of three is considered sufficiently traumatic not only to lay the foundation for later neurosis but also to have decisive influence on woman's character. She must go through life from that time with the feeling either that she was "born short" or that something terrible had happened to her; possibly as a punishment. This feeling of biologic lack, Freud feels, so overshadows all other details in the picture that he is constrained to express a note of complete pessimism about the cure of women. In his paper "Analysis Terminable and Interminable," published in English in 1937, he says the following: "The feminine wish for a penis . . . is the source of acute attacks of depression . . . because . . . they [women] feel analysis will avail them nothing. We can only agree when we discover that their strongest motive in coming for treatment was the hope that they might somehow still obtain a male organ." Such pessimism would only be warranted if it were assumed that it is the actual physical male organ which women are demanding from analysis, whereas it seems to me that when such a wish is expressed the woman is but demanding in this symbolic way some form of equality with men.

According to Freud, because of the little girl's discovery that she has no penis she enters the Oedipus complex with castration already an accomplished fact, while in the little boy the threat of castration arises as a result of the Oedipus complex and brings about its repression. Out of this situation in the little boy Freud believes much that is important in the superego takes its origin. Since the little girl, feeling herself already castrated, need fear no further threat she has less tendency to repress her Oedipus complex and less tendency to develop a superego.

Furthermore, according to Freud, one fact which reinforces the high evaluation of the penis by the little girl is that she is at the time of its discovery unaware that she has a vagina. She therefore considers her clitoris her sole sexual apparatus and is exclusively interested in it throughout childhood. Since she believes this is all she has in place of a penis this emphasizes her inferiority. In addition, the ignorance of the vagina makes for her a special hazard at puberty because the onset of menstruation brings awareness of her female role and requires her to give up her interest in the clitoris and henceforth to seek sexual satisfaction by way of the vagina. With this comes a change in her character. She gives up her boyish aggressiveness and becomes femininely passive.

These are the highlights of the more strictly biologic aspects of Freud's theory of the development of women. I shall touch presently on some other details, but now I wish to review the gross outline in the light of my first consideration, the problem aspect of the biology of woman. The question must be asked: Is this the true story of the biologic sexual development of women? Penis envy dating from an experience in early childhood is sometimes recalled by women patients. In my experience, however, this memory is not recalled by all patients—not even by all of those who present in other respects the clinical picture of penis envy. While a negative finding is not conclusive it suggests that other factors may also contribute to envy of the male. Also, quite frequently, one finds women patients who are not aware of the clitoris as a separate organ and learned it only later in studying biology. This was true even though they had exploited the pleasurable sensations in the region of the clitoris. Although ignorance of the vagina, sometimes until far into adolescence, has been observed especially in hysterics, equally often one finds knowledge of the vagina from an early age and often a history of vaginal masturbation. These facts certainly cast doubt on the idea that the clitoris is always the center of the little girl's interest. It seems that one is in fact entitled to question whether there is, even now, any adequate information concerning the innate sexual interests of women.

However, Freud was usually a keen clinical observer and it may therefore be assumed that his theory was based upon certain facts which he observed. The probable nature of these facts and the principal sources of error in his interpretation of the observations may be considered.

Of the latter, there seem to have been two. In the first place, he saw the problem entirely from a masculine point of view. Horney draws attention to this in her paper "Flight from Womanhood,"[3] published in 1926. In it she marshalls data to show that the attitude prevalent in the male about his own genitals was accepted by Freud as the attitude of both sexes on the matter. She indicates that Freud based his theory on the assumption that the penis is the sexual organ most highly valued by both sexes and at no point in his work showed any recognition of the possibility of there being a female biologic function in its own right. He saw the woman primarily as the negative of the male. The most extreme example of this appears in his theory that woman accepts her ability to produce a child as a compensation for her lack of a penis. Childbearing is a sufficiently important biologic function to have value for its own sake. Surely, only a man could have thought of it in terms of compensation or consolation.

The second source of error in Freud's thinking is the fact that he studied only women in his own or closely related cultures, that because he had no comparative study of other cultures he believed that what he observed was universal woman. Current studies show that this is clearly not the case.

The women observed by psychoanalysts are distinctly women living in a particular culture, the Western culture, a patriarchal culture in a state of transition. It is impossible to separate from the total picture something which one can safely call biologic woman. It is assumed that she exists, that she has her reactions to her particular organic make-up, but it is increasingly clear that not all that seems biologic is biologic. That women behave differently in different types of culture is now beginning to be known, although intensive analyses of women in other cultures have not yet been made. Freud, ignoring these considerations thought the attitudes, interests, and ambitions of the middle- and upper-class women whom he analyzed to be the characteristic attitudes, interests, and ambitions of women in general.

Today one realizes that much which even woman herself may attribute to the fact of her sex can be explained as the result of cultural pressures. At the same time, the fact that bearing children must influence women's personality development cannot be denied. Also the type of sexual response characteristic of a woman conceivably has its influence on her character.

For example, it seems probable that the very fact that the male must achieve an erection in order to carry out the sexual act and that any failure in this attempt cannot be hidden while the female can much more readily hide her success or nonsuccess in intercourse, may well have an effect in the basic character patterns of both. Even here, however, more complete understanding of the cultural pressures is necessary before it can be stated in what way or to what extent biology plays a part. But one thing seems fairly certain; namely, that to the extent to which a woman is biologically fulfilled— whatever that may mean—to that extent she has no tendency to envy man's biology, or to feel inferior about her biologic make-up.

In certain cultures woman can meet with difficulties which would make her biologic make-up appear to be a handicap. This would be true when her drives are denied expression or when fulfillment of the role of woman puts her at a disadvantage. Both of these situations are true in many respects in the United States today. This is essentially a patriarchal culture and although many values are changing and these changes on the whole are working to the advantage of women, the patriarchal situation still presents limitations to a woman's free development of her interests. Also, the newer situations have their hazards in that they usually throw women into unequal competition with men. By unequal, the reference is not to biologic inequality, but an inequality resulting from prejudice and the greater advantages offered the male.

The official attitude of the culture toward women has been and still is to the effect that woman is not the equal of man. This has led to the following things: until very recently woman was not offered education even approximately equal to that given a man; when she did secure reasonably adequate education, she found more limited opportunities for using the training than did a man; woman was considered helpless, partly because she was not given an opportunity to work, and partly because she had no choice but to be economically dependent on some man; and social restrictions were placed on her, especially in connection with her sex life. These restrictions seemed to work to the advantage of the man.

The assumption of woman's inferiority was a part of the prevalent attitude of society and until very recently was accepted by both sexes as a biologic fact. Since there is obvious advantage to the male in believing this, he has proved much more resistant to a new point of view on the matter than have women. Women, at the same time, have had difficulty in freeing themselves from an idea which was a part of their life training. Thus it has come about that even when a woman has become consciously convinced of her value she still has to contend with the unconscious effects of training, discrimination against her, and traumatic experiences which keep alive the attitude of inferiority.

The women whom Freud observed were women in this situation and it was easy for him to generalize the effects of the attitude of the culture as a fact of biology.

It seems justifiable therefore not only to consider Freud's theory in the light of his masculine bias but to examine closely the particular cultural pressures which may have produced the picture of woman as he saw her.

He found that the central problem in the neurotic difficulties of most women was penis envy. If this is interpreted symbolically it will be agreed that in this culture where the advantages go to the possessor of the penis women often find themselves in situations which arouse their envy of men, and so, in their relations to men, they show an attitude which can be called "penis envy."

An awareness of the advantage of a penis might be vaguely conscious in a little girl's mind at the age of three—for already at that age evidences that the son is more privileged are apparent in many middle-class families. Before one can settle the question of whether this early experience takes place in terms of actual envy of the penis, or whether the boy is envied in a more general way, it must be noticed that until very recently the average girl at puberty was made decidedly aware of the disadvantages of being female. In the Victorian era the transition from the freedom of childhood to the restrictions of adolescence must have been especially conducive to unhappiness. An experience of a patient as recently as fifteen years ago shows vividly the still existing cultural situation. Two children, a boy and a girl, the boy a year and a half older than the girl, grew up in a family where freedom of development was encouraged. They were both very fond of outdoor life, and went on long hikes together, often camping out overnight. At the age of twelve suddenly a great change was introduced into the girl's life. She was told that now since she was about to become a woman she could no longer go away with her brother on overnight trips. This was only one evidence, but one very important to her, of the beginning limitation of her activities. She was filled with bitterness and envy of her brother and for several reasons centered her whole resentment on the fact of menstruation. This seemed to her to be the sign of her disgrace, the sign that she had no right to be a person. She became withdrawn and depressed. Her one strong feeling was that she hated to be a woman and did not want to grow up. The condition developed decisively because of the restrictions of adolescence, restrictions which actually changed her whole way of life. I do not wish to imply that this pathologic reaction to the situation at puberty developed in a hitherto healthy girl. Envy of her brother had existed in childhood because of her mother's marked preference for him, but a long period of equality with him had done much to restore her self-esteem. The situation at puberty re-established the idea that he was the more favored person.

The changes brought about by cultural restrictions at the girl's puberty are not of a superficial nature. At this time in the Victorian picture a girl passed from a position of relative equality with boys to one of inferiority. This inferiority was shown in several ways. An outstanding point of the picture was the inhibition of natural aggression. A girl might no longer make demands and go about freely. If she was interested in a boy she must not show it directly. She must never expose herself to possible rejection. This would mean she had been unwomanly. She might no longer pursue her own interests with the same freedom as a boy. Obstacles were placed in the way of her education, her play, and social life. But especially in her sexual life her freedom of development was curbed. The punishment for spontaneous expression of sexual interests was very great. One impulsive act resulting in pregnancy could ruin a girl's whole life. Her training was in the direction of insincerity about her sexual interests. She was taught to be ashamed of menstruation. It was something to be concealed and any accident leading to its discovery was especially humiliating. In short, womanhood began with much unpleasantness. It was characterized by feelings of body shame, loss of freedom, loss of equality with boys, and loss of the right to be aggressive. The training in insincerity, especially about her sexual being and sexual interests, has undoubtedly contributed much to a woman's diminished sense of self. When something so vitally a part of her must be denied it is not a great step further to deny the whole self. The fact that much of this has noticeably changed in the last fifty years seems sufficient proof that this situation was due to a cultural attitude and had nothing to do with innate femininity. Freud, observing this cultural change in the girl's status at puberty, attributed it to the necessity of accepting her feminine passivity, which as he said she could not do without a struggle. Is it not more accurate to say that at puberty it became necessary for the girl to accept the restrictions placed on women, and that this was usually unwelcome. In a word, the difficulties of adjustment found in the girl at puberty are the results of social pressures and do not arise from the difficulty of giving up the clitoris in favor of the vagina.

The cultural attitude about the sexual life of women has been one of denial. In former years there was denial almost of its very existence. Today there is still some tendency to deny that it is as important or urgent as the sexual life of men. Passivity and masochism are usually considered essential characteristics of a woman's sexual drive. Passivity was clearly forced upon her by the inhibition of the right to aggression. Her masochism also often proves to be a form of adaptation to an unsatisfactory and circumscribed life.

Not only in her sexual life has the woman had reason to envy the man. The circumscribing of her intellectual development and the discouragement of personal initiative have been frustrating. Partly from lack of training and partly because of man's desire for ownership woman has had to accept a position of economic dependence on man, and this is still the rule.

Out of this situation come several personality traits which are generally considered typically feminine and which have even been described in psychoanalytic literature as the outcome of woman's biologic make-up. Women are supposed to be more narcissistic than men, to have a greater need to be loved than men, to be more rigid than men and to have weaker superegos than men, these in addition to the already mentioned attitudes of passivity and masochism.

A review of the actual position of economic helplessness of women of the recent past and the relative economic helplessness of many women today leads one to question the innateness of these personality traits. The function of childbearing cannot but have some effect on the personality of woman, but when this function is accompanied by the necessity to legalize the process by marriage and economic dependency—with the only alternative social ostracism and added difficulties in the economic sphere, if she does not marry —one cannot help thinking that woman's greater need to be loved and to have one meaningful sexual relation rather than the more casual sexual life of the man comes about chiefly because she lives in a culture which provides no security for her except in a permanent so-called love relationship. It is known that the neurotic need of love is a mechanism for establishing security in a dependency relation. In the same way to the extent that a woman has a greater need of love than a man it is also to be interpreted as a device for establishing security in a cultural situation producing dependency. Being loved not only is part of woman's natural life in the same way as it is part of man's but it also becomes of necessity her profession. Making her body sexually attractive and her personality seductive is imperative for purposes of security. In the past centuries she could feel safe after she had married and could then risk neglecting her charms, but today, with the present ease of divorce, the woman who depends on a man for her means of support and social position must continue to devote a great deal of her time to what may be called narcissistic pursuits, that is, body culture and concern about clothes. One sees that woman's alleged narcissism and greater need to be loved may be entirely the result of economic necessity.

The idea that women must have weaker superegos than men, as stated by Freud, derives from the notion that in the little girl the Oedipus complex is usually not repressed. Because she enters the Oedipus phase after accepting the fact of castration she has no fear to drive her to repression and the formation of a superego. Not only Freud but other writers, notably Sachs, have pointed out that women therefore often lack strong convictions, strong consciences, but rather tend to take on the convictions and standards of any men on whom they become dependent in the course of their lives. This is said to be especially noticeable in women who have loved several men. Such a woman is supposed to adopt in succession the attitudes of the various men.

Undoubtedly there are many women who answer this description, but the character trait of having no strong beliefs or convictions is not found universally in women and also occurs frequently in men in this culture.

It is an attitude typical of people who have found that their security depends on approval of some powerful person or group. It is relatively easy to become converted to any ideology which will bring one advantage, especially if one has never for neurotic or reality reasons been able to achieve sufficient independence to be able to know one's own mind. This could scarcely but be the case with the Victorian girl who was not permitted to free herself from her father until she was safely entrusted to the protection of another man. For cultural reasons, the girl had to continue to be dependent on her father and emancipation from the childhood tie was not encouraged. Such a situation is not conducive to the development of independent standards. That some women despite this became independent is remarkable.

One other statement of Freud's requires consideration: the idea that women are more rigid than men and lose their capacity for intellectual and emotional growth earlier. He points to the fact that a woman of thirty often seems already incapable of further development while a man of the same age is at the beginning of his best period of achievement. Although he does not explain just how this is the result of a woman's sex, the implication is that it is the outcome of the difficulties of her sexual development. To quote him: "It is as though the whole process had been gone through and remained inaccessible to influence for the future; as though in fact the difficult development which leads to femininity had exhausted all the possibilities of the individual."[4] One might be tempted to believe that because a woman's period of sexual attractiveness is shorter than that of a man she grows old mentally and emotionally earlier. However, here too the cultural factors so dominate the picture that it is hard to see anything else. As long as a woman's sole opportunity for success in life was in making a successful marriage her career was made or lost by the age of thirty. A woman of thirty in the Victorian era and even in some situations today has no future. It is well known in psychoanalytic therapy that for successful outcome of treatment an actual opportunity for further development of the person must exist. This consideration would seem to offer an adequate explanation of the greater rigidity of women, if in fact any such greater rigidity can be demonstrated. I believe that there is no dearth of inflexible personalities among men who have reached the height of their development by the age of thirty, whether because of inferior mental equipment, unfortunate early training, or lack of opportunity. Moreover, today there are many examples of women not dependent on their sexual value for security who remain flexible and capable of development. All that may be said with certainty is that woman's lack of opportunity and economic dependence on men can lead to early rigidity and a narrowed outlook on life, as can any situation which curbs spontaneous development in either sex.

What I have said thus far shows that the characteristics of women which Freud has explained as the result of her biologic vicissitudes beginning with the discovery that she has no penis can be quite as satisfactorily explained in terms of the cultural pressures to which she is subjected. The latter hypothesis must certainly be entertained—if only for economy's sake—before separating the female of man from the realm of general biologic principles and making her something biologically unprecedented.

It is clear that Freud's theories were originally developed about Victorian women. Let me now discuss in contrast the woman of today. The position of women has changed greatly and if the cultural factors are important she is no longer as sexually inhibited and restricted, her opportunities for self-development are greatly increased and marriage is no longer the only means of economic security. These facts have undoubtedly influenced the character of women. So much so that a new type of woman is emerging, a woman capable of independence and whose characteristics differ from those described by Freud. However, the present is still a situation of transition. It takes a long time for a cultural change to come about, especially in its psychologic implications for nondependent persons. Something of the Victorian attitude still persists in the psychology of most women. One finds several remnants of it; for example, the notion that it is more womanly for a woman to marry and let a man support her. The majority of women still accept this idea, to be sure not as early in their lives as their grandmothers did. They often have a few years of independence first. For some the alternative of marriage with economic dependence, or independence with or without marriage, presents a serious conflict. Also under the influence of tradition and prejudice many women are convinced that their adequate sexual fulfillment, including children, and an adequate self-development are not to be reconciled. Men have no such tradition and with them the two interests usually reinforce each other. In this, certainly, women still have real grounds for envying men.

In this specific, limited sense Freud's idea that women have envy because they have no penis is symbolically true in this culture. The woman envies the greater freedom of the man, his greater opportunities, and his relative lack of conflict about his fundamental drives. The penis as a symbol of aggression stands for the freedom to be, to force one's way, to get what one wants. These are the characteristics which a woman envies in a man. When this envy is carried to a more pathologic degree the woman thinks of the man as hostile to her and the penis becomes symbolically a weapon which he uses against her. In the pathologic picture called penis envy by Freud the woman wishes to have the destructive qualities she attributes to the man and she wishes to use this destructiveness against him.

There remains to be dealt with the ways in which women have met the problem of feeling inferior to and hating men, or to use the Freudian language, have dealt with their penis envy. Freud outlined three solutions: a woman may accept her feminine role; she may develop neurosis; or her character may develop in the direction of a "masculinity complex." The first of these seemed to him to be the normal solution.

Here again the problem arises as to what is biologic woman and what is cultural woman. Certainly biologically woman can only find her fulfillment as a woman and to the extent to which she denies this she must be frustrated. However, there are other implications in the idea of accepting the feminine role—it may include the acceptance of the whole group of attitudes considered feminine by the culture at the time. In such a sense acceptance of the feminine role may not be an affirmative attitude at all but an expression of submission and resignation. It may mean choosing the path of least resistance with the sacrifice of important parts of the self for security.

The solution of envy of the male by way of neurosis may be considered a solution by evasion, and although many interesting facts could be considered here the influence of the cultural pressures does not differ greatly from that found in the next type of situation.

The solution by way of developing a masculinity complex deserves careful consideration. One significant difference of neurotic character structure from neurosis arises from the fact that the character pattern is in many ways acceptable to the culture. It represents not only a working compromise of the person's conflicting trends, but also takes its pattern directly from the culture. The culture invites masculinity in women. With the passing of the old sheltered life, with the increasing competition with men growing out of the industrial revolution as well as out of women's restlessness, it is not strange that her first steps toward equality would be in the direction of trying to be like men. Having no path of their own to follow women have tended to copy men. Imitating a person superior to one is by no means unusual. The working man seeking to move up the social and economic scale not only tries to copy the middle-class way of life but may try to adopt the middle-class way of thinking. He may try so hard that he becomes a caricature of the thing he wishes to be, with the loss of sight of his real goals in the process.

In the same way women, by aping men, may develop a caricature situation and lose sight of their own interests. Thus, one must consider to what extent it is profitable for a woman to adopt the ways of a man. To what extent can she do it without losing sight of her own goals. This leads inevitably to a consideration of what characteristics are biologically male and what have developed secondarily as a result of his way of life. Here, as in the consideration of femininity, the same difficulty in separating biologic and cultural factors is found. Not many years ago a woman's decision to follow a profession—medicine, for example—was considered even by some analysts to be evidence of a masculinity complex. This rose from the belief that all work outside the home, especially if it called for the exercise of leadership, was masculine, and anyone attempting it therefore was trying to be a man.

It is true, practically speaking, that in the business and professional world it often paid to act like a man. Women were entering a domain which had been in the possession of men, in which the so-called masculine traits of decisiveness, daring, and aggression were usually far more effective than the customarily ascribed traits such as gentleness and submissiveness. In adaptation to this new way of life, women could not but tend to change the personality traits acquired from their former cultural setting. The freedom which economic independence brought to women also had its influence in developing characteristics hitherto found only in men. It seems clear, however, that such changes are not in themselves in any fundamental sense in the direction of masculinity. It is not useful to confuse the picture of the independent woman with that of an essentially pathologic character structure, the masculinity complex.

By this, I mean that the culture now favors a woman's developing certain characteristics which have been considered typical of men; but that in addition she may be neurotic and may exploit the cultural situation to protect herself from certain anxieties which have arisen in part from her difficulties of self-development because she is a woman and in part from other privations and traumata. Obviously, if a woman develops characteristics which indicate that she unconsciously considers herself a man, she is discontent with being a woman. It would be fruitful to inquire what this "being a woman" means to her. I have suggested the possibility of several unpleasant meanings. Being a woman may mean to her being inferior, being restricted, and being in the power of someone. In short, being a woman may mean negation of her feeling of self, a denial of the chance to be an independent person. Refusal to be a woman therefore could mean the opposite, an attempt to assert that one is an independent person. The woman with a masculinity complex shows an exaggerated need for "freedom" and a fear of losing her identity in any intimacy.

It has become clear in the treatment of some related situations that the development of this character pattern is not solely the result of conditioning against being a woman. More basic may be a threat to the personality integrity from an early dependency, a domineering selfish mother, for example, or from the undermining of self-esteem by a destructive mother. In short, many of the forces which make for the development of neurotic mechanisms in general can contribute to this one. These women fear dependency because dependency has been a serious threat to them. Such women are often unable to have any intimate relationship with men; and if they marry, show a hostile revengeful attitude toward the husband. The marriage relationship is sometimes, however, quite successful when circumstances leave them free to work and at least partially support themselves after marriage. Pregnancy is apt to be a special difficulty because of its at least temporary threat to this independence. And they are always afraid of getting into someone's clutches and losing control of the situation.

If the masculinity complex is not developed primarily as a defense against a feeling of biologic lack, if the feeling of cultural inferiority at being a woman is not the sole cause of its development, but on the other hand any difficulty in any important dependency relation can contribute to its formation, why then does it take the particular form of wishing to be or pretending to be a man with associated hatred of men?

Two things in the situation encourage this type of character defense. First, because of the general cultural trend there is secondary gain in such an attitude. It looks like progress and gives the woman the illusion of going along in the direction of the freedom of her time. Second, it offers a means of avoiding the most important intimacy in life, that with a man. This relationship because of its frequent implication of dependency and subordination of the woman's interests especially reactivates all of the dangers of earlier dependencies. The struggle for some form of superiority to men is then an attempt to keep from being destroyed. Men are punished for all that women have been suffering in all sorts of dependency situations.

So it would seem that solution of envy of the male by the development of the masculinity complex does not have a simple origin and that sources not simply relating to sexual comparisons are important in it.

In conclusion, let me say that psychoanalysis thus far has secured extensive acquaintance with the psychology of women in only one type of culture. Facts observed in a particular part of the Western world have been interpreted by Freud as an adequate basis for an understanding of female psychology in general and as evidence for a particular theory about specific biologic factors in the nature of woman. I have pointed out that characteristics and inferiority feelings which Freud considered to be specifically female and biologically determined can be explained as developments arising in and growing out of Western woman's historic situation of underprivilege, restriction of development, insincere attitude toward the sexual nature, and social and economic dependency. The basic nature of woman is still unknown.

NOTES

1. C. Thompson, "The Role of Women in this Culture," *Psychiatry* IV (1940), 1–8.
2. Karen Horney, *The Neurotic Personality of Our Time* (New York: W. W. Norton, 1937).
3. Karen Horney, "Flight from Womanhood," *International Journal of Psycho-Analysis,* VII (1926), 324–339.
4. Sigmund Freud, *New Introductory Lectures on Psychoanalysis* (New York: W. W. Norton, 1933), p. 183.

10. Masochism—A Defense Reaction of the Ego

Esther Menaker

In scientific investigation it is often the study of the anomalous, the atypical, that points the way to the discovery of deeper truths. Those phenomena which are not readily explained by our basic theories lead us to question them, to expand or modify them, and often to add new dimensions to the fundamental structure. Masochism, whether it be expressed in the form of a sexual perversion or in a general life attitude which Freud has called 'moral masochism', and to which Reik refers as 'social masochism', is just such an atypical phenomenon. The individual who behaves masochistically seemingly contradicts the basic psychological principle that the important motivating force in human behavior is the attainment of pleasure—if not directly, at least through the achievement of equilibrium or a freedom from tension. Even if such pleasure is postponed under the aegis of the reality principle, the ultimate goal of typical normal behavior is gratification and fulfilment rather than the pain, suffering and unhappiness which are the apparent goals of the masochistic reaction.

It would seem reasonable to conclude, therefore, that in masochism the apparent goal of suffering is not the real goal, but merely a way station to it. What then is the ultimate goal, and why has the individual chosen this particular way station as a means of its realization?

According to Freud the masochistic response is the expression of the death instinct (primary masochism) and has as its aim the gratification of an unconscious need for self-punishment, arising from guilt about forbidden impulses. In sexual masochism the punishment eventuates in direct sensual satisfaction (orgasm). The pleasure principle is still served, for the sexual gratification is obvious even though it is achieved through the way station of pain. The pain is but the condition under which pleasure is permitted; it is not the end-pleasure itself. The gratification is not so clear in moral masochism. Here the repeated, unconsciously provoked failures, suffering, and

Reprinted with permission from *Psychoanalytic Quarterly* 22 (1953):205–21.

unhappiness in the life history are never experienced as pleasurable, although an unconscious need for punishment may be satisfied.

The apparent discrepancy between the pleasurable aim of the sexual masochist and the punishment sought by the moral masochist led Reik to question the basic character of pleasure in moral masochism and through his answer to reconcile the two forms of masochism as having a common instinctual root. The origin of the masochistic response, be it sexual or moral, lies, according to Reik, in the 'psychic transformation of a sadistic fantasy'. The sadistic wish is 'to seize and destroy an object'. In sexual masochism the ego is the passive object of this sadistic drive; in moral masochism the fantasy of final victory, of the ultimate carrying out of one's own will, the conquering of all one's enemies despite the failures and defeats one suffers in the present, represents both the expression and gratification of the hidden sadistic wish. Were we to agree that such is a correct description of the dynamics of masochism, we would still be left with the question of its basic purpose. Why the psychic transformation of which Reik speaks, and to what end and under what conditions does it occur?

Reik gives only a partial answer to these questions, and that in a somewhat vague and incomplete form. He sees masochism as a 'particular way of avoiding anxiety and of gaining pleasure'. He reminds us that for the masochist 'any approach to success is avoided because then the forbidden aggressive and imperious tendencies could break through and the inevitable punishment threaten'.

According to Wilhelm Reich all masochism is derived from the sexual instincts and in moral masochism, the typical expression of the masochistic character structure, suffering is accepted as one order of punishment for forbidden sexual wishes which protects the individual from an even greater punishment (castration). The pleasure comes from relief because castration has not take place. The punishment is further an expression of love, and thus its unconscious provocation becomes a provocation of love.

Karen Horney equates neurotic suffering and moral masochism and sees them as ways of relinquishing the self, thus avoiding anxiety and conflict.

The observation that masochism is a way of avoiding anxiety, a point on which a number of analysts agree, is a clue to the fact that one of its important aspects is its function of defending the ego. Important psychoanalytic contributions to the understanding of masochism, however, have thus far been too exclusively concerned with its libidinal meaning. The point of departure has been how gratification is achieved for the individual through masochistic behavior, rather than examining the way in which it serves the ego.

We find that viewing the problem of masochism from the standpoint of the self-preservative functions of the ego leads to new insights. As might be expected the ego function of the masochistic attitude is most clearly discernible in the study of moral masochism. Berliner, confining his observations primarily to moral masochism, has made an important contribution to the concept of masochism as a defense mechanism of the ego. He takes masochism out of the sphere of the instincts and views it as a function of the ego. It is 'a pathologic way of loving' in which the ego through processes of introjection, identification, and superego formation turns the sadism of the love object (not its own sadism) on itself. The motivation for so doing is the need to cling to a vitally needed love object. The dependent child accepts the suffering emanating from the rejecting love object as if it were love, failing to be conscious of, or denying the difference between, love and hate. Once the hating love object has become part of the superego, the constant wish to please and placate the superego causes the individual to lose his identity and to 'make himself as unlovable as he feels the parent wants him to be'.

Analytic experience confirms Berliner's view of masochism as a function of the ego in the service of maintaining a vitally needed love relationship to a primary object. It would seem, however, that the basis for the loss of identity and the conception of one's own worthlessness, which are so characteristic of the moral masochist, is to be found in a much more archaic level of ego development than the identification and superego formation to which Berliner refers.

The awareness of the self is one of the earliest ego experiences. It occurs in infancy, simultaneously with the perception of external objects, through the perception of one's own functions. The unfolding of the ego functions is phylogenetically determined, and in the human infant, because of the long period of biological dependence, the development takes place within the mother-child framework. It has been pointed out in psychoanalytic theory that the basis for the ambivalent feelings of love and hate toward the mother have their beginnings at this early level of differentiation between self and object, and are an outgrowth of the gratification and deprivation of the instinctual needs of the child. There is an additional dimension which depends on the mother's relationship to the developing ego functions of the child. If the mother is indifferent, or if her care and upbringing interferes with the normal development of the child's ego, the ego drives, even at the earliest and most primitive levels of expression, become sources of frustration and are experienced as painful *(unlust),* rather than as enjoyable. The mother must affirm and, through love, further the development of the child's ego. That this is a necessity for physical as well as psychological survival has been amply proven by the studies on hospitalism in infants. It should be noted that what is needed is the expression of love by the mother not only through the satisfying of the instinctual needs of the child (feeding and oral erotism, for example) but through the affirmation of the growing ego functions. Failing this, the demands of the developing ego are associated with pain *(unlust),* become in themselves a source of deprivation rather than of fulfilment and gratification, and are ultimately hated.

The potentiality for loving or hating the self is thus contained in the destiny of the development of the ego functions, which in turn depends on the mother's attitude toward them. When such elemental functions as walking, speaking, feeding oneself, etc. are not permitted to develop normally because of neurotic attitudes of the mother, self-hate and the feeling of powerlessness of the ego appear very early in the life history of the individual. Since the self can no longer be regarded as a source of pleasure, the mother is felt as the only source of pleasure; since the ego is felt as powerless, the mother is experienced as the sole source of survival long after this ceases to be a biologic fact.

The hatred of the self, originating at the earliest level of ego differentiation, and the accompanying feeling of powerlessness become the prototype for later feelings of worthlessness which characterize the moral masochist. These very feelings are used in the service of the ego to protect it from the fear of being abandoned, and to gain for it a fantasied gratification of love. This is the essence of moral masochism as a defense reaction of the ego. Self-devaluation is a decisive characteristic of moral masochism. The psychoanalytic study of its origin and function leads inevitably to a broader understanding of ego psychology, the therapeutic implementation of this understanding to an amelioration of the masochistic reaction.

The analyses of a number of patients have confirmed for me the hypothesis that masochistic self-devaluation originates at the oral level of infantile development, that it is the outcome of traumatic deprivation, that it functions as a defense against experiencing this deprivation with its concomitant anxiety and aggression, and that it is a means of perpetuating whatever bond there is to the mother.

The structure and dynamic of this aspect of masochism as a defense reaction is clearly illustrated in the analysis of a young woman of twenty-five who came into analysis because of an unhappy marriage, sexual frigidity, psychogenic gastric symptoms, and vocational maladjustment. She was an intelligent, gifted young woman who constantly, and with firm conviction, underestimated her own capabilities, and consequently suffered from a chronic inhibition of activities. The same devaluation expressed itself in her conception of her own body. Despite the fact that objectively she was an attractive person, and that her life experience had in innumerable ways and on many occasions proven her attractiveness to men, she regarded herself as being deficient as a woman. In her estimation her body was immature, unwomanly. Unconsciously she perceived the truth about her emotional infantility which she projected onto her body. From the standpoint of her superego, she regarded herself as morally inferior. Actually there was no area of her being which she had not invested with self-depreciation.

It was through the analysis of her social responses that the first understanding of the depth, nature and function of the patient's masochistic reaction was gained. The patient had invited a young couple to live with her and her husband. These people neither shared the expenses, gave their helpful cooperation, nor displayed basically friendly attitudes. The invitation was even more striking in view of the fact that the patient had recently married and had scarcely begun to work out the problems of marital adjustment. She behaved like someone who felt that she was undeserving either or a home or a husband of her own, and rationalized this masochistic attitude in terms of her philosophy of life which demanded that she share everything with others. In spite of her apparent generosity, measured in conscious, rational terms, she constantly berated herself for the least trace of possessiveness, for the slightest insistence on her reasonable rights, and for any unwillingness to inconvenience herself to the utmost for the sake of others. Thus, if she had to study for an examination and was disturbed by the singing or merrymaking of a houseful of guests, she blamed herself for not being able to concentrate despite these distractions—never the inconsiderations of her husband or their friends to take her needs into account. Since this mechanism was so easily rationalized in terms of her ideology, it was at first difficult to show her its neurotic character and to convince her that she had rights as an individual, that she was, in fact, an individual at all.

It soon became clear why she had so weak an ego. Her childhood was spent in a completely symbiotic relationship to her mother. She had been the possession, the extension, the tool of her mother from the beginning of life. A frankly unwanted child, her birth was regarded as the cause of her mother's 'nervous illness' which followed it. For the first four or five months of her life she was turned over to a maternal aunt, who had just had a child of her own, and who in turn handed her over to her husband who operated a small factory. There, bedded in a box amid the noisy clamor of a factory, she spent the earliest months of her infancy. The gratification of only her minimal needs from the beginning imposed on her great frustration and deprivation which appeared in frequent dreams, the content of which was a fear of starving. Always there was some huge, insuperable object which stood between her and the gratification of her hunger. Consciously, too, she experienced fears of starving, especially in adolescence when she made her first tentative attempts to be away from home. These were visits to friends or camping trips which were regularly accompanied by the fear that she would find herself without food or, more accurately, that she would not *be fed*. At that point it was inconceivable to her that she could feed herself, that is, be responsible for getting her own meals.

The passive attitude of the ego as reflected in the wish to be fed was also expressed in the patient's mental activity. Uncertain, unable to make decisions—to be sure of the truth of her own processes of reasoning—she could also never trust the judgment of others. How could she be sure that the ideas 'fed' her by others were true, good. Yet, reflecting her enormous desire to be fed, she was always searching for 'the person' whom she could trust and to whose superior judgment she could submit.

A minor incident accurately illustrates the nature of this submissive masochistic reaction. She entered a dress shop one day to price a dress in the window which had attracted her. The dress had been reduced considerably from its original price because it was somewhat soiled and shopworn. She could not make up her mind and finally decided to see what was available elsewhere. In a second store close by, she came upon an identical dress which she was quite shocked to find cost twenty dollars more than it was priced in the first shop. In the childlike, naïve manner which often characterized her questioning approach to adults, she told the shopkeeper that she had seen the same dress for twenty dollars less in a nearby store and asked him why he charged more. He, feeling accused, became angry and protested that his dress was not identical with the one she had seen elsewhere. In her provocative, compulsive way she insisted on proof of this difference and finally succeeded in annoying the storekeeper to such an extent that he asked her to leave the store, saying he would not sell her the dress if she were willing to pay his price.

At the time of the incident, and even after narrating it in analysis, she was completely unaware of the provocative nature of her behavior; she could not understand why she should not have asked the questions she did, nor could she see why the shopkeeper should have felt threatened, accused or insulted, or why his behavior was a logical outcome of hers. In fact, her reason for reporting the incident was her puzzlement at the frequency with which she precipitated reactions in others that put her in the wrong in their eyes. At home, no matter what she said or did, she was always wrong. Consciously she was aware of an all-consuming desire to prove that she was right—in this instance that the two dresses were identical and that therefore the price should be the same. As we talked, however, it became clear that she wished the burden of proof to be on the shopkeeper: he must either admit that they were the same or prove that his dress was superior. She felt incapable on the basis of her own perception and judgments to decide definitely that the two dresses were alike even though they had identical labels. How could she tell by feeling the material that the cloth was the same quality in both; how could she tell by looking at the workmanship that it was equally good in both? It developed that what she really wished, when she asked the aggressive question about the discrepancy in price, was for the shopkeeper to prove to her the superiority of his garment, to convince her firmly of this fact, so that she could then pay the higher price and get the better dress. However, she clearly did not wish to achieve this through the use of her own critical faculties or her own testing of reality, but rather, as in hypnosis, through the masochistic obedience to the will and judgment of a stronger, superior being. Her questioning was not a provocation of rejection on a libidinal level, as one might think at first. It was a provocation to induce the other individual to prove his superiority, but to give her, at the price of her submission, the libidinal gratification which she wished—in this case, consciously, the better dress— the symbolic significance of which is the love of the good imago. It would seem that the masochistic individual gives up the independent, assertive position of the ego, in extreme cases even to the point of giving up the accurate perception of reality, in order to achieve passive oral gratification, and to retain the illusion of the superiority of the person to whom he submits and from whom he gets this gratification.

The early oral frustrations crippled the budding ego, and left it with a feeling of powerlessness that persisted throughout the patient's life. These primary deprivations were subsequently re-enforced by the nature of the mother's attitude toward the girl during her entire childhood. The mother, overwhelmed by unconscious guilt for her lack of maternal feeling, infantilized and overprotected this daughter at every point, representing this anxious overconcern to the world as mother love and at the same time depriving the child of every opportunity to develop an independent ego. Thus the daughter was literally spoon-fed until she was ten years of age. All active play with children was forbidden lest she be injured. She had no toys whatsoever. One day during her analysis, in describing a recent visit to a family in which there were children whose parents not only gave them toys but shared their play with them and helped them in the mastery of the play material, it became painfully clear to her that no one had ever shared her activities, that a complete separation existed between the world of adults and her own world, and that no opportunities had existed for her to bridge this gap through mutual activities with adults, which might have given her chances for imitation and later for identification.

The deprivations on the oral level were re-enforced by analogous experiences on each subsequent level of libido development. Her adult toilet habits give us a picture of the complete subjugation which she must have experienced as a child. So obedient was she to the will of her mother that throughout her life she had never deviated in the regularity of her excretory habits. She awoke each morning, as a young infant might, with an impatient, demanding hunger, and the need to move her bowels immediately. This was an invariable routine. In fact, she was not only surprised but perturbed by her discovery as an adult that not all people functioned in this manner.

Her first tentative genital strivings suffered the same fate as all other attempts at the expression of any independence. A painful memory, from about the age of four, was of being found masturbating by her mother, who immediately threatened that if she ever did this again, mother would cut off her genitals, frame them, and hang them on the wall for all to see. The child was haunted throughout childhood by a vivid image of her labia, cut off and hung up in a picture frame. Needless to say she never again masturbated. It became clear later in her analysis that her inability to be alone, especially to be without a sexual relationship with a man for even a very short period, was at least in part due to a need to defend herself against the impulse to masturbate, the consequences of which would be as terrible as her mother had predicted.

Only in the intellectual sphere—in her studies at school and of music for

which she had distinct talent—was her development not only encouraged but
demands for superior performance were made upon her, so that even in those
areas, in which her ego seemingly functioned, the activity was not her own
but belonged to her mother, so to speak. The child's achievements served the
narcissistic gratification of the mother, not the ego development and satisfaction of the daughter.

Such a weak ego could survive only in a parasitic relationship to the
mother; it could have no life of its own. To maintain the dependent bond the
mother's basically unloving attitude had to be denied, for the perception of
this reality would mean the emergence of hostile feelings toward the mother
which in turn would mean separation and loss. To avoid separation, therefore, the mother image had to be maintained as good and loving, and all
frustration experienced in the mother relationship was attributed to the worthlessness of the self.

Self-depreciation is characteristic of one type of moral masochism. The
ego image or self-conception is built principally from two sources: first,
through the experiences and awareness of the ego's functioning; second,
through identification with the attitudes and judgments of significant love
objects. To the extent that such identification reflects attitudes, it becomes
ego; to the extent that it reflects judgments, it becomes superego. In this
instance, the masochistic self-conception represents not so much the aggressive, punitive attitude of the superego toward the ego, characteristic of the
compulsion neurosis, but a self-conception derived from the earliest oral
level through the ego's elaboration of the perception and experience of its
own inadequate, if not nonexistent, functioning. This early conception is
then re-enforced by an identification with the mother's attitude toward the
child as weak, helpless, dependent, and by a precipitate in the superego of a
critical attitude toward the ego through identification with whatever were the
mother's strictures in her attitudes toward the child.

The masochistic self-conception can be thought of as a primitive way of
establishing and maintaining an object relationship with a 'good' imago, as
well as of avoiding separation, and therefore as a defense against psychosis
(entire loss of the outside world).

It is significant that this patient throughout her childhood and adolescence
never experienced conscious hostility toward her mother; that although she
could perceive the differences between her own and the upbringing of her
contemporaries, she neither felt nor expressed resentment for the limitations
imposed upon her activities. Only in the course of analysis, as her ego gained

more strength and the nature of the masochistic reaction began to be understood, did she begin to insist on her rights as an individual, to react with appropriate aggression to the aggressions of others, and to refuse to assume responsibility for the projected guilt of others.

The gradual emergence of her ego, with the consequent abatement of the masochistic reaction, brought about radical changes in her marital and in her social relationships. The transference character of her relationship to her husband in terms of her mother relationship became clear to her. Previously she had tended to take full responsibility for any sexual inadequacy in the relationship, failing completely to be aware that her husband had clearly definable disturbances of potency, that he tended to be somewhat depersonalized during the sexual act, and had certain fetishistic tendencies. Whenever he had exhibited interest in other women, it had previously been for her a measure of her own inadequacy, attributable by her to her physical inferiority (her breasts were 'not large enough', her figure 'not curving enough') or a defect of personality, but never to her husband's immaturity. As she began to perceive him more realistically, the tensions in the marital relationship increased, since he was neurotically dependent on her masochistic response, and ultimately the marriage dissolved.

Her social relationships during this period altered similarly as she began to emerge as an independent person and was accordingly free of a phobic reaction to being alone. She had throughout her life been fearful of being alone, and her childhood was a torment whenever her parents left her in the care of someone else.

Prior to the analysis of the character of her relationship to her mother, the patient had acted out this symbiosis, and the accompanying masochistic position of the ego, in practically all other relationships. Had such a symbiosis been established in the transference, the problem of helping this patient to achieve sufficient ego strength to give up the masochistic defense and to attain independence would have been a grave one indeed. Two important factors militated against this eventuality. The first was the patient's tendency to 'act out' her neurotic character traits, a trend which is generally regarded as detrimental to the progress of an analysis. In this and similar cases, however, the fact that so much libido is actively invested, however neurotically, in personal relationships leaves little surplus for the transference. In this respect the analyses of such patients resemble those of children in which the precipitates of the processes of identification are not yet formed, the ego is still incompletely developed, and conflicts are acted out in the child's life rather than as fantasies in the transference. The second important factor in averting the masochistic reaction in the transference is the management of the analytic situation in such a manner as to make it extremely difficult for the patient to create an imago of the analyst that would correspond to the idealized, all-powerful, all-good mother image on which the masochistic ego feeds.[1]

The patient herself expressed an awareness of a new quality in her relationship to the analyst: 'You are the first and only adult', she said, 'toward whom I feel equal'. Although she was adult in years, her world was divided into two antagonistic camps: children and adults. She, of course, always regarded herself as one of the children, 'put-upon' and rendered helpless by the powerful adults. Through an attitude of respect for her personality, an avoidance of any hint of authoritarianism in the analytic procedure, an expressed belief in her potentialities for growth as an independent person, a genuine sympathy for her plight, and a conscious presentation of myself as definitely human and fallible, I was able to create this atmosphere of equality. Thus the analytic relationship had sufficient measure of reality and provided no fertile soil in which the masochistic ego could take root, making a new type of identification with the analyst possible. Such identification with the analyst strengthened the ego, making possible a discontinuance of the old, symbiotic relationship to the mother out of which the masochistic position of the ego had grown.

In the course of analysis she temporarily changed her work and for a time taught young children. She was constantly impressed by the rebelliousness and self-assertiveness of these children, especially as the extent of her own submissiveness and self-abnegation became clearer to her, and she questioned me about the meaning of the complete absence of self-assertion in her own childhood, wondering, again masochistically, if its absence were not an innate deficiency. It seems to me that in the answer to this question lies the special instructiveness of this case for an understanding of the origins of the masochistic defense mechanism. Psychobiologically, except in instances of organic inferiority, the potentiality for the psychological development of the ego and its functioning is inherent, just as are the potentialities for sphincter control, for motility, for speech, etc. However, the normal development of the ego is as directly dependent on getting love from the mother at the earliest infantile level, as is the physical development on getting milk. If mother love on the oral level is absent or insufficient, the individual suffers a psychic trauma which must eventuate in a malformation and malfunction of the ego.

The masochistic reaction is one form of an attempt on the part of the ego to deal with this trauma. It sacrifices itself, that is, its own independent development and the sense of its own worth, to sustain the illusion of mother love —an idealized mother image—without which life itself is impossible. Actually the ego, in its weakness, has little choice and perhaps no alternative reaction. In this patient both the early absence of her mother's love, in the form of actual physical rejection, and the child's subsequent deprivation, in the form of extreme infantilization and overprotection, did not permit the existence of the child as a separate entity. Her ego was thus rendered so weak that separateness from the mother was inconceivable. Therefore the one who held her in bondage had to be conceived of as good, for the awareness of any hostile feelings would have meant a rift between the ego of the mother and that of the child. A child who could not tolerate the absence of her mother even for a few hours had to think of her mother as all-powerful, infallible and just, and to regard all fluctuations in the dispensation of her love as due to her own faults or unworthiness. This absence of the development of a critical faculty in the estimation of others and being compelled to blame herself characterized all her significant relationships with people.

In addition to preserving the idealized mother image—and thereby sustaining the gratification that arises from the symbiotic bond between mother and child and avoiding the fears that would result from separation—the masochistic reaction of the ego serves still another, subtler and perhaps more basic function. The fact that there is a mother image and a masochistic reaction to it means that, despite the symbiotic relationship to the mother, sufficient ego development has taken place in the child to make possible an awareness of its own ego as distinct from that of the mother. Were this not so, were the mother completely incorporated and fused with the ego of the child, we would have a psychotic confusion of identity. By maintaining the good image of the mother on a preambivalent level, the ego of the child, masochistically and at its own expense, tries to establish and maintain a primitive object relationship. In this way the masochistic ego reaction serves as a defense against a psychosis, that is, as a defense against the entire loss of the outside world, since at this level of development the mother represents the total world outside the ego.

The ego's ability to differentiate between itself and the mother in terms of what might be called a 'system of values', namely the aggrandizement of the mother and the debasement of the self which we have called a masochistic defense reaction of the ego, can be thought of as a mechanism of psychological survival. Faced with insufficient love, the ego survives on the illusion of love—the potentiality of which is vested in the mother—and simultaneously accounts for its absence in reality by the conception of its own worthlessness.

NOTE

1. Menaker, Esther: *The Masochistic Factor in the Psychoanalytic Situation. Psychoanalytic Quarterly*, XI, 1942, pp. 171–187.

BIBLIOGRAPHY

1. Bergler, Edmund: *The Basic Neurosis*. New York: Grune & Stratton, Inc., 1949.
2. Berliner, Bernhard: *On Some Psychodynamics of Masochism. Psychoanalytic Quarterly*, XVI, 1947, pp. 459–471.
3. Buehler, Charlotte: *Kindheit und Jugend*. Leipzig: Verlag von S. Hirzel, 1931.
4. Buehler, Karl: *Die geistige Entwicklung des Kindes*. Sixth ed. Jena: Gustav Fischer, 1930.
5. Fenichel, Otto: *The Psychoanalytic Theory of Neurosis*. New York: W. W. Norton & Co., Inc., 1945.
6. Freud, Anna: Indications for Child Analysis. In: *The Psychoanalytic Study of the Child, Vol. I*. New York: International Universities Press, Inc., 1945.
7. Freud: *Beyond the Pleasure Principle*. London: Int. Psa. Press, 1922.
8. ———: *The Economic Problem of Masochism*. Coll. Papers, II.
9. Greenacre, Phyllis: The Biological Economy of Birth. In: *The Psychoanalytic Study of the Child, Vol. I. Loc. cit.*
10. Horney, Karen: *The Neurotic Personality of Our Time*. New York: W. W. Norton & Co., Inc., 1937.
11. Menaker, Esther: *The Masochistic Factor in the Psychoanalytic Situation. Psychoanalytic Quarterly*, XI, 1942, pp. 171–186.
12. Reich, Wilhelm: *Charakteranalyse: Technik und Grundlagen*. Vienna: Published by the author, 1933.
13. Reik, Theodor: *Masochism in Modern Man*. New York: Farrar and Rinehart, 1941.
14. Spitz, René A.: Hospitalism. In: *The Psychoanalytic Study of the Child, Vol. I. Loc. cit.*

11. Outside and Inside, Male and Female

Judith Kestenberg

Both in therapeutic and in character analyses we notice that two themes come into especial prominence and give the analyst an unusual amount of trouble. It soon becomes evident that a general principle is at work here. The two themes are tied to the distinction between the sexes; one is as characteristic of males as the other is of females. In spite of the dissimilarity of their content, there is an obvious correspondence between them. Something which both sexes have in common has been forced, by the difference between the sexes, into different forms of expression. (Freud, S. 1937, p. 250)

We often have the impression that with the wish for a penis and the masculine protest we have penetrated through all the psychological strata and have reached bedrock, and thus our activities are at an end. This is probably true, since, for the psychical field, the biological field does in fact play the part of the underlying bedrock. The repudiation of feminity can be nothing else than a biological fact, a part of the great riddle of sex. It would be hard to say whether and when we have succeeded in mastering this factor in an analytic treatment. We can only console ourselves with the certainty that we have given the person analyzed every possible encouragement to reexamine and alter his attitude to it. (Freud, S., 1937, pp. 252–53)

Ever since Freud tried to unravel the riddle of female sexuality, the interest of psychoanalysts has periodically turned to this subject (Barnett, 1966; Benedek, 1952, 1960; Bonaparte, 1953; Brierley, 1932; Deutsch, 1925, 1944–45; Eissler, 1939; Erikson, 1950; Freud, S., 1905, 1925, 1931, 1933, 1937; Greenacre, 1950; Heiman, 1963; Hitschmann and Bergler, 1934; Horney, 1933; Jacobson, 1936; Jones, 1927; Kestenberg, 1956a; Lampl-de Groot, 1928; Marmor, 1954; Moore, 1964; Müller, 1932). In contrast, Freud's theory of male development has remained essentially unchanged throughout decades of psychoanalytic experience. But the repudiation of femininity,

Adapted with permission from Judith Kestenberg, *Children and Parents: Psychoanalytic Studies in Development* (New York: Jason Aronson, 1975). First published in 1968.

common to both sexes, is still a riddle that poses a challenge to psychoanalysts and biologists.

In trying to do justice to the complexity of factors that cannot be reduced to a simple formula, I shall survey psychoanalytic literature and pertinent data from biology and expand on my own views on female sexuality (Kestenberg, 1956a, 1956b, 1961, 1967a, 1967b, 1968). I shall propose that the universal repudiation of femininity is based on the anxiety-provoking nature of inner-genital sensations, and that, because man can more persistently externalize these sensations, he is less vulnerable than woman to fears of injury and loss of the inside genital.

Using clinical material from the analyses of children and adults, I shall compare the development of inner and outer genitality in women and men, distinguish adult from infantile genitality, and normality from pathology. After surveying similarities and dissimilarities in male and female development, I shall attempt to demonstrate the role of man in helping woman complete her sexual development. Lastly, I shall try to throw some light on the question why psychoanalysis cannot do more to help women achieve vaginal orgastic fulfillment than to restore her awareness of vaginal sensations.

INTRODUCTION

Psychoanalytic and Biological Views on Feminine Functioning

Freud persistently emphasized penis envy as a central feminine complex (Freud, S., 1925, 1931, 1933, 1937, 1940). He held that the vagina was awakened in puberty and not fully libidinized until adult genitality was established through the experience of coitus; the vagina was dormant in childhood and the occurrence of vaginal sensations before puberty was due to early seductions. The young boy, shocked by the discovery of the female opening, not only denied its existence but reinforced this denial by endowing women with a phallus. Beginning with Horney (1933), a great many, especially female analysts, could show that the "denial of the vagina" occurred regularly in feminine development as well, and that hyperchathexis of the clitoris as a small phallus, penis envy, and fantasies about an inner female phallus were all mechanisms that reinforced this denial. There remained the controversy whether or not girls experienced vaginal sensations before puberty, whether they had to transfer their genital interest from the clitoris to the vagina and even had to condemn the clitoris to do so (Bonaparte, 1953).

Freud did acknowledge the role of the clitoris in adult genitality in a poetic reference to it as sparking the fire of the vagina (Freud, S., 1905). In discussing vaginal anesthesia, most analysts felt that the persistence of clitoral sensations was due to the typical feminine castration complex, to penis envy (Hitschmann and Bergler, 1934), and that the cultural suppression of women and the emphasis of phallic supremacy contributed in a great measure to the prevalence of frigidity. H. Deutsch (1925, 1944–45) emphasized the complementary roles of maternality and sexuality and felt that much of feminine genitality was spent in reproductive functioning. Both she and Bonaparte (1953) stressed that feminine masochism led women to endure rather than enjoy coitus and contributed to the pain in reproductive functioning. Freud attributed woman's greater vulnerability to the more complex demands made on her, since she had to transfer her love from the mother to the father and her organ cathexis from the clitoris to the vagina.

Data from biology tended to confirm Freud's view on the role of the vagina in childhood. It is indeed an undeveloped organ in early childhood and its capacity to develop mucosal changes and vascularization is as limited as that of the "steroid-starved" postmenopausal woman (Huffman, 1959; Masters and Johnson, 1966; Kestenberg, 1967b, 1968). In addition, the surface of the vagina has few nerve endings and thus, compared to the clitoris, could not be considered a "live" organ even in adulthood. This view, especially propagated by Kinsey et al. (1953), became very popular and many a knowledgeable man spent time in trying to find the clitoris he was supposed to excite. The controversy became as intense as if there were two warring camps, the pro-vagina and the pro-clitoris factions (Bergler, 1947). Both women and men demanded vaginal orgasm as the ultimate achievement of female sexuality. Analysts stood by helplessly, acknowledging that they had not been too successful in helping patients to achieve vaginal orgasm (Benedek, 1961; Deutsch, 1961; Sherfey, 1966). Much of the hue and cry proved in analysis to be a renewal of the old demand that women should be given a penis, if not an outer one, at least an inner one (Jacobson, 1936; Rado, 1933).

Masters and Johnson's (1965, 1966) new discoveries about female sexuality help to correct the error made by Kinsey and others before him, who confused discriminatory sensibility dependent on somatic nerve endings with visceral sensibility, dependent on: sympathetic and parasympathetic innervations of genital organs; the nerve supply to the unique genital vascular system; and the mixed innervation of striate and nonstriate muscles involved in orgastic experiences. Analysts were aware of this difference just as they were of the fact that feminine functioning depended on a specifically feminine integration rather than on simply quantitative variations in the importance of one organ or another (Barnett, 1966; Benedek, 1952; Bonaparte, 1953; Brierley, 1932, 1936; Deutsch, 1944–45, 1961; Erikson, 1950, 1964; Greenacre, 1950; Harley, 1961; Kestenberg, 1956a, 1961; Moore, 1964; Payne, 1935).

Some analysts singled out orality as essential in feminine integration (Brierley, 1936; Deutsch, 1944–45; Heiman, 1963), but the claim of the latter two that the vagina has a sucking function has not been substantiated by Masters and Johnson (1966). Lorand (1939) and Langer (1951) presented cases of frigidity in which frustrated orality was an important factor. This is a frequent finding of experienced clinicians (Brierley, 1932). It may reflect an increasingly greater role of orality in both sexes rather than a selective influence of orality on vaginal functioning. With bottle feeding replacing breast feeding, the period of sucking has been extended beyond the oral phase. This mixture of deprivation and overindulgence of childhood oral needs has enhanced fixations in the oral phase. The vagina becomes endowed with the qualities of mouth, anus, urethra, baby, and phallus in fantasies derived from successive developmental phases, and individual differences in the importance of these representations stem from the individuality of constitution and early experience. Exaggerated emphasis on any one factor leads to an imbalance in feminine integration (Kestenberg, 1956a, 1961).

Whichever factor is singled out as cause of frigidity, there is a consensus that once denial and repression are removed, vaginal sensations impinge upon woman's awareness with full force. It does not necessarily follow that orgastic discharge will develop automatically.

The Orgastic Discharge

In normal development toward adult femininity, sensations from both clitoris and vagina become more integrated in an overall experience in which the inner genital is dominant (Masters and Johnson, 1966). But the vagina cannot achieve dominance in the same way as the clitoris and phallus. The latter organs can serve as "sensual foci" (Masters and Johnson, 1966) because of their abundant supply of superficial nerve endings. In contrast, visceral genital sensations are characterized by a "spreading" tendency, lack of localization, and refractoriness to verbal description. Diffusion of sensations, anesthesia to outer stimuli, and near or real loss of consciousness (Keiser, 1947, 1952; Masters and Johnson, 1966) involved in the total organismic response during orgasm break down the differentiation between inside and outside, between self and object. It is likely that at the peak of orgasm, both men and women who are not unduly afraid of surrender to primary-process functioning lose the awareness of a sensual focus. Nevertheless, a fundamental difference between the sexes remains: the female's sexual experience is inwardly oriented and is permeated more by purely visceral, inner genital sensations than by sensations from external genitals; the male's sexual experience is outwardly oriented and makes greater use of outer phallic sensations than of the purely visceral, inner genital sensations that initiate ejaculation.

The female orgasm may be felt as initiated by a clitoral sensation which resonates deep vaginal-pelvic feelings or as a diffuse spreading of inner general excitement over the entire genital. This culminates in rhythmic contractions of the "orgastic platform" (Masters and Johnson, 1965, 1966) that evolve from gradually ascending and descending waves of deep sensuous tension in the vagina, and merge with spasms and sensations from all over the body, ending in dimming of consciousness. The male orgasm may be experienced as initiated by the inner pelvic sensations of "ejaculatory inevitability" (Masters and Johnson, 1966), but is quickly transformed into a hypercathexis of the vascular and muscular changes in the phallus that occur during expulsion of the ejaculate. The generalized contractions and the merging of sensations from the whole body are shrouded by a loss of consciousness that is often equated with death—*le petit mort* (Keiser, 1947, 1952). A masterful presentation of fantasies of attack and injury, lust and fear, loss of identity between partners, and loss of distinction between life and death in orgasm is given in Ross's (1968) interpretations of Ahab's struggle with the whale in Melville's *Moby Dick:*

The conflict culminates in a raging orgasm spewing forth "mountain torrents" and leaving as aftermath a "closing vortex . . . subsided into a creamy pool" out of which emerges a "coffin life buoy." It is orgasm yielding death, not life, or, if life, life is the object of death.

When the orgastic experience of partners coincides, boundaries between them break down as their outsides and insides unite, bringing them close to the yearned-for union with the mother or to the archaic image of hermaphroditic symbiosis (Ferenczi, 1924). The dimming of consciousness is akin to primary repression, which helps to repudiate these fantasies when the ego's control reestablishes individual sexual identity. But the state of shock in the woman may be more intense and last longer than in the man, and the loss of body boundaries more readily evokes the image of loss of the sex organ (vagina), which at that moment merges with the self-representation. Not only women but also many men fail to reach such loss of control in orgasm, and even those individuals who can experience it do not do so always. Individual integration of pregenital, inner and outer genital drives under the dominance of a sex-specific zone (outer in the male and inner in the female) does not assure a high degree of orgastic fulfillment. An integrated relationship between love objects, based on mutual trust and predicated on successful identification with a nonincestuous partner, is an important prerequisite, especially for the woman. Furthermore, states of fatigue, anxiety, depressive feelings, and alertness to outer stimuli detract from the intensity of the orgastic experience or prevent its occurrence. Female object relationships and moods are more subject to fluctuation because women are more influenced by hormonal changes than men, more easily lose self-esteem, and more frequently feel a split between feelings for the mate and the children. Man's relationship to young children is more consistently desexualized than that of the woman; he is less tempted to regress to pregenital and early genital phases than is the woman, who is prone to relive the phase of childhood corresponding to the age of the child she is caring for. To be an "ordinary devoted mother" (Winnicott, 1949) she needs to desexualize her genital feelings and externalize her impulses upon her baby.[1] To fill her role as a sexual partner she needs to resexualize her genitals and give up externalization. Man can continue desexualization of his inside genitalia and externalization of inner genital impulses up to the moment of imminent ejaculation. Only for that brief moment does he cope with inner genital sensations and only then must he accept the passivity and helplessness that are brought about by the realization that he is losing control.

Man's adaptive task is easier and less subject to failure than that of woman; he can maintain ego control more consistently and more uniformly than she. His experience with orgastic discharge during masturbation is more successful. But the primary reason for his greater capability in orgastic discharge is his higher differentiation and his correspondingly lesser fear of an irreversible loss of control during orgasm. Nevertheless it is a fallacy to assume that frigidity is so much more frequent than impotence. It is more correct to say that total frigidity and vaginal anesthesia are more frequent than total impotence and failures of erections. Extreme denial of the "inside" makes the man unable to identify with women; it motivates him to seek out phallic women and makes him more prone to perversions based on externalization. Much of the present-day demand for woman's orgasm comes from man's feeling of failure; he feels that her deficiency may be due to his inability to delay ejaculation long enough. But the hyperpotent male, envied for his *ejaculatio retardata* or for his capacity to reinstate erection soon after ejaculation, is as much a victim of defensive externalization and compensatory overcathexis of the external genitals, as is the oversexed woman (Sherfey's [1966] "satiation in insatiation" type). Both are afraid of losing control and facing the sensations that are requisite for sexual fulfillment.

The similarity between the sexes is specific to *Homo sapiens*. It is based on externalization of inner sensations, without which secondary-process thinking and the formation of the human ego could not be achieved. Secondary-process thinking is derived from perceptions that aid localization, discrimination, and orientation in space, time, and in relation to gravity (Kestenberg, 1965); primary-process thinking is closer to visceral and protopathic global sensations. The repudiation of femininity (Freud, S., 1937) common to both sexes stems from the repudiation of the confusing visceral sensations from inside the body. Externalization of sensations from the inside protects the individual from overwhelming floods of excitation leading to regressions and states of shock.

The dissimilarity between the sexes is based on the higher differentiation of the male, leading to the enlargement of the outer genitalia and a greater development of musculature, both of which facilitate externalization and adjustment to reality. The fact that woman's reproductive organs are hidden helps her protect the young, but at the same time makes her more vulnerable to the breakdown of secondary-process thinking. Man, on the other hand, is more vulnerable to physical mishaps; engaged as he is in coping with the forces of nature and combating other males, he must remain aware of the danger to his exposed outer genitals.

Inner and Outer Genitality

Analysis of children and adults reveals that the outer and inner parts of the genitals play different roles in different developmental stages, that fantasies reinforce or diminish the cathexis of one or another genital zone, and that a transfer from inside to outside and vice versa occurs repeatedly. This two-way traffic between external and pelvic organs is not easily accessible to conscious awareness because its main connections are conducted by autonomic nerves:

In the male, the extensions from the prostatic plexus reach the erectile tissues of the penis, and in the female similar nerves proceed to the clitoris from the vaginal plexus. It is suggested that the pudental nerve also carries autonomic fibres, both sympathetic and parasympathetic, to the penis or clitoris. (Cunningham, 1964, p. 780)

Throughout development there is a trend toward externalization of inner sensations which reaches its peak before sexual differentiation is accomplished. Puberty brings about a reversal in this trend in both sexes, but the cathexis of the inside genital plays a role in woman different from that in man. That woman's identity is based on her inner genital core is best expressed by Erikson (1964):

When we speak of biologically given strengths and weaknesses in the human female, we may yet have to accept as one measure of all difference the biological rockbottom of sexual differentiation. In this, the woman's productive inner space may well remain the principal criterion whether she chooses to build her life partially or wholly around it or not (p. 598) . . . in women the basic schema exists within a *total optimum configuration* such as cultures have every reason to nurture in the majority of women, and this for the sake of collective survival as well as individual fulfillment. (p. 599)

How this total configuration is achieved in development, and where fixations and distortions interfere, can best be shown through examples from literature and analytic practice. A presentation of the development of attitudes toward outside and inside in children, women, and men will serve to highlight sources of the repudiation of femininity.

INSIDE AND OUTSIDE IN FEMALE DEVELOPMENT

Infantile Genitality

Adult human genitality differs greatly from that of other mammals who respond only during estrus. Estral genitality is indiscriminate; any male will do. It is insatiable for the duration of the estrus. The engorgement of the sex skin of female animals persists after coitus, and full resolution of engorgement occurs only after the estrus. Some primate females solicit in a manner reminiscent of human prostitutes. They are "hypersexed" and demand repeated service from the male. Aberrant human genitality, because of its infantile traits, may retain traces of behavior of ancestral adults (Bradley, 1961).

The human female before puberty is safeguarded against indiscriminate genital activity by the concealed location of the vagina, its inanimate quality, the hymen that "locks the door," and the low hormonal supply in childhood, which keeps the vaginal mucosa as thin and bloodless as that of an aging female (Huffman, 1959; Masters and Johnson, 1966). However, the undeveloped genitals of the girl before puberty are as susceptible to sexual excitation as the target organs of the aging female (Masters and Johnson, 1966). When seduced, she may develop orgasms (Kramer, 1954). Under ordinary circumstances, maternal care brings about direct and indirect stimulation not only to the outside but to the inside genitals as well (as, for instance, through bath water). It is the task of the mother to stimulate and prime all bodily functions. Enough genital stimulation is provided during child care that, coupled with excitations triggered by small doses of hormones and those arising from pressure by adjoining organs, the genitals are prepared well enough for their use in adult genital behavior at the onset of sexual maturity.

Kittens and puppies that have not been licked by their mother in the appropriate zones will neither defecate nor urinate (Beach and Ford, 1952). Harlow's primates, raised by an artificial mother and isolated from playmates, did not know how to copulate or nurture their young (Harlow, 1965). Domesticated animals often require assistance from the breeder to perform coitus. Animals raised in zoos, deprived of the opportunity to observe adult mating (primal-scene deprivation), have to be taught how to copulate when they mature, but the vagina can be reawakened in maturity without exposure to mating behavior, as exemplified in the behavior of a young zoo primate who introduced twigs into her vagina, even though she did not know how to act in mating (Hediger, 1965). Conversely, in cases of congenital atresia of the vagina, the artificial vagina requires a great deal of priming before it becomes functional (Kaplan, 1963; Masters and Johnson, 1966). In normal development, maternal and hormonal priming of the vagina in childhood is reinforced in adulthood by successful coital techniques. These need to be taught in cultures characterized by "primal-scene deprivation."

Direct stimulation of the vagina during child care is minimal, but excitations of the external genitals spread to the inner genitals via nervous and vascular connections; in addition, nonstriate muscles of inner organs contract simultaneously with striate perineal muscles (Kinsey et al., 1953). Inner and outer genitals are also supplied with connections to other parts of the body, which participate in sexual excitement from early childhood (Cunningham, 1964).

Modes of Genital Excitation in Childhood

Children usually do not masturbate to the point of orgasm, comparable to adult acme. Genital pleasure often occurs as a by-product of exploration or manipulation, designed to reaffirm the persisting presence of the organ. Lack of sensations makes the child fearful that the valuable organ is lost or changed.

Direct observation of masturbatory practices suggests that much of infantile genital handling is performed with rhythms that only rarely lead to orgasm comparable to that of an adult.

Light tapping or pulling of the genitals has the character of an "oral" rhythm; playful tensing and releasing of perineal muscles evokes genital pleasure, associated with rhythmic sphincter contractions; prolonged contractions culminating in an explosive release may simulate orgasm, but this terns out to be an anal-sadistic type of discharge associated with holding and explosive discharge of feces; a passive surrender to dribbles of excitation is urethral in nature; a series of interruptions and cessations of contractions in which the control of continuity and discontinuity is the main source of pleasure is a urethral-sadistic discharge form (Kestenberg, 1965, 1967a). An "inner-genital" rhythm of discharge, I believe, is characteristic for children between two-and-a-half and four years of age. It can be discerned in wavelike and spreading movement of thighs or pelvis. The tension is low, it rises and falls gradually, and the rhythmic contractions are kept up for a long time. Sometimes it can be seen in slight pelvic writhing, reminiscent of the irregular rhythmic changes seen by Masters and Johnson (1966) in the expanding upper portion of the vagina of the adult woman.[2] In contrast, masturbation in the phallic phase is concentrated rather than spreading; it ends quickly, but is repeated quite often (Kestenberg, 1965, 1967a).

In latency, masturbation is either concealed or disguised and not accessible to direct observation. One can find its derivatives in latency stories which graphically represent the rhythmic inner genital discharge which is interspersed and coordinated with sudden spurts of activity derived from clitoral impulses. Direct communication about vaginal sensations and impulses occurs more frequently in prepuberty, but the "silent" organ of the latency girl is symbolized in accounts of dolls who are alive only when no one looks (Burnett, 1898). Of special import are the recurrent sudden initiations and cessations of all activity when the child pays attention to the doll. Both initiations and cessations seem to be derived from clitoral discharge forms that spark the "gentle fire" of the child's vaginal excitement or take over when the vagina yields to the clitoris, which acts as its resonance organ (Weiss, 1962).

Derivatives of Genital Discharge Forms Illustrated by the Theme in Children's Literature

The following excerpts from a popular story for girls illustrates the nature of the genital excitation processes which underlie fantasies of girls in latency and in transition to adolescence (Burnett, 1898). To distinguish between quotations from the story of nine-year-old Sara and my own comments, the latter will be bracketed.

> *The Vanishing Doll.* "What I believe about dolls," she said, "is that they can do things they will not let us know about. Perhaps Emily [the doll] can read, talk and walk, but she will only do it when people are out of the room. That is her secret."
>
> [As we shall see, Magda, whose case is presented later, complained that there was nothing in the vagina even though there was activity in it when she masturbated externally. Similarly, women who masturbate externally and do not allow themselves to acknowledge the activity "inside the room," even during coitus, are not aware of vaginal activity, whose existence during external genital excitation has been clearly established by Masters and Johnson.]
>
> "You see [Sara continued], if people knew that dolls could do things, they would make them work. So, perhaps they have promised each other to keep it a secret. If you stay in the room, Emily will just sit there and stare; but if you go out, she will begin to read perhaps or go and look out of the window. Then if she heard either of us coming, she would just run back and jump into her chair and pretend she had been there all the time."
>
> [In this passage we may recognize the well-known fear that once the vagina is discovered, its denial undone, and its representation freed from repression, it may be prematurely "put to work" by the adult seducer. "Looking out of the window" as if yearning to go outside may be taken

as an invitation to come in, which stimulates the child to "open the door" and engage in sex play with a friend.]

"Let us go very quietly to the door" she whispered, "and then I will open the door quite suddenly; perhaps we may catch her."

She was half-laughing, but there was a touch of mysterious hope in her eyes which fascinated Ermengarde [the girl friend], though she had not the remotest idea what it meant, or whom it was she wanted to "catch," or why she wanted to catch her.

[We see here an instance of denial and virginal innocence of the seduced which, in the next passage, is followed by a gradual building up of anticipatory excitement, characteristic of sensations in the labia minora and the introitus. An influx of a clitoral type of discharge initiates the entrance into the "room."]

Whatsoever she meant, Ermengarde was sure it was something delightfully exciting. So, quite thrilled with expectation, she followed her on tiptoe along the passage. They made not the least noise until they reached the door. Then Sara suddenly turned the handle, and threw the door wide open.

[We are reminded here of the widening of the vagina in response to stimulation, characteristic of the stage of excitation in adult women. But, as is often the case when adult women retain features of infantile genitality, the "gentle fire" of the vagina does not make up for the disappointment experienced when the budding awareness of its activity suddenly ceases, to be replaced by clitoral sensations.]

Its opening revealed the room quite neat and quiet, a fire gently burning in the grate, and a wonderful doll sitting in a chair by it, apparently reading a book.

"Oh, she got back to her seat before we could see her!" Sara exclaimed. "Of course, they always do. They are as quick as lightening." [This seems to symbolize the suddenness with which vaginal sensations can disappear when transferred to the clitoris.]

The Last Doll. In prepuberty, pregenital, early vaginal, and phallic discharge forms are gradually reorganized under the primacy of a more mature form of genitality. The hormonal influx and the growth of innergenital structures begun in latency (Freud, S., 1905) bring on spurts of inside excitement, which contrast with the gentler activity of the vagina characteristic of latency. As early genital discharge forms become incorporated into phases of the menstrual cycle, initiated by the irregular influx of hormones in prepuberty, the girl retains a "respect" and a liking for the doll that helped her to desexualize cryptic vaginal excitations. Her early experiences with switching genital excitement on and off, in which the clitoris acts as a trigger and a shut-off valve, with fantasies of the live doll (sexualization of the vagina) and the quietly reading doll (desexualization of the vagina), prepare her not only for the impatient waiting in puberty, but also for adulthood, when she must alternate between sexualization of the vagina in coitus and its desexualization during the care of children and home. The last doll often signifies a turning point in the girl's life, a landmark that separates childhood sexuality from growing up to adult womanhood.

[In thanking her father for the last doll he gave her, Sara conveyed to him what it meant to be eleven:] "I am getting too old" she wrote, "you see, I shall never live to have another doll given to me. This will be my last doll. There is something solemn about it. . . . No one can take Emily's place. But I should respect the last doll very much, and I am sure the school would love it. They all like dolls, though some of the big ones —the almost fifteen ones—pretend they are too grown up."

The Lost Doll. The detachment from the doll in prepuberty is preceded by several phases in which the girl's experiences with the loss and the recovery of a loved doll symbolize her struggles with the loss and recovery of the inner genital impulses which she had externalized upon the doll. A whole series of girls' stories deals with a long-lost doll that is found again (Gates, 1905; Lownsberry, 1956; McGinley, 1950). These show the despair of the child and the joy of finding what was once hers. Nothing comparable can be found in boys' literature. One may think that the "lost doll" represents the penis and in some passages of some stories it does. But this typically feminine theme relates to the loss and recovery of inner genital sensations.

In analysis, the recovery of memories about childhood dolls often precedes the recovery of vaginal sensations. It is then that one can see how diffuse inner sensations evoke a yearning for a focus that was once found in the "mothering" of dolls. The loss of the doll represents the loss of the inner genital. Vaginal sensations shift to the clitoris in an incomplete externalization that makes it possible for the patient to experience a sensual focus on an external part of the genital rather than on an external object. But the dominance of the clitoris also implies a loss of the vagina as an organ. Lost and recovered in the working through of repeated repudiations and reacceptances of femininity, vaginal sensations eventually unite and coordinate with sensations from the introitus, the labia, the prepuce, and the clitoris.

Most dramatic is the feeling of loss at the end of the early maternal (inner-genital) phase at the age of four. In repudiating her femininity the girl denies the existence of her introitus and recognizes with sorrow that the "live doll" she had treated like a real baby is only an inanimate object (Kestenberg, 1956a, 1956b). She transfers all feelings to the clitoris which, in the phallic phase, becomes hypercathected at the expense of inner genital sensations. In oedipal games, the girl plays house with dolls, girls and boys, acknowledging that babies need not only a mother but a father too. With her turning to her father, and her fantasies of being penetrated and delivering a baby, she comes very close to the recovery of vaginal sensations. But the denial of the vagina persists, and the reawakening of vaginal sensations is counteracted by the repression that ushers in latency. In latency, genital feelings from inside and outside are expressed in drive-derivative fantasies, games, and stories. In prepuberty the onrush of genital feelings calls for a renewed repudiation of the inside and once more the child gives up the doll. The theme of the lost and recovered doll in stories comes to an end; prepuberty stories shift from the loss of the doll to the loss and recovery of friendships. The cherished doll is replaced by the cherished girl friend.

Clashes Between Inside and Outside: Case Reports

The three-year-old integrates her pregenital and early genital urges before she can externalize her inner sensations upon the clitoris. This "inner-genital" phase is revived in prepuberty. The return of the vaginal cathexis, which had been shifted to the clitoris, breasts, and other external parts of the body, ushers in periodic variations in the ratio of inside and outside genital excitations in various phases of the menstrual cycle. Adolescent genitality emerges from the integration of regressive pregenital, early genital, and new forms of sexuality. At the end of adolescence another phase of integration precedes the emergence of adult genitality (Kestenberg, 1961).

Examples from analyses in phases of transition from pregenitality to phallicity, from latency to adolescence, and from adolescence to adulthood will best illustrate the developmental crises which, though exaggerated and distorted by pathology, can give us insight into the struggles between inside and outside, between the acceptance and rejection of femininity that precede feminine integration in normal development.

Transition from Pregenitality to Phallicity

"My vagina hurts"

Gigi's case illustrates how excessive genital excitations in early childhood prevent externalization on substitute objects, interfere with the integration of pregenital, inner-genital, and phallic drive components, and produce an excitability comparable to that of adult women who are never satisfied.

Gigi was a delicate four-year-old girl who took on a witchlike quality when she quarreled, whined, and clung to her mother. Although very bright, Gigi had difficulties taming her pregenital drives. She was neither completely weaned nor trained before the age of three and a half. She demanded special foods and screamed to get what she wanted. She was a nail biter and also bit the inside of her mouth. She threw things around in a provocative way and staged temper tantrums. Gigi dealt with genitality directly and indirectly. She pulled her brother's penis and referred to the time "when I will be a man." At the same time she like to twirl like a ballerina and would amuse herself stuffing little things in her purse, but she never really enjoyed doll play for any length of time. She masturbated externally and vaginally, but also anally. During the day she seemed beset by divergent urges which interfered with her adjustment to reality. At night the focus of her distress was clearly centered on genital irritations. She would wake up and complain: "My vagina hurts."[3] She would be bathed in the middle of the night or else an ointment would be applied, outside and in the vagina, to alleviate the irritation that was due to congestion and aggravated by scratching and rubbing.

Gigi was beset by clashing pregenital, inner-genital, and outer-genital urges. Unable to bring order into this avalanche of confusing excitations, she repeatedly demanded relief from her mother. It was hard to know in advance when she would become excited, and it was not possible to help her when she attached the causes for her frustration to insignificant events of everyday life that could not be helped. When I suggested to her that she clung to her mother and pulled on her because she could not by herself alleviate what bothered her, she released her mother and proceeded to watch me for signs of excitement. She demonstrated to me dramatically that she expected me to get excited, which would take the excitement away from her. She tore up paper in tiny little strips and threw them all over the floor, all along looking up at me to see how I reacted. Turning from passivity to activity, she indicated that she would not pick anything up from the floor because she did not want to do it. This defensive anal-sadistic pattern was also used to express the wish to eject all the clashing stimuli from her body and transfer them outside. Everything was in pieces, beyond relief, and it was up to the adult to restore harmony in her body and mind by picking up the scattered fragments.

It was striking that Gigi seldom used play and toys to externalize inner-genital impulses, as children between three and four usually do. Because she used the genitals and pregenital zones as avenues of genital discharge, she was not able to desexualize any of her bodily functions. My first task was to eliminate current sources of genital excitement, which prevented externalization and interfered with the organizing forces that would enhance a transition into the phallic stage. Only after this was accomplished was I able to assist her in the process of the integration she herself was striving to achieve, as if driven by progressive developmental forces (Freud, A., 1965).

Among past sources of excitation was a fungus infection at the age of sixteen months which involved the genitals and the perianal area; recurrent sources of irritation were pinworms and very sensitive mucous membranes. By the institution of proper medication Gigi's current genital distress was removed. When she calmed down, she became creative, could tell stories and draw, play with dolls and doctor sets, and thus become both analyzable and acceptable to her mother and playmates. This also helped her to renounce an imaginary companion, an alter ego who was responsible for all her misdeeds. She became maternal rather than ferociously jealous and destructive to her baby sister.

Instead of dealing with the inside genital directly, Gigi now produced memories of her third year of life, when she was frightened by workmen in her home who made windows and doors where none had existed before. The alteration of the house served to symbolize Gigi's discovery of her introitus, which had prevented externalization on dolls, initiated intense penis envy and a depression. The mother had mistakenly interpreted Gigi's preoccupation with her vagina as due to a congenital absence of a hymen and, I suspect, was as distressed as Gigi when the walls of her house were taken down and gaping holes were exposed to view. With the working through of these and other memories and fantasies, Gigi's depression lifted and she was dismissed from treatment as she was entering the phallic-oedipal phase with a more successful denial of the introitus than she was able to achieve by herself.

Since describing the maternal preoccupation of the girl between two and four, I have come to realize that the maternal play with dolls, in identification with the active mother, is only one of the manifestations of externalization, typical for that stage. Externalization on substitute objects serves the integration of pregenital, inner-genital, and phallic drives before a focused phallicity can be established as a safeguard against the intrusion of inner-genital sensations during the oedipal phase. Passive wishes to be penetrated and given a penis or a child are projected upon men before the repression of oedipal fantasies reinforces the denial of the vagina with the beginning of latency. But throughout these phases, the doll continues to be used as a preferred object on which inner-genital sensations can be externalized. When, toward the end of latency and in prepuberty, forbidden fantasies and impulses are lifted from repression, externalization once more becomes the principal mechanism by which reintegration of various drive components can be established. Prepuberty reorganization is least disturbed when previous attempts at externalization can be used as models for its more mature forms. Analysis of prepuberty fantasies often leads to the recovery of memories from the "inner-genital" phase between two and a half and four (Kestenberg, 1966). In cases where earlier attempts at externalization were not satisfactory, the child must struggle with inner-genital strivings in latency.

Transition from Latency to Adolescence

"Sit" in the "upstairs room"

The account of Magda's analysis covers the period between the end of the latency at nine through her early teens. Magda was an underachiever in school, did not get along with peers, and was persistently quarrelsome and excited at home. In the beginning, her analysis focused on her relationship to her parents, especially her mother, to the analyst, and to her girl friend, all of whom made her feel dissatisfied and frustrated. The solution to all her troubles, she felt, was either a large live horse (Freud, A., 1965) or a hobbyhorse. This wish was connected with the feelings she had had as a child of about three when her father gave her piggyback rides and let her swing on his leg. Some of her current play with the girl friend, which always culminated in quarrels, was of a similar nature.

Magda's overwhelming excitement, unrelieved by masturbation, resembled that of Gigi, but was even more intense and spreading. It was contagious and disturbing to the environment. She herself could not tolerate her own disorganizing excitement and tried to discharge it by oral, anal, urethral, and clitoral routes, by nagging, sadistic attacks and masochistic surrender, by passing on her excitement to others, and by projecting all blame. As prepubertal changes occurred, she became at once more excited, more diffuse and disorganized. But she herself began to want to be better organized and could focus more clearly on the source of her excitement. She discovered that her excitement was "inside," and named it "Sit" in continuation of her fantasy of an illusory penis, of her need to blame all genital feelings on men, and in acknowledgment that her "inside" was foreign and frightening. "Sit" was a cripple who tortured and pursued her relentlessly. He tried to entice her to enter the "upstairs room"; he forced her to trap women to enter and be trapped there with him. He was very much afraid of me, the analyst, lest I catch him, take him out of hiding and cure him of his lameness. On one level he was an imperfect penis, unsatisfactory to women; on another level he represented inner-genital excitement, which Magda tried to "lame" for fear that it might go away and be lost. "Sit" also unified pregenital, inner-genital, and phallic urges, as he directed everything in the inside and outside of her body. Magda could not manage without his advice. In a way, he acted like a husband or father, cruel to be sure, but powerful and self-assertive. He enslaved Magda, swallowed people she liked, and made them do anything "he" pleased.

While "Sit" concealed from me what was going on inside, Magda was better able to describe what she experienced on the outside of her genitals. She would shift her excitement further and further away from the introitus, upward and laterally and to a special focused point on the side of the clitoris where she could reach orgasm (see similar descriptions in Masters and Johnson, 1966). She called her clitoris "skin and bones," which probably referred to the foreskin and to the pressure she exerted on the pubic bone when she tried to reach the retracted clitoris (Masters and Johnson, 1966; Sherfey, 1966). Whenever she hurt herself or feared to do so, she shifted her manipulations lower down "to give the skin and bone rest," perhaps to lure it out from concealment. "Sit" was an occupant of the "inside" and there was no link between him and the clitoris. But her clitoral and labial masturbation fantasies were masochistic, about men who enslaved and tortured her, much as "Sit" did from inside.

When Magda demonstrated her image of her anatomy in a drawing, I helped her understand that her inside was structured and contained useful organs. She blamed me for her attempts to explore her inside and denied any "good feelings" there, but said she was playing "that I am getting a baby and it's coming out." Playing delivery, she succeeded in externalizing and desexualizing her vaginal excitement. But she complained that she could not penetrate very far, and once more she blamed it on "Sit": "He wants to stay there, he does not want the box in which he hides to be broken." She became sulky and responded to my remark that there was a door to the inside by telling me she did not want any Christmas present from me. Her wish for a penis became intensified as she refused to accept the "door" that would not open widely enough to admit her to the depth of the "box." She said sadly: "But when you put the tip of your finger there, there is nothing." She could not see how excitement could come from "nothing at all." When I told her that the inside had walls as she knew from her own drawings, she acknowledged that she knew she could control it by movements that made it tighter or wider. Through the puppets with which she played during these discussions, she made clear that rubbing the clitoris produced movement inside and vice versa, something inside made the clitoris move. "Look, look," she said with amazement, recognition, and exhilaration, "you don't even touch the tip of his nose, you must move your hand inside his neck and the nose moves. If you take his mane off, he will be a lioness. Look, look you can make his ears move and you don't even touch them." I agreed that unseen feelings and movements from inside influenced all parts of outer genitals. Yet she was still distressed by her inability to experience the vagina as an active, outer organ she could touch and feel. She demanded and received the "last doll," but rejected one as too small: "But that will be nothing at all, I need a babysize doll which I can hold in my arms like a real baby." Sewing clothes for the doll, she worked through her worries about the size of the vagina, about its expansion and contraction. After entering puberty she ceased to masturbate, became calmer, and began to feel very intensely about boys whom she dated.

In the transition from adolescence to adulthood the young girl reexperiences more intensely the feelings, familiar to her from the later oedipal phase, that her sexual needs cannot be satisfied without the help of a man as guide and unifier of outside and inside genitality. Excerpts from the analysis of an eighteen-year-old girl show her struggles with the acceptance of her femininity, struggles that were greatly intensified because earlier attempts to integrate inner-genital impulses with more focused external sensations had failed. To alleviate her tensions she manipulated men rather than allowing them to teach her.

Transition from Adolescence to Adulthood

"I wish I were a doll"

Fern never masturbated by herself. Instead she quarreled with boyfriends and ended the mounting excitement by allowing them to masturbate her. She limited their manipulations to genital zones furthest removed from the vagina. When a boy put his finger inside it, she became irritable and stopped him abruptly for fear that he would hurt her. She admitted sheepishly that boys had hurt her by rubbing the clitoris too violently, but that had not deterred her from sex play. She would prefer to have no genitals at all. "I wish I were a doll," she said repeatedly.

Fern insisted that she never wanted a penis, because its possession would bring even more trouble. She had masturbated boys and seemed to know that they were troubled too. When separated from a boyfriend for a short time, she began to masturbate on her own and achieved orgasm on the clitoris but claimed that there was no feeling in the vagina. With the vagina she maintained a continuous warfare. Every exercise, she believed, affected her hymen so that it eventually became all used up. Each time she had to remove a tampon, her vagina stubbornly refused to cooperate; it would not open on command and she had to use force. She tolerated the liquid menstrual blood, but the brown particles were "awful" and proof of being used up inside. Her vagina was always leaking somehow, spilling brown secretions when she "forgot" to remove the tampon, secreting a whitish discharge when she was not menstruating. Thus it was slowly approaching the state of nothingness which Fern yearned for and dreaded (Jones, 1927). She wanted relief from inner tensions, but was afraid that the loss of excitement would indicate the loss of her "inside." She maintained her excitement as if it were a precious possession she might lose if it slipped out of sight. She habitually lost articles of clothing, parcels, and handbags. She felt that she could not find them herself and waited until someone returned them. She demanded detailed and clear instructions as to how to go about the search. She never knew exactly what was in the parcel or bag she had lost. She gave few clues, but was never satisfied with any suggestions given. She constantly demanded directions and explanations and then refused to understand what she was told.

Although she was fully enlightened and knew anatomy, Fern felt that her ovary floated freely in the abdomen and there was no opening to the uterus. She closed up her uterus from above and her vagina from below to protect them from being used up or swelling into an unhealthy growth.

After an interpretation of the way she blamed men for everything she dreaded, she accused me of forbidding her the "use" of men to free herself from uncomfortable feelings. She now had to face what was going on inside of her. She became aware that her genitals were exciting her and the excitement spread all over her body, making her so irritable that she had to get rid of the feeling immediately. Her hostility to her own inner genital tension also became apparent to her. She quarreled with it and treated it as an adversary who would overwhelm her if she did not get rid of "him" first.[4] She yearned for a boy who would direct her, take responsibility for everything, and restore her balance. She began to realize that the boyfriend could not really do what she expected because she prescribed what he was to do and never really yielded control. She had to accept her vagina with all its qualities before she could allow a male to teach her how to use it.

All three of these patients had a trait that accounted for their dissatisfaction and their need for treatment: they were unteachable. It was the task of analysis to restore psychic balance so that they could function appropriately, in keeping with their developmental phases. Whether they would continue to develop their potentials depended in good measure on environmental forces to stimulate growth, hinder regression, and assist progressive reintegration toward adult functioning.

Pseudoadult and Adult Feminity Distinguished

With children, the role of the teacher and guide must be assumed by the parents; young adult women transfer their dependence on the parent to their new love objects, who become their teachers. Women who are teachable, but unsuccessful in meeting and attracting men able to teach and assume dominance in a relationship, frequently adapt to the habits, neurotic attitudes, and unconscious fantasies of the men they do find. Treatment of the husband may produce striking improvement in the wife. Conversely, overzealous men may chose doll-like infantile women, whose readily awakened sexuality appears to be very promising and satisfying until they realize that they are dealing with "playthings" rather than with teachable adults.

A case of a twenty-three-year-old woman will illustrate a pseudoacceptance of feminity, in which multiple orgasms stimulated maturity but betrayed their source from infantile sexuality, nor easily convertible into adult form.[5]

Multiple Orgasms

"We giggled a lot in bed"

Peg failed in everything she undertook, except in sex, which she professed to enjoy very much. She would always manage to lose the man who satisfied her and loved her. Yearning for children, she had to undergo an abortion and expended her maternal feelings in playing with dogs and watching horses she was "crazy about." She failed in her career despite great talent. Depressed, harassed, and forever badly treated by men, she failed even in a suicide attempt. After that she longed to sleep all day and have fun all night. The last of her lovers was an older, experienced man who seriously considered marrying her. But she clung to him so tenaciously that she exhausted his patience. She called him day and night demanding that he tell her where he was every minute. She felt well only when he embraced her and told her that she was a "good girl," not a tramp. Their relationship was so good, she said, that she could not understand why he would not marry her. He finally gave up explaining, saying that she ought to go to a psychiatrist. It seemed obvious that he loved her as a father might love a little girl but could not succeed in educating her to play the role of a grown woman, fit to be his wife.

When I asked how she felt about sex relations, she begged me not to tell her mother. With glee she reported that she had not only one orgasm but several during one coitus. She could not tell exactly where they were focused, but the implication was clear that her vagina played a role in the experience. Her face lit up and her depression lifted when she explained to me, as if in answer to my question about orgasms, that they giggled a lot in bed and rolled around, even fell on the floor. The playful nature of her multiple orgasms, which reflected her immaturity, attracted men who wanted to protect her and help her grow up. She made them feel powerful and her enjoyment of sex gratified them, but none of her suitors could really gratify the infantile needs which she presented under the guise of adult femininity.

All patients described here felt mistreated and frustrated; all went through life martyred, unsuccessful in play and work, crying, excited, argumentative or depressed, driven, illogical, puzzles to their environment, and happy only when they could maneuver others into alleviating their excitement. In many ways their feelings were identical with those described in premenstrual distress, but their states were chronic. What I have described comes close to a caricature of woman as she appears in popular belief, cartoons, and jokes.[6] One can readily classify this syndrome as "satiation in insatiation" which, Sherfey (1966) postulates, is the prototype of womanhood. Every analyst is familiar with the complaints of dissatisfied women as well as with their nagging of husbands and children. There is usually some foundation for the complaints but they are aggrandized out of proportion to the misdeed, and the role of the patient in provoking others is obscured. These patients take a long time before they can realize that they externalize their need to control genital impulses and project the blame upon others. Quite often, penis envy and competition with men appear to be at the center of the dissatisfaction, but the analysis of the determinants of penis envy brings on manifestations of oral, anal, and urethral fantasies. A lack of integration between pregenital and genital drives becomes apparent, and attempts to discharge vaginal tensions through pregenital and phallic channels become especially noticeable in premenstrual phases. Diffusion of thought processes, physical discomfort, and states of psychic disequilibrium become intensified, and there is corresponding urgency to find a focal form of discharge to escape the feeling of dissolution and annihilation of ego boundaries (Jones, 1927; Keiser, 1952; Lorand, 1939). Analysis of this typically feminine fear reveals *woman's dread of losing the "'inside genital"'—the core of the feminine body ego.*

Acceptance of the vagina as a source of pleasure without fear is an important, but not the only, factor in adult feminine integration. Throughout development, the girl goes through phases of sexualization and desexualization of the vagina, of transfers of cathexis from inside to outside or vice versa. These all converge in a unified image of external and internal genitals, in which parts of the genitals function in specific ways but in consonance with each other. Moreover, some parts become more dominant in sexual functions and others in reproductive functions. The more proximal, the more internal the organ, the more it serves reproductive functions and the more removed it is from sensuous awareness (ovaries, tubes). The more distal the genital organ, the more it serves as a "sensual focus," a "receptor," a "transformer" (Masters and Johnson, 1966) of vectors of genital discharge, a resonance organ (Weiss, 1962) of deep inner sensations, and the more removed it is from reproductive functioning (clitoris). The introitus, the labia, the distal and proximal portions of the vagina and the uterus partici- pate, to varying degrees, in sexual discharge and reproduction. The vagina, as a middle organ with qualities of expansion and shrinking, and a readiness to be desexualized when it serves expulsion and to be sexualized when it serves reception, is uniquely and sensitively calibrated to shift from external- ization to internalization and vice versa. The many transfers from inside to outside and outside to inside, which development provides before the vagina can assume its dual function in sexuality and reproduction, serve as prepara- tions for optimal functioning. The transfer from the clitoris to the vagina in adolescence is only one instance of many similar earlier and later transfers. An adult woman must be able to desexualize her total genitals and to externalize her sexual impulses in adaptive and sublimatory activities. In optimal functioning, she becomes capable of resexualizing the genitalia under conditions of effective and undisturbed stimulation, which promotes an inte- grated unification of all portions of her genitalia. In order to achieve an adult feminine orgastic discharge, woman is just as dependent on man's perfor- mance as teacher and organizer of her sexuality as she is dependent on his performance as effective intruder into her body and giver of semen. This double dependence is anticipated in development in the many phases in which a girl yearns for an outside agent to relieve her genital tensions and to bring on an effective discharge.

The frequency of vaginal frigidity, statistically significant as it may be (Benedek, 1961; Deutsch, 1961; Kinsey et al., 1953; Marmor, 1954; Moore, 1964), is a by-product of this organ's sensitive calibration and a by-product of its dependency on the man as organizer. The causes of frigidity range widely between phase-specific disturbances of the development of vaginal calibration and failures of men to act as final organizers of feminine sexu- ality.

PATHOLOGY AND NORMALITY IN WOMEN

Since the vagina's existence as an organ can be established only in states of sexual excitement, woman's feelings range from an overwhelming dread of loss to confident expectation that the "absent" organ will eventually return. Defense mechanisms, originated in childhood to counteract the fear of inner-genital excitation and of disintegration of the body ego, are perpetuated in adulthood in various forms of feminine pathology:

1. *Regressive shift of cathexis* from the genitals to pregenital zones which may lead to somatization, persistence of infantile habits, and poor control over bodily functions. The genital itself may function as a zone of discharge for regressive pregenital discharge forms that invade genital functioning, as seen in pseudogenital multiple orgasms, vaginismus, profuse spontaneous lubrication, and spontaneous orgasm akin to spontaneous emissions (wet dreams) of immature men.

2. *Passing on excitement* to others by "contagion" or provocation leads to its perpetuation. Excitement is treated like an object that can be tossed back and forth between partners. This is expressed in teasing and arguments.

3. *Externalization of "inside" impulses* onto children or child substitutes in mildly seductive, adaptive mothering activities. When this mechanism is successful, the vagina becomes desexualized and maternal activities are sublimatory in nature; when it fails, maternal behavior becomes explicitly seductive and genital sensations and impulses break through in nursing, diapering and fondling activities (Heiman, 1963; Masters and Johnson, 1966; Sarlin, 1963).

Irreversible or only mildly reversible desexualization of the vagina creates a permanent split between maternality and sexual adjustment, as seen in women who are frigid, or only mildly interested in sex, but are truly maternal to their children and husbands (Deutsch, H., 1961).

Persistence of externalization on transitional objects, associated with infantile desexualization of the vagina, can be seen in certain forms of spinsterhood and infertility (Kestenberg, 1956b, 1967b, 1968). Deficient externalization with desexualization of the vagina, or with its opposite, hypersexuality, weakens the integrative function of the ego, hinders adjustment to reality, and fosters the persistence of infantile genitality. Examples are: "child brides" (Greenacre, 1947), promiscuity (Glover, E., 1943), sexual delinquency, prostitution, and subordination to phallic women in overt homosexuality (Weiss, 1962).

4. *Denial or isolation* of the vagina promotes: masculine identification and penis envy, transfer of inner sensations upon the clitoris, intolerance of passivity and repudiation of femininity. In extreme forms it leads to a condemnation of the clitoris not only as an inadequate penis substitute but also as a trigger and resonance organ of the vagina, whose phobic avoidance may progressively enlarge the area of "safe distance." This syndrome can be seen in cases of inveterate forms of total or partial genital anasthesia, voluntary spinsterhood, defensive devotion to careers away from the home, and agenital forms of homosexuality.

In some cases an illusory penis serves to aggrandize the clitoris or promotes the acceptance of the vagina as a hidden penis (Jacobson, 1936; Rado, 1933). These syndromes manifest themselves in a defensive insistence that the clitoris is the prime organ of female sexuality (Bergler, 1947; Kinsey et al., 1953) or in unattainable demands that the vaginal orgasm must be equivalent to the male orgasm. These mechanisms are grossly exaggerated in promiscuity, based on masculine identification, and in dominant forms of overt homosexuality.

5. *Projection* of aggressive and sexual wishes may lead to: masochistic surrender to men; provocation of attack; enduring all feminine functions as a burden rather than a pleasure; passive submissive attitudes toward men and children which only stimulate true womanhood and motherhood. These syndromes are usually associated with a continuation of infantile dependency on preoedipal or oedipal objects, a failure of internalization, and an insufficient differentiation of the superego.

6. *Repression* of perceptions and representations of the genitalia and of connected fantasies leads to total frigidity. In partial frigidity the remainder of the genital is isolated from the cathected part. Where repression and isolation are weakened, a scattering of sensations and their displacement bring on conversion symptoms.

This classification has listed defense mechanisms in chronological order as they seem to appear during development from pregenitality to latency. In further development, drive derivatives undergo modifications, and temporary breakdowns of repression and regressions give the child a chance to reorganize constellations of defenses. In normal development the onset of sexual maturity enhances growth and differentiation of drives, adaptation to a new reality, and acceptance of femininity (Kestenberg, 1967b, 1968).

Feminine integration is completed when woman learns to adjust to her role as wife and mother. In this she can succeed only if she is teachable and can accept her husband and children as organizers of her femininity.

A constellation of feminine defense mechanisms in an individually varying ratio of intensity, combination, and sequence is representative of woman's character formation. However, fluctuations and shifts in pattern occur in response to: internal and external changes, cyclic hormone fluctuations, states of alertness, fatigue and stress (Masters and Johnson, 1965).

Primacy of the inner genitalia cannot be achieved or maintained in face of the typically feminine castration anxiety that the inner genital will disappear (Benedek, 1961; Deutsch, 1961). This fear evokes denial and repression which, so to speak, put the vagina to sleep to safeguard its intactness. But through externalization of inner-genital sensations and impulses the activity of the vagina is perpetuated on substitute objects and organs.

The vagina of the normal adult woman becomes fully functional and capable of being awakened by man without prolonged conditioning when the following requirements have been met:

There must be sufficient priming of the vagina in critical developmental phases. Denial and repression of genital-pelvic sensations and their reinforcement by hypercathexis of the clitoris must not be so strong as to become almost irreversible. Not only the vagina, but all other parts of the genitals must be accepted and allowed to function in coordination with each other.

The male's acceptance of his own inside genitals, projected on the woman, must be expressed in his fearless interest in the woman's inside genitals so that he will not defensively libidinize the clitoris as a homologue of his penis. To be regarded as a valuable organ and not an object of aggression, the vagina must be libidinized by the man's continuing interest in its penetration (Masters and Johnson, 1965, 1966), without intent to injure it.

Both partners must be relatively free of incestuous ties and capable of object constancy which motivates them to mutual adjustment and satisfaction.

Pregenital components in foreplay as well as in the three phases of the sexual cycle (Freud, S., 1905; Masters and Johnson, 1966) must be so encompassed within the dominant sphere of genitality that they cannot become dominant themselves. Their integration with the genital complex must not be so rigid, however, that they cannot be rearranged in intensity or sequence to adjust to the partner's needs.

There must be a flexible balance between desexualization and sexualization so that sexualization develops only under conditions appropriate in time and place.

There must be an ego-syntonic balance between activity and passivity and between inner- and outer-genital stimulation, so that masculine and feminine rhythms in each individual can operate in harmony with each other and with those of the partner. A conflict between partners or a competition between body parts leads to interruptions in excitation, shifts in cathexis, and scattering of sensations, all incompatible with a harmonious total genital experience. Mutual trust and identification must be based on sensitive attunement between sex partners so that foreplay is mutually satisfactory, rhythms of tension flow compatible, and body parts shaped in complementary alignment to each other (Kestenberg, 1967a).

For orgastic discharge, both men and women must be prepared for a regression in which the ego voluntarily and fearlessly relinquishes control and surrenders to drive pressure. Such a surrender must not be masochistic to the point that painful sensations sharpen the experience and prevent regressive abandon to visceral sensations; it must not be coupled with relegating sole responsibility to the partner for the timing of the discharge in substitution for mutual attunement.

Female sexuality cannot be understood in isolation from the sexuality of man; it is important to review male feelings toward inside and outside genitality. In the following section I shall confine myself to discussing those aspects of man's sexuality which influence his attitude toward woman. The case reports will illustrate how disturbances in these areas affect the quality of his performance as her teacher and his ability to help her achieve adult female integration.

INSIDE AND OUTSIDE IN MALE DEVELOPMENT

[The author acknowledges the existence of inner sensations in the little boy, which arise not only from testicles and the prostate but also from accessory genital pelvic organs. These inner genital drives are the source of feminine and motherly feelings.

[In the boy's development, the denial of the "inside" and the externalization to the phallus become a requisite for the establishment of the phallic phase. The denial of the awareness of inside tensions and of diffuse sensations is later reinforced in men by the equation of all inside structures with femininity, the projection of feminine wishes upon women and the displacement of curiosity about his own inside to that of women. The shift of emphasis from inside to outside in male genitality is reflected in mythology and it has been confirmed in clinical findings. — ED.]

SURVEY OF SIMILARITIES AND DISSIMILARITIES IN MALE AND FEMALE DEVELOPMENT

This brief survey is based on clinical material from analyses. The reconstruction of developmental stages and the views on the role of outer- and inner-genital organs in the development of sexuality fit into the framework of psychoanalytic theory and do not require an emendation of its basic principles. Where they differ in some respects from prevailing opinion they must be looked upon as tentative formulations subject to reevaluation and critical scrutiny by other investigators of psychoanalytic child psychology (Barnett, 1966; Bradley, 1961.)[7]

Similarities

In the *pregenital* phases, both sexes cope with genital tensions by incorporating them into phase-specific pregenital discharge forms. The relief experienced after the intake of food or the expulsion of products from the inside provides a model for the child's wish to eat or expel all sources of tension.

In identification with the preoedipal mother, children of both sexes feel that they too have babies. They animate the world around them with beings like themselves, "babies." At the same time, they preserve and enliven the lifeless products that gave rise to "live" sensations when they were inside or about to enter or leave the body. Images of babies are condensed with images of oral, anal, and urethral products but their derivation from early genital tensions becomes dominant only when pregenital wishes to play with food and excreta are repudiated.

The *"inner-genital"* phase is initiated by the spreading of genital excitement from the inside of the body, which increases the need for externalization. The toddler is vaguely familiar with sources of tension, unrelieved by intake or expulsion of visible products. The two- to three-year-old imagines that the inside is composed of food, feces, and urine. He is puzzled by the discovery that handling of external genitalia resonates vague sensations from the inside of his body. During this early "inner-genital" phase the child becomes more aware of genital tensions which come and go without leaving traces in the outside world. He begins to formulate the thought that there is something unknown inside him that he would like to take out and examine. In an effort to cope with this unknown "something" he externalizes the diffuse inner-genital impulses upon objects such as dolls, teddies, trucks, and trains, whose origin is to him equally mysterious, but which can be handled and examined. He animates these objects and pretends that they are babies that came from his inside. All things unknown seem to emanate from his inside, which is there although one can neither see nor touch it.

As the "inner-genital" phase progresses, the spreading of genital excitement from the inside of the body increases the need for externalization. This readily available mechanism is put in the service of integration of conflicting trends. Externalization helps the child to repudiate regressive pregenital wishes, to distinguish them from inner- and outer-genital impulses and, eventually, to coordinate them under the dominance of the outwardly oriented phallic drive. With the progressive increase of unfulfilled genital drives, the three- to four-year-old's externalization fails periodically. From time to time he becomes disillusioned with the inanimate objects which substituted for live babies and helped him create an image of his inside. He acknowledges periodically that they are only playthings and reinvests his genitals with the cathexis withdrawn from them. With the recathexis of the "inside," disquieting, unproductive, inner-genital tensions evoke fears of bursting, exploding, becoming eviscerated, empty, and "dead." To protect himself against attacks from the inside, the four-year-old focuses his excitement on the external genitals and denies the existence of the threatening inner-genital organs. The discovery of the difference between sexes reinforces the child's conviction that the inside is dangerous, dark, bloody, and full of strange attackers who must be locked up and not allowed out. Femininity becomes associated with bloody holes and masculinity with intactness. The phase of identification with the preoedipal mother is terminated by denial of femininity, renunciation of the wish for a live baby, and repudiation of the inside as babyish and feminine (Kestenberg, 1956a, 1967b, 1968).

In the *phallic* phase, masturbatory activities allow for a focal form of discharge on the penis or clitoris which resonates deeper pelvic tensions, but prevents anxiety-provoking spreading and diffusion of sensations. The positive and negative oedipal fantasies that accompany masturbation reflect the child's conflicting wishes to penetrate sadistically and to be penetrated masochistically. The wish to give the mother a baby and the wish to receive one from the father arouse fears of injuring the mother and being injured by the father. The boy projects his wish to be penetrated onto women, and the girl projects all genital impulses onto men, who, she feels, want to penetrate and injure her.

The repression of sexuality in *latency* does not permit a direct expression of genital fantasies. It upholds the denial of feminity and perpetuates the trend toward externalization of inner-genital sensations in drive-derivative activities.

In *prepuberty,* the rapid growth of inner-genital structures increases inner tensions. The child tries to relieve them by a renewal of externalization, which protects him from overwhelming visceral sensations. But the onset of menses and emissions introduces new forms of discharge for inner-genital tensions and presents a concrete proof of the existence of inner-genital structures in both sexes. The renewed attempt to identify the inside with femininity and pregenitality and the outside with masculinity is counteracted by integration of pregenital, inner-genital, and outer-genital drives—a reorganization which initiates the sex-specific genital primacy in puberty.

In *biological puberty,* when reproduction becomes possible, the adolescent is faced with a reality which overshadows earlier fantasies. The boy projects infantile representations of his inside as feminine upon woman; the girl projects infantile representations of her inside structures as an inner phallus upon men.

At the end of puberty in a *preadult* developmental phase a reintegration of infantile and adolescent trends into adult genitality becomes the basis for sex-specific identity.

Dissimilarities

The sex-specific organs of the newborn are adultlike at birth and involute during the first weeks or months of extrauterine life. In the *pregenital* phases, the differences between the sexes are accentuated or blurred by maternal reactions evidenced in bodily care.

Internal genital organs are stimulated indirectly by pressures from the bladder and rectum. The exposed introitus of the baby girl accounts for the frequency of vaginal infections and inflammations in childhood (Nelson, 1959). Secretions from the vagina evidence the activity of this organ in childhood. Washing and swabbing of the introitus stimulate the vagina, urine may drip into it and bath waters suffuses it. Through the intrinsic nervous and vascular connections between clitoris, vestibular bulb, vagina and uterus, the continuity between inside and outside is maintained. There are similar connections in the male (Cunningham, 1964), but the spreading of pelvic sensations is counteracted by the continuous influence of epicritic sensibility in the skin covering of the penis which has no parallel in the female. The penis is accessible to manipulation and manual exploration earlier than the clitoris. Toward the end of the first year the boy discovers his penis as an organ by connecting what he can feel with what he can see. Very early he fuses scrotal and deep testicular sensations with the more acute and localizable sensations of his penis. The girl discovers her vulva later. She fuses it with anal and urethral images.

In the *"inner-genital"* phase, the boy erects an image of his inside based more on mechanical models than on baby-dolls. This representation is derived from experimentations on his own body and on outside objects (trains, balls, etc.); it constitutes the core of the "masculine inside." It condenses and overlaps with images of the inside, based on the identification with the preoedipal mother. In contrast, the girl's image of her own inside is more uniformly feminine, its principal model being the baby. The boy's fantasies about impregnation and delivery are repudiated because of their connection with regressive pregenital impulses and fears of injury.

Anorectal representations provide a connection between the scrotum, the perianal region, the rectum, and the prostate—a route which, by its discontinuity and organ division, is less suitable for access to the inside than the direct route from the external labia, the introitus, and the vagina, to the uterus. By identifying the rectoanal-scrotal route with the birth canal, the boy shifts his representation of the anal baby to the testicular baby; as he repudiates anality, equated to feminity, he denies the importance of the scrotum and testicles and transfers their cathexes to the adjoining phallus, which in its flaccid state also comes to represent a baby. The girl who fuses anal, perianal, and introital sensations also repudiates her inside genital as she repudiates anality and the anal baby; she derives from it not a fear of loss of the clitoris, but rather a fear that all of her inside will fall out during defecation (delivery), which parallels the fear of the boy that he may lose his testicles in the toilet (Bell, 1964).

The urethral route inside the boy's body is also associated with birth fantasies and culminates in the equation of the erect penis with a baby boy. Before he can establish his penis as symbol of activity and maleness, the boy is frightened by the invisible forces that stiffen the penis or soften it, erect it, or let it hang again. These are condensed with fears of testicular elevation, turgidity of the scrotum, and the unaccounted "falling" of the testicles with scrotal relaxation. The internal route from the testicles to the penis is equated with the female birth canal and with the tube that connects the bladder to the outside. But the boy recognizes the groin as the place of entry of the spermatic cord inside his body and also imagines that the baby is delivered on the *side* of the body through the inguinal ring which he equates with the birth canal. The girl fuses vesical-urethral sensations with clitoral, introital, and vaginal sensations and imagines being impregnated by urine entering her. She also thinks that the boy's bags may contain urine or babies and by identification with the boy may endow her external labia with these representations. But the boy's fantasy of the inguinal route (side, Nunberg, 1947) as passage of impregnation and delivery is unparalleled in the girl.

Girls externalize their dissatisfactions and inner tensions upon the preoedipal mother much more than boys, because they are more beset by "nagging" inner-genital tensions than boys. The denial of the inside and the transfer of cathexis to the outside genitals is much more successful in the boy than in the girl.

With the onset of the *phallic* phase, the connection between testicular movements and genital excitement is obscured, but the fear that the penis will be transformed into a baby and be cut off is perpetuated in oedipal fantasies of impregnation through the rectum. The phallic boy is satisfied that his whole body supports his penis; the phallic girl transfers her dissatisfactions with her inside to her clitoris. She dimly perceives that the clitoris arouses and resonates innermost tensions which are impossible to control.

The girl envies the boy for his penis because he continues to have an organ before, during, and after sexual excitation. She can neither see nor feel her clitoris all the time; even that organ keeps appearing and disappearing in consonance with the arousal and abatement of diffuse inner-genital tensions. The fantasy that she will grow a penis is imparted to her by the boy, who feels more confident that he could grow a new penis if he lost the external end of it. The girl herself is more apt to think that she has an inside penis, connected to the clitoris, whose "jumpy" qualities, retractability, and sensory connections to pelvic organs promote such a fantasy. However, she readily gives up this imaginary organ in exchange for a penis introduced into her and making a baby there, which will come out. This wish helps her to think that she really has nothing inside, just as she has nothing outside, and that she is merely a carrier for the penis-baby her father will give her. He might lose his penis and she will gain a baby rather than lose what is inside of her. Her wish to penetrate her mother with a penis, as father can, is based on identification with the nursing mother. The intrusiveness, experienced as an active quality of the phallus, promotes positive oedipal fantasies in the boy. Since neither clitoris, tongue, finger or nipple have the intrusive qualities of the penis, the girl's negative oedipal fantasies lack the support from somatogenic sources. The girl does not know what it feels like to have a penis, although she continuously demands one in expression of her dissatisfaction with her sexual tensions, which cannot be fully resolved by clitoral masturbation.

The projection of sexual impulses upon men and the repression of sexuality make the girl's *latency* more peaceful than that of the boy. But the urgency of her feelings is expressed in her continued preoccupation with dolls, dogs, and horses, on which she can externalize her genital impulses. The two-way traffic between vaginal sensations and clitoral discharge forms is usually latent and becomes apparent only in typically feminine forms of sublimation. In latency, boys in our culture are surrounded by women who are in charge of taming their impulses. Feminine identification is fostered in both sexes, and in contrast to boys', girls' modes of externalization receive full support from the environment. The growth of internal and external reproductive organs in late latency is more apparent to the boy, and the increase of androgen production favors masculinization, independence, and outward orientation. The boy starts his battle to free himself from the feminizing influence of his home very early. In this process he repudiates femininity and denigrates feminine sexual organs. In the battle of the sexes in latency, the girl envies the boy's independence and is greatly influenced by the image of femininity imparted to her by the boy.

In *prepuberty,* the boy feels vague inner sensations—growing pains—which no one can explain satisfactorily. He regressively revives pregenital feminine representations of the inside of his body and connects them with the new internal sensations. Overwhelmed by fears that the understructure of his phallus has become endangered by mysterious forces from within, he looks to his peers and older boys for reassurance. By comparing himself with other boys, he finds out that emissions are masculine and not the result of injury to his inside. He tries out new forms of masturbation, plays tricks with his scrotum, his testicles, and exerts pressure on the perineum. Sometimes he attempts anal masturbation to see "what it is like to be a woman." He tries to squeeze out emissions or prevent them. He worries that someone, especially his mother, will discover that he is abusing himself and wasting himself. Although proud of his first emissions, he also worries that he is depleting his inside. The change in his scrotum and testicles bothers him greatly (Bell, 1964). The pendulousness of his scrotum seems to him a sure sign that his inside is "falling" lower. He externalizes his worries and his curiosity onto substitute objects. He uses pseudoscientific theorizations to conceptualize what is inside his body and to rid it of pregenital and feminine attributes, with which he has endowed his inside at the end of the early inner-genital phase. Eventually the boy succeeds in accepting the fact that the inside of his body contains structures essential to masculine functioning. He integrates pregenital inner- and outer-genital sensations in his masturbatory experience in such a way that they become subordinated to the genital primacy in puberty. He concentrates his libido on the phallus, but, instead of endowing the whole body with phallic qualities, he accepts the contribution of other parts of his body to the total genital experience.

The tremendous increase of estrogen production in prepuberty makes the girl especially vulnerable to inner-genital excitations. Shifting of libidinal cathexis from the vagina to the clitoris and to breasts reduces her fears and reinforces the equations of these organs with the penis. But neither nipples nor clitoris prove to be safe islands which remove her from the dreaded inner genitality. Genital sensations seem to float all over her body and shift rapidly from one organ to another. Externalization of genital impulses on substitute objects helps her to reestablish the image of her body and regain control over desexualization of her vagina. But menstruation forces her to accept the existence of the vagina and uterus as feminine organs.

The repeated experience of internal upheaval with resulting blood flow helps her to reorganize the image of her inside which she had erected in the early inner-genital phase. It is becoming clearer to her that what she has inside is neither a baby nor a penis but a container and a receptacle for both. She reorganizes her concepts about femininity and pregenitality. She looks to boys for the alleviation of her inner distress and for signs of admiration which imply the acceptance of her newfound femininity. But she still uses the clitoris as a sensual focus, as an organ that responds to stimulation from various parts of the body and resonates her inner-genital sensations, to which she cannot respond by direct manipulations.

With the onset of *biological puberty,* progesterone production regularizes the girl's cycles, brings on uterine cramps, and effects changes in the consistency of the menstrual flow. The regular changes in her vagina affect the girl's moods and attitudes. She becomes aware of feelings in the clitoris, whose association with deep vaginal sensations can no longer be ignored. The role of the clitoris recedes as the girl's wishes for penetration and direct contact with a penis increase. In sex play the girl allows the boy to help her find new discharge forms. When he manipulates and examines her, he gradually loses his fear of female genitalia.

In biological puberty, the boy seems to feel a new strength in the expulsive quality of his urethra and the strong contractions of pelvic muscles. He becomes proud of the ejectile propulsion of his semen but also worries about impregnating the girl. The new masculine experiences promote the identification with his father and reinforce the battle against infantilization (feminization) by the mother. The girl's approval of the boy as seducer and protector helps him to free himself from oedipal bonds.

To accept his inside genitality as masculine, the young man must weaken the link between the inside of his body and his mother. He can no longer hold on to her "apron strings" to keep him free from injury from within. In contrast to the girl, his detachment from his mother proceeds rather abruptly. The repression of his incestuous wishes is reinforced by his need to protect himself against his mother's persistent demands that he remain her baby.

Puberty brings the girl closer to her father. Deep vaginal sensations revive oedipal wishes to be penetrated and impregnated. But these wishes are now realizable and the girl intuitively understands that her projection of these wishes upon her father meets his own wishes halfway. To accept her vagina as a real organ, the girl needs the experience of being accepted by her father as a woman, when she has finally become one. Too strong a repression of adolescent ties to the father tends to desexualize the vagina. The more intolerant the woman's superego, the more difficult it is for man to relibidinize her vagina.

During the *preadult* reintegration period, the young man shifts his allegiance from his home to the social milieu he selects as his own. His ego-ideal and his actual place in society become the narcissistic core of his identity before he can safely invest his object-cathexis in a permanent relationship. In contrast, the preadult young woman molds and organizes her own identity to fit the ego-ideal and social aspirations of her love object. Her readiness for feminine object-ties evolves directly from her relationship to her parents. Her place in society is the niche created by man, who shelters her like her mother did, and provides for her like her father did.[8]

Vaginal sensations in childhood were linked to the wish for a baby, and thus were desexualized. To resexualize her vagina during coitus the adult woman must postpone her wish to receive a live baby when she feels the intromission of the phallus. The biological readiness of the vagina to accommodate the male organ in response to sexual stimulation and in preparation for impregnation is reflected in the woman's fears that she may become empty when exposed to vaginal excitement without impregnation. On the basis of past experiences she holds on to her excitement for fear that at the end of coitus she will again have nothing inside. Her fear lessens when she feels assured that man will neither injure her while she is helpless nor abandon her when her excitement subsides.

To fill the role of a lover and protector man must overcome fears of the inside as dangerous. Confident of his masculinity, he can doubly libidinize the vagina, which he has denied and dreaded for so long: as an organ essential to the full unfolding of male sexuality and as an organ which he yearned to explore in its deepest parts. If he has rid himself of the sadistic components of his curiosity and of his desire to attack and destroy what is foreign to him, he ceases to regard his semen as dangerous and can also accept and adjust to the retentive aspects of female orgasm.

Woman can accept the expulsive qualities of orgasm when she is ready to relinquish her own excitement and release the phallus. The end phase of female orgasm represents her struggle between expulsion and retention. The successive rise and ebb of excitement (sometimes confused with multiple orgasms) that distinguishes feminine orgasm from the abrupt release gained by man corresponds to the much less abrupt way woman relinquishes her oedipal ties as compared with man.

Woman's orgasm cannot be initiated without the participation of the vagina. Vaginal sensations are no longer dependent on their resonance in the clitoris when they can be directly experienced through repeated contact with the penis. In the process of reorganization of woman's sexuality the man unifies her past and present, her outside and her inside; thus he gives her a chance to incorporate all parts of her genitals in the sexual experience or to emphasize some and minimize the role of others. When woman loses confidence in the man as protector of her femininity, she safeguards her vagina from injury and loss by a rapid transfer of vaginal cathexis to the clitoris which acts as a safety valve.

Restoration of Function and Learning in Men and Women

Psychological impotence and frigidity can be successfully treated by psychoanalysis. But even men and women who have resolved the conflicts that had invaded genital functioning can achieve an adult form of constancy of self-representations and object-relatedness only in actual experience with real nonincestuous objects. This involves a learning process predicated on a freedom to learn which, if lost, can be restored by psychoanalysis. In psychoanalytic treatment, the patient becomes teachable, but the treatment situation does not allow for training, which only performance of function can give.[9] That must be relegated to the physical sphere of learning, practiced by mutually devoted men and women, or, if need be, taught by those practitioners who devise pedagogical methods to inculcate skills. But here we encounter significant differences in the learning process of men and women.

Not only do men in our culture create institutions and customs which allow them to learn the mechanics of sex before they teach them to their constant love objects, but by virtue of their outwardly oriented male sex anatomy and physiology they can learn much faster than women. Women require a great deal of priming of their principal sex zone, the vagina, because they lack direct experience with it earlier in life and because the vagina is an internal, visceral organ. Moreover, conditioning of the vagina in adulthood is more successfully accomplished with a constant love object so that the conflict-laden areas of unwanted pregnancy and the threat of infanticide do not impede the learning process.

It is too early to determine whether the premarital sexual activity of young women, freed from fear of pregnancy by the newly introduced contraceptive drugs, will facilitate vaginal conditioning and the achieving of orgasm. In predicting the outcome of these social changes one must be aware of the physical and psychological differences in ovulatory and anovulatory cycles. The latter may well enhance regression to early adolescence which is not compatible with adult genital functioning. Moreover, one must remember that contraception to the unconscious implies infanticide, equated with the loss of the inner-genital and with the loss of feminine identity. These deeply rooted feminine fears may not be easily counteracted by the conscious realization that prevention of ovulation does not constitute ''germ killing.''

Masters and Johnson (1966) report success in treating frigidity with the method of frequent and prolonged vaginal excitation, borrowed from techniques of awakening the artificial vagina. The setting for this form of physical therapy is conducive to conflict-free learning. It is taught to married women who desire children and are motivated to learn, with the full cooperation of their husbands whose role as conditioners of the vagina is sanctioned by parental figures, represented by the therapists.

Analysts treat their patients in an atmosphere of physical deprivation. By alleviation of conflicts analysis restores functions, but the ensuing improvement in these functions is to be sought in the patient's life experience. Analysis restores the awareness of tensions, sensations, and impulses emanating from the genitalia. It liberates infantile fantasies and fears and confronts the patient with the infantile demands of the superego which impede functioning on an adult level. By allowing the patient to reorganize his personality structure, analysis facilitates an adult sex-specific integration which, in the woman, is dominated by adult inner-genital drives and interests. Thus, analysis can remove the obstacles that psychological maladaptations pose in the way of orgastic fulfillment. It can neither teach nor institute the requisite setting for normal adult orgastic discharge, in which freedom from fear is provided by a constant love object. The self-imposed limitations, intrinsic to psychoanalytic technique, promote the therapeutic process. Analysts must leave methods of conditioning and teaching to the natural teachers of women, their adult love objects—men.

SUMMARY AND DISCUSSION

Analyses of children and adults reveal the obstacles encountered in the development of the external orientation of men and inward orientation of women. Both sexes fear the destruction of their insides, but this more archaic form of the castration complex is typical for women.

There seem to be two ''inner-genital'' stages in which anxiety-provoking inner-genital impulses give rise to a reorganization of pregenital, inner-genital, and outer-genital component drives. The first ''inner-genital'' stage ends with the subordination of all component drives to phallic dominance. The second ''inner-genital'' stage in prepuberty ends with the integration of all component drives, including the phallic, in the sex-specific genital primacy that begins with the onset of biological puberty. Adult genital organization cannot be achieved without the acceptance of the role of internal genital organs in coitus and reproduction.

The developmental trend toward externalization, common to both sexes, promotes adjustment to reality and facilitates the formation of psychic structures at the expense of sexualization of internal genital organs. However, this very trend obscures and retards the developmental steps that prepare the acceptance of the vagina as the primary erotogenic zone of the adult woman.

Throughout development the girl depends on external objects to alleviate her inner-genital tensions. Completely to overcome her fear of losing her ''inside,'' woman depends on man to protect her against the danger of ego dissolution, represented in the loss of contact with reality at the peak of orgastic experience.

Analysis can free man from the fears and defenses which prevent him from accepting and carrying out his role of teacher and organizer of feminine sexuality. Analysis can free woman from the defensive masculinization that supports her externalization, denial, and repression of the vagina, and prevents the cathexis of vaginal excitation. Analysis can make woman teachable, but it cannot teach her. Woman's orgastic capacity develops to its full potential only when man can help her to achieve it.

NOTES

1. In my first accounts of externalization of inner genital tensions upon the baby-doll and later the child, I failed to realize that the tensions and vague sensations I was describing must evoke impulses that lead to maternal activity. It was Bradley (1961) who pointed out my error. My early presentations also erred in the use of projection and externalization interchangeably. Inner genital impulses are externalized into maternal activities beginning with the early maternal stage, which I now subsume under the heading of an ''inner-genital'' stage or the early stage of integration (Kestenberg, 1966). Sexual and aggressive wishes are projected upon the male in a late oedipal stage. Corresponding stages of development in the male are discussed in later sections of this chapter.
2. A rhythm of this kind can also be observed in the scrotum of neonates. The movement appears wavelike or wormlike, spreads from one side of the scrotum to the other, and may be followed by rotatory movements in the testicles (Robbins, 1964).
3. The reference to the vagina need not be taken as indication of inner sensations. ''Modern'' mothers, in their zeal to be enlightened parents, introduce this word for the female genital before the child is aware of her inner organ. As a result, they refer to the vulva as ''vagina'' and this semantic confusion serves the externalization of the vagina rather than enhancing its acceptance. Gigi called both inner and outer genitals ''vagina.''
4. Reich's (1927) patient Lotte, whose feelings were even stronger than Fern's, talked to her vagina as if it were her child and promised it relief while she masturbated.
5. Curves drawn to represent multiple orgasms (Reich, 1927) suggest that the rhythms involved are similar to pregenital and early inner-genital rhythms, characterized by small changes and a frequency of repetition that is unsuitable for adult genital discharge. Repeated high waves or peaks which eventually lead to disengorgement and relief (Dickinson, 1949) should not be construed as multiple orgasms but as phases of orgastic discharge, typical for women.
6. Nagging women, who particularly blame their husbands and ''pick'' on them, sometimes become aware of their problem without analysis, as the following excerpt from a letter illustrates: ''I swore if I ever found a good man I would be the best wife in the world. Well, I found a real jewel. . . . So, will you please tell me why my mouth is never shut? I nag constantly, I'm forever picking on this marvelous man and I'm so sick of listening to myself that I can't stand it. What is wrong with me anyway?''
7. The primary differences pertain to the question whether inner-genital impulses and drives play a role in childhood sexuality. The reconstruction of ''inner-genital'' phases can be validated only by pooling psychoanalytic material and examining it for evidences of fantasies derived from inner-genital impulses and drives in early childhood and in prepuberty.
8. Recurring protests against subjugations by men and calls for equalization of sexes, are based, no doubt, on the wish to abolish discriminatory practices against women. However, they are frequently reinforced by disappointments in men, who failed to provide for and shelter women and their children. Feeling unloved and unprotected, women tend to repudiate womanhood altogether and to identify with men who look down on child- and home-care as inferior.

9. Child analysts are continuously faced with the fact that, once functions are restored, skills are not automatically acquired. Stutterers or asthmatics often require retraining by speech therapists or physiotherapists, once analysis frees them from conflicts that prevented normal breathing. An old joke may serve to clarify the dilemma of the analyst who cannot "teach" a patient a skill he never possessed. A patient asks a surgeon who put a cast on his fractured wrist: "Doctor, will I be able to play the piano?" Doctor: "Of course." Patient: "That's wonderful, I never could play before."

BIBLIOGRAPHY

Barnett, M. C. Vaginal awareness in the infancy and childhood of girls. *J. Amer. Psychoanal. Assoc.*, 14:129–141,1966.

Beach, F. A. & Ford, C. S. *Patterns of Sexual Behavior*. New York: Paul Hoeber, 1952.

Bell, A. Bowel training difficulties in boys. *J. Amer. Acad. Child Psychiat,* 3:577–590, 1964.

Benedek, T. *Psychosexual Functions in Women*. New York: Ronald Press, 1952.

Benedek, T. The organization of the reproductive drive. *Int. J. Psycho-Anal.,* 41:1–15, 1960.

Benedek, T. In Panel: Frigidity in women, rep. B. E. Moore. *J. Amer. Psychoanal. Assoc.,* 9:571–584, 1961.

Bergler, E. Frigidity in the female: Misconceptions and facts. *Marriage Hygiene,* 1:16–21, 1947.

Bonaparte, M. *Female Sexuality*. New York: International Universities Press. 1953.

Bradley, N. The doll: Some clinical, biological and linguistic notes of the toy-baby and its mother. *Int. J. Psycho-Anal.,* 42:550–556, 1961.

Brierley, M. Problems of integration in women. *Int. J. Psycho-Anal.,* 13:433–448, 1932.

Brierley, M. Specific determinants in feminine development. *Int. J. Psycho-Anal.,* 17:163–180, 1936.

Burnett, H. F. *A Little Princess* (1898). New York: Scribner's, 1953.

Cunningham, D. J. *Cunningham's Textbook of Anatomy*, ed. G. J. Romanes. London: Oxford University Press, 10th ed., 1964.

Daiken, L. *Children's Toys Throughout Ages*. New York: Praeger, 1953.

Deutsch, H. The psychology of women in relation to the functions of reproduction. *Int. J. Psycho-Anal.,* 6:405–418, 1925.

Deutsch, H. *The Psychology of Women,* 2 Vols. New York: Grune & Stratton, 1944–45.

Deutsch, H. In Panel: Frigidity in women, rep. B. E. Moore. *J. Amer. Psychoanal. Assoc.,* 9:571–584, 1961.

Dickinson, R. L. *Atlas of Human Sex Anatomy*. Baltimore: Williams & Wilkins, 1949.

Eissler, K. R. On certain problems of female sexual development. *Psychoanal. Quart.,* 8:191–210, 1939.

Ellis, H. *Studies in the Psychology of Sex,* 4 Vols. New York: Random House, 1936.

Erikson, E. H. *Childhood and Society*. New York: Norton, 1950.

Erikson, E. H. Reflections on womanhood. *Daedalus,* 2:582–606, 1964.

Federn, P. Beiträge zur Analyse des Sadismus und Masochismus: I. Die Quellen des männlichen Sadismus. II. Die libidinösen Quelen des Masochismus. *Int. Z. Psychoanal.,* 1:29–49, 1913; 2:105–130, 1914.

Fenichel, O. *The Psychoanalytic Theory of Neurosis*. New York: Norton, 1945.

Ferenczi, S. *Thalassa: Theory of Genitality* (1924). Albany, N.Y.: Psychoanalytic Quarterly, 1938.

Freud, A. *Normality and Pathology in Childhood.* New York: International Universities Press, 1965.

Freud, S. Three essays on the theory of sexuality (1905). *Standard Edition,* 7:125–245. London: Hogarth Press,1953.

Freud, S. Totem and taboo (1913). *Standard Edition,* 13:1–161. London: Hogarth Press, 1955.

Freud, S. Some psychical consequences of the anatomical distinction between the sexes (1925). *Standard Edition,* 19:243–258. London: Hogarth Press, 1961.

Freud, S. Female sexuality (1931). *Standard Edition,* 21:225–243. London: Hogarth Press, 1961.

Freud, S. New introductory lectures on psycho-analysis (1933). *Standard Edition,* 22:3–182. London: Hogarth Press, 1964.

Freud, S. Analysis terminable and interminable (1937). *Standard Edition,* 23:209–253. London: Hogarth Press, 1964.

Freud, S. An outline of psycho-analysis (1940). *Standard Edition,* 23:141–207. London: Hogarth Press, 1964.

Gates, J. S. *The Story of the Lost Doll.* Indianapolis: Bobbs-Merrill, 1905.

Glenn, J. Sensory determinants of the symbol *three. J. Amer. Psychoanal. Assoc.,* 13:422–434, 1965.

Glover, E. The psychopathology of prostitution (1943–1957). In: *Roots of Crime.* New York: International Universities Press, 1960, pp. 244–267.

Greenacre, P. Child wife as ideal: Sociological considerations. *Amer. J. Orthopsychiat.,* 17:167–171, 1947.

Greenacre, P. Special problems of early female sexual development. *The Psychoanalytic Study of the Child,* 5:112–138. New York: International Universities Press, 1950.

Halverson, H. M. Infant sucking and tensional behavior. *J. Genet. Psychol.,* 53:365–430, 1938.

Harley, M. Some observations on the relationship between genitality and structural development in adolescence. *J. Amer. Psychoanal. Assoc.,* 9:434–460, 1961.

Harlow, H. F. Sexual behavior in the rhesus monkey. In: *Sex and Behavior,* ed., F. A. Beach. New York: Wiley, 1965, pp. 234–265.

Hediger, H. Environmental factors influencing the reproduction of zoo animals. In: *Sex and Behavior,* ed. F. A. Beach. New York: Wiley, 1965, pp. 319–355.

Heiman, M. Sexual response in women: A correlation of physiological findings with psychoanalytic concepts. *J. Amer. Psychoanal. Assoc.,* 11:360–387, 1963.

Hitschmann, E. & Bergler, E. *Die Geschlechtskälte der Frau.* Vienna: Ars Medici. 1934.

Horney, K. The denial of the vagina. *Int. J. Psycho-Anal.,* 14:57–70, 1933.

Huffman, J. W. The structure and bacteriology of the premenarcheal vagina. *Ann. N. Y. Acad. Sci.,* 83:227–236, 1959.

Jacobson, E. Beitrag zur Entwicklung des weiblichen Kindeswunsches. *Int. Z. Psychoanal.,* 22:371–379, 1936.

Jacobson, E. Development of the wish for a child in boys. *The Psychoanalytic Study of the Child,* 5:139–152. New York: International Universities Press, 1950.

Jones, E. The early development of female sexuality (1927). *Papers on Psycho-Analysis.* London: Baillière, Tindall & Cox, 5th ed., 1948, pp. 438–451.

Kaplan, E. Observations on the congenital absence of the vagina. Read at the Long Island Psychoanalytic Society, June, 1963.

Keiser, S. On the psychopathology of orgasm. *Psychoanal. Quart.,* 16:378–390, 1947.

Keiser, S. Body ego during orgasm. *Psychoanal. Quart.,* 21:153–166, 1952.

Kestenberg, J. S. Vicissitudes of female sexuality. *J. Amer. Psychoanal. Assoc.,* 4:453–476, 1956a.

Kestenberg, J. S. On the development of maternal feelings in early childhood. *The Psychoanalytic Study of the Child*, 11:257–291. New York: International Universities Press, 1956b.

Kestenberg, J. S. Menarche. In: *Adolescents*, ed. S. Lorand & H. I. Schneer. New York: Hoeber, 1961, p. 19–50.

Kestenberg, J. S. Rhythm and organization in obsessive-compulsive development. *Int. J. Psycho-Anal.*, 47:151–159, 1966.

Kestenberg, J. S. The role of movement patterns in development: I. Rhythms of movement; II. Flow of tension and effort; III. The control of shape. *Psychoanal. Quart.*, 34:1–36; 34:517–563, 1965; 36:356–409, 1967a.

Kestenberg, J. S. Phases of adolescence: with suggestions for a correlation of psychic and hormonal organizations. Parts I, II, III. *J. Amer. Acad. Child Psychiat.*, 6:426–463, 6:557–614, 1967b; 7:108–151, 1968.

Kinsey, A. C. et al. *Sexual Behavior in the Human Female*. Philadelphia: Saunders, 1953.

Klein, M. *The Psycho-Analysis of Children*. London: Hogarth Press, 1932.

Kramer, P. Early capacity for orgastic discharge and character formation. *The Psychoanalytic Study of the Child*, 9:128–141. New York: International Universities Press, 1954.

Lampl-de Groot, J. The evolution of the oedipus complex in women. *Int J. Psycho-Anal.*, 9:332–345, 1928.

Langer, M. *Maternidad y Sexo*. Buenos Aires: Editorial Nova, 1951.

Lorand, S. Contribution to the problem of vaginal orgasm (1939). *Clinical Studies in Psychoanalysis*. New York: International Universities Press, 1950, pp. 148–158.

Lownsberry, E. *Marta the Doll*. New York: Longmans, Green, 1946.

McGinley, P. *The Most Wonderful Doll in the World*. New York: Lippincott, 1950.

Marcus, H. & Berlowe, J. Erections in newborn infants. Research of the Movement Study Group (in preparation).

Marmor, J. Some considerations concerning orgasm in the female. *Psychosom. Med.*, 16:240–245, 1954.

Masters, W. H. & Johnson, V. E. The sexual response cycle of the human male and female: Comparative anatomy and physiology. In: *Sex and Behavior*, ed. F. A. Beach. New York: Wiley, 1965, pp. 512–535.

Masters, W. H. & Johnson, V. E. *Human Sexual Response*. Boston: Little, Brown, 1966.

Mead, M. *Male and Female*. New York: William Morrow, 1949.

Mead, M. Personal communication.

Moore, B. E. Frigidity: a review of psychoanalytic literature. *Psychoanal. Quart.*, 33:323–349, 1964.

Müler, J. A. A contribution to the problem of libidinal development of the genital phase in girls. *Int. J. Psycho-Anal.*, 13:361–368, 1932.

Nelson, W. E. *Pediatrics*. Philadelphia: Saunders, 1959.

Nunberg, H. Circumcision and problems of bisexuality. *Int. J. Psycho-Anal.*, 28:145–179, 1947.

Payne, S. A. Conception of femininity. *Brit. J. Med. Psychol.*, 15:18–33, 1935.

Rado, S. Fear of castration in women. *Psychoanal. Quart.*, 2:425–475, 1933.

Reich, W. *Die Funktion des Orgasmus*. Vienna: Internationaler psychoanalytischer Verlag, 1927.

Robbins, E. Rhythmic scrotal contractions in the newborn. Research of the Movement Study Group, 1964.

Róheim, G. Aphrodite, or the woman with a penis. *Psychoanal. Quart.*, 14:350–390, 1945.

Rosenblum, L. Personal communication.

Ross, J. M. *Pierre As Sequel to Moby Dick: A Study of Herman Melvile* (1968, unpublished).

Sarlin, C. N. Feminine identity. *J. Amer. Psychoanal. Assoc.*, 11:790–816, 1963.

Sherfey, M. J. The evolution and nature of female sexuality in relation to psychoanalytic theory. *J. Amer. Psychoanal. Assoc.*, 14:28–128, 1966.

Silving, H. The oath. *Essays on Criminal Procedure.* Buffalo: Dennis, 1964.

Talbot, N. B., et al. *Functional Endocrinology from Birth Through Adolescence.* Cambridge: Harvard University Press, 1952.

Tausk, V. On the origin of the "influencing machine" in schizophrenia (1919). In: *The Psychoanalytic Reader,* ed. R. Fliess. New York: International Universities Press, 1948, pp. 52–85.

Van der Leeuw, P. J. The preoedipal phase of the male. *The Psychoanalytic Study of the Child,* 13:352–374. New York: International Universities Press, 1958.

Van Ophuijsen, J. W. H. On the source of feeling persecuted. *Int. J. Psycho-Anal.*, 1:235–239, 1920.

Veszy-Wagner, L. The equation: baby = girl = doll. Read at British Psycho-Analytical Society, February, 1965.

Weiss, E. Theoretical and clinical aspects of female homosexuality. In Panel: Theoretical and clinical aspects of overt female homosexuality, rep. C. W. Socarides. *J. Amer. Psychoanal. Assoc.*, 10:579–592, 1962.

Winnicott, D. W. *The Ordinary Devoted Mother and Her Baby.* London: Tavistock Publications, 1949.

Winnicott, D. W. Transitional objects and transitional phenomena (1953) *Collected Papers.* New York: Basic Books, 1958, p. 229–242.

Yazmajian, R. W. Reactions to differences between prepubertal and adult testes and scrotums. *Psychoanal. Quart.*, 35:368–376, 1966.

12. The Sense of Femaleness

Robert J. Stoller

In 1965 I suggested (12) that in normal boys the sense of maleness comes from the attitudes of parents, siblings, and peers toward the child's sex, from the anatomy and physiology of his genitalia, and from a biological force that can more or less modify the effects of the attitudes of others. Some of the data I presented, however, indicated that even boys born without penises do not doubt that they are males if their parents also believe this without question. Such a defect may cause many problems in the later development of their masculinity, yet they take for granted that they are males. In the present paper I shall show that the conclusions apply equally well to the development of the sense of femaleness.

Boys born without penises but recognized at birth to be males have their equivalent in girls who are genetically, anatomically, and physiologically normal except for being born without vaginas. Discovery of such a defect may cause a girl or woman great pain, but I have not seen or heard of any such woman who had a disturbance in core gender identity (that is, a fundamental uncertainty whether she was female or male). Gynecologists, with much more extensive experience with such women, concur; they do not see severe gender defects.

The anatomical defect may make a woman feel flawed; she may question whether she is feminine enough, or she may wonder whether the vagina the surgeons gave her is not the real thing, but she does not think she is a male and she does not wish to be converted into a male.[1] It may be taken as evidence that they feel themselves females that these women seek to have a vagina constructed and then can use it enthusiastically; Masters and Johnson report that in such women a surgically constructed vagina is not only physiologically and biochemically essentially normal, despite the fact that its 'mucosa' is created from a skin graft, but they have demonstrable evidence of orgasms which are physiologically indistinguishable from those of women with natural vaginas (9). I think it can be shown that the sense of being a

Reprinted with permission from *Psychoanalytic Quarterly* 37(1968):42–55.

female develops out of the same roots (parental attitudes and ascription of sex, genitalia, and a biological force) as does the sense of being a male and that this core gender identity persists throughout life as unalterably in women as in men.

If this is correct, there is good reason to question Freud's remark about women: 'Their sexual life is regularly divided into two phases, of which the first has a masculine character, while only the second is specifically feminine' (3, p. 228). In fact, an important purpose of this paper is to support those who believe that Freud may have distorted his whole description of the development of 'sexuality' in both boys and girls by his insistence on beginning the story (in certain regards) only after the onset of the phallic phase. He gradually came to see the tremendous significance of preoedipal relationships and especially the great importance of mothers for their developing children; yet his discussion of sexuality (by which he seems to have meant both development of the capacity for erotism and that related but still rather different quality—gender) is distorted; for there is evidence that what he considers the first phase of gender development in a little girl is in fact a secondary phase, the result of a growing awareness that there are people whom the little girl thinks luckier than she, whom she recognizes as belonging to the classification 'male'.

This question was raised a long time ago, most clearly by Horney (4, 5) and Jones (6), in the 1920s and most movingly in 1944 by Zilboorg (13). These three led others in stating that Freud was influenced by personal bias in constructing his theory. In 1933, Jones said: '. . . in Freud's description of the phallic phase the essential feature common to both sexes was the belief that only one kind of genital organ exists in the world—a male one' (7, p. 2). Zilboorg, in agreement, says: 'The point at issue at first appears rather trivial, and yet it is fundamental, for it involves the question of whether femininity is primary in the civilized human female or secondary and subsequent to the rudimentary masculinity' (13, p.272).

However, such issues are not resolved by setting up the authorities face to face against each other. Clinical data are less stirring but more helpful. Most recently Sherfey (11) has given us an extensive review of the anatomical and physiological findings of Masters and Johnson.

CLINICAL EVIDENCE[2]

If we were to design an experiment to help us understand the development of the sense of femaleness, we should want to study several types of patients: 1, females without vaginas but otherwise biologically normal; 2, females who are biologically neuter but whose external genitalia at birth looked normal so that no doubt was raised in their parents' minds as to the sex of the infant; 3, females biologically normal except for masculinization of their external genitalia (but with vaginas) who were reared unequivocally as girls; 4, females who are biologically normal except for masculinization of their external genitalia (but with vaginas) who were reared unequivocally as boys; 5, females who are biologically normal but without a clitoris.

The first category is familiar to gynecologists. Its outcome is a sense of femaleness with an accompanying femininity that leads as frequently as it does in anatomically normal women to women's tasks and pleasures, including marriage, vaginal intercourse (in the artificial vagina) with orgasm, childbearing (when a uterus is present), and appropriate mothering.

This is illustrated by a seventeen-year-old feminine, pretty, intelligent girl who appeared anatomically completely normal at birth although behind her external genitalia there was no vagina or uterus. Her parents, having no doubts, raised her as a girl, and female and feminine is what she feels she is. Breasts, public hair, and feminine subcutaneous fat distribution began developing at age ten (because she has normal, ovulating ovaries), but, although she had bouts of monthly abdominal pain, no menstruation occurred. At age fourteen, a routine physical examination—including for the first time examination of the genitalia—revealed that she had no vagina and subsequent studies demonstrated that the uterus was missing but the ovaries were present and functioning normally. She was told these findings. 'What shocked me most was I wanted to have kids . . . and I wanted a vagina. I wanted to feel like everybody else. I wanted to use mine. I mean, when the time came around, I wanted to use it. I didn't want to feel different from anybody . . . which I did. . . .' When given the opportunity for a vaginoplasty, she insisted on it instantly. When asked how she felt about now having a vagina, she said, 'It's different; it's better; it's a step further. I feel like anybody else now.' This is not literally true; at another time she made it clear that she felt almost like other girls and that this was deeply gratifying, but she could not escape her awareness that her vagina is not one she was born with.

Her reaction was what we should expect of a female who has no question as to her sex and who has the desires and fantasies (hopes) of a feminine woman. The absence of vagina and uterus had not damaged her sense of being a female, though since age fourteen the knowledge of this absence had made her feel like a defective female. She never felt she was a boy nor ever wanted to be a male.

The second category can be represented by a biologically neuter girl (the syndrome of ovarian agenesis): chromosomally XO, without gonads or any physiologically significant levels of female hormones. She is feminine, wants to be and works at being attractive in the ways that other girls do; she wants marriage, intercourse, and babies. While she knows she is anatomically defective, as with the non-neuter girl in the first case, she does not question that she is female.

When this girl was first seen at age eighteen, she was unremarkably feminine in her behavior, dress, social and sexual desires, and fantasies, indistinguishable in this regard from other girls in the community. There was one troubling condition which made her less than average to herself. Her breasts had not begun to develop by the time she was eighteen, nor had menstruation started. She was found to have no vagina, though her external genitalia looked normally female; her clitoris was small. She had no uterus, no ovaries, no tubes, no testes.

Her first response on being told she was sterile was to weep. 'I wonder what my kids would have looked like.' Later, when asked if she could recall any dreams from any time in her life, she could remember only one, from a time a year or two before, when she was seriously concerned about not having grown breasts or started to menstruate: 'I was getting married. I had to marry the fellow because I was pregnant.'

When told she would need to have an artificial vagina created, she fought against all the efforts of her family to delay this till she was ready to marry, insisting that they permit the operation immediately. Since the operation she has remained grateful for it. (I presume the reader can only say at this point, 'Of course'.)

What about her feminine interests and role? Her oldest sister told us that the patient when a child was pretty, interested in dresses and dolls and in using cosmetics to play at being a grown-up. The patient reported that on her dates with young men she liked to go dancing, bowling, or to the movies. Her greatest interest had always been stylish clothes, on which she would spend all her spare money. When in her late adolescence she first went to work, she did so only to have extra money for clothes. She did little reading and that exclusively movie and romance magazines. Her daydreams had the same content—interest in feminine ways—as her reading. This is certainly not a list of activities that strikes one as unique, bizarre, carefully thought out to accomplish a plan, or especially worthy of report, were it not that it is my design to underline the unspecialness, the naturalness of her gender identity.

Subjects in the third category (masculinized females reared as girls) and fourth (masculinized females reared as boys) were of key importance in the work of Money and the Hampsons (10). They studied differences in gender identity that arose in infants with the adrenogenital syndrome. In this condition, the external genitalia of the otherwise normally-sexed female infant have been masculinized *in utero* by excessive adrenal androgens. They describe two such children, both biologically normal females, genetically and in their internal sexual anatomy and physiology, but with masculinized external genitalia. The proper diagnosis having been made, one child was reared unequivocally as a female (category three); she turned out to be as feminine as other little girls. The other, not recognized to be female, was reared without question as a male (category four), and became an unremarkably masculine little boy.

In the fifth category is the female normal in all regards except for congenital absence of a clitoris. I have never seen such a case, but should guess that such a child would have no question that she is a female and so during infancy and childhood would develop an essentially intact sense of femaleness, although like a girl without a vagina the part of this sense that results from body sensations of that part of the anatomy would be missing. But we have a clue in regard to such people. It is the practice in certain parts of the Moslem world to excise the clitoris of every female, some in infancy and some not till years later. Despite the fact that there are today millions of such women, they do not fail to develop their sense of being females; they do not lose it; nor do they or their men report that their femininity is reduced (e.g.[1]).

DISCUSSION

Except in the very rare situation where they are uncertain from the birth of their child whether they have a boy or a girl, the parents of the infants we have described have not doubted that the child was a female. And barring some fanciful explanation, such as that she has an inherited racial uncon-

scious awareness of creatures who have penises, the infant will unquestioningly develop her sense of the dimensions and sensations of her body from
her own sensory experiences, which confirm for her the parents' conviction
that she is female. In this way an unquestioned sense of belonging to the
female sex develops. As with males, it is fixed in the first few years of life
and is a piece of identity so firm that almost no vicissitudes of living can
destroy it. Even a severe psychosis or the deterioration of organic brain
disease will not loosen the core gender identity. Other aspects of gender
identity may be severely distorted in the symptomatology of such illnesses,
but the severe disruptions of gender identity we often see in psychotics
(Schreber is an extreme example) are not evidence that the sense of maleness
or femaleness has been destroyed. The patient still knows his sex and in
unguarded moments behaves appropriately for his sex, though his delusions
and hallucinations reveal the force of his *wish* to be a member of the opposite
sex.

It seems to be well established that the vagina is sensed, though probably
not erotized, in little girls, yet I believe that it is not the essential source of
femininity. Just as the sense of maleness of little boys is augmented by the
presence of a penis, but exists even if there is no penis, little girls without
vaginas develop an unquestioned sense of femaleness. They do so because
their parents have no doubt that they are females. Awareness of their biological femaleness coursing below the surface of consciousness no doubt augments this development, but, as we have seen even in the neuter (XO) child
who is not biologically female, a feminine gender identity develops if the
infant is unquestioningly assigned to the female sex.

By adhering to the faulty premise that little girls believe themselves to be
castrated boys, Freud deduced unwarranted conclusions.[3] For instance, he
says, 'the first steps towards definitive femininity' (3, p. 232) occur only
after following a 'very circuitous path' (3, p. 230), by which he means that
no *first* definitive femininity has appeared before the phallic stage, around
age three or four, a statement which simple observation contradicts. Elsewhere (3, p. 234) he states that working out the rage produced by penis envy
on one's first husband is the reason that 'as a rule, second marriages turn out
much better', an opinion we should find hard put to prove a rule. And Freud
said, as everyone knows, that as a result of the anatomical distinction between the sexes he 'cannot evade the notion (though I hesitate to give it
expression) that for women the level of what is ethically normal is different
from what it is in men. Their superego is never so inexorable, so impersonal,

so independent of its emotional origins as we require it to be in men. Character-traits which critics of every epoch have brought up against women —that they show less sense of justice than men, that they are less ready to submit to the great exigencies of life, that they are more often influenced in their judgments by feelings of affection or hostility—all these would be amply accounted for by the modification in the formation of their superego which we have inferred above. We must not allow ourselves to be deflected from such conclusions by the denials of the feminists, who are anxious to force us to regard the two sexes as completely equal in position and worth . . .' (2, pp. 257–258).[4] One gets the impression from observing little girls —and I cannot believe that others have not seen the same—that they show definitive signs of femininity long before the phallic and oedipal phases and that one can trace these early traits of femininity from at least the first year or so of life, not ever seeing them disappear as the little girl grows up and becomes mature. If the observation is correct, then this fundamental building block in Freud's theory of the development of femininity—penis envy and castration complex—becomes only one aspect of the development rather than the origin of it, and opinions like those of Freud quoted above must stand or fall on demonstrable evidence, no longer buttressed by the theory that women are by nature inferior to men, their personalities simply variants on the theme of their being castrated males.

Before closing, let us return to our first case, biologically normal except for having no vagina and uterus. I am not alleging that the body ego of this girl is the same as that of an anatomically normal female, for she has not had that vaginal awareness dimly present in anatomically normal little girls. I suppose that the latter have a sense of space within, of indefinite dimensions but definite significance, produced especially by the vagina and more vaguely by the uterus, this sense being brought in time by use into the sensed body ego, in a way comparable to the building up of the infant's body ego by the felt use of the various parts of his body.

For this girl, however, such sensed representation of these parts could not exist even dimly, and therefore her sense of femaleness could not be exactly the same as that of anatomically normal girls.[5] Her own words indicate how, despite her femininity and her unquestioned sense of being female, that part of her core gender identity produced by body sensations was formed a bit differently from the anatomically normal girl.

'We were taught in school about menstruation [at age ten, four years before she was told she had no vagina or uterus]. I never understood it at all.

I even read books, and I still didn't understand it. I just didn't figure . . . nothing fitted in. My mind was just a blank on it. Then in the eighth grade, I recognized more—that there was a vagina. Yet I still never knew what was intercourse. I didn't know I was different from other people.' She was asked whether, after the school lectures describing the vagina and uterus, she became aware that she was lacking. 'No, in fact you may think it a little ridiculous, but I'll tell you how I thought girls menstruated: from the breasts. But they *had* explained how menstruation really occurred. I don't know *how* I thought that.'

She says she looked as normal as other girls she saw nude; however, when her girl friends began talking about their first sexual experiences in adolescence and she began picturing more clearly what a vagina is, she did not, as far as she could recall, explore for hers, although she was now masturbating.

Then, still speaking of the time before she was told that she had no vagina and before she had any conscious thought that she might not—'I'll tell you what happened the first time when I realized something must be wrong: this boy tried to rape me. He had me down and there was nothing I could do. He started to have intercourse with me—and he just stopped. I thought maybe he was just stopping because he felt bad. Then [much later] for some reason or another, I came out and told somebody I thought I was never going to have kids—and yet I still did not know anything [about the abnormality] and I've never been able to explain that. I felt I couldn't have kids and I wanted kids and I felt I couldn't and yet I don't know what gave me those feelings. *I did not know a thing.*'

In other words, a girl's conviction that she is a female comes from her parents' conviction, but that part of her awareness of being a female which comes from sensing her genitalia will vary according to the anatomy and physiology of these tissues (but will not vary to the degree that she does not believe herself female).

As with little boys, in time the increasingly complicated structure of the personality will overlay the core gender identity with complications and subleties of gender that are not now to be our concern. (I refer to the varying degrees of masculinity that can be found in little girls; their identifications with their fathers and brothers and the development of masculine traits; fantasies of being like boys; envy of the masculine role and of the prized insignia of that role, a penis; disturbances in resolving the oedipal situation; and other traits.) As with the clearly masculine behavior of little boys, however, one can see evidences of gratifying, unquestioned femininity in little girls often by the time they begin to walk. These vary from culture to culture (and from family to family), but even though they are learned attitudes by this early age they are nonetheless already rather firm parts of the child's identity.

These ideas may have some relevance for treatment. It is possible that the analyst has an incorrect criterion for the success of an analysis if he believes he has reached the core of a woman's femininity when he is able to get her to share with equanimity his belief that she is really an inferior form of male.

CONCLUSION

Freud says, 'We have found the same libidinal forces at work in it [female sexuality] as in the male child, and we have been able to convince ourselves that for a period of time these forces follow the same course and have the same outcome in each. Biological factors subsequently deflect those libidinal forces [in the girl's case] from their original aims and conduct even active and in every sense masculine trends into feminine channels' (3, p. 240). Strangely, in the face of what they must have observed daily in their own small children, there are still analysts who are committed to Freud's supposition. Yet it is hard to conceive that such an observer as Freud really believed that the development of masculinity and femininity is the same in boys as in girls until the phallic phase. It may be that having committed himself to his theory ('We have been able to convince ourselves'), Freud tended to ignore his observations. There are hints that he was aware of an earlier phase before the little girl discovers penises, a phase before femaleness has been depreciated: '*When* the little girl discovers her own deficiency, from seeing a male genital, *it is only with hesitation and reluctance that she accepts the unwelcome knowledge.* As we have seen, she clings obstinately to the expectation of one day having a genital of the same kind too, and her wish for it survives long after her hope has expired. The child invariably regards castration in the first instance as a misfortune peculiar to herself; only later does she realize that it extends to certain other children and lastly to certain grown-ups. When she comes to understand the general nature of this characteristic, it follows that femaleness—and with it, of course, her mother—suffers a great *depreciation* in her eyes' (3, p. 233). I have italicized parts of this quotation, for therein Freud hints at the earlier phase of primary femininity. 'When' means that that time has already passed and that there was a time before 'the little girl discovers her own deficiency'; the word 'depreciation' indicates a process that started at a happier point and then retreated.

Therefore, I think that Freud also knew of a time in the little girl's life when she did not feel depreciated but rather accepted herself unquestioningly as a female.

SUMMARY

It is possible that Freud's view of the development of femininity in women is incorrect. He looked upon femininity as a secondary, reparative stage always following upon an earlier awareness of genital inferiority and penis envy. It is suggested, however, that the earliest phase of women's femininity—the core gender identity—is the simple acceptance of body ego, 'I am female'. Only later will this be covered over by penis envy, identification with males, and the other signs of femininity in disrepair with which analysts are so familiar.

This core of femininity develops regardless of chromosomal state or anatomy of the genitalia so long as the parents have no doubt their infant is a female. To explore this thesis, several types of patients are described: 1, females without vaginas but otherwise biologically normal; 2, females who are biologically neuter but whose external genitalia at birth looked normal so that no doubt was raised in their parents' minds as to the sex of the infant; 3, females, biologically normal except for masculinization of their external genitalia (but with vaginas), who were reared unequivocally as girls; 4, females who are biologically normal except for masculinization of their external genitalia (but with vaginas) who were reared unequivocally as boys. Some speculations and anthropological data are presented with regard to a fifth category, females who are biologically normal but without a clitoris.

In the first three types, those unequivocally thought to be females developed a female core gender identity—'I am a female'. Evidence suggests that type four regard themselves as boys. Females of the first three types continued to regard themselves as female even after learning that they were anatomically defective.

NOTES

1. If Freud had treated a woman without a vagina, I think he would have seen that the only thing a woman wants more than a penis is a vagina. It is only when a woman has normal genitalia that she can afford the luxury of wishing she had a penis.
2. That the findings described do not come from women in analysis is a weakness that may be offset by the consistent femininity observed in these patients' behavior: speech, movements, dress, daydreams, and object choices, and in the appropriate affects accompanying these manifestations.
3. Cf. Zilboorg (13, p. 268): 'All agree that in the examination of natural phenomena the introduction of values is perilous to truth. I am inclined to believe that it is the introduction of the concept of the superiority of man in the psychoanalytic theory of sexual development —a concept of values—that is responsible for the general lack of clarity.'
4. Prof. Henry Higgins maintains the same position (8).
   'Why can't a woman be more like a man?
   Men are so honest, so thoroughly square;
   Eternally noble, historically fair;
   Who when you win will always give your back a pat.
   Why can't a woman be like that?
   Why does ev'ryone do what the others do?
   Can't a woman learn to use her head?
   Why do they do everything their mothers do?
   Why don't they grow up like their fathers instead?
   Why can't a woman take after a man?
   Men are so pleasant, so easy to please;
   Whenever you're with them, you're always at ease. . . .'
5. I am certainly not trying to say that all women have exactly the same sense of femaleness, but only that one anatomically normal girl whose parents do not question her sex assignment has much the same core gender identity as another, and that these girls have a very different core gender identity from those reared as boys or as hermaphrodites and not much different from those without vaginas but with sureness of sex assignment.

REFERENCES

1. Bettelheim, Bruno: *Symbolic Wounds, Puberty Rites and the Envious Male*. Glencoe, Ill.: The Free Press, 1954.
2. Freud: *Some Psychical Consequences of the Anatomical Distinction Between the Sexes* (1925). Standard Edition, XIX.
3. ———: *Female Sexuality* (1931). Standard Edition, XXI.
4. Horney, Karen: *On the Genesis of the Castration Complex in Women*. Int. J. Psa., V, 1924, pp. 50–65.
5. ———: *The Flight from Womanhood: The Masculinity Complex in Women, as Viewed by Men and by Women*. Int. J. Psa., VII, 1926, pp. 324–339.
6. Jones, Ernest: *The Early Development of Female Sexuality*. Int. J. Psa., VIII, 1927, pp. 459–472.
7. ———: *The Phallic Phase*. Int. J. Psa., XIV, 1933, pp. 1–33.
8. Lerner, Alan Jay: *My Fair Lady*. New York: Coward-McCann, Inc., 1956.

9. Masters, William H. and Johnson, Virginia E.: *The Artificial Vagina: Anatomic, Physiologic, Psychosexual Function.* W. J. Surg., Obstr., and Gynec., LXIX, 1961, pp. 192–212.

10. Money, John and Hampson, J. G. and J. L.: *Imprinting and the Establishment of Gender Role.* Arch. Neurol. and Psychiatry, LXXVII, 1957, pp. 333–336.

11. Sherfey, Mary Jane: *The Evolution and Nature of Female Sexuality in Relation to Psychoanalytic Theory.* J. Amer. Psa. Assn., XIV, 1966, pp. 28–128.

12. Stoller, Robert J.: *The Sense of Maleness.* Psychoan. Q., XXXIV, 1965, pp. 207–218.

13. Zilboorg, Gregory: *Masculine and Feminine: Some Biological and Cultural Aspects.* Psychiatry, VII, 1944, pp. 257–296.

13. Penis Envy: From Childhood Wish to Developmental Metaphor

William I. Grossman and Walter A. Stewart

None of Freud's theories of female sexuality and psychology has been subject to more severe criticism than his concept of penis envy. The persisting controversy over this issue suggests that the basic theoretical questions have not yet been clarified. And because the theory lacks clarity, its clinical application does not always produce the results expected. Our presentation centers on two such instances, offering clinical vignettes wherein problems in the interpretation of penis envy are demonstrated.

Both patients were in second analyses. In both first analyses, because the patients expressed envy of men and an inability to accept femininity, both analysts interpreted the unconscious penis envy to their patients. Both patients accepted the interpretation with apparent conviction, yet the analyses became stalemated. Freud's (1937) famous dictum that, ". . . with the wish for a penis and the masculine protest we have penetrated through all the psychological strata and have reached bedrock, and thus our activities are at an end" (p. 252) seemed at first to have been vindicated.

Neither of the second analyses, however, confirmed this view. In the second analyses of both patients it became clear that the central conflicts involved a sense of identity, narcissistic sensitivity, and problems of aggression. These conflicts were expressed in terms of a general envy, a sense of worthlessness, inadequacy, damage, and deprivation. The patients apparently easily accepted the reductionism of the interpretation of penis envy in the first analyses primarily because it fitted into their own tendency toward this type of understanding. They regularly explained any unhappiness they experienced as due to some unfair deprivation. This led, of course, to a constant state of envy. The inexact interpretation (Glover, 1931)—or at least the incomplete interpretation—of their penis envy reinforced their sense of being defective and deprived and increased their sense of injustice.

Reprinted with permission from the *Journal of the American Psychoanalytic Association* 24(1976):193–212.

As we hope to show in our clinical examples, *the interpretation had an organizing effect, but not a therapeutic one.* The interpretation, in our view, functioned like a delusion: it brought order into what was otherwise a type of "free-floating envy" or a ready tendency to become envious. The idea of a wish for a missing and unobtainable organ provided a concrete and understandable explanation for dissatisfaction.

CASE PRESENTATIONS

The first patient, Mrs. A., diagnostically a narcissistic character, began her first analysis when she was 21 years old, shortly after she had graduated from college. In the last few months of her college career she had developed an obsessional concern with the meaning of words. This symptom, plus an intense shyness and depression, led to her treatment. She was the first child, four years older than her sister. She described her father as a shy man, successful in business and impatient with and critical of women. He was undemonstrative and objected to being touched. He patronized women and disliked what he considered their hyperemotionality. He was a chronic tease. The patient wanted to impress him and often entered into long aimless arguments with him, which ended in her feeling defeated and running away in tears. Her mother was preoccupied with appearances and hid her anxiety under an aggressive, dominating facade. Insensitive to the feelings of others and often given to sudden enthusiasms for various life styles, she was self-indulgent and was indulged by her husband. Both drank considerably, and dinner often ended in angry recriminations.

The mother constantly criticized the patient for her shyness, her poor posture, and general awkwardness. The mother found these faults particularly irritating because she set such high value on popularity and social success. She liked to recall her social life abroad and recount the number of proposals she had had. Neither the father nor the mother felt there was any reason for a woman to acquire an education; they had no intellectual interests and never had any open discussions about ideas.

The avenue toward a successful feminine development was partly closed by the patient's feeling she couldn't compete with her mother. The mother's craving to be indulged and her self-indulgences meant she wanted to have and had all the advantages of being fed and catered to that belong to babyhood.

Little is known about the first analysis except that the analyst felt that the patient's penis envy was the central issue. In fact, it became so central an obsessional preoccupation that the patient seriously considered going to Denmark for a transsexual operation in which she expected the transplant of a penis could be accomplished. This bizarre response notwithstanding, the patient appeared to have benefited from the first analysis. For the first time in her life she was seeing a man her parents found acceptable. Partly to gain their further approval, she impulsively decided to marry him. Because of this decision and with some satisfaction with the apparent improvement, the analyst decided to terminate the analysis—a decision the patient accepted. The analyst later mentioned to one of us that he felt pleased that the analysis had led the patient to give up her Bohemian ways and to marry a respectable man of her own class.

After the marriage, the patient adopted the role of the upper middle-class "devoted wife and mother with healthy outside interests." This role-playing did not prevent her from becoming progressively more depressed and dissatisfied. She returned to analysis for short periods of time over the next ten years. Her dissatisfaction finally reached such a pitch, she wanted to separate from her husband. She felt he was totally self-absorbed and that their sexual life was an empty ritual. She decided to re-enter analysis, and, because her first analyst was not available, he referred her to one of us.

In the first few sessions she complained that her husband dominated all social gatherings so that by comparison she felt totally unimportant and neglected. He became an overnight expert on a wide variety of subjects, particularly any in which she showed an interest.

In retrospect, she felt the marriage had been a mistake, that she had married because her analyst seemed to approve. She recalled that soon after the termination she felt a sense of surprise and anger that the relationship with the analyst had ended. It seemed that in her mind the marriage was meant to make her more acceptable to the analyst; that he would continue to see her, protect her, and recognize her true but hidden values. Later she came to feel that she had too readily and indiscriminately accepted the interpretation that she wanted a penis.

Mrs. A. was a shy woman who spoke in clichés. She tended to see all issues in black or white, and as having cosmic implications which were not clear to her. Similarity implied an identity, and difference of tastes, opinions, or interests implied a total misfit. Because she disliked a picture in the analyst's waiting room, she felt she and her analyst were so different and incompatible that he would never understand her or be able to analyze her.

She saw herself as a radical and a feminist and felt her difficulties stemmed primarily from the social discrimination against women. She saw the analyst as an uncritical disciple of Freud's who would only see her social protests as penis envy and would attempt to influence her to return to the kitchen and find fulfillment in submission to a man. She felt that, if she agreed to anything the analyst said, she would have to agree with everything.

It became apparent that she had taken the interpretation of her "penis envy" in the first analysis simply as the "proof" of her worthlessness. She had not seen it as an interpretation, but rather as an accusation and a confirmation of her worst fears that she was in fact hopeless and worthless. To the extent that she admired any quality in a man, she became depressed and felt despair. The only solution she could envisage was that she should admit and accept her degraded state.

Her emotional responses were positive and negative extremes. Her affection became infatuation, her admiration, idealization. In the analysis, her sense of worthlessness and her need for love and admiration were central issues. She was rivalrous with and envied both men and women.

The admiration-rivalry conflict reminded her of her feelings for a male cousin who lived with the family when she was in her early teens. She loved and admired him and was impressed by the fact that he could go to the village and date girls there. She looked up to him, but felt he could never be interested in her. She felt awkward, shy, and inarticulate in his presence. This awe of men was still present when she entered the second analysis. She admired men "who could travel to Chicago on business." The patient's awe of men and her sense of relative worthlessness led to the analysis of her masochistic trends, which took the form of spanking fantasies and fantasies of anal rape. The focus of her complaints about being a woman dealt more with the fear of humiliation and ridicule than with the sense of castration— that is, anal and masochistic features were the most prominent. Since admiration always led to rivalry and envy, and sexual interest to aggression, the only permanent tie to the object was of a sadomasochistic nature. She chose the masochistic role and the defense of a mild paranoid attitude. Indeed, the "helpless acceptance" of the penis envy interpretation in the first analysis seemed masochistically gratifying.

Even to interpret her masochism posed the threat that the interpretation would be experienced as a "put down" and gratify her masochistic impulse; all interpretations, if not narcissistically gratifying, gratified masochistic wishes. They were felt as attacks in which her worthlessness, her defectiveness, and her aggression were unmasked. The analysis threatened to become interminable, one in which the relationship to the analyst was maintained, but only at the price of an analytic stalemate.

Over many years the patient was able to recognize her need to be a mistreated little girl, rather than to face her disappointments as a grown woman. The emphasis on the male-female dichotomy gradually lessened and focused more on the problem of her status. As she increasingly experienced the positive values in being a woman rather than a victimized child, she became less clinging, more outgoing, and her sense of humor increased. The sadistic impulses behind the masochistic submission have become clear to the patient. Finally, interpretations were experienced as illuminating and helpful. The case is now in a terminable phase.

In summary, the issue of wanting a penis never came up in that form. Rather, the conflict appeared more widely narcissistic in terms involving the patient's importance and value, although it was expressed chiefly in terms of the disadvantages of being a woman. When, in the first analysis, an interpretation of her penis envy was offered, she took the interpretation quite literally and concretistically, as shown by her plan to go to Denmark for a transsexual operation. Her envy of men was only one aspect of an envy that dominated her life. Her complaints were that in all situations she had been cheated. Her sister got her mother's breast. Her mother had the baby, was loved and indulged by the father, and had everyone's love and admiration, even the patient's. Mrs. A. felt doomed to be the one who has nothing, and has no claim to love or fame.

She could not do what many of our patients can do: see the emotions and experiences that lie behind this way of expressing their conflicts. *As analysts we may also on occasion have similar difficulties in knowing how concretely the metaphors of development are to be understood.*

Our second case, Mrs. B., a 28-year-old married secretary, had begun her analysis with a woman analyst. She stated, with seeming unconcern, that she was homosexual and alcoholic. She subsequently reported a doll phobia. She had been married for one and a half years when she confessed her homosexual interests and activities to her husband. He insisted she see the family physician, who referred her for analysis.

The patient was the oldest of three children and the only girl. Her brothers were two and a half and five years younger. The father was an angry, anxious man. The patient said that if he looked at a lovely view, the only thing that caught his attention would be the garbage dump. The mother was a flirtatious woman, the life of the party. She paid little attention to the patient except when the father was away, when she would take the patient into bed with her. The patient recalled lying in "spoon position" next to her, stiff with fear. Mrs. B. had had almost no direct contact with the father, all communications being routed through the mother. The father's father had been an improvident man with many get-rich-quick schemes. She recalled with a great sense of loss and guilt that he had taken her sledding, caught pneumonia, and died. She had felt she would be accused of murder. This grandfather had three children, the patient's father being the youngest. There were two older sisters, both of whom had been promiscuous, possibly prostitutes, and certainly alcoholic. The father held up his sisters as bad examples of what would happen to the patient if she ever did anything of which he disapproved.

During adolescence, she recalled "playing dead," for a long period of time and frightening her playmates. She also remembered cutting her wrists, which she claimed was in order to get attention, thinking it was the equivalent of the injuries boys got when they played football. She had always had the wish and expectation of becoming a priest, ignoring the fact that, at that time, this was not possible. She had consciously wished to be a boy because boys had greater freedom and companionship. Her dreams had a bizarre quality and were full of injuries and bleeding. In one dreams she became radioactive and was therefore a threat to all who came near her. In another dream a young man had his tongue cut out.

The first analyst felt the patient was identified with men and that she was pretending to be a man. When asked if she really wanted to be a man, the patient replied, yes, she did, but then added, "Of course, not consciously." She felt her brothers were better off, being stronger, able to win medals and admiration. A dream stating that "All people should have medals that no one was stupid!", along with other material, convinced the first analyst that the patient resented being the "only one in the family who did not get a penis."

The first analyst interpreted the patient's penis envy to her. The patient quickly agreed that this was the issue and, in fact, the only reason for her coming into analysis. Since her wish could not be fulfilled, there was no point in her continuing the analysis. A sadomasochistic impasse developed in which the patient felt the analyst treated her as if she were a criminal. In response, the patient refused to listen to anything the analyst said or to tell her anything meaningful about herself. This was the situation after one year; in the face of this impasse, she was referred to one of us.

Mrs. B. was a short, stocky woman who looked younger than her stated age. She was obviously under great tension, which she handled by acting in a pseudotough manner. When asked about her feelings at suddenly being transferred to a new analyst, she said she felt it was "just in time," and that she was "lucky to get out alive." She "interpreted" this to mean that in her "unconscious she must be murderously angry," and then added, "but this is only one interpretation . . . there may be others."

It was apparent that in the first analysis Mrs. B. had experienced all interpretations, including the one of penis envy, as accusations and as an assault. During her second analysis she recalled that her younger brother by two and a half years, had had severe colic as a baby and had cried constantly. On one particular occasion, he was left to "cry it out" in the patient's room. She recalled being afraid of her wish to strangle him. When he finally stopped crying and fell asleep, she was afraid he was dead or, even more frightening, that he had crawled out of his crib and was snaking across the floor, creeping toward her with the intention of eating her up.

Her dreams and associations suggested that she was the illegitimate daughter of one of the father's sisters. This suspicion was confirmed, and then the fact of her extraordinary early neglect emerged. Her biological mother, the more delinquent of the two sisters, had been totally incapable of taking care of her. The patient had been so severely neglected, she had to be hospitalized in a starved condition. She remained in a Catholic home between the ages of fourteen and eighteen months. In an eerie manner she recalled a number of experiences from this time, and one particularly traumatic event. She recalled an evening when a child in the crib next to her was crying inconsolably. She refused to stay down in the crib and had to be tied down. When the patient woke next morning, she saw that the girl in the crib had died, having suffocated in her own vomitus. This was the incident screened by the memory of the brother's crying and was the major contributing experience to her doll phobia.

The diagnostic category of borderline seemed quite clear when she reported that she bathed each evening because she might meet the analyst in her dreams. This type of thinking also illustrated the patient's inability to distinguish between the reality of an experience and its possible symbolic meaning. On one occasion, when at the beach with her nieces, she wanted to keep them warm by wrapping the terry cloth robe she was wearing around them. She felt she could not do this because it would signal her wish to be pregnant and she couldn't afford to let anyone know of this.

In the analysis, the central issue was the patient's fear of aggression. The pseudotough demeanor and the conscious wish to be a man were her defenses against her fear of the man's aggression. This in turn was based, of course, on the projection of her own aggressive and destructive impulses which she quite correctly felt she couldn't control. As a consequence she was constantly tense, frightened, and on guard. When her mother once asked her about her analysis and if her analyst was handsome, the patient had a fantasy that the mother would storm into the analyst's office, break up the furniture, and either kill or seduce the analyst.

The patient's "wish to be a man" was in part a response to her father's feeling that most women were dirty and unable to exert any self-control. It was also an effort to overcome some envy of her brothers. Of much more significance was the role of the "penis envy" as a defense against castration. In regard to the man's phallic aggression, penis envy represented an identification with the aggressor. But the patient was afraid of impulses from all stages of psychosexual development. She was perhaps most afraid of being devoured and of her own cannibalistic impulses. These fears were based, of course, on the early neglect and frequent abandonment. The early neglect contributed to poor ego boundaries and poor self-object differentiation. The consequent projective identification is clear—in her fear of her brother's cannibalistic impulse, the aggressive sexuality of all men, and the firm belief that she was lucky to have "gotten away alive" from her first analyst. Her chronic panic was also illustrated by her fear of being close to or touched by her mother. One can say that she lived in a perpetual state of panic that she would be eaten, beaten, or penetrated. The fantasy of being radioactive, dangerous, and not to be touched was one defense. The other was to depersonalize. The alcoholism was a way of diminishing the panic, as was also the homosexuality, in which she took the male role, since men appeared to be less vulnerable.

The interpretation of the penis envy exploited a metaphor, which seemed to represent both her fears and her defense against them. It created a type of delusional formation that brought order into her thoughts. It is reminiscent of Schreber's (Freud, 1911) delusional system, which also involved homosexuality and self-transformation, and which was intended to act as a defense against aggression.

These two cases help to explain why a woman's "wish for a penis" or "envy of the penis," whether inferred and interpreted as an unconscious wish during analysis or stated openly by the patient, must be treated—like the manifest content of a dream or a screen memory—as a mental product. It is not to be regarded as an ultimate, irreducible, and even genetically necessary truth, impenetrable to further analysis. This is most obviously true in patients who come for analysis having interpreted their own dissatisfactions as "penis envy." It is particularly and more significantly true in patients such as ours, whose envy is conscious and where the narcissistic injury and fear of aggression are more central to the illness. In these cases, the "wish for a penis" is but one highly condensed representation of these critical concerns. We have been told of other cases in which the interpretation was made that what the patient "really wanted was a penis, a penis of her own," in which the envy of men hid a sense of deprivation, worthlessness, and fear of abandonment. These feelings and the experiences that led to them were the critical issue. The interpretation of penis envy, even when it referred to real experiences, reduced the multiple sources of dissatisfaction to a single cause. Whether intentionally or unintentionally, a clinical metaphor was thus created.

DISCUSSION

For over 50 years the role of penis envy in feminine psychosexual development and in pathology has been questioned. For Freud, the discovery of the anatomical distinction between the sexes marked the real beginning, or more accurately, the nodal point, in the differences between male and female psychosexual development. He regarded libidinal development prior to this moment as essentially similar in boys and in girls and did not concern himself with other factors—for example, the effect on development of the different ways in which parents treat their sons and daughters. Freud may not have recognized the importance of these particular environmental determinants in psychosexual development or, more likely, he may have been primarily interested in reconstructing the *typical* ways in which the child's distorted understanding of reality influenced his development. In any event, he seems to have focused on the route by which object relations developed out of narcissism and how the succession of libidinal goals resulted from the transformation of instincts. He saw the little girl's observation of a penis as marking a turning point in her psychosexual development, observing that girls react to this discovery with a feeling of damage, deprivation, and envy. Their response is a narcissistic injury and an envy that is concerned with genital differences and often focuses on the penis. Freud felt the wish for a penis had to be transformed into a wish for a baby if normal feminine development was to be accomplished. More precisely, he stated that the wish for a penis added to the wish for a child, which originated in other sources (1917, 1933). The optimal solution to the penis-baby transformation, in Freud's view, was one of the *forces* that led to the change from the girl's preoedipal attachment to the mother to the oedipal attachment to the father.

Freud's formulation of the girl's development was based on a comparative approach to the development of both boys and girls. It seemed to highlight the ubiquitous factors common to both sexes (Freud, 1931), while sharply contrasting the differences entailed in the development of masculinity and femininity. Freud's examination of early female sexuality led him to emphasize certain aspects of the preoedipal period. He stressed the role of early disappointment, narcissistic injury, fixation, and penis envy in the development of women's psychosexual pathology. He thought that the failure to resolve in an optimal way the developmental challenges posed by penis envy would of necessity impair the change of object and the change of leading genital zone. Character disorders, neurosis, genital inhibition, and the rejection of femininity would almost inevitably be the result.

In contrast to these views was a series of papers by Horney which led to an apparently irreconcilable difference between the two. She (1967) acknowledged an early 'narcissistic" penis envy, but discounted its importance in pathology. In her view, penis envy did not promote development, but was the result of the girl's disappointment in her naturally developing attachment to her father. Penis envy could help to repress the little girl's fears of penetration of the vagina by the large penis of the father. Horney's approach thus had the value of pointing to the need to clarify the origins of penis envy, its defensive function, and its role in early object relations.

We shall not pursue here the ramifications of this interesting controversy. The important point for clinical and theoretical understanding of penis envy is that we need to resolve the false antithesis generated by the apparent disagreement. "Penis envy" and the "denial of the vagina," "early narcissistic injury" and "disappointment in object relations," are different facets of the same issues of normal and pathological development. The overemphasis of one facet or the other promotes the tendency to reductionism in clinical interpretation, as occurred in the first analysis of each of the patients we presented.

Freud and Horney agreed that penis envy could occur during development on a narcissistic basis and as a result of oedipal disappointment. They differed with regard to which type was more important for pathology. The differing views can be reconciled with an epigenetic approach, an approach that enables us to recognize that the child's awareness of the genital differences is an important organizer of experiences at many levels of psychic differentiation and integration (Grossman, 1975).

We suggest that, of the two distinctly recognizable phases (see Greenacre, 1953), in the earlier phase, the awareness of the genital differences becomes meaningful in terms of the child's sense of her worth and in terms of her attempt to differentiate herself from her mother. Narcissistic needs and self-object differentiation are then the critical development issues (Galenson and Roiphe, 1976; Mahler, 1975; Mahler et al., 1975). In the later phase, the relationships to both parents as a function of the sexual difference is the important issue and leads to the familiar fantasies of the phallic stage and the oedipal period; conflicts having to do with object relations and drive impulses are central, along with the formation of the ego ideal and superego. Once the genital differences are discovered, and once penis envy appears, the latter becomes enmeshed in those relations that give it meaning. The working out of the oedipal relations will have an important influence in determining to what extent both conscious and unconscious penis envy come to stand as the representation of earlier and later conflicts.

Thus, to the child, the meaning of the discovery of the "anatomical distinction" will depend on a complex variety of preparatory experiences. The timing of this discovery will be important, since the child's cognitive and libidinal levels will naturally play a part in his interpretation of this new information. Narcissistic conflicts and the child's relations to both parents will determine the final result. Parental attitudes toward the sex of the child, toward their own genitals and sexual relationships, will aid or disrupt the child's integration of the awareness of the genital differences.

We think the awareness of the importance of these factors, which is forced upon us by the clinical examples we have presented, helps to resolve some current criticisms of the penis envy concept.

Finally, it follows from our discussion that, in the clinical setting, the emergence of "penis envy" must be treated as a manifest content, the significance of which will only emerge in the analysis. Narcissistically fixated patients, for example, when they confront the fact of the genital differences, will experience this awareness as a further narcissistic injury. To narcissistically oriented patients, "penislessness" can at any time in the psychosexual development become a prime example of deprivation, and they experience this in the same way as when they were eighteen months old. A severe disturbance in the narcissistic development will create a traumatic vulnerability to the discovery of the genital differences and to all experiences of deprivation. Thus, the primal scene, too, will be traumatic because, as another instance of stimulation without gratification or resolution, it is experienced as a narcissistic affront.

Clinically, the problem is to distinguish penis envy as it represents an attempted regressive solution to oedipal conflicts from penis envy as part of a general narcissistic character disorder. As in the cases we have presented, the penis envy is apt to be merely one means of representing the narcissistic injuries of all levels of development.

Whether penis envy is, in a particular instance, a contributing factor in the development of narcissistic character pathology, or whether it is a consequence of this pathology or otherwise implicated in it, the attendant ego disturbances present technical problems. We have observed other patients similar to those presented and have recognized certain factors making the analysis of "penis envy" difficult. Commonly found factors include global identifications and the associated fears of merging and abandonment, domination-submission conflicts, fear of overwhelming aggression, masochistic fantasies, primitive defenses, and extreme sensitivity to narcissistic injury. Patients with narcissistic character disorders also responded in a remarkably similar way to any interpretation of "penis envy" or their "wish for a penis" in particular. They seemed unable to distinguish fantasy, metaphor, or symbolic representation from reality. This is very clear in Mrs. B.'s fear of warming her nieces by wrapping them in the terry cloth bathrobe she was wearing—not permissible because it meant a wish to be pregnant. The original wish to warm the children was totally ignored because the symbolic meaning of the act became the only "reality."

The patients clearly did not respond to the interpretation of their "penis envy" in a way that was useful to them. They heard it as a final immutable truth. Although they readily agreed to the interpretation, it was with a feeling of despair—for it confirmed their worst fears of being worthless.

Is the problem of interpretation one of technique, in the sense that the interpretation was, for example, incorrect or poorly timed? Or is the stalemate that occurred in these cases due to a lack of clarity in our clinical theory?

We believe that the interpretation of the penis envy was correct in the sense that it described the patient's defensive effort toward the resolution of an inner conflict, and, yet, in some sense it must be incorrect, since it was not helpful (mutative) to the patient.

Perhaps the issue can be more clearly seen from another perspective. We wish to focus on the way theoretical constructs and developmental models are sometimes applied to clinical situations. Certainly, examples such as ours can serve only as illustrations. Furthermore, our understanding of these cases can be enriched if countertransference and other technical problems are considered as well. Still, there is a problem of the application to interpretation and reconstruction of theory and developmental understanding. The analyst's understanding of his patient is informed by psychoanalytic theory, especially conceptions of drive and defense and their role in development. We have a shorthand for describing patients' conflicts that we use in presenting cases, and penis envy is part of that shorthand. When we speak of penis envy we may be referring to a number of things simultaneously, including experiences, fantasies, wishes, derivatives, and so on. In this sense, then, the concept of penis envy may be said to be a metaphor belonging to the theory, since the concept derives its name from a specific experience. To classify clinical material under the heading of penis envy is to "interpret" the case, according to one way we use the word interpretation.

What about the patient's "wish for a penis"? It may be conscious from the start of treatment as an intellectualization. It may, as in the cases presented, be a conscious wish as the result of a prior analysis. In that instance, it needs to be analyzed, for it is a conscious mental content whose unconscious meaning must be understood.

We are suggesting that in these cases, the analysts lent the patients their theoretical metaphor and the patients accepted it. In these cases, too, much that was important in the patient's conflicts was condensed under this heading. For them, the metaphor was an apt one in that it represented one of their desires and sources of dissatisfaction. However, the wish for a penis was not their own developmentally derived metaphor, their own unconscious shorthand for representing their childhood disappointments. Nor was the disappointment over the discovery of the genital difference the starting point of the derivatives later to be interpreted as penis envy. The misapplication of the theoretical metaphor to the clinical situation was a confusion of theory and clinical situation which reduced the patient's conflicts to the "bedrock" of a concretely apprehended metaphor. We believe that, in development as well, the wish for a penis may also become the unconscious concretely apprehended metaphor for childhood disappointments that are associated with the recognition of the genital difference.

The tendency to use theoretical formulations directly in clinical interpretations, in a sense, like a theoretical cliché, undoubtedly arises with the failure of clinical understanding. It is a misuse of theory that is common and to which theory easily lends itself. The analyst may then explain his lack of success as due to the fact that the interpretation involves the "bedrock" wish, or that there is faulty reality testing, a thought disorder, or other defect. Thus he explains the "immutability" of the wish.

The interpretation of the patient's wish for a penis is correct in that it makes conscious the metaphoric representation of the conflict. It offers a frame of reference from which the patient can look at the experience. It is incorrect as a clinical interpretation because it forces a theoretical impersonal form onto the material. It has only an organizing function; not a therapeutic one. This miscarriage of the purpose of an interpretation seems to have characterized the analytic approach in the first analyses of the patients presented.

Some patients, primarily those with neurotic conflicts, are not misled by the metaphor and will make the interpretation meaningful and therapeutic. These patients, quite unlike the category of patients our examples illustrate, generally resist the interpretation at first. Indeed, it takes hard and time-consuming analytic work to convince the neurotic patient that the unconscious fantasy of possessing a penis is derived from childhood, but is active as a determinant of her current life activities and the nature of her object relations. We think these clinical differences can be accounted for if the early narcissistic syndromes of penis envy are distinguished from the later object-related forms.

We believe this distinction rests on and also supports the theoretical formulations presented earlier in the paper. Finally, we hope the theoretical distinction helps in understanding why the early controversy concerning penis envy and the current criticisms of the concept have not been resolved.

SUMMARY

Two phases of penis envy are considered. The first regularly occurs early in development and is registered as a narcissistic injury which can be resolved under optimal conditions and can contribute to female psychosexual development. If, however, it is not favorably resolved or, even more significantly, if the basic character disorder is of a narcissistic type, the awareness of the genital difference becomes one of many narcissistic traumas.

A later phase of penis envy usually represents a regressive effort to resolve oedipal conflicts. In the past, these two phase-oriented forms of penis envy have not been adequately distinguished.

Two clinical examples are presented in which the envy of men was only part of the tendency to envy in a narcissistic character disorder. In the analysis, the interpretation of the penis envy offered a metaphor around which all of the "free-floating" envy could coalesce. The cases illustrate the necessity to consider penis envy as the manifest content of a symptom that needs analysis, rather than as "bedrock" or ultimate conflict.

REFERENCES

Freud, S. (1911), Psychoanalytic notes upon an autobiographical account of a case of paranoia. *Standard edition*, 12:3–82. London: Hogarth Press, 1958.
——— (1917), On transformations of instinct as exemplified in anal eroticism. *Standard edition*, 17:126–133. London: Hogarth Press, 1955.
——— (1931), Female sexuality. *Standard edition*, 21:223–243. London: Hogarth Press, 1961.
——— (1933), Femininity. *Standard edition*, 22:112–135. London: Hogarth Press, 1964.
——— (1937), Analysis terminable and interminable. *Standard edition*, 23:216–253. London: Hogarth Press, 1964.
Galenson, E. and Roiphe, H. (1976), Some suggested revisions concerning early female development. *JAPA*, 24(5):29–57.
Glover, E. (1931), The therapeutic effect of inexact interpretation; a contribution to the theory of suggestion. *Internat. J. Psycho-Anal.*, 12:397–411.
Greenacre, P. (1953), Penis awe and its relation to penis envy. In: *Drives, affects, behavior*, ed. R. M. Loewenstein. New York: International Universities Press, pp. 176–190.
Grossman, W. I. (1975), Discussion on "Freud and female sexuality." *Internat. J. Psycho-Anal.*, in press.
Horney, K. (1967), *Feminine psychology*, ed. H. Kelman. New York: Norton.
Mahler, M. S. (1975), Discussion of "Some suggested revisions concerning early female development" by E. Galenson and H. Roiphe. Presented at the New York Psychoanalytic Society, 11 February 1975.
——— , Pine, F. and Bergman, A. (1975), *The psychological birth of the human infant*. New York: Basic Books.

14. The Influence of Values in Psychoanalysis: The Case of Female Psychology

Ethel S. Person

Introduction

At the heart of the psychoanalytic enterprise is the purpose of examining the ways in which thoughts and behaviors, beliefs, preferences, and values are influenced by unconscious mental processes. Psychoanalysis is a discipline that fosters skepticism about the apparent and self-evident meaning of surface phenomena, thereby challenging the certainty of either revealed or objective truth, the first (religion) explicitly and the second (science) implicitly. Like philosophy, psychoanalysis alerts us to the fact that we must look for the values and ideology underlying any body of knowledge, including psychoanalysis itself.

No cultural enterprise is value free, including science. Science values objective knowledge. Objectivity is fundamental to the pursuit of science, as is evident in the historical fact that science is an achievement of Western culture, not an autonomous development in every culture. Yet as Kuhn (1962) has pointed out, scientific research is based on beliefs about the nature of the world. While these beliefs appear to be objective and truthful, they may be superceded when new findings or anomalies arise to contradict the existing set of beliefs, assumptions, or traditions. Thus, despite its objectivity, science is both the product of cultural values and a contributor to the cultural evolution of values. According to Hogan and Emler, "Science supports the myth of developmental progress. Innovation, experiment, the rebuilding of theory, all these are justified because they will make things better . . . the extraordinary success of science in the modern era has contributed to the influential position of individualism and rationalism" (Hogan and Emler, 1978, 486).

A similarly complex relationship exists between cultural values and psychoanalysis. Psychoanalysis, beginning with Freud's assumptions, embodies

Reprinted with permission from *Psychiatry Update* 2 (1983):36–50.

values central to Western culture. Chief among these are an interest in the individual and his or her welfare and a commitment to self-knowledge as an end unto itself. Rieff claimed that "Freud created the masterwork of the century, a psychology that . . . unriddled—to use Emerson's prophetic catalogue of subjects considered inexplicable in his day—'language, sleep, madness, dreams, beasts, sex' " (Rieff, 1961, xx). In insisting that nothing human was alien to him, Freud revealed a commitment to the worth of the individual, no matter how marginal or mad. Freud's work is thus an integral part of an intellectual tradition that elevates individualism to an ideology.

In turn, psychoanalysis has given a distinctive shape to intellectual life in the twentieth century. According to Rieff, "Freud's doctrine, created piecemeal and fortunately never integrated into one systematic statement, has changed the course of Western intellectual history; moreover, it has contributed as much as doctrine possibly can to the correction of our standards of conduct" (Rieff, 1961, xx). Indeed, some psychiatrists and critics of culture have raised the objection that individuals living in an era of declining objective moral authority attempt to substitute the goals of mental health and normalcy for a comprehensive moral system (Rieff, 1966; Morgenthau and Person, 1978; Gross, 1978). Psychoanalysis and values, then, like science and values, ply a two-way street.

This discussion is meant to emphasize the fact that no *cultural* enterprise can be value free. A cultural enterprise must, by definition, be value laden and embody a set of beliefs. Values are not always easily separated from prejudice and bias. Values may be generally defined as highly abstracted ideas about what is good or bad, right or wrong, desirable or undesirable. Prejudice and bias carry a particularly pejorative connotation. To be prejudiced or biased means to judge without adequate knowledge or examination and to come to a premature conclusion, usually unfavorable. Therefore, it is important to distinguish values that are implicit in the context and framework of any cultural enterprise from values and prejudices that contaminate either the application or the theoretical assumptions of an enterprise.

In psychoanalysis, as in the other behavioral sciences, observations and hypotheses are inevitably distorted by historical bias and sometimes, more pervasively, by values buried in major theoretical assumptions. As Macklin (1973) has pointed out, values are implicit in psychoanalysis in at least three ways. Values are held by the patient. Values are held by the therapist. And values are implicit or explicit in the theory. As long as those values coincide, they go virtually unnoticed. Cultural biases become most apparent during times of social change, times when they no longer coincide.

Freud sincerely but mistakenly believed that analysts were ethically neutral and that the observations of analysis were value free. Freud himself, however, offers an example of the influence of bias in his own beliefs about the nature of femininity.

Under the impact of changing cultural norms, we have become aware of the presence of sexism in all of the psychotherapies, including psychoanalysis, and of the theoretical justifications for sexism in fundamental psychoanalytic assumptions. Changing prescriptions and changing concepts of the female role(s), as well as the persistence of outdated theories, have led us to scrutinize value biases implicit in practice and theory.

This chapter describes changes in the definition of normative femininity and in psychoanalytic formulations of female psychology. Reformulations of female development seem to have lagged unduly, given the considerable countervailing data and the serious critiques of early formulations. As the chapter demonstrates, the reasons for this lag illustrate the methodological problems and value biases in psychoanalytic theory making that transcend the special case. The chapter employs a dual concept of values, examining some of the perversions of values (biases, prejudices) that have developed and also exploring the beliefs and commitments (general values) that underlie psychoanalytic formulations. By focusing on one example, the author intends to demonstrate how new data, both from psychoanalysis and from other fields, have forced a reexamination of the methodology of psychoanalysis and of the values embedded in its major theoretical assumptions.

SEXISM AND CHANGING GOALS IN THERAPY

Many feminist scholars and mental health professionals have used the theme of sexism in psychotherapy to illustrate value bias underlying therapeutic decisions, practices, and theoretical formulations. The concept of "normalcy" or appropriate femininity necessarily colors the assessment of both pathology and treatment goals. According to Broverman et al. (1970), mental health professionals, rather than challenging gender stereotypes, shared popular biases. Dependency and passivity were seen as normal female qualities and assertiveness and independence as normal male qualities. Accordingly, mental health professionals attributed role dissatisfaction in women to psychopathology. The debate about normal female development and femininity relates to the more general debate in psychiatry about the distinction between difference (or deviation) and mental illness. Arguments about "what women want" and whether these goals reflect health or neurosis are analogous in form to arguments about homosexuality or political dissidence.

Because psychoanalytic theory proposes mental health norms, it also implies therapeutic goals. This is true regardless of what one proposes should be the primary mental health objective—genital maturity, motherhood as the ultimate resolution of penis envy, the cult of true femininity, mature object relations, or generativity. For clinicians, knowledge of this existential dilemma, what has been called the dual descriptive-normative role of theory (Macklin, 1973), translates into vexing clinical problems. Clinicians no longer have the certainty of fixed, external definitions of abnormality and mental health, previously conceptualized as mature genitality or as the achievement of gender-appropriate behavior. And the therapeutic community stands charged "with fostering traditional gender roles, stereotyping of women, biased expectations and devaluation of women, sexist use of theoretical constructs, and responding to women as sex objects, including seduction" (Vaughter, 1976, 140).

What Women Want: Changing Treatment Goals

Analysts disagree strongly about whether the nature of psychological illness has changed or whether a new language has simply developed for describing old problems. Some classes of clinical problems do seem virtually unchanged, such as the biologically derived mental illnesses. But a decisive shift has occurred in the problems of living that patients predominantly complain about and in the goals they seek.

Attitudinal changes toward sex, gender, and pair-bonding implicit in the sexual revolution, the women's movement, and the crisis of the family have complex and contradictory implications for opportunity and security in women's lives. With the changing definitions of femininity, women have assumed greater latitude in their lives, and the modern woman does not entirely resemble her more traditional counterpart. Many goals have changed radically, while some remain the same. In any case, we can no longer be dogmatic about what are the appropriate choices in women's life trajectories. A greater range of plausible and acceptable adaptations exists, stemming from the dramatic changes that have taken place in the cultural milieu.

Whatever the major presenting symptom, newer treatment goals, insofar as they are articulated, are cast in terms of enabling a woman's individual enhancement in the professional, sexual, or relational sphere. The emerging pattern is one of activity and achievement, not one of passive acceptance, and while underlying conflicts may be the same, different adaptive resolutions are sought.

Increasingly, women are seeking treatment as an explicit aid to their search for autonomy and self-realization, and they believe that the vehicle for this is their professional or creative achievement. This stands in marked contrast to goals commonly stated twenty years ago. At that time, such ambitions were often believed to represent masculine aspirations and hence to be misguided. Penis envy and its attendant anxieties were considered to lie at the heart of a woman's work problems. Today, the goal is to work through any inhibition of assertion or achievement motivation.

Women today are also seeking greater sexual fulfillment. They are looking for new modes of interpersonal relationships, different from the more traditional role in which submissiveness and ingratiation were deemed so integral to their "femininity." Today, women place increasing value on egalitarian relations, and this new bias extends to the therapy situation. Many more women seek female therapists in order to avoid a stereotypical relationship in which a young and helpless female patient is dependent on an older and authoritative male.

Some goals, of course, are not at all new. Women are still motivated toward stable affiliative relations, as are men. Many seek treatment because they are unable to form permanent relationships, while others seek it to help them through the breakup of a marriage, a deteriorating relationship, or the stresses that accrue from the breakdown of the family.

Shifting goals highlight the intrinsic problem in the dual descriptive and normative roles of theory. The serious potential for therapeutic bias in goal setting is sometimes underestimated. Take, for example, Barglow and Schaefer's (1976) response to a question raised by Marmor (1973). Marmor had posed a hypothetical question about treating Ibsen's Nora. Should an analyst interpret her penis envy and rejection of a normal female role, or should he foster her healthy rebellion? Barglow and Schaefer disavow the dilemma. They ask, "Are these really psychoanalytic problems? Psychoanalysis, after all, is not an ideology (the critics to the contrary), but professes to be a science" (Barglow and Schaefer, 1976, 322). In the author's opinion, Marmor was right, and Barglow and Schaefer have missed the point: an analyst's response (countertransference) must be permeated by his or her world view. Preferences and beliefs influence the therapist's judgment and may thereby slant interpretations or therapeutic emphasis.

Therapists communicate their values not primarily with directives, but with silences, questions, and the very rhythms and cadences of the therapeutic hour. Sometimes, though, their directives are explicit. The author has seen this in consultation and treatment with any number of women, particularly those now in their fifties and sixties. Many of these women were directly advised by analysts and psychiatrists that their feminine obligation, destiny, or duty lay in preserving the marriage, in not threatening their husbands, in modulating their own sexuality, and so forth. Parenthetically, this age group of former patients bears the most hostility to psychiatry. While such inappropriate direct interventions are manifestations of countertransference reactions, the underlying theory has enabled clinicians to remain blind to them. In other words, although such countertransference reactions were individually derived and not theoretically mandated, they were culturally and theoretically reinforced. Furthermore, psychoanalysts may have tended to be more prescriptive with women than with men because of their shared countertransference response toward women. For example, Chodorow (1978) has pointed out the prescriptive quality in Freud's discussion of female psychology: the little girl "must," "has to," and so on. Finally, at a time when dependency was more consonant with the female role, women may have sought such interventions transferentially with more insistence than male patients.

AN OVERVIEW OF CHANGING THEORIES

Freud essentially used only a single concept, that of penis envy, to explain the development of sexuality, normal gender development, and neurotic conflict in women. By ascribing femininity solely by the outcome of thwarted masculinity, his theory doomed women to infantilism and immaturity relative to men. Contemporary psychoanalysis, in contrast, takes a systems approach. Most important, theories of normal sexual development, of the acquisition of femininity (gender), and of the predominant neurotic conflicts have now been revised.

The following sections discuss the changing theories of sexuality, gender identity, and penis envy in some detail, since dramatic theoretical revisions have taken place in these areas. A review of changes in these formulations highlights the faulty methodology and the underlying ideology that for so long locked the old ideas into place. Many other aspects of female psychology must be omitted here because of limitations in the length of the discussion. Despite the importance of changes in conceptions about conscience and morality (Schafer, 1974; Gilligan, 1982) and about early object relations (Chodorow, 1978), for instance, the review cannot extend to these areas.

Changing Theories of Sexuality

It was a tenet of Freudian theory that female sexuality must necessarily be somewhat debilitated or hyposexual, given the need to switch both object and organ. According to Freud, penis envy was decisive in sexual development, as well as in neurotic conflict and the development of femininity. Penis envy was responsible for the girl's turn away from her mother (renouncing the clitoris) and toward her father (to get a penis from him). Such a double switch was believed to result necessarily in a diminished libido. This theory appeared to be substantiated by the inability of many women patients to achieve orgasm. Clara Thompson (1950) was among the first to readdress the apparent problem of female sexuality. She believed that the major sexual dilemma for women was not penis envy, but acknowledging their own sexuality in this culture. Her insight proved prophetic.

It is in the area of sexuality that the most radical changes have occurred, both in women's expectations and in psychoanalytic theory. The continuing role of clitoral eroticism in adult women, as demonstrated by Masters and Johnson (1966) and others, has led to a repudiation of Freud's theory of a clitoral-vaginal transfer, hypothetically triggered by the young girl's sense of clitoral inferiority. No one today holds that true femininity depends on achieving vaginal orgasms. Female sexuality is no longer viewed as intrinsically debilitated: it is now viewed as actively robust.

Along with rhetoric actual sexual practices have also changed. Female sexuality has been liberated in two ways. First, it has been freed from ignorance. The recognition that maximum sexual pleasure in orgasm depends on adequate clitoral stimulation and that it is not an automatic outcome of heterosexual coitus was a crucial insight. Coupled with significant changes in sexual behavior, this knowledge has permitted more women to find sexual fulfillment than ever before, a major benefit of the scientific studies of sex.

Second, sexuality has been freed from an exclusive focus on male preferences and from the traditional idea of female submissiveness in relationships. Female sexual inhibition was often based on deference to the male and fear of him. It included a repertoire of behaviors such as faking orgasm, not insisting on adequate stimulation, assuming that male orgasm terminated the sexual encounter, and paying excessive attention to pleasing rather than receiving pleasure. In many women, these sexual inhibitions begin to resolve themselves when women achieve greater assertiveness and a sense of autonomy. This would not be possible, however, without a significant redefinition of the female-male bond. In fact, many so-called frigid women have no substantive problems with achievement of either arousal or orgasm. They suffer instead from ignorance about what constitutes appropriate stimulation or from interpersonal intimidation.

Somewhat surprisingly, many psychiatrists persist in minimizing the effect of the sexual revolution on women. Frequently, they argue that we only see change in behavior and that unconscious wishes and conflicts remain unchanged. Such an argument utterly neglects the psychological function of orgasm per se, the power of orgasm to reaffirm the "incontrovertible truth" of the reality of personal existence (Lichtenstein, 1961; see also Eissler, 1958; and Person, 1980). The liberated sexual behavior among women thus may open new potentialities which, while sexual in nature, transcend the sexual. Sexual achievement has almost unequivocally benefited women, not only proffering sexual gratification, but often serving as a cornerstone for increased self-esteem.

It would, however, be erroneous to dismiss the suppression or expression of female sexuality as merely cultural in its origin. The critical developmental and psychoanalytic question is why the female erotic impulse is vulnerable to suppression across so many different historical and cultural circumstances (Person, 1980). For example, the inhibited sexuality of many Victorian women has had a permanent validity that poses a theoretical problem to be addressed.

Changing Theories of Gender Identity

Gender identity has also been systematically reevaluated. There is a growing psychoanalytic consensus that classical formulations fail to theorize acquisition of core gender identity ("I am female/male") and gender identity (femininity/masculinity) in accordance with the facts of development. Anatomical differences, while important, are no longer seen as determining per se. According to Howell, "It is the study of gender identity that has offered the most important correction to Freud's theory of feminine development" (Howell, 1981, 16).

Freud (1925; 1931; 1933) believed that prephallic development was essentially congruent for both sexes. Development diverged only with the child's discovery of the anatomical distinction that boys have penises while girls do not. Freud derived his theory of masculinity and femininity, what we now call gender role identity, from the contrast between the behavior of the two sexes after that discovery. In Freud's psychology, penis envy or the masculinity complex was at the center of the female psyche, whereas castration anxiety was central in the male. Freud thus postulated that femininity grew out of thwarted masculinity. He suggested that on discovering the sexual distinction, the little girl was overcome by clitoral inferiority and penis envy and hence developed the compensatory characteristics of passivity, masochism, narcissism, and dependency. These characteristics represented her adaptation to a profound narcissistic wound. Since Freud believed that the problems he saw clinically in women could be traced to the penis envy; he also believed that their treatment was inherently limited: the cause of their problems, genital inferiority, was essentially incurable.

Such a theory is intrinsically odd, because it should be apparent to even a casual observer that girls and boys begin to diverge in behavior, mannerisms, and interests by 12 to 18 months of age. Freud's formulation underscores the danger of deriving developmental theories from adult analyses without validation from child observation. Horney (1924; 1926; 1932; 1933) and Jones (1927; 1933) strongly challenged Freud's theories, noting that the masculine-feminine divergence occurred early in childhood, before the discovery of the anatomic distinction. In contrast to Freud, they proposed that femininity was primary, not derivative, that it antedated the phallic phase and was innate. Horney attributed heterosexual object choice to innate femininity, itself grounded in female biology and awareness of the vagina, not in disappointment over lacking a penis. Jones supported Horney's contention. As he put it, "The ultimate question is whether a woman is born or made" (Jones, 1935, 273). Thus, in the opinion of both Jones and Horney, heterosexual desire was innate. The girl desired the penis libidinally, not narcissistically.

Contemporary theorists confirm Horney's and Jones's observations but have held their explanations to be narrowly derived. Their formulations, like Freud's, gave too much exclusive priority to perceptions of genitals and of genital sensations. Blind children, boys with congenital absence of the penis (Stoller, 1968), and girls with congenital absence of the vagina (Stoller,

314 PSYCHOANALYTIC VIEWS ON FEMALE SEXUALITY

1968) have all been observed to differentiate along gender lines corresponding to their biological sex. Furthermore, current research reveals that sexual object choice is acquired, not innate. These observations prove that gender differentiation cannot be primarily derivative from body awareness, from perception of the sexual distinction, or from innate heterosexuality.

Money and his colleagues (1955a; 1955b; 1956) demonstrated that the first and crucial step in gender differentiation is the child's self-designation as male or female. This self-designation evolves according to the sex of assignment and has unconscious as well as conscious components. Core gender arises out of the very early self-identification as male or female, later symbolized in terms of the external genitals, and is therefore for the most part cognitively and socially constructed. Core gender derives from nonconflictual learning experience, not from conflict. The distinction between gender and biological sex is central to current formulations. Most theorists now believe that the developmental lines of gender precede those of sexuality, a complete reversal of Freud's original formulation.

This change in theoretical formulation has manifold implications for therapy, and many of these have been achieved without being made explicit. The concept of normative femininity is freed from the stereotypes of passivity, masochism, dependency, and narcissism. The content of femininity is now regarded as being multidetermined, with significant input from cultural prescriptions. Femininity and masculinity are seen as parallel constructs, removing any theoretical reason to posit inherent restrictions on women's creativity and autonomy. Consequently, modern theory does not view female prospects as being intrinsically dim.

However, as in the case of sexuality, a critical developmental and psychoanalytic question remains, one that cannot be reduced to a simple cultural perspective. The question remains regarding the universal polarity of gender role(s) that exists despite the plasticity of the content of those roles. One requires a theory that integrates object relations, the symbolic investment of the genitals, and sexual differences, along with the cultural perspective.

Differences in gender role are now attributed to diverse antecedents that include biological differences, learning, power relations, scripting, socialization, sex-discrepant expectations that shape fantasies, and guiding myths, in addition to the standard psychoanalytic emphasis on body awareness, sexual distinction, and the vagaries of the Oedipus complex.

Changing Views on the Centrality of Penis Envy

Feminists have complained bitterly about the damage done by the propagation of the penis-envy doctrine as the irreducible dynamic in female mental
life. They have raised the suspicion that it is not women who are fixated on
penis envy, but psychoanalysis. While analysts of different theoretical persuasions ascribe varying significance to penis envy as an operative dynamic,
few stress it to the same degree as Freud or Deutsch. Many analysts have
since reevaluated the data and come to different conclusions.

According to Blum, "Though very important and ubiquitous, penis envy
can no longer be regarded, if it ever was, as the major organizer of femininity
. . . To derive femininity mainly from penis envy would be developmental
distortion and reductionism" (Blum, 1976, 186). Although Tyson believes
that the awareness of anatomical differences may function as a "psychic
organizer," she has echoed Blum, arguing that "we must look to the early
identifications with the idealized mother-ego ideal in order to understand the
greater portion of the feminine personality organization" (Tyson, 1982, 77).
And Lerner has written, "Today's analyst is less quick to label women's
aggressive, ambitious, and competitive strivings as 'masculine' or to interpret
them a priori as a manifestation of penis envy" (Lerner, 1980, 39).

While Freud put penis envy at the center of the female's neurotic conflicts,
different conflicts are seen as predominant today. One hears much more
today, and much more to the point, about conflicts over the fear of loss of
love or over excessive dependency needs than about conflicts over penis
envy. First alluded to by Freud (1924), the fear of loss of love belongs with
a cluster of traits that are particularly characteristic of women in Western
cultures: dependency needs, fear of independence, fear of abandonment,
unreconstructed longing for love relationships with a man, and fear of being
alone. These problems are viewed not as bedrock, replacing penis envy as a
core, but as preoccupations in the minds of contemporary women. They may,
however, be rooted in early female object relations, socialization, or a
combination of factors. And to some degree, they may reflect the individual's
response to the external situation. Many analysts and psychologists have
come to recognize the need to distinguish contextual responses from internalized stable personality traits.

VALUES AND THEORY MAKING

Recent changes in practice and theory are of inestimable practical benefit to women. From the vantage point of psychoanalysis as an intellectual and scientific discipline, however, we would risk trivializing the theoretical failures of Freud and his followers if we were to restrict our interests solely to correcting the inaccuracies and misperceptions related to the special case of female development. Thus, while we may applaud various corrections in our theories of female psychology, we must also confront the reasons why penis envy for so long retained its power as a monolithic explanation and why sexuality and femininity were essentially seen as meager and distorted. Some have insisted that these early formulations reveal the severe limitations of psychoanalytic theorizing. The emphasis here is on *theorizing* rather than on *theory,* because the whole psychoanalytic enterprise has been challenged, not just one tenet of psychoanalytic theory. The specific questions concern how these theories have persisted for so long and what their persistence reveals both of faulty methodology and of value biases. As the following discussion illustrates, they have persisted so long for at least three reasons: misogyny, the lack of a requirement for verification in psychoanalytic theorizing, and the underlying biological assumptions in psychoanalysis.

Freud's Patriarchal Bias

Feminist scholars and analysts, under the impact of changing social values, have correctly insisted that Freud wrote from the patriarchal stance typical of his cultural milieu. Because he viewed female development simply as a variant of the male counterpart, he failed to achieve a comprehensive or accurate description and theory. Furthermore, they argue, his theoretical biases were automatically translated into therapeutic biases and had profound negative impacts on women patients. Freud not only viewed women as powerless, but also saw them as lacking essential special capacities and a powerful unique sexuality. Penis envy, as doctrine, focusing as it does on female inadequacy, coincided with this traditional perception of the woman as powerless, inferior, and subordinate. A number of feminist writers have eloquently pointed this out, challenging the analytic formulation of the origins of "femininity." In fact, theories of female psychosexual development have, in the past, been misused as theoretical justifications for women's subordinate positions in society.

Horney (1926) literally charted Freud's bias. She drew a close parallel between a small boy's ideas about the sexual difference and psychoanalytic ideas about feminine development. Doing so, Horney was among the first to raise the possibility that Freud's insistence on the centrality of penis envy was related to the male's own envy of the female and particularly of her capacity for motherhood. In a remark which Rohrbaugh (1979) has also quoted, Millett made an interesting and relevant observation. "Freudian logic has succeeded in converting childbirth, an impressive female accomplishment, and the only function its rationale permits her, into nothing more than a hunt for a male organ" (Millett, 1970, 185).

The charge that Freud's psychology of women is infused by patriarchal values has not been restricted to feminists. Consider, for example, Schafer's objection. "Freud's ideas on the development and psychological characteristics of girls and women, though laden with rich clinical and theoretical discoveries and achievements, appeared to have been significantly flawed by the influence of traditional patriarchal and evolutionary values. This influence is evident in certain questionable presuppositions, logical errors and inconsistencies, suspensions of intensive inquiry, underemphasis on certain developmental variables, and confusions between observations, definitions, and value preferences" (Schafer, 1974, 483). Freud's beliefs mirrored those of his culture. His systematic distortion alerts us to the danger of using common sense corroborated by cultural consensus to confirm scientific theory. Value bias lulls us into theoretical complacency.

The Lack of Systematic Verification in Psychoanalytic Theory

Psychoanalytic data are subject to a variety of interpretations. Analysts and therapists of different persuasions encounter the same underlying data from the couch: symbols, dream content, fantasies, and so forth. Yet Freudians, Jungians, culturists, and others use these data to verify their theories, thereby revealing the inadequacy of the couch as the sole source of data for verifying theory.

Biases in perception and interpretation occur all the time. The fact that they persist and become codified in psychoanalytic theory reflects a methodological problem in psychoanalytic theorizing. Misperception does not usually or necessarily take the form of distorting the symbols of conflict. Nor is it based on thin air. Misperception can occur from selective inattention to data or from incorrectly weighing their significance. A random fantasy is different from an organizing fantasy. Most commonly, bias is reflected in a misinterpretation of the meaning of the data. On the one hand, the analyst may view attempted conflict resolution as symptomatic rather than adaptive, in accordance with his or her subjective values. On the other hand, the analyst may interpret certain symbols as being causal, irradicable, or intrinsic rather than as being secondary, maladaptive attempts at conflict resolution.

Grossman and Stewart (1976) have illustrated the latter distortion in their paper, "Penis envy: from childhood wish to developmental metaphor." They presented two clinical examples of analyses in which the interpretation of penis envy, apparently grounded in clinical data, *"had an organizing effect, but not a therapeutic one"* (Grossman and Stewart, 1976, 194). In both examples, the interpretation of penis envy was close enough to the data of the analyses that the women accepted the interpretation and used it to rationalize and consolidate their real pathological constellations. Thus, penis envy is often a symbolic condensation that conceals significant underlying conflicts. As Blum stated, "It is necessary to theoretically distinguish between penis envy as a dynamic issue and as a developmental influence" (Blum, 1976, 186). Freud himself made a peculiar jump from patients' clinical fantasies about castration to his developmental hypothesis about the little girl's discovery of "the fact of her castration." His confusion between fantasy and reality precluded his investigation of the meaning of castration fantasies.

One must distinguish between the meaning of clinical themes and developmental causality (Person, 1974). Meaning can be separated from assumptions of continuity insofar as the latter imply a casual chain. Many analysts have criticized certain of the assumptions of continuity and causality that are routinely made in psychoanalysis, along with those made in the other historical sciences such as history, evolution, or developmental psychology. However, it would be inaccurate to claim that psychoanalysis is simply a science of meaning and that it therefore does not belong to the natural sciences. Psychoanalysis is a natural science insofar as it deals with the composition of self-sustaining characteristics of current mental organization. Thus it addresses the schemata of meaning and their association with affect in a horizontal segment of time (see Modell, 1978). It is out of the correspondence between meaning sets and affects that we generate psychoanalytic hypotheses.

Klerman (1982) made an apt observation that is worth echoing here. Psychoanalysis has been rich in generating hypotheses, but has not been sufficiently committed to their verification. This case study regarding the psychology of women clearly illustrates the dangers of theorizing developmental processes without seeking validation from nonanalytic data. To hold to theories without such validation is to invite contamination by value biases.

The Biological Assumptions of Psychoanalysis

While misogyny has been posited as the culprit responsible for certain inaccuracies in the early psychoanalytic theories about women, misogyny alone does not account adequately for their persistence in the presence of countervailing data. An explanation based on Freud's misogyny is too narrow if his misogyny is seen as emanating solely from simple historical bias. The question really is whether his misogyny is incidental to the basic assumptions of psychoanalysis or whether it is intimately related to the structure of the ideas Freud generated. To the degree that we raise this question, we must move beyond an examination of susceptibility to a particular value bias in psychoanalysis and consider that biases may be even more broadly based in their underlying assumptions.

In 1961, Rieff raised exactly this point. "A denial of the Freudian psychology of women cannot depend on historical reductions of Freud's own psychology . . . His misogyny, like that of his predecessors, is more than prejudice; it has a vital intellectual function in his system . . . And just as sympathetic expositors of Schopenhauer and Nietzsche want to dismiss these philosopher's views on women as idiosyncratic and philosophically irrelevant, so the neo-Freudians (led by eminent women analysts like Karen Horney) would like to omit that part of Freud's work as mere culture-prejudice, maintaining that much of the remaining doctrine can be realigned without damage" (Rieff, 1961, 199–200).

In general, Freud was able to use criticism from both his followers and his defectors by integrating it into his theories. For example, Adler's concepts of masculine protest and power strivings are regarded as having been catalytic in Freud's consideration of aggression. On the other hand, despite cogent contemporary criticisms about his theories of female development (for example, Horney, 1924; 1926; 1932; 1933; Jones, 1927; 1933; 1935), Freud never revised these theories. Later criticisms met the same fate at the hands of Freud's followers. Although Clara Thompson (1943) clearly stated that women envy men at least in part because of women's subordinate position in culture, she had no impact on mainstream psychoanalytic theories about women. Ovesey's observations on the devaluation of women (1956), Moulton's work on primary and secondary penis envy (1973), as well as the work of others, all now well regarded, were originally viewed as merely culturist. Thus, Freud and his followers never really confronted or resolved Freud's schema of female development, and the argument about the critical factors in female development remained dormant until the 1970s.

During the past decade, women's expectations were radically altered, and feminists were extremely vocal in their protests against psychoanalytic theories about women. Parallel with changing cultural directives about appropriate goals and the content of "femininity," psychoanalytic theories about the development of women were fundamentally revised. This is not to say, however, that psychoanalytic theory changed in direct response to the women's movement. Indeed, many of the criticisms leveled against psychoanalysis in the 1970s were the same as those raised by an earlier generation of feminists and dissident analysts. The pertinent question, then, is why psychoanalysis became more receptive to the same critiques.

The delay in incorporating such critiques can only indicate the vital function of misogyny underlying the psychoanalytic theories. Alluding to Freud's problem in theorizing the psychology of women, Schafer has stated that "it . . . was introduced into Freud's theorizing, and thus his comparative view of men and women, by his adhering to a biological, evolutionary model for his psychology . . . This model requires a teleological view of the propagation of the species . . . One observes in this entire line of thought the operation of an implicit but powerful *evolutionary value system.* According to this value system, nature has its procreative plan, and it is better for people to be 'natural' and not defy 'natural order' '' (Schafer, 1974, 468–469). Rohrbaugh (1979) has raised the same question about Freud's theory, provocatively asking whether psychoanalysis can exist without penis envy. She believes that the concept of penis envy is embedded in Freud's insistence on a framework of biologically unfolding psychosexual stages and that his theory cannot account adequately for input from the familial, social, or cultural context.

Although Freud's clinical studies reveal a broad perspective, what has been referred to as his psychological theory or his metapsychology rested on reducing mental processes to biology and on minimizing the influences of experience and learning. By adhering to a strictly instinctual frame of reference, his theory could not offer an adequate means for understanding the influences on female development of early object relations, the prephallic development of personality, or the subordinate societal role of women. In effect, Freud was unable to theorize adequately the interface between individual psychology and cultural injunction.

Toward a Paradigm Shift

Retrospectively, it appears that psychoanalysis was unable to encompass early criticisms about theories of female development until it had developed the ability to theorize the intersection between individual psychology and the cultural milieu. Analysts had objected to the theories of the interpersonal school because they implied that subjectivity simply mirrored the external world. Thus, they viewed the critiques of classical formulations of female development as largely culturist. These analysts were unwilling to embrace a perspective that seemed to undermine their hard-won recognition of the importance of intrapsychic and unconscious factors. Only recently have the theoretical assumptions of psychoanalysis been enlarged to the point that the earlier criticisms could be assimilated. Before this could happen, the question of whether "the unconscious has a history" had to be addressed (the phrase is Marcus's, 1982). More narrowly, this question relates to the way in which external reality is internalized and so organizes individual psychology. What was required, then, was a shift away from a theory which posited that development was exclusively the preordained outcome of libidinal development, that is, a shift away from reducing mental processes to biology, and a shift toward a theory that focused on object relations and internalization as the major psychic organizers. Bias regarding women could apparently not be fully recognized or acknowledged before a more general paradigm shift had occurred.

There is today a growing consensus that libido theory, taken alone, provides an inadequate explanation of human development. While the basic constructs of psychoanalysis (motivation, the important of childhood experiences, unconscious mental processes, and so forth) are still viable and are almost universally accepted, some tenets of metapsychology have been challenged. Given the studies of ego psychology, Ross (1970) and Lichtenstein (1970) have suggested that personality maturation can no longer be seen as the sole dependent variable and sexuality as the sole independent one. Sexuality is considered one independent variable among others, although it is still regarded as the leading one by some theorists. Object-relations theory attempts to formulate those ways in which the experience of the external world is internalized, not just in the organization of perception and affective relationships, but in the very creation of subjectivity. While all psychoanalytic theory acknowledges the internalization of external values and prohibitions in the formation of ego ideal and superego, object-relations theory places more emphasis on the way subjectivity (fantasies, wishes) and the formation of ego are influenced by the experiential. Even sexuality, so clearly grounded in biology, is embedded in meaning and cannot be understood without reference to culture. Individuals internalize aspects of their interpersonal world, albeit in a way that is distorted by infantile mental processes and fantasies. This internalization shapes both their experience of desire and their expression of sexuality (Person, 1980).

These evolutions in psychoanalytic thinking did not occur primarily in response to social movements but in response to new data and the systematic critique of its metapsychological assumptions. The new data were accumulated from the direct observation of children, from studies of intersex patients, from the study of psychoanalytic treatment failures, and from the psychoanalytic therapy of new types of patients (the widening scope). These new data have led to a paradigm shift in psychoanalysis, a shift which in turn can more adequately confront the many apt criticisms raised against Freudian theories about women.

SUMMARY

The case of female psychology stands as a cautionary tale. Not only does it reveal the impact of historical bias on scientific assumptions, but more important, it lays bare some underlying assumptions in early psychoanalytic theories. This special case, in which theories appeared to be verified by clinical data, reveals methodological problems specific to the field of psychoanalysis. The temptation to confuse the symbols and meanings uncovered in analysis with developmental causality is readily apparent. Such confusion causes us to risk mistaking the accidents of historical contingency for eternal underlying truths. Consequently, the case of female psychology encourages us to distinguish systematically between the contingent and the universal. It reveals the impact of beliefs and value biases on both patients and analysts. It forces us to refine our scientific paradigms, first to acknowledge the inevitable dual descriptive-normative role of any psychoanalytic theory (Macklin, 1973), and second to separate hypothesis generating from hypothesis testing (Klerman, 1982).

Finally, the case of female psychology leads us to reexamine certain underlying psychoanalytic assumptions. As the author has argued here, misogyny may be too narrow an explanation for Freud's misunderstanding of women. Freud's misunderstanding and misogyny have broader meaning than simple cultural prejudice. His scheme of female psychosexual development betrays a biological bias that leads to an overemphasis on genitals and reproduction and that lacks an appropriate theoretical scaffolding to support a full understanding of the manifold influences in personality development. It is indeed ironic that in attempting to avoid culturist reductionism, Freud mistook Victorian femininity for eternal femininity.

Given its recent theoretical developments, psychoanalysis can now encompass the issues raised by the study of female psychology. We have made significant revisions in theory. We will no doubt revise the revisions. We will base these on insights into our current blind spots. The acknowledgment that values are pervasive in psychoanalysis, as in other scientific disciplines, ought not to discourage us. Psychoanalysis as a theory and methodology is constantly evolving, and this, indeed, is what distinguishes it from blind ideology.

REFERENCES

Barglow, P., Schaefer, M.: A new female psychology? J. Am. Psychoanal. Assoc. 24:305–350, 1976.

Blum, H. P.: Masochism, the ego ideal, and the psychology of women. J. Am. Psychoanal. Assoc. 24:157–191, 1976.

Broverman, I. K., Broverman, D. M., Clarkson F. E., et al.: Sex-role stereotypes and clinical judgments of mental health. J. Consult Clin. Psychol. 34:1–7, 1970.

Chodorow, N.: The Reproduction of Mothering: Psychoanalysis and the Sociology of Gender. Berkeley, CA, University of California Press, 1978.

Ehrenreich, B., Hess, E., Jacobs, G.: A report on the sex crisis. Ms Magazine, 61–88, March 1982.

Eissler, K.: Notes on problems of technique in the psychoanalytic treatment of adolescents: With some remarks on perversions. Psychoanal. Study Child 13:223–254, 1958.

Freud, S.: The dissolution of the Oedipus complex (1924), in Complete Psychological Works, standard ed., vol. 19. London, Hogarth Press, 1961.

Freud, S.: Some psychical consequences of the anatomical distinction between the sexes (1925), in Complete Psychological Works, standard ed., vol. 19. London, Hogarth Press, 1961.

Freud, S.: Female sexuality (1931), in Complete Psychological Works, standard ed., vol. 21. London, Hogarth Press, 1961.

Freud, S.: Femininity (1933), in Complete Psychological Works, standard ed., vol. 22. London, Hogarth Press, 1964.

Gilligan, C.: In a Different Voice: Psychological Theory and Women's Development. Cambridge, Harvard University Press, 1982.

Gross, M.: The Psychological Society. New York, Random House, 1978.

Grossman, W. I., Stewart, W. A.: Penis envy: From childhood wish to developmental metaphor. J. Am. Psychoanal. Assoc. 24:193–212, 1976.

Hare, R.: The philosophical basis of psychiatric ethics, in Psychiatric Ethics. Edited by Block, S., Chodoff, P. New York, Oxford University Press, 1981.

Hogan, R. T., Emler, N. T.: The biases in contemporary social psychology, in Social Research: An International Quarterly in the Social Sciences 45:(3) 478–534, 1978.

Horney, K.: On the genesis of the castration complex in women. Int. J. Psychoanal. 5:50–65, 1924.

Horney, K.: The flight from womanhood: The masculinity-complex in women, as viewed by men and by women. Int. J. Psychoanal. 7:324–339, 1926.

Horney, K.: The dread of women: Observations on a specific difference in the dread felt by men and by women respectively for the opposite sex. Int. J. Psychoanal. 13:348–360, 1932.

Horney, K.: The denial of the vagina: A contribution to the problem of the genital anxieties specific to women. Int. J. Psychoanal. 14:57–70, 1933.

Howell, E.: Women: From Freud to the present, in Women and Mental Health, Edited by Howell, E. Bayes, M. New York, Basic Books, 1981.

Jones, E.: The early development of female sexuality. Int. J. Psychoanal. 8:459–472, 1927.

Jones, E.: The phallic phase. Int. J. Psychoanal. 14:1–33, 1933.

Jones, E.: Early female sexuality. Int. J. Psychoanal. 16:263–275, 1935.

Klerman, G. L.: Testing analytic hypotheses: Are personality attributes predisposed to depression? In Psychoanalysis: Critical Explorations in Contemporary Theory and Practice. Edited by Jacobson, A. M., Parmalee, D. X. New York, Brunner/Mazel, 1982.

Kuhn, T. S.: The Structure of Scientific Revolutions. Chicago, University of Chicago Press, 1962.

Lerner, H.: Penis envy: Alternatives in conceptualization. Bull. Menninger Clin. 44:39–48, 1980.

Lichtenstein, H.: The changing concept of psychosexual development. J. Am. Psychoanal. Assoc. 18:300–318, 1970.

Lichtenstein, H.: Identity and sexuality. J. Am. Psychoanal. Assoc. 9:179–260, 1961.

Macklin, R.: Values in psychoanalysis and psychotherapy: A survey and analysis. J. Am. Psychoanal. Assoc. 33:133–150, 1973.

Marcus, S.: Culture and psychoanalysis. Partisan Review 2:224–252, 1982.

Marmor, J.: Changing patterns of femininity: psychoanalytic implications, in Psychoanalysis and Women. Edited by Miller, J. B. New York, Brunner/Mazel, 1973.

Masters, W. H., Johnson, V. E.: Human Sexual Response. Boston, Little, Brown, & Co., 1966.

Millett, K.: Sexual Politics. New York, Doubleday, 1970.

Modell, A. H.: Affects and the complementarity of biologic and historical meaning, in The Annual of Psychoanalysis, vol. 6. New York, International Universities Press, 1978.

Money, J., Hampson, J. G., Hampson, J. L.: An examination of some basic sexual concepts: The evidence of human hermaphroditism. Bull. Johns Hopkins Hosp. 97:301–310, 1955a.

Money, J., Hampson, J. G., Hampson, J. L.: Hermaphroditism: Recommendations concerning assignment of sex, change of sex, and psychologic management. Bull. Johns Hopkins Hosp. 97:284–300, 1955b.

Money, J., Hampson, J. G., Hampson, J. L.: Sexual incongruities and psychopathology: The evidence of human hermaphroditism. Bull. Johns Hopkins Hosp. 98:43–57, 1956.

Morgenthau, H., Person, E.: The roots of narcissism. Partisan Review 3:337–347, 1978.

Moulton, R.: A survey and re-evaluation of the concept of penis envy, in Psychoanalys and Women. Edited by Miller, J. B., New York, Brunner/Mazel, 1973.

Ovesey, L.: Masculine aspirations in women: an adaptational analysis in psychiatry. J. Study Interpersonal Processes 19:341–351, 1956.

Person, E. S.: Some observations on femininity, in Women and Analysis: Dialogues on Psychoanalytic Views of Femininity. Edited by Strouse, E. New York, Grossman, 1974.

Person, E. S.: Sexuality as the mainstay of identity: Psychoanalytic perspectives. Signs: J. of Women in Culture and Society 5:605–630, 1980.

Person, E. S.: Women working: fears of failure, deviance and success. J. Am. Acad. Psychoanal. 10:67–84, 1982.

Rieff, P.: Freud: The Mind of the Moralist. New York, Anchor Edition, Doubleday, 1961.

Rieff, P.: The Triumph of the Therapeutic: Uses of Faith after Freud. New York, Harper & Row, 1966.

Rohrbaugh, J. B.: Women: Psychology's Puzzle. New York, Basic Books/Harper Colophon Books, 1979.

Ross, N.: The primacy of genitality in the light of ego psychology. J. Am. Psychoanal. Assoc. 18:267–284, 1970.

Schafer, R.: Problems in Freud's psychology of women. J. Am. Psychoanal. Assoc. 22:459–489, 1974.

Stoller, R.: Sex and Gender. New York, Science House, 1968.

Thompson, C.: Some effects of the derogatory attitude towards female sexuality. Psychiatry 13:349–354, 1950.

Thompson, C.: Penis envy in women (1943), in Psychoanalysis and Women. Edited by Miller, J. B. New York, Brunner/Mazel, 1973.

Tyson, P.: A development line of gender identity, gender role, and choice of love object. J. Am. Psychoanal. Assoc. 30:61–86, 1982.

Vaughter, R. M.: Review essay on psychology. Signs: J. of Women in Culture and Society 2:120–146, 1976.

PART II

FEMINISM AND PSYCHOANALYSIS

I came to explore the wreck.
The words are purposes.
The words are maps.
I came to see the damage that was done
and the treasures that prevail.

ADRIENNE RICH

In Europe

15. Psychoanalysis and Women

Juliet Mitchell

PSYCHOANALYSIS AND THE UNCONSCIOUS

No understanding of Freud's ideas on femininity and female sexuality is possible without some grasp of two fundamental theories: firstly, the nature of unconscious mental life and the particular laws that govern its behaviour, and secondly, the meaning of sexuality in human life. Only in the context of these two basic propositions do his suggestions on the psychological differences between men and women make sense. It is necessary to make sure of their meaning before any specific theses can be comprehended and assessed.

It is also, I would suggest, a characteristic of most attacks on Freud's work that, though the criticism *seems* to be over specific issues, what is really being rejected is this whole intellectual framework of psychoanalysis. Most hostile critics pay tribute to Freud's discovery of the nature of unconscious mental life and of infantile sexuality, and of the importance of sexuality in general. Most politically revolutionary writers would outbid Freud in their stress on the final indivisibility of normality and abnormality, forgetting that this was one of Freud's starting points. There is a formal obeisance to Freud's theories, yet behind most criticism of details there lies an unacknowledged refusal of every major concept. Time and time again, one dissident after another has repudiated singly or wholesale all the main scientific tenets of psychoanalysis.[1] For the same reason that these critics unconsciously deny the unconscious, it is difficult to offer an explanation of it: it *is* unconscious. But, obviously, it would be worse than inadequate just to suggest that we take Freud's word for it, that we just *believe* in its existence. Although we *can* have a subjective knowledge of our own unconscious mental life, it is only in its random expressions that we can recognize it. Symptoms of the unconscious manifest themselves in latent dream-thoughts, slips of pen and memory, etc., and these are all we can ever know of it in this subjective sense. But Freud, in systematizing these manifestations, offers objective knowledge. We can see how it works and understand the need for it to exist to explain what is happening in the symptom. In one sense, Freud found the unconscious because nothing else would explain what he observed—and he certainly tried everything anyone could think of first. Once, after much doubt, he had postulated its existence, he set out to determine how it worked. This makes the process sound too sequential: an instance of how it worked, of course, would also help convince him of its existence. In other words, unlike the poets and story-tellers to whom he always gave credit for their recognition of the unconscious, Freud could not *believe* in the unconscious, he had to *know* it. To be convinced of his knowledge, we cannot believe it either, but if the laws by which he claimed it operated can be shown to have an internal consistency, then we can give up a faith for a science—imperfect as it may be.

The unconscious that Freud discovered is not a deep, mysterious place, whose presence, in mystical fashion, accounts for all the unknown, *it is knowable and it is normal*. What it contains is normal thought, utterly transformed by its own laws (which Freud called the primary process), but nevertheless only transformed and hence still recognizable if one can deduce the manner of the transformation, that is, decipher the laws of the primary process to which the thought is subjected. For instance, an unconscious wish originating in infancy becomes attached to the wish in the present time which has evoked it, but if it is unacceptable to consciousness, it is pushed down (repressed) into the unconscious where it is transformed and where it remains —until re-evoked, or until it breaks out (as a symptom), or until it is analysed. The point for our purpose here is that unconscious thoughts are repressed and thus transformed 'normal' ones, and that they are always there, speaking to us, in their way.

It is within the understanding of the unconscious that all Freud's observations are made—even those that seem not directly to impinge on it. Leaving aside again those questions that relate to his other great discovery, the role of sexuality, what he is therefore saying, for instance, about the nature of femininity, relates to how femininity is lived in the mind. If we take in advance an illustration from the heart of the feminist opposition to Freud, we can see how crucial is this framework of the concept of the unconscious. In a number of places, Freud refers to his statement that for the woman the baby is a substitute for the missed penis; I will give the version that tends to offend most:

So far there has been no question of the Oedipus complex, nor has it up to this point played any part. But now the girl's libido slips into a new position along the line—there is no other way of putting it—of the equation 'penis=child'. She gives up her wish for a penis and puts in place of it a wish for a child: and *with that purpose in view* she takes her father as a love-object. Her mother becomes the object of her jealousy. The girl has turned into a little woman.[2]

The process being discussed here can be re-described within the terms of the mental structures outlined above. Accepting for the moment the assertion that the girl wants a penis, the desire for one is incompatible with actual possibilities. It is therefore repressed into the unconscious, whence probably on many occasions it emerges transformed. The only legitimate form (or the only form legitimated by culture) is that the idea (the representation of the wish) is displaced and replaced by the wish for a baby which is entirely compatible with reality. The two wishes are in fact one, and will continue to be active in different parts of the mental apparatus: the penis-wish will remain repressed in the unconscious, the baby-wish will be consciously expressed. When, as probably later in life, the woman actually comes to have a baby, the emotions she feels will also have attached to them the repressed unconscious penis-wish; the actual baby will therefore satisfy a very deep-seated, unconscious desire and if it is a baby boy the reality offered will give even greater satisfaction as it will coincide still more pertinently with the unrecognized wish. I know that for the moment we are leaving aside what is for the anti-Freudian feminists the massive stumbling-block of the original wish for the penis—but I think the main problem arises because the suggestion is taken outside the context of the mechanisms of unconscious mental life—the laws of the primary process (the laws that govern the workings of the unconscious) are replaced by these critics by those of the secondary process (conscious decisions and perceptions), and as a result the whole point is missed.

Most hostile critics of Freud implicitly deny the very notion of an aspect of mental life (expressed in its own 'language') that is different from conscious thought-processes. Other psychologies are about consciousness, psychoanalysis is dealing with the unconscious—this was a point on which Freud had to insist even before the first of the important breakaways that came within the psychoanalytic movement. Thus, in 1907, when they were still very much colleagues, we find Freud rebuking Alfred Adler for not realizing the distinction and for offering an analysis of mental life based only on conscious thought-processes. In the light of Adler's penchant for Marxism and future foundation of a school of sociological psychology, it is an interesting rebuke.

Freud's discovery of the unconscious was, of course, completely bound up with his attempts to understand neurotic disturbances, in the early days most particularly the symptoms of hysteria. When he first began to realize that the bodily symptoms of hysteria (paralysis, contortions and so on) were physical expressions of mental ideas, he started to listen more carefully to what the patients had to say.

Studying hysteria in the late eighties and nineties, Freud was stunned to hear women patients over and over again recount how, in their childhood, their fathers had seduced them. At first he gave an explanation in which the repressed memory of *actual* childhood incest was reawakened at puberty to produce the neurosis. He then realized that the whole thing was a phantasy.[3] And in essence this is the step that, pertinently here, neither Reich nor his feminist critics will take with him, nor allow him to take. Freud found that the incest and seduction that was being claimed never in fact took place. The fact that, as Freud himself was well aware, *actual* paternal seduction or rape occurs not infrequently, has nothing to do with the essential concepts of psychoanalysis. Once Freud had acknowledged that he must abandon what he called the 'trauma theory' of actual incest, the notion of phantasy was bound to come in. Whatever the facts and figures of the situation, the desire was far more prevalent than the act. From the notion of unconscious phantasy, Freud's theories moved in one direction to the formulation of unconscious desire and, in another direction, to an understanding of infantile sexuality. Psychoanalysis deals with aspects of the drive: the repression of its psychic representation and its expression in demands, wishes, desires and phantasies—with the interaction of the unconscious, the preconscious and the conscious. Desire, phantasy, the unconscious or even unconsciousness are absent from the social realism of, amongst others, Reichian and feminist critiques. These criticisms are, therefore, in this respect not so much anti-Freudian as pre-Freudian.

In the symptoms of hysteria (and with variations, those of the other two neuroses—obsessionality and anxiety) what is being expressed in another language is the repressed sexual idea which some crisis has re-evoked; a symptom is an alternative representation of a forbidden wish which has broken through from the unconscious, whence it was banished, into consciousness—but in an 'unrecognizable' form. Condensed into the symptom are all the energies of the sexual drive and those that were used originally to repress it: it is both the thoughts attached to the drive and its denial. It can be seen why Freud said that the neuroses were the negative of perversions: perversions are the acting out by the adult of one or other of the undirected, hence polymorphously perverse, sexual drives that the child manifests, neurotic symptoms are the failure of the effort *not* to thus act out such drives and desires. As Freud further pointed out, a man has more opportunity to engage in so-called sexual perversion—a woman, whose sexual activity is more restricted by society, must content herself with a neurotic symptom. As we shall see later, it was because the desires of the child want satisfaction in socially forbidden ways and have to be repressed when, at the time of the Oedipus complex, and the closely connected castration complex, he or she desires either or both parents (incest), that Freud claimed that this moment was 'the nucleus of the neurosis'—it is the resolutions and irresolutions of the Oedipus complex that are re-expressed in the neurotic symptom. (The formation of psychosis is somewhat different.) Because some people resolve the Oedipus complex—the entry into human culture—more thoroughly than others, there is an unequal chance of a later neurosis. (Freud did refer to the possibility of constitutionally determined unequal strength of the drives—but this, he stated firmly, was a question for biology, not psychoanalysis.)

There is, however, obviously, another tenet behind many hostile criticisms of Freud's work. It is claimed that Freud was prescribing a correct 'normal' pattern of behaviour. Yet time and again, during his life, Freud had to point out that so-called 'normality' is only relative and is itself 'neurotic', 'pathogenic', 'psychotic' and so on. Indeed, the very nub of his work was the elimination of an absolute difference between abnormality and normality.[4] Cases of neuroses gave him the clues to normal mental formations, dreams were everybody's everyday, or every night psychoses; sexual perversions or inversions were both widespread and could constitute a choice. In 1905, Freud wrote in his 'shocking' case-study of a young hysterical girl, Dora: 'The less repellent of the so-called sexual perversions are very widely diffused among the whole population, as everyone knows except medical writers upon the subject.',[5] and in 1935, to a mother so overwhelmingly distraught by her son's inversion that she could not bring herself even to mention it:

. . . Homosexuality is assuredly no advantage, but it is nothing to be ashamed of, no vice, no degradation; it cannot be classified as an illness; we consider it to be a variation of the sexual function . . . Many highly respectable individuals of ancient and modern times have been homosexuals, several of the greatest men among them

. . . It is a great injustice to persecute homosexuality as a crime—and a cruelty too . . .

By asking me if I can help you, you mean, I suppose, if I can abolish homosexuality and make normal heterosexuality take its place . . .

What analysis can do for your son runs in a different line. If he is unhappy, neurotic, torn by conflicts, inhibited in his social life, analysis may bring him harmony, peace of mind, full efficiency, whether he remains homosexual or gets changed . . .[6]

'Normality;' is a useful marker on a continuum, no more . . . 'a normal ego . . . is, like normality in general, an ideal fiction . . . Every normal person, in fact, is only normal on the average. His ego approximates to that of the psychotic in some part or other and to a greater or lesser extent . . .'[7] The notion of normality is neither tenable for psychoanalytic theory, nor is its attainability a desideratum of analytic practice:

Our aim will not be to rub off every pecularity of human character for the sake of a schematic 'normality', nor yet to demand that the person who has been 'thoroughly analysed' shall feel no passions and develop no internal conflicts.[8]

It is not just Freud's liberal benevolence speaking through these statements: any other conception would have prevented his foundation of psychoanalysis. Only if we can see that the same mechanisms operate in psychotic, neurotic and normal states (in differing degrees and ways, of course), can we see that normal life, like the other two conditions, is a compromise with reality. Feminist criticisms of Freud claim that he was denying what really happens, and that the women he analyzed were simply responding to really oppressive conditions. But there is no such thing as a simple response to reality. External reality has to be 'acquired'. To deny that there is anything other than external reality gets us back to the same proposition: it is a denial of the unconscious. Such a denial also affects the concept of the child. Without the notion of an unconscious mind, there are only three possibilities for a presentation of infancy. The child can be a miniature and perfectly rational adult, correctly appraising social reality. Or it can become the absent centre of a world of other people: it is seen only as others relate to it. Or, finally, the child can simply vanish from the story. In this last case we have an instance at the conceptual level of 'infantile amnesia'—the problem that, as Freud discovered, we forget our early childhood.

Freud, on the other hand, proposed that the new-born infant was dominated by what he eventually designated 'the pleasure-principle'—a process in which pleasure is striven for and unpleasure withdrawn from. The infant in the earliest infant-mother nexus lives almost entirely within the terms of the satisfaction or otherwise of its needs. If its wishes are unsatisfied it expresses unpleasure and then hallucinates the satisfaction it has been denied (as in later life, we fulfil our wishes in dreams). But repeated non-satisfaction leads to the abandonment of hallucination and the registration of what is *real* —in this case real deprivation. This is the introduction of the reality principle. But the reality principle by no means takes over entirely from the pleasure principle, nor is its introduction uniform and unbroken; it hardly seems to touch some aspects at all. For instance, the pleasure principle remains dominant as a means of translating reality, in phantasy, in children's play, in adult day-dreaming. Nor does the reality principle maintain a strong hold on the sexual drives which, because they can achieve their pleasure in auto-eroticism, are not at first very dependent on external reality. All people not only retain the pleasure principle but also, and this goes with it, are constantly engaged in unconscious processes, both in their untenable desires and in their frequent flights from and refusal of reality, their daily acts of repression. (Unconscious processes and the pleasure principle behave in much the same way.)

The strangest characteristic of unconscious (repressed) processes, to which no investigator can become accustomed without the exercise of great self-discipline, is due to their entire disregard of reality-testing; they equate reality of thought with external actuality, and wishes with their fulfilment—with the event—just as happens automatically under the dominance of the ancient pleasure principle. Hence also the difficulty of distinguishing unconscious phantasies from memories that have become unconscious. *But one must never allow oneself to be misled into applying the standards of reality to repressed psychical structures,* and on that account, perhaps, into undervaluing the importance of phantasies in the formation of symptoms on the ground that they are not actualities, or into tracing a neurotic sense of guilt back to some other source because there is no evidence that any actual crime has been committed. *One is bound to employ the currency that is in use in the country one is exploring*—in our case a neurotic currency [my italics].[9]

We shall see later how radical feminist critics have told Freud he is a fool for not applying the standards of reality to repressed psychical structures; by doing so, they have misunderstood his language. Freud found that an understanding of neurotic mechanisms gave him an understanding of normal mental processes (in other words, they were not different); because both the symptoms of neuroses (in particular in the early days, hysteria) and the normal-psychoses, in other words, dreams, were his 'royal' road to the unconscious (though he used the phrase only of dreams), it was their language they had to use—this was the currency of the land he was mapping.

The snag with Freud's presentation of his discoveries and, therefore, of any attempted simplification and re-presentation of them, is that a description *reverses* the analytic procedure. Freud was listening to the *recollected* history of his patients, he reconstructed infantile life from the fragmentary stories the patient told in which time past and time present are one. He read the history of the person *backwards*—as it is always essential to do; but in retelling it, he describes it as a march forwards, a process of development where it is in fact a multi-level effort of reconstruction. This distinction becomes very important when, as I believe, post-Freudian analysts of femininity continued to describe a process and forgot the historical nature of the events—their work is thus developmental, not analytical. This was a dilemma too, faced later by child analysis. Again, what can be forgotten is that at every moment of a person's existence he is living and telling in word, deed or symptom the story of his life: a three-year-old child has a past that he lives in his present, just as does the octogenarian. It is the crucial acquisition of the story of his life that that person is undergoing at the Oedipal moment, and that repeats itself in different ways throughout his time on earth—or rather within his days in human culture. Freud's discovery of infantile sexuality, and of sexuality as a key factor in mental life, is a perfect example of this difficulty: the person *does* develop and change sexually, but not with ruthless sequential logic and never so that the past is 'past'; even a person's account of his change is a coherent story of himself, it is the way men and women and children 'live' themselves in the world.

A WOMAN'S PLACE

The feminist critics whose work has been discussed, and Wilhelm Reich in his early sociological writings, all praise Freud for the accuracy of his *observations* on the psychological characteristics of middle-class women who are oppressed under patriarchy. They condemn, however, his *analysis* on the grounds of its biological determinism and lament that he did not see the reality of social causation that was staring him in the face. There is justification for this attack only in so far as Freud often gave up on this question when he reached the 'biological bedrock' that underlay his psychoanalytic investigation. But what Freud did, was to give up precisely because psychoanalysis has nothing to do with biology—except in the sense that our mental life also reflects, in a transformed way, what culture has already done with our biological needs and constitutions. It was with this *transformation* that Freud was concerned. What we could, and should, criticize him for is that he never makes his repeated statements to this effect forcefully enough in the context of his accounts of psychological sexual differences. To the contrary, disastrously as it turned out for the future of the psychoanalysis of femininity, it is just at these points that he most frequently turned back from the problem, leaving the reader with a nasty feeling that Freud's last word on the subject referred her to biology or anatomy.

But clearly it was just a taste of biology that 'post'-Freudian analysts savoured. As a criticism of this aspect of *their* work, the condemnations of Freud hold good. If any analysis of feminine psychology is to take place, it is high time that a decisive break was made both with biologism in general and with the specific contribution it makes here: that a so-called biological dualism between the sexes is reflected in mental life. Psychoanalysis is about the inheritance and acquisition of the human order. The fact that it has been used to induce conformity to specific social mores is a further abuse of it that largely has been made possible on the theoretical level by the same biological preoccupation of some post-Freudians. If anatomy were indeed destiny, as Freud once disastrously remarked, then we might as well all get on with it and give up, for *nothing* would distinguish man from the animals. But Freud made this fatal remark in the context of a science concerned with exploring human social laws as they are represented in the unconscious mind.

Both Reich and the feminist critics attack Freud for his ignorance of the determining effects of patriarchal culture, but ironically, in their own analyses, they forget exactly what they have remembered in their denunciatory rhetoric. In all the accounts the asymmetrical specific of a *father-dominated* social structure is forgotten in favour of male-female opposition with male domination. The general notion of opposition and social dualism is likewise an important feature of Laing's work. If such social dualism replaces biological dualism, circularity will be the inevitable result of the debate. The principle of dialectics is *contradiction,* not simple unity: elements contradict one another, resolve themselves, join together, and enter into further contradictions with other aspects—any 'unity' is a complex one containing contradictions. Even looking at the concept from a simplified, formalistic viewpoint, there must be at least *three* elements and the third cannot be the simple unity of the two, as Reich, Firestone and Laing (the authors who are interested in dialectics) would have it.

Freud's analysis of the psychology of women takes place within a concept that it is neither socially nor biologically dualistic. It takes place within an analysis of patriarchy. His theories give us the beginnings of an explanation of the inferiorized and 'alternative' (second sex) psychology of women under patriarchy. Their concern is with how the human animal with a bisexual psychological disposition becomes the sexed social creature—the man or the woman.

In his speculative works on the origins of human culture and man's phylogenesis, in particular in *Totem and Taboo* and *Moses and Monotheism,* Freud shows quite explicitly that the psychoanalytic concept of the unconscious is a concept of mankind's transmission and inheritance of his social (cultural) laws. In each man's unconscious lies all mankind's 'ideas' of his history; a history that cannot start afresh with each individual but must be acquired and contributed to over time. Understanding the laws of the unconscious thus amounts to a start in understanding how ideology functions, how we acquire and live the ideas and laws within which we must exist. A primary aspect of the law is that we live according to our sexed identity, our ever imperfect 'masculinity' or 'femininity'.

The determining feature of Freud's reconstruction of mankind's history is the murder of the primal father in a prehistorical period. It is this dead father that is the mark of patriarchy. In an imagined pre-social epoch, the father had *all* the power and *all* rights over *all* the women of the clan; a band of sons—all brothers, weak on their own, but strong together, murdered the father to get at his rights. Of course, they could not all have his rights and, of course, they must feel ambivalent about the deed they had committed. Totemism and exogamy are the dual signs of their response: in the totem, or symbolic substitute for the father, is guaranteed that no one else may kill him, or by then his heirs (each one of the brothers). Furthermore, not one of the brothers can inherit this father's right to all the women. For as they cannot *all* inherit, none shall. This is the start of social law and morality. The brothers identify with the father they have killed, and internalize the guilt which they feel along with the pleasure in his death. The father thus becomes far more powerful in death than in life; it is in death that he institutes human history. The dead, symbolic father is far more crucial than any actual living father who merely transmits his name. This is the story of the origins of patriarchy. It is against this symbolic mark of the dead father that boys and girls find their cultural place within the instance of the Oedipus complex.

In the situation of the Oedipus complex (which reiterates the rules of the totem and of exogamy) the little boy learns his place as the heir to this law of the father and the little girl learns her place within it. The Oedipus complex is certainly a patriarchal myth and, though he never said so, the importance of this fact was doubtless behind Freud's repudiation of a parallel myth for women—a so-called Electra complex. Freud always opposed any idea of symmetry in the cultural 'making' of men and women. A myth for women would have to bear most dominantly the marks of the Oedipus complex because it is a man's world into which a women enters; complementarity or parallelism are out of the question. At first both sexes want to take the place of both the mother and the father, but as they cannot take *both* places, each sex has to learn to repress the characteristics of the other sex. But both, as they learn to speak and live within society, want to take the father's place, and *only the boy will one day be allowed to do so*. Furthermore both sexes are born into the desire of the mother, and as, through cultural heritage, what the mother desires is the phallus-turned-baby, *both* children desire to be the phallus for the mother. Again, *only the boy can fully recognize himself in his mother's desire*. Thus *both* sexes repudiate the implications of femininity. Femininity is, therefore, in part a repressed condition that can only be secondarily acquired in a distorted form. It is because it is repressed that femininity is so hard to comprehend both within and without psychoanalytic investigation—it returns in symptoms, such as hysteria. In the body of the hysteric, male and female, lies the feminine protest against the law of the father.[10] But what is repressed is both the representation of the desire and the prohibition against it: there is nothing 'pure' or 'original' about it.

The girl only acquires her secondary feminine identity within the law of patriarchy in her positive Oedipus complex when she is seduced/raped by, and/or seduces the father. As the boy becomes heir to the law with his acceptance of symbolic castration from the father, the girl learns her feminine destiny with this symbolic seduction. But it is less important than the boy's 'castration', because she has to some extent perceived her situation before it is thus confirmed by the father's intervention. She has already acquired the information that as she is not heir to the phallus she does not need to accept symbolic castration (she is already 'castrated'). But without the father's role in her positive Oedipus complex she could remain locked in pre-Oedipal dilemmas (and hence would become psychotic), for the Oedipus complex is her entry into her human heritage of femininity. Freud always said that a woman was 'more bisexual' than a man. By this he seems to have been hinting at the fact that within patriarchy her desire to take the father's place and be the phallus for the mother is as strong as is the boy's ultimate right to do so. The bisexual disposition of her pre-Oedipal moment remains strong and her Oedipus complex is a poor, secondary affair. An affair in which she learns that her subjugation to the law of the father entails her becoming the representative of 'nature' and 'sexuality', a chaos of spontaneous, intuitive creativity. As she cannot receive the 'touch' of the law, her submission to it must be in establishing herself as its opposite—as all that is loving and irrational. Such is the condition of patriarchal human history.

With the ending of his Oedipus complex and the internalizing of the 'castrating' father as his authoritative superego, the boy enters into the prospect of his future manhood. The girl, on the contrary, has almost to build her Oedipus complex out of the impossibilities of her bisexual pre-Oedipal desires. Instead of internalizing the mark of the law in a superego to which she will live up, she can only develop her narcissistic ego-ideal. She must confirm her pre-Oedipal identification (as opposed to attachment) with the mother, and instead of taking on qualities of aggression and control she acquires the art of love and conciliation. Not being heir to the law of culture, her task is to see that mankind reproduces itself within the circularity of the supposedly natural family. The family is, of course, no more 'natural' than the woman, but its place within the law is to take on 'natural' functions. For sexuality, which supposedly unites the couple, disrupts the kingdom if uncontrolled; it, too, must be contained and organized. Woman becomes, in her nineteenth century designation, 'the sex'. Hers is the sphere of reproduction.

This is the place of all women in patriarchal culture. To put the matter in a most generalizing fashion: men enter into the class-dominated structures of history while women (as women, whatever their actual work in production) remain defined by the kinship patterns of organization. In our society the kinship system is harnessed into the family—where a woman is formed in such a way that that is where she will stay. Differences of class, historical epoch, specific social situations alter the expression of femininity; but in relation to the law of the father, women's position across the board is a comparable one. When critics condemn Freud for not taking account of social reality, their concept of that reality is too limited. The social reality that he is concerned with elucidating is the mental representation of the reality of society.

NOTES

1. Here I am only going to refer to points of psychoanalytic theory that seem to me to be persistently denied or misunderstood by those critics of Freud whose theses on the psychol-

ogy of women concern me. Thus I am omitting many crucial concepts, an understanding of which would be essential for a less specific use of psychoanalysis.

2. Freud, 'Some Psychical Consequences of the Anatomical Distinction Between the Sexes', 1925, S.E., Vol. XIX, p. 256.

3. O. Mannoni (*Freud*, Pantheon, 1971) points out how Freud preserved the trauma theory (as this hypothesis came to be called) for himself by dreaming that he as a father desired his own daughter, Mathilde (not vice versa which would have entailed the notion of infantile sexual desire and its 'return' in the symptoms of his hysterical patients). Writing of the dream to Fliess, Freud said, 'The dream of course fulfils my wish to pin down a father as the originator of neurosis and put an end to my persistent doubts.' Letter to Fliess, 31 May 1897, *The Origins of Psychoanalysis*, Imago, London, 1954, p. 206.

4. Normality should mean corresponding to whatever norm is being discussed. But normality is frequently equated with health. If we want a rough definition of the signs of a state of mental health: health is the uninhibited quest for knowledge, mental illness the painful pursuit of secondary ignorance—a need not to know, though the knowledge will insist on making its presence felt. Platonists believe that the soul's progress through the world is the search for knowledge; early on in his career Freud contended that an aspect of the psychoanalytic 'cure' was the release in the patient of the ability to work at intellectual and creative pursuits, and the regaining of the curiosity which had been repressed by the difficulties of the Oedipus complex. This regaining could not be innocent, it had to acknowledge and know all that had happened. Nor, of course, can health ever be absolute—for psychoanalysis likewise, it is a platonic ideal.

5. Freud, 'Fragment of an Analysis of a Case of Hysteria', 1905 (1901), S.E., Vol. VII, p. 51 (otherwise known as 'The Case of Dora').

6. 9 April 1935, *Letters of Sigmund Freud, 1873–1939*, ed. Ernest Freud, Hogarth Press, London, 1961, pp. 419–20.

7. Freud, 'Analysis Terminable and Interminable', 1937, S.E., Vol XXIII, p. 235, or: '. . . a healthy person, too, is virtually a neurotic . . . The distinction between nervous health and neurosis is thus reduced to a practical question and is decided by the outcome—by whether the subject is left with a sufficient amount of capacity for enjoyment and of efficiency.' *Introductory Lectures on Psychoanalysis*, Lecture XXVIII, 'Analytic Therapy', S.E., Vol. XVI, 1916–17 (1915–17), p. 457.

8. Freud, 'Analysis Terminable and Interminable', op. cit., p. 250.

9. Freud, 'Formulations on the Two Principles of Mental Functioning', 1911, S.E., Vol. XII, p. 225.

10. It is the language or graphology of the body symptomatology, the traces of repressed femininity in hysteria, that the French women's liberation group, *Psychanalyse et Politique*, is deciphering. It was here in the analysis of the hysterical symptom in his earliest psychoanalytic days that, they consider, Freud stopped short. I am not sure that I would agree with the stress that I understand they put on the father's Oedipal 'rape' of his daughter, as it seems to me that the girl precisely has to learn to arts of seduction, of *winning* love.

16. This Sex Which Is Not One

Luce Irigaray

Female sexuality has always been theorized within masculine parameters. Thus, the opposition "viril" clitoral activity/"feminine" vaginal passivity which Freud—and many others—claims are alternative behaviors or steps in the process of becoming a sexually normal woman, seems prescribed more by the practice of masculine sexuality than by anything else. For the clitoris is thought of as a little penis which is pleasurable to masturbate, as long as the anxiety of castration does not exist (for the little boy), while the vagina derives its value from the "home" it offers the male penis when the now forbidden hand must find a substitute to take its place in giving pleasure.

According to these theorists, woman's erogenous zones are no more than a clitoris-sex, which cannot stand up in comparison with the valued phallic organ; or a hole-envelope, a sheath which surrounds and rubs the penis during coition; a nonsex organ or a masculine sex organ turned inside out in order to caress itself.

Woman and her pleasure are not mentioned in this conception of the sexual relationship. Her fate is one of "lack," "atrophy" (of her genitals), and "penis envy," since the penis is the only recognized sex organ of any worth. Therefore she tries to appropriate it for herself, by all the means at her disposal: by her somewhat servile love of the father-husband capable of giving it to her; by her desire of a penis-child, preferably male; by gaining access to those cultural values which are still "by right" reserved for males alone and are therefore always masculine, etc. Woman lives her desire only as an attempt to possess at long last the equivalent of the male sex organ.

All of that seems rather foreign to her pleasure however, unless she remains within the dominant phallic economy. Thus, for example, woman's autoeroticism is very different from man's. He needs an instrument in order to touch himself: his hand, woman's genitals, language—And this self-stimulation requires a minimum of activity. But a woman touches herself by and within herself directly, without mediation, and before any distinction between activity and passivity is possible. A woman "touches herself" constantly without anyone being able to forbid her to do so, for her sex is composed of two lips which embrace continually. Thus, within herself she is already two—but not divisible into ones—who stimulate each other.

This autoeroticism, which she needs in order not to risk the disappearance of her pleasure in the sex act, is interrupted by a violent intrusion: the brutal spreading of these two lips by a violating penis. If, in order to assure an articulation between autoeroticism and heteroeroticism in coition (the encounter with the absolute other which always signifies death), the vagina must also, but not only, substitute for the little boy's hand, how can woman's autoeroticism possibly be perpetuated in the classic representation of sexuality? Will she not indeed be left the impossible choice between defensive virginity, fiercely turned back upon itself, or a body open for penetration, which no longer recognizes in its "hole" of a sex organ the pleasure of retouching itself? The almost exclusive, and ever so anxious, attention accorded the erection in Occidental sexuality proves to what extent the imaginary that commands it is foreign to everything female. For the most part, one finds in Occidental sexuality nothing more than imperatives dictated by rivalry among males: the "strongest" being the one who "gets it up the most," who has the longest, thickest, hardest penis or indeed the one who "pisses the farthest" (cf. little boys' games). These imperatives can also be dictated by sadomasochist fantasies, which in turn are ordered by the relationship between man and mother: his desire to force open, to penetrate, to appropriate for himself the mystery of the stomach in which he was conceived, the secret of his conception, of his "origin." Desire need, also, once again, to make blood flow in order to revive a very ancient—intrauterine, undoubtedly, but also prehistoric—relation to the maternal.

Woman, in this sexual imaginary, is only a more or less complacent facilitator for the working out of man's fantasies. It is possible, and even certain, that she experiences vicarious pleasure there, but this pleasure is above all a masochistic prostitution of her body to a desire that is not her own and that leaves her in her well-known state of dependency. Not knowing what she wants, ready for anything, even asking for more, if only he will "take" her as the "object" of *his* pleasure, she will not say what *she* wants. Moreover, she does not know, or no longer knows, what she wants. As Freud admits, the beginnings of the sexual life of the little girl are so "obscure," so "faded by the years," that one would have to dig very deep in order to find, behind the traces of this civilization, this history, the vestiges of a more archaic civilization which could give some indication as to what woman's sexuality is all about. This very ancient civilization undoubtedly would not have the same language, the same alphabet—woman's desire most likely does not speak the same language as man's desire, and it probably has been covered over by the logic that has dominated the West since the Greeks.

In this logic, the prevalence of the gaze, discrimination of form, and individualization of form is particularly foreign to female eroticism. Woman finds pleasure more in touch than in sight and her entrance into a dominant scopic economy signifies, once again, her relegation to passivity: she will be the beautiful object. Although her body is in this way eroticized and solicited to a double movement between exhibition and pudic retreat in order to excite the instincts of the "subject," her sex organ represents the horror of having nothing to see. In this system of representation and desire, the vagina is a flaw, a hole in the representation's scoptophilic objective. It was admitted already in Greek statuary that this "nothing to be seen" must be excluded, rejected, from such a scene of representation. Woman's sexual organs are simply absent from this scene: they are masked and her "slit" is sewn up.

In addition, this sex organ which offers nothing to the view has no distinctive form of its own. Although woman finds pleasure precisely in this incompleteness of the form of her sex organ, which is why it retouches itself indefinitely, her pleasure is denied by a civilization that privileges phallomorphism. The value accorded to the only definable form excludes the form involved in female autoeroticism. The *one* of form, the individual sex, proper name, literal meaning—supersedes, by spreading apart and dividing, this touching of *at least two* (lips) which keeps woman in contact with herself, although it would be impossible to distinguish exactly what "parts" are touching each other.

Whence the mystery that she represents in a culture that claims to enumerate everything, cipher everything by units, inventory everything by individualities. *She is neither one nor two.* She cannot, strictly speaking, be determined either as one person or as two. She renders any definition inadequate. Moreover she has no "proper" name. And her sex organ, which is not *a* sex organ, is counted as *no* sex organ. It is the negative, the opposite, the reverse, the counterpart, of the only visible and morphologically designatable sex organ (even if it does pose a few problems in its passage from erection to detumescence): the penis.

But woman holds the secret of the ''thickness'' of this ''form,'' its many-layered volume, its metamorphosis from smaller to larger and vice versa, and even the intervals at which this change takes place. Without even knowing it. When she is asked to maintain, to revive, man's desire, what this means in terms of the value of her own desire is neglected. Moreover, she is not aware of her desire, at least not explicitly. But the force and continuity of her desire are capable of nurturing all the ''feminine'' masquerades that are expected of her for a long time.

It is true that she still has the child, with whom her appetite for touching, for contact, is given free reign, unless this appetite is already lost, or alienated by the taboo placed upon touching in a largely obsessional civiliza-tion. In her relation to the child she finds compensatory pleasure for the frustrations she encounters all too often in sexual relations proper. Thus maternity supplants the deficiencies of repressed female sexuality. It is pos-sible that man and woman no longer even caress each other except indirectly through the mediation between them represented by the child? Preferably male. Man, identified with his son, rediscovers the pleasure of maternal coddling, woman retouches herself in fondling that part of her body: her baby-penis-clitoris.

What that entails for the amorous trio has been clearly spelled out. The Oedipal interdict seems, however, a rather artificial and imprecise law— even though it is the very means of perpetuating the authoritarian discourse of fathers—when it is decreed in a culture where sexual relations are imprac-ticable, since the desire of man and the desire of woman are so foreign to each other. Each of them is forced to search for some common meeting ground by indirect means: either an archaic, sensory relation to the mother's body, or a current, active or passive prolongation of the law of the father. Their attempts are characterized by regressive emotional behavior and the exchange of words so far from the realm of the sexual that they are com-pletely exiled from it. ''Mother'' and ''father'' dominate the couple's func-tioning, but only as social roles. The division of labor prevents them from making love. They produce or reproduce. Not knowing too well how to use their leisure. If indeed they have any, if moreover they want to have any leisure. For what can be done with leisure? What substitute for amorous invention can be created?

We could go on and on—but perhaps we should return to the repressed female imaginary? Thus woman does not have a sex. She has at least two of them, but they cannot be identified as ones. Indeed she has many more of them than that. Her sexuality, always at least double, is in fact *plural*. Plural as culture now wishes to be plural? Plural as the manner in which current texts are written, with very little knowledge of the censorship from which they arise? Indeed, woman's pleasure does not have to choose between clitoral activity and vaginal passivity, for example. The pleasure of the vaginal caress does not have to substitute itself for the pleasure of the clitoral caress. Both contribute irreplaceably to woman's pleasure but they are only two caresses among many to do so. Caressing the breasts, touching the vulva, opening the lips, gently stroking the posterior wall of the vagina, lightly massaging the cervix, etc., evoke a few of the most specifically female pleasures. They remain rather unfamiliar pleasures in the sexual difference as it is currently imagined, or rather as it is currently ignored: the other sex being only the indispensable complement of the only sex.

But *woman has sex organs just about everywhere*. She experiences pleasure almost everywhere. Even without speaking of the hysterization of her entire body, one can say that the geography of her pleasure is much more diversified, more multiple in its differences, more complex, more subtle, than is imagined—in an imaginary centered a bit too much on one and the same.

"She" is indefinitely other in herself. That is undoubtedly the reason she is called temperamental, incomprehensible, perturbed, capricious—not to mention her language in which "she" goes off in all directions and in which "he" is unable to discern the coherence of any meaning. Contradictory words seem a little crazy to the logic of reason, and inaudible for him who listens with ready-made grids, a code prepared in advance. In her statements —at least when she dares to speak out—woman retouches herself constantly. She just barely separates from herself some chatter, an exclamation, a half-secret, a sentence left in suspense—When she returns to it, it is only to set out again from another point of pleasure or pain. One must listen to her differently in order to hear an *"other meaning" which is constantly in the process of weaving itself, at the same time ceaselessly embracing words and yet casting them off to avoid becoming fixed, immobilized.* For when "she" says something, it is already no longer identical to what she means. Moreover, her statements are never identical to anything. Their distinguishing feature is one of contiguity. They touch *(upon)*. And when they wander too far from this nearness, she stops and begins again from "zero": her body-sex organ.

It is therefore useless to trap women into giving an exact definition of what they mean, to make them repeat (themselves) so the meaning will be clear. They are already elsewhere than in this discursive machinery where you claim to take them by surprise. They have turned back within themselves, which does not mean the same thing as "within yourself." They do not experience the same interiority that you do and which perhaps you mistakenly presume they share. 'Within themselves" means *in the privacy of this silent, multiple, diffuse tact*. If you ask them insistently what they are thinking about, they can only reply: nothing. Everything.

Thus they desire at the same time nothing and everything. It is always more and other than this *one*—of sex, for example—that you give them, that you attribute to them and which is often interpreted, and feared, as a sort of insatiable hunger, a voracity which will engulf you entirely. While in fact it is really a question of another economy which diverts the linearity of a project, undermines the target-object of a desire, explodes the polarization of desire on only one pleasure, and disconcerts fidelity to only one discourse—

Must the multiple nature of female desire and language be understood as the fragmentary, scattered remains of a raped or denied sexuality? This is not an easy question to answer. The rejection, the exclusion of a female imaginary undoubtedly places woman in a position where she can experience herself only fragmentarily as waste or as excess in the little structured margins of a dominant ideology, this mirror entrusted by the (masculine) "subject" with the task of reflecting and redoubling himself. The role of "femininity" is prescribed moreover by this masculine specula(riza)tion and corresponds only slightly to woman's desire, which is recuperated only secretly, in hiding, and in a disturbing and unpardonable manner.

But if the female imaginary happened to unfold, if it happened to come into play other than as pieces, scraps, deprived of their assemblage, would it present itself for all that as *a* universe? Would it indeed be volume rather than surface? No. Unless female imaginary is taken to mean, once again, the prerogative of the maternal over the female. This maternal would be phallic in nature however, closed in upon the jealous possession of its valuable product, and competing with man in his esteem for surplus. In this race for power, woman loses the uniqueness of her pleasure. By diminishing herself in volume, she renounces the pleasure derived from the nonsuture of her lips: she is a mother certainly, but she is a virgin mother. Mythology long ago assigned this role to her in which she is allowed a certain social power as long as she is reduced, with her own complicity, to sexual impotence.

Thus a woman's (re)discovery of herself can only signify the possibility of not sacrificing any of her pleasures to another, of not identifying with anyone in particular, of never being simply one. It is a sort of universe in expansion for which no limits could be fixed and which, for all that, would not be incoherency. Nor would it be the polymorphic perversion of the infant during which its erogenous zones await their consolidation under the primacy of the phallus.

Woman would always remain multiple, but she would be protected from dispersion because the other is a part of her, and is autocrotically familiar to her. That does not mean that she would appropriate the other for herself, that she would make it her property. Property and propriety are undoubtedly rather foreign to all that is female. At least sexually. *Nearness,* however, is not foreign to woman, a nearness so close that any identification of one or the other, and therefore any form of property, is impossible. Woman enjoys a closeness with the other that is *so near she cannot possess it, any more than she can possess herself.* She constantly trades herself for the other without any possible identification of either one of them. Woman's pleasure, which grows indefinitely from its passage in/through the other, poses a problem for any current economy in that all computations that attempt to account for woman's incalculable pleasure are irremediably destined to fail.

However, in order for woman to arrive at the point where she can enjoy her pleasure as a woman, a long detour by the analysis of the various systems of oppression which affect her is certainly necessary. By claiming to resort to pleasure alone as the solution to her problem, she runs the risk of missing the reconsideration of a social practice upon which *her* pleasure depends.

For woman is traditionally use-value for man, exchange-value among men. Merchandise, then. This makes her the guardian of matter whose price will be determined by "subjects": workers, tradesmen, consumers, according to the standard of their work and their need-desire. Women are marked phallically by their fathers, husbands, procurers. This stamp(ing) determines their value in sexual commerce. Woman is never anything more than the scene of more or less rival exchange between two men, even when they are competing for the possession of mother-earth.

How can this object of transaction assert a right to pleasure without extricating itself from the established commercial system? How can this merchandise relate to other goods on the market other than with aggressive jealousy? How can raw materials possess themselves without provoking in the consumer fear of the disappearance of his nourishing soil? How can this exchange in nothingness that can be defined in ''proper'' terms of woman's desire not seem to be pure enticement, folly, all too quickly covered over by a more sensible discourse and an apparently more tangible system of values?

A woman's evolution, however radical it might seek to be, would not suffice then to liberate woman's desire. Neither political theory nor political practice have yet resolved nor sufficiently taken into account this historical problem, although Marxism has announced its importance. But women are not, strictly speaking, a class and their dispersion in several classes makes their political struggle complex and their demands sometimes contradictory.

Their underdeveloped condition stemming from their submission by/to a culture which oppresses them, uses them, cashes in on them, still remains. Women reap no advantage from this situation except that of their quasi-monopoly of masochistic pleasure, housework, and reproduction. The power of slaves? It is considerable since the master is not necessarily well served in matters of pleasure. Therefore, the inversion of the relationship, especially in sexual economy, does not seem to be an enviable objective.

But if women are to preserve their auto-eroticism, their homo-sexuality, and let it flourish, would not the renunciation of heterosexual pleasure simply be another form of this amputation of power that is traditionally associated with women? Would this renunciation not be a new incarceration, a new cloister that women would willingly build? Let women tacitly go on strike, avoid men long enough to learn to defend their desire notably by their speech, let them discover the love of other women protected from that imperious choice of men which puts them in a position of rival goods, let them forge a social status which demands recognition, let them earn their living in order to leave behind their condition of prostitute—These are certainly indispensable steps in their effort to escape their proletarization on the trade market. But, if their goal is to reverse the existing order—even if that were possible — history would simply repeat itself and return to phallocratism, where neither women's sex, their imaginary, nor their language can exist.

Translated by Claudia Reeder

17. Inquiry into Femininity

Michèle Montrelay

Like all women you think with your sex, not with your mind. — A. Artaud

Why was the theory of femininity in psychoanalysis articulated from the start in the form of an alternative? What does it mean for analysts that they must choose between two contradictory conceptions of women: that of Jones and that of Freud?

The posing of these questions makes it necessary to recall briefly the contents of the two doctrines and the basis of their incompatibility.

For Freud, libido is identical in the two sexes. Moreover, it is always male in essence. For it is the clitoris, an external and erectile part of the body, and hence homologous to the penis, which is the girl's erotic organ. And when, at the moment of the Oedipus complex, she desires a child from the father, this new object is again invested with a phallic value: the baby is nothing but a substitute for the penile organ of which the girl now knows she is deprived. Thus feminine sexuality is constantly elaborated as a function of phallic references.[1]

For Jones, and for the English school (Klein, Horney, Muller), feminine libido is specific. From the start, the girl privileges the interior of the body and the vagina: hence the archaic experiences of femininity which leave an indelible trace. It is therefore not enough to give an account of feminine sexuality from a 'phallocentric' point of view. It is also necessary to measure the impact that anatomy, and the sexual organ itself, has on the girl's unconscious.[2]

Thus Jones and his school were answering the Viennese school when they proposed the precocious, even innate character of femininity. Freud spoke of one libido, whereas Jones distinguishes two types of libidinal organization, male and female.

Forty years have passed: the problem of femininity continues to be posed

Reprinted with permission from *m/f*, no. 1 (1978): 83–101. First published in 1977.

on the basis of the Jones-Freud contradiction. Can this contradiction in fact be surpassed?

PHALLOCENTRISM AND CONCENTRICITY

The investigations conducted by Smirgel and a team of analysts, published as the *Recherches psychanalytiques nouvelles sur la sexualité féminine* have recently shown that it is possible to get past the contradiction. It is an advance which is possible from the moment one abandons all polemical preoccupation and sticks to clinical practice.

Predictably, the book starts with a detailed analysis of the confrontation of the two schools. But having completed the history of this long and burning dispute and disengaged its parameters, the authors do not take sides. Leaving the scene of the debate, they take us to the analyst's: there where the one who speaks is no longer the mouth-piece of a school, but the patient on the couch.

It is rare to be given an account of large fragments of the cures; still more rare for it to be given à propos of feminine cases. Here we have the freedom to follow the discourse of feminine patients in analysis in its rhythm, its style and its meanderings. We are taken into the interior of the space that this discourse circumscribes, a space which is that of the unconscious where, as Freud has seen, negation does not exist, where consequently the terms of a contradiction, far from excluding one another, coexist and overlap. In fact, anyone who tries to take bearings from these researches is referred to Freud *and* to Jones. For this book not only talks of femininity according to Freud, but it also makes it speak in an immediate way that one does not forget. An *odor di femina* arises from it, which cannot be explained without reference to the work of the English and Viennese.

Thus the *Recherches* calls for a double locating, which is worth explicating at greater length here. Let us return to Freud: the essential modalities of the organization of feminine desire cannot be grasped without taking up in its own right the idea of phallocentrism so decried by Freud's contemporaries. The book makes constant and explicit reference to it—but specifying that the phallus cannot be identified with the penis. In fact, far from signifying an anatomical reality, the phallus designates, according to this book the ideas and values that the penile organ represents. By freeing the concept of the phallus from the organic context with which it is still often confounded, the authors enable us truly to grasp the nature of phallocentrism: 'There is every reason for separating the study of penis-envy from any consideration of the penis itself as a thing'.[3] It is necessary, on the contrary, to specify the ideal dimension to which the male organ refers: 'penis-envy is always envy of the idealized penis. . . .'[4]

Simultaneously, the models that are put forward in order to account for feminine desire make clear on the clinical level the real implications of 'phallocentrism': the authors are not fooled by a patient who declares herself impotent and humiliated on the pretext that she is 'only a woman'. The penis-envy latent in these remarks is not reducible to an instinct. It is impossible to legitimate it 'through an alleged state of castration for which phylogenesis would bear the responsibility'.[5]

On the contrary, the desire for the penis can be analysed only in as much as it arises from a complex elaboration, constructed in order to maintain the phallic power of the father. Only those patients whose fathers' prestige and symbolic status had been threatened, posit the possession of the penile organ as indispensable. Their sufferings and their symptoms appear in order to make plain that the essential is withdrawn from them, namely, the penis confounded in the imagination with the phallus. Thus the phallic power of the father is phantasmatically assured.

In the other accounts of homosexual or 'normal' women, in every case, a particular form of relation to the paternal phallus can be traced; in which it is always a question of maintaining an inaccessible term, so that desire can subsist. A subtly constructed relation, but one which does not differ in its nature from that set up by the man: as the detailed account of a masculine case of perversion makes clear enough.[6]

In showing that desire is only ever pure artifice, the book thereby discards the hypothesis of the innateness of desire that the English school had advanced in relation to femininity. It confirms the correctness of Freud's reservations in regard to this 'natural' femininity on which Jones insisted so much.[7]

And yet the *Recherches* takes up the main point of the clinical work of the English school. The article by Grunberger, especially, insists on the specifically *concentric* organization of feminine sexuality.[8] He shows that it is as if the woman, more so than the man, remains dependent on the drives, in which the authors see, like Jones, the intricate patterns of archaic, oral, anal and vaginal schemas.

'Often, for the little girl, it is the mouth which takes up symbolically, and for reasons on which Jones has insisted, the value of a vaginal organ', Luquet-Parat remarks.[9] And further on Maria Torok develops the theory of the English school:

M. Klein, E. Jones and K. Horney have indicated, long before we did, the precocity of the child's discovery and repression of vaginal sensations. We, for our part, have observed that the encounter with the other sex was always a reminder of the awakening of our own. Clinically, penis-envy and the discovery of the sex of the boy are often seen associated with a repressed memory of orgasmic experiences.[10]

Thus two theoretical positions, hitherto considered incompatible, are both verified within the framework of a clinical study. The Jones-Freud contradiction therefore appears to be surpassed.

THE CONTRADICTION DISPLACED

But this transcendence remains implicit. The authors never formulate it as the outcome or culmination of their work. Let us look at these few lines where Grunberger analyses feminine narcissism, 'That which', characterizes '. . . the libidinal cathexis of the woman, is its concentric character *and* at the same time the phallus'.[11]

To simultaneously affirm the 'concentric' and phallic character of feminine sexuality, is to declare that both Freud and Jones are right. But surely it then becomes necessary to formulate a new point of view through which the truth of the two schools would be maintained?

This point of view is not formulated within the framework of the book; rather, the Freud-Jones contradiction seems to gradually lose its relevance in the face of clinical practice. And yet the verification of two incompatible propositions does not do away with the contradiction which links them. The fact that phallocentrism and concentricity may be equally constitutive of feminine sexuality does not prove that they make up a harmonious unit. It is my contention that, on the contrary, they coexist as incompatible and that it is this incompatibility which is specific to the feminine unconscious.

Thus the most important thing about this work, that is, the displacement to which the authors submit the basic contradiction, is not sufficiently brought out. They should have stressed that the Freud-Jones incompatibility, although it was first articulated as a polemic, is far more than a disagreement of two schools. For, once this disagreement and the passions it arouses have subsided, the contradiction emerges again as a play of forces which structures the feminine unconscious itself. Phallocentrism and concentricity, both simultaneously constitutive of the unconscious, confront each other according to two modes: the first, the more spectacular, appears as *anxiety;* but the same relation of forces plays, inversely in *sublimation.* Each of these determining processes of the unconscious economy will be seen at play in the incompatibility of the two aspects of femininity analysed by Jones and Freud.

I. THE DARK CONTINENT

The Representation of Castration

Let us start with anxiety in general, from what we know of this state in so far as it is common to both sexes. This global approach will allow us to situate better in what follows the specifically feminine processes of anxiety.

Anxiety in psychoanalysis is most often described as 'castration anxiety', that is to say, as the horror that seizes the child on discovering the penis-less body of the mother. It is this discovery which engenders the fear of one day undergoing the same fate.

It is true that in each cure the analyst must reckon with the 'imprescriptable' force of this fear of mutilation.[12] But this is not anxiety: to represent to oneself the motive of one's fear is already to give a reason for it. But anxiety is *without reason.* What we mean is that it supposes the impossibility of any rational thought. In other words, anxiety appears as the limit-moment when conscious and unconscious representation are blocked off.

How are we to analyse this blockage? By specifying at first the nature of the representation which is its object. Three positions based on Lacanian theory will serve as points of reference:

1. The unconscious is a structure or combinatory of desires articulated as representations.
2. These representations can be called representations of castration, in as much as their literal articulation effectively deprives the subject of a part of *jouissance.*[i]
3. The stake is this *jouissance,* whose loss is the price of representation.

Let us take these three propositions:

1. Unconscious representation, which is what this article is concerned with, refers to different processes from those currently designated by the term

'representation'. The latter, ordinarily, concerns the conscious; it explains the reflexive activity which applies itself to the reality of the (philosophic) subject and to objects. Unconscious representations, on the contrary, neither reflects nor signifies the subject and its objects. It is a pure cathexis of the word as such. How is this possible? An example will make it clear to us: consider the distinction between conscious and unconscious representations of castration.

2. The conscious representation of castration in the child does not designate any real mutilation. It is am imaginary evocation: either it is the one who threatens by uttering a prohibition (the case of the boy); or the little girl in order to explain the absence of the penis to herself imagines: 'someone must have taken it from me'.

Such a representation take on an unconscious status at the moment at which it no longer refers to anything but the words which constitute it. Taken out of reality, it no longer refers to anything other than its form: what is now cathected, both in the prohibiting utterance and the phantasmatic imagination, is their specific articulation and the multiple puns, the play of sonorities and images that this articulation makes possible. But how can words become the objects of such a cathexis? Why do they mobilize all the strength of the unconscious? Leaving these questions open and referring the reader back to Freud,[13] let us remark only that the words, in the first moments of life, extended the body of the mother and simultaneously circumscribed the place of *suspension* (suspense) of her desire. In words, therefore, the most real of *jouissance* and the furthest of the phallus were conjoined. Perhaps, in the unconscious, the power of words remains the same?

3. Consequently, the unconscious representation is only a text. But the text produces effects: since sexuality is organized as we have seen, not according to some instinct, some 'tendency', but according to what has been said. Consequently, discourse makes impossible any direct and peaceable relation to the body, to the world and to pleasure. It turns away from *jouissance:* it is in this sense that it is castrating. In other words, the unconscious representation of castration is, in the first place, a castrating representation.

But at the same time, the term representation must be taken in a second sense. For the sequence of discourse, having once marked us, endlessly reproduces itself. And we can define the unconscious as the place where these re-presentations are indefinitely staged. This fact of repetition, of the eternal return of words, has been sufficiently demonstrated for us to take it as given here: if the representation then does not cease to represent itself, how can it disappear? Yet, the analyst must reckon with this effacement. For the patient, who expresses anxiety after the event, is speaking of a time when nothing was thinkable: then, the body and the world were confounded in one chaotic intimacy which was too present, too immediate—one continuous expanse of proximity or unbearable plenitude. What was lacking was a lack, an empty 'space' somewhere. Indeed, it seems in these clinical cases that the castrating dimension of representation is missing. Consequently, it is as if representation, at least in its effects, had wiped itself out.

Oedipus and the Stake

To explain the persistence of the representation as well as its vacillation in anxiety, let us pause at the hypothesis we set out a moment ago. Let us imagine that at certain moments, the representation is indeed produced, but without castrating effects: emptily circulating, it would lose the power of turning the subject away from *jouissance*. This, not as a function of facts inherent in representation itself, but from an intrusion, a violence, emanating from the real. Perhaps a reading of Sophocles' drama, *Oedipus Rex,* will serve as clarification.

At the beginning of the drama, Oedipus appears as he whose relations to representation is sufficiently assured to unravel the enigmas of the sphinx. And yet, the tragic action will progressively disclose the ruin of this representation.

The ancients used to say that this ruin was willed by the gods. The analyst declares that Oedipus was led to it by his incestuous desires. We must hold simultaneously to the idea of gods who persecute and to that of the subject who desires. For the theme of the fateful mistake, of the plan controlled by external forces, emphasizes this essential fact: that the realization of unconscious desire is always so catastrophic that the subject can never bring it about on its own.

It is one thing to desire, another to realize this desire. We have seen that to desire is to represent the lacking object (the other), that is to say, to 'enjoy' *(jouir)* exclusively in the form of words. To satisfy this desire is, on the contrary, to decathect words to the profit of reality: in other words, enjoyment of the mother leads back to a recuperation of the stake which, endlessly replayed, is normally the guarantee of representation.

This is why it is necessary that desire should not be realized. Hence the repression that ensures that one does not think, nor see, nor take the desired object, even and above all if it is within reach: this object must remain lost.

But in Oedipus, the gods or chance restore the object of desire: Oedipus enjoys Jocasta. But, simultaneously, repression continues to take place, and in an ever more pressing manner: the successive recourses to Tiresias, to sacrifices and to the law show a desperate effort to avoid seeing the cause of the pestilence. An effort which is ineffectual: repression is no longer anything but a gigantic pantomime, powerless to assure the throwing back into play of the stake of desire. We know that, for want of a stake, representation is not worth anything.

Thus Oedipus' tragedy enables us to emphasize both the economy and the failure of representation at the same time. But it also suggests the cause of this failure. Why does the encounter with the sphinx take place immediately before the drama? To what does the sphinx refer, this reasoning and devouring hybrid being, which beats its wings as it talks? Why does this monster, a woman with the body of a beast, take up her place at the gates of Thebes?

Does not the encounter with this enigmatic figure of femininity threaten every subject? Is it not she who is at the root of the ruin of representation?

Freud, asking himself about feminine sexuality and assessing the small purchase that it offers analytic investigation, compared it to a 'dark continent'.

The *Recherches nouvelles* begin by recalling this formula. How appropriate! And yet it is as if the authors do not see the threatening shadows that they call forth by these words. For feminine sexuality is not a dark, unexplored continent through any provisional insufficiency of research: it is unexplored to the extent that it is unexplorable.

Of course one can describe it, give an account of it in clinical or theoretical work. But it is elsewhere, in the framework of the cure, that femininity stubbornly resists analysis. On the couch, a discourse analogous to that whose style the book renders so well, is enunciated: 'live' discourse, whose very immediacy seems to be a sign of life. But it is this immediacy, this life, which is an obstacle to analysis: the word is understood only as the extension of the body which is there in the process of speaking. It seems no longer to be hiding anything. To the extent that it does not know repression, femininity is the downfall of interpretation.

It is femininity, not women, that can take on such a status. Let us specify what meaning will be given here to the three terms: *woman, femininity, repression:*

—the word *woman* will designate the subject who, like the man, is an effect of unconscious representation;

—by *femininity* will be understood the set of the 'feminine' drives (oral, anal, vaginal) in so far as these resist the processes of repression;

—finally, *repression* will be distinguished from *censorship;*[14] the latter is always submitted to; the former, on the contrary, has the value of an act. In fact, the obstacles the censor opposes to libidinal development appear as the result of the experiences of the Other's desire. Regressions or fixations have made it impossible for the mother or the father to symbolize this or that key-event in the child's sexuality. And from then on, this 'blank', this un-spoken, functions like a check: the censor which is set up appears as the effect of an absence of representation. It is therefore unrepresentable, and consequently 'uninterpretable'. Repression, on the contrary, presupposes a symbolization: as we have seen, it allows the representation to be cathected as such, while the real satisfaction, re-nounced, becomes its stake. Repression is always a process which structures on the level of the psychic economy.

As we will see, feminine eroticism is more censored, less repressed than that of the man. It lends itself less easily to a 'losing itself' as the stake of unconscious representation. The drives whose force was demonstrated by the English school circumscribe a place or 'continent' which can be called 'dark' to the extent that it is outside the circumference of the symbolic economy (forecluded).

What are the processes which maintain femininity 'outside repression', in a state of nature as it were?

The first, of a social order, concerns the absence of prohibitions: the girl is less subject than the boy to the threats and to the defences which penalize masturbation. We keep silent about her masturbation, all the more as it is less observable. Françoise Dolto[15] has shown that, sheltered by their privacy, the girl, the woman, can live a 'protected' sexuality. One tends to refer to the anxiety of rape and penetration without emphasizing that, in reality, on the contrary, the girl risks little. The anatomy of the boy, on the other hand, exposes him very early to the realization that he is not master either of the manifestations of his desire or of the extent of his pleasures. He experiments, not only with chance but also with the law and with his sexual organ: his body itself takes on the value of stake.

In relation to castration, therefore, the position of the man differs from that of the woman whose sexuality is capable of remaining on the edge of all repression. Under certain circumstances then, the stake of castration for the woman finds itself displaced: it consists in the sexuality and the desire of the other sex, most often that of the father and then, of the masculine partner. Which is why Perrier and Granoff have been able to show '. . . the extreme feminine sensibility to all experiences relating to the castration of the man.' [16]

Yet other processes, of an instinctual and not a social order, maintain feminine sexuality outside the economy of representation—the intrication of the oral-anal drives with vaginal pleasure. Jones, Klein and Dolto have insisted on the fact that the girl's archaic experiences of the vagina are organized as a function of pre-established oral-anal schemas. At the further extreme, precocious sexuality 'turns' around a single orifice, an organ which is both digestive and vaginal, which ceaselessly tends to absorb, to appropriate, to devour. We find again here the theme of concentricity disengaged by the authors of the book.

If this insatiable organ-hole is at the centre of precocious sexuality, it inflects all psychic movement according to circular and closed schemas, it comprises woman's relation to castration and the law: to absorb, to take, to understand, is to reduce the world to the most archaic instinctual 'laws'. It is a movement opposed to that presupposed by castration: where the *jouissance* of the body loses itself 'for' a discourse which is Other.

Here, we will not therefore question the truth of the clinical observations produced by the English school: all experience of child analysis confirms the precocity of the 'knowledge' of the vagina. More generally, it is quite true that the very small girl experiences her femininity very early. But, simultaneously, it must be stressed that such a precocity, *far from favouring a possible 'maturation', acts as an obstacle to it,* since it maintains eroticism outside the representation of castration.

Anxiety and the Relation to the Body

A third series of processes stands in the way of repression: those concerning the woman's relation to her own body, a relation simultaneously narcissistic and erotic. For the woman enjoys her body as she would the body of another. Every occurrence of a sexual kind (puberty, erotic experiences, maternity, etc.) happens *to* her as if it came from an other (woman): every occurrence is the fascinating actualization of *the*[ii] femininity of all women, but also and above all, of that of the mother. It is as if 'to become a woman', 'to be woman' gave access to a *jouissance* of the body as feminine *and/or* maternal. In the self-love she bears herself, the woman cannot differentiate her own body from that which was 'the first object'.

We would have to specify further what is only intimated here; that the real of the body, in taking form at puberty, in charging itself with intensity and importance and presence, as object of the lover's desire, re-actualizes, re-incarnates the real of that other body, which, at the beginning of life was the substance of words, the organizer of desire; which, later on, was also the material of archaic repression. Recovering herself as maternal body (and also as phallus), the woman can no longer repress, 'lose', the first stake of representation. As in the tragedy, representation is threatened by ruin. But at the root of this threat there are different processes: for Oedipus, the restoration of the stake proceeded by chance, from the gods; it was effected *in spite* of a prohibition. Nothing, on the contrary, is forbidden for the woman; there is no statement or law which prohibits the recovery of the stake since the real which imposes itself and takes the place of repression and desire is, for her, the real of her own body.

From now on, anxiety, tied to the presence of this body, can only be insistent, continuous. This body, so close, which she has to occupy, is an object in excess which must be 'lost', that is to say, repressed, in order to be symbolized. Hence the symptoms which so often simulate this loss: 'there is no longer anything, only the hole, emptiness. . .'. Such is the *leitmotif* of all feminine cure, which it would be a mistake to see as the expression of al alleged 'castration'. On the contrary, it is a defence produced in order to parry the avatars, the deficiencies, of symbolic castration.

The analyst often finds a 'fear of femininity' in connection with feminine anxiety, especially in the adolescent. We have tried to show that this fear is not a result of phantasies of violation and breaking in (effraction) alone. . . . At bottom, it is fear of the feminine body as a non-repressed and unrepresentable object. In other words, femininity 'according to Jones,' i.e. femininity experienced as real and immediate, is the blind spot of the symbolic processes analysed by Freud. Two incompatible, heterogeneous territories co-exist inside the feminine unconscious: that of representation and that which remains 'the dark continent'.

Defences and Masquerade

It is rare for anxiety to manifest itself as such in analysis. It is usually camouflaged by the defences that it provokes. It is a question of organizing a representation of castration which is no longer symbolic, but imaginary: a lack is stimulated and thereby the loss of some stake—an undertaking all the more easily accomplished precisely because feminine anatomy exhibits a lack, that of the penis. At the same time as being her own phallus, therefore, the woman will disguise herself with this lack, throwing into relief the dimension of castration as *trompe-l'oeil*.

The ways in which this can occur are multiple. One can play on the absence of the penis through silence just as well as through a resounding vanity. One can make it the model of erotic, mystical, and neurotic experiences. The anorexic refusal of food is a good example of the desire to reduce and to dissolve her own flesh, to take her own body as a cipher. Masochism also mimes the lack, through passivity, impotence and doing nothing *('ne rien faire')*. The observations of Hélène Deutsch and those of the *Recherches nouvelles* could be understood in this way. Castration is similarly disguised in the register of erotic fiction: where the feminine orifice, O, is 'falsely' represented in its successive metamorphoses.

Here, I would rather turn to the poets, those who have written in the novelistic or made films out of the feminine drama *('cinéma')*, since the limitations of this article rule out any detailed consideration of clinical cases.

Take Fellini, the director of *Juliette of the Spirits,* a film so baffling, no doubt, because it brings out the presence of the 'dark continent' so well. The dimension of femininity that Lacan designates as masquerade, taking the term from Joan Riviere,[iii] takes shape in this piling up of crazy things, feathers, hats and strange baroque constructions which rise up like so many silent insignias. But what we must see is that the objective of such a masquerade is to say nothing. Absolutely *nothing.* And in order to produce this nothing the woman uses her own body as disguise.

The novels of Marguerite Duras use the same world of stupor and silence. It could be shown that this silence, this non-speech, again exhibits the fascinating dimension of feminine lack: Duras wants to make this lack 'speak' as cry *(Moderato Cantabile),* or as 'music'. Here, let us simply recall what is said in the *Ravishment of Lol V Stein:* 'what was needed was a word-absence, a word hole . . . it could not have been spoken, it could only be made to resound.[17]

Thus the sex, the vagino-oral organ of the woman, acts as obstacle to castration; at the same time, 'falsely' representing the latter in its effects of allurement which provoke anxiety. This is why man has always called the feminine defences and masquerade *evil*.

Woman is not accused of thinking or of committing this evil, but of incarnating it.[iv] It is this evil which scandalizes whenever woman 'plays out' her sex in order to evade the word and the law. Each time she subverts a law or a word which relies on the predominantly masculine structure of the look. Freud says that Evil is experienced as such when anxiety grips the child in front of the unveiled body of his mother. 'Did his desire then refer only to this hole of flesh?' The woman affords a glimpse of the Real, by virtue of her relation to nothing—that is to say, to the Thing. At this moment, the Symbolic collapses into the Real. Freud also says that the pervert cannot see the castrated body of his mother. In this sense, every man is a pervert. On the one hand, he enjoys without saying so, without coming too close—for then he would have to take upon himself a terrible anxiety, or even hate—; he enjoys by proxy the things he glimpses through the mother. On the other hand, he does not appear to understand that her relation to the thing is sublimated. It is this evil which has to be repressed.

A film like *Days of Wrath*[v] bare all the masculine 'defences' against femininity and woman's direct relation to *jouissance*. The man is terrorized by the threat that femininity raises for 'his' repression. In order to reassure him and convince him, the woman always advances further along her own path by explaining herself, wishing to speak the truth. But she does not understand that her discourse will not and cannot be received. For the fact of bypassing the law of repression precisely by *saying all* contaminates the most precious truth and makes it suspect, odious and condemnable. Hence masculine censure.

The frustrations, interdictions and contempt which have weighed on women for centuries may indeed be absurd and arbitrary, but they do not matter. The main thing is the fact of imposing the definitive abandonment of *jouissance*. The scandal can then come to an end—the feminine sex bears witness to castration.

The analyst, for his part, cannot define feminine castration simply as the effect of his strictures. If the examplar of the hysterical, neurotic woman is *one who never lets up wishing to be her sex*, inversely, isn't the 'adult' woman *one who reconstructs her sexuality in a field which goes beyond sex?*

The principle of a masculine libido upheld by Freud could be clarified as a function of this 'extraterritoriality'.

II. *JOUISSANCE* AND SUBLIMATION

1. Feminine Castration: Hypotheses

Once again, let us take an example from literature. Klossowski's portraits of women easily lend themselves to a clinical commentary. We might be surprised at the astonishingly virile attributes (both anatomical and psychical) with which the author endows his heroines and deduce from them some perversion. It is also possible to see in these attributes the material of a moral fable outlining a type of perfected femininity: the 'true' woman, the 'femme' woman would be drawn as she who has *'forgotten' her femininity*, and who would entrust the *jouissance* and the representation of it to an other. For this reason, Klossowski's heroine, Roberte, could in no way talk about herself, her body or 'the work that it conceals'.[18] It is someone else's task to hold the discourse of femininity, in love and/or in a novel.

Under the sign of this forgetting, a second economy of desire, where the stake is no longer the same, can effectively be described. The stake is now precocious femininity and not the penis or masculine sexuality: precocious femininity becomes the material of repression. 'According to Jones' one or several periods of latency correspond to this decathexis of sexuality, periods during which the little girl and the woman disentangle themselves from their own bodies and their pleasures. This is why periods of frigidity in analysis can often be considered as an index of progress: they mark the moment when the patient decathects the vaginal-oral schemas which till then were alone capable of providing access to erotic pleasure.

The decisive step by which the feminine unconscious is modified lies not so much in the change of love object[19] as in the change in the unconscious representative. Masculine, phallic representatives are substituted for the first 'concentric' representatives. The law and the paternal ideals of the father which are articulated in her discourse constitute the new representatives capable of supplanting the models of archaic representations (feminine Oedipus).

Let us note that this substitution does not mutilate the woman and deprive her of a penis which she never had, but *deprives her of the sense* of precocious sexuality. Femininity is forgotten, indeed repressed, and this loss constitutes the symbolic castration of the woman.

For clarity's sake, let us draw a diagram of these hypotheses on the economy of the feminine unconscious.

	Stake	*Representative*	*Relation to Jouissance*
Economy I (according to Jones)	masculine sexuality (phallocentrism)	vagino-oral orifice (concentricity)	anxiety
Economy II (according to Freud)	precocious femininity (concentricity)	signifying order (phallocentrism)	sublimation

This diagram calls for three comments.

1. The parameters of the feminine economy still refer to Jones and to Freud, but in opposite directions.
2. In clinical practice, such a clear-cut distinction is not observed. The two forms of economy usually coexist, with one predominating (provisionally or definitively) over the other.
3. The notion of sublimation has been introduced.

If we can show that in an economy of type II all relation to *jouissance,* including sexual pleasure, is of a sublimatory kind, then not only will a specific dimension of feminine sexuality be clarified, but a misinterpretation of sublimation will also be avoided: that which consists in seeing in sublimation a passage from the sexual to the nonsexual.

2. Sublimation and Metaphor

In the cure and more specifically, in the transference (i.e. the set of unconscious modifications produced by the enunciation of discourse on the couch), the dimension of pleasure can emerge.

In the *Recherches* M. Torok speaks of its manifestation: 'when one of my patients has "understood" an interpretation, when, consequently, an inhibition is lifted, a frequent indication of this advance is that the patient dreams and in this dream she has an orgasm' (a description of one of these dreams follows).[20]

M. Torok, by insisting on the fact that pleasure arises when a new representation is elaborated, tells us what is essential about this pleasure. Contrary to what one might think, this pleasure does not lie in the lifting of an inhibition, i.e. in the releasing of a tension, contained for too long. On the contrary, the pleasure, far from being explicable by the cliché of release ('défoulement'),[vi] arises from the putting in place of *new* representations. Let us note that these were first enunciated by the other, the analyst, who, in interpreting, verbally articulates something of a sexuality maintained till then in the state of nature, in the 'dark'.

Here, therefore, pleasure is the effect of the word of the other. More specifically, it occurs at the advent of a structuring discourse. For what is essential in the cure of a woman is not making sexuality more 'conscious' or interpreting it, at least not in the sense normally given to this term. The analyst's word takes on a completely different function. It no longer explains, but from the sole fact of articulating, it structures. By verbally putting in place a representation of castration, the analyst's word makes sexuality pass into discourse. This type of interpretation therefore *represses,* at least in the sense given to the word here.

Understood in this way, interpretation can perhaps help us to locate a certain cultural and social function of psychoanalysis. The Freudian theory of sexuality was developed *(mise en place)* in relation to women and femininity. We can ask whether psychoanalysis was not articulated precisely in order to repress femininity (in the sense of producing its symbolic representation). At the same time, Freud's reservations about Jones would make sense: the attempts to 'make' femininity 'speak' would surely jeopardize the very repression that Freud had known how to achieve.

Let us return to our example. What pleasure can there be in the repression that is produced at the moment of interpretation? First; let us say that interpretation, as it is analysed here, does not consist so much in explaining and commenting, as in articulating. Here again, it is the form of words which must be emphasized. In response to the analysand's phantasy, the analyst enunciates a certain number of signifiers necessarily relating to his own desire and his listening-place. These words are *other:* the analyst's discourse is not reflexive, but different. As such it is a *metaphor,* not a mirror, of the patient's discourse. And, precisely, metaphor is capable of engendering pleasure.

First Freud and then Lacan analysed the motives of this pleasure with regard to the joke. We laugh when we perceive that the words speak a text other than that which we thought. And if the other laughs, if the misapprehension plays on one more register, the pleasure becomes keener still. What function does this other text, this other ear, have? It has the function of engendering a metaphor, that is to say, of substituting itself for the preceding text and listening-place. Pleasure arises the moment this metaphor is produced. Lacan says that it is identified with the very meaning of the metaphor.[21]

In what then, does this meaning, bereft of signification, consist? We can define it as the measure of the empty 'space' induced by repression. The metaphor, by posing itself as that which is not spoken, hollows out and designates this space. Freud said that the pleasure of the joke lies in the return of the repressed. Does it not, rather, lie *in putting the dimension of repression into play on the level of the text itself?*

It is this pleasure of the joke that can be evoked in relation to all sublimation. For it is an operation which consists in opening up new divisions and spaces in the material that it transforms. In the transference, the patient's orgasm took note of an interpretation. Surely this is best represented as a breath of air between two signifiers, suddenly opened up by the metaphor?

The orgasm, like a burst of laughter, testifies to the meaning—insignificant—of the analyst's word. We must now try to rediscover this dimension of 'wit' in pleasure and *jouissance*. Feminine erotic pleasure varies considerably in its nature and effects. There is variety in the places of the body cathected, in the level of intensity, in the outcome (orgasm or not), and in the effects: a 'successful' sexual relation can cause calm or anxiety. Let us also remember that a neurosis cannot necessarily be inferred from frigidity; and that, reciprocally, psychotics and very immature women have intense vaginal orgasms.[22]

How are we to make sense of the exuberance, the bizarreness and the paradoxes of these pleasures? By referring less to the varieties of form and intensity than to their function in the psychic economy. Here again, we will distinguish two types of sexual pleasure: the precocious and the sublimated.

The first was earlier seen to be the effect of the experience of archaic sexuality. Even if it involves two people, even if it presents the appearance of an adult sexuality, it merely re-actualizes or raises to the highest pitch in orgasm, the *jouissance* that the woman has of herself.[23] In this type of pleasure, the other's look and his desire further reinforce the circularity of the erotic relation. Hence the anxiety that arises before and after the sexual act.

Inversely, pleasure can be structuring in its effects. The sort of 'genius', of inspiration which the woman discovers after love, shows that an event of an unconscious nature has occurred, which has enabled her to take up a certain distance from the dark continent.

We will call sublimated pleasure that which takes the same forms as incestuous pleasure while nonetheless presupposing and confirming woman's access to the symbolic. This pleasure is no longer derived from femininity as such, but *from the signifier,* more precisely, *from the repression that it brings about:* this is why sublimated pleasure is identified with the pleasure derived from the joke.

Such a transformation is on a par with the mutation which has been outlined above as the passage from Type I to Type II sexual economy. The latter assumes, on the one hand, the forgetting of precocious femininity, and on the other, the setting in place of a new representative or signifier of castration. Does not the sublimated sexual act constitute for the woman one of the ways of putting a Type II economy into place, where:

1. the signifier would be actualized in the rhythm, the periodic return of the penis;
2. the stake would consist of the repressed feminine drives,[24] inseparable from the penis itself.
3. pleasure would be the meaning of the metaphor through which the penis 'would repress' the body, feminine sexuality.

Let us be more precise: the penis, its throbbing, its cadence and the movements of love-making could be said to produce the purest and most elementary form of signifying articulation. That of a series of blows which mark out the space of the body.

It is this which opens up rhythms all the more ample and intense, a *jouissance* all the more keen and serious in that the penis, the object which is its instrument, is scarcely anything.

But to state this is to state a paradox: the penis produces *jouissance* because it incarnates a finitude. Sublimation always implies a deidealization. The phallic signifier, detached from the terrifying representations of the superego which revolve around the imaginary phallus, must appear as an object of not-much-meaning.[25]

This step, usually suspended during childhood, takes place after the first sexual experiences of adulthood. Is it a question of unconscious processes? Provided the ground has been prepared, life and a certain ethic undertake this work. To the extent that romantic idealization is successfully mourned (relinquished), to the extent that the dimension of the gift predominates, the penis can objectify, by its very insignificance, the 'difficulty to be' of the couple, in which *jouissance* is lost. Thus it can no longer be separated in its consistency from the material of this archaic, feminine *jouissance* which has been renounced. It embodies it as lost, and all of a sudden restores it a hundredfold. For it deploys this *jouissance* in direct proportion to the forgetting, which is in itself infinite.

Thus, ethics is indissociable from a 'certain' relation to *jouissance*. The de-idealization that it implies alone makes possible the occasional coming together and binding of two perfectly distinct, heterogeneous spaces. The voluptuous sensation of an aspiration of the whole body in a space absolutely Other and consequently, infinite, cannot simply be explained as the effect of the perception of the vaginal cavity. It implies that this cavity is hollowed out by repression, that is to say, by a symbolic operation.

Consequently, pleasure, far from being reduced to the excitation of an organ, on the contrary *transports* the woman into the field of the signifier. Sublimated pleasure, like the dream and hypnosis, like the poetic act, marks a moment when the unconscious representation takes on an absolute value: in other words, when the act of articulating produces on its own the meaning of discourse (meaning nothing). Sweeping away all signification, it lays hold of the woman and catches her in its progression, and its rythms.[26]

For the man, exceptions aside,[27] this transportation into the signifier cannot be produced in so violent and radical a way. In fact, how could he abandon himself to that which he himself controls, and from whose play he gives pleasure (*jouissance*). Moreover, this game (play) involves the risk of detumescence,[28] and also the vertigo and anxiety aroused by the absolute of feminine demand: the woman expects and receives all there is of the penis at the moment of love.

If we no longer consider what is properly called pleasure, but the orgasm usually designated as '*jouissance*' by the analyst, a similar distinction must be made between *jouissance* of Type I and the orgasm which is produced in a sublimated economy. In the former, the residue of pleasure comes to a dead end, since the woman again finds herself powerless to maintain the unconscious economy. This form of orgasm, registering pleasure outside significance *(signifiance)*, bars access to the symbolic. Sublimation, on the contrary, transports not only pleasure but the orgasm into metaphor. Orgasm, endlessly renewed, brought to a white heat, explodes at the moment of pleasure. It *bursts* in the double sense of the French term *éclater:* the sense of deflagration and that of a revelation. There is therefore a continuity of the ascent of pleasure and of its apogée in orgasm: the one carries the signifier to its maximum incandescence; the other marks the moment when the discourse, in exploding under the effect *of its own force,* comes to the point of breaking, of coming apart. It is no longer anything.

To break *itself,* in other words, to articulate itself through a meaning which endlessly escapes. Orgasm in discourse leads to the point where feminine *jouissance* can be understood as *writing (écriture).* To the point where it must appear that this *jouissance* and the literary text (which is also written like an orgasm produced from within discourse), are the effect of the same murder of the signifier.

Isn't this why Bataille, Jarry and Jabès speak of writing as the *jouissance* of a woman? And why that which she is writing is the Name?[vii]

NOTES

1. S. Freud; cf. on this subject in particular: 'Three Essays', *Standard Edition,* vol. VII; 'New Introductory Lectures', vol. XXII; 'The Dissolution of the Oedipus Complex', vol. XIX.
2. E. Jones, 'The Early Development of Female Sexuality' in *The International Journal of Psychoanalysis,* 1927, vol. VIII; 'The Phallic Phase', 1933, vol. XIV; 'Early Female Sexuality', 1935, vol. XVI.
3. J. Chasseguet-Smirgel, C.J. Luquet-Parat, B. Grunberger, J. McDougall, M. Torok, C. David, *Recherches psychanalytiques nouvelles sur la sexualité féminine,* Payot, 1964. M. Torok, 'La signification de l'envie de phallus chez la femme,' p. 184. Translated as *Female Sexuality,* London: Virago, 1981.
4. Chasseguet-Smirgel et al., *Recherches psychanalytiques nouvelles,* p. 186.
5. Ibid., p. 132.
6. Ibid., pp. 65–90.
7. On phallocentrism and the innateness of desire, see 'La phase phallique' *Scilicet* I, Seuil: a rigorous restatement of the theoretical positions of Freud and of Jones on femininity from the position of Lacanian theory. (Translated in: *Feminine Sexuality: Jacques Lacan and the École Freudienne,* eds. J. Rose and J. Mitchell, Macmillan. 1982).
8. Chasseguet-Smirgel et al., *Recherches psychanalytiques nouvelles,* p. 103.
9. Ibid., pp. 124–5.
10. Ibid., p. 191.
11. Ibid., p. 103 (author's emphasis).
12. Ibid., p. 67.
13. S. Freud, 'Repression' and 'The Unconscious', *Standard Edition,* vol. XIV.

14. This distinction is not always made. These two types of process are usually designated by the term *repression* (primary and secondary).
15. F. Dolto, 'La libido et son destin féminin', *La psychanalyse*, VII, Presses Universitaires Françaises.
16. W. Granoff and F. Perrier, 'Le problème de la perversion chez la femme et les idéaux feminins', *La Psychanalyse*, VII. This article is essential for theoretical work on feminine sexuality.
17. Marguerite Duras, *Le Ravissement de Lol V Stein*, Gallimard, p. 54.
18. P. Klossowski, *Les Lois de l'hospitalité*, p. 145.
19. The 'change of object' designates the renunciation of the first love object, the mother, in favour of the father. On this problem, cf. J. Luquet-Parat, 'Le changement d'objet', *Recherches psychanalytiques nouvelles*, pp. 124ff.
20. Ibid., p. 192.
21. A propos of metaphor, cf. J. Lacan, 'The agency of the letter in the unconscious', *Ecrits. A Selection* (trans A. Sheridan), Tavistock, 1977 and Les formations de l'inconscient', *Séminaire 1956–7*. On pleasure by the same author: 'Propos directifs pour un congrès sur la sexualité féminine', in *Écrits*, Seuil. (Translated in: *Feminine Sexuality*, eds. J. Rose and J. Mitchell, Macmillan.)
22. Cf. F. Dolto, 'La libido'.
23. Cf. P. Aulagnier, *Le Désir et la perversion*, Seuil.
24. Drives repressed both in the course of earlier Oedipal experiences, and in the *present*, by the very fact of the *presence* of the penis.
25. This paragraph and the following one were added to the earlier *Critique* article in 1976. It was necessary to clear up a misunderstanding. Only someone who idealizes the signifier could interpret the fact of relating *jouissance* to an operation of sublimation and to the putting into play of the 'signifier' as 'frenzied idealization' (C. David). I take as a tribute— no doubt involuntary—what someone exclaimed à propos of this article: 'So, the *jouissance* of the woman is produced by the operations of the Holy Ghost!' It can happen!
26. If the woman, at the moment of orgasm, identifies herself radically with an unconscious representation, articulated by the Other, then does she not find herself again precisely in the archaic situation where the maternal representation was the sole organizer of phantasy? Isn't the orgasm, by this fact, a 'regressive' process for her? The reply could be in the affirmative for orgasms of the psychotic or neurotic (acute hysteria) type. In these cases, pleasure and orgasm are nothing more than the manifestation of, among other things, a sort of *direct seizure* of the woman by the Other's discourse. For the woman, who, on the contrary, assumes her castration, this relation is *indirect:* it passes through the (paternal) metaphor of the maternal discourse, a metaphor which, as we have seen, presupposes an economy of desire where the woman puts herself at stake *(enjeu)*.
27. Except in the case of actual homosexuality. However, we must be careful not to set up too clear-cut a distinction between the sexuality of the man and that of the woman. Without pretending to settle the whole problem of bisexuality here, let us only say that every masculine subject is cathected as the object and product of his mother: he was 'part' of the maternal body. In relation to the masculine body and unconscious cathexis then, one could also speak of 'femininity' as implied in maternal femininity. Would not the sexual act be structuring for the male subject to the extent that, putting into play the repression of femininity, he would produce each time the *coupure* which separates the man from his mother, while 'returning' to her the femininity of his partner?
28. On the question of detumescence cf. Lacan, *Séminaire 1967–8*. See also, 'The signification of the phallus', *Ecrits. A Selection*, Tavistock and 'Propos directifs pour un congrès sur la

sexualité féminine', *Ecrits,* Seuil. The latter has been translated in *Feminine Sexuality,* eds J. Rose and J. Mitchell, Macmillan, 1982.

TRANSLATOR'S NOTES

i. The word *jouissance* is impossible to translate. Its meanings include: enjoyment; enjoyment of property or privilege; pleasure; and the pleasure of orgasm. It is necessary, however, to distinguish between *jouissance* and *plaisir* (pleasure) which are two theoretically distinct concepts in Montrelay's text.

ii. The article *la* of *la féminité* is italicized in the French; cf. J. Lacan, 'Dieu et la jouissance de *la femme' in Séminaire XX.*

iii. In 'Womanliness as a Masquerade' in *Psychoanalysis and Female Sexuality,* ed. Henrick M. Ruitenbeek, New Haven, 1966.

iv. In the earlier version of this article which appeared in *Critique* 278 this sentence ends with 'since it consists in confronting desire with a bodily lack (which is carnal)'.

v. Director Carl Dreyer, made in 1943.

vi. The French gives *défoulement* which is a direct inversion/pun on the French word for repression: *refoulement.*

vii. *Nom* puns on the French negative *non* and also refers to *Le Nom du Père* (Name-of-the-Father).

Translated by Parveen Adams,
with acknowledgement to Jacqueline Rose for her invaluable advice

18. Women's Time

Julia Kristeva

The nation—dream and reality of the nineteenth century—seems to have reached both its apogee and its limits when the 1929 crash and the National-Socialist apocalypse demolished the pillars that, according to Marx, were its essence: economic homogeneity, historical tradition and linguistic unity. It could indeed be demonstrated that the Second World War, though fought in the name of national values (in the above sense of the term), brought an end to the nation as a reality: it was turned into a mere illusion which, from that point forward, would be preserved only for ideological or strictly political purposes, its social and philosophical coherence having collapsed. To move quickly towards the specific problematic that will occupy us in this chapter, let us say that the chimers of economic *homogeneity* gave way to *interdependence* (when not submission to the economic superpowers), while *historical* tradition and *linguistic* unity were recast as a broader and deeper determinant: what might be called a *symbolic denominator,* defined as the cultural and religious memory forged by the interweaving of history and geography. The variants of this memory produce social territories which then redistribute the cutting up into political parties which is still in use but losing strength. At the same time, this memory or symbolic denominator, common to them all, reveals beyond economic globalization and/or uniformization certain characteristics transcending the nation that sometimes embrace an entire continent. A new social ensemble superior to the nation has thus been constituted, within which the nation, far from losing its own traits, rediscovers and accentuates them in a strange temporality, in a kind of 'future perfect', where the most deeply repressed past gives a distinctive character to a logical and sociological distribution of the most modern type. For this memory or symbolic common denominator concerns the response that human groupings, united in space and time, have given not to the problems of the *production* of material goods (i.e., the domain of the economy and of the human relationships it implies, politics, etc.) but, rather, to those of *reproduction,* survival of the species, life and death, the body, sex and symbol. If it is true, for example, that Europe is representative of such a socio-cultural ensemble, it seems to me that its existence is based more on this 'symbolic denomination', which its art, philosophy and religions manifest, than on its economic profile, which is certainly interwoven with collective memory but whose traits change rather rapidly under pressure from its partners.

It is clear that a social ensemble thus constituted possesses both a *solidity* rooted in a particular mode of reproduction and its representations through which the biological species is connected to its humanity, which is a tributary of time: as well as a certain *fragility* as a result of the fact that, through its universality, the symbolic common denominator is necessarily echoed in the corresponding symbolic denominator of another socio-cultural ensemble. Thus, barely constituted as such, Europe finds itself being asked to compare itself with, or even to recognize itself in, the cultural, artistic, philosophical and religious constructions belonging to other supra-national socio-cultural ensembles. This seems natural when the entities involved were linked by history (e.g., Europe and North America, or Europe and Latin America), but the phenomenon also occurs when the universality of this denominator we have called symbolic juxtaposes modes of production and reproduction apparently opposed in both the past and the present (e.g., Europe and India, or Europe and China). In short, with socio-cultural ensembles of the European type, we are constantly faced with a double problematic: that of their *identity* constituted by historical sedimentation, and that of their *loss of identity* which is produced by this connection of memories which escape from history only to encounter anthropology. In other words, we confront two temporal dimensions: the time of linear history, or *cursive time* (as Nietzsche called it), and the time of another history, thus another time, *monumental time* (again according to Nietzsche), which englobes these supra-national, socio-cultural ensembles within even larger entities.

I should like to draw attention to certain formations which seem to me to summarize the dynamics of a socio-cultural organism of this type. The question is one of socio-cultural groups, that is, groups defined according to their place in production, but especially according to their role in the mode of reproduction and its representations, which, while bearing the specific socio-cultural traits of the formation in question, are *diagonal* to it and connect it to other socio-cultural formations. I am thinking in particular of socio-cultural groups which are usually defined as age groups (e.g., 'young people in Europe'), as sexual divisions (e.g., 'European women'), and so forth. While it is obvious that 'young people' or 'women' in Europe have their own particularity, it is none the less just as obvious that what defines them as 'young people' or as 'women' places them in a diagonal relationship to their European 'origin' and links them to similar categories in North America or in China, among others. That is, in so far as they also belong to 'monumental history', they will not be only European 'young people' or 'women' of Europe but will echo in a most specific way the universal traits of their structural place in reproduction and its representations.

Consequently, the reader will find in the following pages, first, an attempt to situate the problematic of women in Europe within an inquiry on time: that time which the feminist movement both inherits and modifies. Secondly, I will attempt to distinguish two phases or two generations of women which, while immediately universalist and cosmopolitan in their demands, can none the less be differentiated by the fact that the first generation is more determined by the implications of a national problematic (in the sense suggested above), while the second, more determined by its place within the 'symbolic denominator', is European *and* trans-European. Finally, I will try, both through the problems approached and through the type of analysis I propose, to present what I consider a viable stance for a European—or at least a European woman—within a domain which is henceforth worldwide in scope.

WHICH TIME?

'Father's time, mother's species', as Joyce put it; and indeed, when evoking the name and destiny of women, one thinks more of the *space* generating and forming the human species than of *time,* becoming or history. The modern sciences of subjectivity, of its genealogy and accidents, confirm in their own way this intuition, which is perhaps itself the result of a socio-historical conjecture. Freud, listening to the dreams and fantasies of his patients, thought that 'hysteria was linked to place'.[1] Subsequent studies on the acquisition of the symbolic function by children show that the permanence and quality of maternal love condition the appearance of the first spatial references which induce the child's laugh and then induce the entire range of symbolic manifestations which lead eventually to sign and syntax.[2] Moreover, anti-psychiatry and psychoanalysis as applied to the treatment of psychoses, before attributing the capacity for transference and communication to the patient, proceed to the arrangement of new places, gratifying substitutes that repair old deficiencies in the maternal space. I could go on giving examples. But they all converge on the problematic of space, which innumerable religions of matriarchal (re)appearance attribute to 'woman', and which Plato, recapitulating in his own system the atomists of antiquity, designated by the aporia of the *chora,* matrix space, nourishing, unnameable, anterior to the One, to God and consequently, defying metaphysics.[3]

As for time, female[4] subjectivity would seem to provide a specific measure that essentially retains *repetition* and *eternity* from among the multiple modalities of time known through the history of civilizations. On the one hand, there are cycles, gestation, the eternal recurrence of a biological rhythm which conforms to that of nature and imposes a temporality whose stereotyping may shock, but whose regularity and unison with what is experienced as extra-subjective time, cosmic time occasion vertiginous visions and unnameable *jouissance.*[5] On the other hand, and perhaps as a consequence, there is the massive presence of a monumental temporality, without cleavage or escape, which has little to do with linear time (which passes) that the very word 'temporality' hardly fits: all-encompassing and infinite like imaginary space, this temporality reminds one of Kronos in Hesiod's mythology, the incestuous son whose massive presence covered all of Gea in order to separate her from Ouranos, the father.[6] Or one is reminded of the various myths of resurrection which, in all religious beliefs, perpetuate the vestige of an anterior or concomitant maternal cult, right up to its most recent elaboration, Christianity, in which the body of the Virgin Mother does not die but moves from one spatiality to another within the same time via dormition (according to the Orthodox faith) or via assumption (the Catholic faith).[7]

The fact that these two types of temporality (cyclical and monumental) are traditionally linked to female subjectivity in so far as the latter is thought of as necessarily maternal should not make us forget that this repetition and this eternity are found to be the fundamental, if not the sole, conceptions of time in numerous civilizations and experiences, particularly mystical ones.[8] The fact that certain currents of modern feminism recognize themselves here does not render them fundamentally incompatible with 'masculine' values.

In return, female subjectivity as it gives itself up to intuition becomes a problem with respect to a certain conception of time: time as project, teleology, linear and prospective unfolding: time as departure, progression and arrival—in other words, the time of history. It has already been abundantly demonstrated that this kind of temporality is inherent in the logical and ontological values of any given civilization, that this temporality renders explicit a rupture, an expectation or an anguish which other temporalities work to conceal. It might also be added that this linear time is that of language considered as the enunciation of sentences (noun + verb; topic-comment; beginning-ending), and that this time rests on its own stumbling block, which is also the stumbling block of that enunciation − death. A psychoanalyst would call this 'obsessional time', recognizing in the mastery of time the true structure of the slave. The hysteric (either male or female) who suffers from reminiscences would, rather, recognize his or her self in the anterior temporal modalities: cyclical or monumental. This antimony, one perhaps embedded in psychic structures, becomes, none the less, within a given civilization, an antimony among social groups and ideologies in which the radical positions of certain feminists would rejoin the discourse of marginal groups of spiritual or mystical inspiration and, strangely enough, rejoin recent scientific preoccupations. Is it not true that the problematic of a time indissociable from space, of a space-time in infinite expansion, or rhythmed by accidents or catastrophes, preoccupies both space science and genetics? And, at another level, is it not true that the contemporary media revolution, which is manifest in the storage and reproduction of information, implies an idea of time as frozen or exploding according to the vagaries of demand, returning to its source but uncontrollable, utterly bypassing its subject and leaving only two preoccupations to those who approve of it: Who is to have power over the origin (the programming) and over the end (the use)?

It is for two precise reasons, within the framework of this article, that I have allowed myself this rapid excursion into a problematic of unheard-of complexity. The reader will undoubtedly have been struck by a fluctuation in the term of reference: mother, woman, hysteric . . . I think that the apparent coherence which the term 'woman' assumes in contemporary ideology, apart from its 'mass' or 'shock' effect for activist purposes, essentially has the negative effect of effacing the differences among the diverse functions or structures which operate beneath this word. Indeed, the time has perhaps come to emphasize the multiplicity of female expressions and preoccupations so that from the intersection of these differences there might arise, more precisely, less commercially and more truthfully, the real *fundamental difference* between the two sexes: a difference that feminism has had the enormous merit of rendering painful, that is, productive of surprises and of symbolic life in a civilization which, outside the stock exchange and wars, is bored to death.

It is obvious, moreover, that one cannot speak of Europe or of 'women in Europe' without suggesting the time in which this socio-cultural distribution is situated. If it is true that a female sensibility emerged a century ago, the chances are great that by introducing *its own* notion of time, this sensibility is not in agreement with the idea of an 'eternal Europe' and perhaps not even with that of a 'modern Europe'. Rather, through and with the European past and present, as through and with the ensemble of 'Europe', which is the repository of memory, this sensibility seeks its own trans-European temporality. There are, in any case, three attitudes on the part of European feminist movements towards this conception of linear temporality, which is readily labelled masculine and which is at once both civilizational and obsessional.

TWO GENERATIONS

In its beginning, the women's movement, as the struggle of suffragists and of existential feminists, aspired to gain a place in linear time as the time of project and history. In this sense, the movement, while immediately universalist, is also deeply rooted in the socio-political life of nations. The political demands of women; the struggles for equal pay for equal work, for taking power in social institutions on an equal footing with men; the rejection, when necessary, of the attributes traditionally considered feminine or maternal in so far as they are deemed incompatible with insertion in this history—all are part of the *logic of identification*[9] with certain values: not with the ideological (these are combated, and rightly so, as reactionary) but, rather, with the logical and ontological values of a rationality dominant in the nation-state. Here it is unnecessary to enumerate the benefits which this logic of identification and the ensuing struggle have achieved and continue to achieve for women (abortion, contraception, equal pay, professional recognition, etc.); these have already had or will soon have effects even more important than those of the Industrial Revolution. Universalist in its approach, this current in feminism *globalizes* the problems of women of different milieux, ages, civilizations or simply of varying psychic structures, under the label 'Universal Woman'. A consideration of *generations* of women can only be conceived of in this global way as a succession, as a progression in the accomplishment of the initial programme mapped out by its founders.

In a second phase, linked, on the one hand, to the younger women who came to feminism after May 1968 and, on the other, to women who had an aesthetic or psychoanalytic experience, linear temporality has been almost totally refused, and as a consequence there has arisen an exacerbated distrust of the entire political dimension. If it is true that this more recent current of feminism refers to its predecessors and that the struggle for socio-cultural recognition of women is necessarily its main concern, this current seems to think of itself as belonging to another generation—qualitatively different from the first one—in its conception of its own identity and, consequently, of temporality as such. Essentially interested in the specificity of female psychology and its symbolic realizations, these women seek to give a language to the intra-subjective and corporeal experiences left mute by culture in the past. Either as artists or writers, they have undertaken a veritable exploration of the *dynamic of signs,* an exploration which relates this tendency, at least at the level of its aspirations, to all major projects of aesthetic and religious upheaval. Ascribing this experience to a new generation does not only mean that other, more subtle problems have been added to the demands for socio-political identification made in the beginning. It also means that, by demanding recognition of an irreducible identity, without equal in the opposite sex and, as such, exploded, plural, fluid, in a certain way non-identical, this feminism situates itself outside the linear time of identities which communicate through projection and revindication. Such a feminism rejoins, on the one hand, the archaic (mythical) memory and, on the other, the cyclical or monumental temporality of marginal movements. It is certainly not by chance that the European and trans-European problematic has been poised as such at the same time as this new phase of feminism.

Finally, it is the mixture of the two attitudes—*insertion* into history and the radical *refusal* of the subjective limitations imposed by this history's time on an experiment carried out in the name of the irreducible difference—that seems to have broken loose over the past few years in European feminist movements, particularly in France and in Italy.

If we accept this meaning of the expression 'a new generation of women', two kinds of questions might then be posed. What socio-political processes or events have provoked this mutation? What are its problems: its contributions as well as dangers?

SOCIALISM AND FREUDIANISM

One could hypothesize that if this new generation of women shows itself to be more diffuse and perhaps less conscious in the United States and more massive in Western Europe, this is because of a veritable split in social relations and mentalities, a split produced by socialism and Freudianism. I mean by *socialism* that egalitarian doctrine which is increasingly broadly disseminated and accepted as based on common sense, as well as that social practice adopted by governments and political parties in democratic regimes which are forced to extend the zone of egalitarianism to include the distribution of goods as well as access to culture. By *Freudianism* I mean that lever, inside this egalitarian and socializing field, which once again poses the question of sexual difference and of the difference among subjects who themselves are not reducible one to the other.

Western socialism, shaken in its very beginnings by the egalitarian or differential demands of its women (e.g., Flora Tristan), quickly got rid of those women who aspired to recognition of a specificity of the female role in society and culture, only retaining from them, in the egalitarian and universalistic spirit of Enlightenment Humanism, the idea of a necessary identification between the two sexes as the only and unique means for liberating the 'second sex'. I shall not develop here the fact that this 'ideal' is far from being applied in practice by these socialist-inspired movements and parties and that it was in part from the revolt against this situation that the new generation of women in Western Europe was born after May 1968. Let us just say this in theory, and as put into practice in Eastern Europe, socialist ideology, based on a conception of the human being as determined by its place in *production* and the *relations of production,* did not take into consideration this same human being according to its place in *reproduction,* on the one hand, or in the *symbolic order,* on the other. Consequently, the specific character of women could only appear as non-essential or even non-existent to the totalizing and even totalitarian spirit of this ideology.[10] We begin to see that this same egalitarian and in fact censuring treatment has been imposed, from Enlightenment Humanism through socialism, on religious specificities and, in particular, on Jews.[11]

What has been achieved by this attitude remains none the less of capital importance for women, and I shall take as an example the change in the destiny of women in the socialist countries of Eastern Europe. It could be said, with only slight exaggeration, that the demands of the suffragists and existential feminists have, to a great extent, been met in these countries, since three of the main egalitarian demands of early feminism have been or are now being implemented despite vagaries and blunders: economic, political and professional equality. The fourth, sexual equality, which implies permissiveness in sexual relations (including homosexual relations), abortions and contraception, remains stricken by taboo in Marxian ethics as well as for reasons of state. It is, then, this fourth equality which is the problem and which therefore appears *essential* in the struggle of a new generation. But simultaneously and as a consequence of these socialist accomplishments —which are in fact a total deception—the struggle is no longer concerned with the quest for equality but, rather, with difference and specificity. It is precisely at this point that the new generation encounters what might be called the *symbolic* question.[12] Sexual difference—which is at once biological, physiological and relative to reproduction—is translated by and translates a difference in the relationship of subjects to the symbolic contract which *is* the social contract: a difference, then, in the relationship to power, language and meaning. The sharpest and most subtle point of feminist subversion brought about by the new generation will henceforth be situated on the terrain of the inseparable conjunction of the sexual and the symbolic, in order to try to discover, first, the specificity of the female, and then, in the end, that of each individual woman.

A certain saturation of socialist ideology, a certain exhaustion of its potential as a programme for a new social contract (it is obvious that the effective realization of this programme is far from being accomplished, and I am here treating only its system of thought) makes way for . . . Freudianism. I am, of course, aware that this term and this practice are somewhat shocking to the American intellectual consciousness (which rightly reacts to a muddled and normatizing form of psychoanalysis) and, above all, to the feminist consciousness. To restrict my remarks to the latter: Is it not true that Freud has been seen only as a denigrator or even an exploiter of women? as an irritating phallocrat in a Vienna which was at once puritan and decadent—a man who fantasized women as sub-men, castrated men?

CASTRATED AND/OR SUBJECT TO LANGUAGE

Before going beyond Freud to propose a more just or more modern vision of women, let us try, first, to understand his notion of castration. It is, first of all, a question of an *anguish* or *fear* of castration, or of correlative penis *envy;* a question, therefore, of *imaginary* formations readily perceivable in the *discourse* of neurotics of both sexes, men and women. But, above all, a careful reading of Freud, going beyond his biologism and his mechanism, both characteristic of his time, brings out two things. First, as presupposition for the 'primal scene', the castration fantasy and its correlative (penis envy) are hypotheses, a priori suppositions intrinsic to the theory itself, in the sense that these are not the ideological fantasies of their inventor but, rather, logical necessities to be placed at the 'origin' in order to explain what unceasingly functions in neurotic discourse. In other words, neurotic discourse, in man and woman, can only be understood in terms of its own logic when its fundamental causes are admitted as the fantasies of the primal scene and castration, even if (as may be the case) nothing renders them present in reality itself. Stated in still other terms, the reality of castration is no more real than the hypothesis of an explosion which, according to modern astrophysics, is at the origin of the universe: nothing proves it, in a sense it is an article of faith, the only difference being that numerous phenomena of life in this 'big-bang' universe are explicable only through this initial hypothesis. But one is infinitely more jolted when this kind of intellectual method concerns inanimate matter than when it is applied to our own subjectivity and thus, perhaps, to the fundamental mechanism of our epistemophilic thought.

Moreover, certain texts written by Freud *(The Interpretation of Dreams,* but especially those of the second topology, in particular the *Metapsychology)* and their recent extensions (notably by Lacan),[13] imply that castration is, in sum, the imaginary construction of a radical operation which constitutes the symbolic field and all beings inscribed therein. This operation constitutes signs and syntax; that is, language, as a *separation* from a presumed state of nature, of pleasure fused with nature so that the introduction of an articulated network of differences, which refers to objects henceforth and only in this way separated from a subject, may constitute *meaning.* This logical operation of separation (confirmed by all psycho-linguistic and child psychology) which preconditions the binding of language which is already syntactical, is therefore the common destiny of the two sexes, men and women. That certain biofamilial conditions and relationships cause women (and notably hysterics) to deny this separation and the language which ensues from it, whereas men (notably obsessionals) magnify both and, terrified, attempt to master them— this is what Freud's discovery has to tell us on this issue.

The analytic situation indeed shows that it is the penis which, becoming the major referent in this operation of separation, gives full meaning to the *lack* or to the *desire* which constitutes the subject during his or her insertion in to the order of language. I should only like to indicate here that, in order for this operation constitutive of the symbolic and the social to appear in its full truth and for it to be understood by both sexes, it would be just to emphasize its extension to all that is privation of fulfilment and of totality;

exclusion of a pleasing, natural and sound state: in short, the break indispensable to the advent of the symbolic.

It can now be seen how women, starting with this theoretical apparatus, might try to understand their sexual and symbolic difference in the framework of social, cultural and professional realization, in order to try, by seeing their position therein, either to fulfil their own experience to a maximum or —but always starting from this point—to go further and call into question the very apparatus itself.

LIVING THE SACRIFICE

In any case, and for women in Europe today, whether or not they are conscious of the various mutations (socialist and Freudian) which have produced or simply accompanied their coming into their own, the urgent question on our agenda might be formulated as follows: *What can be our place in the symbolic contract?* If the social contract, far from being that of equal men, is based on an essentially sacrificial relationship of separation and articulation of differences which in this way produces communicable meaning, what is our place in this order of sacrifice and/or of language? No longer wishing to be excluded or no longer content with the function which has always been demanded of us (to maintain, arrange and perpetuate this socio-symbolic contract as mothers, wives, nurses, doctors, teachers . . .), how can we reveal our place, first as it is bequeathed to us by tradition, and then as we want to transform it?

It is difficult to evaluate what in the relationship of women to the symbolic as it reveals itself now arises from a socio-historical conjuncture (patriarchal ideology, whether Christian, humanist, socialist or so forth), and what arises from a structure. We can speak only about a structure observed in a socio-historical context, which is that of Christian, Western civilization and its lay ramifications. In this sense of psycho-symbolic structure, women, 'we' (is it necessary to recall the warnings we issued at the beginning of this chapter concerning the totalizing use of this plural?) seem to feel that they are the casualities, that they have been left out of the socio-symbolic contract, of language as the fundamental social bond. They find no affect there, no more than they find the fluid and infinitesimal significations of their relationships with the nature of their own bodies, that of the child, another woman or a man. This frustration, which to a certain extent belongs to men also, is being voiced today principally by women, to the point of becoming the essence of the new feminist ideology. A therefore difficult, if not impossible, identification with the sacrificial logic of separation and syntactical sequence at the foundation of language and the social code leads to the rejection of the symbolic—lived as the rejection of the paternal function and ultimately generating psychoses.

But this limit, rarely reached as such, produces two types of counter-investment of what we have termed the socio-symbolic contract. On the one hand, there are attempts to take hold of this contract, to possess it in order to enjoy it as such or to subvert it. How? The answer remains difficult to formulate (since, precisely, any formulation is deemed frustrating, mutilating, sacrificial) or else is in fact formulated using stereotypes taken from extremist and often deadly ideologies. On the other hand, another attitude is more lucid from the beginning, more self-analytical which—without refusing or sidestepping this socio-symbolic order—consists in trying to explore the constitution and functioning of this contract, starting less from the knowledge accumulated about it (anthropology, psychoanalysis, linguistics) than from the very personal affect experienced when facing it as subject and as a woman. This leads to the active research,[14] still rare, undoubtedly hesitant but always dissident, being carried out by women in the human sciences; particularly those attempts, in the wake of contemporary art, to break the code, to shatter language, to find a specific discourse closer to the body and emotions, to the unnameable repressed by the social contract. I am not speaking here of a 'woman's language', whose (at least syntactical) existence is highly problematical and whose apparent lexical specificity is perhaps more the product of a social marginality than of a sexual-symbolic difference.[15]

Nor am I speaking of the aesthetic quality of productions by women, most of which—with a few exceptions (but has this not always been the case with both sexes?)—are a reiteration of a more or less euphoric or depressed romanticism and always an explosion of an ego lacking narcissistic gratification.[16] What I should like to retain, none the less, as a mark of collective aspiration, as an undoubtedly vague and unimplemented intention, but one which is intense and which has been deeply revealing these past few years, is this: The new generation of women is showing that its major social concern has become the socio-symbolic contract as a sacrificial contract. If anthropologists and psychologists, for at least a century, have not stopped insisting on this in their attention to 'savage thought', wars, the discourse of dreams or writers, women are today affirming—and we consequently face a mass phenomenon—that they are forced to experience this sacrificial contract against their will.[17] Based on this, they are attempting a revolt which they see as a resurrection but which society as a whole understands as murder. This attempt can lead us to a not less and sometimes more deadly violence. Or to a cultural innovation. Probably to both at once. But that is precisely where the stakes are, and they are of epochal significance.

THE TERROR OF POWER OR THE POWER OF TERRORISM

First in socialist countries (such as the USSR and China) and increasingly in Western democracies, under pressure from feminist movements, women are being promoted to leadership positions in government, industry and culture. Inequalities, devalorizations, underestimations, even persecution of women at this level continue to hold sway in vain. The struggle against them is a struggle against archaisms. The cause has none the less been understood, the principle has been accepted.[18] What remains is to break down the resistance to change. In this sense, this struggle, while still one of the main concerns of the new generation, is not, strictly speaking, *its* problem. In relationship to *power,* its problem might rather be summarized as follows: What happens when, on the contrary, they refuse power and create a parallel society, a counter-power which then takes on aspects ranging from a club of ideas to a group of terrorist commandos?

The assumption by women of executive, industrial and cultural power has not, up to the present time, radically changed the nature of this power. This can be clearly seen in the East, where women promoted to decision-making positions suddenly obtain the economic as well as the narcissistic advantages refused them for thousands of years and become the pillars of the existing governments, guardians of the status quo, the most zealous protectors of the established order.[19] This identification by women with the very power structures previously considered as frustrating, oppressive or inaccessible has often been used in modern times by totalitarian regimes: the German National Socialists and the Chilean junta are examples of this.[20] The fact that this is a paranoid type of counter-investment in an initially denied symbolic order can perhaps explain this troubling phenomenon; but an explanation does not prevent its massive propagation around the globe, perhaps in less dramatic forms than the totalitarian ones mentioned above, but all moving towards levelling, stabilization, conformism, at the cost of crushing exceptions, experiments, chance occurrences.

Some will regret that the rise of a libertarian movement such as feminism ends, in some of its aspects, in the consolidation of conformism; others will rejoice and profit from this fact. Electoral campaigns, the very life of political parties, continue to bet on this latter tendency. Experience proves that too quickly even the protest or innovative initiatives on the part of women inhaled by power systems (when they do not submit to them right away) are soon credited to the system's account; and that the long-awaited democratization of institutions as a result of the entry of women most often comes down to fabricating a few 'chiefs' among them. The difficulty presented by this logic of integrating the second sex into a value-system experienced as foreign and therefore counter-invested is how to avoid the centralization of power, how to detach women from it and how then to proceed, through their critical, differential and autonomous interventions, to render decision-making institutions more flexible.

Then there are the more radical feminist currents which, refusing homologation to any role of identification with existing power no matter what the power may be, make of the second sex a *counter-society*. A 'female society' is then constituted as a sort of alter ego of the official society, in which all real or fantasized possibilities for *jouissance* take refuge. Against the socio-symbolic contract, both sacrificial and frustrating, this counter-society is imagined as harmonious, without prohibitions, free and fulfilling. In our modern societies which have no hereafter or, at least, which are caught up in a transcendency either reduced to this side of the world (protestantism) or crumbling (catholicism and its current challenges), the counter-society remains the only refuge for fulfilment since it is precisely an a-topia, a place outside the law, utopia's floodgate.

As with any society, the counter-society is based on the expulsion of an excluded element, a scapegoat charged with the evil of which the community duty constituted can then purge itself;[21] a purge which will finally exonerate that community of any future criticism. Modern protest movements have often reiterated this logic, locating the guilty one—in order to fend off criticism—in the foreign, in capital alone, in the other religion, in the other sex. Does not feminism become a kind of inverted sexism when this logic is followed to its conclusion? The various forms of marginalism—according to sex, age, religion or ideology—represent in the modern world this refuge for *jouissance,* a sort of laicized transcendence. But with women, and in so far as the number of those feeling concerned by this problem has increased, although in less spectacular forms than a few years ago, the problem of the counter-society is becoming massive: It occupies no more and no less than 'half of the sky'.

It has, therefore, become clear, because of the particular radicalization of the second generation, that these protest movements, including feminism, are not 'initially libertarian' movements which only later, through internal deviations or external chance manipulations, fall back into the old ruts of the initially combated archetypes. Rather, the very logic of counter-power and of counter-society necessarily generates, by its very structure, its essence as a simulacrum of the combated society or of power. In this sense and from a viewpoint undoubtedly too Hegelian, modern feminism has only been but a moment in the interminable process of coming to consciousness about the implacable violence (separation, castration, etc.) which constitutes any symbolic contract.

Thus the identification with power in order to consolidate it or the constitution of a fetishist counter-power—restorer of the crises of the self and provider of a *jouissance* which is always already a transgression—seem to be the two social forms which the face-off between the new generation of women and the social contract can take. That one also finds the problem of terrorism there is structurally related.

The large number of women in terrorist groups (Palestinian commandos, the Baader-Meinhoff Gang, Red Brigades, etc.) has already been pointed out, either violently or prudently according to the source of information. The exploitation of women is still too great and the traditional prejudices against them too violent for one to be able to envision this phenomenon with sufficient distance. It can, however, be said from now on that this is the inevitable product of what we have called a denial of the socio-symbolic contract and its counter-investment as the only means of self-defence in the struggle to safeguard an identity. This paranoid-type mechanism is at the base of any political involvement. It may produce different civilizing attitudes in the sense that these attitudes allow a more or less flexible reabsorption of violence and death. But when a subject is too brutally excluded from this socio-symbolic stratum; when, for example, a woman feels her affective life as a woman or her condition as a social being too brutally ignored by existing discourse or power (from her family to social institutions); she may, by counter-investing the violence she has endured, make of herself a 'possessed' agent of this violence in order to combat what was experienced as frustration—with arms which may seem disproportional, but which are not so in comparison with the subjective or more precisely narcissistic suffering from which they originate. Necessarily opposed to the bourgeois democratic regimes in power, this terrorist violence offers as a programme of liberation an order which is even more oppressive, more sacrificial than those it combats. Strangely enough, it is not against totalitarian regimes that these terrorist groups with women participants unleash themselves but, rather, against liberal systems, whose essence is, of course, exploitative, but whose expanding democratic legality guarantees relative tolerance. Each time, the mobilization takes place in the name of a nation, of an oppressed group, of a human essence imagined as good and sound; in the name, then, of a kind of fantasy of archaic fulfilment which an arbitrary, abstract and thus even bad and ultimately discriminatory order has come to disrupt. While that order is accused of being oppressive, is it not actually being reproached with being too weak, with not measuring up to this pure and good, but henceforth lost, substance? Anthropology has shown that the social order is sacrificial, but sacrifice orders violence, binds it, tames it. Refusal of the social order exposes one to the risk that the so-called good substance, once it is unchained, will explode, without curbs, without law or right, to become an absolute arbitrariness.

Following the crisis of monotheism, the revolutions of the past two centuries, and more recently Fascism and Stalinism, have tragically set in action this logic of the oppressed goodwill which leads to massacres. Are women more apt than other social categories, notably the exploited classes, to invest in this implacable machine of terrorism? No categorical response, either positive or negative, can currently be given to this question. It must be pointed out, however, that since the dawn of feminism, and certainly before, the political activity of exceptional women, and thus in a certain sense of liberated women, has taken the form of murder, conspiracy and crime. Finally, there is also the connivance of the young girl with her mother, her greater difficulty than the boy in detaching herself from the mother in order to accede to the order of signs as invested by the absence and separation constitutive of the paternal function. A girl will never be able to re-establish this contact with her mother—a contact which the boy may possibly rediscover through his relationship with the opposite sex—except by becoming a mother herself, through a child or through a homosexuality which is in itself extremely difficult and judged as suspect by society; and, what is more, why and in the name of what dubious symbolic benefit would she want to make this detachment so as to conform to a symbolic system which remains foreign to her? In sum, all of these considerations—her eternal debt to the woman-mother—make a woman more vulnerable within the symbolic order, more fragile when she suffers within it, more virulent when she protects herself from it. If the archetype of the belief in a good and pure substance, that of utopias, is the belief in the omnipotence of an archaic, full, total englobing mother with no frustration, no separation, with no break-producing symbolism (with no castration, in other words), then it becomes evident that we will never be able to defuse the violences mobilized through the counter-investment necessary to carrying out this phantasm, unless one challenges precisely this myth of the archaic mother. It is in this way that we can understand the warnings against the recent invasion of the women's movements by paranoia,[22] as in Lacan's scandalous sentence 'There is no such thing as Woman'.[23] Indeed, she does *not* exist with a capital 'W', possessor of some mythical unity—a supreme power, on which is based the terror of power and terrorism as the desire for power. But what an unbelievable force for subversion in the modern world! And, at the same time, what playing with fire!

CREATURES AND CREATRESSES

The desire to be a mother, considered alienating and even reactionary by the preceding generation of feminists, has obviously not become a standard for the present generation. But we have seen in the past few years an increasing number of women who not only consider their maternity compatible with their professional life or their feminist involvement (certain improvements in the quality of life are also at the origin of this: an increase in the number of daycare centres and nursery schools, more active participation of men in child care and domestic life, etc.), but also find it indispensable to their discovery, not of the plenitude, but of the complexity of the female experience, with all that this complexity comprises in joy and pain. This tendency has its extreme: in the refusal of the paternal function by lesbian and single mothers can be seen one of the most violent forms taken by the rejection of the symbolic outlined above, as well as one of the most fervent divinizations of maternal power—all of which cannot help but trouble an entire legal and moral order without, however, proposing an alternative to it. Let us remember here that Hegel distinguished between female right (familial and religious) and male law (civil and political). If our societies know well the uses and abuses of male law, it must also be recognized that female right is designated, for the moment, by a blank. And if these practices of maternity, among others, were to be generalized, women themselves would be responsible for elaborating the appropriate legislation to check the violence to which, otherwise, both their children and men would be subject. But are they capable of doing so? This is one of the important questions that the new generation of women encounters, especially when the members of this new generation refuse to ask those questions seized by the same rage with which the dominant order originally victimized them.

Faced with this situation, it seems obvious—and feminist groups become more aware of this when they attempt to broaden their audience—that the refusal of maternity cannot be a mass policy and that the majority of women today see the possibility for fulfilment, if not entirely at least to a large degree, in bringing a child into the world. What does this desire for motherhood correspond to? This is one of the new questions for the new generation, a question the preceding generation had foreclosed. For want of an answer to this question, feminist ideology leaves the door open to the return of religion, whose discourse, tried and proved over thousands of years, provides the necessary ingredients for satisfying the anguish, the suffering and the hopes of mothers. If Freud's affirmation—that the desire for a child is the desire for a penis and, in this sense, a substitute for phallic and symbolic dominion —can be only partially accepted, what modern women have to say about this experience should none the less be listened to attentively. Pregnancy seems to be experienced as the radical ordeal of the splitting of the subject:[24] redoubling up of the body, separation and coexistence of the self and of an other, of nature and consciousness, of physiology and speech. This fundamental challenge to identity is then accompanied by a fantasy of totality— narcissistic completeness—a sort of instituted, socialized, natural psychosis. The arrival of the child, on the other hand, leads the mother into the labyrinths of an experience that, without the child, she would only rarely encounter: love for an other. Not for herself, nor for an identical being, and still less for another person with whom 'I' fuse (love or sexual passion). But the slow, difficult and delightful apprenticeship in attentiveness, gentleness, forgetting oneself. The ability to succeed in this path without masochism and without annihilating one's affective, intellectual and professional personality —such would seem to be the stakes to be won through guiltless maternity. It then becomes a creation in the strong sense of the term. For this moment, utopian?

On the other hand, it is in the aspiration towards artistic and, in particular, literary creation that woman's desire for affirmation now manifests itself. Why literature?

Is it because, faced with social norms, literature reveals a certain knowledge and sometimes the truth itself about an otherwise repressed, nocturnal, secret and unconscious universe? Because it thus redoubles the social contract by exposing the unsaid, the uncanny? And because it makes a game, a space of fantasy and pleasure, out of the abstract and frustrating order of social signs, the words of everyday communication? Flaubert said, 'Madame Bovary, c'est moi'. Today many women imagine 'Flaubert, c'est moi'. This identification with the potency of the imaginary is not only an identification, an imaginary potency (a fetish, a belief in the maternal penis maintained at all costs), as a far too normative view of the social and symbolic relationship would have it. This identification also bears witness to women's desire to lift the weight of what is sacrificial in the social contract from their shoulders, to nourish our societies with a more flexible and free discourse, one able to name what has thus far never been an object of circulation in the community: the enigmas of the body, the dreams, secret joys, shames, hatreds of the second sex.

It is understandable from this that women's writing has lately attracted the maximum attention of both 'specialists' and the media.[25] The pitfalls encountered along the way, however, are not to be minimized: for example, does one not read there a relentless belittling of male writers whose books, nevertheless, often serve as 'models' for countless productions by women? Thanks to the feminist label, does one not sell numerous works whose naïve whining or market-place romanticism would otherwise have been rejected as anarchronistic? And does one not find the pen of many a female writer being devoted to phantasmic attacks against Language and Sign as the ultimate supports of phallocratic power, in the name of a semi-aphonic corporality whose truth can only be found in that which is 'gestural' or 'tonal'?

And yet, no matter how dubious the results of these recent productions by women, the symptom is there—women are writing, and the air is heavy with expectation: What will they write that is new?

IN THE NAME OF THE FATHER, THE SON . . . AND THE WOMAN?

These few elements of the manifestations by the new generation of women in Europe seem to me to demonstrate that, beyond the sociopolitical level where it is generally inscribed (or inscribes itself), the women's movement—in its present stage, less aggressive but more artful—is situated within the very framework of the religious crisis of our civilization.

I call 'religion' this phantasmic necessity on the part of speaking beings to provide themselves with a *representation* (animal, female, male, parental, etc.) in place of what constitutes them as such, in other words, symbolization —the double articulation and syntactic sequences of language, as well as its preconditions or substitutes (thoughts, affects, etc.). The elements of the current practice of feminism that we have just brought to light seem precisely to constitute such a representation which makes up for the frustrations imposed on women by the anterior code (Christianity or its lay humanist variant). The fact that this new ideology has affinities, often revindicated by its creators, with so-called matriarchal beliefs (in other words, those beliefs characterizing matrilinear societies) should not overshadow its radical novelty. This ideology seems to me to be part of the broader anti-sacrificial current which is animating our culture and which, in its protest against the constraints of the socio-symbolic contract, is no less exposed to the risks of violence and terrorism. At this level of radicalism, it is the very principle of sociality which is challenged.

Certain contemporary thinkers consider, as is well known, that modernity is characterized as the first epoch in human history in which human beings attempt to live without religion. In its present form, is not feminism in the process of becoming one?

Or is it, on the contrary and as avant-garde feminists hope, that having started with the idea of difference, feminism will be able to break free of its belief in Woman, Her power, Her writing, so as to channel this demand for difference into each and every element of the female whole, and, finally, to bring out the singularity of each woman, and beyond this, her multiplicities, her plural languages, beyond the horizon, beyond sight, beyond faith itself?

A factor for ultimate mobilization? Or a factor for analysis?

Imaginary support in a technocratic era where all narcissism is frustrated? Or instruments fitted to these times in which the cosmos, atoms and cells—our true contemporaries—call for the constitution of a fluid and free subjectivity?

The question has been posed. Is to pose it already to answer it?

ANOTHER GENERATION IS ANOTHER SPACE

If the preceding can be *said*—the question whether all this is *true* belongs to a different register—it is undoubtedly because it is now possible to gain some distance on these two preceding generations of women. This implies, of course, that a *third* generation is now forming, at least in Europe. I am not speaking of a new group of young women (though its importance should not be underestimated) or of another 'mass feminist movement' taking the torch passed on from the second generation. My usage of the word generation implies less a chronology than a *signifying space,* a both corporeal and desiring mental space. So it can be argued that as of now a third attitude is possible, thus a third generation, which does not exclude—quite to the contrary—the *parallel* existence of all three in the same historical time, or even that they be interwoven one with the other.

In this third attitude, which I strongly advocate—which I imagine?—the very dichotomy man/woman as an opposition between two rival entities may be understood as belonging to *metaphysics.* What can 'identity', even 'sexual identity', mean in a new theoretical and scientific space where the very notion of identity is challenged?[26] I am not simply suggesting a very hypothetical bisexuality which, even if it existed, would only, in fact, be the aspiration towards the totality of one of the sexes and thus an effacing of difference. What I mean is, first of all, the demassification of the problematic of *difference,* which would imply, in a first phase, an apparent de-dramatization of the 'fight to the death' between rival groups and thus between the sexes. And this is not in the name of some reconciliation—feminism has at least had the merit of showing what is irreducible and even deadly in the social contract—but in order that the struggle, the implacable difference, the violence be conceived in the very place where it operates with the maximum intransigence, in other words, in personal and sexual identity itself, so as to make it disintegrate in its very nucleus.

It necessarily follows that this involves risks not only for what we understand today as 'personal equilibrium' but also for social equilibrium itself, made up as it now is of the counterbalancing of aggressive and murderous forces massed in social, national, religious and political groups. But is it not the insupportable situation of tension and explosive risk that the existing 'equilibrium' presupposes which leads some of those who suffer from it to divest it of its economy, to detach themselves from it and to seek another means of regulating difference?

To restrict myself here to a personal level, as related to the question of women, I see arising, under the cover of a relative indifference towards the militance of the first and second generations, an attitude of retreat from sexism (male as well as female) and, gradually, from any kind of anthropomorphism. The fact that this might quickly become another form of spiritualism turning its back on social problems, or else a form of repression[27] ready to support all status quos, should not hide the radicalness of the process. This process could be summarized as an *interiorization of the founding separation of the socio-symbolic contract,* as an introduction of its cutting edge into the very interior of every identity whether subjective, sexual, ideological, or so forth. This in such a way that the habitual and increasingly explicit attempt to fabricate a scapegoat victim as foundress of a society or a counter-society may be replaced by the analysis of the potentialities of *victim/executioner* which characterize each identity, each subject, each sex.

What discourse, if not that of a religion, would be able to support this adventure which surfaces as a real possibility, after both the achievements and the impasses of the present ideological reworkings, in which feminism has participated? It seems to me that the role of what is usually called 'aesthetic practices' must increase not only to counterbalance the storage and uniformity of information by present-day mass media, data-bank systems and, in particular, modern communications technology, but also to demystify the identity of the symbolic bond itself, to demystify, therefore, the *community* of language as a universal and unifying tool, one which totalizes and equalizes. In order to bring out—along with the *singularity* of each person and, even more, along with the multiplicity of every person's possible identifications (with atoms, e.g., stretching from the family to the stars)— the *relativity of his/her symbolic as well as biological existence,* according to the variation in his/her specific symbolic capacities. And in order to emphasize the *responsibility* which all will immediately face of putting this fluidity into play against the threats of death which are unavoidable whenever an inside and an outside, a self and an other, one group and another, are constituted. At this level of interiorization with its social as well as individual stakes, what I have called 'aesthetic practices' are undoubtedly nothing other than the modern reply to the eternal question of morality. At least, this is how we might understand an ethics which, conscious of the fact that its order is sacrificial, reserves part of the burden for each of its adherents, therefore declaring them guilty while immediately affording them the possibility for *jouissance,* for various productions, for a life made up of both challenges and differences.

Spinoza's question can be taken up again here: Are women subject to ethics? If not to that ethics defined by classical philosophy—in relationship to which the ups and downs of feminist generations seem dangerously precarious—are women not already participating in the rapid dismantling that our age is experiencing at various levels (from wars to drugs to artificial insemination) and which poses the *demand* for a new ethics? The answer to Spinoza's question can be affirmative only at the cost of considering feminism as but a *moment* in the thought of that anthropomorphic identity which currently blocks the horizon of the discursive and scientific adventure of our species.

NOTES

1. Sigmund Freud and Carl G. Jung, *Correspondance* (Paris: Gallimard, 1975), vol. I, p. 87.
2. R. Spitz, *La Première Année de la vie de l'enfant* [First year of life: a psychoanalytic study of normal and deviant development of object relations] (Paris: PUF, 1958); D. Winnicott, *Jeu et réalité* [Playing and reality] (Paris: Gallimard, 1975); Julia Kristeva, 'Noms de lieu', in *Polylogue* (Paris: Seuil, 1977), translated as 'Place names' in Julia Kristeva, *Desire in Language: A semiotic approach to literature and art,* ed. Leon S. Roudiez, tr. Thomas Gora, Alice Jardine and Leon Roudiez (New York: Columbia University Press, 1980).
3. Plato, *Timeus* 52: 'Indefinitely a place; it cannot be destroyed, but provides a ground for all that can come into being; itself being perceptible, outside of all sensation, by means of a sort of bastard reasoning; barely assuming credibility, it is precisely that which makes us dream when we perceive it, and affirm all that exists must be somewhere, in a determined place . . .' (author's translation).
4. As most readers of recent French theory in translation know, *le féminin* does not have the same pejorative connotations it has come to have in English. It is a term used to speak about women in general, but, as used most often in this chapter, it probably comes closest to our 'female' as defined by Elaine Showalter in *A Literature of Their Own* (Princeton, N.J.: Princeton University Press, 1977). I have therefore used either 'women' or 'female' according to the context.—AJ.
5. I have retained *jouissance*—that word for pleasure which defies translation—as it is rapidly becoming a 'believable neologism' in English (see the glossary in *Desire in Language*). —AJ.
6. This particular mythology has important implications—equal only to those of the Oedipal myth—for current French thought.—AJ.
7. See Julia Kristeva, 'Stabat Mater', first published as 'Héréthique de l'amour', *Tel Quel,* 74 (1977), pp. 30–49.
8. See H. C. Puech, *La Gnose et le temps* (Paris: Gallimard, 1977).
9. The term *identification* belongs to a wide semantic field ranging from everyday language to philosophy and psychoanalysis. While Kristeva is certainly referring in principle to its elaboration in Freudian and Lacanian psychoanalysis, it can be understood here as a logic, in its most general sense (see the entry on 'identification' in Jean Laplanche and J. B. Pontalis, *Vocabulaire de la psychanalyse* [The language of psychoanalysis], Paris: Presses Universitaires de France, 1967; rev. ed., 1976).—AJ.
10. See D. Desanti, 'L'autre sexe des bolcheviks', *Tel Quel,* 76 (1978); Julia Kristeva, *Des Chinoises* (Paris: des femmes, 1975), translated as *On Chinese Women,* tr. Anita Barrows (London: Marion Boyars, 1977).

11. See Arthur Hertzberg, *The French Enlightenment and the Jews* (New York: Columbia University Press, 1968); *Les Juifs et la révolution française*, ed. B. Blumenkranz and A. Seboul (Paris: Editions Privat, 1976).

12. Here, *symbolic* is being more strictly used in terms of that function defined by Kristeva in opposition to the semiotic: 'it involves the thetic phase, the identification of subject and its distinction from objects, and the establishment of a sign system'.—AJ.

13. See, in general, Jacques Lacan, *Ecrits* (Paris: Seuil, 1966) and in particular, Jacques Lacan, *Le Séminaire XX: Encore* (Paris: Seuil, 1975).—AJ.

14. This work is periodically published in various academic women's journals, one of the most prestigious being *Signs: Journal of Women in Culture and Society*, University of Chicago Press. Also of note are the special issues: 'Ecriture, féminité, féminisme', *La Revue des Sciences Humaines* (Lille III), no. 4 (1977); and 'Les femmes et la philosophie', *Le Doctrinal de sapience* (Editions Solin), no. 3 (1977).

15. See linguistic research on 'female language': Robin Lakoff, *Language and Women's Place* (New York: Harper & Row, 1974); Mary R. Key, *Male/Female Language* (Metuchen, N.J.: Scarecrow Press, 1973); A. M. Houdebine, 'Les femmes et la langue', *Tel Quel*, 74 (1977), pp. 84–95. The contrast between these 'empirical' investigations of women's 'speech acts' and much of the research in France on the conceptual bases for a 'female language' must be emphasized here. It is somewhat helpful, if ultimately inaccurate, to think of the former as an 'external' study of language and the latter as an 'internal' exploration of the process of signification. For further contrast, see, e.g., 'Part II: Contemporary Feminist Thought in France: Translating Difference', in *The Future of Difference*, ed. Hester Eisenstein and Alice Jardine (Boston: G. K. Hall, 1980); the 'Introductions' to *New French Feminisms*, ed. Elaine Marks and Isabelle de Courtivron (Amherst, Mass.: University of Massachusetts Press, 1980); and for a very helpful overview of the problem of 'difference and language' in France, see Stephen Heath, 'Difference', in *Screen*, 19 no. 3 (Autumn 1978), pp. 51–112.—AJ.

16. This is one of the more explicit references to the mass marketing of 'écriture féminine' in Paris over the last ten years.—AJ.

17. The expression *à leur corps défendant* translates as 'against their will', but here the emphasis is on women's bodies: literally, 'against their bodies'. I have retained the former expression in English, partly because of its obvious intertextuality with Susan Brownmiller's *Against Our Will* (New York: Simon & Schuster, 1975). Women are increasingly describing their experience of the violence of the symbolic contract as a form of rape.—AJ.

18. Many women in the West who are once again finding all doors closed to them above a certain level of employment, especially in the current economic chaos, may find this statement, even qualified, troubling, to say the least. It is accurate, however, *in principle:* whether that of infinite capitalist recuperation or increasing socialist expansion—within both economies, our integration functions as a kind of *operative* illusion.—AJ.

19. See *Des Chinoises*.

20. See M. A. Macciocchi, *Eléments pour une analyse du fascisme* (Paris: 10/18, 1976); Michèle Mattelart, 'Le coup d'état au féminin', *Les Temps Modernes* (January 1975).

21. The principles of a 'sacrificial anthropology' are developed by René Girard in *La Violence et le sacré* [Violence and the sacred] (Paris: Grasset, 1972) and esp. in *Des choses cachées depuis la fondation du monde* (Paris: Grasset, 1978).

22. Cf. Micheline Enriquez, 'Fantasmes paranoiaques: Différences des sexes, homosexualité, loi du père', *Topiques*, 13 (1974).

23. See Jacques Lacan, 'Dieu et la jouissance de la femme', in *Encore* (Paris: Seuil, 1975), pp. 61–71, esp. p. 68. This seminar has remained a primary critical and polemical focus for

multiple tendencies in the French women's movement. For a brief discussion of the seminar in English, see Heath (n. 15 above).—AJ.

24. The 'split subject' (from *Spaltung* as both 'splitting' and 'cleavage'), as used in Freudian psychoanalysis, here refers directly to Kristeva's 'subject in process/in question/on trial' as opposed to the unity of the transcendental ego.—AJ.

25. Again a reference to *écriture féminine* as generally labelled in France over the past few years and not to women's writing in general.—AJ.

26. See Seminar on *Identity* directed by Lévi-Strauss (Paris: Grasset & Fasquelle, 1977).

27. Repression *(la refoulement* or *Verdrängung)* as distinguished from the foreclosure *(la forclusion* or *Verwerfung)* evoked earlier in the article (see Laplanche and Pontalis).—AJ.

Translated by Alice Jardine and Harry Blake

In the United States

19. "Sometimes You Wonder if They're Human"[1]

Dorothy Dinnerstein

When I was a child, people sang a popular song that foreshadowed for me, in an oddly disturbing way, a certain helpless, resigned adult astonishment.

> I never thought that anyone in his right mind
> Could treat a fellow human bein' so unkind.
> You went away and never left a note behind—
> Was that the human thing to do?

The singer, a woman, is in some muffled way shocked—as women somehow are, again and again, even when they have had plenty of time to get used to it—to find herself treated as if she were not an actual fellow creature. And she wonders without sharp anger whether the man himself is human, whether he is in his right mind. Women friends of mine say to me, in the same tone of dull surprise, *"You know, I think they're all crazy!"* And men draw cartoons, the meaning of which women understand so immediately and so deeply that acute indignation, for inner reasons which they tend not to explore, is hard to mobilize.

Men's feelings that we are not really human originates in their infancy. It resonates, moreover, with the atmosphere of our own infancy: this is what most centrally muffles our shock, dulls our indignation, when we encounter it. Our own reactive feeling—that it is men who are not really human, "not all there"—comes later and is far less primitive.

The earliest roots of antagonism to women lie in the period before the infant has any clear idea where the self ends and the outside world begins, or any way of knowing that the mother is a separately sentient being. At this stage a woman is the helpless child's main contact with the natural surround, the center of everything the infant wants and feels drawn to, fears losing and feels threatened by. She is the center also of the non-self, an unbounded, still unarticulated region within which the child labors to define itself and to discover the outlines of durable objects, creatures, themes. She is this global, inchoate, all-embracing presence before she is a person, a discrete finite human individual with a subjectivity of her own.

When she does become a person, her person-ness is shot through for the child with these earlier qualities. And when it begins to be clear that this person is a female in a world of males and females, femaleness comes to be the name for, the embodiment of, these global and inchoate and all-embracing qualities, qualities very hard indeed to reconcile with person-ness as one has begun to feel it inside oneself.

One result of female-dominated child care, then, is that the trouble every child has in coming to see that the magic parental presence of infancy was human, a person, can be permanently side-stepped: Women can be defined as quasi persons, quasi humans; and unqualified human personhood can be sealed off from the contaminating atmosphere of infant fantasy and defined as male.

This is why, so long as the hand that has rocked every cradle is female, psychoanalytic theorists and taxi drivers will go on, in their respective ways, complaining that the minimal, irreducible individualism of women is unwomanly, and pontificating about the masculine protest, and wondering angrily who wears the pants. Operetta stars will go on warbling about "a little list" of people who "never would be missed" which includes "the lady novelist." For whatever core of clear self-feeling a mother-raised woman does manage to muster is inevitably perceived by her mother-raised associates as objectionably, presumptuously male; it cannot possibly be seen simply as human.

When men start participating as deeply as women in the initiation of infants into the human estate, when both male and female parents come to carry for all of us the special meanings of early childhood, the trouble we have reconciling these meanings with person-ness will finally be faced. The consequence, of course, will be a fuller and more realistic, a kinder and at the same time more demanding, definition of person-ness.

Until then, women will continue to bear the brunt of our failure to face this trouble. Our gender arrangements, in other words, will go on making it possible for us to act out our early feelings toward the first parent in terms almost wholly unmodified by what we are later able to learn about this parent's actual human capacities, needs, and boundaries.

The discussion that follows examines the felt quasi humanity of woman from three perspectives. (Some overlap is unavoidable, but each needs separate consideration.) First, she is the object of deeply conflicting feelings toward existence itself. Second, we have trouble perceiving her as either wholly possessing or wholly lacking a subjectivity like our own. Third, she embodies the original non-self, a part of the infant's world which is both "it" and "you," and which feels both vitally necessary and vitally threatening to the formation of the "I."

THE MOTHER AS REPRESENTATIVE OF NATURE: PRE-RATIONAL AMBIVALENCE TOWARD THE SOURCE OF LIFE

One basis for our species' fundamental ambivalence toward its female members lies in the fact that the early mother, monolithic representative of nature, is a source, like nature, of ultimate distress as well as ultimate joy. Like nature, she is both nourishing and disappointing, both alluring and threatening, both comforting and unreliable. The infant loves her touch, warmth, shape, taste, sound, movement, just as it loves dancing light, textured space, soft covers, and as it will come to love water, fire, plants, animals. And it hates her because, like nature, she does not perfectly protect and provide for it. She is the source of food, warmth, comfort, and entertainment; but the baby, no matter how well it is cared for, suffers some hunger or cold, some bellyaches or alarming sudden movements or unpleasant bursts of noise, some loneliness or boredom; and how is it to know that she is not the source of these things too?

The mother, then—like nature, which sends blizzards and locusts as well as sunshine and strawberries—is perceived as capricious, sometimes actively malevolent. Her body is the first important piece of the physical world that we encounter, and the events for which she seems responsible the first instances of fate. Hence Mother Nature, with her hurricane daughters Alice, Betty, Clara, Debbie, Edna. Hence that fickle female Lady Luck.

The Envy-Gratitude Split

Melanie Klein provides an intense, poetically vivid account of this infant situation in her short, profound, controversial psychoanalytic treatise *Envy and Gratitude*.[2]

Her efforts to reconstruct "the patient's feelings as a baby at the mother's breast" have convinced her, she says, of the fundamental, lifelong consequences of the simple fact that in this situation, "together with happy experiences'' there are ''unavoidable grievances.'' The infant, for example, ''may have a grievance that the milk comes too quickly or too slowly; or that he was not given the breast when he most craved for it, and therefore, when it is offered, he does not want it any more.''[3] She writes of ''the infant's desire for the inexhaustible, ever-present breast . . .'' and of its ''feeling that the mother is omnipotent and that it is up to her to prevent all pain and evils from internal and external sources . . .'' The resulting attitude of destructive rage, which she calls envy, ''spoils and harms the good object which is the source of life,'' for the child believes—and on some level will always believe—that angry thoughts damage their target. ''If envy of the feeding breast is strong . . . full gratification is interfered with because . . . envy . . . implies robbing the object of what it possesses, and spoiling it.'' As a result, ''a part of the self is felt as an enemy to the ego as well as to the loved object'' and the child feels ''recurrent anxiety that his greed and his destructive impulses will get the better of him . . .''

Envy, in Klein's sense, also engenders another kind of worry. The sense of having harmed ''the breast'' leads by a process of projection to ''persecutory anxiety'': ''. . . the object that arouses guilt is turned into a persecutor,'' becomes the ''earliest internalized persecutory object—the retaliating, devouring, and poisonous breast.''

Threatened by bad feelings from within and (projected) hostility from without, the child is in danger of being cut off from its ''good object''—that is, from its sense of connectedness to a benevolent and lovable outside force. The child handles this danger with what Klein calls a ''splitting'' mechanism: Its hateful feelings are sharply dissociated from its loving ones; the menacing, vengeful aspects of the mother (as she exists in the child's mind) are walled off from her comforting, providing aspects. The child comes to feel ''that a good and a bad breast exist.'' The good breast remains intact, unsullied by badness, but it disappears altogether from time to time and a bad breast is there instead: ''. . . early emotional life is characterized by a sense of losing and regaining the good object.''

Later, when the infant is more able emotionally to endure the anxiety of experiencing such contrasting feelings toward a single object (and, I would add, more able cognitively to conceive of a single object so complex), the early splitting is to some degree overcome. A patient who has not managed to do this in infancy can sometimes do it afterward, Klein says, in psychotherapy. Such a patient achieves the insight that ''the object's badness is largely due to his own aggressiveness and the ensuing projection.'' It is then possible to realize that the object "is not so bad as it was felt to be in its split-off aspects." This paves the way for "the urge to make reparation," which normally arises when the infant tries to integrate the good and bad "breasts." Reparation "involves counteracting destructive impulses by mobilizing feelings of love."

Klein's reconstruction of very early emotional life does not pretend to bridge the gap between the actual texture of the infant's experience and the terms in which psychoanalytic patients (and psychoanalysts) express themselves. Still, the feeling constellations that she describes correspond recognizably in their quality and their general shape with feeling constellations which are central in adult life, emotional states so inarticulate, so global, so profound that they do—in the same way that sexual joy does, for example, or the sense of desertion, or the experience of beatific mutual gazing—seem clearly to have roots in pre-verbal infancy.

Indeed, one of the core problems with which religion (whether it is labeled "religion" or not) tries to cope is precisely the interplay between "envy" and "gratitude." Dostoyevsky is writing, I think, about this basic interplay when he tells us how Alyosha Karamazov feels after his saintly teacher has died and begun—to the malicious delight of people who have all along been jealous of his sweet, joyous spiritual power—to stink.

"I am not rebelling against my God," says he to a spiteful friend. "I simply 'don't accept his world.' " Characteristically cheerful, gentle, and mild, he is now irritable and depressed, ironical and reckless. Angrily, he violates his rules of diet with sausage, pollutes himself with vodka, and goes to a woman who in his mind stands for lust and vindictiveness. But while he is there she suddenly shows him her pain, her emotional generosity, and her need. The tide of his feeling for life begins to turn. Soon afterward he dreams of the wedding at which Christ turned water into wine, where his dead teacher, alive, takes his hand and pulls him toward kindness and rejoicing; then he goes out into the autumn night. He stands gazing—"and then suddenly threw himself down upon the earth. . . . He could not have told why he long so irresistibly to kiss it, to kiss it. But he kissed it . . . and vowed passionately to love it, to love it forever and ever. 'Water the earth with the tears of your joy and love those tears.' His elder's words echoed in his soul."

Though it is seldom felt so purely and directly as Alyosha felt it, his swing between bleak dislike and utter love for what he thought of as God's world is humanly characteristic. Coleridge's Ancient Mariner felt it too.

In his opening comments nature goes back and forth, even within a stanza, from persecutory to alluring: the storm blast was "tyrannous"; but when "ice, mast-high, came floating by," he notes that it was "green as emerald."

The companionable albatross, a "sweet bird," is welcomed. "As if it had been a Christian soul." But wholly without warning, the narrator is moved to destroy it. Feeling toward him shifts from initial approval to heavy blame; his mates hang the corpse of his victim around his neck. Becalmed, all start to die of heat and thirst, and the horror of nature fills Coleridge's canvas: "The very deep did rot: O Christ! That ever this should be! Yea, slimy things did crawl with legs Upon the slimy sea." An uncanny skeleton ship bears down on them against an ugly sunset, without wind. Her crew, especially its female member, is ghastly: "Is that a DEATH? And are there two? Is DEATH that woman's mate? Her lips were red, her looks were free, Her locks were yellow as gold: Her skin was as white as leprosy, The Night-mare LIFE-IN-DEATH was she, Who thicks man's blood with cold." The two play dice. Death wins his comrades, and Life in Death wins the narrator. Accursed and alone, he loathes the world and himself: "A thousand thousand slimy things Lived on; and so did I." His heart, "dry as dust," cannot pray. "For the sky and the sea, and the sea and the sky Lay like a load on my weary eye, And the dead were at my feet." For a week he yearns to die. But then one night, like Alyosha, he looks at the sky, and suddenly, in what before had been "the rotting sea," in which "death-fires danced at night," he sees the "charmed water" burn red in the ship's shadow; he sees the water snakes that were "slimy things" before, and for him, as for Alyosha, the deep turn toward life begins: "They moved in tracks of shining white, And when they reared, the elfish light Fell off in hoary flakes. Within the shadow of the ship I watched their rich attire: Blue, glossy green, and velvet black, They coiled and swam; and every track Was a flash of golden fire. O happy living things! no tongue Their beauty might declare: A spring of love gushed from my heart, And I blessed them unaware . . . The self-same moment I could pray; And from my neck so free The Albatross fell off, and sank Like lead into the sea."

To me, the passionate depth of this swing away from the world and back, and its inaccessibility to will or reason, fit well with Klein's suggestion that it is originally experienced by the nursling, that it is first felt in relation to a parental being whose human qualities are sensed, but only indistinctly sensed: an omnipotent parental being, personal and purposeful enough to earn love for what she provides and blame for every misfortune, and too vastly contradictory to make any steady, integrated sentiment toward her possible. The infant develops strong feeling for this being long before it is able to recognize her—even partially—as the finite, limited, vulnerable creature that she actually is. And this special feeling seems to survive, and to seek an appropriate object, long after its original object has evolved into a mere person (or in any case into that compromised version of a mere person, a mere woman).

Rapacity and Greed, Responsibility and Compunction

The early mother's apparent omnipotence, then, her ambivalent role as ultimate source of good and evil, is a central source of human malaise: our species' uneasy, unstable stance toward nature, and its uneasy, unstable sexual arrangements, are inseparable aspects of this malaise. Both toward women and toward nature as a whole—as originally toward the mother, who was half human, half nature—we feel torn between two impulses: the impulse, on the one hand, to give free rein to the nursling's angry greed, its wild yearning to own, control, suck dry the source of good, its wish to avenge deprivation; and the impulse, on the other hand, to make reparation for these feelings, which threaten to destroy what is most precious and deeply needed.

The balance between infantile destructiveness toward the source of life, and the reciprocal surge of anxiety and good will that keeps this destructiveness within bounds, varies from person to person, and from culture to culture. This balance is sometimes tipped more toward hostility and rapacity, sometimes more toward respect, concern, awe. It need not always be tipped in the same direction for women and for nature. The degree to which destructive and loving impulses are split off from each other is also variable. The main point is that there is always a balance, inherently tense and unstable, and that the destructive side of it is always lively.

What I have just said needs to be qualified in two ways. First, women are obviously not the only human targets of our central destructiveness. Men, and even children, are also treated as natural resources to be mined, reaped, used up without concern for their future fate;[4] as sources of labor to be drawn on with only our own interests in mind; as property to be seized, held, disposed of for our own profit. Men and children, however, are less adequate targets than women for this kind of feeling: they are not so readily classifiable with the early mother; it is harder—though of course possible—to overlook their humanity.

Men, moreover, are likely to feel internally less identified with the early mother, so that even when they cannot escape being treated exploitatively—

indeed, even when they, like women, have been taught by society that as members of a given caste this is their appropriate lot—they are less apt to accept such treatment without clear-cut resentment. Women have, in some deeper sense, expected it all along.

Women, then, are both the most acceptable and the most accepting victims of the human need for a quasi-human source of richness and target of greedy rage. If this were not the case, if there did not exist a special category of human being who seems on an infant level of thought naturally fit to fulfill this infantile need, our species might be forced to outgrow it. Under present conditions, the availability of women as especially suitable victims encourages people to indulge the need, which then extends—since it is inherently insatiable—to embrace other victims as well.

Many other writers have pointed to the connection between the universal exploitation of women and the survival of an atmosphere in which the idea of exploitation in general remains acceptable. What I am trying here to add to this old insight is another, and doubtless stickier, point: The universal exploitation of women is rooted in our attitudes toward very early parental figures, and will go on until these figures are male as well as female. Only when this happens will society be forced to find ways to help its members handle the impulses of greed and rapacity that now make man "wolf to the man." *It is at this point that the human projects of brotherhood, of peace with nature, and of sexual liberty interpenetrate.*

A second qualification must be added to my statement that we all use women as targets of the primitive envy-gratitude ambivalence described by Klein. Both sexes do use women in this way. But the feelings women have about doing so are modulated by the fact that the early mother eventually does, at least to some degree, evolve for the growing child into an actual person. The girl child is likely to come to identify with this actual person more closely than the boy child. She is therefore apt to develop a livelier sense of compunction for her, and also for the figure of the early mother than remains, on archaic levels of awareness, connected with this later, more actual mother. In this compunction—particularly if the split-off antagonism that goes with it is recognized and integrated—lies a strong potential basis for solidarity among women. Men's affection for each other does not include anything like this tender, healing solicitude. They do not need to make reparation to each other for early feelings of greed and rage.

Neither, moreover, are men's solicitous impulses toward women the same as those that women feel toward women. The boy's restitutive urges toward the early mother—as echoed in later relations with her and with other females—are less tinged than the girl's with fellow-feeling. For him, the mother to whom reparation must be made is mainly an idol that has been flouted and must now be mollified lest she exact vengeance, a natural resource that has been assaulted and must now be restored lest it cease to provide, a living source of delight that has been tampered with, perhaps destroyed, and must now be coaxed back to life. For the girl, too, she is all these things; but she is also—more vividly than for the boy—a creature who has suffered injury just as one can suffer it oneself, and who needs to be soothed and protected just as one needs her to soothe and protect one's vulnerable self. (Colette's Renée in *The Vagabond* sees in a lesbian pair "the melancholy and touching image of two weak creatures who have perhaps sought shelter in each other's arms, there to sleep and weep, safe from man who is so often cruel, and there to taste, better than any pleasure, the bitter happiness of feeling themselves akin, frail and forgotten." But what has to be added to her account is that these "women enlaced" are sheltering each other not just from what men want to do to them, but also from what they want to do to each other.)

It seems to me possible that this component of the girl's reparative feeling extends to nature as well as to other women. What has kept women outside the nature-assaulting parts of history—what has made them (with striking exceptions, to be sure) less avid than men as hunters and killers, as penetrators of Mother Nature's secrets, plunderers of her treasure, outwitters of her constraints—may well be not only the practical procreative burden that they have carried, but this special compunction too. Certainly it seems reasonable to suppose that if men had felt all along more closely identified with the first parent—as they will if time permits us to make the necessary change in our child-care arrangements—we would not now be so close to the irrevocable murder of nature.

That we are in fact now so close to this final murder must, I think, have to do with the predominantly self-interested character of male reparative feeling.[5] Men's exploitation of Mother Nature has so far been kept in check largely by their conception of the practical risk they themselves ran in antagonizing, depleting, spoiling her. (In preliterate societies, we are told, ritual apologies are offered by hunters to the animals they kill, and by woodcutters to the spirits who inhabit the trees they chop down.) As technology has advanced, and they have felt more powerful, one part of this sense of risk—the fear of antagonizing her—has abated. A euphoric sense of conquest has replaced it: the son has set his foot on the mother's chest, he has harnessed her firmly to his uses, he has opened her body once and for all and may now help himself at will to its riches. What remains is the danger that she will be depleted, spoiled. Men's view of this danger has been fatally short-sighted; it has not kept pace with the actual growth of their destructive power. What has kept it so short-sighted has been, at least in part, the strength of their vindictive, grabby feelings. To maintain a longer, more enlightened view, these feelings—unleashed by their sense of conquest—would at this point have to be pulled back in, and kept under control, by a more powerful effort of will than they seem to be able to muster.

But our ambivalence toward the parent who is the first representative of nature consists not only of unstable, conflicting feelings of envy and gratitude, rapacity and compunction. It consists also of unstable, conflicting perceptions of her sentience. A central reason for woman's anomalous image, which (even in her own mind to some degree) combines, or fluctuates between, omniscient goddess and dumb bitch, lies in the trouble we have totally accepting the discovery—which cannot be totally rejected, either— that this parent has definable, understandable subjectivity; that she embodies an autonomous awareness corresponding to our own.

THE MOTHER AS REPRESENTATIVE OF NATURE: THE SEMI-SENTIENT "SHE"

Mead and Hays, among others, have documented the tendency, expressed by people under a wide range of cultural conditions, to see in woman a mystic continuity with non-human processes like rain and the fertility of plants. The question is why this should be so much more the case for woman than for man, who has his own metaphoric continuity with these non-human forces. Rain and sun, for example, have been represented in myth as male sources of life that kindle and fertilize the female earth; the sea and its winds have been thought of as male; the upthrusting of trees and green shoots is often viewed as a phallic event. And yet such metaphors dominate people's everyday sense of what men are far less than their sense of what women are. D. H. Lawrence was right, I think, to complain that the animal mystery of men, the cosmic (or—to use the term broadly—religious) impact of their physical maleness, is on the whole underplayed in our life.

Mead suggests that it is the more visible, sustained drama, the more conspicuous mystery, of woman's role in procreation that makes her concrete presence seem so much more a center of magic non-personal force than man's. To Hays, the superstitious awe, often loathing, that surrounds menstruation and parturition, and links them to wider natural events, expresses the human male's ambivalent response to otherness, a response that connects what is not male (woman) with what is not human (nature). Both these explanations seem true as far as they go.[6]

What is also true, however, is that woman is the creature we encounter before we are able to distinguish between a center of sentience and an impersonal force of nature: it seems extremely unlikely that the flavor of this early encounter could fail to survive as a prominent ingredient of our later feeling for her. The ambiguity in our perception of the mother's subjectivity is not explicitly mentioned in Klein's exposition, but it is implicit in the emotional events she describes; without it, they could not occur. This ambiguity seems to me an important part of the reason why people—men especially, but women too—have such a partial, unsteady grasp on the fact that women are human, and find it so hard to show ordinary human respect for them.

"It"ness and "I"ness

Every "I" first emerges in relation to an "It" which is not at all clearly an "I." The separate "I"ness of the other person is a discovery, an insight achieved over time. Small children do not completely have it (an example is the tendency of three- or four-year-olds to assume that you, whom they have just met, must somehow already know by name all the people they know) and the reader need not be told that there are many adults who have only a gross, rudimentary mental grasp of it. This fact of infancy, together with our female-dominated child-care arrangements, guarantees a more or less lopsided view of male and female "I"ness. The mother is first experienced by every one of us as "It," while the father, who is a much more peripheral presence at the beginning, becomes a significant figure only after the concept of an independent outside "I" has begun to be established. It would be strange if this early difference did not carry over, on a prerational level of feeling, into adult life.

A ship, a city, any entity that we half-seriously personify, is called "she." "She" designates the borderline between the inanimate and the conscious. De Beauvoir splendidly describes this quasi-human connotation of "she." In her account, man's assignment of the role of "other" to woman is a way of mitigating the loneliness of his place in nature. He commandeers woman's services as intermediary between his conscious self and the natural surround. And she accepts the role because it relieves her of primary responsibility for a burden he is willing to assume with her assistance: the burden of lonely subjectivity in a world that is otherwise (except as human imagination inhabits it with phantom subjectivities) soulless.

This analysis of de Beauvoir's seems to me entirely valid, but—like any analysis—incomplete. Here, what I want to add to it is the observation that woman, no matter what other changes take place in her situation, will remain fitted for this role as half-human "other," and can never escape it, so long as she agrees to go on being the goddess of the nursery.

The girl's difficulty in coming to accept the "I"ness of women is likely in one sense to be less serious than the boy's, since she comes to feel more identified with the first parent, and of course cannot help being "I" to herself. Unhappily, however, this difference also works in the opposite direction: her sense of continuity with the mother—who to some degree, on some level, remains "It" to all of us—makes her seem less of an "I" to herself.

Even to the daughter, the mother may never come to seem so completely an "I" as the father, who was an "I" when first encountered. The "It"ness that colors her perception of her mother colors her perception of every female presence, including her own.[7] And this view of herself is confirmed by what she sees reflected back in the eyes of others: if she is unamazed, unaffronted, to find herself looked at as "It," the original reason for this monstrous composure of hers (a composure which in turn revalidates the other person's view of her, legitimizes it by failing to challenge it) is the gender of the hand that rocks the cradle.

Conceptions of Female Sentience and Demands on the Natural Surround

Our difficulty in coming to grasp the fact of the mother's separate human subjectivity (like our related difficulty in outgrowing the early feeling that she is omnipotent and responsible for every blessing and curse of existence) has central consequences not only for the way we look at women, but also for our stance toward nature. Because the early mother's boundaries are so indistinct, the non-human surround with which she merges takes on some of her own quasi-personal quality. In our failure to distinguish clearly between her and nature, we assign to each properties that belong to the other: We cannot believe how accidental, unconscious, unconcerned—i.e., unmotherly —nature really is; and we cannot believe how vulnerable, conscious, autonomously wishful—i.e., human—the early mother really was.

Our over-personification of nature, then, is inseparable from our under-personification of woman. We cannot listen to reason when it tells us that the mother—who was once continuous with nature—is a fully sentient fellow person; nor can we listen when it tells us that nature—which was once continuous with the mother—is wholly impersonal, non-sentient. If we could outgrow our feeling that the first parent was semi-human, a force of nature, we might also be able to outgrow the idea that nature is semi-human, and our parent.

But we will do this only when we are forced to do it, and we will be forced to do it only when both sexes have started to carry the emotional aura of the first parent. When all of us come to carry it, full human status can no longer be reserved for those who do not: Our conception of humanness will have to be expanded to embrace this early emotional aura; and our understanding of what the aura really is deepened to make it compatible with humanness. The feelings we all have toward the magic nurturer of infancy will have to be confronted, because they will have to be assimilated into our sense of what can be expected from, and what is owed to, a human person. *It is at this point that the human project of reconciliation between the rational and the pre-rational layers of our sentience interpenetrates with the projects of sexual liberty and of peace with nature.*

Meanwhile, unfortunately, the basic infantile belief that nature is our parent has not at all abated as our power to grab what we want from her has increased. As science and technology advance, formal theological belief in a parental deity has of course come to seem less plausible. But what has changed in the stance most people take toward nature-the-parent is not the destructive infantilism of this stance. What has weakened is a later-born feeling toward parental authority, a feeling which lies closer to the rational surface of awareness, and which is apt to be focused in good part on the father, who represents the more mature human world: that a parent can state valid moral imperatives, and impose predictable penalities if they are not met. The fading away of God the Father, the righteous judge, should in principle motivate his lopsidedly developed offspring to learn how to judge and govern themselves, but so far this has not happened. The loss of supernatural moral guidance in the light of scientific reason has not made people more grown-up; it has only unleashed the amoral greed of infancy.

Inextricable from the notion that nature is our semi-sentient early mother is the notion that she is inherently inexhaustible, that if she does not provide everything we would like to have it is because she does not want to, that her treasure is infinite and can if necessary be taken by force. This view of Mother Earth is in turn identical with the view of woman as Earth Mother, a bottomless source of richness, a being not human enough to have needs of an importance as primary, as self-evident, as the importance of our own needs, but voluntary and conscious enough so that if she does not give us what we expect she is withholding it on purpose and we are justified in getting it from her any way we can. The murderous infantilism of our relation to nature follows inexorably from the murderous infantilism of our sexual arrangements. To outgrow the one we must outgrow the other.

There is an additional way in which the early mother's continuity with nature contributes to our sexual situation. Not only is her own "I"ness ambiguous in the mind of the child; she also acts, for the child, as a central representative of that from which the self must be carved out.

THE MOTHER AS REPRESENTATIVE OF NATURE: THE NON-SELF

Woman and the Formation of the Self

Each subjective self starts forming itself in a world which is both a stimulus and an obstacle to the self-forming venture. In this world, the mother is the most vivid and the most active presence.

On the one hand, her interested awareness is essential to the child's developing selfhood, which finds its own existence reflected, confirmed, in her recognition of it. The child's first experiments in action, its first efforts to see how its own voluntary behavior can bring about change in the environment, are crucially supported by her response to them. It discovers on its own that it can make something interesting come into view by moving a limb, make interesting sounds happen by exercising its vocal apparatus, and so on. But with her it discovers that the movements, sounds, and so on that it is able to produce at will can elicit different, but meaningfully related, movements, sounds, and so on from another creature: it can initiate events in which she will participate. Just as importantly, the way in which she initiates events assumes, recognizes, invites exercise of, the child's capacity for active, conscious, voluntary response. The child thus becomes aware of itself as an influential social being, important and attractive to those who are important and attractive to itself.

As Asch shows in eloquent detail, the human self develops in a social field consisting of mutually interpenetrating subjectivities: there can be no full-blown "I" without a "you" which is perceived as recognizing the "I," and as aware of being recognized by it as another "I." Paradoxically, the mother is never an unqualified "you" in this sense because she always retains some of the "It"ness that she had at the outset; yet she is the first—and for the original formation of the self the all-important—"you."

On the other hand, even while she provides this vital support for the early growth of the self, the mother is inevitably felt as a menace to that self. She is the outstanding feature of the arresting, sometimes overwhelming, realm within which the self's boundaries must be defined. The multiple rhythms of this outside realm, its pulls, pressures, and distractions, can threaten to swamp the nascent self's own needs and intentions, to blur its perception of its own outlines, to deflect its inner sense of direction and drown out its inner voice.

There is also the fact that when the active project of selfhood feels too strenuous or too dangerously lonely the temptation is strong in all of us to melt back into that from which we have carved ourselves out. The mother supports the active project, but she is also on hand to be melted into when it is abandoned. She may, indeed, even encourage the child's lapses from selfhood, for she as well as the child has mixed feelings about its increasing separateness from her. There is of course no such thing as a wholly benevolent mother, with no antagonism whatsoever to the child as an autonomous being.[8] But even if there were, she would be experienced by the child, in its struggle to become such a being, both as an interfering influence and as a lure back into nonbeing.

Adult Consequences

So long as the first parent is a woman, then, woman will inevitably be pressed into the dual role of indispensable quasi-human supporter and deadly quasi-human enemy of the human self. She will be seen as naturally fit to nurture other people's individuality; as the born audience in whose awareness other people's subjective existence can be mirrored; as the being so peculiarly needed to confirm other people's worth, power, significance that if she fails to render them this service she is a monster, anomalous and useless. And at the same time she will also be seen as the one who will not let other people be, the one who beckons her loved ones back from selfhood, who wants to engulf, dissolve, drown, suffocate them as autonomous persons.

In adult life as we know it, it is of course women who are in reality most likely to be distracted, drowned, suffocated as individuals. What they are expected to provide for others, and to suppress in themselves, makes this axiomatic. Yet even so, it is they who are perceived as the naggers and the engulfers, the main menace to the autonomy, the human selfhood, of others. It is true, and by now widely understood, that woman's limited opportunity to develop her own self does in fact often make her batten on, and sabotage, the autonomy of others. But what I am pointing to is another, deeper-lying truth: that the threat to autonomy which can come from a woman is felt on a less rational, more helpless level, experienced as more primitively danger-ous, than any such threat from a man.

The possibility that a man will interrupt a woman's train of thought, interfere with her work, encourage her to sink back into passivity, make her an appendage of himself, does not engender the same panic in most of us as the possibility that she will do this to him. The original threat that we all felt in this connection was felt as emanating from a woman, and we lean over backward in our heterosexual arrangements to keep this original threat at bay. We will have to continue to do so, in some way, until we reorganize child care to make the realm of the early non-self as much a male as a female domain.

NEW WAYS

When we have achieved this reorganization, men will be less afraid of being drowned by women; but a fact which must be faced—and probably few of us are ready to face it without some sense of painful loss—is that they will not need women in the same way either. The precious captive female ''other'' that de Beauvoir has described and that men now need is the maternal ''you'' of infancy, kept on hand to go on helping the ''I'' in its continuous rediscov-ery and redefinition of its boundaries, but penned in, bottled up, so that it cannot suffocate or swallow the ''I'' as it once threatened to do. When the early parental ''other'' is no longer exclusively female, woman will no longer be peculiarly qualified to provide this kind of company.

Correspondingly, woman will be freed of her dependence on the vicarious experience of "I"'ness now provided by man. She will be released from her present obligation to recreate in herself the maternal "you," and to lavish its benefits on man, whose need to protect himself from its dangers she is then forced to respect out of concern for his autonomy, which she is in turn privileged to enjoy second-hand. She will be no more worried than man about the possibility of drowning out or engulfing another person.

Under these conditions she will be as eager as man is to find some direct re-access to emotional contact with the original "other." The nourishment of individuality offered by this magic non-self will inhere as deeply in men as in women, and so will its dangers; new ways will therefore have to be found for coping with these dangers—ways less expensive, and less explosive, than banning the selfhood of half the members of our species.

We already have inklings of what these ways will be. When the magic richness and the magic dangerousness of the first parent are embodied inside every person, male and female, when they are contained within the same skin that contains the subjective, vulnerable, limited human "I," the emotional uses of this magic will change. What now serves as a chronic focus of greed, a chronic source of terror, will be transformed into a wild place to be visited for pleasure, a special preserve where old, primitive regions of human personality can be rediscovered. The "I" will turn to this part of itself, and of the other person, as it turns to forest or flame or moving water: to replenish its energies in contact with something less tidy and reasonable, more innocent and fierce, more ancient and mystifying than itself.

The ways we find, then, will be ways of drawing more flexibly on the emotional resources of infancy, of dealing more openly with our need to regard each other half as fellow creatures, half as magic parents. Our concept of the human person will deepen to do justice to the complex truth of human experience. The actual finite individual in each of us will learn to affirm itself to other people while still allowing them, on some playful level, to endow it with early parental magic.

Until we learn to do this, what should be felt as play will continue to be self-deluded play-acting, lived out in grim earnest. And in this living out we will continue to prey on and terrorize each other; also to gobble up, poison, and chop to lifeless bits the world that we nevertheless love, the world that nurtures us, the only world we have.

NOTES

1. Old saw.
2. Many readers miss the point of this deeply startling little essay, mostly, I think, because it is threatening to them, but partly because of the difficult language in which it is couched. A reader afraid of the essay's emotional challenge can easily escape it by ridiculing what is vulnerable in Klein's exposition. A reader interested in facing the challenge will try harder to hear the main things she is saying. The mental processes that Klein seems to attribute to three- or six-month-old infants, for example, should not be taken literally; her formulations are based on the play, dreams, and transference behaviors of older children and adults, who have recast memories of very early feelings into words and images that the infant did not possess. For this same reason, the term "breast" as she uses it must be understood not solely in its literal sense but also as a metaphor for "source of good."
3. Interestingly, the experimental psychologist Hebb has made the same observation on a young chimpanzee. Finally offered a cup of milk for which she had been clamoring in vain, she dashed it to the floor. What this anecdote suggests is that as creatures approach the human level of complexity, their behavior takes on some of that destructiveness toward the self and what the self loves that we think of as human.
4. Indeed, women themselves are quite capable of transferring to men some of the attributes that originally belonged to the early mother, and of behaving accordingly. A classic literary example of this voracious using up of a husband's creative resources by a heartless wife is George Eliot's portrait of Lydgate and Rosamond in *Middlemarch*. The point is, however, that what seems monstrous when a wife here and there does it to her husband seems simply male—normally, heedlessly male—when a husband as a matter of course does it to his wife.
5. This is not to suggest that it is *the* explanation, of course. Our predicament clearly also has to do with societal factors of the blind kind that Tolstoy described in *War and Peace*— historical and sociological processes whose overall shape does not at all coincide with any participant's motives, and only fragments of which are represented in any participant's awareness. But psychological processes of the kind referred to here—processes rooted deep in "normal" personality, and mutable only if confronted—must be an important *part* of the explanation.
6. Hays, though, does not explain how women, to whom femaleness is not otherness, are persuaded to lend themselves to the uncomfortable rituals that dramatize the male response he describes: are they bullied? brainwashed? just humoring their menfolk?
7. This outcome is modified to the extent that she manages—as many gifted women do—to preserve her "I"ness by thinking of men, not women, as her real fellow creatures. This is a problem for political solidarity among vigorous women that cannot be wished away by denial or pushed safely underground by moral-ideological disapproval. On the other hand, once recognized for what it is, it may provide easier to surmount than certain obstacles to solidarity among men. For the impulse toward reparation, toward the passionate bridging of rifts, has older roots in infancy between women than between men.
8. Quite apart from the ultimate impossibility of human perfection, our gender arrangements militate in an immediate way against the chance that such a mother could exist. The early developmental situation under discussion here makes it hard for any of us—and mothers, too, were infants once—to come to real terms with the independent existence of other subjectivities.

BIBLIOGRAPHY

Asch, Solomon E. *Social Psychology*. New York, 1952.

Beauvoir, Simone de. *The Second Sex*. Paris, 1949. Quoted from the H. M. Parshley translation.

Coleridge, Samuel Taylor. "The Rime of the Ancient Mariner." London, 1798.

Colette. *The Vagabond*. Paris, 1929. Quoted from the Enid McLeod translation.

Dostoyevsky, Fyodor. *The Brothers Karamazov*. 1881. Quoted from the Constance Garnett translation.

Eliot, George. *Middlemarch*. London, 1872.

————. *The Mill on the Floss*. London, 1860.

Hays, H. R. *The Dangerous Sex: The Myth of Feminine Evil*. New York, 1964.

Hebb, D. O., and Thompson, W. R. "The Social Significance of Animal Studies." In *Handbook of Social Psychology*, ed. G. Lindzey. Reading, Mass., 1954.

Klein, Melanie. *Envy and Gratitude*. London, 1957.

Mead, Margaret. *Male and Female*. New York, 1949.

Tolstoy, Leo. *War and Peace*. 1869.

20. Gender, Relation, and Difference in Psychoanalytic Perspective

Nancy Julia Chodorow

I would go so far as to say that even before slavery or class domination existed, men built an approach to women that would serve one day to introduce differences among us all.—Claude Lévi-Strauss[1]

In both the nineteenth- and twentieth-century women's movements, many feminists have argued that the degendering of society, so that gender and sex no longer determined social existence, would eliminate male dominance. This view assumes that gender differentiating characteristics are acquired. An alternate sexual politics and analysis of sexual inequality has tended toward an essentialist position, posing male-female difference as innate. Not the degendering of society, but its appropriation of women, with women's virtues, is seen as the solution to male dominance. These virtues are uniquely feminine, and usually thought to emerge from women's biology, which is then seen as intrinsically connected to or entailing a particular psyche, a particular social role (such as mothering), a particular body image (more diffuse, holistic, nonphallocentric), or a particular sexuality (not centered on a particular organ; at times, lesbianism). In this view, women are intrinsically better than men and their virtues are not available to men. Proponents of the degendering model have sometimes also held that ''female'' virtues or qualities—nurturance, for instance—should be spread throughout society and replace aggression and competitiveness; but these virtues are nevertheless seen as acquired, a product of women's development or social location, and acquirable by men, given appropriate development, experience, and social reorganization. (Others who argue for degendering have at times held that women need to acquire certain ''male'' characteristics and modes of action

—autonomy, independence, assertiveness—again, assuming that such characteristics are acquired.)

This essay evaluates the essentialist view of difference and examines the contribution that psychoanalytic theory can make to understanding the question of sex or gender difference. It asks whether gender is best understood by focusing on differences between men and women and on the uniqueness of each and whether gender difference should be a central organizing concept for feminism. The concept of difference to which I refer here, is abstract and irreducible.[2] It assumes the existence of an essence of gender, so that differences between men and women are seen to establish and define each gender as a unique and absolute category.

I will not discuss differences among women. I think we have something else in mind when we speak of differences in this connection. Differences among women—of class, race, sexual preference, nationality, and ethnicity, between mothers and nonmothers—are all significant for feminist theory and practice, but these remain concrete differences, analyzable in terms of specific categories and modes of understanding. We can see how they are socially situated and how they grow from particular social relations and organization; how they may contain physiological elements (race and sexual preference, for example) yet only gain a specific meaning in particular historical contexts and social formations.

I suggest that gender difference is not absolute, abstract, or irreducible; it does not involve an essence of gender. Gender differences, and the experience of difference, like differences among women, are socially and psychologically created and situated. In addition, I want to suggest a relational notion of difference. Difference and gender difference do not exist as things in themselves; they are created relationally, that is, in relationship. We cannot understand difference apart from this relational construction.

The issues I consider here are relevant both to feminist theory and to particular strands of feminist politics. In contrast to the beginning of the contemporary women's movement, there is now a widespread view that gender differences are essential, that women are fundamentally different from men, and that these differences must be recognized, theorized, and maintained. This finds some political counterpart in notions that women's special nature guarantees the emergence of a good society after the feminist revolution and legitimates female dominance, if not an exclusively female society. My conclusions lead me to reject those currents of contemporary feminism that would found a politics on essentialist conceptions of the feminine.

There is also a preoccupation among some women with psychological separateness and autonomy, with individuality as a necessary women's goal. This preoccupation grows out of many women's feelings of not having distinct autonomy as separate selves, in comparison, say, to men. This finds some political counterpart in equal rights arguments, ultimately based on notions of women exclusively as individuals rather than as part of a collectivity or social group. I suggest that we need to situate such a goal in an understanding of psychological development and to indicate the relationship between our culture's individualism and gender differentiation.

Psychoanalysis clarifies for us many of the issues involved in questions of difference, by providing a developmental history of the emergence of separateness, differentiation, and the perception of difference in early childhood. Thus it provides a particularly useful arena in which to see the relational and situated construction of difference, and of gender difference. Moreover, psychoanalysis gives an account of these issues from a general psychological perspective, as well as with specific relation to the question of gender. In this context, I will discuss two aspects of the general subject of separateness, differentiation, and perceptions of difference and their emergence. First, I will consider how separation-individuation occurs relationally in the first "me"–"not-me" division, in the development of the "I," or self. I will suggest that we have to understand this separation-individuation in relation to other aspects of development, that it has particular implications for women, and that differentiation is not synonymous with difference or separateness. Second, I will talk about the ways that difference and gender difference are created distinctly, in different relational contexts, for girls and boys, and, hence, for women and men. The argument here advances a reading of psychoanalysis that stresses the relational ego. It contrasts with certain prevalent (Lacan-influenced) feminist readings of psychoanalysis, in particular with the views advanced by French theorists of difference like Luce Irigaray and with the Freudian orthodoxy of Juliet Mitchell.

DIFFERENTIATION

Psychoanalysis talks of the process of "differentiation" or "separation-individuation."[3] A child of either gender is born originally with what is called a "narcissistic relation to reality": cognitively and libidinally it experiences itself as merged and continuous with the world in general, and with its mother or caretaker in particular. Differentiation, or separation-individua-tion, means coming to perceive a demarcation between the self and the object world, coming to perceive the subject/self as distinct, or separate from, the object/other. An essential early task of infantile development, it involves the development of ego boundaries (a sense of personal psychological division from the rest of the world) and of a body ego (a sense of the permanence of one's physical separateness and the predictable boundedness of one's own body, of a distinction between inside and outside).

This differentiation requires physiological maturation (for instance, the ability to perceive object constancy), but such maturation is not enough. Differentiation happens *in relation to* the mother, or to the child's primary caretaker. It develops through experiences of the mother's departure and return, and through frustration, which emphasizes the child's separateness and the fact that it doesn't control all its own experiences and gratifications. Some of these experiences and gratifications come from within, some from without. If it were not for these frustrations, these disruptions of the experi-ence of primary oneness, total holding, and gratification, the child would not need to begin to perceive the other, the "outer world," as separate, rather than as an extension of itself. Developing separateness thus involves, in particular, perceiving the mother or primary caretaker as separate and "not-me," where once these were an undifferentiated symbiotic unity.

Separateness, then, is not simply given from birth, nor does it emerge from the individual alone. Rather, separateness is defined relationally; differentia-tion occurs in relationship: *"I"* am *"not-you"*. Moreover, *"you,"* or the other, is also distinguished. The child learns to see the *particularity* of the mother or primary caretaker in contrast to the rest of the world. Thus, as the self is differentiated from the object world, the object world is itself differ-entiated into its component parts.

Now, from a psychoanalytic perspective, learning to distinguish me and not-me is necessary for a person to grow into a functioning human being. It is also inevitable, since experiences of departure, of discontinuity in han-dling, feeding, where one sleeps, how one is picked up and by whom, of less than total relational and physical gratification, are unavoidable. But for our understanding of "difference" in this connection, the concept of differentia-tion and the processes that characterize it need elaboration.

First, in most psychoanalytic formulations, and in prevalent understand-ings of development, the mother, or the outside world, is depicted simply as the other, not-me, one who does or does not fulfill an expectation. This perception arises originally from the infant's cognitive inability to differentiate self and the world; the infant does not distinguish between its desires for love and satisfaction and those of its primary love object and object of identification. The self here is the infant or growing child, and psychoanalytic accounts take the viewpoint of this child.

However, adequate separation, or differentiation, involves not merely perceiving the separateness, or otherness, of the other. It involves perceiving the person's subjectivity and selfhood as well. Differentiation, separation, and disruption of the narcissistic relation to reality are developed through learning that the mother is a separate being with separate interests and activities that do not always coincide with just what the infant wants at the time. They involve the ability to experience and perceive the object/other (the mother) in aspects apart from its sole relation to the ability to gratify the infant's/subject's needs and wants; they involve seeing the object as separate from the self *and* from the self's needs.[4] The infant must change here from a "relationship to a subjectively conceived object to a relationship to an object objectively perceived."[5]

In infantile development this change requires cognitive sophistication, the growing ability to integrate various images and experiences of the mother that comes with the development of ego capacities. But these capacities are not enough. The ability to perceive the other as a self, finally, requires an emotional shift and a form of emotional growth. The adult self not only experiences the other as distinct and separate. It also does not experience the other solely in terms of its own needs for gratification and its own desires.

This interpretation implies that true differentiation, true separateness, cannot be simply a perception and experience of self-other, of presence-absence. It must precisely involve two selves, two presences, two subjects. Recognizing the other as a subject is possible only to the extent that one is not dominated by felt need and one's own exclusive subjectivity. Such recognition permits appreciation and perception of many aspects of the other person, of her or his existence apart from the child's/the self's. Thus, how we understand differentiation—only from the viewpoint of the infant as a self, or from the viewpoint of two interacting selves—has consequences for what we think of as a mature self. If the mature self grows only out of the infant as a self, the other need never be accorded her or his own selfhood.

The view that adequate separation-individuation, or differentiation, involves not simply perceiving the otherness of the other, but her or his selfhood/subjectivity as well, has important consequences, not only for an understanding of the development of selfhood, but also for perceptions of women. Hence, it seems to me absolutely essential to a feminist appropriation of psychoanalytic conceptions of differentiation. Since women, as mothers, are the primary caretakers of infants, if the child (or the psychoanalytic account) only takes the viewpoint of the infant as a (developing) self, then the *mother* will be perceived (or depicted) only as an object. But, from a feminist perspective, perceiving the particularity of the mother must involve according the mother her own selfhood. This is a necessary part of the developmental process, though it is also often resisted and experienced only conflictually and partially. Throughout life, perceptions of the mother fluctuate between perceiving her particularity and selfhood and perceiving her as a narcissistic extension, a not-separate other whose sole reason for existence is to gratify one's own wants and needs.

Few accounts recognize the import of this particular stance toward the mother. Alice Balint's marvelous proto-feminist account is the best I know of the infantile origins of adult perceptions of mother as object:

Most men (and women)—even when otherwise quite normal and capable of an "adult," altruistic form of love which acknowledges the interests of the partner— retain towards their own mothers this naive egoistic attitude throughout their lives. For all of us it remains self-evident that the interests of mother and child are identical, and it is the generally acknowledged measure of the goodness or badness of the mother how far she really feels this identity of interests.[6]

Now, these perceptions, as a product of infantile development, are somewhat inevitable as long as women have nearly exclusive maternal responsibilities, and they are one major reason why I advocate equal parenting as a necessary basis of sexual equality. But I think that, even within the ongoing context of women's mothering, as women we can and must liberate ourselves from such perceptions in our personal emotional lives as much as possible, and certainly in our theorizing and politics.[7]

A second elaboration of psychoanalytic accounts of differentiation concerns the affective or emotional distinction between differentiation or separation-individuation, and *difference*. Difference and differentiation are, of course, related to and feed into one another; it is in some sense true that cognitive or linguistic distinction, or division, must imply difference. However, it is possible to be separate, to be differentiated, without caring about or emphasizing difference, without turning the cognitive fact into an emotional, moral, or political one. In fact, assimilating difference to differentiation is defensive and reactive, a reaction to not feeling separate enough. Such assimilation involves arbitrary boundary creation and an assertion of hyperseparateness to reinforce a lack of security in a person's sense of self as a separate person. But one can be separate from and similar to someone at the same time. For example, one can recognize another's subjectivity and humanity as one recognizes one's own, seeing the *commonality* of both as active subjects. Or a woman can recognize her similarity, commonality, even continuity, with her mother, because she has developed enough of an unproblematic sense of separate self. At the same time, the other side of being able to experience separateness and commonality, of recognizing the other's subjectivity, is the ability to recognize differences with a small "d," differences that are produced and situated historically—for instance, the kinds of meaningful differences among women that I mentioned earlier.

The distinction between differentiation/separateness and difference relates to a third consideration, even more significant to our assessment of difference and gender difference. Following Mahler, much psychoanalytic theory has centered its account of early infant development on separation-individuation, on the creation of the separate self, on the "me"–"not me" distinction. Yet there are other ways of looking at the development of self, other important and fundamental aspects to the self: "me"–"not-me" is not all there is to "me." Separation, the "me"–"not-me" division, looms larger, both in our psychological life and theoretically, to the extent that these other aspects of the self are not developed either in individual lives or in theoretical accounts.

Object-relations theory shows that in the development of self the primary task is not the development of ego boundaries and a body ego.[8] Along with the earliest development of its sense of separateness, the infant constructs an internal set of unconscious, affectively loaded representations of others in relation to its self, and an internal sense of self in relationship emerges. Images of felt good and bad aspects of the mother or primary caretaker, caretaking experiences, and the mothering relationship become part of the self, of a relational ego structure, through unconscious mental processes that appropriate and incorporate these images. With maturation, these early images and fragments of perceived experience become put together into a self. As externality and internality are established, therefore, what comes to be internal includes what originally were aspects of the other and the relation to the other. (Similarly, what is experienced as external may include what was originally part of the developing self's experience.) Externality and internality, then, do not follow easily observable physiological boundaries but are constituted by psychological and emotional processes as well.

These unconscious early internalizations that affect and constitute the internal quality of selfhood may remain more or less fragmented, or they may develop a quality of wholeness. A sense of continuity of experience and the opportunity to integrate a complex of (at least somewhat) complementary and consistent images enables the "I" to emerge as a continuous being with an identity. This more internal sense of self, or of "I," is not dependent on separateness or difference from an other. A "true self," or "central self," emerges through the experience of continuity that the mother or caretaker helps to provide, by protecting the infant from having continually to react to and ward off environmental intrusions and from being continually in need.

The integration of a "true self" that feels alive and whole involves a particular set of internalized feelings about others in relation to the self. These include developing a sense that one is able to affect others and one's environment (a sense that one has not been inhibited by overanticipation of all one's needs), a sense that one has been accorded one's own feelings and a spontaneity about these feelings (a sense that one's feelings or needs have not been projected onto one), and a sense that there is a fit between one's feelings and needs and those of the mother or caretaker. These feelings all give the self a sense of agency and authenticity.

This sense of agency, then, is fostered by caretakers who do not project experiences or feelings onto the child and who do not let the environment impinge indiscriminately. It is evoked by empathic caretakers who understand and validate the infant as a self in its own right, and the infant's experience as real. Thus, the sense of agency, which is one basis of the inner sense of continuity and wholeness, grows out of the nature of the parent-infant relationship.

Another important aspect of internalized feelings about others in relation to the self concerns a certain wholeness that develops through an internal sense of relationship with another.[9] The "thereness" of the primary parenting person grows into an internal sense of the presence of another who is caring and affirming. The self comes into being here first through feeling confidently alone in the presence of its mother, and then through this presence's becoming internalized. Part of its self becomes a good internal mother. This suggests that the central core of self is, internally, a relational ego, a sense of self-in-good-relationship. The presence or absence of others, their sameness or difference, does not then become an issue touching the infant's very existence. A "capacity to be alone," a relational rather than a reactive autonomy, develops because of a sense of the ongoing presence of another.

These several senses of agency, of a true self that does not develop reactively, of a relational self or ego core, and of an internal continuity of being, are fundamental to an unproblematic sense of self, and provide the basis of both autonomy and spontaneity. The strength, or wholeness, of the self, in this view, does not depend only or even centrally on its degree of separateness, although the extent of confident distinctness certainly affects and is part of the sense of self. The more secure the central self, or ego core, the less one has to define one's self through separateness from others. Separateness becomes, then, a more rigid, defensive, rather fragile, secondary criterion of the strength of the self and of the "success" of individuation.

This view suggests that no one has a separateness consisting only of "me"–"not-me" distinctions. Part of myself is always that which I have taken in; we are all to some degree incorporations and extensions of others. Separateness from the mother, defining oneself as apart from her (and from other women), is not the only or final goal for women's ego strength and autonomy, even if many women must also attain some sense of reliable separateness. In the process of differentiation, leading to a genuine autonomy, people maintain contact with those with whom they had their earliest relationships: indeed this contact is part of who we are. "I am" is not definition through negation, is not "who I am not." Developing a sense of confident separateness must be a part of all children's development. But once this confident separateness is established, one's relational self can become more central to one's life. *Differentiation is not distinctness and separateness, but a particular way of being connected to others.* This connection to others, based on early incorporations, in turn enables us to feel that empathy and confidence that are basic to the recognition of the other as a self.

What does all this have to do with male-female difference and male dominance? Before turning to the question of gender difference, I want to reiterate what we as feminists learn from the general inquiry into "differentiation." First, we learn that we can only think of differentiation and the emergence of the self relationally. Differentiation occurs, and separation emerges, in relationship; they are not givens. Second, we learn that to single out separation as the core of a notion of self and of the process of differentiation may well be inadequate; it is certainly not the only way to discuss the emergence of self or what constitutes a strong self. Differentiation includes the internalization of aspects of the primary caretaker and of the caretaking relationship.

Finally, we learn that essential, important attitudes toward mothers and expectations of mother—attitudes and expectations that enter into experiences of women more generally—emerge in the earliest differentiation of self. These attitudes and expectations arise during the emergence of separateness. Given that differentiation and separation are developmentally problematic, and given that women are primary caretakers, the mother, who is a woman, becomes and remains for children of both genders the other, or object. She is not accorded autonomy or selfness on her side. Such attitudes arise also from the gender-specific character of the early, emotionally charged self and object images that affect the development of self and the sense of autonomy and spontaneity. They are internalizations of feelings about the self in relation to the *mother,* who is then often experienced as either overwhelming or overdenying. These attitudes are often unconscious and always have a basis in unconscious, emotionally charged feelings and conflicts. A precipitate of the early relationship to the mother and of an unconscious sense of self, they may be more fundamental and determining of psychic life than more conscious and explicit attitudes to "sex differences" or "gender differences" themselves.

This inquiry suggests a psychoanalytic grounding for goals of emotional psychic life other than autonomy and separateness. It suggests, instead, an individuality that emphasizes our connectedness with, rather than our separation from, one another. Feelings of inadequate separateness, the fear of merger, are indeed issues for women, because of the ongoing sense of oneness and primary identification with our mothers (and children). A transformed organization of parenting would help women to resolve these issues. However, autonomy, spontaneity, and a sense of agency need not be based on self-other distinctions, on the individual as individual. They can be based on the fundamental interconnectedness, not synonymous with merger, that grows out of our earliest unconscious developmental experience, and that enables the creation of a nonreactive separateness.[10]

GENDER DIFFERENCES IN THE CREATION OF DIFFERENCE

I turn now to the question of gender differences. We are not born with perceptions of gender differences; these emerge developmentally. In the traditional psychoanalytic view, however, when sexual difference is first seen it has self-evident value. A girl perceives her lack of a penis, knows instantly that she wants one, and subsequently defines herself and her mother as lacking, inadequate, castrated; a boy instantly knows having a penis is better, and fears the loss of his own.[11] This traditional account violates a fundamental rule of psychoanalytic interpretation. When the analyst finds trauma, shock, strong fears, or conflict, it is a signal to look for the roots of such feelings.[12] Because of his inability to focus on the preoedipal years and the relationship of mother to child, Freud could not follow his own rule here.

Clinical and theoretical writings since Freud suggest another interpretation of the emergence of perceptions of gender difference. This view reverses the perception of which gender experiences greater trauma, and retains only the claim that gender identity and the sense of masculinity and femininity develop differently for men and women.[13] These accounts suggest that core gender identity and masculinity are conflictual for men, and are bound up with the masculine sense of self in a way that core gender identity and femininity are not for women. "Core gender identity" here refers to a cognitive sense of gendered self, the sense that one is male or female. It is established in the first two years concomitantly with the development of the sense of self. Later evaluations of the desirability of one's gender and of the activities and modes of behavior associated with it, or of one's own sense of adequacy at fulfilling gender role expectations, are built upon this fundamental gender identity. They do not create or change it.

Most people develop an unambiguous core gender identity, a sense that they are female or male. But because women mother, the sense of maleness in men differs from the sense of femaleness in women. Maleness is more conflictual and more problematic. Underlying, or built into, core male gender identity is an early, nonverbal, unconscious, almost somatic sense of primary oneness with the mother, an underlying sense of femaleness that continually, usually unnoticeably, but sometimes insistently, challenges and undermines the sense of maleness. Thus, because of a primary oneness and identification with his mother, a primary femaleness, a boy's and a man's core gender identity itself—the seemingly unproblematic cognitive sense of being male—is an issue. A boy must learn his gender identity as being not-female, or not-mother. Subsequently, again because of the primacy of the mother in early life and because of the absence of concrete, real, available male figures of identification and love who are as salient for him as female figures, learning what it is to be masculine comes to mean learning to be not-feminine, or not-womanly.

Because of early developed, conflictual core gender identity problems, and later problems of adequate masculinity, it becomes important to men to have a clear sense of gender difference, of what is masculine and what is feminine, and to maintain rigid boundaries between these. Researchers find, for example, that fathers sex-type children more than mothers. They treat sons and daughters more differently and enforce gender role expectations more vigorously than mothers do.[14] Boys and men come to deny the feminine identification within themselves and those feelings they experience as feminine: feelings of dependence, relational needs, emotions generally. They come to emphasize differences, not commonalities or continuities, between themselves and women, especially in situations that evoke anxiety, because these commonalities and continuities threaten to challenge gender difference or to remind boys and men consciously of their potentially feminine attributes.

These conflicts concerning core gender identity interact with and build upon particular ways that boys experience the processes of differentiation and the formation of the self.[15] Both sexes establish separateness in relation to their mother, and internalizations in the development of self take in aspects of the mother as well. But because the mother is a woman, these experiences differ by gender. Though children of both sexes are originally part of herself, a mother unconsciously and often consciously experiences her son as more of an "other" than her daughter. Reciprocally, a son's male core gender identity develops away from his mother. The male's self, as a result, becomes based on a more fixed "me"–"not me" distinction. Separateness and difference as a component of differentiation become more salient. By contrast, the female's self is less separate and involves a less fixed "me"–"not-me" distinction, creating the difficulties with a sense of separateness and autonomy that I mentioned above.

At the same time, core gender identity for a girl is not problematic in the sense that it is for boys. It is built upon, and does not contradict, her primary sense of oneness and identification with her mother and is assumed easily along with her developing sense of self. Girls grow up with a sense of continuity and similarity to their mother, a relational connection to the world. For them, difference is not originally problematic or fundamental to their psychological being or identity. They do not define themselves as "not-men," or "not-male," but as "I, who am female." Girls and women may have problems with their sense of continuity and similarity, if it is too strong and they have no sense of a separate self. However, these problems are not the inevitable products of having a sense of continuity and similarity, since, as I argue here, selfhood does *not* depend only on the strength and impermeability of ego boundaries. Nor are these problems bound up with questions of gender; rather, they are bound up with questions of self.

In the development of gender identification for girls it is not the existence of core gender identity, the unquestioned knowledge that one is female, that is problematic. Rather, it is the later developed conflicts concerning this identity, and the identifications, learning, and cognitive choices that it implies. The difficulties that girls have in establishing a "feminine" identity do not stem from the inaccessibility and negative definition of this identity, or its assumption by denial (as in the case of boys). They arise from identification with a negatively valued gender category, and an ambivalently experienced material figure, whose mothering and femininity, often conflictual for the mother herself, are accessible, but devalued. Conflicts here arise from questions of relative power, and social and cultural value, even as female identification and the assumption of core gender identity are straightforward. I would argue that these conflicts come later in development, and are less pervasively determining of psychological life for women than are masculine conflicts around core gender identity and gender difference.

Men's and women's understanding of difference, and gender difference, must thus be understood in the relational context in which these are created. They stem from the respective relation of boys and girls to their mother, who is their primary caretaker, love object, and object of identification, and who is a woman in a sexually and gender-organized world. This relational context contrasts profoundly for girls and boys in a way that makes difference, and gender difference, central for males—one of the earliest, most basic male developmental issues—and not central for females. It gives men a psychological investment in difference that women do not have.

According to psychoanalytic accounts since Freud, it is very clear that males are "not females" in earliest development. Core gender identity and the sense of masculinity are defined more negatively, in terms of that which is not female or not-mother, than positively. By contrast, females do not develop as "not-males." Female core gender identity and the sense of femininity are defined positively, as that which is female, or like mother. Difference from males is not so salient. An alternative way to put this is to suggest that, developmentally, the maternal identification represents and is experienced as generically human for children of both genders.[16]

But, because men have power and cultural hegemony in our society, a notable things happens. Men use and have used this hegemony to appropriate and transform these experiences. Both in everyday life and in theoretical and intellectual formulations, men have come to define maleness as that which is basically human, and to define women as not-men. This transformation is first learned in, and helps to constitute, the Oedipal transition—the cultural, affective, and sexual learnings of the meaning and valuation of sex differences.[17] Because Freud was not attentive to preoedipal development (and because of his sexism), he took this meaning and valuation as a self-evident given, rather than a developmental and cultural product.

We must remember that this transformed interpretation of difference, an interpretation learned in the Oedipal transition, is produced by means of male cultural hegemony and power. Men have the means to institutionalize their unconscious defenses against repressed yet strongly experienced developmental conflicts. This interpretation of difference is imposed on earlier developmental processes; it is not the deepest, unconscious root of either the female or the male sense of gendered self. In fact, the primary sense of gendered self that emerges in earliest development constantly challenges and threatens men, and gives a certain potential psychological security, even liberation, to women. The transformed interpretation of difference is not inevitable, given other parenting arrangements and other arrangements of power between the sexes. It is especially insofar as women's lives and self-definition become oriented to men that difference becomes more salient for us, as does differential evaluation of the sexes. Insofar as women's lives and self-definition become more oriented toward themselves, differences from men become less salient.[18]

EVALUATING DIFFERENCE

What are the implications of this inquiry to psychoanalytic understandings of differentiation and gender difference for our understanding of difference, and for our evaluation of the view that difference is central to feminist theory? My investigation suggests that our own sense of differentiation, of separateness from others, as well as our psychological and cultural experience and interpretation of gender or sexual difference, are created through psychological, social, and cultural processes, and through relational experiences. We can only understand gender difference, and human distinctness and separation, relationally and situationally.[19] They are part of a system of asymmetrical social relationships embedded in inequalities of power, in which we grow up as selves, and as women and men. Our experience and perception of gender are processual; they are produced developmentally and in our daily social and cultural lives.

Difference is psychologically salient for men in a way that it is not for women, because of gender differences in early formative developmental processes and the particular unconscious conflicts and defenses these produce. This salience, in turn, has been transmuted into a conscious cultural preoccupation with gender difference. It has also become intertwined with and has helped to produce more general cultural notions, particularly, that individualism, separateness, and distance from others are desirable and requisite to autonomy and human fulfillment.[20] Throughout these processes, it is women, as mothers, who become the objects apart from which separateness, difference, and autonomy are defined.

It is crucial for us feminists to recognize that the ideologies of difference, which define us as women and as men, as well as inequality itself, are produced, socially, psychologically, and culturally, by people living in and creating their social, psychological, and cultural worlds. Women participate in the creation of these worlds and ideologies, even if our ultimate power and access to cultural hegemony are less than those of men. To speak of difference as a final, irreducible concept and to focus on gender differences as central is to reify them and to deny the reality of those *processes* which create the meaning nd significance of gender. To see men and women as qualitatively different kinds of people, rather than seeing gender as processual, reflexive, and constructed, is to reify and deny *relations* of gender, to see gender differences as permanent rather than as created and situated.

We certainly need to understand how difference comes to be important, how it is produced as salient, and how it reproduces sexual inequality. But we should not appropriate differentiation and separation, or difference, for ourselves and take it as a given. Feminist theories and feminist inquiry based on the notion of essential difference, or focused on demonstrating difference, are doing feminism a disservice. They ultimately rely on the defensively constructed masculine models of gender that are presented to us as our cultural heritage, rather than creating feminist understandings of gender and difference that grow from our own politics, theorizing, and experience.

I am very grateful to Susan Weisskopf, Michelle Z. Rosaldo, Jessica Benjamin, and Sara Ruddick for criticisms and comments on an earlier version of this essay.

NOTES

1. From *The Elementary Structures of Kinship,* quoted in Adrienne Rich, *On Lies, Secrets and Silence* (New York: W. W. Norton, 1979), p. 84.
2. See, for example, Alice Jardine, "Prelude: The Future of Difference," in *The Future of Difference* (New Brunswick: Rutgers University Press, 1985). Josette Féral, "The Powers of Difference," in *The Future of Difference* (New Brunswick: Rutgers University Press, 1985). "Women's Exile: Interview with Luce Irigaray," *Ideology and Consciousness* 1 (1977): 57–76; and Monique Plaza, " 'Phallomorphic Power' and the 'Psychology of Woman,' " *Ideology and Consciousness* 4 (1978): 4–36.
3. The work of Margaret S. Mahler, *On Human Symbiosis and the Vicissitudes of Individuation* (New York: International Universities Press, 1968), is paradigmatic. For a more extended discussion of the earliest development of the self along lines suggested here, see Nancy Chodorow, *The Reproduction of Mothering: Psychoanalysis and the Sociology of Gender* (Berkeley: Univ. of California Press, 1978), chs. 4 and 5.
4. Ernest G. Schachtel, "The Development of Focal Attention and the Emergence of Reality" (1954), in *Metamorphosis* (New York: Basic Books, 1959), provides the best discussion I know of this process.
5. D. W. Winnicott, "The Theory of the Parent-Infant Relationship" (1960), in *The Maturational Processes and the Facilitating Environment* (New York: International University Press, 1965).
6. Alice Balint, "Love for the Mother and Mother Love" (1939), in Michael Balint, ed., *Primary Love and Psycho-Analytic Technique* (New York: Liveright Publishing, 1965), p. 97.
7. The new feminist/feminine blame-the-mother literature is one contemporary manifestation of failure in such a task. See esp. Nancy Friday, *My Mother/My Self* (New York: Dell Publishing, 1977). Of course, this is not to ignore or pass over the fact that men have been past masters of such perceptions of women.
8. In what follows, I am drawing particularly on the work of D. W. Winnicott and Michael Balint. See Winnicott, *The Maturational Processes,* and *Playing and Reality* (New York: Basic Books, 1971); and Balint, *Primary Love,* and *The Basic Fault: Therapeutic Aspects of Regression* (London: Tavistock Publications, 1968). See also W. R. D. Fairbairn, *An Object Relations Theory of the Personality* (New York: Basic Books, 1952), and Hans Loewald, "Internalization, Separation, Mourning and the Superego," *Psychoanalytic Quarterly* 31 (1962): 483–504.
9. See Winnicott, "The Capacity to Be Alone" (1958), in *The Maturational Processes.*
10. My interpretation here of differentiation, the self, and the goals of psychic life contrasts with the traditional Freudian view, which stresses ego and superego autonomy. For an excellent discussion of questions of ego autonomy and psychic structure, see Jessica Benjamin, "The End of Internalization: Adorno's Social Psychology," *Telos* 32 (1977): 42–64.
11. See Sigmund Freud, "The Dissolution of the Oedipus Complex" (1924), in *Standard Edition of the Complete Psychological Works* (SE) (London: The Hogarth Press), vol. 19, pp. 172–79, "Some Psychical Consequences of the Anatomical Distinction between the Sexes" (1925), SE, vol. 19, pp. 243–58; and "Femininity" (1933), in *New Introductory Lectures on Psychoanalysis,* SE, vol. 22, pp. 112–35.
12. See Roy Schafer, "Problems in Freud's Psychology of Women," *Journal of the American Psychoanalytic Association* 22 (1974): 459–85.

13. See Robert Stoller, "Facts and Fancies: An Examination of Freud's Concept of Bisexuality," in Jean Strouse, ed., *Women and Analysis* (New York: Grossman, 1974), and other Stoller writings.
14. For reviews of the social psychological literature on this point, see Miriam Johnson, "Sex Role Learning in the Nuclear Family," in *Child Development* 34 (1963): 319–34; Johnson, "Fathers, Mothers and Sex-Typing," *Sociological Inquiry* 45 (1975): 15–26; and Eleanor Maccoby and Carol Jacklin, *The Psychology of Sex Differences* (Stanford: Stanford Univ. Press, 1974).
15. For further discussion, see Chodorow, *Reproduction of Mothering, The Future of Difference* (New Brunswick: Rutgers University Press, 1985).
16. Johnson, "Fathers, Mothers," makes this suggestion, and suggests further that the father's masculinity introduces gender difference.
17. See Juliet Mitchell, *Psychoanalysis and Feminism* (New York: Pantheon Books, 1974).
18. I have not dealt in this essay with the male and female body, and I would like to say a few words about these before concluding, since they clearly have relevance for the question of gender difference. We live an embodied life; we live with those genital and reproductive organs and capacities, those hormones and chromosomes, that locate us physiologically as male or female. But, to turn to psychoanalysis once again, I think it is fair to say that Freud's earliest discovery showed that there is nothing self-evident about this biology. How anyone understands, fantasizes about, symbolizes, internally represents, or feels about her or his physiology is a product of development and experience in the family and not a direct product of this biology itself. These feelings, moreover, may be shaped by completely nonbiological considerations. Nonbiological considerations also shape perceptions of anatomical "sex differences" and the psychological development of these differences into forms of sexual object choice, mode, or aim; into femininity or masculinity as defined by psychoanalysis; into activity or passivity; into one's choice of the organ of erotic pleasure; and so forth. We cannot know what children would make of their bodies in a nongender or nonsexually organized world, what kind of sexual structuration or gender identities would develop. But it is not obvious that there would be major significance to biological sex differences, to gender difference, or to different sexualities. There might be a multiplicity of sexual organizations, identities, and practices, and perhaps even of genders themselves. Bodies would be bodies (I don't think we want to deny people their bodily experience). But particular bodily attributes would not necessarily be so determining of who we are, what we do, how we are perceived, and who are our sexual partners.
19. See Barrie Thorne, "Gender . . . How Is It Best Conceptualized?" (paper presented at the Annual Meeting of the American Sociological Association, San Francisco, August 1978).
20. For a discussion of these general cultural preoccupations and their psychological origins, see Evelyn Fox Keller, "Gender and Science," *Psychoanalysis and Contemporary Thought* 1 (1978): 409–33.

21. The Development of Women's Sense of Self

Jean Baker Miller

The concept of the self has been prominent in psychological theory, but perhaps this is so because it has been one of the central ideas in Western thought. While various writers use different definitions, the essential idea of "a self" seems to underlie the historical development of many Western notions about such vast issues as the "good life," justice or freedom. Indeed, it seems entwined in the roots of several delineations of the fundamental human motive or the highest form of existence, as in Maslow's self-actualizing character.

As we have inherited it, the notion of a "a self" does not appear to fit women's experience. Several recent writers have spoken to this point, for example, literary critic Carolyn Heilbrun (1979), and psychologist Carol Gilligan (1982). A question then arises, "Do only men have a self, and not women?" In working with women, the question is quite puzzling, but an examination of the very puzzle, itself, may cast new light on certain longstanding assumptions.

Modern American workers who write on early psychological development and, indeed, on the entire life span, from Erikson (1950) to Daniel Levinson (1978), tend to see all of development as a process of separating oneself out from the matrix of others, "becoming one's own man," in Levinson's term. Development of the self presumably is attained via a series of painful crises by which the individual accomplishes a sequence of allegedly essential separations from others, and thereby achieves an inner sense of separated individuation. Few men ever attain such self-sufficiency, as every woman knows. They are usually supported by numbers of wives, mistresses, mothers, daughters, secretaries, nurses, and others (and groups of other men who are lower than they are in the social-economic heirarchy, if they are higher). Thus, there is reason to question whether this model accurately reflects men's lives. Its goals, however, are held out for all, and are seen as the preconditions for mental health.

Reprinted with permission from *Work in Progress*, no. 12, 1984.

Almost every modern psychiatrist who has tried to fit women into the prevalent models has had much more obvious difficulty, beginning with Freud, going through Erikson and others. Some haven't tried. In Erikson's scheme, for example, after the first stage, in which the aim is the development of basic trust, the aim of every other stage, until young adulthood, is some form of increased separation or self-development. I am not referring at this point to the process by which each aim is attained (although that is an intimately related point, see below), but the aim, itself, the goal. It is important to note that the aim is not something like development of greater capacity for emotional connection to others; or for contributing to an interchange between people; or for playing a part in the growth of others as well as one's self. When the individual arrives at the stage called "intimacy," he is supposed to be able to be intimate with another person(s), having spent all of his prior development geared to something very different.

Recently, a large amount of writing, which deplores men's incapacity to engage in intimacy, has come from the women's movement. But men have been making the same testimony. Almost all of modern literature, philosophy, and commentary in other forms portrays men's lack of a sense of community—indeed, even of the possibility of communicating with others.

Thus, the prevailing models may not describe well what occurs in men; in addition, there is a question about the value of these models even if it were possible to fulfill their requirements. These two questions are related, as I will try to suggest. It is very important to note, however, that the prevalent models are powerful because they have become prescriptions about what *should* happen. They affect men; they determine the actions of mental health professionals. They have affected women adversely in one way in the past. They are affecting women in another way now, if women seek "equal access" to them. Therefore, it behooves us to examine them carefully. It is important not to leap to the only models available.

THE BEGINNINGS

What are some of the questions which arise when we try to bring women's experience into the picture? We can take Erikson's theories as a starting point, not in order to attempt a thorough examination of them, but to use his formulations as a framework for consideration of a few of the many features in women's development.

In the first stage of life, Erikson says that the central goal is the infant's development of a sense of basic trust. There is another important dimension. Even at that early stage in all infants, but encouraged much more so in girls, the young child begins to be like and act like the main caretaker who, up until now, has usually been a woman—not to "identify" with that person as some static figure described only by gender, but with what that person *actually* is doing. I think that the infant begins to develop an internal representation of her/himself as a kind of being that, for the moment, I will call by a hyphenated term—a "being-in-relationship." This is the beginning of a sense of "self" which reflects what is happening *between* people, as known by the relation between people. The infant picks up the feelings of the other person, that is, it has an early sense that "I feel what's going on in the other as well as what's going on in myself." Really, it is more complex because it's "knowing"—feeling—what is going on in that emotional field between us. The child experiences a sense of comfort only as the other is also comfortable, or, a little more accurately, only as they are both engaged in an emotional relationship that is moving toward greater well-being, rather than toward the opposite, i.e., only as the interactions in the emotional field between the infant and the adult are moving toward a "better" progression of events.* In this sense, the infant, actively exerting an effect on the relationship, begins to develop an internal sense of her/himself as one who changes the emotional interplay for both participants—for good or ill.

The beginnings of a mental construction of self are much more complicated than those suggested by such commonly used terms as fusion, merger, and the like for the mental constructions of the first stages of infancy, as drawn from Mahler (1975), object relations theorists and others. New research on infant-caretaker interactions also indicates the inappropriateness of those terms (see, for example, Stern, 1980, Stechler and Kaplan, 1980; Klein, 1976).* research suggests that these constructs are not likely to describe adequately the complex internal representations of the self and "the other," or rather the internal self-other relational patterns that the infant is likely to create even from the earliest age.

When we talk about a sense of self in this field, we have been referring to a "man-made" construct meant to describe an internal mental representation. The suggestion here is that from the moment of birth this internal representation is of a self which is in active interchange with other selves. Moreover,

---

*These points have been made in various ways by many theorists, such as M. Klein and several others. The features which they emphasize, however, are different.

the kind of interaction has one central characteristic, and that is that people are attending to the infant—most importantly attending to the infant's core of being, which means the infant's emotions—and the infant is responding in the same way, i.e., to the other person's emotions. The beginning of mental representations of the self, then, is of a self whose core—which is emotional—is attended to by the other(s); and who begins to attend to the emotions of the other(s). Part of this internal image of oneself includes feeling the other's emotions and *acting on* the emotions coming from the other as they are in interplay with one's own emotions. This means that the beginnings of the concept of self are not those of a static and lone self being ministered to by another (incidentally, this construct has a strongly suggestive male flavor), but much more of a self inseparable from a dynamic interaction. And the central character of that interaction is one of attending to each other's mental states and emotions.

This early "interacting sense of self" is present for infants of both sexes, but the culturally induced beliefs of the caretakers about girls and boys enter the scene from the moment of birth. These beliefs are, of course, internalized even in the woman caretaker, although more so in fathers, according to suggestions from some studies (e.g., Rubin et al. 1974, Block 1978, and others). Girls are encouraged to augment their abilities to "feel as the other feels," and to practice "learning about" the other(s). Boy infants are systematically diverted from it, to their deprivation and detriment in my opinion. (In my opinion, this responds, too, to the detriment of the whole construction of societal structure and of our models of thinking.)

Out of this interplay of experience one certainly develops a sense of one's self, that is an internal or mental representation of one's self. Moreover, one develops a sense of one's self as a person who attends to and responds to what is going on in the relationships between two or more people.

Much of the prevalent literature tends to suggest that because she is the same sex as the caretaker, the girl cannot develop an internal sense of self; that is, that boys develop a sense of self because they separate themselves from the female caretaker. This is truly an incredible notion. First, it ignores all of the complexity of the interaction between caretaker and infant. It is as if there were no interaction because they are both of the same sex, i.e., female, an amazing negation of the very idea of girls and women.

Second, the prevalent literature has ignored the extraordinarily important character of the interaction—that of attending to and responding to the other. This is the essential feature of what comes to be called "caretaking." It is also the basis of all continuing psychological growth, i.e., all growth occurs within emotional connections, not separate from them. Current theories ignore, too, the likelihood that the early self is built on the model of this very process—as opposed to the very different kinds of interaction which exist in the current world. The very notion of true caretaking precludes anything that would lead the infant to feel submerged, fused or merged with the other. These are words which may describe some of the phenomena observed after *distortions* in caretaking have occurred, but they are unlikely to characterize the infant's prototypic sense of self.

Third, the current notions tend to ignore the very likelihood that the only possibility of having any sense of self at all is built on this core process. As suggested above, I believe that this is true for both sexes, but it is not allowed to flourish in boys. Instead, it begins to be discouraged early. For girls, it is encouraged, but complications are added at this and at each succeeding phase of development.

Surrey has suggested that this early mental representation of the self can be described as a more *encompassing* sense of self by contrast with the more boundaried, or limited, self that is encouraged in the boy from a very young age. She suggests, too, the term "oscillating" sense of self as compared to the more linear current mode; and that the "oscillation" would follow from the ongoing growth of empathy in the child as well as in the mother. (Surrey 1984; Jordan, Surrey, and Kaplan 1982). Many implications follow. To mention just a few: Certain events in later life which are seen as detracting from the self, according to other models, are seen as satisfying, motivating and empowering. For example, to feel "more related to another person(s)" does not mean to feel one's self threatened, but enhanced. It does not feel like a loss of part of one's self, but the prospect of a step toward more pleasure and effectiveness—because it is the way the girl and woman feel "things should be," the way she wants them to be. Being in relationship, picking up the feelings of the other and attending to the "interaction between" becomes an accepted, "natural-seeming" way of being and acting. It is learned and assumed. It is not alien or threatening. Most important, it is desired; it is a *goal*—by contrast to a detraction or a means to some other end, such as one's own self-development. Thus, it forms a *motivation*.

We have come to think of this whole experience as so "foreign," I believe, because our cultural tradition has emphasized such a different direction. In the dominant and official culture, attending to the experience of others and of the relationships between people has been so lacking as a usual basis and *requirement* of all of life. It has been relegated to the alien and mysterious world of mothers and infancy—and misunderstood. Sometimes, when I have tried to talk about this, some psychiatrists have said, "Oh, I see what you mean. All right, I agree that women are more altruistic." That is not what I mean. That is attempting to slot this description into the old categories. It suggests a "sacrifice" of parts of a kind of self which has developed in a different fashion. To engage in the kind of interaction I am discussing is not a sacrifice; it is, in fact, a source of feeling better and more gratified, as well as more knowledgeable—about what is really happening. I believe it is closer to elementary human necessities from which our dominant culture has become unnecessarily removed.

Another implication relates to the topic of self-esteem or the sense of self-worth. The girl's sense of self-esteem is based in feeling that she is a part of relationships and is taking care of the relationships. This is very different from the components of self-esteem as usually described and, incidentally, as measured by most available scales. Another ramification involves the issue of competence or effectiveness. The girl and woman often feel a sense of effectiveness as arising out of emotional connections and as bound up with and feeding back into them. This is very different from a sense of effectiveness (or power) based on the sense of lone action and especially from acting against others or over others. This sense of effectiveness can develop further in the next and all subsequent ages, but it grows upon this base.

AGENCY WITHIN COMMUNITY

To move quickly through the next ages of life, I will sketch a few suggestions about each of them, leading here only as far as adolescence. Erikson speaks about the second stage of childhood as one in which the goal is autonomy; others have spoken about separation and individuation. I would suggest, instead, that we could think of this as a period when the child has more abilities, more possibilities "to do" and more physical and mental resources to use. S/he also has an enlarged "point of view" on all events, as it were, i.e., a more developed sense of how s/he sees things. There is not, however, nor need there be, any increased separation. Instead, there are new configurations and new "understandings" *in the relationship*. Maintaining the relationship(s) with the main people in her/his life is still *the* most important thing.

We might think of this as something like a phase called "agency-in-community.'' These words are borrowed from Bakan (1966), but not used with his definitions. Instead, by "agency," I am searching for a word again, a word that means being active, using all of one's resources, but without the connotations of aggression, another large topic, but one that cannot be developed here (Miller 1983). Here, again, what the "doing" is, is different from what has been described. Often for little girls, it is doing *for*—again, for the mother (and others)—following the model of what the mother is doing (Jordan, Surrey, and Kaplan 1982; Surrey 1984). What the mother is still doing with little children is attending to their feelings and *"doing for"* them, although not totally. So the action, again, has a different character—it is doing for other(s) within a relationship, with the little girl using very increased powers and increased "opinions" about how and what she wants "to do," and an increased assertion of what she can do.

In her internal representation of herself, I would suggest that the girl is developing not a sense of separation, but a more developed sense of her own capacities and a sense of her greater capability to put her "views" into effect. That is, she has a sense of a larger scope of action—but still with an inner representation of a self that is doing this in relation to other selves. A larger scope of action is not equivalent to separation; it requires a *change* in her internal configuration of her sense of self and other, but not a separation.

The child can move on not only to a larger, but a more articulated sense of herself *only because* of her actions and feelings in the relationship. These may—inevitably are—actions and feelings different from the other person's. They are obviously not identical. The point is that she is attuned to the feelings of the other person and that her feelings are also in response to the others' feelings and, in turn, influence them as theirs influence hers. She has a wide range of feelings and actions, and they vary at different times with one or another in ascendancy, but they occur within the relational context.

Of course, the character of the relationship differs from that of infancy; new qualities come in. But this does not lead to a "separate" sense of self. It leads to a more complex sense of self in more complex relationships to other selves.

The whole notion of describing human interaction in geographic or spatial terms, along a scale of close or distant (i.e., separated) seems questionable. Surely it is the *quality* of the interaction that is the question—the interplay of "conceptualized feelings" (i.e., feelings *cum* concepts), the doing of good or bad to the other—in relation to the nature of each's needs. A growing child has the possibility to do more that s/he could do before. The caretaker who recognizes and supports this enlarged ability does not become more distant. S/he becomes one step *more caring* in one more way—i.e., *more related*—and the child does, too.

CHILDHOOD

When we move to the next stage, which is based on the Oedipal stage, we may ask whether one reason that people, beginning with Freud, have had such trouble delineating this stage in girls is that it may not exist. There is no big crisis of "cutting off" of anything, and especially relationships. And there is no need to fulfill the goal of "identifying with an aggressor," i.e., the threatening and dominant male figure. (Several theorists believe that all of society, culture, and thought is built on this Oedipal moment of identification with the aggressive father. It is interesting to think about the possibility that society need not be built on this base.) However, there is a message which may come in more forcefully at this time (though it begins earlier and it continues later, too), that the girl should now focus all of her attunement to the other person on the well-being and the growth and development of men. But, the relationship to the mother and to other women continues. A pronounced turning away from the mother and toward the father may occur because of particular conditions in particular families, especially when the mother, herself, encourages and models this way of being. Western culture has dictated that mothers should uphold the superior importance and the power of the man. These forces begin to affect deeply the girl's sense of herself and her relationship to her mother, and to complicate the relationship in many ways. However, the relationship to the mother and to other women continues, although it may be less obvious and it may be made to seem less important. There are ethnic, class, and historical variations in the degree of influence of the mother or father within the family, but the greater importance, value, and power of the father—and the devaluation of the mother—seems to come through psychologically, in general.

In latency, or the period which, according to Erikson, has "industry" as its goal, there is increasing evidence that girls are not very latent. What girls may do is learn to hide more, if we are talking about sexuality, as Freud was when he initiated the use of the term. But certainly if we are talking about relationships, this is the time when the girls are very intensely involved in all of their relationships, especially with other girls. Many girls are very interested in men and boys, too, but the boys are often either not interested or actively deprecating and destructive to girls. The boys are out learning "industry," which others have talked about as "learning the rules of the game and how to play them" (Gilligan 1982). Most of these, incidentally, seem directly traceable to war games. In a study of this period, Luria (1981) describes the events in a grade school playground. She talks about the boys' learning not only how to be "warlike" and to win out over others, but how to cheat and get away with it. If she asks the girls what they are doing, they often say, "Nothing." The girls are hanging around the edges of the playground "just talking." What are they talking about? They are talking about the issues in their families and how to solve them. In discussing their families, the girls are, of course, very involved in an emotional interaction with each other. Surrey (1984) has pointed out that the vast amount of psychological development which occurs within the relationships between girls at this time has been one of the major neglected areas in psychological study.

ADOLESCENCE

Now, adolescence. Adolescence has been seen as a time when the individual has greatly increased capacities. Traditionally, psychologists have *divided* them in several ways: for example, sexual capacities, aggressive capacities —which I will call for the moment, agentic (the ability to act); cognitive capacities, with the development of formal thought which does greatly expand the universe. However, many studies still indicate that this is a time when the girls begin to "contract" rather than expand. Clara Thompson (1942) noted this long ago. She said that for boys, adolescence was seen as a period of opening up, but for girls it is a time for shutting down. In his terms, Freud said this too. Freud believed that girls now had to learn for good that they were not to use actively all of themselves and all of their life forces from a base centered in their own bodies and in their own psychological constructions. For Freud, this meant, of course, the derivatives of their sexual drive. Instead, these forces are to be turned, now, to the use of others —men, in the first instance, and to the service of the next generation, childbearing. That is, girls had to resolve their psychological issues by becoming passive and masochistic—i.e., to accomplish the necessary submission to the man and to "sacrifice" themselves for children.

Freud's observations may have reflected much of what happened—and still happens. That is, in regard to sexuality, most girls still learn that their own sexual perceptions, sensations, impulses are not supposed to arise from themselves, but are to be brought forth by and for men. Thus, girls still tend to experience their physical and sexual stirrings as wrong, bad, evil, dirty, and the like. This is to say that part of what has been going on in the girl's earlier internal representations of herself has included several problematic parts. One of these involves bodily and sexual experience. This situation can lead to an attempt to deal with this experience by turning to passivity and submission. The girl picks up the strong message that her own perceptions about her bodily and sexual feelings are not acceptable. They acquire connotations of badness and evil. They become parts of her self which are shameful and wrong. She has sought to bring these parts of herself into relationships with others all along, but has had difficulty in doing so. She still seeks to act on these desires within relationships with others. But she meets opposition. In the face of this, the solution of "doing it for others" can seem to offer a ready answer. The problem is that this solution is one which attempts to leave her, and her sense of herself with all of her own psychological constructions, out of the relationship.

In heterosexual relationships, if the girl or young woman tries to have her own perceptions, to follow her own desires, and to bring them into sexual experience with boys, she still is destined for conflict. Despite all of the recent talk, the girl's attempt to act on the basis of her own sexuality still leads to conflict with her potential male partners. It will lead, also to internal conflict with certain components of her sense of self. One is the part that says she should—and that she wants to—be attuned to others, which leads to a conflict if the other is behaving in ways which are excluding her perceptions and desires from the relationship. Another is the part that has made sexuality an unacceptable aspect of her internal sense of self and therefore prevents her from bringing a large part of herself into the relationship.

It is similar in regard to "agency," that is, the girl's whole capacity to perceive and to use her powers in all ways. Women were not supposed to do this, and have incorporated the idea that to do so is wrong and shameful. The girl has learned and done many things, until now, within a relationship. However, because of societal influences, she has also incorporated a sense— again to varying degrees—that she is not fully and freely to use all of her powers. At adolescence, however, she receives this as a much stronger message.

Thus, her sense of self as an active agent—in the context of acting within a relationship and for the relationship—has been altered to some degree all along by a sense of a self who must defer to others' needs or desires. However, at adolescence she experiences a much more intense pressure to do so. Her sense of self as developed so far now faces a more serious conflict with the external forces she confronts.

The question is how she will deal with this conflict. As with sexuality, I believe that the major tendency is for the girl to opt for the relationship both in her overt actions and also in an alteration of her internal sense of self. She will tend to want most to retain the self that wants to be a "being-in-relationship," but she will begin to lose touch with the definition of herself as more active "being-within-relationships." If one part has to go, and until now it did, most girls lose more of the sense that they can bring their agency and sexuality, as they experience it, into the relationship.

To restate some of these points, at adolescence the girl is seeking fulfillment of two very important needs: to use herself, including her sexual and all of her capacities, but seeking to do so within a context that will fulfill her great desire to be a "being-in-relationship." This wish to do so has developed all through earlier ages. She wishes that the other person(s) will be able to enter into a relationship in this fashion. I believe that the boy really has the same needs, at bottom. However, he has been much more preoccupied with trying to develop "himself" and a sense of his independent identity. This culture has made the very heavy demand that he be so preoccupied. It has been doing so all along, but it does so at adolescence in an even more forceful way. He has also picked up the idea that the girl should adapt to him, and he has not been encouraged to continue the development of the sense that he is primarily a boy-in-relationship with a primary responsibility for others and a desire to concentrate on the relationship between him and others.

Thus, girls are not seeking the *kind* of identity that has been prescribed for boys, but a different kind, one in which one is a "being-in-relation," which means developing all of one's self in increasingly complex ways, in increasingly complex relationships.

The model of a "being-in-relationship" which women are seeking is not easy to attain in present conditions. As I have tried to suggest, it is a very valuable model and, I believe, a model more related to reality, the reality of the human condition. In the current situation, however, it still tends to mean for women the old kind of relationship with the suppression of the full participation of the woman's way of seeing and acting. This has been the historical pattern, certainly. For most women it is still the case. Even so, the woman's struggle continues into later life, but many more factors now complicate it.

PRACTICAL IMPLICATIONS

The practical implications are many. To suggest just a few, women probably do talk about relationships more often, and this is often misinterpreted as dependency. It is very important to listen carefully to what women are saying. Often it is not about wanting or needing to be dependent *or* independent, but about wanting to be in relationship with others, and again, to really comprehend the other; to understand the other's feelings; to contribute to the other; wanting the *nature* of the relationship to be one in which the other person(s) is engaged in this way (see Stiver 1984; Surrey 1984; Jordan, Surrey, and Kaplan 1982). Thus, very often I've heard women described as dependent who are taking care of (and still developing psychologically from taking care of) about six other people. Sometimes they were doing so within a framework which contained many factors of realistic dependency, i.e., economic dependency or social dependency. Sometimes they had to adopt the psychological framework of the other because that is what their partners expected or demanded. But that is better described as the condition of a subordinate (Miller 1976), which is still the social condition. This distinction is important.

It is not because of relationships, per se, that women are suppressed or oppressed. The issue is the *nature* of the relationships. In fact, without the recognition of the importance of relationships to women, we do not help women to find a path that leads them to growth and development. Some psychologists fall into a tendency to encourage "independence" or "separation," which is not what many women want. In the past, mental health professionals encouraged dependency with submission. The point is that the construction of concepts on that axis is inappropriate and misleading.

Perhaps I can illustrate these points by referring briefly to parts of the therapeutic work with one young woman, Ms. D. Ms. D., a twenty-three year-old woman had been depressed and had felt worthless in an extreme way since about the age of thirteen. She was clearly very intelligent and also had a profound quality of thought. She was exceptionally physically attractive.

She did not know where all of the troubles were coming from, and could not connect their onset with any specific events. She saw her father as a sort of nice guy; he was light, humorous, and the parent she liked. By contrast, she perceived her mother as a difficult, agitated, "screaming" person— someone no one would want to be like or even to be around. This is one description of parents that therapists hear frequently.

There was one thing that seemed related to the trouble beginning at age thirteen, although Ms. D. did not make this connection initially. The main part of her relationship with her father appeared to center around her tagging along with him in what seemed his major interest, football. From about age twelve or thirteen, he did not let her tag along anymore, and did not let her play with him and her brothers, and the other boys around. This also is one fairly common occurrence.

She had two brothers, two and four years younger, to whom she felt very devoted. She had always been very sympathetic to them, felt she understood them, did a great many things for them, and always had, from young childhood.

Something else began around age thirteen: many boys began to pursue her, some clearly making a straightforward dash for sex; others seeming to seek her ability to hear their needs, to understand them, to be responsive, sympathetic, to help them, all of which she did. In neither case, however, were the boys interested in her feelings and concerns if she tried to bring these into the relationship. By the time of therapy, she had lost much of her ability to do so.

I will highlight in abbreviated fashion some of the features which emerged in therapy. Ms. D. came to see that she had developed in many ways, even with all that was bad and lacking in her life. She had related to others in a way that fostered their development. She did this and did it with pleasure and willingness, but she, herself, was not given much sense of self-worth and self-validation for the doing of it. No one recognized it fully, or gave her much affirmation for it. Thus, for one thing, she missed a huge portion of a basis for self-esteem which she could and should have had. Second, almost no one did this for her, that is, wanted to know and to respond to her needs and desires as she perceived and felt them.

Only after a while in therapy did she see that she, indeed, had worked at bolstering her father (which she felt was her task) and her brothers; most important, she connected some of this to the "life's work" that had preoccupied her mother all along, She could see, for instance, that a great part of her mother's "ranting and raving," as she called it, resulted from the attempt to "shore up" her father and help her more valued brothers. Her father always had been shaky in his work, and there was a lot to do in the effort to help him "succeed." Her mother had been trying to do that. A large part of her mother's behavior was, however, both a cry for help at her felt obligation to accomplish an impossibility, and a "protest" against having to accomplish that impossibility. Late in therapy, Ms. D. could begin to feel a sense of connection to her mother in the recognition that they both had been engaged in that task. Both had gained little sense of value from it. Simultaneously, her mother had not been able to value her daughter as she had not been able to value herself.

After this recognition, Ms. D. was able to alter some of her resentment toward her mother, although acknowledging the ways that her mother failed her. Later, too, she came to see her father as someone who had never been prepared or able to hear her concerns, or to be responsive to her. She was able to perceive this only after she had first become able even to *think* of seeking this kind of interaction with him. When she tried to bring her own needs into discussions with him, she perceived his ability to relate to her in this way. It was not like football.

Ms. D. had to confront her anger. She had a large amount of anger at both her father and her mother, for different reasons. It took a long time, but she became more able to allow herself her anger, as she also became able to see how much she had really contributed to others' development. That is, she had first to feel some sense of value before she could tolerate a view of herself as a person with anger (see Miller 1983). Then the understanding and redirection of her anger further relieved her sense of worthlessness. Very importantly, she came to see that she would not have had a large amount of anger if she, indeed, had not had her own set of perceptions, expectations, wishes, desires, and judgments, that is, the sense of self that she had thought she never had. She was angry because of the violation of the self she really had. She, like many people, particularly women, had said originally that she had no sense of self at all; she was able to discover one and then to go on to build on it.

Her biggest problem in a way remains: how to be the kind of self she wants to be, a being-in-relationship, now able to value the very valuable parts of herself, along with her own perceptions and desires—and to find others who will be with her in that way. She still encounters situations, particularly but not only, with men, in which she feels annihilated as a person. I think she is experiencing situations which are common to all of us.

RICHER MODELS

To generalize from this example, then, the model of self-development as it has been defined so far does not help us to understand or to help women well. Many women perceive the prospects held out by this model as threatening, for good reason. I think their perception reflects at bottom a fear of forfeiting relationships. By contrast, men's fears occur in different forms. Indeed, most men see the prospect of self-development as not only desirable, but a basic definition of what they must do in life. Moreover, seeking to understand women opens paths to enlargement of a model of "a self" to one which encompasses more truthfully the range of human necessities and possibilities.

For Ms. D. there had been problems in relationships, especially in having directed a large portion of her life to relationships which benefitted others, primarily. However, to have overlooked their value, and her value in them, would have robbed Ms. D. of the major source of her strength and her potential for greater strengths.

The features I have suggested are present even in many highly accomplished women, and women who, like Ms. D., do not care for families in the concrete sense. There is a small group of women today who seek a sense of self similar to that which has been advocated for men. But even many of these women express many of the same themes. They are often the relatively advantaged women who feel very pressured to advance in careers. They often find that their desires to live and work in a context of mutually enhancing relationships conflict with male norms. There is pressure to believe that the latter are better and to devalue the relational desires in themselves.

Importance evidence is emerging from other parts of the psychological field. Notably, Gilligan's (1982) work in developmental psychology suggests that women's sense of self and of morality revolves around issues of responsibility for, care of, and inclusion of other people. It is embedded in a compelling appreciation of context and an insistent unwillingness to make abstractions which violate their grasp of the complexities of the connections between people. Women were previously seen as deficient or at a low level of development as a consequence of their encompassing these realms of context and of psychological connection. These features are found even in as accomplished a group as current women Harvard students. In other studies, McClelland finds that women tend to define power as having the strength to care for and give to others, which is very different from the way men have defined power.

As always, the artists have said it long ago. It is interesting to note that in much of literature the man has been in search of his self, as in many examples: *David Copperfield, Portrait of an Artist* and many others. Women express desires, but they have tended to cast them in the overarching terms of wanting to make deep connection with another (others) and usually to enhance another, as in G. Eliot's *Middlemarch* or C. Bronte's *Villette*.

In the overall, then, the concept of a "self" as it has come down to us, has encouraged a complex series of processes leading to a sense of psychological separation from others. From this there would follow a quest for power over others and power over natural forces, including one's own body. This would seem to be inevitable if one cannot be grounded in *faith* in the kind of interconnections I have tried to suggest. Have such definitions of a separated self become conceivably *only* because half of the species has been assigned to the realm of life which involve such necessities as attending to the complex particularities of building the day-to-day emotional connections with others? This means, in effect, primary attention to participating in and fostering the development of other people—and even direct concentration on the sustenance of the sheer physical life of others. Simultaneously, these realms delegated to women have been granted less value. They have not been incorporated into our perceptions as sources of growth, satisfaction, and empowerment. It then becomes difficult to conceive of them as the wellsprings of true inner motivation and development. But they are.

Another way to put this, perhaps, is to say that women's actual practice in the real world and the complex processes which those practices entail have not been drawn upon, nor elaborated on, as a basis of culture, knowledge, theory, or public policy. They then come to sound almost unreal or idealistic, but they are real; they are going on every day. If they were not, none of us would have lived and developed at all. But they have been split off from official definitions of reality.

An underlying question may be, Has our tradition made it difficult to conceive of the possibility that freedom and maximum use of our resources—our initiative, our intellect, our powers—can occur within a context that requires simultaneous responsibility for the care and growth of others and of the natural world—that we cannot hope that this will develop *after* the person develops first as a separated "self," as currently defined? Thus, I believe that the search for the more appropriate study of women in women's own terms can lead us all not only to understanding women, certainly valid in itself, but to clues to a deeper grasp of the *necessities* for all human development, and simultaneously to a greater realization of the realities of the vast untapped human capacities. This is not an easy thing to do because our whole system of thought, our categories, the eyes by which we see and the ears by which we hear have been trained in a system removed from this activity.

We have all been laboring under only one implicit model of the nature of human nature and of human development. Much richer models are possible. Glimpses of them have always been struggling to emerge, through the artists and the poets, and in some of the hopes and dreams of all of us. Now, perhaps, we can work at learning about them in this field.

REFERENCES

Bakan, D. 1966. *The Duality of Human Existence: An Essay on Psychology* and *Religion*. New York: Rand McNally.

Block, J. 1978. Another Look at Sex Differentiation in the Socialization Behaviors of Mothers and Fathers. In *Psychology of Women: Future Directions of Research* edited by Julia A. Sherman and Florence L. Denmark. New York: Psychology Dimensions.

Erikson, E. 1950. *Childhood and Society*. New York: W. W. Norton.

Gilligan, C. 1982. *In a Different Voice*. Cambridge: Harvard University Press.

Heilbrun, C. 1979. *Reinventing Womanhood*. New York: W. W. Norton.

Jordan, J., Surrey, J., and Kaplan, A. 1982. Women and Empathy. *Work in Progress* 82-02. Wellesley: Stone Center Working Papers Series.

Klein, G. 1976. *Psychoanalytic Theory*. New York: International Universities Press.

Levinson, D. 1978. *The Seasons of a Man's Life*. New York: Alfred A. Knopf.

Luria, Z. 1981. Presentation. Stone Center Dedication Conference, Wellesley, Massachusetts, October 1981.

McClelland, D. 1979. *Power: The Inner Experience*. New York: Irvington.

Mahler, M. 1975. *The Psychological Birth of the Human Infant: Symbiosis and Individuation*. New York: Basic Books.

Maslow, A. H. 1973. *Dominance, Self-Esteem, Self-Actualization* Monterey, Calif.: Brooks/ Cole.

Miller, J. B. 1976. *Toward a New Psychology of Women*. Boston: Beacon Press.

———. 1983. New Issues, New Approaches. In *Psychoanalysis and Women*, edited by J. B. Miller, Baltimore: Penguin.

Rubin, J. Provenzano, F., Luria, Z., 1974. The Eye of the Beholder: Views on Sex of Newborns. *American Journal of Orthopsychiatry* 44:512–19.

Stechler, G. and Kaplan, S. 1980. The Development of the Self. *Psychoanalytic Study of the Child* 35:85–105.

Stern, D. 1980. The Early Differentiation of Self and Other. Presentation at the Symposium, Reflections on Self Psychology, Boston Psychoanalytic Society, Boston, Massachusetts, October 1980.

Stiver, I. 1984. The Meaning of "Dependency" in Female-Male Relationships. *Work in Progress* 83–08. Wellesley: Stone Center Working Papers Series.

Surrey, J. 1984. "The Self-in-Relation": A Theory of Women's Development. *Work in Progress* 84–02. Wellesley: Stone Center Working Papers Series.

Thompson, C. 1942. Cultural Pressures in the Psychology of Women, *Psychiatry* 5:331–39.

22. The Alienation of Desire: Women's Masochism and Ideal Love

Jessica Benjamin

The growing consensus that girls achieve gender identity not by repudiating an initial masculine orientation toward the mother but by identifying with her maternal attributes appears finally to discredit many problematic assumptions in Freud's original ideas about women. The idea of core gender identity (Stoller, 1968)—the preoedipal assimilation of gender identity based primarily on identification and object relations, mediated through parental assignment of gender—paves the way for a multifaceted reappraisal of female development (Chodorow, 1978; Fast, 1984). The problems that have aroused most controversy in regard to femininity, in this case masochism, can now be discussed without the rearguard arguments against notions of anatomy as destiny and feminine nature that so shaped earlier debates. On the other hand, we now require fresh explanations for the problems of femininity that do not have recourse to nature.

The theory of penis envy and the feminine Oedipus complex as Freud (1924b, 1925, 1931, 1933) bequeathed it provided compelling answers to the question of why women might have a propensity to masochistic fantasies, or why femininity might be associated with masochism. It may seem ungrateful to challenge a theory that has rescued femininity from its association with envy, narcissism, masochism, and passivity. But the new view of femininity based on maternal identification offers a less seamless explanation for the appearance of such phenomena. Rejecting Freud's view of penis envy as the organizer of femininity in favor of the theory of maternal identification, we may relinquish the idea that the little girl begins as a little boy, that femininity is characterized by the transformation from active to passive love. Yet we are still faced with a lacuna, an unsolved problem: the problem of *woman's desire*.

The problem begins with the fact that the mother is not articulated as a

Reprinted with permission from Judith L. Alpert, ed., *Psychoanalysis and Women: Contemporary Reappraisals* (Hillsdale, N.J.: The Analytic Press, 1986), 113–38.

sexual subject; she is the woman without desire. That is to say, in culture and theory alike, she is always refracted through the lens of the child's experience, in which passion, with all its implications of selfishness and independent subjectivity, is denied. Mother is there to serve the interests of the child; the image of her sexual power is too frightening for this denial to be challenged directly. The identification with her thus seems an ill-fated beginning for the developing sense of sexual agency. Whence, if not through the phallus, through masculine orientation, do women derive their sense of sexual agency? And what represents it? There is no equivalent symbol of female desire that, like the phallus, suggests activity and potency. And the actual evidence about the cultural representation of women's sexuality is disheartening: the sexy woman is object, not subject, able to attract and ignite the passion of others. Her desire is known as a function of her physical desirability.

The alternative to the female sex object is seemingly the active or "phallic" mother. But the mother is not regarded as a sexual subject even in psychoanalysis—her emblem of power is the borrowed phallus that she loses when she becomes the oedipal, castrated mother. Phenomenologically speaking, she is not someone who actively desires something for herself; her power consists not of the freedom to do as she wills, not of control over her own destiny, but at best control over others. By contrast, the power of the father, signified by the phallus and expressed as sexual agency and potency, is clearly the power of a sexual subject. Even without attributing the ultimate power of desire to the phallus, it appears nonetheless associated with father and masculinity and so still at odds with the primary feminine identification.

The frequent occurrence of woman's submission confirms the old idea that women enter into love relationships with men in order to acquire vicariously something they have not got within themselves. That women often try to protect their autonomy by avoiding intense involvement with men implies the same predicament: woman's desire too often conflicts with her sense of agency and is bound up with the fantasy of submission to an ideal male figure. This search for ideal love, the eroticization of submission in fantasy or reality, points us back to the problem of masochism. Underlying the wish for submission to an idealized other can be seen the issues of separation-individuation and self-other recognition. These issues, I shall demonstrate, are intricately bound up with the establishment of early gender identity and the search for an object of identification. Masochism, especially the variant I call ideal love, can be seen as an alienated attempt to resolve the difficulty of representing female desire—a difficulty that arises out of the tension between identifying with and separating from a desexualized mother, between wishing and being unable to identity with a father who stands for desire. Unable to create a representation of desire based on maternal identification, a sense of sexual agency that is active and feminine, the girl turns to idealizing love for a male figure who represents desire.

THE CONCEPT OF FEMININE MASOCHISM

Let us first briefly review the history of the concept of feminine masochism in the early psychoanalytic movement. The association of femininity with masochism derived both from the inherent suppositions of Freud's view of feminine development (1924b, 1925, 1931, 1933) and from his explicit statements about feminine masochism (1919, 1924a). Masochism "as an expression of feminine nature" was the form "most accessible to our observation" (1924a, p. 161). What masochism expresses that is "natural" to women appears to be the passive sexual stance assumed toward the father in the Oedipus complex. Masochistic fantasies generally "place the subject in a characteristically female situation; they signify, that is, being castrated, or copulated with, or giving birth to a baby" (p. 162). Freud thought that both feminine masochism and moral masochism are derived from a primary erotogenic masochism that is defined as pleasure in pain. As it turns out, this understanding of pain and pleasure is as problematic as his construction of femininity.

Freud's exposition of feminine masochism was far less influential in promulgating the idea than the work of Helene Deutsch (1930, 1944) and Marie Bonaparte (1953). It was they, especially Deutsch, who elucidated the idea more fully in lengthy works on female sexualism. Deutsch has become notorious for her view that masochism, narcissism, and passivity are the decisive tendencies in women's sexual and psychic life. The acceptance of the notion of feminine masochism was of course influenced by the widely held fantasies of submission and rape these analysts found among their female patients. The problem, as Horney (1933) argued, lies not in this finding, but in an explanation that has primary recourse to nature. In turning to Freud's theory of femininity for an explanation of such fantasies, Deutsch found the logical psychoanalytic explanation in women's lack of a penis. In realizing that she has no penis, in relinquishing her active-aggressive sexual stance that was associated with the clitoris, the oedipal girl makes the decisive step toward masochism (Deutsch, 1930). It is now inevitable that she will turn her aggression against herself and transform her sexuality into the wish to be castrated by the father in the act of being penetrated by him (Deutsch, 1930). Without a turn to an alternative view of femininity and female psychosexual development, an alternative explanation for these widespread fantasies could not emerge.

Deutsch's conception of masochism did not really comprehend the distinction between the reality of pain and the symbolic meaning of the fantasy of pain: extrapolating from erotic fantasy life, she generalized about pain in actual life. Deutsch (1945) argued that women's acceptance of pain, humiliation, and lack of gratification is not only crucial to sexual relations with men but also comprises an important part of mothering and childbirth. Thus, the idea of feminine masochism drew its force from two sources: first, the prevailing view of femininity as determined by the lack of the penis; second, the psychoanalytic postulate that a symbolic relation in fantasy (giving birth stands for painful castration) also represents an unconscious wish. It was a short step from the idea of the wish as the underlying motive of fantasy and reality alike to the conclusion that women derive masochistic pleasure from the pain of childbirth.

The idea of "pleasure in pain" has also misled Freud's critics. Most recently, Paula Caplan (1984) has contended that women continue to be seen as masochistic by clinicians and that this represents a mislabeling: what women do is not pleasureful but merely the performance of their assigned role. She correctly points out that the capacity to endure pain has been confused with the wish to undergo it and enjoyment of it. Altruism and nurturance have been confused with self-abnegation and martyrdom. As de Beauvoir (1952) and Blum (1977) have also pointed out, the classical view of masochism did not distinguish the willingness to bear pain in the service of a higher goal from perverse, self-destructive acquiescence to abuse. Having disputed that women enjoy pain, Caplan wrongly concludes that she has refuted women's proclivity to masochism. In any case, she must still explain women's acceptance of submission. Caplan proposes as explanation that what is "called masochistic has tended to be the very essence of trained femininity in western culture" (p. 137). This implies that social learning of a cultural myth about womanhood suffices to explain the presence of masochistic fantasies in women, or that the association of femininity with masochism is the result merely of a pejorative view of women's nurturance and altruism. Undeniably, femininity and motherhood as we know them have been tainted with submission, self-abnegation, and helplessness even if sub-mission works to conceal or deny a certain kind of power that woman as mother exercises). But from a psychoanalytic point of view that is interested in unconscious motivation, it is unsatisfactory to attribute the pervasiveness of submission fantasies in erotic life merely to cultural labeling or to dero-gation of women and their attributes. The alternative to a biological explana-tion must be sought not only in culture, but in the interaction of culture with intrapsychic processes.

The Freudian theory of feminine masochism reflects, no doubt, both the ideology and some of the painful reality of female sacrifice and subordina-tion. One important aspect of Freud's notion of masochism as dictated by the pleasure principle was that the original sexual drive is reversed into passivity and the original aggression is turned against the ego. Both phenomena, passivity and the internalization of aggression, are quite readily observable in people who display what Freud called moral masochism, what Horney simply summed up as the masochistic person. Horney (1933) synthesized the atti-tudes of erotic and moral masochism with a description of what we now see as narcissistic pathology—low self-esteem, difficulty in separation, helpless-ness, and passivity. In this sense, she was moving toward the more compre-hensive understanding of masochism that has developed in the last twenty years. Horney contended that the girl's discovery that she does not have a penis does not suffice to explain her abdication of active pursuit of sexual pleasure. But Horney tried to replace Deutsch's (1930) theory of feminine masochism as feminine nature with an explanation derived directly from sociocultural factors, such as woman's dependency and inhibited aggression. In order to explain the origins of woman's condition, she then resorted to woman's biological vulnerability, winding up with a position she wished to refute. While Horney's perceptions of culture are accurate, her argument reveals the absence of both an alternative theory of female psychosexual development and of self or ego pathology that could compete with the Freud-Deutsch's interpretation.

The confusions that arose from the concepts of erotogenic masochism as "pleasure in pain" could be dispelled only by the evolution of theories of object relations and ego development. The question now became: what does masochism do for the ego in its struggle to individuate from the primary object (Menaker, 1973)? The concept of erotogenic masochism pointed to a highly significant phenomena—in this case the apparently fascinating contra-diction that people can derive pleasure from pain. I do not mean to dismiss

Freud's suggestions about the eroticization of negative stimuli and the internalization of aggression. But the idea of "pleasure in pain" is misleading insofar as the crucial point in masochism is not the experience of pain, but of submission. Submission may involve eroticized pain, but more often pain is a symbol or metaphor for submission. Indeed, pain may be associated not with submission but with erotic frenzy or physical performance of a clearly triumphant nature—it is only masochistic when it is "wanted as proof of servitude" (de Beauvoir, 1952). As has been shown in regard to the original Masoch, the enjoyment of pain required the context of submitting to a woman he idolized (Smirnoff, 1969). The fantasy of pleasure in pain has less to do with enjoyment of pain than enjoyment of submission, the annihilation or loss of will under what appear to be conditions of control and safety.

The desire for submission—for release from annihilation and loss of self —directs us to the ego issue in masochism: the issue of sustaining separation from the object, independence of the self. The symbolic significance of pain is violation, a rupture of ego boundaries; its aim is the loss of self through submission to an idealized other (Benjamin, 1983). How much concrete pain a person seeks depends on the capacity for symbolization, whether the person tends to somatize, act out, fantasize, or sublimate symbolic meanings. But without the surrounding experience of the master's power, without the idolatry and ritual, without the sense of submission to a higher authority or purpose, the infliction of pain loses its meaning and becomes unsupportable or disgusting (Smirnoff, 1969; Khan, 1979). When the analysis of masochism shifts from the concept of pleasure in pain to submission, the focus moves to the ego or self. Contemporary discourse on masochism has therefore emphasized such issues as object loss and separation (Stoller, 1975, 1979; Khan, 1979), the idealization that results from inability to separate from the primary object (Menaker, 1973), and the attempt to ward off self-dissolution and supply missing self-structure through merger with an ideal object (Kohut, 1971; Stolorow and Lachmann, 1980). This perspective on masochism is essential to any reinterpretation of the association of femininity with masochism. It allows us to reformulate the problem by asking, what are the vicissitudes of feminine development that predispose women to seek out relationships of submission?

The question—what is woman's desire and how does it become a desire for submission?—is still valid and provoking even though we are not satisfied by the answer Freud gave. Freud (1924a) associated both moral masochism and feminine masochism ultimately with the wish to be beaten by the father, which stands for the wish to have a passive sexual relationship with him. He argued (1919) convincingly that the guilt experienced by the little girl at wishing to be her father's lover and the wish itself ("father loves only me") are satisfied by a regression to an anal-sadistic, punishing form of eroticism. But in thus unraveling the secret of masochism, Freud implied that submission and passivity are not the true oedipal stance of the little girl but a product of guilt. Why then should the little girl be more prone to guilt and disavowal of oedipal wishes, to passivity and punishment, than the little boy? Why should the fantasy that emerges for the little girl involve the beating of a boy, a fact that Freud (1919) attributes to the spurring of her "masculinity complex" by the regression? The challenge posed by Freud's analysis is to explain woman's greater guilt, that is to say, fear, in regard to active sexuality and her attempt to resolve that predicament by a masculine orientation, without simply attributing it to her lack of phallus, the emblem and entitlement to desire. The perversion of woman's sexual agency, the alienation of desire that is masochism, remains to be explained.

THE FATHER-LIBERATOR OF RAPPROCHEMENT

When an omnipotent mother perpetuates primary love and primary identification in relation to her daughter . . . a girl's father is likely to become a symbol of freedom from this dependence and merging [Chodorow, 1978, p. 121].

Paradoxically, the father seems to occupy a much more important place in the psychosexual development of the boy than of the girl, be it as a love object or as a rival [Chasseguet-Smirgel, 1970, p. 95].

The key to reinterpreting masochism as a feminine experience must be sought in the already worked out consequences of the theory of core gender identity (Stoller, 1968). Nancy Chodorow's book *The Reproduction of Mothering* (1978) is the most comprehensive analysis of how the fact that children of both sexes receive primary care from and find their first object in a woman influences the pattern of identifications and object relations that create individual gender identification. I suggest that the patterns of gender identifications and separation-individuation that arise from female parenting creates a feminine proclivity to masochism. Masochism is here considered in its dimension of submission to an idealized other—ideal love. Ideal love can be seen as rooted in the relationship to the father during separation-individuation. While its occurrence in that phase is normal, its common frustration in girls can lead to a transformation in which the adult search for ideal love becomes the basic content of masochistic fantasy.

The father's role as a figure of separation from the preoedipal mother has been elucidated in reinterpretations of penis envy. In emphasizing the power of the preoedipal mother and early object relations, the French analyst Torok (1970) and Chasseguet-Smirgel (1970) and the American feminists Dinnerstein (1976) and Chodorow (1978) concur that the power of the father and his phallus derives from the role they play in separating from the mother. Standing for difference and separation, the phallus becomes the desired object for children of both sexes, who wish to possess it in order to have that power. The meaning of the penis as a symbol of revolt and separation derives from the nature of the child's struggle to separate from the original maternal power.

The psychological imperatives of early narcissism and separation-individuation conflicts invests the father and the phallus with idealized attributes. The father, not the phallus, is the starting point—but this means that the father as he is internally represented and refracted through the child's psyche. The origins of ideal love and the problem of woman's desire lie in the relation to the father. The unconscious conflicts from which the phallus derives its significance do not begin with oedipal difficulties and regression from the feminine stance, what Horney (1926) called "the flight from womanhood." The development being emphasized is that of the ego (or self), and the conflict is the preoedipal one of separation.

Before the theoretical delineation of preoedipal ego development, the discussion of the father's connection with the phallus was couched in terms of the oedipal phase and the girl's switch in love objects. But as it has become apparent that the issues of separation and of gender identification begin in the second year of life, the girl's early narcissistic interest in the penis must be seen in terms of the conflicts of that phase. Although psychoanalytic theory has not caught up with the observational research suggesting that fathers and infants become attached much as mothers and infants do (Spieler, 1984), psychoanalysis has accepted the idea that the father does not delay his appearance on the scene of male gender development until the oedipal phase. Probably the father's differences from the mother are actually first formulated by the child at the height of separation-individuation, the rapprochement phase (Abelin, 1980). It is here that the struggle to differentiation becomes fatefully intertwined with gender identity. The realization of gender identity—one's own and one's parents—evolves between the ages of

18 and 36 months. This means that the realization of gender identity coincides fatefully with rapprochement.

In the rapprochement phase, the child's awareness of its separate existence intensifies (Mahler, Pine, and Bergmann, 1975). Realizing for the first time that the parent's help is outside its magical control or omnipotence, the child now resents its dependency. A considerable tension now arises between the wish to be independent and the wish to restore magical dependency with the primary parent. Rapprochement can be seen as the great fall from grace, when the conflict between self-assertion and separation anxiety brings forth an essential tension. In rapprochement the child experiences its own activity and will as a counterpoint to a more powerful parent and to its own helplessness. The child's self-esteem can now be damaged by the realization that it does not control mother and that much of what mother does is not an extension of its own power. It must be repaired by the mother's confirmation that the child can do real things in the real world. Thus originates the need to be recognized as independent by the very person upon whom one once depended. This paradoxical need for recognition by the other is a source of the great conflict and tension of this period; it is entangled with the narcissistic vulnerability of recognizing one's own dependency.

But the struggle for recognition is not only a matter of compensation for lost magic. The child is also gaining something new; it is becoming conscious of will and agency in a new way. In becoming conscious of will, of desiring, the child advances a step toward being the subject of desire. The child now wants not simple satisfaction of need. Rather, in each of these wants lies the desire to be recognized as a subject—above and beyond whatever is wanted, the child wants recognition of its will, its desire, its act.[1] Rapprochement inaugurates the first in a long series of struggles to achieve a sense of agency, to be recognized in one's desire.

It is precisely in rapprochement that the awareness of gender identity emerges. The difference between mother and father begins to take hold symbolically in the psyche and to meld with the vital conflict between separation and connectedness, independence, and dependence. The struggle for recognition joins with the moment of differentiation between mother and father; differentiation between self and other, male and female, become structurally intertwined. This conjunction ought to be thought of as the rapprochement complex. It is a nodal point that vies in theoretical importance with the Oedipus complex. In the rapprochement complex the father begins to assume the crucial role of standing for freedom, separation, and desire.

Here begins the child's relationship to the father that has been adduced to explain the power of the phallus.

No matter whose theory you read, the father is always the way into the world. There is rather widespread agreement that the father is the "knight in shining armor" (Abelin, 1980). He appears as powerful, but not as all controlling, all giving, all perfect oneness (Dinnerstein, 1976). The asymmetry of the father's role for boys and girls, the fact that little girls cannot as readily utilize the father in their separation from the mother, has, with some important exceptions by women analysts (Clower, 1977; Lax, 1977; Bernstein, 1983; Levenson, 1984; Spieler, 1984), been uncritically accepted as inevitable in psychoanalytic literature. That little girls in rapprochement become more depressed, lose more of their practicing enthusiasm than boys, is noted as a natural occurrence (Mahler et al., 1975). The family organization and object relationships responsible for this occurrence are simply taken for granted. But once we do challenge a system in which women are always the primary parent, we may also investigate this apparent fact of female development. Similarly, we wonder about the fact that boys escape the depressive mood of rapprochement and deny the feeling of helplessness that comes with the realization of separateness. According to Mahler and her colleagues (1975), the boy succeeds in this denial by virtue of his "greater motor-mindedness," the buoyancy of his body ego feelings, his pleasure in active aggressive strivings. What accounts for this difference?

Ernest Abelin (1980) argues that in rapprochement the father plays the liberating role for the boy more than for the girl. The father was already tuned into his toddler's "wild exuberance" in practicing. He remains exciting, "a stable island of practicing reality," while the mother "becomes contaminated by feelings of intense longing and frustration" (p. 155). Essentially, the identification with the father offers the boy toddler his first model of desire, "the first symbolic representation of the object and the separate self, desperately yearning for that object" (p. 154). The boy now imagines himself to *be* the father, the subject of desire, in relation to the mother. (While Abelin attributes central importance to the wish, "I want Mommy," I suspect that the father's externality and representation of the subject who desires and acts in the world has a more general significance.)

Abelin (1980) suggests that the shift in the child's interest toward being the subject of desire coincides with the transition from the sensorimotor stage to a symbolic perception of the world. Earlier, the sensorimotor child experienced desire only as a property of the object, as in "It is desirable." Now the child can be a subject aware of desiring, as in "I desire it"—hence the importance of the father as a different kind of subject than the mother, a subject of desire. The other subject is not the object of gratification, the supplier of need, but the other who gives recognition. This means that the father's entry is a kind of *deus ex machina* that solves the quandary of rapprochement. Instead of having to get the confirmation of independence from the one he or she still belongs to depend on, the child can turn to the father for that recognition. The father is a vehicle not merely for enabling separation, but for avoiding conflict, denying helplessness and the loss of practicing grandiosity. In the boy's mind, the magical father with whom he identifies is still as omnipotent as he would like him to be. Recognition through identification is now substituted for the more conflictual need to be recognized by the primary parent with whom he feels his dependency. The boy can have the fantasy that he is being the father toward the mother rather than her helpless baby. The father of rapprochement is internalized as the ego ideal of separation and, like the oedipal superego, can be seen as a psychic agency that embodies a specific resolution of the rapprochement conflict.

The upshot of his analysis is that for boys separation-individuation becomes a gender issue: the issues of recognition and independence become organized within the frame of gender. Male gender formation revolves around the gradual replacement of an original, primary identification with the mother by a new identification with the father. This disidentification with mother (Greenson, 1968) is widely held to be crucial at this point for the fate of the boy's masculinity (Stoller, 1975). But the switch to the father, as we now see, is suffused with the rapprochement issues of wanting simultaneously to be independent of mother and yet be recognized as independent by her, of wanting to leave her and yet return to her. On one hand, the assumption of masculine identification allows a defensive resolution of the rapprochement paradox; on the other hand, the rapprochement ambivalence thrusts the child toward his father and shapes the nature of his masculinity. This reciprocal interaction between gender and identity formation within the context of the father-son relationship also contains the core experience of being the subject of desire. It appears that what is crucial to masculinity is not the phallus or the father, but the internal representation of a new relationship toward the mother that cancels the primary identification with her: separateness appears to be the essence of male identity. (Keller, 1978; Chodorow, 1979).

What is striking in psychoanalytic theory is how, in contrast to the boy's, the girl's relationship to the father hinges on the phallus more than on the identification with him. When we turn to the little girl's story, we find no coherent integration of the interlocking elements of gender, individuation, and paternal identification. The question of how successfully the paternal identification is offered by the father, confirmed by the mother, and integrated by the girl has not been endowed with structural meaning in psychoanalysis. Too often we still hear the argument that not having the penis suffices to determine identity. We are likely to find either a denial that the father is as important to the girl's identity (Abelin, 1980) or an assertion that she is really concerned with the penis (Roiphe and Galenson, 1981). In terms of the rapprochement complex, the girl's wish for a penis can be given a more precise meaning. Girls desire it for one of the main reasons that boys cherish it—because they are struggling to individuate. They are seeking what toddler boys recognize in their fathers and wish, through identification, to affirm in themselves—recognition of their own desire. But they find themselves in conflict about this wish to tear themselves from the attachment to mother—often greater than the conflict of boys because of the intense narcissistic bond between mother and daughter—and seek to find another *object* with whom to identify. This other object is the father, and his otherness is guaranteed and symbolized by his other genital.

The rapprochement complex is not simply an earlier version of the Oedipus complex. The early identification with the father includes, of course, the element of active desire toward the mother than Freud originally emphasized. But the meaning of the phallus and of desire here, especially for the girl, leans far more in the direction of separation from than reunion with the mother. This does not mean that the girl's love for her mother is not intense, but that it is not yet associated with the phallus. Possessing a penis with which to woo the mother is a later, genital, oedipal idea. In this phase the representational aspects of the phallus are shaped by the anal tendencies and have more to do with the difference between father and mother, with agency and independence (Torok, 1970). So the girl must make what is *not hers* represent her desire. Can the girl, through a more positive identification with the father, resolve this difficulty and come to feel that desire and agency are properly hers?

Too often, little girls cannot or may not use their connection with the father, in both its defensive and its constructive aspects, to deny helplessness and to forge a genuine sense of separate selfhood. The depressive response to the rapprochement complex may be attributed to the lack of the boy's manic defense. Because girls are more aware of gender and generational differences—less able to deny them as boys do—both the difficulty of separating from mother and their own helplessness confront girls more directly. This deflation of early omnipotence may be viewed positively as generating the ego's capacities for sociability and sublimation (Roiphe and Galenson, 1981; Gilligan, 1982) or the future capacity to be a parent (Abelin, 1980). But we also know that many girls are left with a lifelong admiration for those who get away with their sense of omnipotence intact; they express their admiration in relationships of overt or unconscious submission. They grow up to idealize the man who has what they can never possess, the emblem of power and desire. Putting the other in the place of their own ego ideal, they seek to incorporate him sexually, rather than striving to attain their own ideal.

Much of this problem in girls' development must be attributed to fathers themselves. Fathers often do prefer their boy infants, forming a more intense bond based on identification, which is followed by greater mutual attachment and mutual identification in toddlerhood (Lamb, 1977; Gunsberg, 1982). When the father is not available to the girl, it is can be argued that her helplessness and depression increase, turning inward her aspirations for independence and her anger at being denied recognition. Galenson and Roiphe (1932) sum up one little girl's position thus: she longed for "the missing excitement and erotic nature of their relationship, which had earlier been attached to the father in toto and now was identified as emanating from his phallus in particular" (p. 162). This transformation from excitement and desire in general to the symbol of the phallus in particular may indeed begin in rapprochement, especially enhanced when the father himself is "missing."

Long before the phallic representation is formed by the child, the father is experienced in his total kinesic and affective behavior as the exciting, stimulating, separate other—his play is more active (Lamb, 1977), more stimulating, discrepant, and novel (Yogman, 1982), more fostering of differentiation (Kestenberg et al., 1982; Gunsberg, 1982). From the beginning, then, the father is the representation of excitement, outside, otherness. The rapprochement wish to be like the father, the identificatory impulse, is not only a defense, an alternate route for recognition that avoids the ambivalent mother. It also is rooted in an intrinsic need at this point in development to make desire one's own, to experience it as legitimate and self-originated. New excitement begins to be felt not simply as the property of the object, but as one's own *inner desire* (Abelin, 1980). Desire is now felt as emanating from within; it is a property of one's own will. While the child looks for recognition in both parents at this time, the exciting father is the one who recognizes in the child what the child recognizes in him, recognizes the child as *like* himself. Thus the multiple functions of the rapprochement complex evolve into multiple reasons for the father to become the symbolic figure of recognition—the need to separate, the need to avoid ambivalence, and the need to find a subject who represents desire and excitement.

What I am stressing here is the role of identification in love and desire. Peculiar to this phase of development is a kind of *identificatory love*. Identification—being like—is the chief mode in which a child in this phase can acknowledge the subjectivity of another person, as the well-noted fact of parallel play implies. The first loving of someone as a subject, as an agent not a source, is this kind of identificatory love. Structurally, then, a particular type of relationship of identification intervenes for the male child during his key period of struggle with independence. Inner desire and will are consolidated, the need for recognition is fixed on the paternal object, and masculine identity is established through separation. Identificatory love is the matrix in which these developments occur. The strong mutual attraction between father and son allows for recognition and identification, a special erotic relationship. The practicing toddler's "love affair with the world" turns into a homoerotic love affair with the father, who represents the world. The boy is in love with his ideal. This homoerotic, identificatory love is the boy's vehicle for establishing masculine identity. Through this ideal love he begins to see himself as subject of desire; in this relationship of recognition he finds his sense of self.

Ideal love can be understood through reference to this identificatory, homoerotic love between toddler son and father.[2] We can locate the origins of ideal love in the period when the child is beginning to confront his own helplessness but can still comfort himself with the belief in parental omnipotence (Mahler et al., 1975). He seeks to recognize in this parental power the power of his own desire; he elaborates it in the internally constructed ideal. This love is structurally important not only for masculinity, but for the search for an ideal image of the self. I conclude, then, that this father-son love affair is the model for ideal love; that the rapprochement conflict between independence and helplessness is the model conflict that ideal love is usually called on to solve; and that the wish, or desire, that underlies ideal love is the desire for recognition.

IDEAL LOVE

All my foolish acts and all the good things I have done have the same cause: an aspiration for a perfect and ideal love in which I can give myself completely, entrust my being to another . . . How I envy the ideal love of Mary Magdalene and Jesus: to be the ardent disciple of an adored and worthy master; to live and die for him, my idol . . . [Janet's patient, cited in de Beauvoir, 1952, p. 716–17].

The analysis I have offered to the roots of ideal love in the identification with the rapprochement father of separation affords the possibility of reconstructing and reintegrating theories of masochism and femininity. The failure to appreciate the importance of ideal love in the father-daughter tie and its parallelism with many aspects of the father-son tie has led to many psychoanalytic misunderstandings of women. The boy's early psychic structure is seen as derivative of both mother and father bonds; the girl's psychic structure, whether derived from the maternal identification or organized by penis envy is seen as strangely detached from the father. The current emphasis on maternal identification may ignore the problem that the mother is not articulated as a sexual subject and the crucial role played by the father as a figure of identification. In Freud's understanding of women, the gap in the girl's subjectivity left by the missing father appeared as "the lack" and the theory of penis envy emerged to fill it. The conclusion was drawn that the girl's masculinity complex was an obstacle to femininity and that feminine sexual self-esteem could be drawn from the passive oedipal relation to the father. More recently, Blum (1977) has argued that penis envy should be seen as the organizer not of femininity but of "female masculinity" which may actually impede the development of femininity. Here the danger of accepting the notion of primary feminine identity and rejecting bisexuality becomes apparent. I believe, rather, that this envy represents a desire for important elements of selfhood associated with masculinity: independence, self-esteem, excitement, and agency. What is desirable is the integration of those elements through the girl's integration of maternal and paternal identifications. It is the failure to achieve this integration and the accompanying withdrawal from autonomy and agency, especially sexual agency, that fosters conflict with femininity and, ultimately, masochism.

   A full delineation of the failure of this integration is still the gap in our theory. "In this culture there may be a basic contradiction between sexual liberation and personal liberation (or autonomy) for women insofar as sexuality as constructed expressed dependent or masochistic trends,'' wrote Person (1980). The psychological beginnings of this contradiction may be seen in the girl's struggle at rapprochement—a struggle vastly complicated by the prevalent denial of women's subjectivity. The frustration, or absence, of an ideal identificatory love relationship with someone who represents desire and excitement can be seen to damage any child's sense of agency. But even with successful paternal identification in the early father-daughter tie, conflict may arise between the preoedipal and oedipal love for the father, that is, between identification with the object love for him. Once genital love has entered the picture, in the oedipal phase or in adolescence, the situation becomes more complicated and conflictual for all parties. While these further developments demand a great deal more exploration, some gross patterns deriving from the gender division are obvious: difficulty in integrating agency and love may arise both from the father's ultimate refusal to accept a feminine equal to the mother's inability to model autonomy. A succinct statement of the problem was made by Doris Bernstein (1983):

Analytic literature says little about the relationships of fathers and daughters: primarily the focus is on the father as libidinal object, as protector and rescuer from the mother. Fathers do not seem able to offer themselves as objects of identification to girls as they do their sons—with few exceptions. To the extent that the father's individuation rests on the biological base of difference from mother, to the extent that he mobilized, or continues to mobilize the "no, I am unlike" to maintain his autonomy, the more *unable* he is to permit or welcome his daughter's identification with him as he is his son's. Repeatedly, women have complained that their fathers encouraged intellectual development and education but only up to a certain point [p. 196].

The point is that paternal identification is not merely defensive, but reflects positive strivings that must be fostered through identification and parental recognition. Although it is preferable, under the present gender constellation, that fathers should be as available to their daughters as to their sons, this solution is not without conflict for the girl. In the girl's inner world, the obstacles to paternal identification are reflected in injury to the grandiose self, to narcissistic self-esteem, and to the sense of agency, and in inability to separate from the primary object. This means that love the father will often be associated either with one's own castration, since father's lover must relinquish agency and competition, or with the guilt of castrating him (Chasseguet-Smirgel, 1970). As long as the sexual division persists—the mother representing the primary attachment object, who holds and soothes, and the father representing the separation object identified with the outside world of freedom and excitement—the father will be important to girls as well as to boys in the effort to differentiate and recognize themselves in another subject of desire. The difficulties that attend this paternal identification, as well as its absence altogether, is the basis for adult versions of ideal love.

Ideal love may characterize a whole spectrum of relationships, including those of covert submission and idealization, those featuring persisting unrequited longings in the face of abandonment and rejection, and those that openly erupt into sadomasochistic practices. Most of the issues of separation and recognition, the narcissistic pathology associated with masochism, can be contextualized in terms of rapprochement issues in general and difficulties in consolidating father-daughter identification in particular. Women are often drawn into relationships of submission because they seek a second chance for ideal love, a chance to reconstitute father-daughter identification in which their own desire and subjectivity can finally be recognized. Even in those relationships that involve annihilation of the self, one can often discern the fantasy of resolving the conflict between activity and passivity. As de Beauvoir (1952) wrote, "This dream of annihilation is in fact an avid will to exist . . . when woman gives herself completely to her idol, she hopes that he will give her at once possession of herself and of the universe he represents" (p. 717).

Woman's ideal love, the submission to or adulation of the idealized other in whom one hopes to recognize oneself, parallels the identificatory love of the boy's rapprochement complex. The masculine orientation that Freud (1919) noted in women's beating fantasies—the fact that they were the boy being beaten—may now be seen as modeled on the homoerotic, identificatory nature of the boy's love of the father in this phase. In fantasy, the girl is portraying herself as the boy that is in love with his father; but finally she is punished, castrated, denied that vital link of identity and equality with the father.

Although ideal love is often charged with oedipal fears and guilt and is combined with genital object love for the father, it can also exist by itself as the legacy of the girl's rapprochement complex. The replay of identificatory love for the father is best seen not as regression into masculinity but as a revival of unresolved conflicts and aspirations that attended this earlier phase. In the boy's ideal love he seeks to protect his omnipotence and grandiosity, to establish separateness through identification with someone who is already separate, to recognize his desire in the father's desire and be recognized in return. These aims can also be found as primary motives in woman's ideal love. Perhaps what most distinguishes our approach from Freud's is the notion that these aspirations are legitimate and may hold the key to active femininity, once they are disentangled from the helpless envy and disavowal of womanhood that have filled the lack of her own desire and agency.

By way of illustrating the roots of ideal love in the identificatory love of rapprochement, I shall briefly sketch a case. Elaine was a young woman writer who could not get over her preoccupation with a man who had left her. This man represented the idealized father with whom she wanted to identify in order to disidentify from her mother. Elaine explicitly saw her lover as her ideal, a person like herself as she wished to be: he was magical, outrageous, creative, imaginative, unconventional. He alone understood her, her eccentricity, her outrageousness, her wild and free spirit, her refusal to be a conventional female. After his departure, she began work on a mystery novel in which he was the incestuously loved older brother and she was the tomboyish sidekick whom he took everywhere. She rejected the trappings of femininity, dressed as a boy, performed feats of physical courage and mechanical ingenuity. When her hero deserts her, the heroine struggles to carry on, still living in the shadow of her brother's charismatic abilities. She tries to prove herself to him, to live up to the independence she thinks he embodies, in the hope that he will finally acknowledge her. The story parallels Elaine's actual ideal love affair, which was largely fueled by the need to have a person highly different from her mother who would recognize her. it bore all the features of longing for a homoerotic, narcissistic love affair with the father and the world. Her lover was so vital and attractive to her because of "something to do with freedom." She often said he was "the only one who recognized my true self; he made me feel alive."

Elaine perceives her ambitions to have been thwarted by both parents in a sex-stereotypical way. Her mother, who had many children, was weak and ineffectual, wholly without aspirations for herself or children, and especially paralyzed when it came to helping them with "anything we did *outside*." Her father had never given her the recognition she wanted. He had been too outside—distant, angry, judgmental, and impatient with his children and wife, involved in his own work and failure, and frequently criticizing her for being stupid or timid when she did not meet his expectations. Elaine believes that her mother was valuable as a source of comfort and soothing to her babies and children when they were little, but that she was devoid and discouraging of any excitement or spark—all that is important in life. When Elaine identifies with her mother or sisters, she feels paralyzed, sick, weak. Moreover she is terrified of the depths of submission and self-annihilation her sister reached in her terrible desire to please her father. As a result Elaine refuses to invest the therapist with the power to help her and suffers because of what she terms her inability to have "faith," which she readily admits reflects her fear of devotion to an idol. At the same time, she expresses contempt for any soothing or comfort, although her agitation and inability to self-soothe is flagrant; fearing the debilitating sympathy her mother offered, she must remain separate from her at all costs.

Elaine's memories confirm that the mother withdrew the moment her children began to crawl away from her, returning when a child was injured and required her ministrations. The withdrawal of the holding environment in the face of the child's separation is the commonly cited environmental failure underlying ego pathology of this kind (e.g., Masterson, 1981). The crisis of separation has occurred in a context where all separation is experiences as a threat to attachment, and so the object is both inconstant and potentially engulfing. Elaine became one of the many children who, by rapprochement, are clinging and fearful in mood, making occasional dangerous and disastrous forays out of the mother's orbit. The masochistic ideal love is a simultaneous expression of this helplessness and separation anxiety even while it is an attempt to overcome it by borrowing the other's cohesiveness. On one hand, Elaine is seeking a heroic sadist, one who represents the liberating father rather than the engulfing mother. On the other hand, what she really needs is someone who supplies not only the missing excitement but also the holding environment. Such containment is acceptable only in its most masculine form because it would otherwise threaten to pull her back into the fusion with the helpless, engulfing mother.

The ideal love is chosen to solve the problem posed by frustration of desire and agency and the ensuing rage at nonrecognition—an avenue of escape through a figure of identification. In this sense, it is defensive. But the creation of this father figure, seen in terms of the normal splitting of the rapprochement also entails a wish. This wish should not become invisible to us merely because it appears in the more disturbed version fueled by rage and frustration. Successful treatment involves both aspects. In escaping her mother, Elaine hopes to escape her own tremendous rage at her for failing to withstand her daughter's attack. Unleashed activity and aggression would destroy whatever remains of the good mother within. Thus she regards her anger and desire as highly driven, even monstrous, and can unleash them safely only in the hands of a man who is more powerful, in control, and does not depend on her for his strength. Only when such destruction is permitted can she find her own creativity, she maintains. Here ideal love, sustaining the idealized phallic father image, combines two sets of needs: (1) to achieve what boys get from their fathers in the normal course of rapprochement, a vehicle of solving that conflict between separation and dependency that preserves grandiosity and omnipotence, salvaging self-esteem and independent will and desire; (2) to put her desire finally in another's hands, make him the manager of the highly disturbing and driven need for freedom and self-expression that is permeated with rage and so can be contained only by a figure of supreme independence and power. On one hand, the father's unavailability for identificatory love has led to the effort to recreate it in a masochistic relationship. On the other hand, the inadequacy of the mother as a figure for identification has intensified that longing for identificatory love and combined it with the search for an object that can withstand aggression and separation. The ideal love seeks the never attained synthesis by imbuing the loved man with features of both the ideal mother and the ideal father, containment and excitement.

The need for an object who is truly outside, who does survive destruction in Winnicott's (1971) sense, is crucial to the fantasy of the ideal love. The man who does not depend on her can be truly outside, and it is this fact—not merely the propensity for suffering—that so often makes only the unreliable abandoning figure a safe or attractive one. The ideal lover seems to offer the boundedness and limits within which one can experience abandonment and creativity. The analysis of masochistic fantasy repeatedly shows that in the control of the other, the masochist seeks the freedom of releasing her own desire, as well as the recognition of her deepest self (Benjamin, 1983). Elaine has also described such experience in reference to her teachers, saying that they provide you with the freedom to turn inward and explore, understanding when you have "got it." The element of containment and boundedness that informs this fantasy underscores the important role played by failure of the holding environment in the etiology of masochism. This is the failure of the ideal mother, the containing, holding mother who can support excitement and outside exploration, who can withstand and limit aggression, who can give permission to separate and can recognize the child's independent accomplishments. Her direct recognition is as crucial to the child as the indirect recognition achieved through identification with the ideal father.

In Elaine's history and treatment it is apparent that the need to escape a weak, engulfing mother is at war with the need to turn back to the mother and engage in the struggle for that recognition—the struggle to death for the life of the self. Simply, we are talking about the mother's ability to provide a structure for the child's aggression that makes it possible to integrate that aggression with its close relatives: activity, will, and desire. It is not merely the recognizing response of the exuberant father than ignites the child's own sense of activity and desire. As discussions of the psychoanalytic situation as a holding environment suggest, the function of containment is also important, Or, as Elaine described the good teacher, the need is for an other whose presence does not violate but permits and helps to recognize the experience of one's own *inner* desire.

Behind the ideal love we have seen the early father identification. But this identification is part of a whole complex that includes the ambivalence toward the mother, the struggle to reconcile independence and dependency, the need for recognition from a mother who survives that struggle. In the actual analysis of masochism, returning to the struggle with the mother is as crucial as reexperiencing the disappointment with the ideal father. The problem of woman's desire must finally be situated in the difficulties with mother and father in the rapprochement complex. These difficulties stem from the gender division: the mother is not the active subject of desire for the child, and the father is that subject. For the daughter, the constellation of a mother how is lacking subjectivity and a father who does possess it presents a difficult choice. Particularly if she fails to receive that recognition from her father, but even if she does so, her active subjectivity and her sense of femininity must be in conflict. A frustrated identification with the father is one primary motif in the masochistic relationship. But even a "successful" identification can create conflicts with feminine identity as long as the girl is confronted with the mother's own lack. Usually, this means that she will find herself faced with a conflict between her sexuality and her sense of autonomous self, because the longing for ideal love exerts the greatest pull on her sexuality, if not on her activity in the world. The sense that female sexuality is an active creative force ultimately depends as much, therefore, on the mother's actual realization of subjectivity as on the father.

While the ego and self pathology that underly masochism can readily be aced to failures in the holding environment and the internalization of a containing mother, the gender content of masochism, its association with femininity, involves the dynamic relationship of mother and father in our present gender system. The structural conditions of gender that now exist do not allow for reconciliation of agency and desire with femininity. Although they often fit the common reality of our gender arrangements, we have criticized the theoretical assumptions about early female development that make feminine submission seem inevitable: that mothers cannot be a figure of separation for both children, that fathers cannot offer their daughters what they offer their sons. We must challenge the structure of heterosexuality in which the father supplies the missing excitement and the way out of the dyad, functions defensively to "beat back the maternal power" (Chasseguet-Smirgel, 1976), and denies the mother's subjectivity as too threatening (Dinnerstein, 1976). The normative image of motherhood that psychoanalysis has long adumbrated must be revised: the ideal of a mother who provides symbiosis and then separation "on demand" must be replaced by the mother who also moves under her own steam. The mother's own integration of separateness and agency must be the profound source from which her recognition of the child's autonomy proceeds. Ideally, the adult woman's sense of agency and separateness should mitigate her sense of having to *be* the all-perfect mother of infantile fantasy, and so should help disconfirm the child's fantasy of maternal power and paternal defense.

The drawbacks of the constellation of idealized masculinity as a protection from primitive maternal power have been pointed out by many feminists: the defensive repudiation of the mother by the boy may further his separation but does not help him to resolve intimacy and independence (Miller, 1973; Gilligan, 1982; Chodorow, 1978, 1979). I believe that the idealization of the father resulting from the conventional gender role and parenting constellation is never fully counteracted. Even when reality contradicts this paternal ideal, it remains active inside as a longing, a fallback position whenever real agency and recognition fail. The father remains the figure who stands for subjectivity and desire, so that, culturally speaking, woman's desire must always contend with this monopoly. Both sexes can therefore continue to comply in ideal love the prevalent form of domination and submission in erotic life. The association of femininity with masochism, the submission to an idealized other, derives above all from the early idealization of the father, an idealization charged with the urgency of resolving the crisis of separation and establishing the self. The other side of this idealization is the derogation of femininity and motherhood and the consequent difficulty in reconciling maternal identification with an active sense of self, preventing the emergence of woman's desire.

In the analysis of ideal love an inverse relationship emerges between desire and recognition on one hand and submission on the other. To oversimplify: the more agency and recognition, the less submission. But this does not necessarily mean that the opportunity to exercise agency—as some feminists imply—will reverse the tendency toward submission once it is firmly in place as an internal object relationship that compensates and eroticizes the loss of self. Once the relationship of identification in which the child recognizes her own desire has been marked by failure with the appropriate parent at the appropriate phase, the search for a powerful ideal figure who represents the desiring self begins to replace it. Agency and recognition are achieved vicariously by submitting to this ideal lover, often in conventionally acceptable forms of wifely self-sacrifice. When identification such as that between toddler and father occurs at the appropriate phase with the pleasure of mutual recognition, then identification serves as a vehicle of development. But when identification emerges later in ideal love, it becomes an impediment, a vicarious substitute. Thus ideal love becomes a perversion of identification, an extension of early identificatory love into a substitute form of embodying one's own desire. Ultimately, we can agree with Freud that women's masochism is linked to the retreat from active sexuality; however, this retreat begins not with resignation to anatomical imperatives but with failures in early individuation. And we see in masochism, especially the variant of ideal love, woman's alienated search for her own desire.

NOTES

1. My interpretation of rapprochement places more emphasis on desire and agency than on loss and abandonment as blows to omnipotence. Kohut's (1971) discussion of the child's need for an object that mirrors the grandiose self and an ideal object that allows the self to become cohesive in the image of that ideal is pertinent. Probably both functions contribute to the early representation of the father as an ideal object who can mirror the child's grandiose aspirations.
2. This interpretation obviously resonates with Freud's (1921) discussion of the ego ideal, which he saw as beginning in the boy's preoedipal identification and love for the father. This identificatory love did not conflict with but prepared for the Oedipus complex, Freud thought; but it could be lost sight of if, as in the case of girls and some boys (in the negative Oedipus complex), it were translated into object love for the father.

REFERENCES

Abelin, E. L. (1980). Triangulation, the role of the father and the origins of core gender identify during the rapprochement subphase. In: *Rapprochement,* ed. R. F. Lax, S. Bach, and J. A. Burland. New York: Aronson, pp. 15–170.

Beauvoir, S. de (1952). *The Second Sex.* New York: Knopf.

Benjamin, J. (1983). Master and slave: The fantasy of erotic domination. In: *Powers of Desire,* ed. A Snitow, C. Stansell, and S. Thompson. New York: Monthly Review Press, pp. 280–299.

Bernstein, D. (1983). The female superego: A different perspective. *Internat. J. Psycho-Anal.* 64:187–202.

Blum, H. (1977). Masochism, the ego ideal, and the psychology of women. In: *Female Psychology,* ed. H. Blum. New York: International Universities Press, pp. 157–192.

Bonaparte, M. (1953). *Female Sexuality.* New York: International Universities Press.

Caplan, P. J. (1984). The myth of women's masochism. *Amer. Psychol.,* 39:130–139.

Chasseguet-Smirgel, J. (1970). Feminine guilt and the Oedipus complex. In: *Female Sexuality,* ed. J. Chasseguet-Smirgel. Ann Arbor: University of Michigan Press, pp. 94–134.

——— (1976). Freud and female sexuality. *Internat. J. Psycho-Anal.,* 57:275–286.

Chodorow, N. (1978). *The Reproduction of Mothering.* Berkeley: University of California Press.

——— (1979). Difference, relation and gender in psychoanalytic perspective. *Socialist Rev.* 9(4):51–70. Also published as: Gender, relation, and difference in psychoanalytic perspectives in *The Future of Difference,* ed. H. Eisenstein and A. Jardine. New Brunswick: Rutgers University Press, 1985.

Clower, V. L. (1977). Theoretical implications in current views of masturbation in latency girls. In: *Female Psychology,* ed. H. Blum. New York: International Universities Press, pp. 109–126.

Deutsch, H. (1930). The significance of masochism in the mental life of women. In: *The Psychoanalytic Reader,* ed. R. Fliess, New York: International Universities Press, 1969, pp. 195–207.

——— (1944, 1945). *The Psychology of Women,* Vols. 1 & 2. New York: Grune and Stratton.

Dinnerstein, D. (1976). *The Mermaid and the Minotaur.* New York: Harper and Row.

Fast, I. (1984). *Gender Identity.* Hillsdale, N.J.: Analytic Press.

Freud, S. (1919). A child is being beaten. *Standard Edition,* 17:179–204. London: Hogarth Press, 1955.

——— (1921). Group psychology and the analysis of the ego. *Standard Edition,* 18:67–144. London: Hogarth Press, 1955.

——— (1924a). The economic problem of masochism. *Standard Edition,* 19:159–172. London: Hogarth Press, 1961.

——— (1924b). The dissolution of the Oedipus complex. *Standard Edition,* 19:173–182. London: Hogarth Press, 1961.

——— (1925). Some psychical consequences of the anatomical discussion between the sexes. *Standard Edition,* 19:248–260. London: Hogarth Press, 1961.

——— (1931). Female sexuality. *Standard Edition,* 21:225–246. London: Hogarth Press, 1961.

——— (1933). New introductory lectures on psychoanalysis: Femininity. *Standard Edition,* 22:112–135. London: Hogarth Press, 1961.

Galenson, E., and Roiphe, H. (1982). The preoedipal relationship of a father, mother, and daughter: In: *Father and Child*, ed. S. H. Cath, A. R. Gurwitt, and J. M. Ross. Boston: Little, Brown, pp. 151–162.

Gilligan, C. (1982). *In a Different Voice*. Cambridge: Harvard University Press.

Greenson, R. (1968). Dis-identifying from mother: Its special importance for the boy. *Internat. J. Psycho-Anal.* 49:370–374.

Gunsberg, L. (1982). Selected critical review of psychological investigations of the early father-infant relationship. In: *Father and Child*, ed. S. H. Cath, A. R. Gurwitt, and J. M. Ross. Boston: Little, Brown, pp. 65–82.

Horney, K. (1926).The flight from womanhood. In: *Feminine Psychology*. New York: Norton, 1967, pp. 54–70.

———— (1933). The problem of feminine masochism. In: *Feminine Psychology*. New York: Norton, 1967, 214–233.

Keller, E. F. (1978). Gender and science. *Psycho-Anal. Contemp. Thought*. 3:409–453.

Kestenberg, J., Marcus, J. H., Sossin, K. M., and Stevenson, R. (1982). The development of paternal attitudes. In *Father and Child*, ed. S. H. Cath, A. R. Gurwitt, and J. M. Ross. Boston: Little, Brown, pp. 205–218.

Khan, M. (1979). *Alienation in Perversions*. New York: International Universities Press.

Kohut, H. (1971). *The Analysis of the Self*. New York: International Universities Press.

Lamb, M. E. (1977). The development of parental preferences in the first two years of life. *Sex Roles*, 3:495–497.

Lax, R. (1977). The role of internalization in the development of certain aspects of female masochism: Ego psychological considerations. *Internat. J. Psycho-Anal.*, 58:289–300.

Levenson, R. (1984). Intimacy, autonomy and gender: Development differences and their reflection in adult relationships. *J. Amer. Acad. Psychoanal.*, 12:529–544.

Mahler, M., Pine, F., and Bergman, A. (1975). *The Psychological Birth of the Human Infant*. New York: Basic Books.

Masterson, J. F. (1981). *The Narcissistic and Borderline Disorders*. New York: Brunner/Mazel.

Menaker, E. (1973). *Masochism and the Emerging Ego*. New York: Human Sciences Press.

Miller, J. B. (1973). New issues, new approaches. In: *Psychoanalysis and Women*, ed. J. B. Miller. Baltimore: Penguin, pp. 375–406.

Person, E. S. (1980). Sexuality as the mainstay of identity: Psychoanalytic perspectives. *Signs*, 5:605–630.

Roiphe, H., and Galenson, E. (1981). *Infantile Origins of Sexual Identity*. New York: International Universities Press.

Smirnoff, V. (1969). The masochistic contract. *Internat. J. Psycho-Anal.* 50:665–671.

Spieler, S. (1984). Preoedipal girls need fathers. *Psychoanal. Rev.*, 71:63–80.

Stoller, R. J. (1968). *Sex and Gender*. New York: Aronson.

———— (1975). *Perversion*, New York: Pantheon.

———— (1979). *Sexual Excitement*, New York: Simon and Schuster, 1980.

Stolorow, R. D., and Lachmann, F. M. (1980). *Psychoanalysis of Developmental Arrests*. New York: International Universities Press.

Torok, M. (1970). The significance of penis envy in women: In: *Female Sexuality*, ed. J. Chasseguet-Smirgel. Ann Arbor: University of Michigan Press, pp. 137–170.

Winnicott, D. W. (1971). The use of an object and relating through identifications. In: *Playing and Reality*. Harmondsworth: Penguin, pp. 101–111.

Yogman, M. W. (1982). Observations on the father-infant relationship. In: *Father and Child*, ed. S. H. Cath, A. R. Gurwitt, and J. M. Ross. Boston: Little, Brown, pp. 101–122.

23. Remapping the Moral Domain: New Images of the Self in Relationship

Carol Gilligan

In Book 6 of the *Aeneid,* when Aeneas goes to the underworld he is startled to discover that Dido is dead. He did not believe the story that had reached him: "I could not believe," he tells her, "that I would hurt you so terribly by going." [1] Seeing her wound, he weeps, asking, "Was I the cause?" [2] Yet, explaining that he did not willingly leave her, he describes himself as a man set apart, bound by his responsibility to his destiny. Caught between two images of himself—as implicated and as innocent, as responsible and as tossed about by fate—he exemplifies the dilemma of how to think about the individual as at once separate and connected to others in a fabric of human relationship.

The representation of the self as separate and bounded has a long history in the Western tradition. Consonant with, rather than opposed to, this image of individual autonomy is a notion of social responsibility, conceived as duty or obligation. Yet as Virgil tells his story in the *Aeneid*—of a man apart, devoted to his mission of founding a city and bringing home his gods to Latium—he shadows the story with others that resist expression, of "a sorrow too deep to tell" and "a love beyond all telling," [3] Aeneas's story of the fall of Troy and Dido's of her passion. These stories of sorrow and love have generally been kept apart from discussions of morality and the individual; as in the *Aeneid,* they are considered *infandum,* told in private, known but unspeakable. Interspersing these stories with the account of Aeneas's heroic and arduous journey, Virgil, however, suggests a connection. The uncertainty created by this connection emerges in the underworld meeting of Aeneas and Dido. In this scene, described by T. S. Eliot as one of the most poignant and civilized passages in poetry,[4] an acute psychological wisdom leads to a profound sense of moral ambiguity.

Was Aeneas responsible for Dido's self-inflicted wound? Why couldn't he believe that he would hurt her so terribly by leaving? These questions reflect in their essential tension two ways of thinking about the self in relationship. A psychology of love that can explicate the connection between Aeneas's departure and Dido's action, as well as her subsequent anger and silence, vies with the categories of moral judgment that presuppose a separate and autonomous individual. The two images of self anchored by these two conceptual frameworks imply two ways of thinking about responsibility that are fundamentally incompatible. When Aeneas encounters consequences of his action that he had neither believed nor intended and Dido, once generous and responsive, is rendered by grief cold and impassive, this disjunction momentarily surfaces. The detachment of Aeneas's *pietas* becomes the condition for his ignorance of her feelings, yet his adherence to his mission does not imply the indifference that she in her responsiveness imagined. Thus the simple judgment that would condemn Aeneas for turning away from Dido or Dido for breaking her vow of chastity yields to a more complex assessment that encompasses the capacity for sustained commitment and the capacity for responsiveness in relationships and recognizes their tragic conflict.

The two meanings of the word "responsibility"—commitment to obligations and responsiveness in relationships—are central to the mapping of the moral domain put forth in this chapter.[5] Since moral judgments reflect a logic of social understanding and form a standard of self-evaluation, a conception of morality is key to the construction of the individual. By asking how we come to hold moral values and by tracing the ontogenesis of values to the experience of human relationships, I will claim that two moral predispositions inhere in the structure of human connection. These predispositions— toward justice and toward care—arise from the experience of inequality and of attachment embedded in the relationship between child and parent. Since everyone has been vulnerable to oppression and to abandonment, two stories about morality recur in human experience.

The different parameters of the parent-child relationship—its inequality and its interdependence or attachment—also ground a distinction between the dimensions of inequality/equality and attachment/detachment that characterize all forms of human connection. In contrast to a unitary moral vision and to the assumption that the opposite of the one is the many, these dimensions of relationship provide coordinates for reconstructing the individual and for remapping development. The two connections of responsibility, reflecting different images of the self in relationship, correct an individualism that has been centered within a single interpretive framework. At the same time, the identification of attachment or interdependence as a primary dimension of human experience ties the psychology of love to the representation of moral growth and to identity formation.

The haunting simile that Virgil suspends over the scene of the underworld encounter, comparing Aeneas seeing Dido wounded to "one who sees,/Early in the month, or thinks to have seen, the moon/Rising through cloud, all dim,"[6] catches the uncertainty surrounding the perception of a reality that has been obscured or diminished. As the dim moon recalls the ideals of stoic detachment and hero individualism, it also conveys the fragility of love and its vulnerability to loss and separation. Thus two stories in their shifting configuration create a fundamental confusion; yet one story tends to get lost, buried in an underworld region.

In recent years, two classical scholars, W. R. Johnson and Marilyn Skinner, have noted the continuing tendency of critics to reduce the complexity of Virgil's poetic statement, to override ambiguity in an effort to resolve the central problem of competing loyalties.[7] The same tendency to reduce complexity is evident in contemporary psychology as well, where the ideal of individual autonomy has rendered the reality of love evanescent. In this sense, the current readings of the *Aeneid* by Johnson and Skinner, which focus the significance of the underworld meeting, correspond to efforts within psychology to recover a story about love that is known but dimly apprehended. In both instances, this retrieval reveals an inherent complication by drawing attention to "the ethical dilemma, now perceived, in what formerly had been thought of as a right and proper, albeit painful, course of action."[8] As the perception of this dilemma "requires of Virgil that he shape a new formulation of heroism,"[9] it currently implies a change in our psychological theories about development and about the individual.

The individualism defined by the idea of the autonomous self reflects the value that has been placed on detachment—in moral thinking, in self-development, in dealing with loss, and in the psychology of adolescence. By reconstituting the tension between attachment and detachment, which is dissolved by this representation, I will describe two conceptions of morality and of the self that lead to different ways of understanding loss and thinking about the conflicts of loyalty that arise in the course of human life. The close tie between detachment and dispassion reveals the problem I wish to address by showing how the recovery of a lost story about love changes the image of the self in relationship.

The definition of the self and morality in terms of individual autonomy and social responsibility—of an internalized conscience enacted by will and guided by duty or obligation—presupposes a notion of reciprocity, expressed as a "categorical imperative" or a "golden rule." But the ability to put oneself in another's position, when construed in these terms, implies not only a capacity for abstraction and generalization but also a conception of moral knowledge that in the end always refers back to the self. Despite the transit to the place of the other, the self oddly seems to stay constant. If the process of coming to know others is imagined instead as a joining of stories, it implies the possibility of generating new knowledge and transforming the self in the experience of relationship. The reference for judgment then becomes the relationship between the other and the self. Although the capacity for engagement with others—for compassion and for response to another's pleasure and distress—has been observed in early childhood and even in infancy, this capacity is not well represented in accounts of human development, in part because it is at odds with the image of relationships embedded in the prevailing concept of the self.

From George Herbert Mead's description of the self as known through others' reflection and Cooley's conception of the "looking-glass self," to Erikson's emphasis on the discovery of self in others' recognition and the current psychoanalytic fascination with the process of "mirroring," the relational context of identity formation has repeatedly been conveyed. But the recurrent image of the mirror calls attention to the lifelessness in this portrayal of relationships. When others are described as objects for self-reflection or as the means to self-discovery and self-recognition, the language of relationships is drained of attachment, intimacy, and engagement. The self, although placed in a context of relationships, is defined in terms of separation. Others disappear, and love becomes cast in the depersonalized language of "object relations." [10]

A different way of describing the self, generally confused with a failure of self-definition, has been clarified in recent years by attention to the experience of women. [11] In this construction, the self is known in the experience of connection, defined not by reflection but by interaction, the responsiveness of human engagement. The close tie I have observed between self-description and moral judgment illuminates the significance of this distinction by indicating how different images of the self rise to different visions of moral agency, which in turn are reflected in different ways of defining responsibility.

When asked "What does responsibility mean to you?" a high school student replied: "Responsibility means making a commitment and then sticking to it." This response confirms the common understanding of responsibility as personal commitment and contractual obligation. A different conception of the self and of morality appears, however, in another student's reply: "Responsibility is when you are aware of others and you are aware of their feelings. . . . Responsibility is taking charge of yourself by looking at others around you and seeking what they need and seeing what you need . . . and taking the initiative." [12] In this construction, responsibility means acting responsively in relationships, and the self—as a moral agent—takes the initiative to gain awareness and respond to the perception of need. The premise of separation yields to the depiction of the self in connection, and the concept of autonomy is changed. The seeming paradox "taking charge of yourself by looking at others around you" conveys the relational dimension of this self-initiated action.

These two conceptions of responsibility, illustrated here by the definitions of two young women, were focused initially in my research by a dissonance between women's voices and psychological theories. [13] Exploring this dissonance, I defined new categories of moral judgment and self-description to capture the experience of attachment or interdependence, which overrides the traditional contrast between egoism and altruism. This enlarged conceptual framework provided a new way of listening to differences not only between but also within the thinking of women and men. In a series of studies designed to investigate the relationship between conceptions of the self and morality and to test their association with gender and age, two moral voices could reliably be distinguished in the way people framed and resolved moral problems and in their evaluations of the choices they made: one that speaks of connection, not hurting, care, and response; and one that speaks of equality, reciprocity, justice, and rights. Although both voices regularly appeared in conjunction, the tension between them was evident in the confusion that marked their intersection and in the tendency for one voice to predominate. The pattern of predominance, although not gender specific, appeared to be gender related, suggesting that the gender differences recurrently observed in moral reasoning signify differences in moral orientation, which in turn are tied to different ways of imagining the self in relationship. [14]

The values of justice and autonomy, presupposed in current theories of human growth and incorporated into definitions of morality and of the self, imply a view of the individual as separate and of relationships as either hierarchical or contractual, bound by the alternatives of constraint and cooperation. In contrast, the values of care and connection, salient in women's thinking, imply a view of the self and the other as interdependent and of relationships as networks created and sustained by attention and response. The two moral voices that articulated these visions thus denote different ways of viewing the world. Within each perspective, the key terms of social understanding take on different meanings, reflecting a change in the imagery of relationship and signifying a shift in orientation. As the illustration of the ambiguous figure is perceived alternately as vase or faces, so there appear to be two ways of perceiving the self in relation to others, both grounded in reality but each imposing on that reality a different organization. But, as with the perception of the ambiguous figure, when one configuration emerges, the other temporarily vanishes.

The nature and implications of these differences are clarified by the example of two four-year-old children who were playing together and wanted to play different games.[15] In this particular version of a common dilemma, the girl said, "Let's play next-door neighbors." "I want to play pirates," the boy replied. "Okay," said the girl, "then you can be the pirate that lives next door." By comparing this inclusive solution of combining the games with the fair solution of taking turns and playing each game for an equal period, one can see not only how the two approaches yield different ways of solving a problem in relationships but also how each solution affects the identity of the game and the experience of the relationship.

The fair solution, taking turns, leaves the identity of each game intact. It provides an opportunity for each child to experience the other's imaginative world and regulates the exchange by imposing a rule based on the premise of equal respect. The inclusive solution, in contrast, transforms both games: the neighbor game is changed by the presence of a pirate living next door; the pirate game is changed by bringing the pirate into a neighborhood. Each child not only enters the other's imaginative world but also transforms that world by his or her presence. The identity of each separate game yields to a new combination, since the relationship between the children gives rise to a game that neither had separately imagined. Whereas the fair solution protects identity and ensures equality within the context of a relationship, the inclusive solution transforms identity through the experience of a relationship.

Thus different strategies for resolving conflict convey different ways of imagining the self, and these different forms of self-definition suggest different ways of perceiving connection with others.

In 1935 the British psychiatrist Ian Suttie called attention to the representation of love in modern psychology, asking, "In our anxiety to avoid the intrusion of sentiment into our scientific formulations, have we not gone to the length of excluding it altogether from our field of observation?" [16] Noting that science, as generally conceived, "is at a particular disadvantage in dealing with the topic of human 'attachments,' " Suttie observed that love is either reduced to appetite or dismissed as an illusion. [17] Thus he set out to reconstitute love within psychology, defining love as a "state of active, harmonious interplay" and tracing its origins to a "pleasure in *responsive* companionship and a correlative discomfort in loneliness and isolation" that are present in infancy. [18]

This understanding of love was substantially extended by the British psychoanalyst John Bowlby. [19] As Freud found in dreams and free associations a window into men's souls, Bowlby discovered in children's responses to loss a way of observing relationship. From this angle of vision, he came to see in the sorrow of children's mourning a capacity for love that previously was unimagined. The knowledge that this capacity is present in early childhood required a transformation in the account of human development. Tracing the formation of attachment to care giving and responsiveness in relationships, Bowlby rendered the process of connection visible as a process of mutual engagement. On this basis, he challenged the value psychologists have placed on separation in describing normal or healthy development, arguing instead that in separation lies a pathogenic potential for detachment and disengagement. Thus he asked how the capacity for love can be sustained in the face of loss and across the reality of separation.

Bowlby's method was essentially the same as the one Freud set forth in his *New Introductory Lectures on Psychoanalysis*. Relying on the magnification of pathology to reveal what otherwise was invisible, Bowlby viewed loss as a fracture that exposes the underlying structure of connection. As Freud observed the psyche fractured in neurotic symptom formation, Bowlby observed in traumatic separation the breaking apart of a relationship. Quoting Gothe's statement that "we see only what we know" and William James's observation that "the great source of terror in infancy is solitude," [20] he set out to describe the phenomena of human attachment and sorrow, to separate the account of loss, mourning, comfort, and love from orthodox psychoanalytic interpretations and to anchor it instead in direct observation. The unit of his analysis was the relationship rather than the individual.

In his essay "Mourning and Melancholia,"[21] Freud describes with a clarity that remains unequaled the symptomatology of depression, attributing it to a failure of mourning, conceived as a failure of detachment. Rather than withdrawing libido from a lost and irretrievable object, the depressed person as it were takes his stand against reality, digging his heels into the argument that the object in fact cannot be lost. The mechanism of this denial, Freud says, is identification, complicated by anger and consequently leading to self-denigration. In an effort to ward off a seemingly unbearable sorrow, the depressed person becomes the lost object of his affections. Rather than abandon the other, he chooses to become the other and abandon himself. Thus, in Freud's exquisite statement, "the shadow of the object fell upon the ego";[22] the self undergoes eclipse.

In charting the natural history of mourning from his observations of children dealing with loss and separation, Bowlby demarcates a three-stage sequence of protest, despair, and detachment.[23] Seeing denial and anger as inevitable responses to loss—the concomitants of normal grieving—he reinterprets detachment as the sign of a pathogenic repression rather than as a signal of mourning completed. Although both Freud and Bowlby stress the importance of remembering, Freud emphasizes remembering the loss and coming to terms with its reality, whereas Bowlby focuses on remembering the love and finding a means for its representation. This divergence leads to opposing predictions about the capacity for love following loss. Freud implies that only when the last shreds of hope and memory have been relinquished will the libido be free to attach again.[24] Bowlby, proceeding from a different conception of relationships and a different model of psychic energy, describes the process of mourning in terms of a separation or tear that must be mended, tying the renewal of the capacity for love to weaving together the broken narrative. The story of love must be told not so that it can be forgotten but so that it can be continued into the present. Although "object-finding" may be "object-refinding," in Freud's famous phrase,[25] attachments—located in time and arising from mutual engagement—are by definition irreplaceable.

Thus Bowlby introduces a new language of relationships into psychology and recasts the process of development as one of elaboration rather than of replacement. Pointing to the visible signs of human engagement, he records the interplay of attachment seeking and care giving by which human bonds are formed and sustained. Yet in drawing the underpinnings of his revised theoretical conception from ethology and the study of information processing, he moves away from the human world of love he set out to describe. Using animal analogies and machine images, he aligns his work with the prevailing metaphors of science; the cost of this assimilation is a reduction in the portrayal of relationships. The mother, casts as "attachment-figure," is seen primarily through the eyes of the child, and the mutality of relationships, although stated, is lost in the way they are presented.

In directing attention to the observable signs of human connection, Bowlby's work recasts the distinction between mourning and melancholia in terms of a distinction between real and fabricated relationships. Seen in this light, mourning signifies grief over the loss of an attachment whose felt reality can be sustained in memory; melancholia signifies the isolation felt when an attachment is found to be fragmentary. If separation exposes the nature of connection, then the melancholia of depression, with its endless argument of self-accusation, may be seen as a response to failure of attachment rather than as a failure of separation. This interpretation offers a new way of reading the stories about sorrow and love in the *Aeneid*.

Dido, discovering that Aeneas is secretly planning to leave her, suddenly sees the love between them to have been imagined. Correcting for distance in light of this perception, she replaces the term "husband" first with "guest" and then with "deserter."[26] Yet, driven by a wavering memory, searching wildly for support and finding only disconfirmation, she turns in the end to enact the destruction of the relationship upon herself. Aeneas's surprise at seeing her dead confirms the reality of his separation. Yet his belated expressions of sorrow reveal the love which he had previously kept hidden. In Book 4, two uses of the word "husband" convey a central misapprehension: Aeneas, saying "I never held the torches of a bridegroom,/ Never entered upon the pact of marriage," refers to the absence of contract; Dido, "humbling her pride before her love," refers to the fact of conjugation.[27] In Book 6, these two perspectives begin to cross and intermingle.

By verbal echoes and situational reversals, Virgil spins a skein of ironic allusion that serves, as Skinner observers, "to recall prior tragedy and examine it from an altered perspective."[28] The compelling poignancy and ultimate futility of Aeneas's and Dido's last meeting arise from the recognition that Aeneas's stoic detachment has lots its heroic quality, "becoming instead pathetically defensive," and that Dido's death has come to appear less tragically necessary, seeming "a wretched, preventable accident."[29]

Thus the costs of detachment—whether undertaken out of a mistaken notion of *pietas* or arising from traumatic separation—become increasingly clear. Dido flees while Aeneas stands pleading, demonstrating her unwillingness now to respond and recognizing that again he will leave her. Aeneas, his "once kindly ears"[30] having been blocked by divinely ordained duty, continues his mission of founding a city. At the end of the epic, he appears "fierce under arms" and "terrible in his anger"; driven by anguish and fury, he enacts a senseless retribution on Turnus in the name of keeping a promise.[31]

The image of a civilization built on detachment returns in Freud's description of adolescent development, where he identifies as "one of the most significant but also one of the most painful psychical accomplishments of the pubertal period . . . detachment from parental authority, a process which alone makes possible the opposition, which is so important for the progress of civilization, between the old generation and the new."[32] This view of detachment as a necessary, although painful, step in the course of normal development casts problems in adolescence as problems of separation. Observing that "as at every stage in the course of normal development through which all human beings ought by rights to pass, a certain number are held back, so there are some who have never gotten over their parents' authority and have withdrawn their affection from them either very incompletely or not at all," Freud concludes that this failure of development occurs mostly in girls.[33]

Seen from a different perspective, however, the resistance of girls to detachment calls attention to the ethical dilemma that the orthodox account of development obscures. Rather than signifying a failure of individuation, the reluctance to withdraw from attachment may indicate a struggle to find an inclusive solution to the problem of conflicting loyalties. Adolescent girls resisting detachment generally have appeared in the literature on adolescence to illustrate the problems that arise when childhood forms of relationship are not changed. But by drawing attention to the problem of loyalty and to a transformation of attachment that resists the move toward disengagement, the experience of girls in adolescence may help to define an image of the self in relationship that leads to a different vision of progress and civilization.

Psychological development is usually traced along a single line of progression from inequality to equality, following the incremental steps of the child's physical growth. Attachment is associated with inequality, and development linked to separation. Thus the story of love becomes assimilated to a story about authority and power. This is the assimilation I wish to unravel in remapping development across two dimensions of relationship to distinguish inequality from attachment. Starting from the child's position of inequality and attachment, one can trace the straight line that leads toward equality and increased authority. But one can also trace the elaborating line that follows the development of attachment, depicting changes in the nature and configuration of relationships and marking the growth of the capacity for love. This two-dimensional framework of interpretation clarifies the problems created by oppression and by detachment. But the interweaving of the two lines of development reveals a psychological ambiguity and ethical tension, which is most sharply focused by two opposites of the word *dependence*.

Since dependence connotes connection, it can be extended along both dimensions of relationship, leading in one direction to independence and in the other to isolation. These contrasting opposites of dependence—independence and isolation—illuminate the shift in the valence of relationships that occurs when connection with others is experienced as impeding autonomy and when it is experienced as protecting against isolation. When dependence is opposed simply to independence, this complexity disappears. Progress becomes equated with detachment, seen as a sign of objectivity and strength; ambiguity vanishes and attachments appear as an obstacle to the growth of the autonomous self.

The opposition of dependence to isolation, retrieving the ethical problem and the psychological tension, was highlighted by adolescent girls' responses to a question about the meaning of dependence. The girls were participants in a study designed to map the terrain of female development that remains largely uncharted in the literature on normal adolescence.[34] In an interview that included questions about past experience, self-description, moral conflicts, and future expectations, the question about dependence was asked at the end of a section about relationships. The study served to underscore the contrast between the view of relationships conveyed by the opposition between dependence and autonomy, which has structured the discussion of adolescent development and appears on most scales of psychological assessment, and the view of relationships conveyed by the opposition of dependence to isolation, implied in the following examples:
What does dependence mean to you?

I think it is just when you can be dependent on or you can depend on someone, and if you depend on someone, you can depend on them to do certain things, like to be there when you need them, and you can depend on people to understand your problems, and on the other hand, people can depend on you to do the same thing.

When you know that someone is there when you are upset, and if you need someone to talk to, they are there, and you can depend on them to understand.

Well, sometimes it bothers me, the word, because it means that you are depending on somebody to make things happen. But also that you are depending on someone else to help you, you know, either to make things happen for you that are good or just to be there when you need them to talk to and not feel that you are cutting into their time or that they don't want you there.

I wouldn't say total dependence but if we ever need each other for anything, we could totally be dependent on the person and it would be no problem. For me, it means that if I have a problem, I can depend on her to help me or anything I need help with, she will be there to help, whether she can help me or not, she will try, and the same goes for me.

Caring. Knowing that the person will always be there. I think there is a word like "painstaking care." You know that the other person would go through all the pain . . . it is so rare, you are really lucky if someone is like that.

That I know if I go to her with a problem or something like that or not a problem but just to see her, even if she has changed and even if I have changed, that we will be able to talk to each other.

Dependence, well, in this case it would be just like I really depend on him to listen to me when I have something to say or when I have something I want to talk about, I really want him to be there and to listen to me.

Here, dependence is assumed to be part of the human condition, and the recurrent phrases—"to be there," "to help," "to talk to," "to listen"— convey the perception that people rely on one another for understanding, comfort, and love. In contrast to the use of the word *dependence* to connote hanging from someone like a ball on a string, an object governed by the laws of physics, these responses convey the perception that attachments arise from the human capacity to move others and to be moved by them. Being dependent, then, no longer means being helpless, powerless and without control; rather, it signifies a conviction that one is able to have an effect on others, as well as the recognition that the interdependence of attachment empowers both the self and the other, not one at the other's expense. The activities of care—being there, listening, the willingness to help, and the ability to understand—take on a moral dimension, reflecting the injunction to pay attention and not to turn away from need. As the knowledge that others are capable of care renders them lovable rather than merely reliable, so the willingness and the ability to care become a standard of self-evaluation. In this active construction, dependence, rather than signifying a failure of individuation, denotes a decision on the part of the individual to enact a vision of love.

I would say we depend on each other in a way that we are both independent, and I would say we are very independent but as far as our friendship goes, we are dependent on each other because we know that both of us realize that whenever we need something, the other person will always be there.

I depend on her for understanding a lot and for love and she depends on me for the same things, understanding and just to be there for each other, we know that we are there for each other.

These portraits of love reveal its cognitive as well as its affective dimensions, its foundation in an ability to perceive people in their own terms and to respond to need. Because such knowledge generates power both to help and to hurt, the uses of this power become the standard responsibility and care in relationships. In adolescence, when both wanting and knowing take on new meanings, conflicts of responsibility assume new dimensions, creating conflicts of loyalty that are not easily resolved. Seeking to perceive and respond to their own as well as to others' needs, adolescent girls ask if they can be responsive to themselves without losing connection with others and whether they can respond to others without abandoning themselves. This search for an inclusive solution to dilemmas of conflicting loyalties vies with the tendency toward exclusion, manifest in the moral opposition of selfish and selfless choice—an opposition in which selfishness connotes the exclusion of others and selflessness the exclusion of self. Thus the themes of inclusion and exclusion, prominent in the childhood games girls play and manifest in their strategies for resolving conflicts, come to be addressed consciously in adolescence, in a line of development that leads through changes in the experience and understanding of attachment.

Within this framework of interpretation, the central metaphor for identity formation becomes dialogue rather than mirroring; the self is defined by gaining perspective and known by experiencing engagement with others. The moral passion that surrounds this quest for self-definition was evident when adolescent girls were asked to describe a situation in which someone was not being listened to. The acuity of their perceptions of not listening, their awareness of the signs of attention, extended across examples that ranged from a problem in international politics to conflicts in personal relationships, making the public as well as the private dimensions of attachment or interdependence clear. The themes of silence and voice that emerge so centrally in female narratives convey the moral dimensions of listening, but also the struggle to claim a voice and the knowledge of how readily this endeavor is foiled. When someone refuses to listen—interpreted as a failure to care— adolescent girls speak of themselves as coming up against a wall. Silence can be a way of maintaining integrity in the face of such disconfirmation, a way to avoid further invalidation. But the willingness to speak and to risk disagreements is central to the process of adolescent development, making it possible to reweave attachment, and informing the distinction between true and false relationships.

"I just wish to become better in my relationship with my mother, to be able more easily to disagree with her." This adolescent's wish to engage with others rather than "making myself in their image" signifies both her temptation to yield to others' perceptions—to become, as it were, the mirror —and the recognition that the exclusion of the self, like the exclusion of others, renders relationships lifeless by dissolving the fabric of connection. With this dissolution, attachment becomes impossible. Given the failure of interpretive schemes to reflect female experience and given the celebration of selflessness as the feminine virtue, girls' resistance to detachment challenges two long-standing equations: the equation of human with male and the equation of care with self-sacrifice. At the base of this challenge lies a story about love that joins opposition and progress to attachment as well as a view of the self as an individual within the context of continuing relationship.

Jane Austin structures the plot of her novel *Persuasion* to reveal a transformation in the understanding of love and duty—a transformation that hinges on a change in self-perception.[35] Anne Elliot, the heroine, yields to the persuasion of her "excellent friend," Lady Russell, and breaks off her engagement to Captain Wentworth in the name of duty and prudence. The suffering brought on by this detachment is chronicled in the course of the novel. The resolution, however, takes an interesting turn: Anne Elliot reconstructs her understanding of relationships in light of her recognition that "she and her excellent friend could sometimes think differently";[36] Captain Wentworth comes to see the impediment created by "my own self." He explains, "I was too proud, too proud to ask again. I did not understand you. I shut my eyes."[37] Two ways of defining the self—by submission and by detachment—have created an obstacle to attachment that begins to give way when dialogue replaces reflection and blind commitment yields to response. Like searchlights crossing, these transformations intersect to form a bright spot of illumination, making it possible to join the self with the other and the other with the self. In this novel, where the engagement of divergent perspectives defines happy marriage, new images of the self in relationship convey a new understanding of morality and love.

NOTES

1. Virgil, *The Aeneid,* trans. Robert Fitzgerald (New York, 1983), 6: 463–64, p. 176.
2. Ibid., 6: 458, p. 175.
3. Ibid., 2: 3, p. 33; 4: 85, p. 98.
4. T. S. Eliot, *On Poetry and Poets* (New York, 1957), p. 63.
5. A similar distinction is made by H. Richard Niebuhr in *The Responsible Self* (New York, 1963).
6. *Aeneid,* 6: 450–52, p. 175.
7. W. R. Johnson, *Darkness Visible: A Study of Virgil's Aeneid* (Berkeley and Los Angeles, 1975); Marilyn B. Skinner, "The Last Encounter of Dido and Aeneas: *A* 6.450–476," *Vergilius,* no. 29 (The Vergilius Society, 1983), pp. 12–18.
8. Skinner, p. 16.
9. Johnson, p. 153.
10. The term object was first used by Freud in *Three Essays on the Theory of Sexuality* (1905) to distinguish sexual objects from sexual aims. It is now widely used by object-relations theorists, psychoanalysts following Melanie Klein and Margaret Mahler who focus on the primacy of relationships. In both contexts, the term refers to a person who has become the object of another's desire.
11. This difference was described in the mid-1970's by Nancy Chodorow, "Family Structure and Feminine Personality," in M. Z. Rosaldo and L. Lamphere, *Woman, Culture and Society* (Stanford, Calif., 1974); by Jean Baker Miller, *Toward a New Psychology of Women* (Boston, 1976); and by Carol Gilligan, "In a Different Voice: Women's Conceptions of the Self and of Morality," *Harvard Educational Review,* 47 (1977). The point has been extended by Chodorow, *The Reproduction of Mothering* (Berkeley and Los Angeles, 1978); Gilligan, *In a Different Voice: Psychological Theory and Women's Development* (Cambridge, Mass., 1982); and Miller, "The Development of Women's Sense of Self," Stone Center Working Paper Series, no. 12 (Wellesley, Mass., 1984); as well as in a variety of other feminist writings.
12. These responses to questions about responsibility were given by students at the Emma Willard School for girls, in Troy, New York. All such quotes in this chapter are from these girls.
13. Gilligan, *In a Different Voice.*
14. C. Gilligan, S. Langdale, N. Lyons, and M. Murphy, "The Contribution of Women's Thought to Developmental Theory," report to the National Institute of Education, Washington, D.C., 1982. See also S. Langdale, "Moral Orientations and Moral Development," Ph.D. diss., Harvard Graduate School of Education, 1983, and N. Lyons, "Two Perspectives: On Self, Relationships and Morality," *Harvard Educational Review,* 53 (1983).
15. For this example, I am grateful to Anne Glickman, the mother of the four-year-old boy.
16. Ian Suttie, *The Origins of Love and Hate* (New York, 1935), p. 1.
17. Ibid., p. 2.
18. Ibid., p. 4; emphasis in text.

19. John Bowlby, *Attachment and Loss,* in three volumes: *Attachment* (New York, 1969), *Separation: Anxiety and Anger* (New York, 1973), *Loss: Sadness and Depression* (New York, 1980).
20. Bowlby, *Loss,* p. 44.
21. Sigmund Freud, "Mourning and Melancholia" (1917), *The Standard Edition of the Complete Psychological Works of Sigmund Freud,* ed. James Strachey (London, 1953–66), XIV, 249.
22. Ibid., p. 249.
23. Bowlby, *Loss.*
24. Freud, XIV, 248.
25. Freud, *Three Essays on the Theory of Sexuality* (1905), VII, 227.
26. *Aeneid,* 4: 323, 4: 421.
27. Ibid., 4: 338–39, 4: 414, pp. 107, 110.
28. Skinner, p. 12.
29. Ibid.
30. *Aeneid,* 4: 440, p. 111.
31. Ibid., 12: 938, 12: 946–47, p. 402.
32. Freud, VII, 227.
33. Ibid.
34. The study was conducted at the Emma Willard School for girls and is part of a larger project on adolescent development. For omission of girls in the literature on adolescence, see J. Adelson, ed., *Handbook of Adolescent Psychology* (New York, 1980).
35. Jane Austen, *Persuasion* (New York, 1964).
36. Ibid., p. 140.
37. Ibid., p. 234.

Name Index

Italic numbers indicate references.

Abelin, E. L., 462, 464, 466, 467, *478*
Abraham, K., 111
Adler, A., 333
Applegarth, A., 25, *34*
Asch, S. E., 415, *419*
Austin, J., 493

Bakan, D., 443, *453*
Balint, A., 425
Barglow, P., 309, *323*
Barnett, M. C., 234, 237, 262, *274*
Beach, F. A., 242, *274*
Beauvoir, S. de, 411, 412, *419*, 458, 460, 469, 471, *478*
Bell, A., 267, *274*
Benedek, T., 234, 236, 237, 257, 260, *274*
Benjamin, J., 26, 32, 33, *34*, 455–77, *478*
Bergler, E., 108, *233*, 234, 236, 259, *274*, *275*
Bergman, A., 29, 32, *37*, 300, *304*, 463, 464, 468, *479*
Berliner, B., 223, *233*
Berlowe, J., *276*
Bernstein, D., 25, *34*, 464, 470, *478*
Bettelheim, B., *288*
Bion, W., 160, *183*
Block, J., 440, *453*
Blum, H. P., 25, *34*, 315, 318, *323*, 458, 469, *478*
Bonaparte, M., 3, 15, *34*, 234, 236, 237, *274*, 457, *478*
Bowlby, J., 8, *34*, 486, 487, 488
Bradley, N., 242, 262, *274*
Brierley, M., 8, 20, *34*, 234, 237, *274*
Broverman, D. M., 307, *323*
Broverman, I. K., 307, *323*
Brunswick, R. M., 3, 6, 14, 19, *34*, 43–64, 106, 108
Buehler, C., *233*
Buehler, K., *233*

Burgner, M., 21, *34*
Burnett, H. F., 244, *274*

Caplan, P. J., 458, *478*
Chasseguet-Smirgel, J., 9, 19, *34*, 88–128, 353, 461, 462, 470, 476, *478*
Chodorow, N., 6, 12, 26, 28, 31, *34*, 310, 311, *323*, 420–34, 455, 461, 462, 465, 476, *478*
Cixous, H., 13, *34*
Clarkson, F. E., 307, *323*
Clower, V. L., 464, *478*
Coleridge, S. T., *419*
Colette, *419*
Cunningham, D. J., 241, 243, 265, *274*

Daiken, L., *274*
Deutsch, H., 3, 6, 15, *34*, 93, 95, 151, 191, *197*, *206*, 234, 236, 237, 257, 258, 260, *274*, 363, 457, 458, 459, *478*
Dickinson, R. L., *274*
Dinnerstein, D., 12, 28, 31, *34*, 401–17, 462, 464, 476, *478*
Dolto, F., 360, 361
Dostoyevsky, F., *419*

Edgcumbe, R., 21, *34*
Ehrenreich, B., *323*
Eissler, K., 312, *323*
Eissler, K. R., 234, *274*
Eliot, G., *419*
Eliot, T. S., 480
Ellis, H., *274*
Emler, N. T., 305, *324*
Erikson, E. H., 25, 32, *34*, 234, 237, 241, *274*, 437, 438, 439, 442, 444, *453*, 483

Fast, I., 27, *35*, 455, *478*
Federn, P., *274*
Fenichel, O., 193, *197*, *206*, *233*, *274*

Feral, J., 13, *35*
Ferenczi, S., 239, *274*
Fermi, L., 11, *35*
Firestone, S., 11, *35*
Fisher, S., *157*
Ford, C. S., 242, *274*
Freud, A., 9, *35*, 150, *157, 233*, 249, 250, *275*
Freud, S., 2, 5, 14, 15, 22, 27, 43, 82–85, 88, 89, 93, 94, 95, 96, 106, 107, 110, 112, 116, 117, 126, 146, 148, 150, 151, *158*, 187, 190, 191, *197*, 208, 209, 210, 211, 215, 217, *220*, 221, *233*, 234, 235, 236, 240, 245, 260, *275*, 286, *288*, 290, 297, 298, 299, *304*, 313, 315, *323*, 331–42, 353, 354, 355, 356, 357, 362, 365, 367, 368, 383, 433, 445, 455, 457, 459, 460, 461, 471, *478*, 486, 487, 489

Gagnon, M., *34*
Galenson, E., 27, *35*, 159, 167, 172, *183*, 300, *304*, 466, 467, *478, 479*
Gates, J. S., 246, *275*
Gebhard, P., *36*
Gilligan, C., 13, 33, 311, *324*, 437, 445, 451, *453*, 467, 476, *479*, 480–94
Glenn, J., *275*
Glover, E., 258, *275*, 290, *304*
Greenacre, P., 4, 25, 27, *35*, 104, *233*, 234, 237, 258, *275*, 300, *304*
Greenson, R., 465, *479*
Gross, M., 306, *324*
Grossman, W. I., 27, *35*, 290–304, *304*, 318, *324*
Grunberger, J., 92, 104, 126, 354, 355
Gunsberg, L., 467, *479*

Haiman, M., *275*
Halverson, H. M., *275*
Hampson, J. G., 282, *289*, 314, *324*
Hampson, J. L., 282, *289*, 314, *324*
Hare, R., *324*
Harley, M., 237, *275*
Harlow, H. F., 242, *275*
Harnik, J., 191, *197*
Hartmann, H., 9, *36*
Hays, H. R., 410, 411, *419*
Hebb, D. O., *419*

Hediger, H., 242, *275*
Heilbrun, C., 437, *453*
Heiman, M., 234, 258
Hermann, I., 95
Hess, E., *323*
Hess, T. B., 157, *158*
Hitschmann, E., 234, *275*
Hogan, R. T., 305, *324*
Horney, K., 3, 4, 15, 16, *36*, 96, 103, 105, 149, 150, 189, 193, *197*, 207, 209, *220*, 222, *233*, 234, 235, *275*, 279, *288*, 299, *304*, 313, 317, 319, *324*, 352, 355, 457, 458, 462, *479*
Howell, E., 313, *324*
Huffman, J. W., 236, 242, *275*

Irigaray, L., 13, 29, 30, *36*, 344–51, 422

Jacobs, G., *323*
Jacobson, E., 24, *36*, 187–97, 234, 236, 259, *275*
Johnson, V. E., *37*, 236, 237, 238, 242, 243, 251, 257, 258, 260, 271, *276*, 279, *289*, 311, *324*
Johnson, W. R., 482
Jones, E., 3, 15, 16, 22, *36*, 90, 91, 105, 106, 109, 234, 253, 256, *275*, 279, *288*, 313, 319, *324*, 352, 353, 354, 355, 356, 361, 362, 365
Jordan, J., 441, 443, 448, *453*

Kaplan, A., 441, 443, 448, *453*
Kaplan, E., 242, *275*
Kaplan, S., 439, *453*
Keiser, S., 238, 256, *275*
Keller, E. F., 465, *479*
Kestenberg, J. S., 4, 25, *36*, 234–73, *275*, 276, 467, *479*
Khan, M., 26, *36*, 460, *479*
Kinsey, A. C., 4, *36*, 236, 242, 257, 259, *276*, 460, *479*
Kleeman, J., 27, *36*
Klein, G., 439, *453*
Klein, M., 15, 16–19, *36*, 65–86, 90, 105, 111, 126, 189, 190, 193, *197, 276*, 352, 355, 361, 403, 404, 405, 406, 408, *419*
Klerman, G. L., 318, 322, *324*
Knights, L. C., 144, *145*

Kohut, H., 26, 27, 28, *36*, 460, *479*
Kramer, P., 242, *276*
Kramer, S., 27, *37*
Kristeva, J., 13, 30, *36*, 374–96
Kuhn, T. S., 305, *324*

Lacan, J., 9, 21, 22, *36*, 152, 153, 155, *158*, 363, 367, 368, 383, 390
Lachmann, F. M., 26, *38*, 460, *479*
Lamb, M. E., 467, *479*
Lampl-de Groot, J., 3, 6, 14, *36*, 95, 126, 234, *276*
Langer, M., 237, *276*
Lawrence, D. H., 410
Lax, R., 464, *479*
Leclerc, A., *34*
Lerner, A. J., *288*
Lerner, H., 315, *324*
Levenson, R., 464, *479*
Levinson, D., 437, *453*
Lichtenstein, H., 312, 321, *324*
Lorand, S., 237, 256, *276*
Lownsberry, E., 246, *276*
Luquet-Parat, C., 91, 112, 355
Luria, Z., 440, 445, *453*

McClelland, D., 451, *453*
McDougall, J., 23, 24, *37*, 90, 159–83, *183*
McGinley, P., 246, *276*
Macklin, R., 306, 308, 322, *324*
Mahler, M. S., 29, 32, *37*, 300, *304*, 439, *453*, 463, 464, 468, *479*
Marcus, H., *276*
Marcus, J. H., 467, *479*
Marcus, S., 321, *324*
Marmor, J., 234, 257, *276*, 309, *324*
Martin, C., *36*
Maslow, A. H., *453*
Masters, W. H., *37*, 236, 237, 238, 242, 243, 251, 257, 258, 260, 271, *276*, 279, *289*, 311, *324*
Masterson, J. F., 473, *479*
Mead, G. H., 483
Mead, M., *276*, 410, *419*
Menaker, E., 26, *37*, 221–33, *233*, 459, 460, *479*
Miller, J. B., 32, *37*, 437–53, *453*, 476, *479*
Millett, K., 317, *324*

Mitchell, J., 29, *37*, 331–42, 422
Modell, A. H., 318, *324*
Money, J., 282, *289*, 314, *324*
Montrelay, M., 30, *37*, 352–71
Moore, B. E., 234, 237, 257, *276*
Morgenthau, H., 306, *325*
Moulton, R., *37*, 320, *325*
Müller, J. A., 105, 234, *276*, 352

Nacht, S., 154, *158*
Nelson, W. E., 264, *276*
Nochlin, L., 157, *158*
Nunberg, H., 266, *276*

Ovesey, L., 320, *325*

Parens, H., 27, *37*
Payne, S. A., 8, 20, *37*, 237, *276*
Person, E. S., 7, 27, 28, *37*, 305–23, *325*, 470, *479*
Pine, F., 29, 32, *37*, 300, *304*, 463, 464, 468, *479*
Pollock, L., 27, *37*
Pomeroy, W., *36*
Provenzano, F., 440, *453*

Rado, S., 188, *197*, 236, 259, *276*
Reich, A., 25, *37*, 198–206
Reich, W., 222, *233*, *276*, 338
Reik, T., 221, 222, *233*
Rich, A., 13, *37*
Rieff, P., 306, 319, *325*
Riviere, J., *37*
Robbins, E., *276*
Roheim, G., *276*
Rohrbaugh, J. B., 317, 320, *325*
Roiphe, H., 27, *35*, 159, 167, 172, *183*, 300, *304*, 466, 467, *478*, *479*
Rose, J., 4, 12, *37*
Rosenblum, L., *276*
Ross, J. M., 238, *276*
Ross, N., 321, *325*
Rubin, J., 440, *453*

Sachs, H., 188, 194, 196, *197*, 215
Safouan, M., 22, *37*, 146–57
Salomé, L. A., 7, *37*
Sarlin, C. N., 258, *277*
Schaefer, M., 309, *323*

Schafer, R., 25, 33, *37,* 311, 317, 320, *325*
Schilder, P., 95
Segal, H., 170, *183*
Sherfey, M. J., 4, *37,* 151, *158,* 236, 240, 251, 256, *277,* 279, *289*
Silving, H., *277*
Skinner, M., 482, 488
Smirnoff, V., 460, *479*
Sossin, K. M., 467, *479*
Spieler, S., 462, 464, *479*
Spitz, R. A., *233*
Stechler, G., 439, *453*
Stein, C., 118
Stern, D., 439, *453*
Stern, J., 27, *37*
Stevenson, R., 467, *479*
Stewart, W., 27, *35*
Stewart, W. A., 290–304, 318, *324*
Stiver, I., 448, *454*
Stoller, R. J., 4, 23, 32, *37,* 159, 167, *183,* 278–87, *289,* 313, *325,* 455, 460, 461, 465, *479*
Stolorow, R. D., 26, *38,* 460, *479*
Strachey, R., 3, *38*
Surrey, J., 441, 443, 445, 448, *453, 454*
Suttie, I., 486

Talbot, N. B., *277*
Tausk, V., *277*
Thompson, C., 3, 25, *38,* 207–20, *220,* 311, 319, *325,* 445, *454*
Thompson, W. R., *419*
Tolstoy, L., *419*
Torok, M., 9, 20, *38,* 355, 366, 367, 462, 466, *479*
Tyson, P., 315, *325*

Van der Leeuw, P. J., *277*
Van Ophuijsen, J. W. H., *277*
Vaughter, R. M., 308, *325*
Veszy-Wagner, L., *277*

Weber, M., 188, *197*
Weiss, E., 190, *197,* 244, 257, 258, *277*
Winnicott, D. W., 8, 20, *38,* 132–45, *145,* 174, *183,* 239, *277,* 474, *479*
Wittels, F., 95

Yazmajian, R. W., *277*
Yogman, M. W., 467, *479*

Zilboorg, G., 279, *289*

Subject Index

Abusive men, submissive women and, 200–201
Achievement
  cultural context, 215–16
  guilt related to, 100–104
  as narcissistic reward, 112
  penis envy and, 111
Active Oedipus complex, 48
Active-passive phase, 47
Activity, as male element, 94–95
Adolescence
  girl's sexuality and, 445–47
  males compared to females, 445
  self development, 445–47
  transition from latency, 250–53
  transition to adulthood, 253–54
Adrenogenital syndrome, 282
Adulthood, transition from adolescence, 253–54
Agency-in-community view, self development, 442–43
Aggression
  genesis of, 49–50
  rejection of and masochism, 226–27, 259
  toward penis, 96
Allergic object relation, 119
American school, 9–11
Anal castration, 102
Anal sadism, 55
  in women's psychosexual development, 93–95
Anal stage, 53
"Analysis Terminable and Interminable" (Freud), 15, 208
Anger, anal stimulation and, 55
Animals
  animal phobias, 68
  genitality of, 241–42
  maternal care and bodily functions, 242
Anorexia nervosa, 7
Antagonism toward women
  ambivalence toward early mother, 403–10
  formation of self and, 414–16

mother as representation of nature and, 410–14
  roots of, 401–2
Anus
  stimulation of, and anger, 55
  vaginal sensitivity and, 58–59
Anxiety, relation to body, 361–62
Attachment. See Mother attachment
Autonomy, self development and, 442

Bedtime rituals, 71
Beyond the Pleasure Principle (Freud), 93–94
Birth fantasies, 56, 57, 75
  of boy, 265–66
Birth of sibling, 60, 67
Bisexuality, 8, 15, 24, 118, 132, 138, 341
  bisexual drive and creative process, 167–68
  as inherent feature, 81
  relationship to homosexuality, 138
Borderline diagnosis, 296
British school, 8
Bulimia, 7

Castration, early fears of boys, 84–85
Castration complex, 5, 15, 21–22, 44, 190, 196
  anxiety as, 356
  female transfer of libido, 50–51, 62, 83, 111
  masochism and, 222
  Oedipus complex and, 83
  representation of, 356–58
  repression of female masturbation and, 57–59, 60–61
  superego and, 188–94, 196, 214–15
"Change of Object, The" (Luquet-Parat), 91, 112
Child brides, 258
Childhood, masturbation in, 243–44
Chronic pain, 297
Claustrophobia, 97, 125

Clinging child, 60–61
Clitoris, as little penis, 149, 150–51
Concentrism, 355, 365
"Contribution to the Problem of Femininity"
    (Lampl-de Groot), 95
Control instinct, dyspareunia and, 100
Conversion symptoms, 259
Core gender identity, gender differences,
    430–31, 432
Counter-society, 387
Creativity
    integration of bisexual wishes and, 167–
    68
    masculine/feminine features, 132
    masculine motivation for, 103
    phallic significance of, 103–4
Cultural context, masochism and, 458–59
Cultural values and psychoanalysis
    biological assumptions and, 319–21
    Freudian bias, 316–19
    penis envy, 315
    shift in paradigm, 321–22
    theories of gender identity, 312–14
    theories of sexuality, 311–12
Culture and women
    achievement, 215–16
    attractiveness/seductiveness and, 214
    cultural context and penis envy, 212
    Freudian theories, limitations of, 209–12,
    214–17
    masculinity complex, 217–20
    in patriarchal society, 211
    puberty and, 212–13
    sexual life and, 213–14
    unequality of women, 211, 212–13
Culturist orientation, 4

Death instinct, 17
    masochism and, 221
Death of parent, dead father and psychic
    trauma, case example, 161–66, 168–82
Defense mechanisms, of sexual pathology,
    258–59
Delusion formation, 89
Dependence, female conception of, 490–92
Depression
    disturbance of Oedipus complex by, 73–
    76
    mourning and, 487

Deprivation, infantile, 337
Deuterophallic phase, 47, 109
Developmental course
    active-passive phase, 47
    masculine-feminine phase, 51
    phallic-castrated phase, 47–51
Developmental impairment, Oedipus com-
    plex and, 62–63
Differentiation phenomenon, gender differ-
    ences, 422–29
Dissociation
    of Hamlet, 143–44
    male-female elements in people, 136–39
    male's nonmasculine elements, case ex-
    ample, 133–37
    split-off of other sex element, 137–39
"Dissolution of the Oedipus Complex, The"
    (Freud), 88
Dolls, sexual development and, 245–47,
    250
"Dread of Women, The" (Horney), 96
Dyspareunia, control instinct and, 100

"Early Female Sexuality" (Jones), 93
Eczema, 119
Ego, masochism and, 222–23, 229–32, 460
Ego and the Id, The (Freud), 94
Ego and the Mechanisms of Defence, The
    (Freud), 150
Ego development, mother and, 222–23,
    225–26, 228–29, 231–32
Ego integrity, penis envy and, 112–16
Ego psychology, 9–10, 12, 321
Electra complex, Freudian view, 341
Enemas, 55
Environmental factors, formation of male/fe-
    male elements, 141–42
Envy and Gratitude (Klein), 91, 403
Erection, male, 210
Estral genitality, 241
Evil, relation to women, 364

Fantasy
    about parental sexuality, 54
    unconscious, 17
    wish for child, 56, 57
    wish for penis, 57
Father
    creativity and, 103–4

dead father and psychic trauma, case example, 161–66, 168–82
  deviant sexual development and, 166–67
  girl's transfer of libido to, 50–51, 62, 83, 111
  guilt related to achievement and, 100–104
  ideal love and, 461–62, 468
  identification with penis by daughter, 116–26
  incorporation of paternal penis, 96–99
  masochism and, 461
  object idealization by girl, 90–93, 96–97, 114–16
  role in puberty, 269
  unavailable father and girl's development, 467
Femaleness, study of
  absence of genitals and, 278–81, 284–85
  masculinized females and, 282
  neuter female and, 281–82
  normal females and, 282
  parental influences, 282–83, 285, 287
Female psychology
  biological assumptions and, 319–21
  Freudian bias in, 313, 316–19, 339–40
  liberation of, 311–12
  misogyny and, 319
  penis envy, 315
  shift in paradigm, 321–22
  theories of gender identity, 312–14
  theories of sexuality, 311–12
  treatment goals and, 307–10
Female sexuality
  autoeroticism in, 345
  masculine interpretation of, 344–50
Female Sexuality (Bonaparte), 3
"Female Sexuality" (Freud), 14, 15, 88, 89, 106, 187
Feminine elements, 12, 13
  artistic portrayal of, 363
  contrasted with male elements, 142–44
  fear of femininity, 362
  in male, case example, 133–37
  masculinization of females, 188, 191, 197
  maternal care and, 141–42
  passivity and, 94–95
  pseudoacceptance of, 254–56
  pure female element, 136, 140–41, 142
  repression and, 360–61
  split-off of other sex element, 137–39
Feminine identification, rejection by boy, 267
Feminine integration, achievement of, 259–60
"Femininity" (Freud), 3, 15, 89
Feminist movement, 4, 11–12, 28
  early, 420
  generations of women and, 379–80
  motherhood and, 390–91
Fetish, role of, 107–8
"Fetishism" (Freud), 107
"Flight from Womanhood" (Horney), 209
French school, 9
Friendships, 247
Frigidity
  cause of, 93
  desexualization of vagina, 258, 269
  compared to impotence, 239–40
  male role in, 257
  orality and, 237
  repression of genitalia, 259
  social determinism of, 191
  treatment of, 270–72

Gender differences
  attachment and, 486–93
  conception of dependence, 490–92
  core gender identity and, 430–31, 432
  differentiation phenomenon, 422–29
  girl's resistance to detachment, 489
  importance in understanding of, 433–34
  moral judgment, 484–86
  mother and, 425, 432
  orgasm, 238–40
  psychoanalytic view, 429–30
  relational creation of, 421, 432
  sexual development
    male/female dissimilarities, 264–70
    male/female similarities, 262–64
  similarity/dissimilarity of sexes, 240
Gender identity, 4, 23, 32
  absence of genitals and, 278
  affecting factors, 314
  boys, development of, 430–32
  changing theories of, 312–14
  core gender identity, 27, 32, 430–31, 455
  crucial age for, 167

Gender identity (*Continued*)
  femaleness, study of, 278–87
  Freudian view, 313
  girls, development of, 432
  homosexual response and, 160
  inner genital core and, 241
  origins of, 166–67
  parental influences, 282–83, 285, 287
  self-designation by child, 314
Genitality
  adolescence to adulthood development,
    253–54
  animals, 241–42
  early genital desires, 78–79, 80
  genital discharge, fantasies of, 244–47
  genital excitation in childhood, 243–44
  latency to adolescence transition, 250–53
  maternal care and, 242–43
  pregenitality to phallicity transition, 247–
    50
  satiation in insatiation syndrome, 256
  sexual pathology, 258–59
Genital phase
  inner genital phase, 262–63, 265
  male/female dissimilarities, 265–66
  male/female similarities, 262–63
Genitals, inner/outer genitals and develop-
    ment, 240–41
*Group Psychology and the Analysis of the
  Ego* (Freud), 107
Guilt
  achievement and, 100–104
  incorporation guilt, 99–100
  masochism and, 125–26, 221
  Oedipus complex and, 91–93, 113–14
  origin of, 84

Hamlet, dissociation of, 143–44
Headaches, chronic, 100, 101, 102, 103
Homosexuality
  dead father and psychic trauma, case ex-
    ample, 161–66, 168–82
  differentiation in women, 22–23
  Greek myth of, 138–39, 141
  libido, nature of, 167
  male, 63
  narcissistic dimension of, 166
  relationship to bisexuality, 138

  response to sexual role, 160
  as temporary strategy, 30
  "Homosexuality in Women" (McDougall),
    90
Hypersexuality, 258
Hysteria, 5
  Freudian view of, 334–35

Idealization
  of father, 90–93, 96–97, 114–16
  of sexuality, 93
Ideal love
  father/daughter, 469–75
  father/son, 468, 469
  origins of, 468
Identificatory love, 468, 470, 472
Impotence, 138
  compared to frigidity, 240
  treatment of, 270–72
In a Different Voice (Gilligan), 33
Incest, 334
Incorporation, paternal penis, 96–99
Infertility, 258
Inhibitions, Symptoms, Anxiety (Freud), 94,
    110
Inner genital phase, 262–63, 265
"Instincts and Their Vicissitudes" (Freud),
    112
Intellectual activity, possession of penis and,
    100–101
Interpretation, pleasure and, 367–68
Interpretation of Dreams, The (Freud), 383

Latency, 51
  characteristics of, 243–44
  genital discharge, fantasies of, 244–47
  male/female dissimilarities, 266–67
  male/female similarities, 264
  self development, 445
  transition to adolescence, 250–53
Libido
  aggression and, 76, 77–78
  development of, 76–80
  pre-Oedipal phase and, 43–64, 76–80
  transferred to father by daughter, 50–51,
    62, 83, 111
Looking-glass self, 483

Love
  conception in modern psychology, 486
  female attitude toward, 116, 117
  ideal love, 461, 468–77
  identificatory love, 468, 470, 472
  loss and, 486–87
  phenomenon of, 116–17
  self-regard and, 116

Male elements
  activity and, 94–95
  contrasted with female elements, 142–44
  development of, 278
  in female, 20–21
  maternal care and, 141–42
  split-off of other sex elements, 137–39
"Manifestations of the Female Castration
    Complex" (Abraham), 111
Masculine-feminine phase, 51
Masculine protest, 319
Masculinity complex, 461, 469
  cultural aspects, 217–20
Masculinization of females, 188, 191, 197,
    469
Masochism
  case example, 225–31
  castration complex and, 222
  cultural context and, 458–59
  death instinct and, 221
  ego and, 222–23, 229, 232, 460
  as female position, 15–16, 19, 25, 26–27,
    32–33, 191–92, 196, 457
  guilt and, 125–26
  historical view of, 457–61
  ideal love and, 461, 468–77
  main aspect of, 125–26
  moral masochism, 26, 221, 222, 229,
    460–61
  mother and, 222–23, 225–26, 228–29,
    230, 232
  origins of, 221–23
  passivity and, 459
  pleasure in pain misconception, 458, 459–
    60
  preservation of ego in, 222–23
  projection of aggression and, 259
  rapprochement phase, 461–68
  self-depreciation and, 229
  self-hate and, 224–25

  sexual masochism, 221–22
  social masochism, 221
  submissiveness and, 460
  views of, 221–23
Masturbation
  characteristics in childhood, 243–44
  child reactions to castration threat, 60–61
  genital discharge, fantasies of, 244–47
  infantile activity, 50, 53, 54
  male vs. female, 95
  phallic stage fantasy, 55
  primal scene and, 54
  repression in girls, 57–59, 60–61
Menstrual cycle, 246
Mermaid and the Minotaur, The (Dinner-
    stein), 31
Mirroring, 483
Misogyny, female psychology and, 319
Moral judgment, gender differences, 484–86
Moral masochism, 26, 221, 222, 229, 460–
    61
Moral reasoning, male compared to female,
    33
Moses and Monotheism (Freud), 340
Mother
  ambivalence toward early mother, 403–10
  boy's relations with women and, 108
  castrated-mother, boy's view of, 107,
    108–9
  child as narcissistic extension of self, 167
  dependency on men and, 31
  deviant sexual development and, 166–67
  domineering mother, 110
  ego development and, 222–23, 225–26,
    228–29, 231–32
  envy/gratitude phenomenon, 403
  formation of self and, 414–16
  girl's expectations of, 151–54
  good-enough/not-good-enough mother,
    141
  masochism and, 222–23, 225–26, 228–
    29, 230, 232
  maternal care and male/female elements,
    141–42
  mother as representation of nature and,
    410–14
  omnipotent mother concept, 106–12
  perception of mother as object, 425
  phallic mother, 52, 456

Mother (*Continued*)
  powerlessness of child and, 107
  rage/exploitation and, 407–10
  self-development and, 439, 440–41, 444
  splitting mechanism and, 404
  stimulation of bodily functions, 242–43
  submissive women's fixation, 201–3
Mother attachment
  detachment, 486–87, 489
  gender differences, 486–93
  inequality and, 490
  preoedipal phase, 45–46
Mother/child relationship
  extinction of, 59
  phallic mother concept, 52, 456
  physical care, 52–53, 54
  traumas to, 60
Motherhood, feminist movement and, 390–91
Mourning, 486–87
  depression and, 487
  remembering and, 487
  stages of, 487
"Mourning and Melancholia" (Freud), 487

Narcissism
  of boy, 148, 149
  enigma of, 149
  penis envy and, 300–301
  phallo-narcissism, 149
  secondary, 117
Narcissistic compensations, lack of genital
    self-esteem, 191
Narcissistic identification, with male penis,
    192
Narcissistic injury, to child, 50
Nature
  male exploitation of, 409–10
  mother as representative of, 410–14
Negative Oedipus complex, 62
Neurosis
  Freudian view, 334–36
  roots of, 43
Neurotic Personality of Our Time, The (Horney), 207
New Introductory Lectures on Psychoanalysis (Freud), 486
Nuclear passivity, 62

Object-relations
  male/female elements and, 139–41
  subjective object, 140
Object relations theory, 12–13, 20–21, 321–22
Oedipal guilt, 113–14
Oedipus complex, 5–6, 14, 17–18, 19, 21
  active Oedipus complex, 48
  comparative view, Freud/Klein, 82–86
  depression, effects on, 73–76
  developmental problems, case example,
    66–75
  early stages of, 76–80
  Freudian view, 340–42
  girl's Oedipus development, 46, 80–82,
    85–86
  male homosexuality and, 63
  negative Oedipus complex, 62, 88
  origin of neurosis and, 43
  passive Oedipus complex, 48–49, 63–64
  positive Oedipus complex, 66, 88
  preoedipal attitude of boy and, 59
  triangle in, 44
Oedipus Rex, events of, 358–59
"On Narcissism: An Introduction" (Freud),
    112
"On Transformations of Instincts as Exem-
    plified in Anal Eroticism" (Freud), 96
Oral desire, breast/penis and, 77–78
Oral phase
  fixations in, 237
  superego and, 83–84
Orgasm
  affecting factors, 239
  male versus female, 238–40
  multiple orgasm, 255–56
  relationship of sexual partners and, 260–61
  requirements of ego, 261
  vaginal, 148
"Outline for a Study of Narcissism in Fe-
    male Sexuality" (Grunberger), 92
Ovarian agenesis, 281

Paranoid psychosis, 63
Passive Oedipus complex, 48–49, 63–64
Passivity
  femininity and, 20, 94–95

masochism and, 459
submissiveness in women, 201
of young child, 49
Patriarchal bias, psychoanalytic theory, 4,
316–17, 339–42
Penis, identification with penis by daughter,
116–26
Penis envy, 5, 14, 15–16, 17–18, 19–20,
27, 28, 74–75, 88, 89, 208, 235–36
basis of, 57
case examples, 291–98
changing theories of, 315
cultural context and, 211–12
domineering mother and, 110
ego integrity and, 112–16
narcissistic patients and, 300–301
phallic mother and, 111
phases of, 300, 303–4
professional women and, 111
vagina and, 105
views of, 104–5, 298–300
Personality
environmental factors, 141–42
male/female elements, contrasting of,
142–44
male/female elements in people, 136–39
male's nonmasculine elements, case example, 133–37
pure male/female elements in people,
139–41
Phallicism, 147, 148, 155, 156
Phallic mother concept, 52, 456
Phallic phase, 15, 16, 21, 50, 53–54
male/female dissimilarities, 266
male/female similarities, 263–64
mutual touching and, 55
phallic-castrated phase, 47–51
phallic-narcissistic phase, 109
transition from pregenitality to, 248–50
"Phallic Phase, The" (Jones), 88, 91, 106
Phallic sexual monism, 104
Phallic woman, 205
characteristics of, 117–25
Phallocentrism, 353–54
Phallus
as paternal metaphor, 22
as symbol, 104
Phobia
animal phobia, 68

engulfment fears, 97, 99–100
sexual problems and, 100
Pleasure in pain misconception, masochism,
458, 459–60
Pleasure principle, Freudian view, 336–37
Preadult period
male/female dissimilarities, 269
male/female similarities, 264
Pregenital phase
male/female dissimilarities, 264–65
male/female similarities, 262
Pregenital zones, 46
Premature ejaculation, 109
Preoedipal phase, 6, 14
analytical difficulties and, 45
attachment to mother, 45–46, 82–83
influence on development, case example,
61–62
libidinal development and, 43–64, 76–80
preoedipal sexuality, 43
relation to oedipal phase, 59
triangle in, 44–45
"Pre-Oedipal Phase of the Libido Development" (Brunswick and Freud), 106
Prepuberty
male/female dissimilarities, 267–68
male/female similarities, 264
Primal scene, 127
effects of, case example, 67, 68, 69–70
masturbation and, 54
screen memories of, 102–3
Projection, of superego, 195–96
Promiscuity, 258
Prostitution, 204, 258
Psychic trauma, elements of, 165–66
Psychoanalysis, women attracted to field, 2
Psycho-Analysis and Feminism (Mitchell),
28–29
Psychoanalytic theory
American school, 9–11, 24–33
analytic procedure in, 338
contributions of, 5
criticism of, 331–32, 333, 338
criticism of Freud's theory, 209–12, 214–
17
cultural contexts, 7
Electra complex, 341
European school, 8–9, 13, 16–24
femininity in, 6–7

Psychoanalytic theory (*Continued*)
  feminist movement and, 11–13
  Freud's writings on women, 3, 14–15
  homosexuality, 22–24
  hysteria in women, 5
  Lacanian position, 21–22
  masochism of female, 15–16
  mother in, 5–6
  neo-Freudians on feminine sexuality, 16–24
  neuroses, 334–36
  object relations school, 20–21
  Oedipus complex, 5–6, 18, 21, 340–42
  patriarchal bias, 316–17, 339–42
  penis envy, 19–20
  pleasure principle, 336–37
  preoedipal phase, 6, 14
  reality principle, 337
  socialism and, 380–82
  theoretical verification, lack of, 317–19
  unconscious, 332–34
  Vienna school/London school split, 3
"Psychogenesis of a Case of Female Homosexuality" (Freud), 22
Psychology of Women, The (Deutsch), 93
Puberty
  girl's cultural status and, 213
  male/female dissimilarities, 268–69
  male/female similarities, 264

Rapproachment phase
  boys compared to girls, 464, 466
  characteristics of, 462–63
  father and, 462, 464–68
  gender identity, 463–64, 465
Reaction formation, 122
Reality principle, Freudian view, 337
Relationships
  female conception of, 481–82, 490–93
  meaning to women, 442, 443, 445, 447–48, 451
  moral dimensions, 482–93
  responsibility in, 481, 482
Remembering, mourning and, 487
Repression
  femininity and, 360–61
  meaning of, 360
Reproduction of Mothering, The (Chodorow), 31–32, 461

Responsibility
  in relationships, 481, 482
  women's conceptions of, 484

Sadistic fantasies, 70, 79, 105–6
Sadistic love, 63
Satiation in insatiation syndrome, 256
Self
  and experience of connection, 483–84
  true self, 427
Self-depreciation, masochism and, 229
Self development
  adolescence, 445–47
  agency-in-community view, 442–43
  autonomy and, 442
  beginning of, 439
  caretaker and, 439, 440–41, 444
  early mental representations in, 439–40, 441
  Erikson's theory, 439, 442
  interacting sense of self, 440, 441
  latency phase, 445
  mother and, 414–16
  new theories of self, 451–52
  oscillating sense of self, 441
  practical implications, 448–50
Self-esteem, 105
  girl's relationship orientation and, 442
  love and, 116
  submissiveness in women and, 199
Self-hate, 26
  masochism and, 224–25
Self psychology, 27–28
Separation-individuation
  attachment and detachment, 486–93
  father and, 462, 464–68
  gender identity and, 422–29
  rapproachment phase, 462–63
Sexual Behavior in the Human Female (Kinsey), 4
Sexual dependency, 196
Sexual development
  adolescence to adulthood development, 253–54
  animals, 241–42
  changing theories of, 311–12
  genital discharge, fantasies of, 244–47
  genital excitation in childhood, 243–44
  latency to adolescence transition, 250–53

male, 261–62
male/female dissimilarities, 264–70
male/female similarities, 262–64
maternal care and, 242–43
pregenitality to phallicity transition, 247–50
Sexual identity, origins of, 166–67
See also Gender identity
Sexual knowledge, origins of, 159–61
Sexual masochism, 221–222
Sexual pathology
denial/isolation of vagina, 259
externalization of inner impulses, 258
passing on of excitement, 258
projection of aggression, 259
repression of genitalia, 259
shifts of cathexis, 258
treatment of, 270–72
Sexual perversion, male versus female, 335
Sexual revolution, 312
Sexual satisfaction
conditions for, 260–61
male role in, 257, 260–61
satiation in insatiation syndrome, 256
Siblings, birth of, 60, 67
"Signification of the Phallus, The" (Lacan), 22
Social dualism, 339
Socialism, psychoanalytic theory and, 380–82
Social masochism, 221
Spinsterhood, 258, 259
Spirituality, female sexuality and, 93
Splitting mechanism, 404
Starving, fear of, 226
Stealing, 145
Sublimation, sexuality and, 93
Submissiveness in women
abusive men and, 200–201
case examples, 198–205
masochism and, 460
meaning of, 198
mother fixation in, 201–3
overvaluation of object by, 203–5
passivity and, 201
self-esteem and, 199
wish to destroy in, 205
Suicide attempt, 114–15
Superego

castration complex and, 188–94, 196, 214–15
changing moral judgments, 187
changing superego and women, 126
of female, 14, 24–25, 33, 81–82, 83
identification with paternal penis and, 126
modern times and women and, 188
of obsessional neurotic child, 71–72
oral phase and, 83–84
projection of superego, 195–96
stages in development in women, 194–96
Symbolic contract, women's place in, 384–86
Symbolization, 30

"Taboo of Virginity" (Freud), 96
Terrorist groups, women in, 388–89
Three Essays (Freud), 14, 93, 94, 95, 107
Toilet training, 54–55, 67
Totem and Taboo (Freud), 340
Totemism, 340
Trauma theory, 334
Treatment goals, female psychology and, 307–10

Unconscious, 29
Freudian view, 332–34
unconscious fantasies, 17

Vagina
acceptance as pleasure source, 256–57
areas of sensitivity, 58–59
biological aspects, 236
clitoris as little penis, 149, 150–51
denial/isolation of, 259
desexualization of, 258
hidden penis concept, 189–90, 193
masculine fear of, 96
modern explorations about, 236–37
orgasmic response, 237–38
penis envy and, 105
post–castration complex status, 191–92, 193
stimulation in maternal care, 242–43
vaginal awareness, 25–26, 27
vaginal orgasms, 148
Values
of cultural enterprise, 306
evolutionary value system, 321

Values (*Continued*)
  scientific, 305
  theory making and, 316
  See also Cultural values and psychoanalysis

War games, 445
Weaning, 60, 67
  depression and, 73–74

Wish for child, in childhood, 56, 57, 75, 265–66
Woman as Sex Object (Hess and Nochlin), 157
"Women's Time" (Kristeva), 30
Writers
  dead father and writer's block, case example, 161–66, 168–82
  relationship to words, 173–74